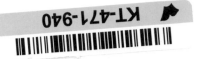

Get a camera...

Get some stock...

Go shoot a Doc...

The Documentary Film Makers Handbook

Avid.

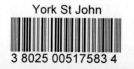

This edition of
The Documentary Film Makers Handbook
is dedicated to

All of our families for all their help and support while making this book.

EALING STUDIOS

With continued support

First published in 2006

The Continuum International Publishing Group Inc
80 Maiden Lane, New York, NY 10038

The Continuum International Publishing Group Ltd
The Tower Building, 11 York Road, London SE1 7NX

www.continuumbooks.com

Printed in the United States of America
Layout and design by Andrew Zinnes
Cover design by Chris Jones & Jim Loomis

ISBN 0-8264-1665-9

The Documentary Film Makers Handbook

1st Edition

by
Genevieve Jolliffe and
Andrew Zinnes

Acknowledgements

We would like like to thank all the contributors in this book for sharing with us their experience and expertise. And to all of the filmmakers in our Case Study section who have been very open and honest about the ups and downs of making their documentaries.

To Chis and Jo Jolliffe, Lynn and Stan Morris and Allen and Ilse Zinnes for their continued support in our choices to persue the oh so safe careers of publishing and filmmaking.

To Chris Jones for his technical wizardry, advice and friendship.

To David Barker our editor for his unending patience and encouragement.

Special thanks to our sponsor for contributing to the cause!

And, Jim, thanks for your illustrations.

LEGAL DISCLAIMER

Nothing in this book should be construed as legal advice. The information provided and the sample forms are not a substitute for consulting with an experienced entertainment lawye and receiving counsel based on the facts and the circumstances of a particular transaction. Furhtermore, case law and industry practice are subject to change and differ from country to country.

The copyright in and to the sample forms and documents in this book is owned and retained by the originator of the work ("the Owner"). These sample forms and documents havebeen created for your general information only. The Owner, the authors of this book and the publishers cannot therefore be held responsible for any losses or claim howsoever arising from any use or reproduction.

The Documentary Film Makers Handbook

Introduction to 1st edition

It's been said that the world is smaller now than it's ever been - that there are no more great frontiers to explore. Documentary filmmakers would passionately disagree as they take on the role of Columbus, Pizzaro and Scott. These storytellers have now become the great explorers of our time. Their stories are where truth and social consciousness can be found. Their work is where those without a voice can be heard. Their films are windows to worlds that people rarely see or speak about. Documentary filmmakers pull no punches or sugar coat things, frequently using their unyielding eye as a call to modern day activism in a post 9/11world. These filmmakers will frequently put themselves in harms way - even losing their lives as James Miller did while shooting *Death In Gaza.*

But not only will these intrepid adventurers fling themselves into the fray at the drop of a hat, they do so on micro-budgets with skeleton crews. They will spend an average of five to ten years in pursuit of their stories, struggling against the odds to bring the truth to light. They are truly guerilla filmmakers.

So given this genre's importance to our culture, we set out to do an exploration of our own. Keeping in *The Guerilla Film Makers Handbook* tradition, we interviewed industry experts and working documentary filmmakers to find out what makes them tick. One thing that kept coming up is that story means much more than technique and form in this genre – especially with technology changing faster than you can read this introduction. And it's this digital revolution spearheaded by DV and now HD that has leveled the playing field and allowed more voices into the mix. The result: myriads of new styles of documentaries that smash the conventions of those that have come before – forcing their way into the theatrical market. Long gone is the notion that docs can only be stuffy and boring!

Although *The Documentary Film Makers Handbook* has a North American slant, documentaries are a global medium – and in fact have always been wildly popular throughout the world. As such, we have devoted a chapter of the book to the Global Perspective in order to create a dialogue between filmmakers from across the planet – even Antarctica!

So it is with great pleasure that we introduce the first edition of *The Documentary Film Makers Handbook.* We hope it will service this important genre to the degree it deserves – the highest, while inspiring a new generation of explorers.

Genevieve Jolliffe and Andrew Zinnes
3:15am, May 25, 2006

Experts Contents

1. Training

2. Legal

3. Research & Development

4. Organizations

5. Writing

6. Funding

7. Broadcasters

8. Production Companies

9. Global Perspective

10. Production & Post

11. Film Festivals & Markets

12. Sales & Distribution

13. The Long View

14. Case Studies

Tips Contents

1. Training

2. Legal

3. Research & Development

4. Organizations

5. Writing

6. Funding

7. Broadcasters

8. Production Companies

9. Global Perspective

10. Production & Post

11. Film Festivals & Markets

12. Sales & Distribution

13. The Long View

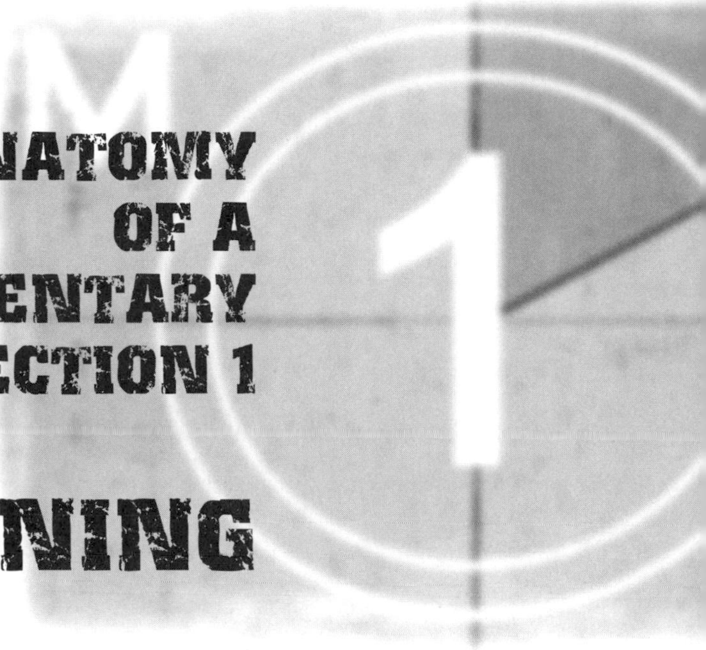

ANATOMY OF A DOCUMENTARY SECTION 1

TRAINING

Pat Aufderhiede
The American University

THE AMERICAN UNIVERSITY

Q – What is the doc program at The American University?

Pat - The Film and Media Arts program allows students to focus on the genre and the subject matter of their choice as they gather their professional skills. We have both an MA (usually 2 years) and an MFA (usually 3 years) program, open to students with no film background and designed to give them enough skills to enter the production world. Many of our students eventually become producers and many do focus on docs. Washington, D.C. is a very good place for docs, with PBS, the Corporation for Public Broadcasting, Discovery, National Geographic and the many federal agencies—all of which, it seems like us, use video. We have gathered a faculty that has special expertise in documentary, especially social docs, public affairs docs, and environmental docs.

Q – What is The Center For Social Media?

Pat – It set up to help look at questions such as - how do you get greater equity in media representation? How do you overcome the bias towards wealth and status that exists in the media? How are people able to participate in the media in their own society? What does a public need from its media, to be informed and active? The Center also puts a spotlight on good documentary work that will hopefully inspire our students at American University. Our Center is entirely grant funded and it serves both the students and the faculty at our school.

Q – How would a new filmmaker start on the path to making a socially oriented documentary film?

Pat – I think it's wise to take a look at the history of documentary film. That way you're not trying to invent something that's already been invented and you can learn from example. I also think a new filmmaker should base themselves in places where there's more focus on social documentary: Washington, DC, Seattle, San Francisco and New York. I'd also encourage people who are starting out to try and get an internship at one of the production houses they admire. That might be Bill Moyers who does public affairs TV in New York. It might be York Zimmerman or Durin Productions or Spark Media or Video Action in Washington, DC or Lumiere Productions in NYC. Look at the credits of really good social documentaries and see where the production houses are based. There are two really great social documentary series on TV that new socially orientated filmmakers should watch – *Independent Lens* and *POV*. Every one of these films has a story behind it of someone who struggled to make it. You can read interviews with those filmmakers on the shows' websites and find out how they got started. Also read Eric Barnouw's book *Documentary*.

Q – How balanced should a filmmaker be when doing a socially oriented documentary?

Pat - When it's a documentary, audiences expect that it's going to be true in some sense. They're going to see something that's about real life and you'll present it honestly from your perspective. However showing it objectively is an unrealistic goal. You have decided to show something for a reason. What is that reason? What do you want to tell people and why is that important? What's your motivation? If you can honestly answer those questions, you should honestly answer them for the viewer, too. No one will ever show the whole story. Nobody ever knows the "whole story." It's the story they wanted to tell and with luck it will be compelling. And that's why you should avoid sticking in stock footage of somebody else's dam for the dam that you are actually talking about. All of those shortcuts are cheating. If it's not true, then don't represent it as true. I know it's easier in storytelling to say let's not do A,B,C as it happened, but instead do A,C, B – but it's cheating.

Q – Are there things a filmmaker should think about when exploring unpopular or negative subjects?

Pat – I think everyone who has a point of view knows the power of the media and uses it to support their point of view. For me, it's trying to do the work that you do with the greatest amount of integrity possible to tell the story you want to tell. I happen to be a pro-abortion person. I can really see someone making an anti-abortion film that's really powerful and helps me understand why this point of view is so very important to them. I might hold onto my beliefs, but be very grateful to that person for making an honestly told story that explains the passion of their convictions. They could only do that if they were trying to clearly articulate that perspective. And with luck they're making it so that people like me could see it. I think the best documentary work is made not only to mobilize your own crowd, but to contribute to a large public conversation. There's a lot of work that's just propaganda on all sides. That comes from efficient persuasion that we've learned from advertising as well as propaganda. People want the bang for the buck and want a mobilizing video to convert and pick up people on the margins. I hope that documentarians strive to reach beyond that advertising or propaganda model.

Q – What are some of the programs and seminars that The Center offers?

Pat – Once a year we do a workshop on strategic design for effective documentary making in production, distribution and exhibition. We want to get people thinking about what they do. Who do they want to reach? What are their goals? People often don't articulate those goals as they are making their film, but they have them. And only when someone asks, *"How do you want to get this out into the world?"* are they thinking about the problems they could have solved if they'd built them into the production. We bring in filmmakers and photographers that we think are excellent examples of this. We hold meetings and activities – one of our projects over the last few years has been to develop a set of collective standards on how to interpret Fair Use for documentary filmmakers. We now have a Documentary Filmmakers' Statement of Best Practices in Fair Use, a project we coordinated with documentarians who worked through five filmmaker organizations throughout the country. This Statement alone has changed industry practice by helping documentarians lower their clearance and legal costs by correctly employing Fair Use. We also have conferences on the future of public media. We think public media is important in terms of having conversations that we believe documentaries fuel - that's conversations between people who may disagree with each other in good faith and share the belief that they have the right to decide the future of their society. We explore big issues like how does public broadcasting deal with a more open environment of the internet.

Q – How did the Fair Use doctrine come about and is it law?

Pat – Fair Use is part of copyright law, but it's recently been very hard for filmmakers to use. The statement is a consensus statement that was created by about 150 filmmakers who worked in small groups across the country with us here at the Center. Where people are able to collectively establish practice, it's very powerful because courts look to what is established and accepted. So until now, if filmmakers wanted to invoke Fair Use they would have had to say, *"Well, I think that's fair. I think that is reasonable."* And their programmer or distributor would go, *"I'm not going to trust you. Filmmakers will say anything."* So we went to five filmmaker organizations and pulled together a group of people who had two national productions. That is to say, they were all invested copyright holders. We asked them what was fair and reasonable in interpreting Fair Use - if somebody did it to you. If someone used your work and used these principles, would that be OK with you? And in fact, everyone had a very easy consensus around what they thought was fair and reasonable. It's not necessarily the standard my co-principle investigator or I'd have drawn, but the standards that copyright holding filmmakers thought was reasonable is in that guide. So it's a powerful document because it instantly lowers any single person's risk. You can get a copy of the document from our website at www.centerforsocialmedia.org/fairuse.htm.

Q – Has anyone had to use it as a defense?

Pat – Not yet - it's brand new. We doubt that we'll see court cases from responsible employment of the document. Several filmmakers at Sundance used it in order to finish their films for the 2006 festival. Public television in principle cleared a film with large amounts of Fair Use - Byron Hurt's *Beyond Beats and Rhymes* on the basis of the Statement and Hurt's lawyer's agreement. Now a cable company is developing an internal fair use code, using the Statement as a guide.

Q – How have the insurance companies and other entities reacted to the doctrine?

Pat – Insurers are still looking at the document E&O insurance is now doing carve outs on Fair Use. In other words, you can use Fair Use, but you'll carry the liability. What'd be great is if you could get E&O insurance companies to compete with each other in offering insurance that recognizes Fair Use. We're talking to them about that now.

Q – Do you feel filmmakers need to go to film school to be documentary filmmakers?

Pat – I think it's true that with today's technology you can walk right out of Best Buy and go film something. However, I think you need some things to help you and films schools make those things easier to get. One of the things you get is the background. What have other great filmmakers done before you? There's also the training but a large part of it is the contacts. Who do your professors know? Where can you intern? Which of your colleagues turns out to be on your crew and someone that you work with from now on? Which of the internships that your colleagues are in look more promising than yours? It shortens up your life voyage a lot. It's possible to do a lot of that on your own, but it's also possible that you might get a much narrower take on things. Very few of those films that are made walking out of Best Buy will be seen. I believe the role of a filmmaker will be increasingly to work in collaborative partnerships with people who have great stories to tell, passionate convictions, inside access, money and equipment but don't have those skills. What you see a lot of now is people getting to post production and faltering saying, *"Well, I guess I need a little more expertise than I have if anyone wants to see it."* We'll see people getting to that point earlier and in a more savvy way.

Q – What are the common mistakes that you see documentary filmmakers make?

Pat – Everything is too long. I see people being afraid to pull in outside advice early and often. I see people afraid to learn what other people are doing. It drives me nuts when my students say, *"I don't want to see so and so's film because I'm making a film on that subject and I don't want to be biased about it."* Go see the movie! Talk to the person. Show them what your interests are. I think people have too great a faith in the technology and they fail to realize that it's all about the story and the narrative. You can't structure a documentary around the chaotic pattern of real life. Stuff happening is not a movie. Yoll tell a story so be honest with yourself about what you are telling.

Q – What advice would you give a new documentary filmmaker?

Pat – Don't do it if it's not fun.

GUERILLA FILM MAKER SAYS!

Fair Use

With the rising costs of archival footage, many documentarians find it difficult to pay the licenses. A the heart of copyright law is the "Fair Use" doctrine that allows someone to use copyrighted material without licensing it under certain circumstances. The two main tests to see if you can invoke "Fair Use" are:

1. If the work is transformative. Meaning if you use the copyrighted material for a purpose other than what it was originally intended for. So if show a clip of a news broadcast to illustrate a point in your documentary, you have changed it from a news clip to a talking point. However, if you use a photograph to show something, it is still a photograph and being used for its original intent and cannot be deemed "Fair Use."

2. How much of the copyrighted material you use. If you use one phrase out of and entire book or 15 seconds of a 15-minute interview, you will probably be covered under "Fair Use." But if you edit in 55 minutes of a 60 minute football game, you probably won't be covered.

Fair use generally doesn't apply to music because you typically use it for what it was intended for and since most compositions are so short, you end up using most of it. Many E&O companies and broadcasters are still a bit funny about "Fair Use," but this may change as more and more cases are decided in the legal system.

To see The Center of Social Media's Best Practices in Fair Use document please go to www.centerforsocialmedia.org/fairuse.htm.

GUERILLA FILM MAKER SAYS!

Documentary Training Programs

American University School of Communication
http://www.soc.american.edu/
Email: communication@american.edu
Phone: (202) 885-2060

Boston University College of Communication
http://www.bu.edu/com/ft/
Email: ftvchair@bu.edu
Phone: 617-353-3483

Brooks Institute of Photography
http://www.brooks.edu/programs/visualj.asp

Center for Documentary Studies (Duke University)
http://cds.aas.duke.edu/
Phone: (919) 660-3663
Email: docstudies@duke.edu

Center of Social Media
www.centerforsocialmedia.com
Email: socialmedia@american.edu
Phone: (202) 885-3107
Fax: (202) 885-1309

Colombia University Graduate School of Journalism
http://www.jrn.columbia.edu/
(212) 854-3828
admissions@jrn.columbia.edu

The Documentary Center at George Washington University
http://www.gwu.edu/doccenter
Phone: (202)994-6787 voice
Email: nlk@gwu.edu
(6 month Institute)

The Documentary Institute, College of Journalism and Communication The University of Florida
http://www.jou.ufl.edu/documentary/
Tel: Journalism Department - (352) 392-0500
Email: gradapps@jou.ufl.edu

Emerson College
http://www.emerson.edu/
Phone: 617-824-8500

Hampshire College
http://www.hampshire.edu
Phone: 413.559.5482,
Email: ethomas@hampshire.edu

The New School
http://www.nsu.newschool.edu/
Phone: (212) 229-5600
Email: nsadmissions@newschool.edu

Rockport College
http://www.rockportcollege.edu/pcert-film.asp
Toll Free: 877.577.7700 | voice: 207.236.8581
Email: info@rockportcollege.edu

Stanford University – The Stanford Program in Documentary Studies
Department of Communication
http://communication.stanford.edu/documentary/
General admissions:
Tel: (650) 723-1941
email: comm-inforequest@lists.stanford.edu
Graduate admissions:
phone: (650) 723-2075
email: comm-studentservices@lists.stanford.edu

Tisch School of the Arts
New York University
http://www.tisch.nyu.edu/
Phone: 212 998 1600

UC Berkeley Graduate School of Journalism
www.journalism.berkeley.edu/program/documentary
Admissions Questions
Phone: 510-643-7928
Email: applysoj@berkeley.edu

UCLA
www.tft.ucla.edu/filmtv
www.uclaextension.edu
Phone: 310-825-5761
Email: info@tft.ucla.edu

USC School of Cinema andTelevision
USC School of Letters. Arts & Sciences: Anthropology
http://www.usc.edu/
Phone: (213) 740-1111
Email: admitusc@usc.edu

University of Montana, Bozeman
Department of Media and Theater Arts
(MFA in Science and Natural History filmmaking)
http://naturefilm.montana.edu/index.php
Tel:(406) 994-5884
Program Coordinator: Julie Isaacs Geyer
jgeyer@montana.edu

Vancouver Film School
http://www.vfs.com/
Phone: 604-685-5808 or toll free in North America 1-800-661-4101

SCHOOL OF JOURNALISM & DOCUMENTARY

Q – What is the program at Berkeley?

Jon – It's a very practical and very much non-theoretical two-year program in producing documentary films. I think it's the only two-year program that's embedded in a journalism school. The students spend the first year learning how to be journalists - going out and finding what's going on in the world, reporting and fact checking it and learning to write and produce print pieces and short TV shows on a deadline. They get a heavy dose of law and ethics. In the first year, they learn basic production mechanics - cameras, sound, editing. In the second year, the students do a Master's thesis project. We really push students to be as daring and experimental as they can be, while at the same time reaching a mass audience; that's a tall order. These things are too hard and expensive to waste your time on unless they're going to be seen by 10 million people. There are no restrictions on the type of films students can do. We have many cinema verité films, plenty of historical essay pieces, personal reflective autobiographical films and hybrid documentaries that combine a bunch of styles. We only ask that they be made for a large media audience and be journalistically sound---all that means is that you can't be foisting off untruth. That what the audience believes to be true after they see the film is in fact true. If the audience believes that Arnold Schwarzenegger is a national hero in Afghanistan, or that a particular man sells bibles for a living, then it better be true.

Q – What kind of equipment do they get to use?

Jon – All our facilities are digital. We use DVCam format cameras. On the high end, DSR-570's and the lower end PD-150's (soon changing over to DVX100A). We're preparing for a change over to HD, but not for a while. We used to do Avid and now we do Final Cut Pro. We see documentary filmmaking as a storytelling enterprise, not so much as a technical enterprise. We're convinced we can take almost anyone and teach them to how to make good picture and good sound.

Q – How do you see documentary filmmaking in the world today?

Jon – It's essential to how democracy functions. Democracy has a free press, and documentary is an increasingly important part of it. I think many people tend to see documentary as the last bastion of unfettered creativity in non-fiction. We try to walk the line between documentary as a hugely popular rambunctious mass medium and documentary as part of serious journalism. Documentary has ascended now in popular culture in a way that hasn't been true in my lifetime until now. It seems routine to have feature docs in theaters now and there are far more docs on TV and cable than then ever were. The democratizing of documentaries with inexpensive cameras and editing systems is great. If that produces 100 lousy films for every one good one, nobody has a problem with that. We work hard to dispel the rumor that young documentary filmmakers have to live hand to mouth, grant to grant. We don't treat it that way we treat it as a wonderful sustainable professional career path. We train them to make a grown up living in that way, but it's not for the faint hearted. You have to tolerate a fair amount of uncertainty.

Q – Do you think it's becoming easier to make documentaries these days?

Jon – It's becoming easier to make documentaries, but I don't know that it's becoming much easier to make a good documentary. Is it any easier to write a good screenplay or a good novel now? Probably not. It's easier for our culture to make world documentaries now. It's certainly true that capital is looking in documentaries as a place to invest and that may be a good and bad thing. That brings a whole set of pressure to documentaries that wasn't there before.

Q – Do documentaries fall under any code of journalism or does anything go?

Jon – No. Anything cannot go. If you want to make a fiction film, make a fiction film. But the fact of the matter is that there's no broad national code for documentaries although there is one for newspapers. If you break the rules of *The New York Times*, you know it, and you'll probably get canned. There are no rules that govern *Grizzly Man, Fahrenheit 9/11* and an episode on The History Channel. That can be good and bad. It allows everyone enormous freedom. But there have been a fair number of shenanigans in documentary throughout history, right from the start, and the ones who get fleeded are the audience. The position I take is that if you make documentaries you are a journalist, whether you like it or not. You can't abdicate responsibility to tell the truth by saying" *I'm not a journalist."* You're stuck with it. People come away from your film believing that Charlton Heston went to a certain city on a certain day and said a certain thing, you are responsible for that. If I make a film that says Robert Oppenhiemer made certain decisions while he was designing the atomic bomb, then I am responsible for that. And that's a pretty simple journalistic baseline; it's not rocket science. Documentaries should be fact checked. We shouldn't fabricate bogus archive footage. We shouldn't exercise a whole lot of shady liberties in shifting footage around. The audience has to know what its getting.

Q – What do you think about one-sided sensationalist political documentaries?

Jon – I love them, as long as they don't pretend to be something else. There' s nothing wrong with sensationalism, there's nothing wrong with propaganda as long as the audience knows that's what it is. An interesting example is *Super Size Me*, which is a very partisan film and in some ways sensational, but it's loaded with vetted, factual material, and the director is very up front about his sentiments. I use it as a teaching tool. The danger comes when documentaries purport to be vetted, objective and factual and in fact aren't. We need advocacy based on evidence.

Q – News in the US seems to be headed towards entertainment so that we never know what the truth really is.

Jon – Nothing wrong with entertainment, but we do need to know what the truth is. I think it has something to do with money. Who pays for the news in the UK? The people. Broadcast TV in the US is so overwhelming driven by ratings and by the commercial monster that it has become suspect. Yet, some of the best documentary work being done in the US is in a very commercial setting, which is HBO; go figure. It's who pays the piper. There was a great watershed 15 years ago when public TV disconnected itself from its original mission, which was to be insulated from the short-term pressures of ratings. PBS embraced the support of advertisers, and in some areas of public TV we have seen stagnation in inventiveness, risk taking, and new ideas. If General Motors or Fed Ex comes along to support a program on public broadcasting, they aren't doing it out of altruism. They're buying eyeballs, so why should it surprise us that challenging edgy, difficult programming gets marginalized? My other life is that I am a documentary producer, and I made a film about the making of the atomic bomb 25 years ago. That film was made entirely from public funds. I'm doing another film now on the same subject and historical characters, and that's only getting 25%-30% from public sources. It has dried up and the Congress doesn't have the political will to support it. A UK citizen pays about $37/year per capita to pay for the BBC. American citizens pay about $3.00/year. You get what you pay for.

Q – Do you feel truth and objectivity are lost?

Jon – You bet. I have done camera work on A-list documentaries that are destined for prime time and the press for high ratings was so great that I've seen my own footage falsified in the interest of pumped up drama and competing in a hellish commercial landscape. There's no question that there's a direct connection between the eroding of truth telling in documentary and the lust for ratings. Don't get me wrong; there are a great number of people in institutions in public and commercial TV, especially in news, who have fierce dedication to doing good journalism and maintaining ethical standards. Some of us have thought about convening and creating a sort of Hippocratic oath for documentary filmmakers. But that's a tricky thing, because documentary in this country has thrived from being unfettered. We undoubtedly have the wildest and most diverse documentary filmmaking community in the world. You want to be really careful before you tinker with it because there's some danger of knocking all the risk and all the fun out of what we do. Myself, I think it's a good idea for a number of institutions, like Sundance, ITVS, HBO, Showtime, to get together and begin to think about a very basic "do no evil" code of ethics.

Q – I believe there's a commission like that in the UK.

Jon – Yes. I know that in the UK, there is a website called docos.com. People get busted, and I think that's probably a good thing. The person viewing the film has no idea what is true and there it's fine to have some oversight. There's an irony in this country in that the most stringent ethical guidelines for veracity in non-fiction are in the commercial sector, not in public TV and that is because they have legal departments who want to shield them from being sued.

Q – Are there any misconceptions about documentaries these days?

Jon – The idea that documentaries are cheaper these days is suspect. Many documentaries are cheaper, but the fact of the matter it's not the cheap camera and digital tape that make up the bulk of a documentary's budget, it's time and people and things like insurance and licensing fees. The cost of making a historical film has gone up because of a vortex of greed around archive materials now. The libraries are consolidating and their rates are going up. And the performing arts communities are beginning to be much tougher as well.

Q – Are many films not able to renew their archival footage licenses because the libraries have upped the rates?

Jon – Sure. I was the series producer on *Eyes On The Prize*, which had that happen to it. That film is out of print and has vanished. It's like a species that has gone extinct. It's a huge problem. I was talking to Orlando Bagwell who was a producer/director on *Eyes On The Prize*, and he can no longer distribute his films. There's this great, heroic work being done by this group at The American University Law School Pat Aufderhiede who started an initiative on Fair Use. We need a similar initiative for ethics and the cost of documentaries. I'm always amused at *Tarnation*, which supposedly was made for $235 on credit cards. But the fact is that in order to premiere that movie at Sundance, to clear the rights for everything, the budget ran up to almost $500,000. We have at Berkeley, The Center for New Documentary and we have been looking at ways to make high quality documentaries really inexpensively. You can make films cheaply if you don't have to license anything and don't have any complicated access to the subject and use small crews. The most important factor is if it's a film that can be started and finished quickly i.e. within a couple of months - to keep the personnel costs reasonable.

Q – Do you think these copyright restrictions are going to cause a very narrow look on the world?

Jon – I think we've reached a point where the people who can make A-list historical films are the people who can raise a million dollars. And that's solely the fault of the consolidation of the archive material. It severely limits the diversity of different voices telling our history, and in the end it's the millions of viewers who suffer, because they only get one version of our history and culture.

Q – Do you think film is a dying format?

Jon – Photo-chemical film is dead. It's gone. Unless you have a couple of oil wells pumping in your back yard, there's no compelling argument to shoot anything on film anymore. I wouldn't have said that a year ago, but the arrival of accessible and affordable HD has changed everything. I'm amused by the cynicism of ads in film magazines which promote 16mm shooting for entry level filmmakers. Film will live on for a while, but the boom may fall when we lose a critical mass of processing laboratories. Walter Murch has pointed out that's going to a happen as soon as theatrical distribution of feature films shifts over to file transfer. Even now, everyone is projecting off HD at festivals, and it looks like a million bucks.

Q – How long do you usually get clearance for from archives?

Jon – It's complicated. We always buy our clearances from the archive at the end of the production, when we're out of money and exhausted. We generally buy the shortest possible license, which is five years. Very few archives are selling rights in perpetuity. So we're making films that are perishable; in some horrible sense they'll just vanish from our shelves five years out, one by one. It's pretty cruel for our kids and our grandkids. I'm trying to do films where there's no archive material, music purchased and artwork purchased. It's a forced resurgence of cinema verité as we have to create everything ourselves, very refreshing actually.

Q – Are docu-dramas the result of the archival footage issue?

Jon – Partly. Recreations are a real sticky wicket. In the 90's, we somehow got stalled in doing reenactments that were maddenly half-baked - all those horses hooves and blurry backs of heads. There was a lot of flirting with just doing straight out drama, but everyone was scared to have an actual actor say an actual line. Now, in hindsight, it all looks so cheesy. It's a relief now that some historical documentaries have sequences in which good actors actually perform good screenplays. I don't care for reenactment, but if it's done so that it's clearly reenactment and the audience knows that this dramatization is just that. That's fine. The rising problem with reenactments is that producers are trying to foist off reenactment footage as real archive footage. It's done very skillfully, but there's a special place in hell for that.

Q – During interviews, what are the ethics in pushing your subject to answering questions?

Jon – We have all the power and to pretend otherwise is silly. All the great documetarians are forthright that they made constructions, even in cinema verité. All we and the audience have is conscience. That sounds high minded, but we all got into this in order to get as close to the truth as we can. Yes, we can debate all day about 'truth,' but in blunt practical terms for those who get up every morning and make documentaries, the difference between truth and untruth is pretty clear. In interviews, that at least means letting people tell their version of the facts. And when we cut the interview, trying to represent in a broad sense what that person's opinion is. There's some sin in here, but not much. You don't put words in people's mouths and you don't tell them what to say. I've adopted a couple of techniques where I think that it's important that the audience hear the interviewer's voice to be reminded that someone is conducting the interview. I always ask the subjects if they have any questions for me, to make it more of a two-way street. It becomes tricky when you are interviewing someone you hate or think is evil. And there is a great temptation to use a different ethical standard for those we detect as the moral other. That's madness. You have to use the same standards on your enemies as your friends. There's a lot of debate on this – is it right to lie to a former concentration camp guard in order to get through the door? It's a slippery slope to apply different morals that way. I have to confess, though, though every single documentary encounter requires us to recheck the whole equation about what's ethical and what's not; it's organic, sort of like the constitution.

Q – At The Center for New Documentary, do you discuss new routes for distribution?

Jon – The elephant in the room is the internet. No one has figured how to successfully stream long form documentaries, either technically or in terms of a revenue stream for it s yet. It appears to be around the corner, but it's a big corner. There's another mess coming as well, since the rights issue is going to rear its head again. If they re-license the rights for *Eyes On The Prize* so it can be seen on TV, they are going to realize they don't have the rights to stream it on the internet. That's going to cost a lot. So there is a certain naiveté to think the archive houses aren't going to go after people trying to stream their footage on the internet. The same thing happened 15 years ago when cheap videotape forms of films were around. You used to have to check out a 16mm print of a film when I was in film school, get a projector and watch a scratchy movie with terrible sound. Now we have DVDs and they are dime a dozen. I wonder if we are going to be able to watch documentaries in any qualitative way on a computer screen. There's a certain jittery, squirrel like attention that we bring to a computer screen. The long form docs are supposed to be viewed as if you were watching a play or a narrative feature in a theater, or the way you would read a few chapters of a novel. They are contemplative events. We're not used to doing that on a computer screen with crappy sound.

Q – What are the common mistakes that documentary filmmakers make?

Jon – There's one practical mistake and one conceptual mistake that we see people make a lot. Audio is shit these days. No one takes sound seriously and they pay for it in the end. Oddly, most documentaries are driven by language but often we see people go out solo and not use a sound recordist. People have become so used to great cameras that make great pictures on autopilot and they confuse that with audio. It's not true. The on-camera mic doesn't work that well, and the mic attached to the camera is often not in the optimal position. In the broad area of what people are making films about, I see a lot of one-dimensional ideas. I see a lot of films with the premise that "life is hard" or that a particular eccentric will be interesting for an hour. If it's good try for more. Audiences are smarter than that and they want complexity and ambiguity and films that work on two or three levels at once. Simply recording something is no longer enough. Another beginner mistake is a lack of understanding of how important story is. I see people who are passionate about doing a film about globalization. *Darwin's Nightmare* is about that, but it's driven by a powerhouse of a story about a place and a cast of characters. Finally, somewhere somehow, filmmakers have gotten the idea that interviews and narration are bad; unfortunate, bad interviews are bad, and bad narration is bad, but the rest can be wonderful.

Q – What advice would you give a new documentary filmmaker?

Jon – Clarity, in all senses. Clarity about the story you want to tell. Clarity in how you are going to get the resources to make this movie. Clarity in what the film is not about. Clarity about your own limits.

GUERILLA FILM MAKER SAYS!

The Documentary Cookbook

In the early 2000's, The Center for New Documentary Graduate School Of Journalism, University Of California, Berkeley realized that the cost of making a documentary film had skyrocketed. They gave three well known documentarians $100,000 each and told them to make a project for a budget and then report back how they did it. The data collected formed a blueprint – or cookbook for filmmakers to follow in order to keep their costs down. Here are some of their findings, but for the whole story go to http://journalism.berkeley.edu/program/courses/dv/cookbook.html.

1. Choose the right story. Find stories that naturally lend themselves to low cost, not stories which will be compromised with short funding.

2. Back into it. Find stories and techniques that can be done with the money readily available, not with money which might someday be available.

3. Exercise Discipline. Be extremely careful and consistent at every stage of planning and production. Make the project all muscle, no fat.

4. Use small format digital video. Use DV/DVCam as starting point to reduce cost from ground up.

5. Exercise consistent technical protocol. Get video and audio close to right in the field.

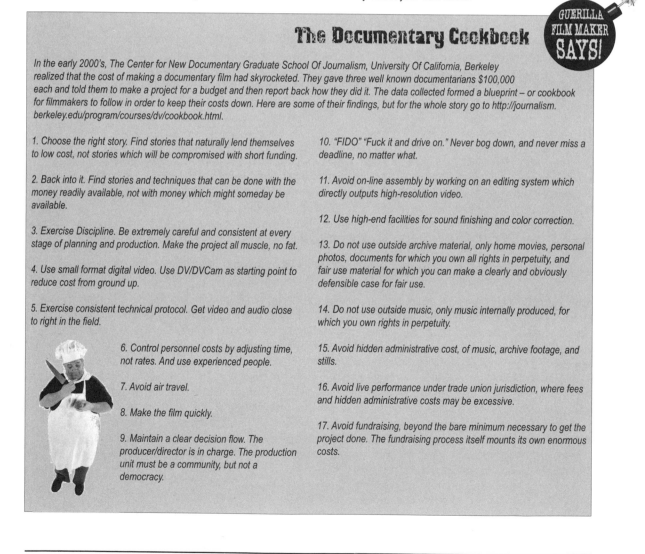

6. Control personnel costs by adjusting time, not rates. And use experienced people.

7. Avoid air travel.

8. Make the film quickly.

9. Maintain a clear decision flow. The producer/director is in charge. The production unit must be a community, but not a democracy.

10. "FIDO" "Fuck it and drive on." Never bog down, and never miss a deadline, no matter what.

11. Avoid on-line assembly by working on an editing system which directly outputs high-resolution video.

12. Use high-end facilities for sound finishing and color correction.

13. Do not use outside archive material, only home movies, personal photos, documents for which you own all rights in perpetuity, and fair use material for which you can make a clearly and obviously defensible case for fair use.

14. Do not use outside music, only music internally produced, for which you own rights in perpetuity.

15. Avoid hidden administrative cost, of music, archive footage, and stills.

16. Avoid live performance under trade union jurisdiction, where fees and hidden administrative costs may be excessive.

17. Avoid fundraising, beyond the bare minimum necessary to get the project done. The fundraising process itself mounts its own enormous costs.

European Documentary Training

You don't have to go to school in North America to learn how to make docs. Go abroad if you can and learn how others do it. At the very least it will give you a chance to find some life experience to make good films!

European Film Schools

The National Film and Television School
Beaconsfield, UK
www.nftsfilm-tv.ac.uk

Metropolitan Film School
London, UK
www.metfilmschool.co.uk

Brunel University
UK
www.brunel.ac.uk

Zelig School for Documentary, Television and New Media
Italy
www.esodoc.com

Maurits Binger Filminstituut
Amsterdam, The Netherlands
www.binger.nl

Netherlands Film and Television Academy (NFTA)
The Netherlands
www.filmacademie.nl

The European Film College
Denmark
www.efc.dk

PCFE Film School
Prague
www.filmstudies.cz

ESEC
Paris, France
www.esec.edu

The European Graduate School
Switzerland/New York/Germany
www.egsuniversity.org
www.egs.edu

Deutsche Film und Fernsehakademie Berlin
Berlin, Germany
www.dffb.de/

Workshops/Forums/programs

The Institute of Documentary Film
Prague, Czech Republic
http://web.docuinter.net/en/

IDFA Forum
Amsterdam
www.idfa.nl

Docs in Thessaloniki Pitching Forum
Greece
www.filmfestival.gr/docfestival

Discovery Campus
Germany
www.discovery-campus.de

European Films Crossing Borders
Spain
www.eufilmscrossingborders.com

Eurodoc
France
www.eurodoc-net.com
Archidoc at La Femis
France
www.femis.fr

Barcelona Film School
Spain
www.ecib.tv/inicio.htm

ESRA - École Supérieure de Réalisation Audiovisuelle
Paris, Nice and Rennes, France
www.esra.edu

APCVL - Atelier de Production Centre Val de Loire
France
www.apcvl.com

Docs Barcelona
Spain
www.docsbarcelona.com

Lisbon Docs
Portugal
www.apordoc.ubi.pt/

Cologne Film House
Germany
www.koelner-filmhaus.de/

Documentary in Europe
Italy
www.docineurope.org/

DocBiz
The Documentary Filmmakers Group and Skillset
UK
www.dfglondon.com

Film Farm
Poland
www.filmfarm.co.uk

Wildeye
Wildlife filmmaking courses
UK
www.wildeye.co.uk

Other programs/workshops and advice for Europe can be found at the following:

MEDIA DESKS around Europe
http://ec.europa.eu/comm/avpolicy/media/desk_en.html

EDN
www.edn.dk

THE DOCUMENTARY CENTER

Q – What is your job?

Nina – I'm the founder and director of The Documentary Center at George Washington University. I'm also a long-time independent filmmaker. As Director of The Documentary Center, I offer a six-month institute that draws students from all over the world. The vast majority of our students don't come from GW. We take students that primarily have been out of college for a while and many have some kind of post-graduate training, so the average age of my students is 26-27. They have been initiated into life and they have decided that they want to be a filmmaker. In addition to teaching the Institute, all of my independent films come through The Documentary Center. The University serves as the platform from which I launch my own documentary work. I usually make one doc at a time and I come out with about a film every year to year and a half. I also have a concurrent appointment at the American Film Institute - I'm the founding director of SILVERDOCS and each year contribute to the festival in some way.

Q – Does GW act as a funder or distributor for your films?

Nina – No, they don't fund or release any of my films, but all of my films carry the University's name. So I have a new film out this year and the final credit reads that it's a production of The Documentary Center at The George Washington University. And that credit goes on the film if it is a broadcast, theatrical, DVD or any other kind of release. In return, the University provides my office space, my legal counsel, they do all my billings – they provide a structure for me to make my films.

Q – Do they see any financial gain from this?

Nina – Sometimes they do. I made a film off an NEH grant and the university has recouped quite a bit of revenue from that project. The university also benefits from residuals or direct payments that I make to them for my work. And the tuition that the students pay goes to the University as well and it is substantial. Between $7,000 and $8,000 for the six months.

Q – What kind of classes can people take?

Nina – There's only one program so once you are in you go through the entire progression. I only take 15-16 students a year. And they come from all over the world, so it's a very diverse group. For the first few months they don't touch any equipment at all. They're purely steeped in learning the language of cinema. They learn a lot about visual literacy, about construction of film. They look at a lot of films. They talk about film conceptualization. We talk about screenwriting. It's a team-taught program, so we have various people come in from different specialties. Somewhere around March, we start technical training in lighting, camera and sound. They learn the Avid after they do a number of shooting exercises. Come May, the group decides on one topic on which they would like to make a film. Then for the last eight weeks of the program, the class brings that film to completion.

Q – Eight weeks is not a lot of time for production.

Nina – They work as a production team. So in that sense, you have more labor to throw against it. To be honest, my goal is not to make them proficient in production. I have been doing this for 25 years and every time I make a film I learn something else about production. It's more to get them to learn the elements of great storytelling and it's to get them to communicate with each other on their creative vision, i.e. *"How do you articulate and use the language of documentary film?"*

Q – What are the more important parts of storytelling that you convey to your students?

Nina – Same as you would in narrative. You've got to have great characters, some kind of story arc and plot points – something has to happen. There has to be some beginning, middle and end. There has to be some kind of transformative experience. And in some way, there has to be a "so what?" What is the film's point of view, perspective? You can make a film about people who go skateboarding, but that is only the topic - you have to know what is the film "about?" I think what my students get from me is being very sharp about knowing their own motivation, their reason for making a film, which may be the most important thing I bring to them.

Q – Do you ever have conversations about subjectivity and objectivity?

Nina – All the time. We talk about how objective can you be and how objective do you really want to be. Every film has to have some kind of POV. Every film has a statement that the filmmaker is making, whether he or she acknowledges it or not. As soon as the filmmaker turns on the camera and decides how he or she is going to shoot a scene and how that scene is constructed and how it is developed in terms of the storyline, it is all very much a construction. And the acknowledgement of that construction – the understanding of the intent of the filmmaker and what is the film trying to convey to the audience – to me is of primary importance. Which is why people who say that they just wait to see what unfolds is actually a self-deception or naïve, or simply untrue.

Q – So you are saying most people who start shooting a documentary film, consciously or subconsciously, know what they are doing.

Nina – Yes. Hopefully, they are following the path to tell a story. I work with Silverdocs: The AFI/Discovery Channel Documentary Festival. We get over 1300 submissions for that film festival a year. I will tell you that 900 of them are terrible because the filmmaker has just gone out and shot without regard for telling a story, of having some kind of intent. Then they get into editing and say, *"Now, I'll figure out what the story is."* It's like that old joke – *"There's so much horse shit, there must be a pony here somewhere!"* Well, unfortunately, they find that there's no story there after all, because they haven't thought about which way to turn the camera to make sure they came back with one. It's a real pity.

Q – Do you get into the business side of filmmaking, such as being able to pitch?

Nina – A little bit and I would say that my students always want a little bit more of the "how to." So we have a very extensive internship program. All our students are eligible and so they go work for independent filmmakers, National Geographic, PBS or other production organizations. We provide some great opportunities to get that real life experience during that six months and then we do some additional in-class work in terms of how you pitch, make a budget, how do you write a treatment for financing, etc. But again, my priority in these six months is to get them to learn about the creative form. The "how to" is such serendipity and ultimately has to do with having credits which none of these students do. So, it's more important for me to tell them how to define their vision such that they can articulate that vision, and perhaps take it to a more senior filmmaker and partner with them, or go out on their own and really get something going.

Q – What kind of equipment is available to your students?

Nina – They shoot DVCam. They shoot functional workhorse cameras because they tend to drop them. My feeling is, and in my advertisement I always say, *"In kindergarten they gave you a crayon and it didn't make you a great artist. In first grade they gave you a pencil and it didn't make you a great writer. Now you can get a DV camera and a desktop editing system, will that make you a great filmmaker?"* From my perspective, I could teach them filmmaking just as well by having them cut advertisements and photos from newspapers and magazines to tell a story. Obviously, we don't do that. We teach cutting on the Avid. OK, that's the state of the art. Big deal. It's so secondary to the act of actually engaging in the ideas and the process of what makes a great film.

Q – Do you discuss the post process beyond the Avid or do you say, "When you get there, you'll learn it."

Nina – I go through the whole post process with them. The online, the music composition, the scoring, sound mixing, color correction – all those things that filmmakers do. A lot of that can be done in the Avid at the rudimentary level so we have them do it. I am sort of a techno nerd when it comes to films so I don't want them to think that that work is not out there to be done.

Q – Do they have to get clearances for what they create?

Nina – No. My feeling is being in school is the only time in your creative life that you can take everything and anything you can find without regard for permissions. Their final film is not for distribution, so I say, *"Take what ever you need and try to make the best film you can."* There're two things that get in the way of you making great films – one is the technology because there are thousands of technical issues that need to be resolved on any shoot, and the second is rights. These two obstacles frequently preclude you from doing so much that when you are in a university setting, you should just be able to revel in the act of creativity. That is a huge ethic of mine. We did take one of the films that came out of one of the Institutes and we did purchase the music rights for that project and it did go into festival distribution. But that is rare. Mostly these are student works and they look like student work, so they may as well be as creative and expansive as possible.

Q – Do you think documentary filmmakers should go to film school?

Nina – I never went to film school. I got on the job training. I think my program balances spending two years of your life in film school that has a $100,000 price tag and a weekend workshop, which isn't enough. The Institute is a taste of what the filmmaking life is like and we encourage you to dive right in. Sitting around in film school talking about it, studying it, pretending you are doing it, is not sufficient. Students come out of film school and they all want to be directors. Well, as it turns out they become production assistants. What I've carved-out as my niche is that I take these 16 students or so and in a pretty short order it's trial by fire. It's very intense and it moves at a tremendous pace. It is sort of like the first two years of medical school where they just overwhelm you with information, so that when you get to the hospital you know basically where the spleen is. That's my approach to teaching documentary filmmaking. Like the film school students, my Institute graduates come out and are production assistants, but they didn't spend an extra year and a half finding out they aren't going to being directors right away. I feel this is a more honest approach.

Q – Do any of the students help you with your films?

Nina – Not really. Every once and a while I'll have them log tapes or make them production assistants. People give me a lot of money to make films and it's not a time for instruction or experimentation. My own film work is done by some of the best people in the profession. I don't see it as a way to educate my students. It is not playtime.

Q – When your students come up with ideas, do you encourage them to go towards one specific genre of documentary?

Nina – No. I teach all genres and really my own work has grown away from historical documentaries and more toward cultural documentaries – more sociologically based. The best test, in my view, is when they do their own film. Each student has to come in with three ideas. So you get about 48 ideas amongst the 15 students and then I force them to do what filmmakers do all the time: you take an idea and you formulate it and then you have to jettison it for one reason or another. I always have 10 to 15 projects in development at any given time. But I only make a film every one or two years. What that "weeding-out" exercise does is to force them to be incisive about how to choose a great film to make. Then they whittle down from 48 ideas to 3 and then they pitch those 3 to me and other members of the faculty of the Institute. I don't tell them what to do, but I help them identify what are the best topics for them. I try to help them see the problems and the opportunities in each one of their pitches. Then they get to decide. It's their movie.

Q – Is the director of the film the person who comes up with the idea?

Nina – Actually, that isn't how it works. Because they are so new at the process - and this is for me the method behind the madness - is that because they each bring something different and personal to the process, at that point there's no auteur. There's a sense of ownership ultimately by everyone who is in the Institute. By the time they get to the final idea, it's barely recognizable from the original idea - which is as it should be - it's now a much better, more formed idea because everyone has had input from their own unique perspective.

Q – Do you find that they sort themselves into the various crew roles based on what interests them?

Nina – We have six editors on the project. I always require that my students work in pairs because I want them to talk things out. Working together forces them to articulate their creative process. We have three teams of two editors and they take different portions of the films and they edit it and therefore they have to connect with each about vision and flow – and again the same things goes for the directors of photography, the producers and the writers. I have never had a year where somebody didn't figure out his or her strength. It always seems to work out.

Q – Who pays for the film?

Nina – We pay for everything. Sometimes they've gotten ambitious and have traveled to other cities to shoot. I don't put them up in nice hotels, but we will pay their mileage. Four people can stay to a room and we work it out.

Q – What are the common mistakes that you see a documentary filmmaker make?

Nina – Students and new filmmakers just go out and they shoot without any sense of intention of story or character development or storyline and they come back with hundreds of hours of footage and just hope that they can find a film in what they shot. They find out they're stuck, because they didn't shoot with any sense of what they wanted to say or do with the film. The craft of a filmmaker is to be in tune with the subjects, the subject matter, and one's own perspective in such as way that you create a piece of work that is an act of intention. What kills me is that young filmmakers get access to astonishing things and people and they bungle it. I think, *"How dare you for wasting that access!"* They think that showing up is sufficient enough, and it's not.

Q – What advice would you give a new documentary filmmaker?

Nina – I think you have to read a tremendous amount. Newspapers, magazines, books, philosophy, history – you need ideas. Nothing is as pitiful as a filmmaker who doesn't understand the notion of having an idea and how to develop it. People major in film as undergraduates and my feeling is don't do that. Major in science, history or philosophy and learn how to research and write. Most films come from some seminal idea and something that has sparked the interest of a filmmaker. And there's nothing like sharing or partaking in the ideas of others that helps you formulate and make your ideas more sophisticated. Also, to make a great film, you need life experience - so travel and engage in life. Working in a coal mine is better than learning the Avid at age 18. Life experience is huge in becoming a great filmmaker.

SUNDANCE LABS

Q – What is your job?

Shannon – I'm the Associate Director of The Documentary Film Program of The Sundance Institute. That's a program within the Sundance Institute that deals with supporting contemporary documentaries from around the world.

Q – What kind of support do you offer?

Shannon – It comes in a few forms. First of all through a film fund called The Sundance Documentary Fund, which gives grants to a number of films per year. And then through an associated program, The Sundance Documentary Labs, which take place a couple of times during the year. They are a space where filmmakers are brought together to receive assistance from peers in the field.

Q – How are you associated with The Sundance Film Festival?

Shannon – The Documentary Program is one program within the Institute, which stands beside the festival. The festival is an exhibition space. It is a platform for new films that are beginning their life in the world and the Documentary Film Program is a space for documentary films that are more in the process of their making. So one comes before the other in terms of the life of a film.

Q – What is the Sundance Documentary Fund?

Shannon – In 1996, The Open Society Institute, whose programs are human rights-oriented, had a fund for documentary film. They actually spearhead a number of international human rights initiatives and film just happened to be one of them. A few years into its existence the fund was brought into the Sundance organization and renamed The Sundance Documentary Fund with the thought that there are other energies and other tools within the Sundance organization that could be brought to bear, and end up providing more services to filmmakers. The chief one is the Lab program.

Q – What can a filmmaker get from the Fund?

Shannon – Chiefly - money. Now the fund is funded both by OSI and by The Ford Foundation. Sundance administers the money of these donors and funnels them to filmmakers. What Sundance does is identify the most exciting documentaries under our mandate that will receive funding in a given year. The mandate itself centers around human rights, social justice, freedom of speech and civil liberties. So we are supporting contemporary documentaries from around the world on these themes. Also documentaries that just by looking at them would have a possibility of a broad international audience, and that could have a viable theatrical life. That's an important distinction in documentary because almost anybody working in documentary these days has TV involvements of some kind. Either they have gotten money from there or that is where they are destined to go. Our interest as a film organization is to support work that is original, challenging, beautiful and artistically driven. That isn't always possible in every TV format.

Q – What grants are available to filmmakers?

Shannon – The Fund supports documentary in two phases – the development phase and as works-in-progress. There are very few funds that support works-in-development. The more common thing that we do is support works that are already under way, and actually most of the proposals we receive are from people that have begun a project and need further support, which is a typical scenario in documentary. The story has already begun and you have to catch up with it. That allows us to see what the film may become as we consider whether we would choose it above other films to contribute to. Also a person who has received support from us before can reapply toward the end of their process for supplemental funding if it is a question of crossing the finish line. There is a dollar amount at which you've maxed out at this fund, but until you reach that amount you can reapply depending at what stage you are at. So a development person can apply for a works-in-progress funding and a work-in-progress person can apply for a supplemental grant.

Q – How does one apply to the Fund?

Shannon – It is very easy. Go to our website, www.sundance.org and under Sundance Documentary Fund where all the specifications are laid out. It gives a little of the history and the philosophy of the Fund and the application procedures. You provide a little sense of what the film is that you are proposing, how you plan on going about capturing it, what your vision is for getting it out into the world, and a little bit about who you are, who your team is, and what have you done in the past. For instance, are you a filmmaker or are you someone who enters from a different door like human rights? What are your commitments so far and what makes you and your project so interesting in comparison of the thousand other projects we see in a given year? Out of the thousand, we fund about 20-25. We also want to see a budget and sample works.

Q – What would get you excited about a proposal?

Shannon – The first thing we look for is the appropriateness to our mandate. So this should be a film that compellingly speaks to contemporary human rights issues. The second thing is a sense of the film itself and is it going to be a film that rewardingly, artistically opens up its issues into beautiful storytelling and image making. Then the third thing is how does it stack up in the field of proposals.

Q – What are the monetary ranges for the three grants?

Shannon – The maximum amount you can make at the development stage is $15,000. $75,000 at the works-in-progress stage. But whether you're funded in one, two or three phases, the maximum you can get is $75,000. If for instance, you got $15,000 in the first round and $40,000 in the second round, you could still come back for $20,000 in the supplemental. You won't always get what you ask for. It is a matter of what your budget is and your need is, and what the selection committee decides.

Q – If a project is funded by Sundance, do you reserve any rights on the film? Does the filmmaker have to put your logo on the film?

Shannon – Every film that comes through the Fund is supposed to credit the Fund on the film print. And those supported at the Labs will also include a logo on the print. However, there is nothing required from the filmmaker besides that acknowledgement and some supporting materials at the end like some video cassettes, stills and a poster. This is an outright grant, so there are no rights reserved by the Sundance Institute or any guarantee of what may happen in the future. We all remain interested in the film and try to remain supportive, but for instance just because we fund something doesn't mean that The Sundance Film Festival will accept it and The Sundance Channel will buy it. But at the same time, we do all talk to one another and it is a good position to be in if you are supported by the Fund.

Q – What are the Documentary Labs?

Shannon – They are very similar philosophically to the feature film Labs, but different in the way they are administered.

Because it's a different craft. So at the feature film Labs, people will learn about shooting with actors who have come in for the exercises, to hone skills in blocking, or getting great performances. In our case, nobody shoots their project at the Labs. They will bring a work in progress and they are provided with an edit suite to work in, with equipment that matches their own equipment. They also get an assistant who can help them with the technical aspects, and advisors that we bring in to give mentorship. One lab is devoted to editing and storytelling. A second lab brings together documentary filmmakers and film music composers. We want people in different crafts to gain experience in working together. Filmmakers in general, because of budget, don't think about music until very late in the process and when they do it is usually too late to do anything interesting or really helpful. So the idea is that you not only begin thinking about it earlier, but experience working with someone and are comfortable with that experience, then you are more apt to factor in music at an earlier point. People in this setting aren't meant to stay together as creative partners, but it sometimes happens. One of the more important assumptions of the Labs, is not necessarily what may happen on this film or this moment, but what it does for you in the long term.

Q – How does one apply to the Labs?

Shannon – Eligibility to the Labs is limited to people who have been funded under the Documentary Film Program. There is not a separate intake process for the Labs. Once you have been funded by us, you are automatically applying to the Labs and we invite a few of those people every year to the Labs.

Q – What makes a great candidate for the Labs?

Shannon – Someone who is in the middle of a very interesting project that might go in one of several ways, and may face challenges in deciding where they go next. It is not uncommon that someone comes back from a period of shooting extraordinary footage and needs to figure out what next. It's often hard to step out of the film and back into the editor's chair with the objectivity required to make hard choices like that. So we can help them with those choices such as helping them figure out what the story is about. Where does it begin and end? What's the tone? What are the key scenes that you must have? What makes a good beginning?

Q – So someone who has a more amorphous project has a better chance of getting into a Lab than someone who has a clear idea of where they are going?

Shannon – Both things are good. It is fantastic to see someone who is full steam ahead. But the Labs ought to be an experience that will make a significant difference to the project.

Q – How long do the Labs last for?

Shannon – Each one of the Labs lasts for a week. Clearly you cannot finish a film in a week or score an entire film in that time, but what often happens is that people come out with a plan and are emboldened by the experience. They have validation and the experience of artistic concentration that is uninterrupted or unfettered by business considerations or daily things like making dinner. Your meals are provided and you're housed and all you are expected to do is be creative.

Q – Where do the Labs take place?

Shannon – At the Sundance Village, which is a resort in Utah just north of Park City.

Q – Can people come to the Labs multiple times?

Shannon – In theory, you can come several times for different projects as long as you are funded by us. It has happened that someone will come to the editing and storytelling lab and then come back to the composer's lab. Again, it depends whether they're the person in a position to benefit the most from the experience.

Q – In either the Fund or The Labs, does it matter what format the film is shot on?

Shannon – It makes no difference between film or video or any digital technology. In fact, almost everything we see is shot digitally. It might look like a million bucks or it might not matter. IMAX might be hard to accommodate technically. Someone may need to bump down to another format in order to edit. But that is an exciting prospect. I'd love to be challenged by it.

Q – Do you have to be an American or based in America to apply?

Shannon – You don't have to be an American to apply to the Fund and you can be an American telling a story about something in Africa – as long as it fits into our mandate. It is meant to be open and fluid. We also want to be a place within America where international voices can come home to roost. Documentary culture in America is pretty fragmented. There is scene in New York, a scene in San Francisco, etc. They have different dynamics involved and not always the most extensive international presence.One of the things that we're always trying to do for the Fund is build a greater synthesis of documentary thinking and activity worldwide. There are a lot of different contexts that people work in and in different national cinemas there are widely varying in their set-up, so that in one country you may have readily availability to a lot of public money and in another country there may be a lot of television commissions. Then there is a country like ours, where there is not much of either. So you end up with national cinemas that look different, and not necessarily for artistic reasons. What we hope for by supporting various films from around the world and by also bringing people together from different contexts, you will see some fertilization of ideas. An American can learn something from a filmmaker in Australia who can learn something from a filmmaker from Israel.

Q – What are the common mistakes you see documentary filmmakers make?

Shannon – Not having read closely what we are about. We are sent lots of fascinating things that we would never fund. I feel badly that people spend as much time as they do preparing those materials for us. I think a mistake that filmmakers make in the construction of their films, and far be it from me to say what is right for a film, because it just may not be a film for me, but I think it can said that people fall into received ideas on how to make a film, rather than exploring new possibilities that may not have been tried yet, or personal impulses. Very often we will get work in that looks extremely professional and significantly unexciting. Invention for its own sake is another extreme and maybe it is a vice, but invention that supports storytelling, narrative ideas, political ideas and helps you get to the heart of the story you're telling is what we hope for, and see very seldom. I think that to get inside of story and feel what it is about, and evoke the most important things about it on the screen, are more important than necessarily adhering to a standard of professionalism.

Q – What advice would you give a new documentary filmmaker?

Shannon – Stick with it. It is hard but please stick with it because these stories are needed.

GUERILLA FILM MAKER SAYS!

Sundance Labs

There are two main programs that The Sundance Institute offers documentary filmmakers. You have to be invited to participate and even if you get money from their Fund, that doesn't mean an automatic invite. Sundance will pick up your travel expenses and pay for your room and board so you don't have to do anything but focus on your project for several days. Go to www.sundance.org to learn about these two labs:

The Documentary Edit and Story Laboratory is an intensive week long program where documentary makers work with accomplished editors and directors on their works-in-progress. You work on your story, characters and dramatic structure. You are encouraged by your mentors to takes risks in order to move your project forward.

The Documentary Composers Laboratory is a four-day program that gives documentarians the opportunity to work with six composers from the Composers Laboratory in relation to musical score. Both sides are mentored by established composers and filmmakers as they tackle a component of storytelling that is often neglected.

DOCS ROCK HIGH SCHOOL

Q – How did the Docs Rock program start?

Thelma – It's a high school program which was initially created by Dr. John Ramirez and myself to reach out to kids about the form of documentary. We began by taking high school students onto college campuses, but we really wanted this to be very curriculum driven and embedded in the school system. Program officers from the City of Los Angeles Cultural Affairs Division were very impressed with the program and at the same time, the IDA proposed for it to be a program. There's a thing called The Percentage for the Arts in Los Angeles where when a developer comes in, 1% of that development fee has to go to the arts. Traditionally, it's been put into creating an art piece at the new development or it supported some sort of communal art thing. In our case, there was a San Pedro development and it was decided that 1% would go toward this project happening in the San Pedro High School. So we began the project with Tony as he's the AP English teacher there. My experience has been that traditionally the good storytellers in high school are English teachers. So along with Tony and John, our goal was to create a curruculum that would involved critical thinking and historical aspects that would meet state standards.

Tony – And we made sure it met the standards for Fine Art and English. What was so exciting about the program is that the standards for California had changed and this was the first class that met the new state standards. And meeting these standards helps the kids if they want to get into a State of California University or UC School.

Thelma – The other thing that we are aware of is that fads come and go. And if it doesn't have a place in the curriculum, principals can decide to offer it or not on a whim. So we need to make it into something legitimate and meet the state requirements.

Q – Are there other Docs Rock programs around the United States?

Thelma – Various school districts seem to want the content, but don't want to be allied with the International Documentary Association. And the IDA as a non-profit organization doesn't have the huge resources to fund a huge program across the country. We need to find an additional funder, so there isn't any Docs Rock across the country yet.

Q – This is a year long program. What is the first semester like?

Tony – The first semester focuses on history and critical thinking. It's an exploration of the fundamentals of art and that documentary is a hybrid of all seven art forms. We introduce them to *The Artist's Way* by Julia Cameron, and at the same time, give them a standard of documentary. Introducing cutaways and archival footage.

Thelma – Introducing the form itself and its elements so they can decode and deconstruct what elements go into a documentary film.

Tony – And that is also coupled with a portfolio piece where the students are paired with an artist in residence and they come up with a two to five minute work. Sometimes it's a vanity piece. It's interesting that documentary is becoming so popular that it's easier to make it more accessible. If you look at the history of documentary, the first ones were so dull. But with this new creativity that's coming out through media access, it's generated some interest and excitement within the students.

Q – How many students are in the class?

Tony – The average class size in the state of California is 40 to 1. So I can have as many as 40 as that is the legal limit .

Q – Do you have industry insiders come in to speak?

Tony – Yes, we have the Speakers Bureau where we invite people from the industry – documentary filmmakers, cinematographers, etc. – to come in and talk to the students on a regular basis about their experience and processes in the film industry. It's a vital part of the curriculum because students see on a practical level what is happening with filmmakers. I think it's essential for me as a teacher to tell them the truth. If they want to go into the film industry, I want them to go with eyes wide open. They are full aware of every facet of it and make their decisions based on that as opposed to an illusion of what they would like to happen.

Thelma – And filmmakers are willing to do this because these types of filmmakers don't make the films that they make unless they want to make an impact on an audience.

Q – So what is the second semester like?

Thelma – It is a filmmaking semester. The students each propose a documentary project. They select a few and they break up into groups. Tony varies the length of them usually around 15 minutes each. They write a proposal. They have to do a pitch. In those groups, once a proposal is decided upon, they have to make the project.

Q – Are they given a budget?

Tony – No. They get use of equipment and an artist in residence. They get tape and editing space. That's it.

Q – What do you teach them about pitching?

Tony – Everybody does a pitch in the first semester. I put them all into two circles – one inner and one outer and everyone has to present their pitch to everybody else. Then the kids vote on which pitch they liked the best. That person is then chosen as producer for that film, which will be the one produced for that group that semester – whether it's the portfolio piece or the longer piece in the second semester. In the first semester, I do what I truly believe to be a real work environment. I pick the groups. I tell them, when you get a job, you don't get an opportunity to pick who the personnel will be. You get who you get. I put them into groups of five and assign who is the producer. In the second semester, after the pitches and the pieces are picked, the kids have fallen into their expertise. Some realize that they really like to edit. Some find out they really like to produce or shoot. And it happens without fail every time. So at that point, when the students have selected those five pieces, the producers and their projects are for sale. They can negotiate and pick their team or people can approach them and say that they want to be on someone's team. Then they start on the films.

Q – What kind of equipment is available to them?

Thelma – Mini-DV. Tony has six cameras, which is a large percentage so there is almost one for every group. And these are consumer level Mini-DV. Unless they go to an affluent high school or a private school, it is doubtful that they would have the money for a PD-150 or a better type of camera. They work on Macs in Final Cut Pro. It is not an incredibly expensive outlay. But look at the quality of the image those cameras make these days. So they create their pieces just as any filmmaker would and they go through the dynamics of dealing with real people and real situations. In the end, they have to sit in the edit room and recreate a story. The wonderful part of this program is that there is a formal presentation of their work at the end of the year. They invite their subjects, friends, faculty and anyone else they would like.

Q – Is there any discussion about the business side of documentary filmmaking such as dealing with releases and music?

Thelma – My standard mantra is they have to have the rights for everything. Some festivals will accept high school students' work with non-cleared music, but usually you are signing a release form. So if the students want to go beyond the venue of that high school, then they need to clear everything. Tony trains them on getting releases and clearing any footage, music and pictures that they use. Does that happen 100% of the time? No. But at least they are aware of it.

Tony – Wendy Croley, the woman who does the music for *Cold Case*, came in to talk to the kids and she tells this great story of how someone didn't get the rights to the master and wound up paying hundreds of thousands of dollars and losing their job in the process. My students didn't even know that there was a financial and legal aspect to the music used in film. That is more powerful than Thelma or I saying it. When the class starts, I give them a letter stating that I am the executive producer. Everything goes through me. I can look at your production folder any time of the day or night to know if you have a shot list in there, that you have your release letters in there, that you have everything that you need to cover yourself legally. And when they start to film, the first thing we do is show them how to get a verbal legal release during an interview.

Q – Do you get into subjectivity versus objectivity of documentary storytelling?

Tony – Yes. All art is subjective and even though documentary is non-fiction, it is an art form. But depending on someone's journalist integrity, subjectivity could be fairly far away or it could be very much in your face. But no matter what film you see, it is someone's subjective opinion. So the first thing I do is empower those students to have an opinion and to firmly believe in it as long as they can back it up intellectually. They have to detach themselves emotionally and make some profound academic statements. That said, we encourage the students to do that very thing because we are dealing with a format that seems objective, but it really is subjective. Therefore they have to be as objective as they can and follow journalistic standards. They have to get their facts right and their statements backed up. It is more than just entertainment.

Thelma – What is really important in that first semester is that they understand the elements of storytelling both visually and in a sound way and construction through editing you create a story. In that, they are really able to decode messages. Once they know that, they are more than capable to go through and watch movies and have the ability to determine if it is objective or subjective. Then as viewers they can look at something and make an educated judgment on something. They pick up on visual key elements. I took in *Fahrenheit 9/11* and I was very surprised that they picked up on visual shots in the beginning that really sets up Michael Moore's perspective. That is very difficult for anyone, regardless of their age.

Tony – The reason why I get surprised that people are so impressed with my students, is that it just makes sense. If you treat them on an intellectual level, you force them into that kind of critical stress. They come up with it.

Thelma – And they are visually savvy because of what world they come form. Visual images bombard them all the time and they have to process them. And watching a movie is different than just seeing the images. They have to know that there is a difference. I got into an interesting conversation with someone who does animation for video games. Gaming has changed how people look at things. In animation, if you have a character that drops something, you would see the close up of the character, then you would have them look down and then maybe cut to the item that they dropped. In gaming, the way that they animate is that they don't give you any of those cues. It is open on how you go into that world and how you respond to something. So if a sword comes at a character, there is no sense that the character is looking up to see it coming at them. It allows them to have any response to it. So those students are visually educated differently than an older group of students. You have to train them to look at things differently based on the media.

Q – Do you notice anything that they have trouble with?

Tony – Organizational skills that are indicative of anyone their age. They are children and they are different people. But they are quite able to understand complex concepts. My kids were doing a film on drug addiction and local homelessness. They thought that when they went into this project that they were going to find some really true meaning and evoke a lot of emotion. And they kind of got swindled by one of their addicts. And the decision they came to was very Emersonian, *"Are these my poor? I begrudge the dollar the dime the cent that I give to someone I do not know."* That was an important life lesson because they learned in making a film that is what real life entails. That some people will just never be successful at living and these kids got it. I also tell them that to be an artist and really lead that life, it is constant. You never stop growing, learning or improving. You are an incredible technician and an insightful human being. And I have seen that with these kids.

Doc Genres

It seems there are as many documentary genres as stars in the sky, but here are a list of the main categories. Keep in mind that cinema verité and phrases like that are styles, not genres.

Criminal Justice – explores injustices, both on the plaintiff and the defendant side.

Pop Culture – Generally lighthearted in nature. Explores current or popular happenings from the past and present. Topics can range from all kinds of artists, to movies, TV, music and trends.

Exploration – Going places that humans rarely get a chance to see, usually scientific in nature.

Socio-Cultural – A wide-ranging genre. Usually encompasses topics of race, sexuality, women's rights and other inequalities as well as daily life of underrepresented cultures.

Nature – Chronicling the lives of our plant and animal friends.

Sports – Follows the heroes and villains of athletic competition. They usually are in conjunction with another genre. The Life And Times of Hank Greenberg is a sports and Jewish rights socio-culture mixture.

Political – Looks at and often deconstructs the goings on of government to find out why they do what they do. Can anyone say Michael Moore?

Travel – The on the beaten path version of exploration.

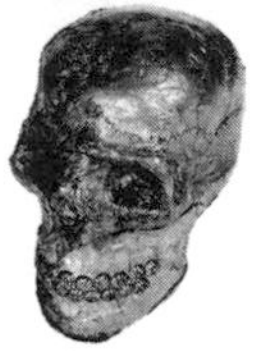

Historical - Looks at events from the past, uses a lot of interviews, archival footage and sometimes recreation.

Scientific - Anything from the natural or physical sciences to medical subject matters.

GUERILLA FILM MAKER SAYS!

Documentary Shorts Film Festivals & Websites

Festivals:

Palm Springs International Short Film Festival
Palm Springs, CA, USA
ww.psfilmfest.org

Yorkton Short Film & Video Festival
Canada's Golden Sheaf Awards
Yorkton, Saskatchewan, Canada
www.yorktonshortfilm.org

The Hollywood SHORTS Film Festival
Beverly Hills, CA , USA
www.hollywoodawards.com

***Cinematexas International Short Film** Festival*
Austin, Texas, USA
www.cinematexas.org

Toronto World Short Film Festival
Toronto, ONT Canada
www.worldwideshortfilmfest.com

Crested Butte Reel Fest
Crested Butte CO, USA
www.crestedbuttereelfest.com

***Antimatter Festival of Underground** Short Film and Video*
Victoria, BC, Canada
www.antimatter.ws

New York Expo
New York, NY , USA
www.nyexpo.org

Uppsala International Short Film Festival
Uppsala, Sweden
www.shortfilmfestival.com

Flickerfest
Sydney, Australia
(02) 9365 6888
www.flickerfest.au.com

Encounters Short Film Festival
Bristol, UK
www.encounters-festival.org.uk

Sao Paulo International Short Film Festival
Sao Paulo, Brazil
kinoforum.locaweb.com.br

CON-CAN Movie Festival (online)
Tokyo, Japan
www.con-can.com

Zinebi
Bilboa, Spain
www.zinebi.com

Hamburg International Short Film Festival
Hamburg, Germany
www.shortfilm.com

Websites:

Atom Films
www.atomfilms.com

Ifilm
www.ifilm.com

Hypnotic
www.hypnotic.com

BMW Films
www.bmwfilms.com

Cyber Film School
www.cyberfilmschool.com

Catatonic
http://www.catatonicfilms.com/films9/

Zap2It
http://alliance.zap2it.com

Nibblebox (animated)
www.nibblebox.com

Urban Entertainment
www.urbanentertainment.com

Bijou Café
www.bijoucafe.com

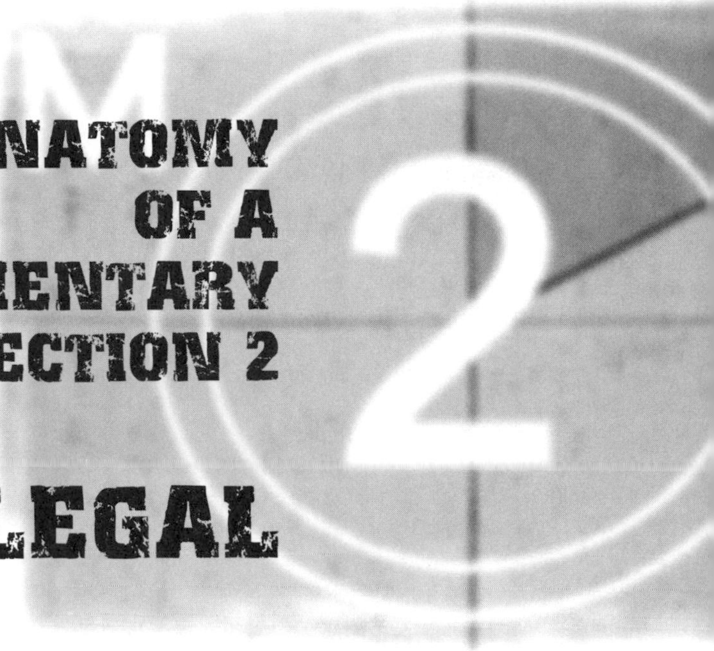

ANATOMY OF A DOCUMENTARY SECTION 2

LEGAL

SETTING UP A COMPANY

Q – Should a documentary filmmaker form a company prior to starting their film?

Stephen – Yes. I always suggest that a filmmaker do that for a couple reasons. Mostly because the filmmaker is going to be taking some one else's money to make their film - either a network, a motion picture company or an investor. It's important for the filmmaker to shield themselves from personal liability either with respect to the money or the content of the film.

Q – What are the kinds of companies they can form?

Stephen – Basically, there are two structures that get used. One is the corporation and the other is a limited liability company or LLC. They both have very similar if not identical benefits in terms of acting as a protection against personal liability. And in terms of the tax treatment, they can be easily structured so that they have the same tax implications and consequences. You want to structure them so that the money coming into the company isn't taxed until it comes out into the hands of the owner of the company – the member. Both of these entities are treated by the law as separate people. So the government will normally tax money when it's received by the company and then again when it's paid out to the shareholder. There's a structure called Subchapter S-Corporation, which provides that the government doesn't get two bites. LLCs are treated the same way. LLCs have become more popular lately. There are additional costs involved, at least in New York in setting up an LLC, that don't apply to a corporation, which can be meaningful for a small entrepreneur or filmmaker. It runs into the four figures in the process for setting up LLCs.

Q – Are there any differences in where investment in the companies can come from? For example, can only LLCs receive foreign money?

Stephen – I'm not a tax lawyer, but I don't think that's correct. It used to be that in order to apply for Subchapter S treatment, all the shareholders had to be US citizens and individuals. But I think that's no longer true. What's true is that the shareholders have to be individuals, but they don't have to be US Citizens. With LLCs, neither of those are true. The members, which is the functional equivalent of the shareholders, can be individuals, other companies, corporations or other LLCs – there are no restrictions in the nature of a member.

Q – Is it possible for someone to get a 501 (c) 3 designation and would you recommend it?

Stephen – It's very difficult to do it by yourself because what's involved for qualifying for a 501(c) 3 treatment not only involves setting up the entity, which is not that complicated, but it's a different kind of entity than the normal for profit corporation or the LLC. Beyond that once you have it set up there is a fairly elaborate IRS process that you have to go through in order to qualify. It's not magic or mumbo jumbo, it's just complicated. It's more advantageous to use a company that is already set up as a 501 (c) 3 organization and come in under their banner especially for a one off project. It's also very expensive. Those companies can receive grants on your behalf because they have non-profit tax status and then they will charge an administrative fee, which varies. Shop around and find the best one.

Q – Are Private Placement Memorandums, PPMs, used a lot in documentary films?

Stephen – The fact that a film is a documentary as opposed to a narrative feature film is not relevant to the applicability of the PPM. It's a mechanism by which money is raised for a film. They're used in circumstances where money is being raised from a number of potential investors. That process itself adds a certain level of expense as it's a form of securities offering and has to be done carefully. There's a body of law attached to those so you tend to do them in circumstances when you're talking about raising enough money to make it worth incurring the cost of them.

Q – Do you have any advice or tips on releases in documentary films?

Stephen – A documentary filmmaker needs to make sure that anybody who appears in their film, who speaks on camera – any interview subject – signs a personal release. Any Errors and Omissions Insurance carrier will require that you have them. In terms of the form, there're lots of them around and very often they need to be crafted for the specific circumstances of the film. Networks have their forms they like the filmmakers to use. There are books that have forms in them. You have to be careful. I have a circumstance now where a well-known documentary filmmaker is making a film and has been working on it for months. The network finally looked at the release that he had been using that I drew up and said that they needed it to say this and this, in certain language. So we will put it in. Sometimes they use the language, sometimes they don't. I usually choose not to for strategic reasons in terms of how the release is going to be used and the people who are going to be asked to sign it. Then I work on ones that change releases to make it happen.

Q – Would you recommend that filmmakers create deal memos for their crew?

Stephen – Yes. People are better off if there's a simple piece of paper that lays out what they think they've agreed to. They don't have to be complicated. I had a client the other day who had put together a one page, couple of paragraphs document that she gave to someone who was going to be her associate producer. It didn't work out. So it was one of those things where she said, *"I wish I had called you before so I hadn't had these problems."* We worked it out, it was not a big deal. But there should be a deal memo that says I will do this and you will do that; this is how much you will get paid; I own everything that you do.

Q – What things should a filmmaker be looking out for in a contract with a distributor or sales agent?

Stephen – What you want to pay attention to in such a document is what you're going to have to pay that person. If it's a distributor, are they paying you an advance for the rights in your film? Most distributors are wary about doing that especially with new filmmakers and documentaries. What kind of distribution fees are they going to charge? What kind of expense are they going to deduct? Is there any limit on the expenses? What territories are they distributing the film in? Is it worldwide? Just for Europe or specific countries? What kind of control does the filmmaker have over the kind of deals that get made? Do the deals require his or her approval? What kind of rights, if any, does the distributor have to edit the film? What about dubbing costs for foreign language? There are other things as well, but that's a good laundry list. For a sales agent who is going to go out and find a distributor, those terms are a little different. Normally, the sales agent will work on a commission – so what is that commission? That can range, based on who the sales agent is and what services they are providing, as little as 10% to up to 20%. But it could be more depending if they are providing legal services to negotiate and paper the distribution deals. With sales agents, they're going to probably take worldwide as their territory. With both sales agents and distributors, one thing you want to pay attention to is time. How long does the contract last? It should never be forever. Is there a term in the contract?

Q – What type of split can a filmmaker expect from the distributor?

Stephen – Their fee is usually between 25%-35% depending on the territory. 50%/50% splits are very rich to the distributor and rarely happen unless they are putting up production money.

Q – What is cross-collateralization?

Stephen – It's when a distributor puts up costs for more than one film, and does not pay out any revenue until all of the expenses from all of the films have been recouped. So if one film is selling like gangbusters and the other is a dog, you are not going to get money on the successful film until all of the costs on both films are earned out. The more successful film is carrying the less successful film. Normally one would resist cross-collateralized accounting. You want each film to stand or fall on its own.

Q – What percentage of the budget should a filmmaker set aside for legal expenses?

Stephen – Figure that the line item for legal will run between 1.5%-2% of the budget. I have seen slightly over if it's a very complicated budget and it can get up to 2.5%.

Q – When should a filmmaker approach you?

Stephen – Instantly. In order to structure the contracts right, in order to structure the release correctly, in order to make the necessary deals and that they're papered correctly, I think it's important for a filmmaker involved earlier rather than later. I recognize that there're economical consequences to that and that lawyers are expensive and budgets are limited. It's a legitimate concern. But it's to the filmmakers benefit to have a lawyer involved sooner rather than later.

Q – How is new media affecting distribution and contracts?

Stephen – That's the biggest moving target of all. Technology is changing so fast, it's hard to be specific about that other than to say as a practical matter, if a filmmaker makes a deal with one of the cable networks for example, the prospect of the filmmaker being able to hold onto internet rights is non-existent. No cable network is going to allow that to happen. They're just too important.

Q – Is it not possible for you to sell your own film off your own website?

Stephen – It's possible. But again from the network's perspective they're going to insist on having the internet and streaming rights and the video on demand rights. They aren't going to be willing to let the filmmaker compete with them in exploiting those rights. That's not to say the filmmaker shouldn't get paid for the exploitation that they do.

Company Pros & Cons

GUERILLA FILM MAKER SAYS!

Corporation

Pros:

1. Limited Liability
2. You may leave up to $250,000 in business account with no tax penalty.
3. Capital generation – i.e may sell stock, issue bonds, borrow money, mortgage assets or contract for financing.
4. Taxed at corporate rates, which are less than personal income rates.
5. The entity may live forever. No need to close a corporation if an owner or manager dies.

Cons:

1. Double Taxation.

Subchapter S-Corp.

Pros:

1. Limited Liability
2. Easy management; much less formalities than C corp.
3. Tax benefits and revenue pass through to the owners.
4. Corporate income tax payments are not required. Taxed as partnerships.
5. Early loss benefit. Corporations may operate at a loss in their first 5 years. Shareholders may benefit from a reduction in personal taxable income by receiving their share of corporate losses.
6. Self-employment tax is either reduced or eliminated.

Cons:

1. Shareholder restrictions – corporations, foreigners and partnerships disallowed.
2. May have 75 shareholders or less.

LLC (Limted Liability Company)

Pros:

1. Limited Liability
2. Corporate income tax payments are not required. Taxed as partnerships.
3. Early loss benefit. LLCs may operate at a loss for first 5 years. Members may benefit from a reduction in personal taxable income by receiving their share of corporate losses.
4. Shareholders can be corporations, foreigners and partnerships.
5. No limit on how the amount of members.
6. Members don't have to be US citizens.

Cons:

1. Life of corporation has a set ending date.
2. Some states will not allow an LLC to have only one member.

Q – Are you noticing sales agents being bypassed and filmmakers going right to the distributors or the public?

Stephen – No. That's not to say it's not possible, but as a practical matter, the likelihood of that happening in any meaningful economic way or in terms of reaching an audience, doesn't seem likely. You are competing in this welter of opportunities for the consumer so it's like vanity publishing.

Q – Is there anything else a filmmaker should be considering when it comes to contracts?

Stephen – It kind of goes back to when should a filmmaker get a lawyer? There's a universe that every filmmaker needs to be careful of. There are copyright issues. I have done a lot of work in Fair Use and copyright in documentary film, which is a very complicated area. And different kinds of issues come up with different films with different purposes. There is a whole laundry list of things to be aware of and that is why I say go to a lawyer as soon as possible. You need someone who has their eye out for the more obvious issues, but the peculiar ones as well.

Q – What are the common mistakes that you see documentary filmmakers make?

Stephen – Documentary filmmakers out of frustration take short cuts to clearing stuff. It's understandable, not because it's complicated, but it certainly qualifies as a pain in the ass. It's difficult to find who owns what rights and it may be expensive. It's like spring cleaning – nobody wants to do it. They takes their chances and don't clear things and hope that nobody will come along. That you see a lot.

Q – What advice would you give a new filmmaker?

Stephen – Try as much as you can to tell stories that you're really interested in. That sounds kind of obvious, but what makes documentary film wonderful when it's wonderful is that documentary filmmakers tell stories that they care about. They're really invested in it and want to tell their version of what they think is true. You want to try not to make a film just because it's there to be made. It's too hard and nobody is going to get rich making documentary films. So tell the stories that you're passionate about telling.

GUERILLA FILM MAKER SAYS!

Your Accountant

Documentaries just like features have budgets and you need to stick to them as best as you can. But when you are running around getting footage or dealing with archive houses, it can be difficult to keep your receipts in order. Consider hiring an accountant to make sure you're not going over in any area. They will need all your receipts and the budget of the film for starters. Make sure you hire someone who has entertainment or production experience so they know what all the phrases mean and can anticipate when problems or opportunities will arise.

Additionally, accountants can do things like set up corporations, handle the forms needed for certain tax relief schemes and of course, do your company's taxes when needed.

Michael Donaldson
Lawyer

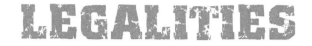

LEGALITIES

Q – When would be a good time for a documentary filmmaker to approach a lawyer for his project?

Michael – At the conception stage. The later you wait – it just drives the bills up. Find someone that you like and then stick with that person.

Q – When should people consider when hiring a lawyer?

Michael – The first thing a filmmaker ought to do is educate themselves about the issues they are likely to run into. If they are working on a movie with a lot of clearances issues, they should get a book like *Clearance And Copyright* to get them up to speed, so that when they go talk to a lawyer, they have the language and vocabulary to listen well and understand what the conversation is about. Also you'll not be asking fundamental questions at $400 an hour that you could have gotten out of a $25 book. I'm shocked at how many filmmakers think a one-on-one consultation with a lawyer is the best way to learn about the fundamentals of clearance and copyright. It is a waste of the lawyer's time and the lawyer might get paid, but they don't get a lot of satisfaction out of it. When a filmmaker is informed, they'll be able to separate the baloney from the real thing as far as choosing a lawyer is concerned.

Q – What is Fair Use and to what extent does it go?

Michael – Fair Use is a concept that exists in all copyright law all around the world. It recognizes the fundamental truth that every creation is built upon something that goes before it. Fair Use is expressly stated the United States where we deal with copyright as a property – as an asset. It's generally looked at as a defense. What that means is that if you take from other people's work you have to meet certain tests. One of the tests is that you have to do something different with it. That's called being transformative. For instance, you're doing a film on the rating system for the MPAA and you need to show certain scenes that cause movies to get certain ratings. You need to show those scenes to tell your story. So you have a right to go into those films and cut out those scenes and put them into your documentary. This kind of use is totally transformative. You have taken these narrative passages pieces and changed them into an intellectual examination of a ratings system. Another thing the courts look at is how much you took compared to the length of what you took it from. If you took five lines from my *Clearance and Copyright* book, it would be Fair Use no matter what you did with it. There are a lot of lines in that book. But if you took five lines from a haiku poem, there wouldn't be anything left. So it's the percentage of the underlying work that you take. And finally a concept that confuses a lot of people is replacing the market. For instance, if you take something that was shot for a news clip and use it on another news program you are replacing the market for it. Even if it's very fast-breaking news that is very important and raises public awareness, taking from one news story to use in another news story is not Fair Use. There are a couple of very clear cases on that around the taping of the Reginald Denny beating. Another example is the 19-hour Elvis Presley documentary where they took almost all of his appearance on *The Steve Allen Show* and put it in the documentary. That replaces the market for the original because it's just a repeat of *The Steve Allen Show*.

Q – What are some of the ramifications of breaking these three rules?

Michael – If your use of someone else's copyrighted work fails to meet the fair use test, you infringe their copyright. And their case is usually pretty strong because it's obvious that what you used came from their work. In fact, you admit that at the opening of the fair use argument.

Q – What if you license the footage?

Michael – Then it's a matter of contract law and whatever your license contract states is what is enforced.

Q – So if the footage that you take passes these three tests, then you do not have to pay to clear them?

Michael – If you have a legitimate Fair Use there's no requirement to pay anyone. If there were no fair use in the copyright law, no one would be able to write a very interesting critique. In fact the first Fair Use case some 150 years ago came up in that exact context. There was a very harsh criticism of a book and the critic used quotes to show how bad a piece of writing the book was. The author sued and lost.

Q – Does Fair Use cover music?

Michael – Yes, but music is very difficult because it's so much shorter. By the time you have taken what you want, you have taken a pretty big piece. Secondly, it's very hard to say that music is transformative as far as a film is concerned. There have only been a few cases where music survived the Fair Use test. Recently, the Beastie Boys won a Fair Use case where they intentionally didn't license the composition because they took only one note or three notes (depending on whom you talk to.) It amounted to less than 2%. The Beastie Boys had licensed the master, but didn' t license the composition.

Q – What should you be aware of when using photographs in a documentary?

Michael – When you bring a photo up you are showing 100% of it. Not good. And typically you are not transforming it – you are using it for exactly the purpose it was intended. So photos are tough. There was a case a few years ago in a New York court where they found a poster of a quilt that was up for a couple minutes in a TV show to be copyright infringement. But the court went on to say that if the poster was in a documentary about the museum or a documentary about the woman who made the quilt, it might have been fair use. So the door is open, but there are no cases yet. A picture in the background of an interview should be Fair Use.

Q – How was Morgan Spurlock able to use the McDonald's logo and advertising throughout Super Size Me and not pay a fortune?

Michael – You want to separate logos from copyrighted material. Trademarks are the opposite of copyright. In copyright, the owner creates it and owns it 100%. They can put it in their drawer and say nobody can use it. A trademark only exists through use. Trademarks are to tell people the source of whatever it is that they are buying. People make soap and put Ivory on it – that's a trademark and it is only good for that line of products. Look at the Universal logo. You see that and you know they are selling movies. But you could have a Universal Hair Salon. So a filmmaker can show any logo in a movie without clearing it as long as they show it accurately and it's being used the way it was intended to be used.

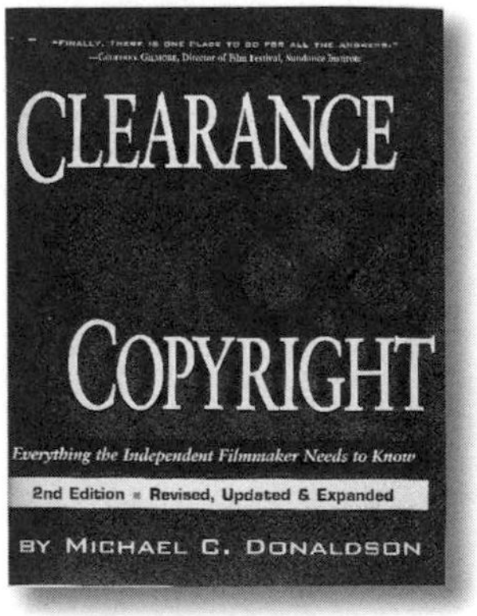

Q – Are there any privacy issues that documentary filmmakers should be aware of and can you probe public figures further than private figures?

Michael – The answer to both of those questions is yes. You want to think of privacy like a balloon. Private people have a very big bubble that you cannot get into. Public people who go out and try to get press have a very small bubble. If you run for President of the United States, it's like there is no bubble at all. And if you are President of the United States, your sex life becomes everybody's business. But if you are a very private person, the same information would be a real invasion of privacy. Privacy is about the expectation of a reasonable person. Defamation of character is part of this as well. That's when you say something that is not true in a factual nature that harms somebody.

Q – What is False Light?

Michael - False Light is a when you misrepresent someone. This all came about because Clint Eastwood was out having dinner with a woman and a reporter said he was having an affair. It wasn't true. The reporter said if people didn't believe it, then it didn't hurt him because it enhanced Clint's image as a leading man. But Clint sued and won. False light. Of all the ones that documentary filmmakers must be most careful, it is that one. You must be accurate in what you say, even if your inaccurate statement does not harm the person.

Q – What is De minimus Copyright Doctrine?

Michael – It is a kissing cousin to the Fair Use Doctrine. If you go into a courtroom and sue over 5 lines out of over 5,000, the judge will not even go through the analysis. It's de minimus. That means that it's too small to bother the courts with. There are some things that you should just let be.

Q – When do documentary filmmakers need to have signed releases and whom do they need them from?

Michael – You want to get them from the person that you're interviewing unless the person is a minor. Then you need to get it from their parent or guardian. Most insurance companies and broadcasters want to see those releases.

Q – If you get someone on camera giving you their permission to film them, does that hold up?

Michael – Absolutely. However, insurance companies and broadcasters like to see it on paper, even though the on-camera release is often better for court.

Q – If you're shooting an interview and there are people walking around in the background, do you need to get all of their releases?

Michael – In the example you just gave, the answer would be "no". However, broadcasters and insurance companies will often require you to get them. They don't want to bother with the litigation.

Q – Does E&O Insurance cover you if you break the Fair Use rules?

Michael – The answer is yes and no. It's handled on a case by case basis.

Q – If you've gotten someone's permission to use their likeness and then they change their mind, do they have any legal recourse?

Michael – They have a right to change their mind, but that doesn't cancel their permission. Too bad. The release covers it.

Q – What is the most common mistake that documentary filmmakers make?

GUERILLA FILM MAKER SAYS!

Exceptions to Limited Liability

Even if you have Limited Liability, there are times when an owner of a corporation or a member of an LLC can be held personally liable. Here are some of those instances:

1. If they personally and directly injure someone.

2. If they personally guarantee a bank loan or a business debt on which the corporation defaults.

3. If they fail to deposit taxes withheld from employee's wages.

4. If they are negligent in hiring or supervising their employees.

5. If they do something fraudulent, illegal that causes harm to the company or someone else.

6. If they treat the corporation as an extension of their personal affairs, rather than a separate legal entity. This might happen if you do not conduct your business in order to the formalities required of running a corporation or company.

Making a Contract

GUERILLA FILM MAKER SAYS!

Contracts are extremely important for they are often the only thing protecting the poor and downtrodden filmmaker. In its simplest terms a contract is an agreement between two or more parties to do certain things for one another, and if one party should fail to live up to their end of the deal, the contract spells out the penalties that will be imposed. You should always consult a lawyer to help you sort out the legalese that is needed to make a contract ironclad and always get everything in writing. A verbal agreement can often be disputed and could ultimately be worthless. Here are some other things to think about when dealing with contracts.

1. Remember a contract is just a piece of paper and if someone is intent on doing something which breaks the contract, there is nothing you can do short of legal action - something that you may not be able to afford, particularly if you're an independent film maker, and also something that the other party may realize to their advantage.

2. If money is involved, get as much up front (on commencement of contract) as possible. If you can get it on the signing of the contract, even better. You don't know what might happen a little down the line – your investor or distributor might die, go bankrupt, get bored etc.

3. ALWAYS have a contract for everything, even if it's between friends and family. Many friendships have disintegrated because there was no partnership agreement in place defining the boundaries of each party. Pay that extra for a lawyer to draw up a contract to save your friendships.

4. When entering a deal with a company where they will supply you with goods or services, make sure they put the quote down on paper and fax it or email it to you. Many deals have fallen through because the company employee who struck the deal with the production company has either left the company or died.

5. Follow your instincts – if something is too good to be true, it probably is.

6. ALWAYS sign a contract before work begins (especially with actors).

7. Read and understand all the text of the agreement, including the infamous fine print. Never sign right away, take the contract home with you and sleep on your decision. Beware of loop holes for in one section you may be given certain rights, but later on in the contract they may be taken away or nullified.

8. If in doubt, always consult your lawyer.

9. When you do consult your lawyer, make sure that both you and they absolutely understand how you will be charged (i.e. by the hour, by the half hour, a percentage of the film). You want to make sure that each time you make a quick phone call with one simple question, that you're not going to be charged for a half hour/consultation fee etc.

10. If push comes to shove (and, by that we mean you are in DIRE STRAIGHTS – the rent is due, you're hungry and your cat is dying...), and it comes to the choice of either signing a not so great deal and getting to make your doc, OR not signing and not making your doc, sign. You will walk away with a very valuable experience - your first documentary film. Remember, docs can have a long shelf life – you may end up seeing some money back in the long run.

Michael – They don't educate themselves on these kinds of issues until they're deep into it. They know all about the subject matter they're investigating. They know how to operate the camera and how to do the lighting and the sound. They can stretch a dollar until you can hear it squeal all across the country. And they just don't educate themselves on these clearance and copyright issues. That gets them into trouble.

Q – What advice would you give a documentary filmmaker?

Michael – Don't think you have to ask anyone's permission to go out and make a film. Pick up your camera and start shooting. If there is a story you want to tell, go for it. There is always a way to get your project finished.

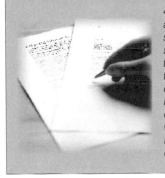

MUSIC RIGHTS

Q – How can The Rights Workshop help documentary filmmakers?

Brooke – We provide music supervision, music licensing and clearance. We do film clearance, art clearance, photography clearance image and likeness. We also do composer contracts, and represent two new music record labels but we mainly pertain to music rights issues.

Q – What type of music rights are there that a filmmaker should be concerned about?

Brooke – There are three types of music that are used in a film. One type is created by a composer and that should be a work for hire agreement, the other is using a music production library which you usually get in post-production houses and the third way is by using commercial music. That's in the order of how expensive it is to acquire that music. Commercial music tends to be the most expensive and the reason why is that there are two permissions that need to be granted. One is from the songwriter from the song, the second by the performer of the song. To get permission from the writer, you have to go to a publisher to ask permission and a quote is generally given. The performer permission, which is called the master right usually comes from the record label. You have to request it, get permission and receive a quote for it. That's why commercial music is the most difficult and that's why most people use our service. We have good relationships with record labels and publishers that help us either get or tell you very quickly if you can get permission to use these songs.

Q – Of the three examples, which one would you say is the most common to a documentary film and what problems could arise if you don't clear something?

Brooke – I can't say which is more common as in general documentary filmmakers should use a composer most of the time. The problem that documentary filmmakers have more than other filmmakers is that when you're recording on the spot, your microphone is open and you can inadvertently record commercial music. You're still going to have to clear that if you decide to use the clip in your film. So if you're walking down the street taping your subject and there's a Bruce Springsteen song going on in the background and you pick up that song, you're going to have to pay for it. The only time you're not going to have to pay for it is when your lawyer could explain in court that it comes under the Fair Use waiver. But other than that, you're going to have to clear that piece of music and that's when documentary filmmakers really get into trouble.

If you don't clear something you can get something that's called a "Cease and Desist" letter, which means you need to stop using that piece of music in your film and you need to take it out. The cost involved in that is usually a penalty that arises out of using that piece of music and can range from $1500 to $7k to $24k. That fee is based on how many times that film has been exhibited and the medium in which it's being used. Then there's additional cost of actually taking out that piece of music – you have to go back into the edit suite and substitute it in with something. Also if you base your whole film, like the guy who did the Nirvana documentary, on a band and you don't have clearance or permission from the estate or the composer then the whole film is going to be all for not.

Q – What are your thoughts on Fair Use?

Brooke – I don't rely on it. Fair Use for music is an entirely subjective decision. And that decision to claim something might be Fair Use needs to be looked at on a very individual basis. So you can't say, *"I only used four notes from something. I don't need to clear it."* That's simply not true. I've had to clear four notes of Herb Albert before because it's undeniably Herb Albert. It has nothing to do with how many notes you're using. It has to do with if that song is identifiable, is it pertinent, is it pivotal. As a music supervisor, my job is to administer the position of the lawyer who's overseeing the film. If the lawyer says it's not Fair Use, that's when I come in and have to clear the piece.

Q – When you clear something, are you usually clearing it in perpetuity or is it for a certain amount of time? And does it matter whether it's for theatrical or DVD?

Brooke – It totally depends on what the medium is, which could be television, cable, art house theatrical, theatrical, DVD, home video, internet only, conference only, in flight, military bases, etc. There are so many different mediums out there it's incredible, so when I do clear music for a documentary filmmaker, generally, unless the film has been picked up by a distributor already, we do a film festival license with an option for other mediums. Or we do an option for all rights in perpetuity, as sometimes it's more cost effective. It depends on who the client is, how big their pockets are and also where they think their film is going. If their film is going to PBS, then they don't even have to clear the music as the Corporation for Public Broadcasting agreement covers it. But when you have a show air on PBS, generally PBS wants to repackage those shows for DVD. So when you air them on PBS then the only rights you have to get are home video rights for DVD. Or maybe it might be public television outside the US. If that's the case we clear a) the home video/DVD rights and b) the public television outside the US. In those cases DVD rights aren't that expensive. They can range from a few hundred dollars up to a thousand dollars per license. Outside the US, public TV tends to be a lot more expensive but it just depends on where the client is going to be exhibiting their films. So price is entirely dependent on exhibition.

Q – Say you made the mistake of putting in music that you just couldn't clear and now you have to replace it, in your experience have you found that doing this can hamper the sale of the film?

Brooke – I've never been on the sales side so I'd have no idea if it's actually hampered a sale. However, I've been in the situation where a film was sold with a song in it but we did have to take it out. In that case, the filmmakers got the composer to do a song that sounded just like it or we did everything possible to find a song by that artist that we could clear. If HBO likes something with a piece of music, they'll put up the money for it. So it depends who's getting the film.

Q – When filming, your subject starts singing a song – what rights would you have to clear for that?

Brooke – Only the publishing rights or what's called the synchronization rights because the master rights are owned by the person performing it - your friend on camera. You don't have to get permission from them, just a release.

Q – How much is it to clear 'Happy Birthday'?

Brooke – *Happy Birthday* must always be cleared but again it depends on the media. For a film festival it could probably be $500 for one year. For television in the US, it's probably about $1,500 for five years. Outside the US, probably the same. But it also depends on the budget of the film. If you're talking about a major Hollywood motion picture, then you're probably talking about $2,500 or $5,000. But you don't have to generally clear the performance of it, you only have to clear the publishing of it as in a documentary it'll be your subject singing it.

Q – If a filmmaker is making a documentary with lots of music, would you advise the filmmaker to approach a company and make a deal with them early on for clearing the rights?

Brooke – I would say you have to clear the music before you finish the film because you have to know if you can use the song. There're very few films that become moneymakers right off the bat, so I think the licensors, if they're smart and they know that it's being distributed by someone big, they might ask for a step deal where they get a certain percentage if you go over a certain amount of sales. Right now I'm trying to get someone to use a Duncan Shiek song and who knows if he becomes the next big hot thing, next year it'll be a lot more expensive. So yes, it's better to do it ahead of time.

Q – What are some of the things a music supervisor can you do for a filmmaker in suggesting music?

Brooke – A good music supervisor will be able to make good suggestions that will be helpful to support the emotion of the film. First of all, the supervisor should get along with the filmmaker as this is a creative process and there needs to be a lot of respect given to the music supervisor. But a good music supervisor would be able to help provide the director with the right sorts of music they need but they'll also know their prices. So no music supervisor is going to suggest a Ben Harper song when he doesn't license his music in film and TV. If you get somebody like that then you're doomed, as then you can't trust them on anything. Why would they get you excited about something if you can't use it? So be careful - if you use your best friend because they have a cool record collection the reality is that person might not understand the whole licensing process, how to acquire the rights and the nuances involved on getting a musician involved on a project. I was talking to a filmmaker today who was hesitant on bringing a music supervisor on board, but the director is getting in such a crunch that they can't actually see straight due to editing. So if you can't get a piece of music that you like, what you can do is go to a music supervisor and within 24 hours they should be able to turn around and give you some other options of other songs that you can use at a decent price. Another great thing about a music supervisor is they can get you deals like getting you a great song before an artist has hit and therefore it's can cheaper.

Q – Do you help find composers?

Brooke – Yes, we can suggest composers.

Q – Is it common for documentary films to have music supervisors?

Brooke – It depends on the size and level of their documentary. I've worked on *Ballets Russes* as a music supervisor and we cleared 90% of the music, I worked on *The Devil and Daniel Johnson* and it was my relationship with the publisher that enabled them to get a deal with the publisher in 24 hours at a super price.

Q – When should a documentary filmmaker approach you?

Brooke – For music supervision, sooner than later. Most people go to a supervisor in post-production and that's OK. If you can go earlier, that's even better. Same goes for rights clearances. Although it depends if you're doing a documentary on a particular musician or artist then you're going to want to do it sooner because you'll want to make sure you're going to get that music. We're working on a documentary project right now on buying guitars and guitar collectors and I've just tried to clear the *Immigrant Song* by Jimmy Paige and Robert Plant. He has three people in a recording studio recording the song and we just got the "no." If he'd started a month ago, he could've gotten another song. He can use it in the soundtrack, but he can't use it in the film. Things are rejected for two reasons – money and contextual reasons like religion, violence or sex.

Q – Do you negotiate a soundtrack and are they popular for documentaries?

Brooke – Some are and it depends on the film. Yes we do soundtracks. It's a little different but it can be done. It's done with a record label in mind. It does get cleared afterwards but what's interesting is when you're doing a soundtrack you want it to be released at the same time as the film. Record labels need at least 6-8 months before the film's release to put a soundtrack out so you need to have that time in order to clear it. We're doing *The Devil and Daniel Johnson* and there's a soundtrack for that and we're trying to get that out at the same time. It was shown a year earlier at Sundance and there's time there to put a soundtrack together.

Q – Who pays for the soundtrack?

Brooke – The record label. They'll give an advance for the royalty-bearing artists on the soundtrack and to the producer/director. Those percentages range from 3% - 5% for the producer.

Q – What kind of a fee should a filmmaker allow for music supervision?

Brooke – For all music in the budget, I always say you should allow 10% of your overall film budget towards music. That includes music supervisor, music composer and all licensed music.

Q – When you're done clearing everything, is there any paperwork that you have to give to the filmmaker and distributor?

Brooke – Oh my God, my whole desk is paperwork! Everything I do is via fax and email and everything has to printed up and documented. Nowadays, distributors want double signed contracts and it's becoming harder and harder for me to get that from the companies. All they want is their money and they don't give double signed contracts. The filmmakers get a draft memo that's a sign off with the quotes on it, as they need that for their E&O on signoffs. But all the rest of the stuff, research material etc., we don't give them that. We do music cue sheets for certain clients who request them. Usually that's the editor's job but we've done them! They're incredibly important!

Q – Would you recommend using public domain songs?

Brooke – Yes. People can use public domain songs that are free and clear. The only pitfall is to make sure that it's public domain. If it isn't, then you have to go and clear it. You might have to pay for the research on it so to make sure that it is but in essence you really should make sure that it is. You can go to publicdomain.com to check out what's in public domain.

Q – What are the common mistakes that you see documentary filmmakers make?

Brooke – I always feel sad when filmmakers do this, which is not hiring a music supervisor. Because when a filmmaker comes in to see me and they've started to do music clearances themselves, they tend to get higher rates and they tend to have not done it in a straightforward fashion. So they come in to us to almost clear up the mess they've made and it's almost more work for me to step into a project halfway. And I've also seen some filmmakers come in with licenses in place where I've gone, *"Oh my God! You've actually contracted for this amount, I can't believe it!"* Because they don't realize that when you go out and request a license, that person comes back with an answer and a figure but that's still negotiable. It's not something that you actually have to take as the end all price. So the biggest mistake is had they worked with someone like us and paid a little bit of a fee upfront, a) it would have alleviated the frustration that they feel from trying to get these things and b) they get it at a much better price. People hire us and pay us sometimes to get things for free!

Q – What advice would you give a new documentary filmmaker?

Brooke – Don't spend too much time on your subject . You want to know your subject matter well enough to do the task and tell the story, but remember there's life! A better piece of advice would be breathe!!!!

GUERILLA FILM MAKER SAYS!

Music Rights

Synchronization Rights - the right to use music in conjunction with a film where the music is synchronized against the picture. These rights are obtained from the songwriter or composer via the publisher.

Master rights – the right to use an existing sound recording of the music in a film or television project. These rights are from by the performer and are given by the record label.

Work for hire – you contract and pay a songwriter or composer to create original music for your film and in doing so, you own the rights and therefore don't have to get anyone's permission.

Try to get licenses in perpetuity and for all markets and windows (sometimes called a "buy out"). That way you will never have to renegotiate for the rights when their prices may have gone up.

Release Form

Here is a sample release form from the documentary film, Backyard Racers. You will need to have your subjects sign some version of this document so you can use their likeness in your film without them sueing you. Or, it gives you some protection if they decide to sue you anyway! Remember that this is a sample and that the release for your film may need special language depending on whom and what you're filming - so consult with an attorney before using any release. The more specific your release is the more protection you have, while the more general, the more adaptable it is for other situations. Also, try to get people's releases BEFORE you start filming. Otherwise, they may disappear or refuse to sign unless compensated in some way.

RELEASE FORM

Project: BACKYARD RACERS

Company: Crazee Pictures

Shoot Date: 3/19/2005

Performer Name: ______________________

Social Security #: ______________________

Address: ______________________

Address: ______________________

Phone/E-mail: ______________________

In exchange for good and valuable consideration, including but not limited to your appearance in the documentary film (as defined below), the receipt of which I acknowledge, I hereby consent that the above named members of Crazee Pictures ("the Company") may use my filmed/videotaped/performance in the documentary film identified above (the "Film"), including any edited, revised or modified versions thereof, as well as my name, voice and/or likeness, for purposes of advertising, distribution, broadcast or other dissemination and in trade in any and all media anywhere in the world at any time without limitation.

You hereby agree that the Film is a work made for hire for the Company listed above. The Company shall own all the rights therein, including without limitation any copyright therein, throughout the world and in perpetuity, fee of all claims from you. In the event that the Film is not deemed to be a work made for hire, you hereby transfer and assign all of your rights in the Film to the Company.

I hereby waive any right that I may have to inspect and/or approve the finished product or the treatment that may be used in connection therewith or the use to which it may be applied.

I hereby release, discharge and agree to save harmless the Company, their legal representatives or assignees and all persons acting under the permissions or authority or those for whom they are acting, from any liability by virtue of blurring, distortion, alteration, whether international or otherwise, that may occur or be produced in any processing tending towards the completion of the finished project.

I hereby warrant that I am over the age of 18 and have the right to contract in my own name in the above regard. I state further that I have read the above authorization and release, prior to its execution, and that I am fully familiar with the content thereof.

Actor: ______________________

Guardian Name: ______________________

Guardian Signature: ______________________

Date: ______________________

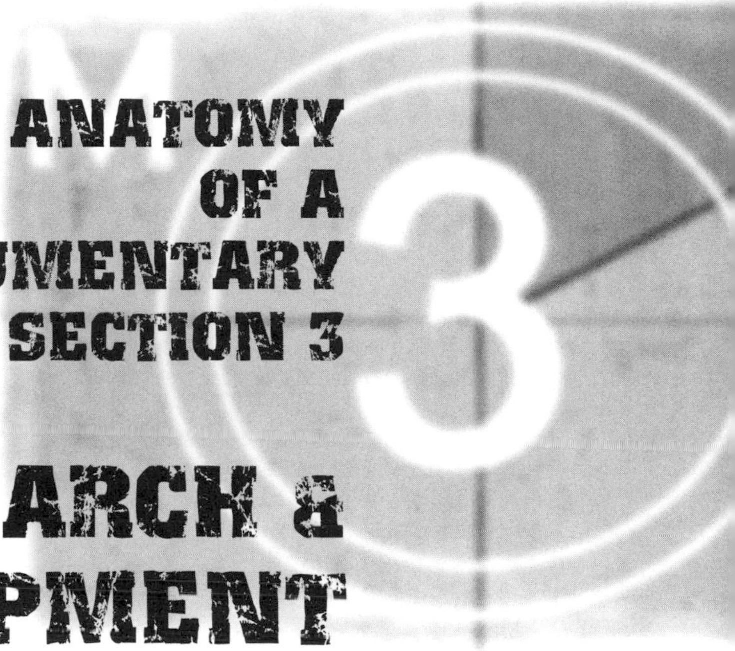

ANATOMY OF A DOCUMENTARY SECTION 3

RESEARCH & DEVELOPMENT

Fernanda Rossi

THE DOCUMENTARY DOCTOR

Q – How do you define doctoring?

Fernanda – Doctoring is interactive troubleshooting. First you spot a problem and help the filmmaker see it. Then you explain why it happens and present tools that will help the filmmaker find solutions consistent with his or her vision. This process is in direct opposition to just presenting solutions unilaterally. Out of fear, insecurity and other things, we get a committee of people around us who make decisions for us, rather than getting people to educate us on how to make better decisions by and for ourselves. I put extra effort in not taking the power away from filmmakers by imposing my vision to their film. It's about how I can be an instrument for change and improvement.

In order to work interactively, sessions are in person and they take all day – as opposed to on the phone, a couple of hours. When filmmakers look for help, they'ill be better off with a methodology that will empower them rather make them dependent on somebody's "expert" advice. I prefer to ask questions and listen attentively. That takes skill, patience and to be egoless, but in my experience the end result is much more satisfactory for the film and everybody involved.

Q – What's the difference between getting opinions, getting feedback and doctoring?

Fernanda – Opinions are what people say about a film from an emotional place. It's an emotional reaction that's immediately rationalized or justified. Someone may like something or not and they tell you why – though that "why" doesn't follow a strict methodical analysis necessarily. I think that opinions are useful for developing marketing strategy. When you get an opinion you're realizing whether that's your target audience or not. I don't think opinions are bad, I think they're just misused. When someone says that they don't like a certain part of the film, I don't think people should change it. They should ask themselves, What are the characteristics of this person? Is this my target audience?

The second tier is where most consultants fall into – feedback. Feedback is useful. It's a step above opinions because they're not only telling you how people feel but rather what they think is or isn't working. They can be sometimes more precise and technical in their approach. I think it's still misleading because it's still putting the center of attention on the other person. But it's useful because sometimes you get lost and it's good to have an outsider saying, "This is the problem". Unfortunately, as soon as we put the authority on someone else, we lose.

My suggestion is that we have to remain quiet and listen to answers from the inside. I help people to find their voice rather than tell them what I would do. My answers – and any outsider's answers - will be limited compared to the research that a filmmaker has done for his or her own film.

There's another type of feedback: those who have gone through the same before you, namely other filmmakers. But they've already attached a sense of success to a specific methodology. If I call a famous filmmaker for feedback, he or she has already a way of doing things that has worked for him/her. So to this filmmaker there are one, two, three ways of doing things that have proven infallible for her. Personally, I've seen all kinds of people succeed with their own method or strategy. In this business you have to be willing to try, be wrong and try again. The minute you are working by formulas – especially other people's formulas – you lose your personal vision and voice. And then, can we call that "our" film?

RESEARCH & DEVELOPMENT

Q – Since most documentaries rarely have a script, isn't it easy for people to get lost?

Fernanda – Yes. Every film is uncharted territory and it gives us that sense of utter despair when we're half way into making it. Opinions are easier to dismiss if we disagree with them, but feedback is much harder to turn down. Because if you're really lost, any lifesaver that they throw at you, you'll grab onto it. That's why I think feedback is so dangerous, it gives you that false feeling that you have resolved something. For real definite solutions you have to dig deep.

Q – When do people usually approach you?

Fernanda – Some people call me as soon as they have an idea. They want to see if it's viable and what it would take to make it happen. That's a very small percentage. Most people come when they have shot some footage and they want to make a trailer or plan for the rest of the project – brainstorm on where they story could go and prepare for that. They also might want help knowing how to fundraise. That's about 20% of people.

Some people call me when they're about halfway through their shooting. They've shot 70 hours and they still don't know where they're standing with the story. That's another 20%. And then the remaining 50% is divided into two groups. Those people who are about to start and want to maximize their post-production budget by not getting lost in the cutting room where they're paying $2,000/week. And those who've been in the cutting room for several weeks and they still don't have anything to show. Or they might have a rough cut but it's not what they wanted.

Also, some people call me after all festivals have rejected them. They've received the same consistent feedback. Unfortunately many times they don't know what to do with such feedback because they're either dealing with a great deal of anger regarding those rejections or are unable to figure out how to transform that feedback into a tangible plan of action. I'm happy to say that in those cases once they've got over the frustration of having to go back to the cutting room, a few structure tweaks landed them into several festivals and even got them a theatrical release. So I join projects at several stages. The nature of what I do changes depending on the phase the film is on, but the methodology is the same.

Q – Do you find that the number of documentaries has increased since the DV revolution?

Fernanda – There're definitely more documentaries being made, although I don't think the films are necessarily better because of it. So the pyramid is just bigger, but it's still a pyramid. There's a small percentage of good films, a larger chunk of
of confused directors! People are just shooting and shooting and not thinking or taking responsibility for it.

Q – What is your process once they hire your services?

Fernanda – People contact me via e-mail and then I send them a questionnaire, which helps me evaluate if I can help them. Some people are not helpable and they don't want to be helped. Then we talk on the phone, discuss the main problems with the film and I explain how I work. If that's what they are looking for, we set a date for an in-person all day session. There, we start with some exercises and depending on the stage they're at, we either do a scene breakdown or story development or whatever needs to happen. And then at the end of day, we do a plan of action. The session includes four weeks of phone support so they can keep asking questions while they're making decisions.

Q – How can you tell if somebody can be helped? And if they can't be helped, what do you do?

Fernanda – Both the questionnaire and the phone conversation tells me if that person and I can work together. I take for granted that all films can be improved no matter the state of it if the person is ready.

There're two types of people who aren't ready for a consultation or aren't suitable for this method. People that want to consult to get approval and those who want to prove to me they know better. In the first case, they don't seem to have any problems with the film. They just want me to watch it and get my… I don't know… blessing? Well my opinion on a film doesn't really matter, I only work with filmmakers who need help. I tell them their film must be great and I'll see it at a regular screening like everyone else.

In the second case, they usually say something like, *"I'm a very experienced filmmaker and I'm having some issues. I don't know whether you can help me."* And I say, *"You're right. I don't know if I can help you."* Those are people who are transferring their fears or anger to others. They're looking for someone to fight with and I don't need to be the punching bag. Most of the time they're just frustrated. Or they've had some tough things said to them. They're defensive. If I see I can work around those emotions I might go ahead. If they only want to prove that they know better, that's ok we don't need a whole day for that, a few minutes on the phone are enough.

Q – How much do you charge?

Fernanda – It varies. A script doctor in LA can charge $1,500 and up for a one-day session. I'm way below that. Even after several consultations I'm in the low four figures. But I'm flexible and I throw in a lot of perks. Let's say someone is really struggling, then I invite them to my lectures and seminars for free. The average filmmaker saves in the range of the five figures after working with me because they cut down the production and their postproduction time significantly. Unfortunately, this is only evident after they are done, but it also means I get a lot of repeat clients.

Q – Do you travel to your clients?

Fernanda – Yes. I'm based in New York and travel to LA five times a year. I also lecture all around the country. People know this in advance and book sessions in their towns or travel to NY or LA.

Q – When a filmmaker gets an idea, should they stop to do research or jump in and begin shooting?

Fernanda – I think it depends a lot on the deadline of the topic. And the funny thing is all filmmakers think their film has an immediate deadline. There are some things like the Kumbamela in India, which happens every 12 years, so you better get on the plane now. Then there are the imaginary deadlines. The problem with making imaginary deadlines real is that the grant makers and everybody around them know better. In my book, I spend a lot of time talking about making the film in your head. And the more you make the film in your head the more things will flow. There's something funny about us humans, we resist change and the unknown. So if you chart the territory, you will go much faster –we fool ourselves into believing is not that unknown after all. I have a few exercises in my book on how to work with that. I don't believe in scripting a doc, but I do believe in seeing yourself making the doc. That is, foreseeing the possibilities and expanding the scenarios and storylines.

Research is a tricky thing, too. It can become a writer's block. You always believe that you have to research one more thing. So the key issue here is balance – listen to yourself. Have I truly researched enough? Or am I getting blocked and research is a safe place? That situation can be avoided by envisioning yourself in the process. I do that when people get scared to release the film. It is the fear of exit 5 – one of the five points where people can drop the film. They're delaying locking picture because they know that the next step is going to be a challenge for them.

Q – Is there anything filmmakers should think about before they begin their film?

Fernanda – Yes. Why they want to make it and what they expect to achieve. All throughout the making of the film, filmmakers fear that there's no story really or the story is not good. It comes up in a number of questions. People want to be certain that they are investing their time, money and enthusiasm into something that will be successful. Success means different things for each person. No matter the definition someone is going by – awards, money, etc. - there're many variables that determine such success and we have control over only one of them – the product. We have no control over the other variables: other films in the market, the need of the market at that moment, the reviews that you will get. So if we can only control one variable of many, how can we predict success? So it's good to have a good story as a starting point, but we have to make films because we want to comment on the world or because we want to bring something to the commonwealth, not because of success.

Q – What about at the midway stage?

Fernanda – They ask if they have the story already. Have they shot enough? In the editing stage, it's if they've left anything out. It's kind of a funny question because they fear that there's a great scene amongst the 100 hours of footage that they don't know about. That's when they've become obsessive. My answer to that is if you have those doubts, then the story structure isn't in place. It's not about having enough; it's about making a decision of what you want to say. And in terms of what was left out, my theory is that if you can't remember it, then it can't be that important.

Q – How important would you say a fundraising trailer is to a documentary film?

Fernanda – Some years ago a piece of paper was enough. The more people make films, the higher the standards. And now that everyone has access to a camera and a desktop editing system, people assume that you can afford to make a trailer. So I 'd say, *"Absolutely"*. There's hardly any grant that goes from production to post-production, which doesn't require a work-in-progress, sample tape or fundraising trailer. Development will give you money to make such demo. But as soon as you get past the development stage, every grant asks for something audiovisual to support the paperwork. And private investors, it drops out of their mouth, *" Do you have something?"* People are more keen to watch even the sloppiest of teasers than read one page. And even if they like to read, images make a stronger impression because after all we're fundraising to make a film not writing a novel.

Q – How long should a fundraising trailer be?

Fernanda – 7 to 10 minutes is a good average for general purposes, that means grants, investors, fundraising parties, etc. People tend to make a fundraising trailer as a cross between a movie preview and a music video, that's a very bad idea. A fundraising trailer, work-in progress or sample work should be a short without an ending. If it has an ending, then grant panelists and investors will say that if it works as a short, why should they fund a feature length piece? With these fundraising demos you want to prove three things. There's a story, you're the one to tell the story and that you have access to that story. For that you need full scenes not a flashy montage.

Q – What are the most common problems that you see in documentaries?

Fernanda – In terms of development, I think filmmakers confuse good topics with good stories. Some topics make great photograph books or magazine articles, but because they're filmmakers, they feel they have to make films out of every topic they like. Once in the editing room, one common problem is trying to cut the film in the order that it's going to be shown. That puts a lot of pressure on both the editor and the director. Another problem is not being able to sustain the story. They have a great first 15 minutes, but then they hit a slump. The middle of a film is a challenge, especially in documentaries where you don't necessarily have a conflict driven structure. And it's a huge mistake to apply a conflict dr[illegible]
think that their film is wrong. That is never the case. It's the model that has been misused.

Q – What advice would you give a new filmmaker?

Fernanda – Look for clarity inside first and the answers will come from outside.

FINDING YOUR SUBJECT

Q – What do you think a documentary filmmaker should bear in mind when choosing their subject matter?

Mark – It should be something that you feel strongly about. It should be meaningful to you, a subject worth spending the time on that it takes to make a film. And that can vary from maybe a year if you get financing right away, to 4-5 years if it takes a long time to raise the money. The older I get, the more I question if I really care deeply about the subject before I start a documentary. I have been very fortunate that most of the films I've done have had a long life. One of the first films I did was about Caesar Chavez and the grape strike. I knew that something important was happening in Delano and I was right because 40 years later the film still has a life. It proved that my instincts were good and that I should trust them.

Q – Once they have chosen their subject, how should filmmakers start on the path?

Mark – A lot of preliminary research. You need to know who are going to be the main characters. I think casting a documentary is one of the most crucial decisions you make as a director. Whom are you going to be focusing on? Through whose eyes is this story unfolding? Casting is as essential for documentary filmmaking as it is for narrative filmmaking. And then the next thing you need to figure out is what is the question you are examining. What am I trying to say? What's your point of view on this? That can change as you go through the film, but I always have some attitude toward my subjects when I start.

Q – Do documentaries tend to have any rules to them regarding form?

Mark – I think documentary films have more in common with fiction films than differences. I write fiction, novels and screenplays. I teach screenwriting. I think there are certain basic narrative rules. When I start out, I don't think so much in three acts, but I do think about a beginning, middle and end. How is this going to unfold? How do I keep the audience involved? The biggest aesthetic issue of documentary is always structure.

Q – How planned can documentaries be?

Mark – It depends on the kind of film you're doing. For the last ten years or so, I have been doing mostly historical documentaries. So the events are over and you can very much plan what's going to happen. History is not going to change. What's important is your interpretation of history. For these, and my observational films. I end up doing a detailed treatment beforehand. It helps me organize my thoughts and they are often based on a lot of research. But there's always a tension between what you think is going to happen and what actually happens. So I sketch out a structure as to how I think the film is going to unfold, but I'm not tied to that. I did a film on Peace Corps groups in South America in the late 1960's. I did a month of research in Colombia trying to figure out which one I was going to focus on. I came back and wrote a 12-15 page treatment based on what I'd seen there. I went back and started shooting and had to throw the treatment away. When I was preparing to cut the film, I looked at the treatment and while the scenes were not the same, the structure was. Treatments help me know what dramatic elements I need for the film.

Q – Is it important to have a specific style in your documentary?

Mark – I think content dictates form or style. A verité film is different from a historical film where you are using a lot of stock footage. I've shot interviews that are against the same kind of textured or black background and I've shot interviews on location in people's homes. It depends on the nature of the film.

Q – How do make your subjects feel comfortable during interviews?

Mark – I spend a lot of time with them beforehand. I always try to establish a relationship with them. That might mean going out to breakfast with them beforehand or a pre-interview phone call. I always spend at least an hour beforehand somehow. I think it's essential that you don't go in cold.

Q – How much time do you block off for an interview?

Mark – At least a couple of hours. For my historical documentaries, if I can do two interviews a day, that's about right. A good interview in a documentary can be very revealing. When people are talking intimately about their lives, I want to see their faces and expression. I try to only use them on camera when they are talking emotionally.

Q – Are there any tips on getting good interviews?

Mark – Besides spending time with them, I think it has to do with how you respond to them. I really listen to the music as much as the words. I'm always trying to listen to the underlying emotions of my subjects. And my interventions are not so much questions of facts as they are questions of emotion. Instead of asking, *"what happened next?"* I might say *"That must have made you really feel sad,"* or something comparable. I suppose my model is more of a therapeutic one. I have been doing a lot of films on the Holocaust where people are talking about extremely traumatic events. When you're in that situation, it's important that the subject know that you aren't going to flinch from their pain. That you're going to sit there and tolerate the pain that they went through. If it makes you at all anxious or uncomfortable, they aren't going to tell you about their lives.

Q – How do you feel about the adage of having the interviewee repeat the question as part of their answer?

Mark – It helps sometimes. I try to train people beforehand to do that. Sometimes they remember and sometimes they forget. I hate to break the flow, so I listen carefully and think if I can pick this up later. If I can't, then I interrupt. But usually you can pick it up. I sometimes give people a hand signal to remember, but when we're talking about emotional things, I don't like to stop the flow.

Q – What are the common mistakes that you see documentary filmmakers make?

Mark – One thing is that they haven't thought clearly through what the audience needs to know to understand this film. They're so immersed in it, they make assumptions that the audience knows what they know. People are afraid of narration. It's sometimes the easiest way to get from point A to point B and to provide the exposition that you need. People are fans of observational film and they don't think you need to set things up.

Q – What advice would you give a new documentary filmmaker?

Mark – You have to really love the process of filmmaking. I've been making documentaries for over 40 years. It's not only my vocation; it's my way of experiencing the world. It's a way for me to discover things about myself. Every film that I've made, successful or not, it has been a great learning process for me. And I love the process.

Kees Bakker
Professor, Consultant

ETHICS

Q – When in the life of a documentary do ethics apply?

Kees – Always. When we consider ethics as a practical philosophy and the conception, writing, producing, shooting, editing, showing and viewing of a documentary are actions, then in all of these stages ethics are an issue. Up till now, ethics in documentary has mainly been discussed when talking about the relation between the filmmaker and his subjects. But the audiovisual representation itself (the truth-claim, questions of objectivity/subjectivity, rhetorical strategies), the distribution, the programming and showing of a film (the selection by cinemas, festivals, broadcasters, etc.) are actions that – thus – imply ethical values. In the same vein, the act of watching a film implies an ethical stance. The spectator isn't that innocent anymore. With the proliferation of audiovisual messages – especially in the so-called Western world – the average spectator knows quite well how to value the images and sound and how to position himself in relation to those audiovisual messages. The spectator's interpretation of documentaries is not free from moral and ideological values, and in my eyes it's to some extent his responsibility to be conscious of the fact that as well the representation he's watching as his own interpretation of it are guided by the world views of respectively the filmmaker and the spectator.

Q – Do documentary filmmakers have a responsibility to their subjects? And what is "informed consent" and would that cover a filmmaker from being sued?

Kees – Documentary filmmakers should be aware that the representation of subjects in a documentary film could have an important impact on the daily life of these subjects. This can be a positive or a negative impact, or hardly any impact at all. The filmmaker has a moral obligation to inform his subjects of how they'll be depicted in the film, and how this might affect them when the film is shown. When the subjects agree to be filmed, after being informed of how and with what possible consequences, this agreement is called 'informed consent'. In theory, this is quite simple, but in practice it's not always that easy. Not necessarily because the subject doesn't want to, but because it depends very much on the moment and situation during the shooting. Informed consent depends on the honesty of the filmmaker, but we have to be aware that the filmmaker can't foresee all possible interpretations and effects of his film on the private life of the subjects.

Q – What are the ethics involved when paying someone to be in your documentary?

Kees – This puts the notion of 'informed consent' under pressure because it's a kind of bribery; the appearance in the film has become a paid contract. Does a documentarist have to pay his actors? In general, I don't think so. And in general documentaries aren't that good investments; they rarely make profit. But there're exceptions, like *Etre et Avoir,* which became a huge box-office success. It led one of the subjects, George Lopez to sue the producers and the director Nicolas Philibert, probably because he wanted to have a part of the pie. He accused the director and the producers of counterfeit (claiming to be co-author of the film because fragments of his courses were depicted in the film) and of infringement of his "image rights". All claims were nonsuit: there was informed consent. Lopez couldn't be considered co-author since he didn't participate in the creative process of the filmmaking itself; the film was not reproducing elements of his courses for which he could claim copyrights; the judge considered that Lopez and the kids had only been filmed in their "natural habitat."

Q – What is 'The Television Without Frontiers Directive" of the European Union and how does this apply to documentaries in Europe?

Kees – It regulates the free movement of television broadcasting services in the European Union. It concerns the production and distribution of European works, television advertising, protection of minors etc. What's interesting in relation to documentary is that the Directive stipulates a quota (10% of broadcast time or 10% of the program budget) that broadcasters have to spend on independent productions (as well as a majority of transmission time on European works, produced by the broadcasters themselves or by independent companies). More interesting is how this Directive relates to national legislations, in which there are often quotas for specific programs, e.g. sports, factual programming, entertainment, fiction, advertising, etc. Reality TV, for example, has been labeled as 'factual programming', instead of "entertainment", in order to meet those quotas with financially lucrative programs instead of with 'boring' documentaries.

Q – In the USA, TV news has gone from news = truth, to news = opinions, entertainment and competition for ratings. Is there a danger of broadcasters imposing this new form of journalism onto documentaries?

Kees – The problem is that broadcasters are the big financers of documentaries. They're in their right when they commission a film to impose some demands. This dependence on television channels makes the documentary very vulnerable. There's less and less space for 'stubborn' documentary filmmakers who think of themselves as artists, and whose documentaries present a distinct way of looking at the world. Audiovisual journalism doesn't have the same force – nor the same mission – to stimulate the spectator to reflect on events or opinions. Its main mission is to inform. In the

documentary. It has become synonymous with audiovisual journalism; an enormous impoverishment of the documentary, in which creativity, subjectivity and aesthetics were the strong points. Of course, they both deal with 'reality', but where newscasts have an informational mission, documentaries normally should go beyond that. Personally, I don't mind that much that news for some channels has become a vehicle for opinions and entertainment, as long as it's presented as such. It becomes more problematic when such 'newscasts' become the only source of information of a spectator. I know there are many people that only stick to a single news source, and then it becomes worrying.

Q – Is it a good idea to have opinionated documentaries out there? How can one ensure balance in the documentary field so it's never one sided?

Kees – Why should there be a balance? I think it's more honest to be one sided than to pretend to know what the world is like. When Joris Ivens had made *The Spanish Earth*, one of the critiques was that it was one sided. He hadn't filmed from the Fascist point of view. His reply was that it would've needed a second film made by someone else. How can you be objective about the other side when you condemn the other side's worldview? Actually, I don't think there are unopiniated documentaries. And those who pretend to be unopiniated should be handled with extreme distrust. The balance one should look for is more in the openness, sincerity and coherence of the arguments and opinions.

Q – Is there a ruling body that can reside over news programs?

Kees – There is, fortunately, not a world wide ruling body, but most countries have some kind of controlling body. Their task is often interesting, but very, very sensitive. Apart from the statistical controlling mechanisms related to quotas, like advertising or the time newscasts spend on political parties in election time, these controlling bodies sometimes lean towards a censorship that is based on an ideology that may not correspond with public opinion, and neither with the law. In the latter case it becomes very problematic. A controlling body should be well defined regarding its missions, and not appropriate a power (of censorship) that goes beyond law.

Q – Is there a journalist code of ethics that has to be adhered to?

Kees – Journalist codes of ethics differ from country to country. That's why the Council of Europe established a resolution on the ethics of journalism to get some unity in it. It's not an obligation to adhere to it, but more a guideline for journalists. In that sense it differs from the European Convention of Human Rights, which has the status of an international treaty to which signatory states adhere to; it has the status of law. It also includes articles on the right to freedom of expression, the right to information and sometimes there can be a tension between these different rights, especially when it comes to public figures. There are journalists that have less respect for the private life of their subjects, but in general my impression is that most journalists respect the major ethical codes related to their profession. When they don't, the subjects may have a case before a tribunal. There's no code of ethics for documentarists, but apart from common law they often implicitly adhere to journalist codes of ethics.

Q – What are the true dangers to documentary filmmakers when they explore something sensitive and should documentary filmmakers hold back or not if their society's morals are different from others?

Kees – Well, the true danger is to be killed by an intolerant bastard. Theo Van Gogh was killed because of his stance against Muslim fundamentalism in his writings and in his film *Submission*. Van Gogh was someone who wouldn't hold back, and sometimes he crossed the borders of decency. The normal legal procedure is to sue the one who offended. Unfortunately, we live in a world where some people think they have the right to play judge, jury and executioner, without following the legal – national or international – procedures. Some people think you can impose respect by using violence. If we let our lives be determined by these kinds of people, we give in to fear and moral weakness. But it's not up to me, nor to the authorities, to decide for others how they should position themselves. If a documentary filmmaker works in a society with different moral standards, he should take them into account, but this does not mean that he may not denounce what he thinks necessary to denounce. But by denouncing people, systems or religions, you make enemies. Some enemies are not that bad: they use their freedom of expression to hit back. Other enemies, often by lack of arguments, have recourse to violence. What's important to know is that the use of our freedom of expression is nevertheless limited (e.g. slander and incitement to discrimination, hatred or violence are not allowed), and definitely guided by ethical considerations.

In the case of the recent Danish cartoons, we've seen a shift in the motivations to publish them. Initially, they were intended to denounce the use of religion to justify terrorism. That may, and did offend people, but in my eyes that was not the primary motivation of these cartoons. But once the riots started, the motivation for republishing these cartoons became different: the attitude of "we want to show you that we stick to our freedom of expression" became more a freedom to offend; republishing the cartoons for the sake of it. From an ethical point of view I find that motivation much more problematic than the initial denunciation. But in both cases, the proper way to protest is by legal procedures. The riots that occurred in protesting against the cartoons laid bare an enormous hypocrisy with many people: for decades they have burned flags, portraits, crucifixes, and the like, so apparently there are people that appropriate rights they want to deny to others. In peaceful protest, I suggest to drop millions of copies of George Orwell's *Animal Farm*.

Q – Should docu-dramas be taken as seriously as documentaries? Can a documentary filmmaker recreate a scene, even rehearse their subject?

Kees – Unless they're parodies, docu-dramas should be taken as seriously as documentaries or fiction films. A filmmaker is free to choose the form in which he wants to put his story. Fiction films should be taken seriously too, because they often can teach us serious things about our own real world. It's not the use of an actor that changes the value of the story; neither does the use of an actor imply that the story isn't about the real world. In the first decades of documentary film it was common practice to use actors and to stage scenes. This wasn't to mislead the spectator, nor to make a fiction film, but to better convey the story.

Ford Transit by Hany Abu-Assad was labeled 'docu-drama' because of the limited knowledge of and view on documentary of the broadcasting organization that commissioned the film. Not because the film is a docu-drama (for me it isn't, it's a documentary), but for the simple fact that the director used an actor to tell his story and to give his view on the effect of Israeli occupation on the daily life of Palestinian people. If we continue to follow that logic, we have to rewrite documentary film history. Everything before was fake or fiction. Unfortunately, television imposes more and more its standards of storytelling onto documentary, leading to a narrowing down of the concept of documentary, based on the idea that documentaries should tell the truth and telling the truth cannot be done by using fictional elements. I find such an attitude very shortsighted: first because it's based on a positivism that thinks there exists only one truth, and secondly because it leads to an enormous impoverishment of the film language. Third, there is sometimes more truth in fiction films than in news programs. And fourth, we should stop thinking of documentary as being the opposite of fiction film – it is not. So yes, when it's up to me, documentary filmmakers may recreate and rehearse scenes if it supports the story they want to tell.

Q – Are there any rules or boundaries that should never be broken in documentary filmmaking?

Kees – No other than defined by law. All other rules are conventional, and I don't mind when films, be they documentaries or fiction films, play with the conventions of the genre. It's often a way to make the spectator aware of the arbitrariness of

Q – What are the ethics of an interviewee nudging their subjects in interviews to go somewhere that might be too sensitive, painful – all for exposing the cause but also sensationalism? What about ethics in using music in documentaries which will manipulate the audience?

Kees – If it's for mere sensationalism it's very disputable. If it's for exposing the cause, it may be defendable. Whether it concerns harsh interviews, or imposing new meanings by adding music or editing the interview, it would be very important to have the subject's consent after he or she has seen the final result of the film and has been explained the possible consequences of showing the film to wide audiences. But when the interviews concern public figures and their public functions there's much more freedom for the interviewer and/or the documentary filmmaker to manipulate without having an informed consent, than with private citizens in the privacy of their lives. Manipulations are sometimes very effective to denounce manipulations. Of course, the spectator may dismiss a film because of this kind of manipulations, but that is probably something the filmmaker is aware of from the start.

Q – What common mistakes do you see by documentary filmmakers in relation to ethics?

Kees – It's difficult to talk about 'mistakes' when it comes to ethics. You might not subscribe to the same ethics as someone else. We may not agree, but that does not mean it's a mistake. In general, I think the deontology of documentary filmmakers is quite reasonable. The thing that disturbs me most, but this is my personal stance, is the attitude or pretension of objectivity that many documentarists have, which in my eyes is more misleading than an explicit subjectivity.

Q – What advice would you give a documentary filmmaker?

Kees – Be sincere. Believe in yourself and in what you want to tell and show.

GUERILLA FILM MAKER SAYS!

Choosing Your Subject

The two most important decisions you are going make on your doc is what is the topic and who are you going to follow. Here are some tips for choosing wisely.

1. Try to choose a topic that hasn't been explored before. Watch as many docs as you can and look at the listings of the major festivals to see if you have any competition.

2. If you choose a topic that's been done before like criminal justice, find a new spin on the subject matter in order to make it stand out. A good way to do this is talk to the experts of the field who can tell you what might be up and coming and hasn't been done yet.

3. Choosing a topic that is very mainstream will be an easier sell than one on the fringe unless the fringe is something that's never been seen before, engaging or just plain shocking.

4. Do research on your subject so you know its intricacies. If you're shooting animals for a nature doc, know when they hibernate or mate so you can prepare your proposal, budget and schedule.

5. When choosing a person to follow, find someone who is open and honest. Closed off interviewees (especially the lead) make for boring docs.

6. Try to ascertain the integrity of your subjects. You don't want someone coming back stating that they didn't mean what they said during an interview.

7. If you can, go after subjects who are underrepresented in mainstream community. They will give you more because they want their voice heard. They can also hook you up with others like them for the same reason.

8. Going after high profile subjects means a lot more red tape, schedule changes and time (even if you know them!). Prepare for it.

THE RESEARCHER

Q – What is your job?

Rosemary – Archival Film Researcher. I'm the professional individual who conducts the search for all and any of the visuals required in your documentary, film, video, or commercial. We search for the perfect visual to match your script in archives in person as well as on-line. My work involves searching in archives, which are worldwide, not only nationwide. An archival film researcher with a highly trained eye can save you days and even weeks of searching, thereby keeping your budget cost down. An untrained eye can only be counted on to obtain the same footage every single other documentarian is using as all archives have certain visuals placed on "sample reels", i.e. the reel may contain archival footage from World War II or from a natural disaster from a particular year. Without digging, every single documentarian or filmmaker creating a new work on that subject matter will receive the same footage as others have before him or her. Expecting an intern to yield the fruits of a highly trained individual is compromising one's artistic and creative vision. We are worth your investment.

Q – How long are you employed for?

Rosemary – It can range from literally one or two days or as long as a six-month period of time.

Q – What resources do you use to find information?

Rosemary – I ask permission of each client to go into archives in person so as to do a better job for them. That usually is a cost today of a $100.00 archive visiting fee, which is usually then deducted off the client's final order. Otherwise, I utilize the internet, scanning the globe that way for images, making connections by both phone and by email with staff in each archive to insure we have gotten the best visuals they can offer.

Q – What does a filmmaker receive from you?

Rosemary – The client will receive a time coded preview videotape, usually VHS, as many archives still do not offer DVD in preview format to clients. That is changing, though. I will collate facts and footage as part of my job for each client.

Q – Do you do any editing of this footage and do you give your clients a shot list?

Rosemary – I don't edit any of the footage that I have researched for a client, as one never knows what piece of footage may inspire the artist or documentarian or filmmaker. I do collate the time coded preview reels for each client and if I believe there's something of particular interest to them, I will notate that in writing. All archives will provide a written shot-list with time code as well, to follow along with. If a client seeks my input, I am always happy to give my views, but overall, I leave the creative driving to my clients.

Q – Do you receive a credit and if so what is it?

Rosemary – I do receive a credit. It has ranged from Archival Film Researcher to Researcher/Post-Production Supervisor or Associate to Production. I usually work alone so there's no assistant that receives a credit.

Q – Does a filmmaker need to cite where his research came from much like one would in a research paper?

Rosemary – Yes, the archives each should be listed one by one, if footage has been obtained, paid for, licensed and utilized in a production.

Q – Why is hiring a researcher an indispensable investment? How do you help your client save money?

Rosemary – Hiring a researcher is indispensable in terms of adding to the quality of your production's values. A trained researcher can find in one day what will take an inexperienced individual days and days to locate, thereby, saving a client monies.

Q – How much information do you like to get from a filmmaker as to what they are after?

Rosemary – As much as they can give me. There's no such thing as too much information to a researcher like myself! I like and I encourage my clients to give me *"what I would like to see, if this were a perfect world,"* list, where they list shot by shot, theme by theme, exactly what their dreams, hopes and needs are for their documentary or production.

Q – How much do you charge?

Rosemary – I charge $250.00 per day

Q – Do you handle obtaining any licenses for footage or information? If so, what do they usually cost?

Rosemary – I do handle that sometimes, but some clients prefer to do it themselves, so as to try to negotiate within their budgets. For a 90 minute production, using 70% archival film footage, one should put aside at least $25,000-$35,000 of their budget, for the images, the licensing fees, permission to utilize and to exhibit on cable television, art cinemas, television, festivals, worldwide and nationwide.

Q – What can a producer do to make your job easier?

Rosemary – Give me as detailed a list of their needs as possible. Answering my queries in emails within 24 hours.

Q – What common mistakes do you come across with filmmakers in regard to your job?

Rosemary – That many still believe that public domain means that the footage is totally and completely free! That there will be imagery available of events, which preceded the birth of the camera. That there were news crews on location for such events like the Triangle Shirt Factory Fire in NYC. There are no mistakes; we're all learning together.

Q – What advice would you give a filmmaker?

Rosemary – My advice to all documentarians and filmmakers is never think putting aside part of your budget to hire a professional researcher will ever, ever be a drain to your budget, or that it is not a worthy investment.

ARCHIVAL FOOTAGE

Q – How far back do your archives go?

Nancy – While the majority of our footage covers 1950 to present, we do have footage from the first half of the 20th century, including the Universal Newsreels from 1920-1960.

Q – Does this include NBC Radio, NBC Entertainment and affiliated stations like Telemundo?

Nancy –Yes. NBC News Archives licenses NBC News Radio, MSNBC and Telemundo, NBC's Spanish language network. NBC Entertainment programs are licensed by Entertainment's clip licensing department. They may be contacted at: 818-840-6618 or fax: 818-526-7821.

Q – How does one go about ordering footage from you?

Nancy – Please visit our website www.nbcnewsarchives.com where one may search for footage and find instructions to order footage. You may also order footage by faxing your request to: 212-703-8558, email: footage@nbc.com or contacting our office: 212-664-3797.

Q – Is it possible to order footage with either the NBC logo on it or voice over?

Nancy – Yes. In both situations, we request a treatment or description of your production and a script. These requests are reviewed on a case-by-case basis.

Q – If you know that something aired on NBC, but can't remember when or can't find it in the database, do you have in-house researchers that can help?

Nancy – Yes. There is a $25/hour fee that goes along with this.

Q – Can you screen footage before ordering?

Nancy – Yes, you may screen film and tape at our office: 30 Rockefeller Plaza, New York, New York. A screening fee may apply. There is no need to visit our offices for research purposes, as our database is online.

Q – On what format do you provide the footage?

Nancy – We provide footage on VHS, Beta, BetaSP, Digibeta, DVCPro and Film.

Q – How fast is the turnaround time once an order is placed?

Nancy – That depends on the amount of footage ordered and the original format of the footage. If the order is a few clips, that can be turned around the same day or within 24 hours. If the order is for a substantial amount of footage, it would take

Archival Houses

GUERILLA FILM MAKER SAYS!

Here's
Library's website under Public Moving Images @ www.loc.gov/film/arch.html.

ABC News VideoSource - NYC
800-789-1250, 212-456-5421
www.abcnewsvsource.com

BBC Motion Picture Gallery
London: 44 (0) 20 8433 2861 / 2862
www.bbcmotiongallery.com
Archives Canada - Ottawa
866-254-1403, 613-565-5445
www.archivescanada.ca

The New Zealand Film Archive - Wellington
64 4 384-7647
ww.filmarchive.org.nz

ITN Archive House, London
www.itnarchive.com

Historic Films - NY
800-249-1940, 631-477-9700
www.historicfilms.com

National Geographic Digital Motion – Wash., DC
877-730-2022
www.ngdigitalmotion.com

WPA Film Library – Illinois and International
800-777-2223, 708-460-0187
UK: 44 (0)207 734 9159
Germany: 49 (0)6131 991313
www.wpafilmlibrary.com

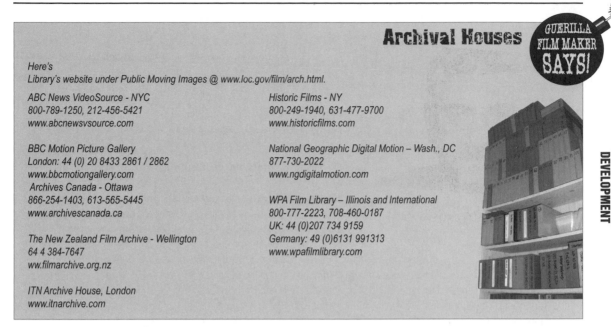

more time to process. If the footage is on film, we'll advise you of the amount of time required to transfer the film

Q – Do you require a producer to credit NBC anywhere in the film if they use your footage?

Nancy – We request an end credit in the production.

Q – How much does a license cost?

Nancy – The licensing fee depends on the market of distribution such as World Wide TV, Cable TV, Theatrical, DVD, etc. and if the production will be distributed in a single market or multiple markets. A single market such as film festivals or TV rights is less expensive than multiple markets.The licensing fee is based on a per-second charge with a 30 second minimum. We do in perpetuity licenses but it costs more. If you buy in bulk, we can give you a better rate on the license.

Q – What are some of the common mistakes filmmakers make when approaching you?

Nancy – I don't know if there are mistakes but I can suggest guidelines to search for footage. First, we license NBC News footage. We don't license sports events, stills or feature film clips, for example. Second, be prepared with as much information as possible such as the rights you require, the format needed, the date you require the footage, the billing and shipping information and the name and address of the licensee. Third, know your footage budget. Fourth, remember it takes time for us to screen and dub the footage and it's important to factor our time to process your order into your deadline. Finally, there is no "dumb" question. Please ask any and all questions. That may save time and eliminate confusion in the long run.

Q – Any tips for filmmakers out there when approaching you?

Nancy – Search our database. If you don't find the exact footage you need, we may have other footage suitable for your production. Or, speak with one of our researchers. We know our footage and are happy to assist with searches.

PROPOSALS

Q – What is a proposal and what are the main sections of it?

Morrie – The best way to answer that question, what is a proposal, is whatever the funder wants. Every funder will want something different. Barring that, there's a general template for what would be in a proposal. It'd include a description of the project, a description or a statement proving that there's a need for the project, which is very important. Then there's always something about the intended audience that you're making the piece for. And then I have every client write a treatment. The treatment is often the most important part of the proposal and for some reason filmmakers have trouble writing treatments. Maybe it's because filmmakers are visual people. But then again, the treatment is totally visual in nature. It doesn't say anything about why I'm doing it or what I intend to prove out of this. In words you describe what people will visually see on the screen. Next in the proposal you need something about your timeline and production plans. You need information about the personnel and a detailed budget. Another important part of the proposal is distribution and outreach plans. Filmmakers screw up this part of the proposal a lot.

Q – What should filmmakers think about with regard to distribution and outreach?

Morrie – They need to think about who the audience is and as many ways as possible to get the project out to those audiences. Funders are looking for very rich, interesting and varied distribution ideas and plans. And they're also looking more and more for community outreach plans as well. Many funders are demanding that you have a website; expecting a website so people can see what you're doing.

Q – What in your opinion makes a proposal stand out from others?

Morrie – The word I like to use is "compelling." Funders are looking for a proposal that grabs them, that says this project has to be made and these people are the ones who have to make it. The writing has to be good and compelling. Another word I say to filmmakers is "story." The proposal has to make a good story - that's what people are looking for.

Q – Do you give any advice on how to create a good story?

Morrie – I tell filmmakers to personalize it. I always look at the level of language and if it's too abstract and theoretical, it is not going to work for a full proposal. You can use it a little bit. You can say, *"Here is why I am making it. To save the planet."* But then you should say, *"And in order to do that I am going to show the story of Juan Valdez in Venice Beach."* Then you're going to tell me a story that really grabs me. Use active verbs and tell them about some very visceral things that they'll see. You want to be very specific and visual. The treatment seals the deal.

Q – How many pages is a typical treatment?

Morrie – I like a two page, single-spaced treatment for a piece that might be as long as two hours. Some funders allow you more room than that and few would allow you less. But, again, the right answer is whatever the funder will allow or prefers.

Q – Is it good to include any awards that you've won, letters of support or video footage?

Morrie – Yes, all of that. I'll always tell filmmakers to get letters of support for a film. Kudos letters, I call them. You always want one or two from a distributor. Those are like gold. And you always want a couple from a potential user of the film - whomever is going to see it or buy it. And if you're going to do a project on a special subject, you want to get an expert in the field to write you a letter of support. So if you're doing a piece on water, then you want a water expert, an author or academic, to write you a letter saying that this is a great project and this person knows what they're doing. All of this stuff is to help shore up your credibility. The funders want to know that you're going to get it done.

Q – What about the budget?

Morrie – Yes, you need to include one. That's often a weak spot for filmmakers because the filmmaker will configure it such a way that it loses the grant for them. It might not be understandable, it might not be detailed enough, it might have squirrelly figures in it that aren't explained. I think it's important every time you see a figure in your budget that people might question, you write a note about it. Most filmmakers don't do that. They just assume you'll know about it. Some filmmakers that come out of the commercial world include things like contingency. That's a mistake because most funders don't understand it. Most budgets fail for me because they don't include distribution, marketing or PR. If I don't see a budget that doesn't have budget for production stills, I get angry. Festival fees, screeners, press kits should be included as well.

Q – Do most funders understand these budgets?

Morrie – The ones that fund media do, but most don't. And that's why you have to write notes for them. And don't forget that if they don't understand it they're smart enough to give it to someone who does.

Q – If you're going to shoot film or video, do you have to explain why?

Morrie – Only if it is important for some reason. Most funders won't care.

Q – Is it important to know people in the organizations, foundations or entity that you are soliciting?

Morrie – Yes. And that is why it's a slow, long process. You have to be strategic about it and about whether or not you want that money. It takes years to establish those relationships. So if you're an emerging filmmaker and you haven't applied anywhere or you don't know anyone, you have to start down that long path of making connections. In my experience, many proposals hinge on some kind of contact. It's a mistake to think that you can just send a proposal in without making any contact at all and stand to have a great chance of getting the money.

Q – Do you find that most people in these entities are amenable to that contact?

Morrie – No! Why should they be? That's the whole trick! If they were amenable that would be easy. But let me differentiate between public funders and private funders. Any government funder like the NEH *has* to talk to you. They can't refuse your phone call by law. They're a public servant. Somebody has to talk to you and give you the information that you need. So there's no reason in the world for any filmmaker not to take advantage of that. Now with private funders, that's not true. They don't have to talk to you and some won't talk to you. Most set up structures to make it difficult for you to talk to them because they don't want to be inundated with conversations with filmmakers. One of the ways that they shield themselves is in their guidelines. They'll say don't call - send a letter of inquiry before a formal proposal. I'm somewhat controversial on this, but I tell people never to send the letter unless there's no way around it. Try to talk to them. It's also important to make the right contact. You have to do a lot of research and know your stuff or you're dead. One of the important things is to really know what the funder is about before you call. If you call up and ask questions that are already in their guidelines or ask things that have nothing to do with them, you're dead.

Q – Should you start at a junior level and work up or start at the top and work down?

Morrie – Get as high in the chain as possible. Get to the decision maker if you can. For many of the private funders, you're going to have to go to a program officer even though the board of trustees will be making the decisions.

Q – If you have written a proposal, can you send it blindly to anybody?

Morrie – NO! That is a big mistake! That is a major error. I call it the shotgun method. If you send one general proposal and send it out to everyone, you're dead. You won't even hear back. You have to tailor each proposal to each funder individually. And that is why I like to have one big file of everything the filmmaker needs and then you jerryrig it and change it and massage it every time.

Q – What is the most important thing to make clear in your proposal?

Morrie – A need for the project to be made. You need to prove that the world needs this program. And that can be done by doing basic research that most filmmakers don't do - like being able to name similar projects and why yours is different. Talk to experts, distributors, Google it. I was just working for a year on a project with a filmmaker and I asked him if he knew if anyone else has done anything like it. He said he didn't know and we did a little research. I get a call from him a week later and he says that someone just made this film. He had to switch gears dramatically and it was a devastating blow. What is weird is that this is not unusual.

Q – Do the funders understand the power of the documentary medium or media in general as far as promotion of their cause or message?

Morrie – No. There's a small handful that do and they like to fund media projects. Most funders don't. They are scared of it. Confused by it. They think it's too expensive. That means that when filmmakers are getting support from a foundation, it is despite the fact that they are making a film not because they are making a film. And what lures them into feeling they have to do it, is that you're covering a subject that they really believe in or are interested in such a powerful manner that they have to support it. So many a funder that says we don't support media has supported a media project because the filmmaker gave them a proposal that was so close to their mission. So I should say they're aware of the power of the medium, they are just not convinced that they need to be involved or can afford to be involved.

Q – Are you getting a sense that these days there is more or less money available for funding documentary projects?

Morrie – It depends if you are looking at the whole pie or slivers of the pie. I think the whole pie is bigger. I think portions of the pie are smaller. Government support is definitely down over the last ten years. No question. Private foundation support, however, has grown. That is only because the private foundation sector has exploded. There are more foundations now than ever and they have more money than ever. Individual money is still around and there's a lot of it. It's just a matter of tapping into it.

Q – Most filmmakers don't think about their careers beyond the here and now.

Morrie – And they should because it is absolutely essential. If a filmmaker wants to consult with me, I send them a stack of materials to fill out. And at the top of the stack is their personal mission statement as a filmmaker. 99% of them don't have one and ask me why they need that. What I've learned is that if you cannot clarify a couple of big issues like mission, you are never going to be good at fundraising and make it through the process of looking for money. You have to show the funder that you have a backbone - that you're a person with a purpose. The competition is so stiff for money that the funder can pick and choose whomever they want to give money to. So you need differentiators and the first one is *"are you a person with a sense of purpose?"* - because if you aren't I don't want to be with you. The second thing is that once you decide on the mission you can focus on the style of the fundraising you want to undertake. There are lots of ways to raise money. So in the non-commercial side of things, you can go to individuals with personal asks or conduct direct mail campaigns. Or you can write grants to public agencies or foundations. Or you could go get corporate money or support from small businesses. But the smart filmmaker will say to him or herself, *"What kind of career do I want to have in filmmaking?"* And, "*What is the right path for looking for money in the path I want to take*?" Once you have a bead on that you can be strategic every time you take on a project. What you are actually doing is thinking two or three projects ahead and you're beginning to build a base of both contacts and learning that you can work off of. Otherwise you will waste a lot of time. An example of this is if I'm working with a filmmaker and the second thing I ask about is vision of career path. If they say that they *"...eventually want to be making narrative feature films, but the project I am working on now is a documentary"* - I say that if that is true, you don't want to spend a lot of time learning how to write grants because what you will be doing later on is raising money from individuals. That's going to be your path. So let's start going down that path and learn those skills.

Q – So for documentarians who want to do social issue projects, you would teach them how to write grants?

Morrie – That's right. And actually for people doing projects on social issue work, they have the largest panoply of ways to get money. Almost all the avenues are open and appropriate save for corporate money. So we'll teach you how to do the research and talk to the funders and teach you how to write grants.

Q – What are the biggest mistakes that documentary filmmaker make in their proposals?

Morrie – Lack of research. The second thing is lack of self-awareness. Sometimes they lowball their budgets. The thinking is that if I come in low enough they may be more likely to fund me, so I will cut this and that and make it look doable. That is a mistake because they will send the budget to someone like me and I will call back and say they can't do it for this. The other thing is what if you get the money? Now you have to do it for that price and you lied. You're in trouble.

Q - What advice would you give a filmmaker?

Morrie – Writing proposals is the tip of the iceberg. And that writing a grant is the lesser art and grant hustling is the greater art. They key to a good proposal is really understanding the project well and being able to articulate it. If you don't have good writing skills, you can always hire a good writer or write a rough draft and have them look at it. On the low end, you are looking at $20-$50/hour and $100-$150/hour on the high end. The other thing is that you want to balance passion with reason. You need both of those in a proposal. And do your research. Think from the mind of the funder. Ask yourself what they want and then you're more likely to be successful.

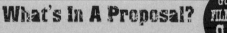

GUERILLA FILM MAKER SAYS!

What's In A Proposal?

Two rules of thumb for proposals: one, that you give the funder whatever they ask for and two, you tailor the proposal to address their needs and concerns. Check with the funder to find out what they specifically require or more importantly, what they absolutely DO NOT want. Here are some basic sections of all proposals.

1. A description of the project stating why the project is important.

2. A descripton of the intended audience.

3. A treatment outlining the narrative of the documentary. Should be visual in nature, not a discussion.

4. A description of what kind of access you have to the subject matter.

5. A budget. This must add up and make sense. Don't under-budget or over-budget and ALWAYS include a fee for yourself.

6. A timeline. A general idea of how production will proceed.

7. Production Team – who are the principles and what have they done. May include your advisory board as well.

8. Distribution plans – the biggie for funders! How do you plan to get your project out into the world? Funders love community outreach as well – so non-theatrical, non-broadcast distribution is something to seriously consider.

9. Work samples – they usually want something to show you can make a film. If you don't have anything, you can use samples from your production team. Careful though, your sample should match the tone and style of the film you propose.

OPEN PITCHING

Michaelle McLean
Toronto Documentary Forum

Q – How long should a pitch be when you're pitching to a broadcaster and/or at a public pitch session?

Michaelle – There are no hard and fast rules, especially as the ideal pitch is a two-way conversation. Some conversations end quickly and some carry on because both parties find it interesting. In a one-on-one situation take your cue from whether they take the bait and ask questions, which prompt you to carry on. In a large public session it will depend on the format's parameters - at the Toronto Documentary Forum each project presentation slot is 15 minutes with half that time for the producer to present and show a brief clip, and the other half for the moderator to garner feedback from the roundtable of broadcasters.

Q – What are the most important points to get across in your pitch?

Michaelle – I'd say you should quickly communicate why you should tell it, what your way in to the story is and why telling it now is relevant for audiences. Beyond that, I think mentioning whatever you have in your pocket that sets the project apart is very good. That could be the exclusive access you have to the subject, existing finance from another source, the critical or commercial success of your last film, etc. all that can build confidence and interest in the project. As far as style, some commissioners are more focused on the material and others appreciate a cinematic or visual style. Do your research.

Q – How can you grab an audience of commissioning editors in the first minute?

Michaelle – Confidence of presentation is important so don't read from notes and instead, speak conversationally. Have a good story line. One of the best I ever heard was for *Offspring* by Barry Stevens. His opening line was *"I just discovered I may have 245 half-siblings. I recently found out my mother was one of the first to use a sperm donor and this film is about my search."* It was a great public pitch.

Q – How important is it to mention the outreach possibilities of the documentary?

Michaelle – It's probably not that important unless you're dealing with a public channel with a strong connection to that community. The private channels' main concern will be their audience.

Q – How important is it to tailor your documentary to the network you are pitching to? And how can you tailor your documentary to certain networks when pitching at a public pitch session?

Michaelle – Always important. And at a public pitch just say *"Yes, I would absolutely love to talk about the possibility of..."* if someone asks for something you hadn't thought about yet.

Q – How important is presentation when giving a pitch? Should you bring visual aids to a pitch?

Michaelle – Over the years broadcasters have told me that seeing clips is immensely helpful. If they don't know you it helps to get a reading of your sensibility, and even if they do know you, it's always useful to show the charisma of your characters, to prove the access you have, and sometimes the scope of the project.

Q – What characteristics are good for pitching

Michaelle – Confidence and an attitude of cooperation. I've seen a number of great sounding projects die on the vine at the TDF because the producer or director rejected every suggestion from the commissioning editors and insisted it was their way or the highway. This may have been due to nerves, but since broadcasters review hundreds of hours of documentaries and have access to ratings and audience feedback, it's incredibly counterproductive for a filmmaker to insist they have all the answers. On the nerves issue, Mark Achbar of *The Corporation* told me he thinks we event organizers should hand out beta-blockers to help with pitchers nerves. I say whatever works for you.

Q – What are the common questions that you should be prepared for when pitching?

Michaelle – Can you do a shorter/longer version for me? Do you have enough money in your budget for all the rights? How is your project on xyz subject different from the one I just broadcast 3 months ago?

Q – If someone likes your pitch, what would the next step generally be?

Michaelle – A big celebratory drink, and a quick follow up email saying it was great to hear you're on board for the xyz project. What would you like next from me?

Q – What are the common mistakes in pitching?

Michaelle – Taking it personally. Unless you're an incredibly unpleasant person, it's really all about the project and not about you. If it's not this project, it could well be the next one, especially if you're able to strike up a bit of a relationship and seem like someone who'd be great to work with. Another mistake might be that the producer believes that just because one or two or even three broadcasters say it's not for them, there isn't a home somewhere for it. There're many channels with diverse needs and interests. That said, there will be a point where you have to assume the market has no place for it.

Q – What advice would you give documentary filmmakers about pitching?

Michaelle – Again, don't take it personally. This is a conversation. A public pitch is a great opportunity to have a preliminary conversation with a lot of people at once, but is the lead-in to a number of possible private conversations about the details. It's an opportunity to introduce yourself. Sometimes a broadcaster may decide they like your approach and thinking but the project isn't a fit for them, but another one might be.

Pitching Tips

1. Do research on the people you are pitching to so you don't tell them something that has no chance of being funded. If it's a broadcaster, watch their channel. If it's an organization, read their mandates! PLEASE!!!
2. Rehearse your pitch and try it out on friends. Everyone is a consumer when it comes to finding out just how good your idea is.
3. Have more than one version of your pitch. A really short one to get people's attention if you have a minute and a 2-3 minute one to really engage them.
4. Try to only pitch people one or two projects at a time. Most broadcasters and funders hate the "shotgun" approach.
5. Stay on the story. Don't tell them about the technical aspects or the style until the end.

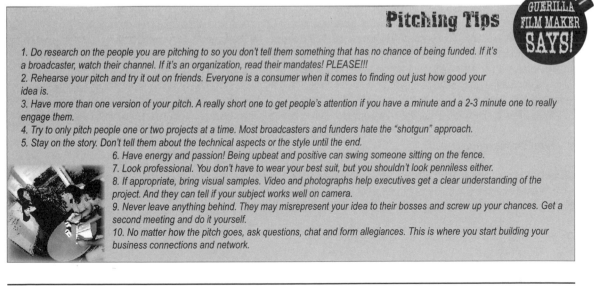

6. Have energy and passion! Being upbeat and positive can swing someone sitting on the fence.
7. Look professional. You don't have to wear your best suit, but you shouldn't look penniless either.
8. If appropriate, bring visual samples. Video and photographs help executives get a clear understanding of the project. And they can tell if your subject works well on camera.
9. Never leave anything behind. They may misrepresent your idea to their bosses and screw up your chances. Get a second meeting and do it yourself.
10. No matter how the pitch goes, ask questions, chat and form allegiances. This is where you start building your business connections and network.

PITCHING FUNDERS

Q – How different is pitching a broadcaster versus a foundation or individual investor?

Carole – In general, you need to create a basic pitch that can be altered depending on whom you're pitching. For example, an investor wants to know if they're going to get a return on their investment – go bottom line. A foundation wants to know if your film fits their guidelines. And a broadcaster wants to know if your film fits their audience. Your pitch must address their needs, not yours.

Q – What tips would you give for pitching?

Carole – The pitch must be a visual description of the film. Stay on the story and don't confuse the issue with technical information because most of those people don't know what a HD camera is. They fund stories so don't give them the history. Tell them the story. They want stories of interesting events with great characters. Another thing is that pitches are verbal, yet you have to write them. And sometimes writing doesn't sound great when spoken. So after you write your pitch, say it out loud to make sure it works.

Q – How long should a pitch be?

Carole – Under three minutes. I like a two-minute pitch. It should engage people. I should be able to see your film as you are talking. You want me to start asking questions that will get you to tell me more. So have an introduction pitch and then have other information ready to give me. Sometimes the person doesn't ask the question that you want them to ask. So I tell my filmmakers to do what the politicians do – tell them what you want them to hear.

Q – Should support material be brought into a pitch?

Carole – It all depends on if they are allowed and where you are. If they are, then definitely use them. The most important part of the pitch is that it's part of you. It comes from the heart not the head. And you can tell the difference when filmmakers are pitching. So it's still most important to be able to give a good verbal pitch because you never know when you are going to be at a cocktail party and someone saunters up and asks you want you're doing. Then you say what film you're working on and they tell you they work for ITVS. Then they want to see the proposal. I've seen that happen a lot. I tell my students that they need to create an elevator pitch. That means that you can get on an elevator and by the time you reach the 10th floor, you have pitched your film, given them your card and have them so engaged that you know they will call you. I know a filmmaker who pitched a woman standing behind her at the grocery store and got a $5,000 donation.

Q – What makes a good pitch?

Carole – Passion. We all want to know why you're making the film and do you have the staying power. Say you're making a film on Alzheimer's, you might say that you're making this film because your father died of Alzheimer's. You can squeeze that in because that will alleviate our fears that you will not finish the film.

Q – How important is your physical presentation?

Carole – Very important. There're a lot of people who look at people's shoes. They want to know where you're coming from. How neat are you? They don't always look at whether you have money or not. I've funded filmmakers who wear thrift store clothes because their passion was finishing the film. So I gave that person all the raw stock she needed to finish it. You affect people through your dress. But how you carry yourself shows your self confidence. When you stand up straight, you show us the pride you have in your project and we are really attracted to that.

Q – How important is a funding trailer?

Carole – Before inexpensive cameras, trailers were a bonus. Now they're a necessity. A good under 7 minute trailer is paramount to getting your film funded. Fernanda Rossi says, *"The trailer has to be long enough to tell the story."* She's absolutely right. You're a storyteller so get in and get out and leave me wanting more so I'll fund you to tell the whole story. I'll fund people from only a proposal and will continue to do so. But if I can see visuals and can see how compelling your characters are, it's much easier to fund. And it should be on DVD so you can show it anywhere. Also you need a lot more than money to make a film. You need support, ideas, guidance, lawyers, accountants, cameramen and soundmen.

Q – How long should a proposal be?

Carole – It should be as long as your funder requests. I tell my filmmaker that when they get the idea for a project they're passionate about, they should write down all their ideas and thoughts they have about it. It may take two weeks, but put all your emotions and feelings in writing. Give it a week and then go back to it. In those thoughts you will find the proposal. Go through and find three words or sentences or paragraphs that fully describe your thoughts because you have to knock me off my feet with a dynamite proposal. If this is for the LA Film Grant, you might be one of a hundred applications. And I read one after another, so if you have something good, it will wake me up. If you're having trouble with the story, then your film is underdeveloped and don't worry, it will emerge through this writing/talking method.

Q – So story should always win out over character?

Carole – Absolutely. You are telling a story. Now I want you to introduce me to the main characters, but no more than three. I can't handle more than that. You want to describe them to me and give me the emotions and feelings of who they are in a way that will touch me. We all communicate through the heart charka. You touch me when it touches my heart. Then I am more likely to give you my resources. Don't talk to my head or I will start analyzing you.

Q – So your proposal should really talk emotionally about how your subject matter fits their mission statement.

Carole – Yes. Let's go back. Once you have written all those pages on your idea – cut it down to about ten pages and now you have your template for your vision. Then edit it down to meet each funders required length. They'll also have certain requirements. Like the Roy W. Dean Grant wants films that are unique and make a contribution to society. I like it when people write in their proposal, *"This film is unique because..."* Or, *"This film makes a contribution to society because..."* That way I know they have read my guidelines and know what the needs are. We like that. You have to think like they think. For investors of documentary films, it's important to get your story down to two pages and give them some visuals of the people and locations you plan to shoot. I love pictures in my proposals. It's branding. I won't forget it.

Q – What should filmmakers know about budgets for proposals?

Carole – I like to see general budgets of under $500,000. It doesn't have to be super-detailed, but I want to know that you know that you can do it for what you think you can do it.

Q – How important is it to show access in the proposal?

Carole – Very important. You have to show that you have the rights to the story so we know that your film can be made without any problems. If it is with a person, we want to know that you have an agreement with that person or their family. If you have letters you should include that.

Q – Is it a good idea to contact people for advice who have previously received grants or funds from particular funders?

Carole – Yes. But some producers can be very closed mouthed about giving out copies of their applications because they may still be in the funding process. One thing you can do is read interviews with people to see how they got their grants.

Q – If you fail to get a grant, is it a good idea to go back to that funder and reapply with changes?

Carole – Yes. I know a filmmaker who went to ITVS three times and failed. Each time she received guidance on how to make it better and by the fourth time, they accepted her. Every person who enters my grants (Roy W. Dean), I promise to give them a 15-minute interview where I go over their proposal and give them guidance on getting funding. I get to know them and can feel into the passion. Of course, I want them to come back, especially when I see that they are committed to making that film. The film *The Flute Player* won on the third time they applied and it was shown on PBS.

Q – Where's a good place to look for individual investors and what's a good way to ask for money or services?

Carole – When you ask for money, you get advice. When you ask for advice, you quite often get money. Remember that people don't give money to films; they give money to filmmakers. They're going to fund you. It's you they're interested in. You could go to an established production company with your project and ask that you work on the film with them as a co-producer. Or if you want to do it on your own, then you have to ask yourself who would be interested in this film. If it's a sports film, then maybe you can find a CPA or an attorney for major sports figures that would be a good fit.

Q – What advice should you ask for?

Carole – Let's say you have a film and you have a list of people who've invested in that type of film. You can get that list easily through the 990 forms from non-profit organizations. That form tells you where the company received their money and who they gave it to. So say you want to do a story on an opera singer. You can easily find donors to the Metropolitan Opera and others. But to walk in and ask them for money is a long shot. Instead, put a lovely proposal together and send it to them with a cover letter stating that you need their advice. *"I know that you"re a patron of the arts and I need help in many ways. Would you be interested in mentoring me?"* Now the best way to get to them is to make friends with their secretary. That's the person who can fund your film. If they take it into their boss and say, *"I think you should really look at this. It's a great concept and the kid needs your help."* They trust their assistants and will listen to them. Once you have good advisors and they see what you're doing, they're more apt to give you money. Invite them to all your meetings – production, scouting, whatever you're doing. And whenever you create paperwork for your proposal run it by them so they see everything you put together.

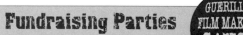

Fundraising Parties

GUERILLA FILM MAKER SAYS!

If you don't have access to or have been turned down by larger funders – all is not lost. You can still attract cash by going right to private investors by holding fundraising parties, giving your pitch and asking for contributions on the spot. Here are some tips –

1. *Have a trailer and other visual aids to get investors excited.*
2. *Have one of your subjects there to make the film seem more personal. It's like having Julia Roberts there!*
3. *Connect with organizations who are interested in your subject matter who might have a place to screen your film and can advertise through their membership.*
4. *Make their donations tax deductible by having 501 (c) 3 status through a fiscal sponsor.*
5. *Food, drink and music all make for a festival atmosphere. Try to tie these to your subject matter or theme.*
6. *Pitch, but don't oversell. And answer everyone's questions!*

Corporate Sponsorship

If you can do it, getting a major company to underwrite your film is a way to go. But be mindful that you are now in an image and politics game. Large brands like Coca-Cola or Quaker Oats probably want non-controversial subject matter and family entertainment. Clearly, they also won't fund anything that puts their company or industry in a bad light. They may want some creative control over your film as well – try to avoid that as much as possible.

Some corporations have foundations that give money to certain causes like breast cancer or children in need. They tend to shy away from funding media, but if you have a topic that means something to them, it doesn't hurt to make a call.

Q – Is it likely that you can raise money from product placement?

Carole – I wouldn't say for first timers that they'd get money. But I'd say product itself is a good idea. Someone I know who works in product placement was able to get a computer for a documentary filmmaker because the computer was used in the film. Also realize the audience of the product needs to be the audience of your film. If you are going after Coca-Cola then you should have a clean, family oriented film.

Q – What are in kind donations?

Carole – That's when you get goods and services for free or at a discount. A good way to do that is to go to the vendor with a one-page proposal and ask them for whatever you need.

Q – What are the grants that you offer?

Carole – We have the New York Film Grant that closes every April 30th that offers goods and services from places in the New York area. You can apply for this grant if you live anywhere in the US, but you get more out of it if you live in and around New York. In LA, I have two grants that close June 30th. The Film Grant and the Video Grant. They're donations from people in the industry and they give you goods and services either free or at a discounts. Plus you get contacts at these top companies and once you get in there, you can work all sorts of deals. I have a grant in New Zealand for Kiwis only and someone who won the grant got 100% of what he needed for the project because they love it! Then I have a writer/researcher grant where I send someone to New Zealand where I have a country cottage on the South island where they can be in solitude and create. I give you a house, a car and some money every week for your food and gas.

Q – What are the common mistakes that you see documentary filmmakers make?

Carole – Clearly defined films get funded. That's my motto. When people start telling me a murky story that I cannot follow, I have to work with them to clear it up. When you can see your film, then you can bring it from that level into the physical.

Q – What advice would you give a new documentary filmmaker?

Carole – Passion powers your film. Commitment to your film is crucial. If you don't want to devote three to five years of your life to this film, then go back to dental school.

GUERILLA FILM MAKER SAYS!

Documentary History and Ethics Books

A New History of Documentary Film
by Jack Ellis & Betsy A. Mclane
A thorough survey/history of documentary films mainly from the US, the UK, and Canada. It outlines the origins of the form and then shows its development over the next several decades. The text is straightforward with hardly any academic jargon or high-level theory.

Documentary Film: A Primer
by Carl Rollyson
A succinct intro to docs covering a range of subjects including the Russian Revolution, the Holocaust, and the worlds of fashion and sports.

Lies, Damn Lies and Documentaries
by Brian Winston
Covers many ethical issues surrounding documentary filmmaking especially in regard to contemporary television forms.

Documentary: A History of the Non-Fiction Film
by Erik Barnouw
A compassionate and ethical history of documentary films providing such breadth that most people will want to reread several times to absorb Barnouw's rich historical information.

New Documentary: A Critical Introduction
by Stella Bruzzi
A comprehensive account of the last two decades of documentary filmmaking in the US, Britain and Europe. Bruzzi explores how issues of gender identity, queer theory, performance, "race" and spectatorship are important to our understanding of contemporary documentary.

Principles of Visual Anthropology
by Paul Hockings
Covers ethnographic filming and its relations to the cinema and television; the uses of still photography, archives, and videotape; and overcoming the funding problems of film production. 27 experts lend their voices to this discussion.

ANATOMY OF A DOCUMENTARY SECTION 4

ORGANIZATIONS

IDA

Q – What is the IDA?

Sandra –The International Documentary Association is a non-profit organization that's 23 years old and our mission is to serve the non-fiction in film, video and TV to keep the genre alive through a variety of services. We publish a magazine, *International Documentary*, ten months a year. We have a very prestigious award competition called the IDA Achievement Awards for best short, feature, limited series, continuing series and we give a student award – the David L. Wolper Student Documentary Achievement Award. We do a Jacqueline Donnet Emerging Filmmaker Award. And emerging means you can be merging at 90 years old or 18 years old. There is no age limit. There's an ABCNews Videosource Award for best use in that medium and also one for best continuing series. We have a Pioneer Award and a Scholarship and Preservation Award. We have two newer awards, the Outstanding Documentary Editing Award and the Outstanding Documentary Cinematography Award. We also qualify documentary films for Academy Awards® eligibility in a screening series called DocuWeek. If you feel your documentary has Oscar® potential and you show at this series, you are eligible. But you have to go by the rules of the Academy – the key one being that your film cannot have been seen anywhere in the world on TV, online, satellite or anywhere if it is going to be eligible. It must only have been seen in a theater. This is a dilemma because sometimes your films are financed by television and cable, so you have to work out your deal accordingly. Also your film has to show for seven consecutive days in Los Angeles county commercial theater or in the borough of Manhattan prior to the end of August of that year. We do DocuWeek™ every year at the Arclight Theater in Los Angeles. We have a opening night party and a Q&A after each screening with the filmmakers. It's a good way for the distributors to see your film.

Q – Can you help documentary filmmakers find resources?

Sandra – Yes. We have a website with a members only site so you can find specific information like if you're going to the Czech Republic and you need a cameraperson, you can find a member there. Or you can call us and we will put you in contact with someone there. So we service documentary filmmakers and fans of the documentary. Not everyone who joins this organization is a filmmaker.

Q – Do you do screenings outside of DocuWeek?

Sandra – Yes. We look at works in progress. We look at trailers. We do just about everything you as a documentarian might need except give you money. And we can help you find ways to get money.

Q – What is fiscal sponsorship?

Sandra – In order to raise money for your film, you often want to go to a foundation or a state or government agency like the NEH. But they can only give monies to non-profit organizations. You can become one yourself by going to the government and filling in the forms and paying a few thousand dollars. Or we can receive money for you – that is a fiscal sponsor. To do so, we require that you become a member of the IDA and charge a $75 fee for processing the paperwork. And then you must provide a proposal for your film. It doesn't have to be a thesis – it just has to be a well-written, concise work that describes your film. What makes it unique? What kind of access do you have to your subject? Is this a realistic proposal? You also have to fill out a budget. You then submit this proposal and budget to a committee who are very experienced documentary filmmakers who review your proposal and your budget for the following things. Is it original? Or are you saying something new about a familiar topic? Do you have access? And with the budget, are you realistic and have accounted for all the contingencies. 99% of the people who apply for fiscal sponsorship get in. It's very rare to reject someone, but they will usually ask that you redo your budget. Once you come on board, you are under the auspices of the IDA. We charge 5% of the monies that we raise to take care of overhead and paperwork. Once you join, an escrow account is opened for you. Any monies that are given are tax deductible, so if your grandmother wants to give you $50,000 she gets a deduction. The checks are made out to the IDA and earmarked for your project. Once they clear, the monies are available for you to use for your project. You get them by calling us and get in touch with our fiscal sponsorship director and she will cut you a check. It usually takes about 24 hours to turn it around.

Q – How detailed does the budget have to be?

Sandra – We send you a fiscal sponsorship packet that has a sample budget in it. But I think what people forget is to budget for a website and PR. Be sure that you have money assigned for stills. Pulling clips from the movie look terrible. Even if it's your younger brother taking stills with his digital camera – budget it in and don't forget to do it. If you get into Sundance, you are going to need them. Websites are good for grass roots marketing. And you should always budget for film festival fees, as that is how most filmmakers get their project seen at first. Also budget in money to attend festivals. Do research and find out which festivals you want to go to and budget accordingly for that.

Q – How long does the process take?

Sandra – Four to six weeks. Many people call and say, *"I'm going to get a grant and the deadline is tomorrow and I haven't applied for my fiscal sponsorship."* We can't turn it around in 24 hours. So plan and have a strategy before you make your film. Not just on the making, but in the marketing. I know that sometimes a film has to be done right then and there and I'm all for someone who doesn't have the money going out and shooting, but be smart and savvy. If you think that you have an idea that's good for Discovery, study that network and see the kind of programming they're doing.

Q – Any tips on making the synopsis of a proposal better?

Sandra – You don't have to present a leather bound proposal. It just has to be succinct enough where I can read that proposal and visualize that film. Also you should show that you have something to say that no one else has on that subject or you have access to someone or something that no one else does. What is your POV? Why should anyone fund this film? Think about who your audience is. Is this a global story that you can international with or is it only interesting to a North American audience? Be realistic about who is going to fund your project when you talk about it in the proposal.

Q – What is an advisory board?

Sandra – Most documentary filmmakers are the editor, cinematographer, the director and producer. What you need is a partner that has skills that you don't have. In other words, you might be great at camerawork and the technical stuff, but you aren't great at producing and raising money. An advisory board should be people who know how to go into corporate America or has been through the process and help you get funds from them. They also tend to be people from the community that you are filming and they can help you gain access to other areas through their contacts. They may help legitimize your project in the eyes of the community. Further they give you some objective eyes when you show the film because you are going to be precious of it.

Q – Is an advisory board required by some funders?

Sandra – Sometimes. Especially if you have a very specialized topic like being bipolar. Then is would help to have a few psychiatrists on your board. And you may want that person in your film. But if you're doing a story like *Born Into Brothels* - who would you have on your advisory board? I suppose you could have someone who knows the culture of India and can help you navigate through that culture.

Q – What advice would you give a filmmaker on approaching funders?

Sandra – Well, if you're going to do a grant, you should study the website of that foundation and understand what their mandate is. You don't want to apply to something and find out that they only give money to people in Minneapolis. What funders really hate is when you send them something that is so off base from what they do. It's like going to a job interview and not knowing anything about the company that you are interviewing for. Just be sure you're prepared. When you're going to personal funders, there are lots of things people do. There are home parties where people have friends over and invite those who might be interested in funding your film. Then you show a five-minute trailer and get people excited about it to write you a check right there on the spot. You should be passionate about your subject. You should be knowledgeable about the subject matter. And you should state why you think this film should be made. Be prepared to show your budget and synopsis.

Q – What advice would you give on approaching broadcasters?

Sandra – There are certain things that you can go to that unfortunately cost money like *Real Screen*, which is a market for broadcasters in Washington, DC. They're all there and they're on panels talking about what they are looking for. Sometimes they even have pitch sessions there. But they all say the same thing – study our network and our programming so that you know what they do. It is difficult to sell your film sometimes because a lot of these shows are formulaic. It may be your subject that you bring to them but it will done in the style of Discovery.

Q – How can you help direct filmmakers towards funding?

Sandra – We have contacts with all the distributors, many of whom are trustees of the IDA. If you think you have a film that would fit one of them, I would see a trailer and then contact the distributor if I felt it was something they might be interested in. If they liked it then they would ask to see the filmmaker. Also there are the ThinkFilms and Magnolias of the world with whom we have contacts and who sometimes give finishing funds. They usually look to acquire finished films, but they do look for that little gold nugget that needs finishing and is something special. We have a listing of distributors that we can share with our members. Our magazine has had over the years some excellent articles on alternative distribution. So for example, you might learn that you should fight to maintain the right to distribute your film on DVD via your own website.

Q – Do you have archival footage?

Sandra – No. But we have contacts with places like ABC News who might give our members discounts. We have lots of member's discounts for vendors around the country. We also have health insurance, production insurance and a relationship with DeWitt Stern who provide a discount on E&O insurance. You also get discounts on Kodak film and Alamo rental cars.

Q – What seminars and workshops do you do?

Sandra – Every year we do a series of seminars called Docs A-Z, which we do in the spring. It's in LA and NY and every week it's on a different subject matter. One week it might be editing documentaries, the next week it could be on sound or composers. And we're going to go to other cities as well.

Q – What kind of networking events do you offer?

Sandra – We do a lot of screenings both here and New York and San Francisco. They are free for members. We have Salon Screenings here in LA at a club called Monroe's and we show a documentary film and have drinks afterwards. It's free for IDA members and they can show their films or works in progress. They don't have to be from IDA members, but if a distributor calls and wants us to screen it for our members, we will. That will go around the country soon, too. We work with sister organizations like Women in Film, AIVF, Film Arts Foundation, etc.

Q – What is DocuDay?

Sandra – It's the day before the Academy Awards®. All day we show the Academy nominated documentary films from 10am to midnight. All the filmmakers are in town and do a Q&A at the Writers Guild in LA. It's always sold out. We also do it in New York two weeks before the Academy Awards® and we are considering doing it in Washington, DC.

Q – Do your Awards have any monetary awards?

Sandra – There are three that do. The Emerging Filmmaker Award has a $2,000 award. The ABCNews Videosource Award has a $2,000 honorarium and a $2,000 worth of research time at their archives in NY. Pare Lorentz has a $2,500 honorarium.

Q – What do you see as the future of documentary filmmaking?

Sandra – I don't think it's flavor of the month kind of thing. I think the world is asking for another genre of entertainment other than Hollywood films. We provide information on a non-fiction basis. These are non-actors. They are real people in real situations. I think many people feel mislead by the media and that documentary will continue to be a source of information that people can believe.

Q – Do you think there has been a change in the US consumer's attitude toward international documentaries?

Sandra – Yes. If you see what's going on at the festivals there are tons of international films there. We need to see more international films. We need to have access to the films from Asia and Africa. There's so much going on there and we don't know about it. Some of it has to do with oppressive governments and they have to go underground. Iran is a perfect example of that. We have a guy from Nigeria who wants to be on our board and we do elect someone from the membership. But he has to be here in LA once a month for meetings and yet he still wants to be on the board.

Q – What common mistakes do you see filmmakers make?

Sandra – Their films are too long. I think it's because when you are a documentary filmmaker you are the director, editor and cameraman and the umbilical cord is hard to cut. So show your film to other people before you make the final cut. Also they don't prepare themselves for what's involved after you 've shot and edited your film. There's no difference between marketing a feature film and a documentary. Well, the only difference is that you don't have the $30 million they give you in Hollywood for P&A. But you have the same problems. You have to get it out to the media. You have to know who the audience for your film is. Is it American? Is it global? Sandi Dubowski who did *Trembling Before G-d*, marketed his film brilliantly. It's about homosexuals who are Orthodox Jews. He had a distributor who gave him a little money and he went to all the markets. Now what did Sandi have going for him? He had a film about homosexuals and Jews. Two major markets. He went to all the synagogues and gay/lesbian groups and used his website to get people to know about it. If you don't know anything about marketing, then hire someone or get some to help you.

Q – What advice would you give a new filmmaker?

Sandra – Be in love with your subject. Also know that the average time it takes to finish a documentary is seven years, so don't get discouraged when you are in your third year. The only way you get it done sooner is to have all your funding up front. If not, you are working a day job or teaching and that is why it takes so long. Also don't get frustrated if things change. That is the nature of documentaries. Andrew Jarecki started making *Capturing The Friedmans* about a clown and then found out about the charges against the clown's father. That is the challenging and exciting part about it – you don't have control.

Milton Tabbot
Doc Funding Programs, Film Series

IFP-NY

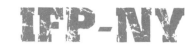

Q – How can IFP help documentary filmmakers?

Milton - Our largest program is the IFP Market. About 50% of the projects in every year's market are documentary works. Completed documentaries, shorts and documentary works-in-progress which can be anywhere from a production that has just recently started to something that is in late post-production. They're all looking for some kind of financing – either finishing, production funding or more development funding. Completed films are basically looking for some kind of distribution - broadcast, theatrical, international. Within the market we do a number of things for documentary filmmakers as well. We do networking meetings and putting industry together with particular projects who ask to meet with them. The other thing that the IFP does for documentaries is give a grant that I manage called the Anthony Radziwill Documentary Fund. That's specifically development money for documentaries. We give ten grants over the course of the year – five every six months. They're small grants of $10,000 to help people start a project such as do some research, shoot some interviews or perhaps shoot enough to start putting together a trailer to do more fundraising. It's generally the first or second money into a project. We started it because there are very few grants that give early money. We also do an exhibition series called Independents Night, which we do six times a year. That's a joint program with the Film Society of Lincoln Center and it's a screening program for completed documentaries that do not have theatrical distribution and have not yet screened in New York.

Q – What stands out in a project to make it eligible for the Development Grant?

Milton – The only restriction is you have to be a US resident. What we're looking for obviously is to have good docs that perhaps won't get initial funding from other large entities. We're hoping for original documentaries - both new voices and established. The first cycle of this program, I expected to get 200-300 submissions - we got 602 proposals for five grants. And they were by and large very good. I wish we had millions more to give away, but now we are five every six months.

Q – Do you give grants to new filmmakers?

Milton – We're open to that. The difference between our grant and some others is that it's not an artist based grant. We aren't just funding a person just because they're good. It's really a project based grant. It really depends on what particular project they want to make and if there's enough there for a feature film. This grant isn't for short documentaries. So does it seem like a valid documentary feature? What is their approach to the work? What is their access? What is their history? Yes, we could be funding someone coming from another discipline or who might be coming right out film school and is making something with little or no film experience at all. It's totally dependent on what's in the proposal and does it seem promising. That said, the people who do the best are people who've been through a grant process before and know how to write a proposal. They know how to make their ideas sound interesting and have something to back it up – meaning they have unique access to a subject or they have experience that gives you confidence that the film will get made.

Q – What do you expect in a proposal?

Milton – It has to set out what the subject matter is. Why it would be an interesting film as opposed to a book? What about the subject matter is important to the filmmaker? What kind of access do they have to whatever they are doing? Are they going to be able to make this effectively? We don't look for other funding because frequently we are the first money. Does it seem like a different take on a familiar topic? Is it something that no one has approached before as a documentary? It really has to come alive on the page and that's something a lot of proposal writers don't think about. Our proposal is not unique, but it's a little different in that at the very first stage as we don't look at previous work or supplementary material. We're strictly reading the proposal. Our application is online. It's a standard format. They're limited in each section to a number of words. Some are quite lengthy such as 1,500-2,000 words, but the maximum would come in at eight pages.

Q – What is the process of selection?

Milton – There are essentially three stages. There's an internal stage, which is mostly me who literally looks at each proposal to say does this meet our criteria. Then there are people who have agreed to evaluate them and they're from all around the country. These are generally are between 20-25 readers who have some direct connection to the documentary world such as documentary programmers for festivals, arts administration type people, other funders and documentary teachers. Each one reads anywhere between 30-40 proposals and then turns in an evaluation on each one. And then each proposal is read by more than one evaluator. They grade them like term papers. We see which ones float to the top and then try to narrow it down. The final stage deals with the ones that are chosen as finalists who now go to a totally different group – a smaller 4-5 person group – where all the panelists meet to discuss the proposals and at that time, at the very last time, they look at previous work from those people.

Q – Is a trailer beneficial?

Milton – Totally depends. Trailers and samples can make or break you. Someone who has made one other film and the panelists don't know the work and want to see the sample. If it is the least bit undermining in terms of confidence, such as the film they propose is visually beautiful and they submit something that is very gritty, then there is a disconnect between what they are making and what they've made. That could hurt you. The converse is true. I've seen proposals where they're not sure but then they put on a previous work and they see that this person knows how to tell a story and make a movie.

Q – Does it matter what they propose to shoot the film on?

Milton – That comes into play in the analysis of the proposal. So if someone has a very on the run, catch it where you can premise and they want to shoot 35mm – why? And they must budget for that. All of these pieces, that's something that these people look at when they're evaluating something. Do they have a general idea of what the budget is going to be? Are they choosing to shoot something on low-end video when cries out for film or vice versa? But, no, we are not looking for film or video specifically.

Q – Does it help to have any finance in place?

Milton – Not with us. It will with other funders and that's why some people would love to get our grant because it'll help them with other funders. If someone shows an initial interest then it's a snowball effect. It could hurt more depending on the amount of funding because if you have a relatively average documentary budget and you've gotten a significant grant that would help you get to the stage that we're trying to get you to, it could hurt you. Generally, if someone has already gotten a grant, they already have a broadcaster in place, then it's very unlikely that we'd give them money.

Q – What is the New York State Council of The Arts Electronic Media and Film Grant?

Milton – It is a small distribution grant that gives $50,000 a year to help people in their distribution efforts. So if they need X number of copies to be submitted to festivals or making flyers. And it's not just film and video, it's web based – anything that uses electronic media and film. But it's for New York based artists only. You need to have a plan for how you use the money. It can be used for festivals. It must be a completed work that you want to get out there. The grant is no bigger than $5,000, but it's a panel of selectors who read the proposals and decide how much to give to each person based on what they're asking for. That isn't specifically documentary.

Q – What time of year is the IFP Market?

Milton – September. It generally follows the Toronto Film Festival by a few days. You can apply online.

Q – How do you choose those films?

Milton – Generally a good part of the screening is done by the artistic director of the market, by me who is in charge of the documentary programs and by senior staff. We have some outside people who help who either program for festivals or they're used to working in the documentary film world. We look at how original is it. Does it seem like there will be a faction that will want to see it? Is this an interesting filmmaker? Is this someone who should be nurtured, supported and get that industry feedback and interaction. It's not just about presenting a film and hoping to sell it or hoping to get additional financing for it. It's about creating a space where the filmmakers, the creative community and industry can mix and interact. We tell people that a lot of what you're doing here is meeting your peers from around the country and they are people that you could be working with in the future. You learn a lot from hearing their experiences.

Q –When is the deadline for the Market application?

Milton – End of May or early June. It changes every year so check our website. The deadline for the Documentary Fund is twice a year March 1st and September 1st. And you don't have to be an IFP member to participate.

Q – Is there a fee for the Market?

Milton – Yes, there's an application fee of around $40. If you get in the market there's a participation fee, which is around $350-400. Check our website for the accurate amounts.

Q – How many distributors come to the market?

Milton – There are usually 400 different types of companies from festivals to production companies. However, in the documentary world it's smaller subset. It's been bigger in the last couple of years because of the success some documentaries have had in the theaters. So you will have ThinkFilm who has made a real commitment to acquiring documentaries. But companies like Lionsgate are now there looking for another theatrical documentary.

Q – Do you have any documentaries that are in the script stage?

Milton – No. There was a very brief period in our co-production market called No Borders where we entertained the idea of taking proposals. It was very hard to run. We weren't equipped for that.

Q – What equipment do you have that filmmakers can use?

Milton – We have a camera package that anybody can use for free. We also have a Final Cut Pro system members can use. If you're a member and your film is playing a one-week engagement, we promote your film – it's called Members on the Screen. We'll promote you through e-mail and put you in the newsletter. There are the various networking things that we do such as Producers POV where you can come in and sit down with a producer if they have questions about their project or production. That's generally once a month. There's a lawyer where you can ask them questions once a month. We have a once a month training session on the camera for those who don't know how to use it. And of course if you have trouble finding some resource, you can call us and we'll help you.

Q – What is the fee to join IFP-NY?

Milton – $100/year for individuals and less for students. Households are $150. Check our website for accurate amounts.

Q – Do you have any budgeting workshops?

Milton – A huge part of the market is called The Filmmaker Conference. This is the conference component that is 40-50 panels and workshops that're happening concurrently during the Market.

Q – What do you offer documentary shorts?

Milton – We have a monthly shorts program that I program at the Pioneer Theater here in New York. It's called IFP Buzz Cuts and it's for documentary and narrative. The Market is the other way we service shorts filmmakers. Short documentaries are a challenged area because there's very little output for them.

Q – What are the most common mistakes that you see with documentaries that have been submitted?

Milton – Some people don't have an awareness of what has come before or what's out there at the moment. So there might be 15 criminal justice stories out there right now and you aren't going to take all of them. Which one seems a little different? We can only take between 90-100 documentaries in the Market. The Market has changed as it has gotten more selective since quality keeps going up in the doc world. The amount you submit is key. If you've just started shooting and you can only put together 3 minutes, it better be a really good 3 minutes because you're competing against things that are almost rough cuts. The other thing about a short trailer if it's a really good trailer is that maybe it will be a good film, but it could also only be the good parts. Another mistake is that there're optional sections in the proposal application, like a filmmaker statement. Take the time to fill it out and explain what you want to do. If you don't take advantage of that, it could hurt you because there is not enough time for us to follow up with you.

Q – What single piece of advice would you give new filmmakers?

Milton – For people who are applying for grants - read the criteria. Understand your funder and really tailor your proposal to that specific grant. It's clear when a generic grant proposal comes in that doesn't address all the issues that we ask for in the proposal or seem to refer to things that some other funder has asked that they didn't take the time to write something new here, they just cut and paste – it hurts.

Independent Feature Project (IFP) Locations

IFP is a nonprofit, membership organization that provides information, support, and education programs to independent filmmakers. Services include seminars, workshops, screenings, advice, and referrals.

Seattle Branch
Independent Feature Project
1001 Lenora Street
Seattle, WA 98121
Tel: (206) 860-8490

Minneapolis Branch:
Independent Feature Project/North
1401 Third Ave. South
Minneapolis, MN 55404
Tel: (612) 870-0156

IFP Phoenix
Phoenix Film Foundation
2345 East Thomas Road, Suite 102
Phoenix, AZ 85016
(602) 955-6444

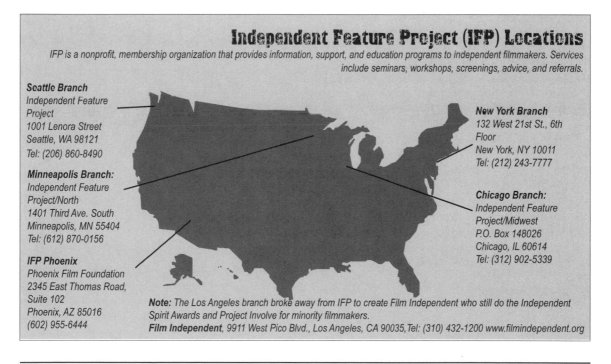

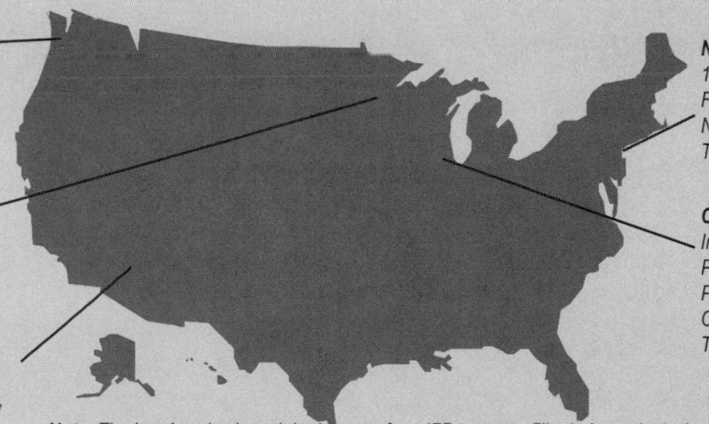

New York Branch
132 West 21st St., 6th Floor
New York, NY 10011
Tel: (212) 243-7777

Chicago Branch:
Independent Feature Project/Midwest
P.O. Box 148026
Chicago, IL 60614
Tel: (312) 902-5339

Note: *The Los Angeles branch broke away from IFP to create Film Independent who still do the Independent Spirit Awards and Project Involve for minority filmmakers.*
Film Independent*, 9911 West Pico Blvd., Los Angeles, CA 90035, Tel: (310) 432-1200 www.filmindependent.org*

DOCUCLUB

Q – What is DocuClub?

Susan – Myself and other documentary filmmakers all felt the isolation of working on a documentary and would talk about the importance of community. After talking to Walter Scheuer, an Academy Award producer of documentaries and the inspiration for DocuClub, I was given the green light to start this grass roots organization. "Wally" loved the idea of filmmakers meeting in our offices to discuss films, network and share works-in-progress. He donated a video projector, a large screen and all the chairs we could possibly need. And then I invited about ten filmmakers and lovers of the form to our office, everyone contributed at least ten names to our mailing list and DocuClub was born. Over the years the list has grown from 60 to over 4,000 names.

Q – Now that is has grown so large can you still facilitate that?

Susan – Well, the popcorn is not on every seat anymore! Yes, I hope we've managed to keep it intimate and about the filmmaking. Our venues have changed over the years, and now we program at the IFC Center and for special events at Makor.

Q – How many members do you have that come to these events?

Susan – Our programs are offered to members and nonmembers. Our events are always well attended. At each event half are usually members. Lets just say we have an enthusiastic membership base, but like every organization we love signing up more members. It's $40 for the season. If a person is interested, he or she should log onto DocuClub.org to find out how to be a member and to learn more about DocuClub.

Q – So to be a member you have to be based in NYC?

Susan – No, we have many members outside of NY. Just recently someone flew in from LA to screen his work-in-progress. One of the major bonuses of DocuClub is the physical contact with fellow filmmakers and industry professionals. Everyone seems to love the networking parties after the screenings.

Q – What is the In-The-Works program?

Mary – In-the-Works helps filmmakers gain perspective on their films when they're in the final stages of production. We offer to show a film on a big screen with an audience of filmmakers and lovers of the form who want to give critical feed back to help filmmakers in the edit room. For the record none of our projects are rejected, we offer every film that is submitted an opportunity to receive feedback through our Home Screening program. We also audio tape all the sessions so the filmmaker can concentrate on the essence of what's being said and not be distracted by taking notes.

Q – What is the Idea Workshop?

Mary - Our Idea Workshop is basically a pitching session where we choose three projects that will be pitched to three industry representatives in front of a live audience. In the past couple of months, we've had people from POV, Showtime, HBO, and Discovery Docs critiquing not just the content of the projects, but the way the filmmakers pitched them. This is a very important, often overlooked, component of pitching – the impression that you personally make on the person you are pitching to. And we have just instituted a new component of the Idea Workshop – the open pitch. We receive many more submissions than we can accommodate, so now you can put your name in a hat at the beginning of the evening and we choose someone at random to pitch at the end of the program.

Q – What is the Home Screening Program?

Mary – We offer filmmakers a list of names of industry professionals who'll watch their films and offer individual critiques. It's basically a more private In-the-Works session for our members who do not want to screen their rough cut in front of a large, public audience.

Q – How do you submit a film to DocuClub?

Mary – Well you have to be a member to submit your film and all the information is on our website. We send out a call-for-entries at the beginning of our season, which starts in September. We also solicit rough-cut projects that would be good for our In-the-Works or Idea Workshop programs.

Q – What other resources do you have?

Susan – We offer advice, contacts, websites and postings on our e-mail blasts. If we don't have the answers we suggest that a filmmaker contact one of the many other film organizations in the city, such as the IFP, AIVF, Women Make Movies, Third World Newsreel, F/VA, Shooting People, Doculink and the list goes on.

Q – What common problems do you see when people make their docs?

Susan – When you make an independent documentary you're often working in a vacuum. I find that in the edit room filmmakers are too attached to their footage and tend to want to keep all their best moments rather than make those very tough editing decisions. Filmmakers need to work with people who are not as attached to their story and/or footage. DocuClub definitely offers that kind of safe exploration with people that care about the process.

Q – What advice would you give a new filmmaker?

Susan – Look for organizations in your hometown that can offer resources and community. Another way to get an overview of the process is to find an apprenticeship with a filmmaker who you respect. If you're in New York City, the IFP is a great place to volunteer during its film market in September. To survive as an independent I also suggest mastering some specific profession in the field, such as being an editor, cinematographer, sound engineer, producer, researcher, and the list goes on.

501 (c) 3

GUERILLA FILM MAKER SAYS!

501 (c) 3 is the US Tax Code for non-profit organizations. Many funders can only give to places that have this designation. If you have this status any contributions to your film become tax deductible for the donors. The easiest way to take advantage of this is to join a non-profit organization that will act as your fiscal sponsor. Foundations and donors will donate to the organization with the funds earmarked for your project. The organization then takes a fee to cover their overhead – usually around 5%.

The other option is to get non-profit status for your own company. It's very possible to do and you won't give up that 5%, which is a big deal if you have a large budget. But the red tape and strict accounting you have to adhere to can be a real pain and means you need a good tax lawyer and accountant (which you should have anyway!)

FILM/VIDEO ARTS

Q – What is Film/Video Arts?

Paul – We work with filmmakers in a variety of ways: first by providing educational support so if you're a director and you don't know anything about the newest cameras and you want to learn about the newest HD camera, then you can take one of our classes. Or if you want to brush up on your cinematography skills, you could take one of our cinematography classes; or take one of our Final Cut Pro or Avid classes. Second, we help people financially, raising funds through our fiscal sponsorship program where we sponsor filmmakers' projects and enable them to get government or private grants by being their fiscal sponsor. Because we're a non-profit, the donations are tax deductible. Thirdly, we have different hands-on programs and support for the filmmakers. We have our resident filmmaker program, which is kind of like when a doctor does a residency before they become a real doctor. It's for people who have a reel and can use our equipment and services here as well as get to work on different projects to learn the various aspects of filmmaking. And lastly we offer equipment. We have two Final Cut studios and an Avid. We have two really nice Canon XL1s, a nice Panasonic and a Sony as well. Then we have all varieties of equipment you would need to shoot. We even have an Arri Super 16mm camera. If you're a member of the organization you get it for a much cheaper price.

Q – Do the residents use it for free?

Paul – Yes. And they take our classes for free. We try to put together a training program for them based upon their skill level and what they know, what they need to know and what their project entails. Once we know that, we recommend which classes they should take. We do works-in-progress screenings for them and give them critique on their projects.

Q – How does one join and how much does it cost?

Paul – For an individual, the membership is $50. For an organization it is $350 and that covers everyone within the organization. If it's over three or four people in an organization, we say do it as an organization so that everyone can become a member. Benefits of membership are discounts at external equipment rental places, post-production facilities, film stock cameras, any kind of equipment, any kind electronic software hardware. We've negotiated for the filmmakers in kind of a collective bargaining agreement to get these great discounts. The benefits also include discounts on the courses - a $100-$200 savings per course.

Q – How many classes do you do?

Paul – It can vary from five different types of classes in a month to thirty-five. It depends on the time of the year. We have a series just on documentaries that include: how to film a documentary, how you write your documentary and how you raise funds for your documentary. We have a have a whole series of classes on editing and equipment.

Q – How many students do you usually have per class?

Paul – We usually try not to go above 6 people in a class. The camera classes could go up to 30 people in a class, but we make sure there's enough equipment so that everyone gets hands-on in class. We like to make sure that there are now more than three people on a camera. They range from about $350 to $500.

Q – And is that $300 for a series of classes?

Paul – It varies on the program. The cheapest classes meet once: like one of the basic camera classes; it might only be $50. You learn how to use the camera. It's more like a seminar than it is a class. The more usual class meets about 5 to 8 times. It could be 5 weeks or two weeks depending on whether they meet once or twice a week.

Q – Do you do a budgeting and proposal class?

Paul – Yes. Budgeting and fundraising go together. It's great once you know how to budget but then the next logical question is: how am I going to get this money? The instructor we have teaching the class really focuses on her experiences having to produce a whole bunch of documentaries. She brings in other people who are documentary film producers and they talk about their experiences. Then it's basically how to write a documentary: the planning to the writing and the actual writing of the documentary itself. How to shoot a documentary: the actual setting of your shots, locations. Even how you should prepare yourself for a documentary.

Q – Do any of your classes deal with interview techniques?

Paul – That's part of the how to prepare, how to write and what questions to ask. There are people who like to talk a lot as they are interviewing. You need to let the other person answer a question; don't direct the person to an answer. You have to be comfortable asking the difficult questions. But you don't want to be a prosecutor either because then you put the person on the defensive and they close off. This is a difficult technique to master. The success of the documentary is dependent on how well you interview the featured people.

Q – What about fiscal sponsorship?

Paul – First you have to submit an application. We need a director's reel and the top peoples reel of the project if they have one. 80% of the time the applicants aren't first time filmmakers.

Q – Is it a disadvantage if you're a first time filmmaker since you wouldn't have a reel?

Paul – We ask a lot more questions of a first time filmmaker. We usually want to see that the other people on the project are experienced and have a reel. So they submit their reel and their CV's, the proposal for the project and a detailed budget. Then there's peer review, which is a filmmaker review, and then there's board review. There are two or three filmmakers on the executive board who will review the application. It's a rolling admission so we're constantly accepting people into the program. Once they're in, they have different needs. The filmmakers will bring their own ideas about where to apply for sponsorship, send us their grant proposals to some of the larger grants and ask us to review their proposals. We'll also write the grant proposal for them for a fee.

Q – Do you help them figure out where to submit their finished films?

Paul – Yes. We also tell people where not to show their films. When you finish your film you want to show it to everyone. Sometimes that's not the best approach. If you show the film at one festival, another festival may not want to see it. For example, we have a once a month show on cable in which we feature our filmmaker films and everyone wants to be on that show. We have to ask where is your film in its life? Where has it gone? Where has it been? We want the ones that you said, *"I'm done with it! No one else wants it!"* We help them with arranging private screenings. If somebody wants to put together a screening for some potential other backers, or to do another project, we'll help them find another location.

Q – Do you do any fundraising for your filmmakers?

Paul – We will participate in their fundraisers and promote fundraisers to raise funds for their projects. We'll have someone from F/VA come down and talk about the project to the audience to give them more support, that is the organization is backing them up. Not enough filmmakers take advantage of the resources that we offer.

Q – Why is that?

Paul – We probably could do a better job letting them know about how to do it. And a lot of people don't plan accordingly. Usually the fewer projects they have, the less planning they've done. Everything is last minute and then it's difficult to coordinate the resources and really do the things you'd like to. An independent filmmaker's success will come down to how well they plan their project. From the budgets, to when you're going to shoot, to your people, your equipment - everything. The more planning you can get done and can bring experienced people in the more success you're going to have.

Q – Are the majority of people who go to these events private investors or organizations?

Paul – The big funding organizations will not show up at a fund raiser. It's private investment. It's friends and family, co-worker and maybe if you're an Italian American filmmaker you'll hit every Italian-American organization and invite their representatives to the showing and try to get them to participate in the funding.

Q – How do you advertise the showing?

Documentary Online Communities

D-Word community
www.d-word.com

Third World Newsreel
www.twn.org

Fractured Atlas
www.fracturedatlas.org

Doculink
www.doculink.org

Downtown Community Television
www.dctvny.com

Shooting People
www.shootingpeople.org

The Forum
www.filmarts.org/theboard

Paul – Manhattan Neighborhood Network advertises, as does the New York State Council for the Arts. A lot of our funders will advertise it as well. Plus if you knew that your film or short were going to be there that night, you'd tell everybody to watch. The number of viewers is directly related to how much the filmmaker cares.

Q – Do you accept first time filmmakers for your Resident Filmmakers Program?

Paul – We're looking for people who have a project or two under their belt. These people have certain specific needs and can lend value to the organization and its members. They help create a filmmaking environment.

Q – How long is the resident filmmakers' program?

Paul – Six months. At the end of six months they can reapply for another six months. In the course of a year, we'll have close to 20 resident filmmakers.

Q – Besides using the equipment what are the advantages to this program?

Paul – Classes and the work-in-progress screenings. At the end of your residency if you've completed your film, we put on a screening for you and promote it as much as possible. You apply by requesting an application and we'll mail it to you. You submit it and it gets reviewed. Then there's an interview process where staff and board members look at the applications. Applicants may go through two or three interviews. Once they get in, they get a monthly stipend that comes from a grant from Con Edison.

Q – What do the filmmakers have to do in return?

Paul – They have to work here a certain number of hours a month. Then they can start enrolling in classes, use the equipment and working on the special projects.

Q – What is the Artists Mentorship Program?

Paul – It takes emerging filmmakers and partners them up, three people at time, with a well-known independent filmmaker who helps them with their projects over a year. The New York State Council On The Arts sponsors it so everyone receives funds for doing it. The well-known filmmaker is paid for their time and the independent filmmaker receives money for their project. They have to stage a big screening at the end.

Q – Can they see this mentor person any time?

Paul – Yes, they meet together as a group and they meet together as individuals. The mentor will review their work and help them with anything related to their work.

Q – Do you have an online service so that not just New York filmmakers can participate?

Paul – Yes. We have filmmakers who are in Arkansas and Kansas and some really remote places within the United States. We have 15 filmmakers in Chicago for some reason. Usually someone goes out there, starts working with us and then they tell their friends.

Q – Do you have anybody that your members can talk to about insurance, legal and other business issues?

Paul – One of our board members, John Johnson, is an entertainment attorney specializing in film and video and distribution, releases. Once every couple of months he runs a seminar on legal issues related to documentary. Most filmmakers don't realize that they really need that information until it's too late.

Q – Do you have production insurance?

Paul – Yes, that's part of the membership. We even discount the production insurance. If you're going to do a shoot, and you don't have your own production insurance, but you need to use equipment we have production insurance. But it's only good on our equipment. We do get discounts from other insurance companies if they need to rent something special.

Q – Do you have a library for accessing information? Like information on a contract or PPM?

Paul – We have digital documents that are examples of things. Plus we have books. If you're filling out a fiscal sponsorship application, we have sample budgets and proposals. We'll even e-mail one to you if you're a member.

Q – What are the most common mistakes you see from filmmakers?

Paul – Not really seeing where their project is taking them. You have to be able to step back and look at it again and say. *"What am I saying now?"* A lot of times documentaries fail because they don't get what they're saying or what they're saying doesn't have an impact you in any way. It's not thought provoking, interesting or engaging. You have to uncover something and make it thought provoking. That's why you need a very strong plan and be able go back to your plan and keep adjusting. Some don't know when to let go when they realize that there is nothing there.

Q – What advice would you give to documentary filmmakers?

Paul – Shoot a lot. You can ponder it and investigate it, but just get out there with the camera and be there around your subject as much as possible. Let your subject tell the story. Don't try to dictate to the subject what to tell.

FILM ARTS FOUNDATION

Q – What is the Film Arts Foundation and how can it help documentary filmmakers?

Donald – The mission of Film Arts Foundation is to support the creation, exhibition, and success of independent film. Film Arts is a resource for filmmakers of all genres, formats, medium, and experience levels. It's a member-driven organization, with more than 3,000 members in over 30 countries. Services include: community events for members, screenings for the public, low-cost and hands-on workshops, affordable access to production and post-production equipment, a highly-reputable fiscal sponsorship program, publication of the award-winning *Release Print* magazine, and vast online resources including the searchable Independent Film Pages with deadlines for funding, festivals and more.

Q – How much is membership and what do you get as a member?

Donald – Membership ranges from $45 - $250 per year. At the $45 membership level, filmmakers receive a subscription to *Release Print* magazine, log-in access to the vast resources in the members-only section of www.filmarts.org, and discounts with more on products and services with more than 40 film-related companies (including film and digital stock, hardware and software, training books, printing, post-production, film processing and more). At the $65 membership level (Filmmaker Level), filmmakers additionally qualify to apply for our fiscal sponsorship program, group dental insurance, steeply discounted legal services, and discounts on classes and equipment rentals.

Q – Do you provide fiscal sponsorship for your members? If so, how does one apply for it?

Donald – Yes, we provide one of the more robust fiscal sponsorship programs for our members. Filmmakers turn in completed proposal materials demonstrating that they are ready to begin fundraising efforts. Then they enter a 1–3 month review process to ensure that they have everything ready to successfully fundraise. Due to this review process, a Film Arts fiscal sponsor may receive extra consideration by some funders.

Q – Do you provide any film grants to documentary filmmakers?

Donald – Our grants program is currently on hold, as we rebuild our endowment. In the past we have given out grants totaling more than $1 million to all types of filmmakers, including documentary.

Q – Do you help projects become eligible for funding?

Donald – By providing fiscal sponsorship we help projects become eligible for funding. We also offer many workshops and classes each year to help documentary filmmakers improve their proposals for funding.

Q – Can you help documentary filmmakers find funding?

Donald – Yes. Our resource, the Independent Film Pages, is famous worldwide for providing the most complete and concise information about funding opportunities. Every issue of *Release Print* magazine includes highlights of upcoming deadlines from the Indepenent Film Pages, and it is searchable 24/7 in the members-only section of www.filmarts.org

Additionally, Film Arts regularly offers workshops, lectures, and panels that provide funding guidance, tips, and skill-building.

Q – Do you offer legal help to your members should they require it?

Donald – Members at the Filmmaker level and above receive a free half-hour of legal services and steeply discounted rates thereafter from our long-standing legal partner.

Q – Do you have to be a member to take part in your education program/classes?

Donald – Anyone can take part in classes and workshops at Film Arts, though membership can provide substantial discounts. Most of our classes take place in the evenings or weekends, to allow the widest access to our programs. We have a regular documentary storytelling class. At the Filmmaker Level and above, members can also include a half-hour consultation with staff to review the project for feedback and advice. In addition, the Film Arts Resource Library has several dozen sample proposals that members can review.

Q – What kind of equipment do your members have access to?

Donald – Anyone can rent our equipment provided they can demonstrate basic technical proficiency. Members at the Filmmaker level and above receive significant discounts on all equipment rentals. Currently our equipment includes: several digital video camera packages, 16mm cameras, sound recording packages, several lighting kits, ProTools editing suite with sound room, and HD-enabled editing suite with Final Cut Pro and Avid Xpress Pro. We also rents out 3 rooms, including a state-of-the-art screening room that seats up to 60 people.

Q – As any level member, do you have access to the editing suites?

Donald – Anyone can access the editing suites, provided they can demonstrate basic proficiency. Members at the Filmmaker level and above receive significant discounts on the rental costs.

Q – What is the STAND program and does it apply to documentary filmmakers?

Donald – STAND is a grant program for first-time filmmakers from underrepresented communities to receive mentorship and in-kind services to help complete a short film. It can apply to documentary filmmakers or those from any genre.

Q – What is the True Stories screening series?

Donald – Film Arts has curated a monthly "sneak peek" of new documentaries for past 10 years at the Yerba Buena Center for the Arts. Designed to create some early "buzz, many of these documentaries have gone on to screen at major festivals, receive national broadcast, and win awards.

Q – How do you help filmmakers network?

Donald – We provide at least one social opportunity per quarter and often many more. Our classes and seminars are excellent opportunities for filmmakers to make connections. Our online community, The Forum (www.filmarts.org/theboard) is an active self-publishing posting board with user profiles. We also promote and co-present many events and screenings throughout Northern California to encourage our members to engage with our vibrant film community.

Q – If a member experiences problems during their productions, can you help?

Donald – Yes. We often provide valuable information, references, or referrals when problems arise in documentary production. If a member calls or stops in with a question, we can usually point them in the right direction if we don't know

Human Rights Organizations

Documentary filmmakers need more than cash to get their films made. You need ideas and support as well. If you're planning on looking at some social issue the places below can help you out with connections, subjects, advisors and in some cases funds.

***Amnesty International**: www.amnesty.org or specifically for the US www.amnestyusa.org*
Amnesty International (AI) is a worldwide movement of people who campaign for internationally recognized human rights.

***Witness:** www.witness.org*
Founded by musician and activist Peter Gabriel and the Reebok Foundation for Human Rights and Lawyers for Human Rights. The organization empowers human rights defenders to use video to shine a light on those most affected by human rights violations.

***Article 19:** www.article19.org*
An organization that defends and promotes freedom of expression and freedom of information all over the world. Their name is taken from Article 19 of the Universal Declaration of Human Rights, which states: Everyone has the right to freedom of opinion and expression; the right includes freedom to hold opinions without interference and to seek, receive and impart information and ideas through any media regardless of frontiers.

***Human Rights Video Project:** www.humanrightsproject.org*
Provides resources for organizations that wish to create effective discussion programs around human rights issues through documentary film screenings.

***Doctors without Borders**: www.doctorswithoutborders.org*
Doctors Without Borders/Médecins Sans Frontières (MSF) is an international independent medical humanitarian organization that delivers emergency aid to people affected by armed conflict, epidemics, natural or man-made disasters, or exclusion from health care in more than 70 countries.

***The Innocence Project:** www.innocenceproject.org*
A non-profit legal clinic and criminal justice resource center. They work to exonerate the wrongfully convicted through postconviction DNA testing; and develop and implement reforms to prevent wrongful convictions. Read about the doc After Innocence in the Case Study section for more info!

***Rights and Democracy**: www.ichrdd.ca*
A Canadian organization whose mandate is to defend and promote the rights and freedoms enshrined in the International Bill of Human Rights and encourage the development of democratic societies.

***United Nations Foundation**: www.unfoundation.org*
A foundation that seeks to support the goals and objectives of the United Nations and its Charter in order to promote a more peaceful, prosperous, and just world - with special emphasis on the UN's work, especially on behalf of economic, social, environmental and humanitarian causes.

***UNICEF (United Nations International Children's Emergency Fund)**: www.unicef.org*
UNICEF is the driving force that helps build a world where the rights of every child are realized.

***UNIFEM (United Nations Development Fund for Women)**:*
www.unifem.org
Provides financial and technical assistance to innovative programs and strategies to foster women's empowerment and gender equality and placing the advancement of women's human rights at the center of all of its efforts.

Human Rights First:
www.humanrightsfirst.org
Human Rights First is a leading human rights advocacy organization based in New York City and Washington, DC. They work to create a secure and humane world – advancing justice, human dignity, and respect for the rule of law.

The America Red Cross:
www.redcross.org
Provides relief to victims of disasters and helps people prevent, prepare for, and respond to emergencies.

the answer ourselves. Our Resource Library contains more than 500 film/video-related books that members can check out at no cost for several weeks at a time. Our online Forum has topic areas to post questions when problems arise. And some of our workshops also address problems that can arise during the documentary production process.

Q – San Francisco has traditionally always been a hotbed for non-fiction filmmaking, what is unique about San Francisco in comparison to the rest of the country that allows for this?

Donald – Due to its economic, geographic, and historical evolution, San Francisco has developed a culture of counter-culture, individual expression, progressive politics, and exploration of the self and spirit. Documentary film is a natural extension of that culture; it's independent voices telling their stories; or telling the stories of those on the margins of society; or telling alternative sides to the stories of the mainstream media. Independent documentary and experimental film in

San Francisco also tends to serve as a rabblerousing, DIY, indie counterpoint to the narrative feature-driven studios in Hollywood. And from what we hear, the documentary community in the San Francisco Bay Area is the most community-oriented, supportive, and collaborative of the epicenters for non-fiction filmmaking in the United States.

Q – What common mistakes do you come across with documentary filmmakers?

Donald – New documentary filmmakers often think that documenting something interesting will result in an interesting documentary – this is usually not the case. Well-made documentaries can make it look simple, but they are very complex. We try to teach the importance of: clear concepts, planning, writing, story structure, realistic budgets, compelling characters, and treating the subject with the most appropriate style and structure.

Q – What advice can you offer new documentary filmmakers?

Donald – Get plugged into a community, whether it's online, at a place like Film Arts Foundation, or a few like-minded friends. Though making documentaries is often times a personally rewarding process, it's also a challenging journey and having support can help keep you going. The more you understand what you're trying to shine your light on and why, the better chance you have to succeed. Documentaries are primarily forged on relationships with real characters, so know yourself, your intentions, and try to always interact with integrity and openness. Try to apprentice and intern with those who have more experience. Study and watch great documentaries to inform your approach. Make short documentaries and practice the entire process. Study narrative story structures and practice your writing skills. Attend festivals and marketplaces, talk to distributors and festival programmers – knowing their thinking and objectives can help you avoid pitfalls later down the road.

IFP Minneapolis/St.Paul

IFP Minneapolis/St. Paul (IFP-MSP) promotes the work of artists who create screenplays, film, video, and photography in the Upper Midwest. Being a member of IFP-MSP does not make you a member of the other IFP chapters, but you may take part in any of their activities. IFP Minneapolis/St. Paul is the only organization in the Central United States that offers such a spectrum of programs and services for independent filmmakers and photographers at such low cost. Here is some of what they offer.

1. A broad curriculum of classes (over 25 quarterly) and seminars annually on various aspects of documentary filmmaking and photography, such subjects as screenwriting, independent producing, technology, cinematography and alternative distribution.

2. Virtual Documentary Conference - An online salon which stimulates conversations on the craft and business of documentary filmmaking. Available to the international documentary filmmaking community at large, the Virtual Doc Conference is held on-line four times per year.

3. Members are allowed to rent facilities and equipment well below local vendor costs. They have 16mm camera equipment, digital video cameras and non-linear editing systems.

4. Through the Minnesota Independent Film Fund, The McKnight Fellowship for Screenwriters, the Annual Access Grant, and MNTV, IFP-MSP allocates more than $152,000 to local artists each year.

5. The Central Standard Film Festival, which showcases 15 documentaries and 29 independent short films from local and national filmmakers.

6. Extensive community outreach programs such as darkroom time for inner city students, teaching youths how to use the equipment and have them capture stories from their own communities, scholarships to all public events, activities and classes, the Equipment & Facility Access grants, which focus on emerging and women artists, and the Native American New Voices Program, a series of classes to teach inner city Native American youth the filmmaking process.

Jane Minton, Executive Director
401 N. 3rd St., Ste. 450, Minneapolis, MN 55401
Tel: (612) 338-0871 Fax: (612) 338-4747
www.ifp.org

Priscilla Grim

AIVF

Q – How can AIVF help a documentary filmmaker?

Priscilla – We provide information about where to go for fiscal sponsorship. We have several different directories on our website, such as a listing of film festivals and our magazine, *The Independent Video And Film Monthly* has listings of calls for submissions for funding nationwide with some international listings as well. We have lawyers that work with our members for discounted rates. We have health insurance information. One program that we have sent off into the world is Festivals 101. It's designed for emerging makers to be educated on film festivals around the world. We are an association so we get discounts on car and hotel rentals. We have a distributor guide where you can match your film to a company who is going to represent you well and understand where you are coming from.

Q – What is the PBS mentorship sessions?

Priscilla – In the spring, we bring in acquisition executives from ITVS, PBS, POV, etc. It is a weekend event. We hold a call for entries among our membership to send in their projects, which they will pitch to these executives. Usually the projects will be about 75% completed. We select 10-15 projects out them and those directors and producers will meet with those executives and pitch their project. We have been doing this for seven years and 90% of the filmmakers have gone on to get either broadcast or distribution through the PBS system.

Q – How do you determine what films get chosen?

Priscilla – You want something that is socially relevant. Something that says something new. Something that's going to mean something down the road. We're looking for meaningful films that are well constructed and tell a meaningful story. And it's based solely on content.

Q – How much is membership?

Priscilla – $70 a year.

Q – How would you say AIVF is different from any other film organization like the IFP?

Priscilla – AIVF is more grass roots. We don't have an awards show that airs on Bravo. We're really open to our membership. People can call us about their projects and get someone on the phone to discuss what their next step should be. We also do a lot of advocacy for documentary filmmakers. One of the things we do is approach companies that we think are giving filmmakers less than a fair shake. I don't know if you have been reading anything on Current Television, which is the new cable network that Al Gore and Leonardo DiCaprio started. Last fall we were in meeting with all the acquisition people from Current to try and convince them that their pricing structure and their licensing deals are exploitative. What they do is they pay you a pittance of money and then you sign away your work to them forever. When we discovered that Current wanted to sell advertising on the channel, our first question was – well what about residuals to the makers? They said they didn't have to do that because of the contract. So we are trying to work on that.

Q – Any tips on how to go about looking for grants?

Priscilla – If you're looking for grants, AIVF is an excellent place to come to because we publish all the grant deadlines in the back of our magazine every month. We aren't a fiscal sponsor, but if you're looking for one you really want to shop around and look for one that's not only going to charge you a low administration fee, but is also going to be helpful to your project. Not that you need hand holding, but you probably need more guidance than you realize. You want to find someone who is going to grow with you and your project. It's a good deal for the sponsor if the film does well because it promotes them as well as the filmmaker.

Q – You mentioned that you have lawyers that can help your members.

Priscilla – We have a list of lawyers that give free consultations to AIVF members. You go in and say these are the issues I'm dealing with – clearances or vet a distribution contract – and they give you a list of what they can do and at what price. If you can't pay that price, they'll tell you where you can go to get those services.

Q – Does AIVF have equipment that your members can rent?

Priscilla – No, we don't, but we have a deal with Downtown Community Television that gives discounts on equipment rental.

Q – What are the common mistakes that documentary filmmakers make?

Priscilla – Clearances! Oh, my God, clearances. I don't care that you have this amazing interview. You don't know where this person is any more and you don't have their clearance. Sure, you can put it into a festival and try to sell it, but no one is going to buy it! They are liable as well. Clearances! Get it on paper. Listen to music that's not in movies. Work with a composer if you've to because it's a really key element that people forget. Sound issues are a problem. Hire a sound person to avoid bad sound issues. Do not do it yourself.

Q – What advice would you give a new documentary filmmaker?

Priscilla – Be compassionate.

Doc Shorts Versus Doc Features

GUERILLA FILM MAKER SAYS!

Should I make a doc short or a doc feature as my first film? An often asked question. Here are some facts to help you make up your mind.

Shorts

1. Less expensive to make because of their length.

2. Good for comedy because it works best in quick spurts.

3. Good calling cards to showcase talent to funders and executives, especially if you have a feature that you want to make.

4. Doc shorts have almost no commercial value as they are hard for broadcasters to program and theater owners to slate.

5. Does not have the glamour of making a feature.

Feature

1. More expensive and takes a long time to produce.

2. The best calling card and more definitive of director's ability.

3. More likely to get work/future financing from a doc feature.

4. Can be sold and for larger sums of money and have long shelf lives, so more likely to get investors.

5. Allows you more time to get into the story and characters.

6. Feature length docs may have problems selling outside of the US where broadcasters want hour-long fare for their TV slots. Be prepared to make more than one version, which means time and money.

Debbie Zimmerman
Executive Director

WOMEN MAKE MOVIES

Q – What kind of programs does Women Make Movies have?

Debbie – We have a distribution program where we're largest distributor of films by and about women in the world and we also have a production assistance program, which currently only is open to American filmmakers. In that program, we are in the middle of helping about 200 filmmakers raise money for their projects. We don't actually raise the money, but we help them in seeking funds from corporations, individuals, government and other non-profit funding sources.

Q – Why the emphasis on women?

Debbie – Just look at the Academy Awards and you will know why. Or look at just about any festival in the world and what you will find is rarely more than 25% representation of women. Women still have a lot tougher time. Their budgets are lower both in production and marketing. Women just don't have the same opportunities men do especially when they're making films about women's subjects.

Q – Why do you think that is?

Debbie – I think it's because the industry is still so male dominated on every single level. And this is true whether it's distributors or production executives, producers, film festival directors, the people on the jury or the film critics. You are often times pitching to men. I really believe that men and women experience film in a different way. They're interested in different things and men aren't as interested in women's subjects. And vice versa is the same too. What we want to see is equality. We want to see an equal number of women in power. And an equal number of women filmmakers.

Q – Does the playing field get level if a woman has a completed film?

Debbie – Absolutely not. We have actually been doing a study in looking at funding patterns over the last five years at government and foundation sources and it's absolutely appalling. With some funders, less than 20% of funding goes to women. And again those percentages go way, way down when you're talking about women making films about women's subjects.

Q – How does your Production Assistance program work?

Debbie – We have deadlines four times a year and any woman can apply to our program. Our application is on our website and they have to be the director of the film. They don't have to be the producer. The films in the Production Assistance program do not have to be about women – they can be about anything. They can be features, documentaries, or shorts. Some of the films that came out of the program were *Boys Don't Cry, The Incredible Adventures Of Two Girls In Love*, and Julie Dash's film *Daughters Of The Dust*, which was the first African American feature that was distributed in the US. We act as a fiscal sponsor. So as long as you're in the program, you don't have to pay taxes on the grants and donations you receive. You can be in any phase of production when you apply. They way it works is you submit a proposal and a sample. The criteria that we use include the quality of the proposed film, whether we think you can really finish the film and whether we think you can raise the money. Once you're accepted into the program we'll consult with you on your proposal as well as your sample and help you get the best materials together so you can present that project to a variety of funders. We will let you know when deadlines are coming up. We have a great diversity of resources on our website – sample proposals and budgets, etc. We have a series of workshops in New York twice a year that focus on the business side of the business and this year we will doing some in LA. The workshops are on fundraising and distribution and we bring in panelists experienced in all phases of production and marketing

Q – What is the overhead percentage you take on the fiscal sponsorship?

Debbie – 5%.

Q – Does the filmmaker get some sort of Women Make Movies stamp when they're in your Production Assistance program or does that only happen when you distribute the film?

Debbie – I think it happens in both programs. I was just at Sunny Side Of The Doc Rendezvous in Washington, DC. It's a French-US co-production market. One of our projects was there and her card was pulled out of a hat to pitch. Since it was her first time, I went up on stage with her. Being able to say that this project is sponsored by Women Make Movies gives you an entrée. People maybe take you a little more seriously. Foundations know there is a non-profit organization with 30 years experience behind you and that will make sure that the funds received will be used in the way the funds were proposed to them.

Q – How does your distribution program work?

Debbie – We distribute to all markets including theatrical. We don't do that with every film, as a theatrical release is not always appropriate. Because we focus on documentaries, it's harder to get them into the theater. A lot of the films that we do aren't even feature length. For those films we try to use the broadcast as a way of getting the film to the general public. This year *Troop 1500* will be broadcast on *Independent Lens*. Each year we have a few films on Sundance Channel, quite a few on PBS, sometimes HBO, Oxygen, etc. We work with many broadcasters. After theatrical and broadcast, the film goes into educational distribution where it goes to universities as well as museums, schools, film societies, community groups, and all kinds of other educational and cultural centers.

Q – Do you take any kind of commission from the sales of these films?

Debbie – Our distribution contracts are the same as any other distributor, but the money we earn has to go back into the organization in order for us to retain our non-profit status. The staff doesn't get a share of the profits. And as a non-profit, we can receive grants. One such grant we received was from the National Endowment of the Arts in order to increase our broadcast sales domestically and to research the international market. Being non-profit also enables us to be able to take on films that are risky because they don't have a commercial market.

Q – What else gets you excited by a film?

Debbie – Quality. We want great films. We're also looking for films that challenge audiences in one of two ways. Either it brings information that you're not getting from the mainstream media or the form is different. Films that are art. When those two things happen together it's a great film.

Q – Where are the places you go to look for your films?

Debbie – Every year I go to Sundance, Toronto and Cannes. We sometimes go to Berlin and Rotterdam. We also go to the Amsterdam International Documentary Festival in November and Hot Docs in Toronto. I usually have to turn down a lot of invitations because there are so many. We also work with a lot of women's film festivals around the world that are just starting up. In the last few years, we worked with the Mexico City Women's Festival, an Israeli Women's Film festival,

Filmor, a Women's Film Festival in Istanbul and a number of others.

Q – Are there any tips on distribution and marketing that you think are important?

Debbie – I encourage filmmakers to learn as much as possible about distribution and marketing before they finish their films. I encourage them to go to film festivals whether or not they have a film in the festival. Festivals are great ways to learn about the industry and make connections. One thing that I tell people all the time in my distribution workshops is there are three things you can get out of distribution: fame, fortune and a good conscience. You aren't always going to get all of them. Sometimes you're making a film to be a calling card in order to build your career. In that case, you want to create a really great festival strategy for your film. If you're making a film for a particular audience you need to be thinking about that while you're in production and you need to come out of production with a really great list of organizations that are going to be interested in the films afterwards. And then create a marketing strategy that will get it out to those groups or individuals.

Q – What are the common mistakes that you see documentary filmmakers make?

Debbie – Not thinking about distribution or marketing. Also, people come up with the same ideas. There are so many subjects that haven't been covered. Use your imagination. And when you get an idea do your research to find out what other films have been made on the subject. You can learn so much from watching those films about what you should and shouldn't put in your film. Look at the end of the film and see who funded it – that's a great place to start in terms of funding your film. Another thing I have to say is be nice. Filmmakers are Type A personalities. They have to work so hard to get their films made and once they're made, they need to shift gears a bit. It's very important to be the kind of person someone wants to go into business with. That's part of our decision-making. When you sign a distribution contract, you're signing a contract that is for five to seven years. I always say that festival programmers have it easy. When they show a film, it's like going out on a date -- and you can go out on one date with almost anybody. But when we acquire a film, it's like you are getting married. It's important not to be so pushy that you alienate the people that you are trying to appeal to. And that is true for filmmakers that accost broadcasters, funders or distributors in bathrooms, or that stick DVDs in your hand. Or people that send us something and call and call and call. I'm not saying don't follow up, but be conscious of treating people how you want to be treated.

Q – What advice would you give a new documentary filmmaker?

Debbie – It's important to understand that you are not going to succeed overnight; it takes a lot of hard work. Also, when filmmakers, especially first time filmmakers, say they don't have enough money to make a trailer, I look at them like they are crazy. You have to invest that. You can barter yourself – you work for free so someone else will do your sound or whatever you need done for free – get that trailer finished.

ANATOMY OF A DOCUMENTARY SECTION 5

DOC WRITING

THE WRITER'S GUILD

Q – How can the Writers Guild help documentary filmmakers?

John – The most viatl thing we can offer documentary filmmakers is the Documentary Screenplay contract. Then we have a Nonfiction Writers Caucus and a Nonfiction Forum where we screen documentary films. If you've written a half hour nonfiction program on cable, the internet or feature film, you can become affiliated with The Writers Guild. It's not full membership – the benefits are similar to an associate membership. You get Guild mailings and get invited to all the Guild events. What you don't get is the right to vote in the major Guild elections. But it does give you a good introduction to the Guild and if you live in or near Los Angeles or New York, there are a lot of advantages especially from an educational standpoint—events, seminars and the like. There is also a discounted health plan filmmakers can join.

Q – What is the Documentary Screeplay contract?

John – The Writers Guild traditionally has not covered the writing of documentaries because the 500-page Writers Guild agreement is too demanding for start up filmmakers. We had to pare it down to make it more useful. The big stumbling block has always been paying writers up front. In about 90% of documentary films, the writer is also the director and the producer. So if that writer-producer-director's company signs this 10 page agreement and if the budget is under $500,000, all money that is owed to them is deferred until production costs are recouped or commercial distribution, whichever comes first. They don't have to pay anything up front. If the film recoups it's money, they'll get a writer's fee and a 14.5% health and pension benefit on top of that. The goal for filmmakers would be to get a distributor to assume the rights of the agreement. So the distributor, when it picks up the film, makes that payment. Distributors do this all the time with low budget fiction films. When the writer is paid, he/she gets pension and health benefits going forward. Through the WGA, if you work 5 years (nonconsecutive) and earn $5,000 in each one of those years, you can earn a pension. The more you earn, the more goes into your pension. Down the line you can build up quite a nice retirement plan.

Q – Does this Caucus apply in your New York branch?

John – Yes. But that's out of Writers Guild of America, East and it's called The Nonfiction Writers Committee. West of the Mississippi is our region and east of the Mississippi is theirs.

Q – How have the distributors reacted to this agreement?

John – In about 3 years, we've signed approximately 100 of these contracts for narrative (fiction) films through our low-budget agreement. As for documentaries, it's too early to know yet. The agreement has only been available since February 2006, and we haven't heard reactions from the distributors yet. It really doesn't alter their business model. The current screenplay minimum is $37,000 and hopefully, the distributor is going to pay the filmmaker much more than that for their documentary. And when that film is bought and distributed to other markets, a residual formula kicks in and that is important because a filmmaker will always get a piece of their film when it's reused for other media.

Q – So the distributor has to pay that?

John – The signatory company does. In many independent films and many studio films, the distributor signs what is known as a distributors assumption agreement. They assume the rights for the documentary from the original (signatory) company and they would assume all payments owed. A smart filmmaker is going to insist on getting piece of the profits as the film goes to other markets. If he works under this agreement, a minimum is guaranteed for him. This contract sets a minimum scale for these filmmakers.

Q – How does this work if a documentary has investors that need to be repaid?

John – We'd recommend that all parties investing know that this agreement exists, and the financial consequences of it. This agreement is contingent on either recoupment of production costs or commercial distribution, without which, the writer doesn't get paid.

Q – So you are guaranteeing that the writer will be getting a little bit of money up front?

John – Yes. There're three ways the contract works. If a writer is also employed as either a producer or director, he can defer his writing fee until the end. If you're a writer employed to write the project and you're doing more than just narration – we've rates for narration, you'd be paid $5,000 up front and the rest upon commercial distribution or upon recoupment of cost. Or in the rarer instance that you write something ahead of time that a documentary is based upon, then you can defer that until recoupment of cost or until commercial distribution. This is all for under $500,000. If the budget is $500,000-$750,000 then $10,000 is owed up front and the rest is paid upon commercial distribution or upon recoupment of costs. If the budget is $750,000 to $1.2 million, then it is $10,000 for the writer/director and $15,000 up front for the writer for hire. We worked with a lot of filmmakers to come up with this agreement that we believe is fair and reflects the market place.

Q – And if it's over $1.2 million, then it goes into the standard WGA agreement?

John – Yes. And that's rare for documentaries.

Q – So if the film doesn't sell at festivals, the monies are not paid until sales come in?

John – Yes. If no monies come in, then no one gets paid. Which is pretty much true whether you work under the WGA agreement or not. Under this agreement, when monies come in you get paid and you get a pension and health benefit - two things that narrative filmmakers have had for years.

Q – How much do you have to earn to get health benefits?

John – Approximately $30,000 a year and that's why we tied it to this almost $37,000 number. The other thing to know is that documentaries are written differently than traditional narratives. They're written throughout the process and sometimes in tandem with the editor. We have seen editors get writing credits. Sometimes it is done ahead of time. That $37,000 number is encompassing of all drafts up to 12 weeks of employment for the writer and that covers most films. What is considered a draft in documentary film is a little more of a grey area than in narrative so we decided to bring it all in under one number.

Q – But most documentary films take an average of five to seven years to make, is it feasible that they can earn $5,000 a year or $30,000 a year to get these benefits?

John – Yes, because it's not just fees that count here. It's all monies earned so royalties and residuals count as well. And you might pick up a couple other jobs while you're making your film. That counts as well. And the $5,000 doesn't have to be consecutive. So if a guy makes a film every seven years and he has a 35-year career. In theory, he only makes $5,000 every seven years; he would still get a pension. But it has to be consecutive for the health care. If you earn the money in one quarter or over four quarters, then you get the next four quarters going forward.

The Treatment

GUERILLA FILM MAKER SAYS!

Every funder is going to want to see your vision on paper. Here are some tips on how to give your treatment a lot of punch.

1. The treatment is a written expression of your visuals, so use a lot of adjectives and adverbs to describe what you plan to show.

2. The treatment should convey the mood of the project. Even if it is a somber subject, you still need to get your funders excited, so be careful with your words.

3. You don't want to put anything business-like in the treatment. So instead of saying that you have access to a person or place imply that you do by mentioning them as part of the story.

4. The treatment shouldn't be any longer than 2-3 pages.

5. Always go for story over character when writing your treatment.

6. Try not to introduce more than three main subjects in the treatment or else it will become confusing.

7. When starting, write down all the things that you like about your subject via free-writing. When you go back and look at your thoughts, you will see the elements of your treatment.

8. Your treatment doesn't have to be precisely what you use to lock picture. Production is fluid and most funders know that.

Q – What happens if you want to start writing fiction?

John – If you work under this contract you would qualify for membership to The Writers Guild. And you could join as soon as the monies come in or just prior to that. That's another benefit of this.

Q – What do you need for people to apply for the agreement?

John – We need an outline of the project. Principal photography has to begin within 90 days – that's important. We don't want to string someone along. We needed a detailed budget and then they sign some paperwork, which is free.

Q – Documentaries have scripts?

John – Yes, they do. One of the things the Guild has dealt with, quite successfully, in my opinion, was dispelling the notion that all nonfiction programming is unscripted. Quite the opposite. Writers show up at the Guild every day saying *"I'm a writer, but I'm not allowed to be called a writer."* So the first thing we did was to create an award that recognizes the writer component of documentary. It was a risk because we didn't know how it was going to be received, but the documentary community has warmly received it. People do recognize the storytelling component – it's more than just narration. There has been a 45% increase in the number of films that take a writing credit since the award was created.

Q – Does the script end up looking like more of a transcript?

John – Sometimes. Sometimes it's similar to a traditional fiction narrative. Sometimes it's done in a two-column screenplay style with the visuals on one side and audio on the other. I was at Sundance and someone said writing a documentary is just like writing a narrative, but you're doing it with narration, interviews, visuals, cinema verité and words. And that can be more complicated. One of the best cinema verité films that I have seen in terms of storytelling is *Control Room.* Jehane Noujaim and Julia Bacha wrote it. From the footage they found those three characters and followed their stories like you would in a narrative. I think we're entering the golden age of documentary film. There has been a 90% increase in documentary films released since 2002. Writing is essential to this increase. The stories are so compelling.

Q – What happens if the contract doesn't quite work for your situation?

John – Call me and we can see if there's some flexibility within the agreement.

Q – What if a foreign filmmaker comes here to work. Could they be covered?

John – It depends on where the writing is being done. The way the WGA agreement works is that if the writing is being done in a foreign country, then it is not in our jurisdiction. But if they are writing here, we can cover the work. We'll sometimes grant waivers say if our members go to work in Canada. So we do work with foreign guilds.

Q – Do other countries have similar documentary agreements to this?

John – I don't think so. This is brand new. If it becomes a success, then hopefully others will follow.

Q – Can documentary filmmakers register their scripts with you?

John – Yes. And we register books, song lyrics, computer games and all kinds of things. We recommend that you register and copyright material, as there's a big difference between the two. In TV and film, when you sell a script to the studio, they assume the copyright. It's not like a novel where the author retains the copyright. Registration is a proof of authorship. It says on this date and time you wrote a screenplay called this and it's good for five years.

Q – What are the networking events and services you offer?

John – We'll do the nonfiction forums, the awards, special screenings and you get discounts from all things WGA members get. We do panel discussions. We do a party at Sundance and other festivals. You get *Written By* magazine. You can join our film society which offers like 70 screenings a year. We can also put you in touch with distributors, publicists and provide a host of networking opportunities.

Q – Can people come to you with a completed film?

John – We might be able to retroactively cover the film. That's a little trickier. If it hasn't been distributed, it's easier. Call us.

Q – What are the common mistakes that you see documentary filmmakers make?

John – Blindly signing a contract without knowing what you're getting into. I've seen a lot of people get raked over the coals. The other is not protecting your ideas before you pitch them. This is more important for fiction filmmakers, than documentarians, because of the time it takes to make a documentary and the smaller amount of money involved. Nonetheless, you should register a treatment or proposal with the WGA, before you start raising funds.

Q – What advice would you give a new documentary filmmaker?

John – I think Sting said, *"You are going to get lucky. And when you get lucky, you have to be smart."* The WGA contract is a way to be smart and protect yourself. Whether you work with us or not, know what you are getting yourself into. Documentaries are beginning to be profitable because there are so many venues, windows and ways to tell them. Be tenacious and innovative.

GUERILLA FILM MAKER SAYS!

Copyrighting Your Doc

Even though it's a documentary and not a script, you can still and should copyright it. You can do this either through The Library of Congress copyright office and the second is the Writers Guild. There is a process involved for each, which typically includes sending a copy of the work, a fee and a registration form. The WGA has set up a very convenient way to do this through their website. For more information contact:

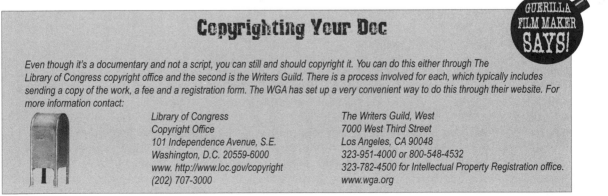

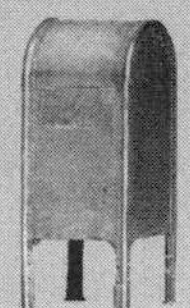

Library of Congress
Copyright Office
101 Independence Avenue, S.E.
Washington, D.C. 20559-6000
www. http://www.loc.gov/copyright
(202) 707-3000

The Writers Guild, West
7000 West Third Street
Los Angeles, CA 90048
323-951-4000 or 800-548-4532
323-782-4500 for Intellectual Property Registration office.
www.wga.org

WRITING NARRATION

Q – Was there anything unique to writing the narration to March Of The Penguins?

Jordan – *March Of The Penguins* was my first participation in a documentary film. And I think this film is very unique. I don't know if others involved in the project have said this, but when I saw the film at Sundance, it was not a documentary. *The Emperor's Journey*, as I believe it was called, was a piece of fiction. Instead of actors, they had penguins, but there was a narrative story that was articulated through the voices of actors, who were acting out the inner feelings and thoughts of the penguins onscreen. And not only did the penguins speak, but they spoke in an extremely poetic manner. So, when we made the decision to lose those penguins voices, and replace them with more traditional voice-over, we essentially turned it into a documentary. In the original French version, there was no sense of objectivity about this penguin family. There was a male, a female and a child. When the film plays around the world, they hire local actors to re-record those voices in the local dialect. So, the US version is the only one that is, technically, a documentary because of our decision to use Morgan Freeman and have him tell the story.

Q – How did you arrive at that decision?

Jordan – I didn't 'get' the movie. It was my experience and that of the other people involved, that the voices, and the overt subjectivity of the film, were taking us out of it. That's a completely subjective opinion. The original was obviously a success; it brought a lot of French people into the theater. But for me, and for many of the people that saw it at Sundance, it didn't emotionally enhance the imagery, it actually did the opposite.

Q – So this is a purely cultural thing.

Jordan – I believe it to be a purely cultural thing. Luc Jacquet, the director, has gone on record saying that he disagrees vehemently with our decision. That, in fact, it would have been a more successful film had we left it, as is, and had American actors play Mr. and Mrs. Penguin and their child, which is a completely legitimate opinion. Both my and Mark Gill's (Warner Independent) concern was that the film, in order to achieve the kind of success that I believed it could, had to be emotionally engaging. But the original, with its high level of anthropomorphism had too much emotion. We decided to diminish some of that emotion and make it a bedtime story.

Q – What were the changes that you made?

Jordan –The story is more or less the same story that was in the film. We took several minutes out and we rearranged the order of two sequences. But the film – footage-wise – was essentially the same. And the story conveyed by the penguins, themselves, in the original film, was the story that I had Morgan tell in ours. We didn't make it about one family. We made it about a tribe of penguins. As for process, I basically wrote to picture. In other words, I wrote what I needed to hear, in order to follow the story I was seeing onscreen. The original film is very short on penguin facts. Temperature, duration of time, time of the year, how much they weigh? There was no science, I suppose, because it couldn't be articulated by the penguins, themselves. But I wanted some. I didn't want much, but I think Warners wanted some as well. That's where National Geographic came in. They would look at the narration I was writing, and then steer me in a more scientific direction. In other words, when I wrote something that was rubbish scientifically, they wrote back that it was rubbish. They'd supply me with the facts and figures, and then I'd incorporate them as best as I could into the story. When I said earlier that this became a documentary at the hands of Warner Independent, that's true – I'm not challenging the validity of it winning the best documentary Academy Award –but it's also not a documentary. It's an extraordinarily subjective film, intentionally. I don't think there's any objective evidence to support the central premise of the film, which is that the penguins' mating ritual is really a love story. That calls into question the very definition of what a documentary is. What I think is interesting about the film is that it exists in an unusual world in the documentary community: subjective and objective, too.

Q – How many drafts would you say you went through before you started working with Morgan Freeman or were you working with him the whole time?

Jordan – No, he didn't come in until the end. I worked with Morgan for one day and he made some changes - maybe there were seven or eight lines that he wanted to adjust the structure of because of his voice. But much of the work wasn't the writing, it was placing the writing onto the existing imagery. I wrote three or four drafts before Warner Independent and National Geographic signed off and approved of how I was telling the story. And then I spent five weeks recording my voice over the film. That was the work. Where Morgan's voice appeared was going to be just as critical. And we didn't have time to make those decisions after Morgan recorded. In a usual circumstance, you would record Morgan Freeman saying five to ten pages of text, and then place that text across the picture as you see fit. We did it the other way. Morgan was given time code as if he was doing ADR on the picture. And he placed the words where I had placed them. We didn't have time because the movie was released four weeks after we recorded Morgan. So I knew we wouldn't have time to dialogue edit and mix and score the film. So we placed the dialogue, in advance, where it now appears in the film.

Q – Did you have contact with Luc Jacquet?

Jordan – No. I wanted to talk to Luc. I think he was understandably disappointed that such drastic alterations were being made to his film, so I think that there's some sense that Warner Brothers kept us a part. I don't know if that's true.

Q – Did you observe anything special about where and how you placed dialogue?

Jordan – Yes. But I'm not sure that I learned anything that wasn't only applicable to the case at hand, to this particular film. What I did learn was that it was a subjective determination because every ear is going to hear it differently. As the author of the words, it was really clear that there was a right place to put voice-over and a bunch of wrong places to put it. But that is not a luxury that any writer in the history of show business is ever going to have again. The two other ingredients that kind of go along with this are sound and music. When I was first hired for the job, they decided to hire a composer as well. They hired Alex Wurman and Alex and I had the dubious honor of sitting down, viewing the film and divvying it up before either of us went to work. This was done because of time. We had to work simultaneously. I think under normal circumstances I would have completed the work of writing and recording the film before Alex got the film to score. In a sense we were working blindly because we made decisions as to where there should be music and where there should be dialogue, or sound, before either of us began our work.

Q – Did you change it at all afterwards?

Jordan – Virtually not at all, which was a big shock and I don't know if I'll ever have that experience again. He and I worked closely and were constantly in communication about how various sequences felt, emotionally. Where it was lighter or darker or dangerous or frivolous or neutral. So when we put all the pieces together, the words actually matched the music.

Q – Were you making any decisions on if the music worked?

Jordan – Both Alex and I commented on each other's work – especially on placement. There were a couple of places, for instance, where a flute melody was emerging in his music and the voice was there at the same time. So we would adjust, in that case, either the music or the voice, since we couldn't 'hear' both.

Public Domain

If the copyright on a work (music, art, photograph, etc.) has expired, it falls into the public domain – meaning you can use that work in your film without getting the copyright owner's permission. You can reproduce the work, sell it and if it's different enough, copyright your version, but you cannot take over the original work's copyright . So, what's in public domain?

1. Any work that was published, but never copyrighted is in the public domain.

2. Any work that cannot be copyrighted, such as government publications, are in the public domain. However, government publications must have credited references to the agency that created them.

3. Any work for which the copyright has expired is in the public domain. As a rule of thumb, any work published prior to 1922 probably is public domain. But, check the copyright date on the work for the copyright may have been renewed and you must go by the most recent date. For music you must go by the date of the recording you wish to use, not the composition's original date. Even if there isn't a date, check anyway as new laws state that a modern work does not have to have a date present to still be copyrighted.

4. Works created outside of the United States should be checked with a copyright lawyer or the United States Copyright Office for something that is public domain in the US might not be in another country.

You can find out if a work is in the public domain by contacting the Library of Congress Copyright Office, and fill out a search form. Submit the form with a search fee (around $80/hr.), and they will contact you with information on the copyright holder and whether the work is in the public domain or not. Or you can also go to www.publicdomain.com to do a search.

Library of Congress, Copyright Office, 101 Independence Avenue, S.E.. Washington, D.C. 20559-6000, 202-707-3000

Q – You were sort of taking over the direction of the film in a way.

Jordan –There's no question that the work that I did more closely resembled the work of a director in post-production.

Q – Did you write the narration on any special software program?

Jordan – I started by writing in Word, writing to pictures. I had the film playing on my computer a hundred times and then I would write down the time code and write a comment. I did that dozens of times. It may never have been converted to Final Draft. Morgan probably read off a Word document. We worked off the time code of the original film, which was kooky because we took several minutes out of the film.

Q – What were some of the things you communicated to Morgan Freeman?

Jordan – When we recorded we tried to make it sound like a bedtime story. I think it was a unique experience for Morgan because here was the writer communicating to him in the recording studio. That isn't something that usually happens, so there was a little give and take with he and I. I understood some of the rises and the falls of the film emotionally, in a way that Morgan, not having seen the film, didn't understand. We just talked about what the scene was about, which he really responded to. There's a quality to Morgan's voice in the film, which is exactly right. He found the right way to convey and balance humor, gravitas and dignity, without ever sounding scientific. He found a place in him to tell this story perfectly. And I think that is something that documentary filmmakers have to pay attention to. You are, in fact, directing the voice.

Q – Were there any other actors considered?

Jordan – No. I heard his voice in my head instantly. He was our first choice.

Q – Is there anything special about narration that struck you during this project?

Jordan –There's a danger of anthropomorphism in the documentary community. Without the projecting of human characteristics onto these birds as is in the French version, it's my belief that the film wouldn't have been as successful a film. But that quality was enormously offensive to many people. And I sit somewhere in the middle. There's no way to write this film without honoring the original film's overt anthropomorphism. The original film literally had birds talking about finding each other, about finding their soul mates. There's no way I could take a film that was endowed with such a level of humanity and just ditch it completely. So we tried to modulate it. But even in modulation, it was still egregious to some people. There are other things about anthropomorphism one needs to be careful about. For starters, if I'm anthropomorphizing, then so are you. I joke sometimes that, while I may have seen these birds as lefty, lesbian and gay Darwinists at a kibbutz in Antarctica, a bunch of religious right folks saw them as marching homophobe Christians at an intelligent design rally. That's the danger of opening the door of anthropomorphic projection, applying human characteristics to animals. They are just animals doing what they are doing. That said, at the very, very beginning of narrative storytelling, animals were endowed with human characteristics because humans were seeing them. If you look at an animal painted on a cave, the animal is invariably going to be articulated with human characteristics. It only becomes questionable when you call that cave painting a piece of documentary. I believe anthropomorphism is ancient and relevant; it's just not scientific.

Q – What advice would you give a new documentary filmmaker?

Jordan – Always tell the truth, whatever your truth is. And don't concern yourself too much with how that truth is heard.

Coverage

Though it seems like a production idea, coverage is something you can be thinking about at the script stage. Good directors know what they want to shoot before they get into an interview or on a location. This way they can focus on getting what they need, getting it quickly and getting out of there so the subject or crew doesn't feel like you are wasting their time. However, like feature films, there are some basic things you are going to have to get in order to tell your story properly. Fortunately, video allows you ample tape to get these shots – just don't overdo it or you will create a nightmare for your editor.

1. Always shoot a master shot of the person or location. This establishes locale and always gives you something to cut back to.

2. Get as many close ups as possible as it will get us into the heads of your subjects, show detail and perhaps create tension.

3. Get as many cutaways and insert shots as possible. Focusing on someone tapping a pencil or a nearby sign can also convey things like tension or information, which can help set up character and story. It will also make your film much more fun to watch.

4. You can get people to repeat themselves if you miss something, but be prepared for it to not have the same energy as the first time.

5. If you are shooting an interview, try to get both eyes of the subject in the shot. It's more engaging.

6. Try to keep your shots as smooth as possible as it makes editing easier. Although, jittery camera is very much acceptable especially if it is clearly a dangerous situation and you are running!

7. Stay on your shots longer than you think, especially with cutaways, as you will give your editor more time to find a good section of a shot.

8. Be careful of getting non-cleared logos, people and songs in your shots. You may have to get the rights to this later, which is a pain, so tell your subjects to put down that beer bottle or turn off their radio.

9. Shooting lots of coverage can wear down a crew. Keep your eye on their fatigue level so you know when to call it a day.

10. Extending the shooting time will also mean extra time with equipment and at locations. Be sure to budget enough time and money for rentals and inform neighbors and communities that you may be inconveniencing them longer than usual or expected.

11. Know the rules before you decide to break them with jump cuts and crossing the parallel line. Not doing so will make you look amateurish and your film like crap.

12. Remember to shoot room tone so your editor or sound mixer has a chance to cover things up.

The Doc Script

Yes, documentary films have scripts. They can either come in the form of a traditional narrative screenplay or a double column format (shown below). Here, the visuals are placed on the left and the corresponding audio (music, narration or dialogue) are placed on the right. Final Draft AV is a good program to use for this. And of course, you can always start by writing narration just on any old word processing program.

Most scripts for docs are used to get funding, in which case you may be guessing what the final product is. That's OK as most funders know that this kind of filmmaking is fluid. The other main reason for them is to create a transcript for your distribution deliverables. From this things like subtitles and foreign language versions will be derived.

6/2/06

Agency	X2	**Writer**	Joe Average
Client	Hello Channel	**Producer**	Jane Doe
Project	WE'RE ALL ONE	**Director**	Frank Muenster
Title	DINNER TIME	**Art Director**	
Subject		**Medium**	
Job #	32N	**Contact**	Frank Muenster
Code #	5678	**Draft**	2

VIDEO	AUDIO
OPEN ON A DINING ROOM TABLE. A GREAT SPREAD OF INDIAN FOOD.	SITAR MUSIC:
A FAMILY OF SIX NOW SIT AT A TABLE IN THE US	BLUES MUSIC: NARRATOR: ALL AROUND THE WORLD, ONE THING THAT IS A CONSTANT IS THAT FAMILES COME TOGETHER FOR DINNER TIME.
A PERUVIAN FAMILY SITS AROUND A HEARTH EATING A MEAL	NARRATOR: IT IS A TIME FOR RECONNECTING WITH THOSE THAT ARE CLOSEST TO YOU. A TIME WHERE THE TRUE COMMUNAL BOND OF FAMILY CAN BE SEEN. THIS HAPPENS ALL THROUGHOUT THE WORLD
MONTAGE OF MORE FAMILIES EATING DINNER. ENDS ON A COUPLE OF KIDS EATING AN EAR OF CORN.	NARRATOR: WHERE DID THIS BASIC INSTINCT COME FROM? AND HOW DOES IT RELATE TO OTHER HUMAN BEHAVIOR? THAT IS WHAT WE INTEND TO EXPLORE OVER THE NEXT HOUR. TO SHOW THAT DESPITE ALL OUR DIFFERENCES, WE ARE ALL ONE.:
START CREDITS	THEME MUSIC:
CAVEMEN HUNTING A DEER. BRINGING IT BACK TO THEIR GROUP. EVERYONE EATS TOGETHER.	NARRATOR: HUMAN BEINGS ARE SOCIAL CREATURES. WE LIKE AND NEED TO BE IN A GROUP FOR SAFTEY AND SANITY. NOWHERE IS THIS CLEARER THAN WATCHING HOW ANCIENT HOMO SAPIENS HUNTED AND FORAGED TOGETHER TO STAVE OFF THE HARSH WORLD AROUND THEM.:
PROF. ARNIE DOBKIN INTERVIEW, TITLED	PROF. DOBKIN: THE WORLD IS A COLD, DANGEROUS PLACE, ESPECIALLY BACK THEN. HUMANS, LIKE ANY ANIMAL PACK, BANDED TOGETHER.:

ANATOMY OF A DOCUMENTARY SECTION 6

FUNDING

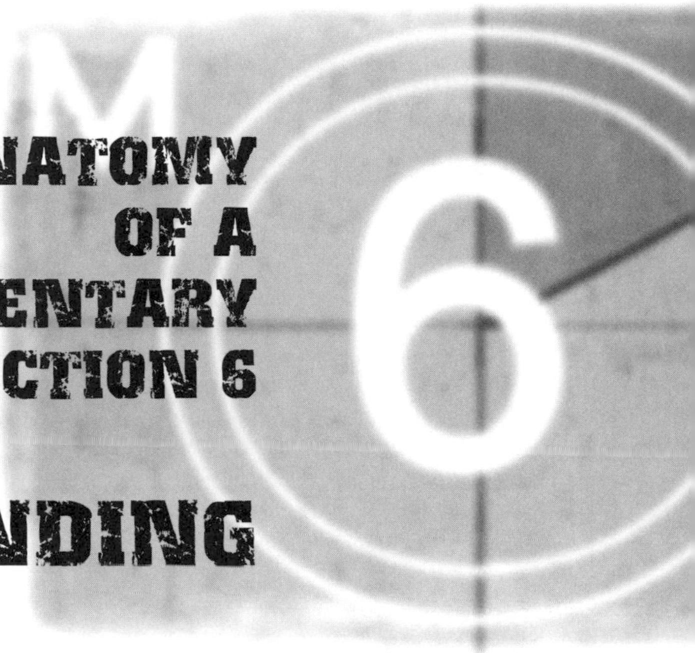

Trinh Duong Aleah Bacquie Vaughn

THE PAUL ROBESON FUND

Q – What's the history of the Paul Robeson Fund?

Trinh –The Paul Robeson Fund started at The Funding Exchange in about 1987. Prior to that there was a fund called the Film Fund and was operating independently. It funded social issue films, documentaries and radio projects. But it had difficulties being a fund on its own. There was a lot of administrative work that needed to be done. And for that reason it became part of the Funding Exchange and we renamed it after Paul Robeson, a legendary civil rights activist, who believed you should use your talent in the pursuit of social change. Every year we raise money to support radio and film projects. Our typical grant making is between $200,000-$250,000 with individual grants of up to $20,000.

Q – Are the grants mostly cash from individual private donations?

Trinh – Yes. They're from progressive donors.

Q – Are there any corporate donors?

Aleah – There're some corporate donors, but it's rare and ther are some corporations we wouldn't accept money from.

Trinh – We do some re-granting of other private foundations. Like for instance, if another foundation wants to support media, but doesn't have the expertise to do so, they'll make a grant to The Paul Robeson Fund and we'll take over from there.

Q – How would people apply to the fund?

Trinh – The first step is either to go through our website or call us for a copy of the guidelines and to read it thoroughly. We're very specific on what we're looking for. If they still have questions, they can call us and we'll answer them. We have a May 15th deadline every year, and that's a real deadline. I should say it must be postmarked by May 15th. Since Paul Robeson is national we realize that someone from California has less of an advantage of getting the proposal into our office. If you're in the area and would like to hand deliver it then it has to be in the office by 6 p.m.

Q – How would you summarize what you're looking for?

Trinh – We fund media that can be used for social change and to build community organizing that's not historical in nature. It must have some sort of organizing portion to it. Also, we also only fund pre-production and distribution. Someone can apply for pre-production and once done, they can come to us for distribution. You could get two grants of up to $20,000 each. But you couldn't get two pre-production grants.

Aleah – This is different from other foundations. It's not the staff making the decisions about who gets the grants. Trinh convenes a meeting every year and she brings activists here. The activists, who are filmmakers themselves, make the decisions about the grants; so you're judged by your peers. They meet in six member panels and they come from across the country with different expertise and experience. Most of them are filmmakers or have done radio programming. They also have some social conscious history with regard to their work.

Q – Are these Michael Moore kind of people?

Aleah – Not quite. We're talking about someone who might be a History professor at San Diego University and might also be a filmmaker. One thing that's important for applicants to understand is it's not just that the issue in the film is really compelling or interesting. The film must be intended to bring about change. That there's some plan during distribution for people to be made aware of the issue and be encouraged to do something about what they've learned.

Q – Does it help if they have distributors in place?

Trinh – They don't have to, but they do have to have a distribution plan. A lot of times people will make a documentary and it will be great, but who's going to see it? What's going to happen with it afterwards? These are often afterthoughts. We want to encourage applicants to think about that up front. That's what we consider the most important part of the project: your distribution. We don't just mean art houses or art festivals. There may be a number of entitles, like school programs or community organizations that do a particular work in the field in which you've done your film, that would be thrilled to use it as a means of educating people and bringing about change.

Q – How long is the decision-making process?

Aleah – By mid-September we announce the grants.

Q – How many eyes are watching them?

Aleah – We get in about 300 to 500 applications and our staff cuts them down to 80. I'll look at all the applications and then we pull other people from our staff that may have expertise in that subject matter. Once we have those 80, the six panel members review them. There're at least three people are involved in the first process. And six people on the second.

Q – Do your guidelines tell what you're supposed to put in your application?

Trinh – Our guidelines are pretty detailed. We tell people exactly what we want, but applicants don't always give us what we're asking for. It's important that people answer all the questions. For instance, even if they're applying for pre-production when they're in pre-production, they'll figure they don't have to answer those questions. They do. We have a standard format, which includes a two-page cover sheet, a section, which allows for a description of the project and a checklist of items we need.

Q – I notice you have a section regarding budget.

Trinh – We ask people for a detailed budget including unit costs. For instance, in distribution they may make 500 copies. Tell us what the cost is. Sometimes their budget is too small or doesn't make sense. If someone is going to hire someone to go on a distribution tour, tell us how long. Sometimes $3,000 is a lot and then sometimes it doesn't make sense to have them working for six months and then only earn that amount. The items need to match up with the money. And the filmmakers should always put the cost of their own labor in.

Q – Why do you not fund production or post-production?

Trinh – We feel pre-production funding is the most difficult to get. We don't ask for a work in progress; we ask for a previous sample work to apply for pre-production. Then they can take that sample to other sources of funding. We fund distribution because that is an important piece for us. We don't fund the parts in the middle because we don't have the funds to do it properly. One project could be $200,000, which would be our entire annual budget.

Fundraising Tips

GUERILLA FILM MAKER SAYS!

Getting cash is the hardest part of making a documentary. Hopefully, these ideas will make that road a little easier for you.

1. Carole Dean said it best, "When you ask for money, you get advice and when you ask for advice you get money." Ask those in the know how to get the cash and they'll put you on the right track.

2. Do research to find out what broadcasters and organizations would be the best fit for your project.

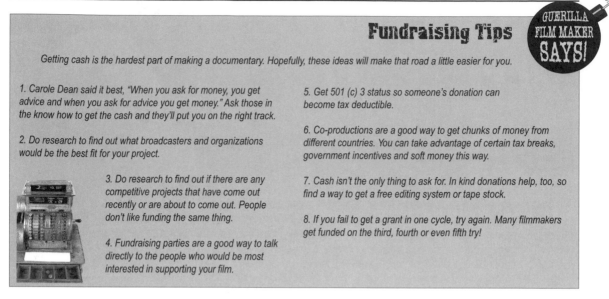

3. Do research to find out if there are any competitive projects that have come out recently or are about to come out. People don't like funding the same thing.

4. Fundraising parties are a good way to talk directly to the people who would be most interested in supporting your film.

5. Get 501 (c) 3 status so someone's donation can become tax deductible.

6. Co-productions are a good way to get chunks of money from different countries. You can take advantage of certain tax breaks, government incentives and soft money this way.

7. Cash isn't the only thing to ask for. In kind donations help, too, so find a way to get a free editing system or tape stock.

8. If you fail to get a grant in one cycle, try again. Many filmmakers get funded on the third, fourth or even fifth try!

Q – What can a first time filmmaker do if they don't have a sample?

Trinh – With new filmmakers we cut them some slack. But we do need something that indicates their potential.

Q – Would it help an emerging filmmaker to show that they had experienced staff?

Trinh – Yes. They could include the sample work of their key production people. And if they had worked with these people before, that would be helpful, too.

Q – What is the Saguaro Fund?

Trinh – The Saguaro Fund is particularly focused on people of color, organized here in the United States. It gets it's name from a cactus from the Sonora Desert, which manages to survive and to produce flowers without many resources. It's a symbol of how people of color are doing here in the U.S. in their struggle for justice. The purpose of the fund is to honor and to assist the work that's being done for social justice in those communities. Often that means they're dealing with racism head-on with regard to policies in people's daily existence. More recently it's playing out in immigration legislation and in environmental justice issues. Most environmental pollution occurs in communities of poor people or people of color.

Q – So if a filmmaker were approaching you for the Robeson Fund could they apply for Saguaro funds, too?

Trinh – Not in the same year. However, it should be known that the Saguaro Fund and The Out Fund could be used for media as long as they fit in the guidelines and they aren't limited to pre-production and distribution. The Out Fund has been formed for liberation of the GTQ community: Gay Lesbian trans-gender bi-sexual and Queer questioning. You can imagine the different types of discrimination or oppression that they face. We've funded films on everything from teens who get kicked out of their homes and have no place to go to agencies that are supposed to address those needs, but don't admit them. Also discrimination in employment, violence against people, organizing around adoption rights, child custody and hate crimes are other subjects. The films might be educating teachers, social workers or student leaders in schools around issues of sexuality and safe environments. The filmmakers might have a national plan to organize in schools and to use film to bring about social change. We want filmmakers to ask *"How can my work change lives?"* with various communities or organizations. But it's not just education; it's about bringing change. So the filmmakers should be teamed up with one or several organizations that will help them make and use the film.

Q – What's the Media Justice Fund?

Aleah – That fund is looking to build long-term media infrastructure in communities and to address media policies. There's another stream of funding through that - the media funding advocacy tool kit. We're funding organizations to create tool kits so that communities can advocate for more just media policies. There's up to $3,000 for individual media makers or organizations who respond to a current crisis. So just to be clear: Robeson is about content; Media Justice is about policy and infrastructure.

Q – Does an applicant have to be 501 (c) 3 backed in order to receive funds?

Aleah – For the Paul Robeson Fund we don't require a fiscal sponsor or that you are a 501 (c) 3 when you are applying, but you must have one when you're awarded the grant.

Q – What are the most common mistakes you see from documentary filmmakers?

Trinh – The biggest problem is that they send their proposals in piecemeal. They separate coversheets from their main work and then send samples. We've several hundred applications to deal with in a week's time and it makes it hard to match up all the parts. When you consider the time we must allow for our panel to evaluate the proposals, when things come piecemeal, it's more likely you won't get funded. Also include your website or email address. Make sure the materials you send us work. Make sure tapes and DVDs are not blank. We watch ten minutes of the sample so queue it for us or tell us the time code or chapter if it's DVD.

GUERILLA FILM MAKER SAYS!

Making Movies On Credit Cards

Jehane Noujaim did it with Control Room as did Ross Kauffman and Zana Briski with Born Into Brothels. They funded their films primarily on plastic. Seems like a good way to go since you don't need that much money to start a doc these days. And with all those pre-approved, low/no interest rates, free balance transfer applications in your mailbox - it seems really enticing. And, if you sell your film (which, we all hope you do) you might escape the daunting possibility of owing $15k at 18% APR.

However, the majority of low budget filmmakers who go down this route of financing find themselves in just this predicament. So, just a word of warning: one thing you really don't ever want to do is destroy your credit rating. This will take years to correct and not only damage any chances of raising money for the next film, but also make it difficult for you to rent that apartment you need to move in to when the production office or set closes and they take your bed away.

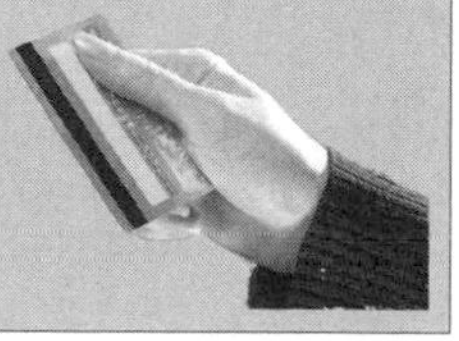

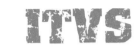

ITVS

Q – What is ITVS?

Claire – ITVS is a funder, presenter and promoter of independent programs by independent producers for public TV. It was founded by the Advocacy of Independent Filmmakers And Producers who mobilized to get their voices on public media. They lobbied Congress very hard and in 1989 got ITVS Congressionally mandated. In 1991, it was open for business. We're a miracle of public policy.

Q – Why just public TV?

Claire – This year we're actually going with other broadcasters because we have a new initiative. But it was originally founded by Congress to get independent filmmakers funded and one of the mandates of that funding is that it gets delivered to public TV. This year we launched an international fund that was funded outside of CPB – the Corporation of Public Broadcasting. This foundation money basically enables us to get international films on any US TV.

Q – Do you have a specific operating budget every year?

Claire – It's about $15 million a year. $10 million of that comes from the Congress allocation. And that's for production funds to give to independents and operational costs.

Q – What kind of funding is available?

Claire – There's the bread and butter funding that people know us for, which is for completion funding for single programs that is via our Open Call program. We try to differentiate the funding because it's not a grant. Grants have generally no strings attached, but this is really a production license agreement. So in exchange for the financial support, we contract with the producer a license for public TV.

Q – Do you get a piece of PBS's license fee?

Claire – No. Basically let's say the project needs $150,000 for completion support. We'd give the producer that amount in exchange for licensing the program for exclusive public TV. It's usually for three or four years. On the other hand, we're able to give that kind of support to a lot of projects. But we also have other initiatives for R&D.

Q – Do you ever get involved in licensing for theatrical or DVD?

Claire – We just want TV, but we have to approve theatrical to make sure that the TV premiere is the first and it doesn't get tied up with waiting for theatrical. That has worked out for films like *Brother To Brother*, which we financed and was a drama, but it had a number of theatrical runs. We don't take any home video or DVD rights.

Q – What kind of film would you fund?

Claire – The mission of ITVS is to find films from independents that are compelling, that tell stories that haven't been told before, that are innovative in either form or content and that push the civic discourse. That means that it's going to spawn debate. So they're usually social issue films and mostly documentaries. We're open to all genres including experimental films and documentaries and animation. We're really interested in drama, but the budgets tend to be very high for us. And with our international shows we're looking for a view on global issues for American audiences that they haven't seen either. One of the first programs we did for that was a story about Arab women living in Israel who started a pickle factory. It's an interesting film because it's about Arab women who are disenfranchised because they're women and they're widows and they're trying to improve their lives by starting a business.

Q – What would you never fund?

Claire – We don't fund any lifestyle kind of television. We don't do "how-to's", nature or entertainment. That said there are a lot of entertaining films that may not seem like they're in the ITVS mandate, but they are. It depends on the show and how you look at it. There's a film that we funded called *King Corn* where these two guys plant an acre of corn in Kansas and they track the corn to where it goes. It goes everywhere from animal feed to high fructose corn syrup for Coca-Cola. It's done in a fun sort of reality show way, but those issues we're interested in.

Q – With the international films, are you doing a similar deal with them as you would the domestic films coming to you for support?

Claire – They're more co-productions than acquisitions. There's a similar license, but since it's international the window is a little longer. On the other hand, we don't control theatrical, home video or other TV markets. We are only interested in American TV and that contains public TV, cable and the free broadcasters.

Q – How does a filmmaker approach you for funding and what is the process?

Claire – There's an application process. Go to our website and go to the "for producers" section in the funding section, look at the guidelines and see if you are eligible. You have to be over 18 and a US citizen or resident. Unless you're international and then it's the opposite. You have to have a prominent role in the film and have completed a previous film where you are the director or producer. It can be a student film – just so long as you have something under your belt. And for Open Call, you have to be in production and have a sample of the program. So a trailer or selects are required. If you qualify for all of that, you send in an application and we have two rounds a year. The deadlines are in February and August and it's a competitive peer panel review process. The other initiatives are for development for diverse producers. One is for a station partnership. The average contracts that we give are $150,000. So the applications go through different rounds of review and it would be read internally and externally. There are three tiers of review and if it goes to the final tier – the final panel review, which is pretty good, there will be 30 projects in that pool and 10 will be funded. If you're chosen, the contract negotiations begin. The whole process takes about six months. We also do some outreach, but most people have heard of us. And there are some filmmakers that we do seek out if we have worked with them in the past or we hear they have a good project. We do answer some questions about how to apply, but we cannot pre-evaluate proposals.

Q – And if it's a filmmaker that you're seeking out...?

Claire – An example is a filmmaker named Stanley Nelson who we've worked with before on a film called *A Place Of Their Own*, which is about his family. He is a middle class black man whose family vacationed in Martha's Vineyard. He came and pitched a program he wanted to work on about black sexuality in Hollywood as it has created controversy ever since *Guess Who's Coming To Dinner* to *Shaft*. We said we would put in some R&D for that so he could come up with a reel and then we'd look at it and decide if we want to put in production funding in the future.

Q – What makes for a good proposal in the eyes of ITVS?

Claire – People have to have to put in a three-page treatment. There's another element, which is a half page synopsis of what the project is about. But with the treatment you hopefully say what the film is about, but how it's going to be told, what is it going to look like, what are the different elements in it. We really want to know if you can visualize the project in words. We look at other things like samples, too, but the treatment is really key. The people who review are internal staff and external people that we engage. They are people just like the applicants, really - independent filmmakers, TV people, educators, outreach people and writers. They have seven criteria that they evaluate the projects on. Is it compelling? Is the treatment clear? Does it speak to an underserved audience - ethnic minorities, the elderly, etc? Does the project have the access that it requires? Why do they want to make the film? Is it going to be something for public TV? If it's more a theatrical film then this is the place to talk about that. Everyone wants to make feature docs and that makes sense, but they are a bit of an oil and water situation with TV. It's hard to schedule 90-minute documentaries. Is the production team strong and is the budget reasonable? Are they first time filmmaker or do they have people on their team that are really good? Is the amount that they are requesting reasonable? And while the treatment is important, we do look at the other materials. If the treatment is beautiful, but the video is really bad or vice versa, we look at them together. We have an essay on our website called "How to Write a Better Treatment" that talks about these issues. How to put into words any visualization and style. And what not to do, such as dropping names.

Q – Do you want to see a classic three-act structure?

Claire – People have said that about us, but I don't think that is the case. On the other hand, when a program definitely has a three-act structure then we have to look at the story that way. And so many documentaries are being structured that way in terms of narrative filmmaking and character based. So if it has that form, then we look to see if it is working. It's really the filmmaker who states that.

Q – What is a way someone can get a character-based doc through?

Claire – Having video on them is really helpful. Sometimes people haven't had a chance to put together any production materials on the main character, but they pull together things like news footage or reportage or something so we know whom they are talking about and if they're going to work on TV.

Q – In your opinion what makes a good documentary program?

Claire – The level of storytelling. Something that's really engaging and talks about things that we would never know before. If you go to a film festival and you read the blurb of a film, you wonder to yourself why you would want to see a 15-year-old girl in the penal system who has bursts of violence. Then you see the film, *Aimee's Crossing*, and you are riveted by the character and the skill of the filmmaker.

Q – If someone was a first time filmmaker and had a good idea, how would they convince you?

Claire – There are different ways. Some people pair up with a more experienced person such as an executive producer or a co-producer. That's usually the way to get into ITVS. There's a great film called *Farmingville*, which was on POV and was produced by two people. One was Catherine Tambini who had done a number of documentaries before and her partner was Carlos Sandoval who was an attorney and an activist. He partnered with her and she was the main applicant. It was his first film and he did a great job. They were funded the first time they came to Open Call because the material was so strong. For an emerging filmmaker, he wasn't emerging in terms of his life. But even if someone has expertise or great access, we hold tight to this rule because so many people that apply just don't have that experience and they need to partner.

Q – Do you do short films?

Claire – We acquire them through *Independent Lens* for American TV rights. We don't go into production funding for shorts unless they are 30-minute pieces that we could put on PBS. People send in shorts through *Independent Lens* and we look at them and then package them into an hour programs. Or if we need them as interstitials to round out the hour, then we look at them. Shorts are so great, there just isn't a lot of room for them. We're going to have an online shorts contest this year and we'll put them on our website.

Q – What is Independent Lens?

Claire – It's a 29-week series of independent programming – everything from documentary to drama to experimental to animation. It was conceived as a way to get independent voices on the air in primetime. It compliments POV, which airs in the same time slot but the rest of the weeks of the year – during the summer. Some of the shows are ITVS funded films and others are acquisitions. Sometimes they follow the PBS calendar themes like February they might have black films on and in June they might do gay and lesbian themes.

Q – When the projects come in do you designate slots right up front or when they are done?

Claire – We try to do it up front, but sometimes it's not possible. We may see something that we want on Independent Lens, but we have to make sure that PBS is on board with that. Some of our shows already have commitments to other PBS shows like *American Masters*, but we try to control the distribution of all our funded shows. And we work with the producers to find the best place for it.

Q – What is ITVS Community and ITVS Community Classrooms?

Claire – It's an outreach program that is the umbrella of all the engagement and outreach programs that we do. That ranges from something called the ITVS Cinema Series where we go to different places and screen ITVS programs to people who are involved with the film and the issues of the film. ITVS Classrooms is where we put out study guides to work with educators to get out the word on certain issues. And not only classrooms, it can be care-givers and people in the health fields. We have a department here that does this and they work with the filmmakers to do the activities.

Q – What is LINCS?

Claire – It is a funding initiative where a filmmaker partners with a public TV station and what ITVS will do is match up to $100,000 of the money that the station puts up. So you would go to WGBH and say I have this program, can you put in $100,000 of post and promotion? Then I could go to ITVS and get $100,000 cash for the project. It's great. It has generated at lot of interesting programs. There was one called *Be Good, Smile Pretty* that won an Emmy that came out of the Kansas City station. It gets all the stations involved from all over the nation including the smaller ones.

Q – Are you seeing any trends in documentary filmmaking?

Claire – There is a huge global trend where American filmmakers are interested in the world. They are doing things that we wouldn't have seen five years ago at ITVS. They'd have been called international shows. There was a program about two women from Kashmir and one is Muslim and one is Hindu. They go on a road trip to Kashmir to see their families and also to see what is the cause of this huge conflict between religions. They were there right before the earthquake. And that's the kind of film we wouldn't have seen. There have been a lot of films about the experience after 9/11. We are seeing a number of films from Arab-Americans and their communities. What is their identity? There are no positive images of Arabs in this country. We are getting a lot of programs that talk about environmental issues. We have always had that, but it is chronic now. Especially about modified food. What we are not getting and what we want are proposals from young filmmakers. We want those perspectives 18-24. Generally, these are more narrative filmmakers because that's what they're interested in. It's hard to get young people interested in documentaries.

Q – Is PBS constrained by the same censoring regulations as the rest of American TV?

Claire – They are now ever since the Janet Jackson incident at the Super Bowl - the wardrobe malfunction. So the FCC really cracked down on what you can show on commercial TV, not cable, but commercial TV, which PBS is part of. Then PBS went and issued a policy statement of what you can and can't show. You can't really get away with anything now. You can't even say "God" on PBS without it insinuating some kind of curse. You can't say "ass" even though Jon Stewart says it

GUERILLA FILM MAKER SAYS!

Other Funding Orgranizations

A.J. Muste Institute
Supports the principles and practice of nonviolent social change in regards to peace and disarmament; social and economic justice; racial and sexual equality; and the labor movement.
www.ajmuste.org

Anthony Radziwill Documentary Fund
Provides grants to emerging and established documentary filmmakers in the form of development funds (seed money) for specific new projects. Run through IFP-NY.
http://market.ifp.org/newyork/docfund

Arthur Vining Davis Foundation
Foundations, Health Care, Public TV, Secondary Education, Private Higher Education.
www.avdfdn.org

Chicago Underground Film Fund
Grants awarded to selected film or video makers for post-production on works-in-progress that are in keeping with the festival's mission to promote works that push boundaries, defy commercial expectations and transcend the mainstream of independent filmmaking.
www.cuff.org

Creative Capital
Supports artists who pursue innovation in form and/or content in the performing and visual arts, film and video, and in emerging fields.
www.creative-capital.org

Crosspoint Foundation
Reducing discrimination and foster understanding and tolerance amongst all peoples. Education, the arts, societal concerns, indigenous issues, intellectual property rights, religion, family, general cultural issues.
www.crosspointfoundation.org

Dance Film Association
Members may apply for DFA's annual postproduction grants for films about dance.
www.dancefilmsassn.org

Ford Foundation
Supports high-quality productions that enrich public dialogue on building democratic values and pluralism.
www.fordfound.org

Frameline Film & Video Completion Fund
Gay and Lesbian themed projects.
www.frameline.org

Guggenhiem Fellowship
Fellowships are awarded through two annual competitions: one open to citizens and permanent residents of the United States and Canada. The otherfor citizens and permanent residents of Latin America and the Caribbean.
www.gf.org

The Jerome Foundation
Must be a resident of Minnesota or NYC to apply.
www.jeromefdn.org

Latino Public Broadcasting
Themes and issues that are relevant to Latinos.
www.lpbp.org

The LEF Foundation
CA: Supports work of creative merit in the fields of contemporary art and architecture, design, environment, literature, the performing arts, film and new media.
NE: Supports contemporary art production and works to enhance environmental conditions.
www.lef-foundation.org

MacArthur Foundation
The Program on Global Security and Sustainability: international peace and security, conservation and sustainable development, population and reproductive health, and human rights.
The Program on Human and Community Development: US community development; regional policy; affordable housing, ducation, juvenile justice, and mental health.
The General Program: public interest media, including public radio and the production of independent documentary film. Grants are made to arts and cultural institutions in the Chicago area.
The MacArthur Fellows Program awards five-year, unrestricted fellowships to individuals across all ages and fields who show exceptional merit and promise of continued creative work. Limited to US citizens and other residents of the US.
www.macfound.org

NAATA
Works that place Asian Americans in the context of an increasingly multicultural society, Issues of national interest but from a unique Asian American perspective.
www.asianamericanmedia.org

Nathan Cummings Foundations
Arts and culture; the environment; health; interprogram initiatives for social and economic justice; and the Jewish life and values/contemplative practice programs.
www.nathancummings.org

National Black Programming Consortium
Supports projects that offer a more realistic, historically accurate, diverse, and non-stereotypical picture of the Black World. ***www.nbpc.tv***

National Fund for Jewish Documentary
Jewish history, culture, identity, and contemporary issues in diverse public audiences.
www.jewishculture.org

Native American Public Television
Projects that illuminate the Native American experience through public television.
www.nativetelecom.org

The North Star Fund
Better schools, housing and health care, protecting civil liberties, stopping domestic violence, creating living wage jobs, and advocating for peace, freedom and human rights.
www.northstarfund.org

Open Meadows Foundation
Cultural and ethnic diversity of our society and promote the empowerment of women and girls.
www.openmeadows.org

Pacific Pioneer Fund
To support emerging documentary filmmakers. Limited to filmmakers who live and work in CA, OR and WA.
www.pacificpioneerfund.com

GUERILLA FILM MAKER SAYS!

Other Funding Organizations cont.

The Playboy Foundation
Civil rights and liberties in the United States.
www.playboyenterprises.com

Puffin Foundation
Encourages emerging artists whose works, due to their genre and/or social philosophy might have difficulty being aired.
www.puffinfoundation.org

Rockefeller Foundation
Agriculture, Arts & Culture, Health, Employment, Housing, Education, Globalization.
www.rockfound.org

Roy W. Dean Film and Writing Grants
Several types of mostly in-kind grants and help writing proposal and treatment.
www.fromtheheartproductions.com

The Sister Fund
Spiritual women and their organizations. Justice and national and international social change agents.
www.sisterfund.org

The Unitarian Universalist Funding Program
Social change.
www.uua.org/uufp

For more information on funding orgranizations and where to find grants, visit www.fdncenter.org.

every night.

Q – What are the common mistakes that documentary filmmakers make?

Claire – They don't read the guidelines or follow the directions. And I can understand in your enthusiasm not doing that, but it is better if you do. Like when we ask for a three-page treatment, don't turn in six pages because you have a lot of material. The other thing is to really think about the material for television. That means an hour show.

Q – What advice would you give a documentary filmmaker?

Claire – It's sort of obvious, but don't give up. Be resolute to what you have to do. And that is the same thing for us. We have to reject 95% of the proposals, but that doesn't mean that the project doesn't have value or that you cannot come back again. That's the spirit of making a film and that is ours as well. Don't take no for an answer.

NEW YORK STATE COUNCIL ON THE ARTS

Q – What kind of grants do you offer documentary filmmakers?

Debby – The New York State Council On The Arts funds documentary filmmakers through its Independent Artists Program for film, video and new media productions. We don't fund documentary filmmakers exclusively. It's open to radio, audio and new media people as well. And they can be working in narrative, documentary, experimental or any new form. We'll fund things at any stage of production and the grants go from $5,000 to $25,000. Artists need to have a fiscal sponsor and live in New York State. They cannot be students, but rather professional independent filmmakers or video artists. There are some other opportunities that are a little less direct in terms of the application process. Through a partnership with The Independent Feature Project we also provide funding for distribution and recently completed work. We support the Experimental Television Center's finishing funds for small-budgeted productions. And with the New York Foundation for the Arts there are fellowships for artists.

Q – How does one apply for one of your grants?

Debby – We aren't able to directly fund individuals so the way we're able to support production in through fiscal sponsorship. There are quite a few non-profits across the state, mostly arts organizations, that apply on behalf of the artist and are allowed to take a small percentage for an administrative fee should the artist be funded. We do this annually and March 1st is our preliminary application deadline where we want kind of sketchy information and then we look at a fuller proposal on April 1st and we make our funding decisions in July.

Q – Does the fiscal sponsor have to be from New York State?

Debby – Yes because we're a state arts agency. We only deal with fiscal sponsors incorporated in New York State.

Q – What are the parts of your proposal and what are you looking for in each section that would get you excited?

Debby – It's a relatively short proposal. At the March 1st deadline all we want to know is what you estimate your budget to be and if you're asking for the full $25,000 or less. We then want a sound bite of what your project is about. This all happens online. Then we do a follow up. We ask for a slightly longer description of the project. I tell people not to boast, but be descriptive. We want to know if it's a short or a feature. What is the topic and how are you going to handle it. And show some awareness of what other information materials are out there on your topic. If you're doing something on a subject that has been approached, before it helps to acknowledge that and state how your project is different. Be specific and focused, but don't give us a rationale of why your issue is important, but talk about why you are doing this particular piece and how you plan to approach it. We also ask for a bit of background on the artist's credentials and for more seasoned artists we want to know how the work advances their approach as an artist. So talk about where their career is going and why this project. If they're a less experienced artist, we like to know how you're going to manage this project. All your previous work may have been student work, so we like to get a sense that all your resources are in place and you're ready to take on your next project. If you come from another arts discipline, it would be good to know about your advisors and crew.

Q – Do you want to see a budget?

Debby – Yes. There are a few other components still. We want to know about your past credentials, any awards you have won and distribution. And we do ask for a production budget. We never fund 100% of any production no matter how small. We typically look at projects that are under $1 million. They can be larger, but we'd be in for a very particular section of it and that there is some evidence that the balance of that budget can be raised. We don't need to have all prior commitments and a fundraising plan. You submit an online budget with a place to put update notes. We're not afraid to be the first money, but we do want to get a sense that the person can go out and complete the work and do it well. I always remind artists to include a salary for themselves. Also give us a sense if you're getting a lot of in-kind equipment or in-kind services as well as the cash expenses. We have some funny little restrictions with government funding in New York. We won't buy plane tickets to go out of state or out of the country and we won't pay for fundraising costs. So we tell artists to not ask us for that. The artists that we look at do cover the whole world, so there is a way to come in without telling us a New York story.

Q – Do you need to see a work sample?

Debby – Yes. We ask for up to ten minutes, but we don't usually watch it all. You can send in two samples. It really makes sense to give us something that really demonstrates your work at its best, but also something that is most relevant to the project. People like to send us trailers sometimes, but trailers don't usually show the person's normal flow of how they approach the craft. So we would rather get a second sample that gives us a better sense of what your approach, sound and pacing are like as well as the trailer. Or if you have some really rough footage of the compelling subject of your new project, you can show us that and then include something more polished. In our application, we ask people how these samples relate to the project. Sometimes samples don't represent the type of work they want to do next and we want to know how they are going to make that leap say from experimental films to documentary. Or if they've done a lot of commercial work and now they want to do independent work. Our process is heavily driven by the production samples and the short description of what the artist wants to do.

Q – Are the work samples the most important part?

Debby – Yes. Sometimes a great narrative and a reason of why we are not looking at better sample work can make up for it. The way our review process works is that we work with a peer panel. And our staff will review all of the information and then they will send off all of the written material to our panel ahead of time. When they come here, they look at the samples after they have read those written proposals. It's after this, that we do our first cut. Some things develop more quickly than others and there is a space to talk to us about it, but we say don't waste time giving us a lot of opening credits and again, if all we get is a punchy trailer, the panel is smart enough to say that they have no sense of what the pacing of the work is going to be. Check our website to see what formats the work samples need to come in because it changes as the technology does.

Q – Do you retain any rights on the films you fund?

Debby – We don't retain any rights on material. We do ask for credit and we provide that information graphically online. We like to know when the work gets done. We require a final report that states how our money was spent. In many cases, the work isn't done and the money is spent but we want it accounted for. In terms of fiscal sponsorship, we ask the artists be certain to have a letter of agreement or a contract with their fiscal sponsor to make sure the sponsor doesn't exercise any rights either unless that's the nature of the project.

Q – Can someone increase their chances of getting a grant with NYSCA?

Debby – We look at 300-325 projects a year and we fund about 20%. We have a budget of about $650,000 to $1 million depending on the year. The way things are selected for funding involves some luck as well as being a good project. Our staff is willing to look at things before the application deadline and can give some guidance, but the panel sometimes does something different. Part of it is the mix that comes in to us. So being aware of other people doing another project on the topic you are doing is important. One year we got three projects in on tap dancing and they were all interesting in their own way and it completely confused the panel. If we had one, it would have been much better for that one moving ahead. So there are certain things that you can't really control in the environment, but if we know that somebody else is working on the same thing and you're on the same grant docket, that makes it harder. You have to be able to make the case that your approach is the one that should be supported now. Other than that, you want to show clarity of what you want to do and a good reason for doing it and a really terrific sample. We fund people that we know and don't know. We try to move the money around a bit among artists. If we fund you, we ask that you sit out for at least two years. We're willing to fund artists more than once, but not every single project.

Q – If someone fails to get funded, do you encourage them to reapply?

Debby – Absolutely. But check with our staff if you haven't been funded to get feedback and see what the reaction was to the proposal and the sample. Also there is slightly different panel and applicants every year and we have seen people not get funded in one year and move ahead in another year.

Q – Are you the only state arts council in the US?

Debby – No. Every state has an arts council. They fund slightly different things. A few do fund production. We are a large arts council and have been around for a long time because New York is such an arts rich state and it is vital to the economy of the state. And if you live in more than one state, we go by where you file your taxes.

Q – What are the common mistakes that documentary filmmakers make?

Debby – They spend too much time describing the cause that they're working on in their work and not so much in what they're going to do as an artist making the piece. It can be in the proposal, but it should not take up several paragraphs. They need to be really smart about work samples. And they need to make sure that someone who's not involved with the project reads over everything that you've written and takes a look at your work samples to see if it talks to people who are not close to the project.

Q – What advice would you give a new documentary filmmaker?

Debby – Find an economy of scale and a medium to get your work done. Don't be held back by fundraising or anything else. Get some work out there and get seen.

Keeping Funders Sweet

GUERILLA FILM MAKER SAYS!

1. Where possible, fulfill any promises made. It may not always be possible to fulfill a promise (one of the disadvantages of low budget filmmaking), but make it a priority to do so at almost any cost.

2. Regular updates on email keeps the funder in touch with what is happening. If the line of communication goes cold, so will the investor.

3. Press – this is great for keeping people happy. Everyone associates press coverage with success, but beware, this may produce a false sense of financial returns on the part of the investors. If press coverage has used artistic license, let funders know.

4. Invite them to a shoot. They love to see the buzz of the actual filmmaking process and especially the chance to meet the actors.

5. Send them a DVD of the final film and invite them to the premiere.

6. If things are going badly, then let them know. As long as there is trust and they can see that you have done everything possible, investors have no real come back (check your agreements though). Funders would rather know things are going badly than hear nothing at all.

7. Give them a credit on the film, either as the Executive Producer (depending on how much money they've put up) or with a special thanks at the end of the film.

8. Pay them properly and quickly when monies come in from deals.

Fundraising Books

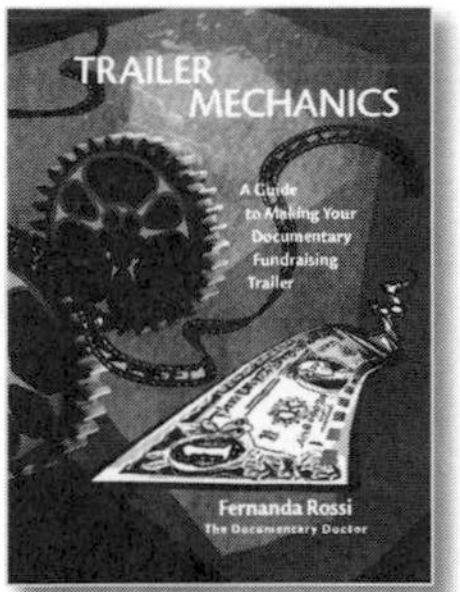

Trailer Mechanics: A Guide to Making Your Documentary Fundraising Trailer
By Fernanda Rossi

The Art of Funding Your Film
By Carole Dean

Get Your Documentary Funded and Distributed
By Jess Search and Melissa McCarthy

The Grass Roots Fundraising Book
By Joan Flanagan

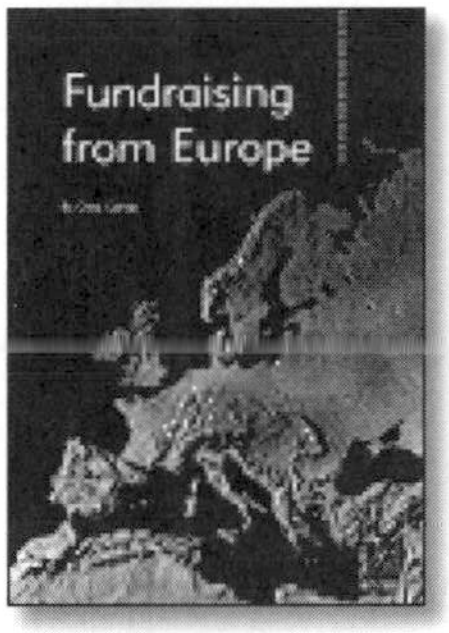

Fundraising from Europe
By Christopher Carnie

Fundraising from America: The Complete Guide for Charitable Organizations Outside the USA
David Wickert (Editor)

Asking Properly: The Art of Creative Fundraising
By George Smith

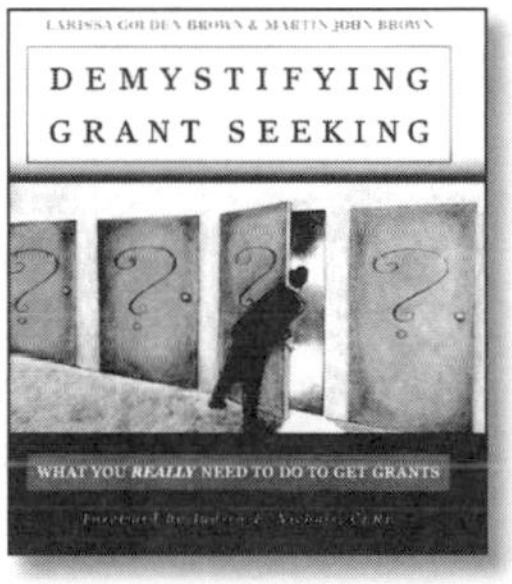

Demystifying Grant Seeking: What You REALLY Need to Do to Get Grants
By Larissa Golden Brown, Martin John Brown

Getting Funded: The Complete Guide to Writing Grant Proposals
By Mary S. Hall

The Fundraising Houseparty: How to Get Charitable Donations from Individuals in a Houseparty Setting,
By Morrie Warshawski.

Shaking the Money Tree: How to Get Grants and Donations for Film and Television
By Morrie Warshawski

Susana Loza
Program Manager

CALIFORNIA DOCUMENTARY PROJECT

Q – What is the California Documentary Project?

Susana – The California Documentary Project is the media grants component of California Stories, the Council's multi-year statewide initiative. The CDP supports high quality documentary work by established documentarians that explore California culture, history and society through telling the stories of individuals and communities. The CDP seeks to fulfill the CCH mission of fostering discussion and dialogue leading to greater understanding and stronger communities.

Q – Is there any subject matter that you typically like to fund?

Susana – Projects must explore California related stories or topics in an entertaining, interesting, thoughtful and nuanced manner. Projects should involve at least two humanities scholars/experts as advisors or consultants. Projects with potential to generate community discussions and to serve larger educational or social purposes are viewed with particular interest. Descriptions of previously funded projects can be viewed at http://www.californiastories.org/programs/doc_intro.htm.

Q – Is there any subject matter that you would never fund?

Susana – Projects that lack a clear California focus, significant humanities content that either take a one-sided approach or an advocate a particular position on an issue aren't eligible for support.

Q – What are the types of grants available and the amounts that one could receive?

Susana – The maximum award from CCH is $20,000 with up to $60,000 in additional support from the Skirball Foundation for projects that clearly demonstrate the potential to reach a significant national audience through broadcast or theatrical distribution. All CCH and Skirball funds must be matched by an equivalent amount of non-federal cash or in-kind support.

Q – How does someone apply for a grant?

Susana – Complete an application form, attach your proposal narrative and budget (using our format), and submit the required supplementary materials (sample work, CV, letters of interest from a distribution and/or broadcaster). California Documentary Project guidelines and application materials are available from the Council website, www.californiastories.org.

Q – Do you need a fiscal sponsor?

Susana – Yes. CCH can only make awards to non-profit or state/local government agencies.

Q – Do you have to be a California resident to apply?

Susana – No, but applications from California institutions are viewed favorably.

Q – Do you require a proposal?

Susana – Yes. Proposals should be tailored to our guidelines, which request information about the subject matter of the project, your approach, humanities content and scholarship, target audience, outreach and distribution, expertise of project personnel, project goals and assessment/evaluation, and a timeline/work plan. The most compelling proposals paint a vivid verbal picture of the story and stories your documentary will tell and are clear, succinct and responsive to the guidelines.

Q – Do you want to see a budget?

Susana – Yes. We also ask that you break down your request using our budget categories using a budget form available on our website.

Q – Do you want to see work samples?

Susana - Yes. Both a completed documentary by the project developmet/project staff and sample work-in-progress are required. Work samples are weighed heavily in the review process, so be sure to submit your very best work!

Q – If you fund a project, do you reserve any rights or does the filmmaker need to credit you in any way?

Susana – CCH must receive on-screen credit as well as acknowledgement in printed and publicity materials; standard language and a logo are provided for your use. CCH reserves the right to use of your completed work for internal purposes, but copyright and full ownership and distribution rights are retained by the filmmaker.

Q – If you fail to get funded, can you reapply?

Susana – Yes. Staff are willing to provide feedback to you and discuss your prospects for resubmission; in some cases, projects are actively encouraged to apply again. If so, up to how many times? That's up to you!

Q – How many times can a filmmaker apply for one of your grants throughout their career?

Susana – There are no limits to the number of applications a filmmaker may submit during their career, although, CCH likes to distribute its resources as widely as possible, consistent with other goals.

Q – What are the common mistakes that you see documentary filmmakers make?

Susana – Not following the guidelines or instructions in preparing their proposals. Insufficient humanities content or not understanding what is meant by humanities content or scholarship (we don't mean humanitarian!). Poor quality work sample. Budgetary miscalculations. Not proofreading proposals before submitting!

Q – What advice would you give a documentary filmmaker?

Susana – Do your homework; find out what types of projects the funder is likely to support. Be tenacious and don't give up; if you believe your project is a good fit, go ahead and apply. Don't wait until the last minute to find out what are the requirements or procedures for applying. Specifically for CCH applicants: Read the guidelines and FAQs, then follow up with a program officer or attend a workshop. To be notified when guidelines and other information is available, please sign up at http://www.calhum.org/programs/grapes_email.epl.

NEH

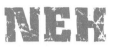

Q – How does the NEH differ from the NEA?

Michael – We fund primarily documentary film that has humanities content, the disciplines of history, literature, religion, philosophy and musicology for example. And it's about interpreting the appropriate scholarship in those disciplines as it relates to a documentary film. We don't fund literary adaptations or performance.

Q – What are the types of grants available to documentary filmmakers at the NEH and how much funding can one get from each one?

Michael – We offer four levels of support at the moment. The initial grant that we offer is The Consultation Grant. That is $10,000. It's a short grant proposal. Only about 7-10 pages and the intention is to enable a filmmaker to put together a board of consultants or humanities advisors who help him or her develop the humanities content of the film that they want to make. That is, identify what the principle humanities themes might be that relate to the given subject. Also, the other resources and other scholars that may be available who the filmmaker may consult for the development of the project. Then we have The Planning Grant, which is $30,000. The purpose of the Planning Grant is to enable a filmmaker to do additional research, and begin to locate primary sources and other material for the film, especially visual materials. And again, to sketch out a preliminary treatment to show what the film would look like. Then there is The Scripting Grants. That varies on the scope and scale of the project. It ranges from $60,000 for a one-hour or two-hour film to $75,000 to $90,000 if it's going to be a series. The grant is for doing additional research and development and to actually write a script that will be a roadmap for the film as it goes into production and editing. And then we have Production Grants, which is the big money. As the name implies it is to fund the production of a film or television series. They go from $400,000 to up to a $1 million depending on the project.

Q – Can a filmmaker apply for more than one of these grants on the same project?

Michael – We need to let people know first that we do not make grants to individual filmmakers. We make grants to non-profit organizations. That means the filmmaker needs to be working through a 501 (c) 3 because that organization will actually be the grantee who would administer the grant. Many of the independent filmmakers that I have worked with have set up their own 501 (c) 3 companies, which is fine as long as they adhere to certain IRS regulations that relate to federal money. The filmmakers can only apply for one grant at a time for the same project. Right now we have a November deadline every year that is for the Planning, Scripting and Production Grants. They are reviewed by staff and peer panels and a decision is made in late May. The Consultation Grants have a March deadline with decisions in July. What this means is that in any grant cycle beginning in either November or in March, an applicant cannot have more than one grant for the project under review at any one time. One or the other. You can choose to come in at any level you want. If you need the Production Grant, then fine, apply for the Production Grant. If you are early in the process and you think you are ready for a Planning Grant, fine, apply for that. You do not need to have one grant to get another grant. You do not have to follow the sequence. And if one year you need a Planning Grant you can apply for that and then in the next cycle you might need a Production Grant and you can apply for that one then. But for a Production Grant we are going to need to see a detailed treatment or script.

Q – What is the We The People Grant Initiative?

Michael – That's a special initiative that's intended to encourage projects that look at American History. They're still reviewed like every other grant. They go to the same panels. They come out of the same budget. There are no special provisions that favor one project as a *We The People* project over another. In other words, the Endowment itself will look at all the proposals that come in and the Endowment will decide what is a *We The People* Project, which carries a certain cache with it and may help with further fundraising.

Q – Are there any subjects that the NEH really likes to fund?

Michael – American history. American literature. That does not mean that foreign culture subjects are not also desired, they certainly are because we recognize the need of the American public to understand the world. We don't consider projects that are based on original performance nor literary adaptations. We don't support films that focus on public policies that might be advocacy of a particular issue - only those that have a historical perspective with an objective view. This is taxpayer's money and we don't want to support projects that are so one way or the other.

Q – How do you apply for a grant with the NEH and what are the sections of the application?

Michael – At the moment we are revising the application guidelines so it's best to look at the NEH website to get an idea of what we want in a proposal when you're ready to apply. But, I think the most important thing for an applicant, especially if they are new to the Endowment is to contact to us. Talk to us about their subject and approach and we might be able to give them some guidance that will be useful to them in navigating the NEH process. We'll read draft proposals and try to offer the best advice we can leading up to the deadline. After the process has run its course, and once the decision has been made and the applicants have been informed, we will send each applicant a letter attached to the evaluation sheets that the review panel filled out and try our best to explain the reasons for the decision made. Our proposal has a number of components, a budget component and a narrative essay that has several components to it. What do they want NEH money for? Why does this matter? They need to tell us something about the visual approach. They need to discuss the humanities themes and the scholarship that informs the development of those films. They need to tell us what progress they have made on the project up until now and what prospective funding they see out there for the project. They also need to tell us who the project staff will be. The production staff and the humanities staff. If they're applying for a Scripting Grant, they need to provide us with a draft treatment that gives us some idea of how they're thinking about the humanities content and the visuals will come together. When they do the Production Grant they'll need a detailed script or treatment to support it.

Q – Do you like other support materials to go along with these applications?

Michael – We require samples of previous work. We would need to see the example of the best work they 've done to date. If it's one program, send it in on DVD or VHS and that becomes part of the application. The filmmaker's experience and background do matter. If we're going to spend $1 million on a project we want to know that this filmmaker can make it happen.

Q – Do you work with first time filmmakers?

Michael – Yes. They need to be consulting with the program staff here and we'll do our best to give them useful advice. It's also useful and smart ot engage a consulting producer.

Q – Do you have any advice on putting together a board of scholars?

Michael – You want to think about people who are appropriate to what ever it is you are trying to do. You want people to have experience and credentials on that subject so that they'll be able to add knowledge to the production team. Certainly, the NEH is going to evaluate the advisors who are engaged in a project.

GUERILLA FILM MAKER SAYS!

Finding Money

1. Production Companies – may have lines of credit with financial institutions or broadcasters to make their own films.

2. Networks/Cable companies (NBC/HBO) – the main way docs get made and shown in the world. They will usually put up a portion of the budget and the filmmaker has to find the rest.

3. Private investors – regular people with money who get a piece of your film for their investment. May have to have a public offering that follows many SEC guidelines, which may cost upwards of $10,000.

4. Grant funding – best for socially oriented documentaries. Modest money from the NEH, the NEA and foundations with certain focuses, but lots of tedious grant writing and long decision making time.

5. Lawyers/Producer Reps – have contacts with producers and financiers and can put you in contact with them.

6. Foreign Equity – foreign private investors. They may ask for some of the rights to the film, especially those for their country.

7. Co-Production – working with a foreign production company and foriegn broadcasters who may have access to monies or tax incentives that you cannot get in your home country. Again, will ask for the rights to their country.

8. Self-Financing – you have the most power because it is your money, but you have the most risk. Be careful of running up huge credit card debt.

Q – Is there anything in particular you look for in a proposal that would really grab your attention?

Michael – What I want to see is a clear statement of why this project is important. What is the public going to learn by seeing this film? I also want to see a clear articulation of the humanities themes and the scholarship that informs those themes. I want to see that the filmmaker has actually done some research and given some thought to the subject matter itself. That they have consulted with some humanities advisors. Then I want to see some indication of how all this might come together as a film. You don't want it to read like a book manuscript proposal. It is a film proposal after all. So you have to tell us how the humanities content it going to have a filmic quality.

Q – If a filmmaker seeks a theatrical release for their film, is that a concern of yours?

Michael – No. We've had a couple projects do that. We want our projects to be seen by the widest possible audience and we feel that is TV. We support projects with the intention for first presentation to PBS or Discovery or whatever – TV. What we will allow is if a producer wants to take their film on the film festival circuit prior to broadcast, like Sundance or whatever, we are fine with that. A large number of our films had their premiere at Sundance. But we are not necessarily unhappy if someone like Lionsgate came in to pick it up. The producer is free to negotiate the best deal they can get, but we do have to sign off on all the distribution agreements. We're usually looking at technical matters about revenue recovery and so forth, because the NEH does have a claim on some of the revenues up to a certain amount of money depending on the size of the grant. That's something that can be negotiated with our Grants Department.

Q – What are matching funds and how do they apply to NEH Grants?

Michael – Matching funds are funds that are offered to a project by the NEH, but are contingent on that project matching those funds from non-federal sources. The NEH budget has two components to it: outright funds and matching funds. My advice to producers is to seek outright funds, especially independent producers. It is difficult for independent producers to raise money these days and so you're better off applying for outright funds. And then the NEH always has the option of offering matching funds. That is unless they have a lot of money from non-federal sources in the bank that can be charged against matching.

Q – What are the common mistakes that you see people make when applying for NEH grants?

Michael – Not reading the guidelines. I think every organization would tell you that. People apply to organizations, including the NEH, not really understanding what that organization does and the projects that they fund. People don't read the guidelines and then they send in projects that don't fit within our guidelines.

Q – What advice would you give a new filmmaker?

Michael - Talk to an NEH staff because we can help them write a better proposal.

GUERILLA FILM MAKER SAYS!

Private Investors

Private investors are simply individuals who want to invest in your film company personally, as opposed to investing in a company. These are typically friends, relatives and other wealthy people you meet (doctors, lawyers, car dealership owners, etc.) who either want to do you a favor or wish to be part of the glamour and adventure that is filmmaking. Some things to keep in mind, and that you must make clear is that there is a good chance people will lose their investment due to the risky nature of filmmaking. Also, it's a legal requirement that you have a business plan (Private Placement Memorandum) containing resumes, attachments to the project, a budget, etc. to give these potential investors. However, you can receive "gifts" either directly from your friends or family (but they must check with their accountant on how much they can give as a "gift" before they are taxed on it), or they can donate to a non-profit organization (501 (c) 3) that you have set up. Finally, be aware that when you take money from friends or relatives, personal relationships and emotions can come into play – make sure you have signed agreements clearly spelling out the terms of the deal with everyone! You don't want to be in a position where you dread catching up with family and friends at Christmas because you burnt their fingers very badly. They can't complain however, if they had ALL the facts before they parted with their cash.

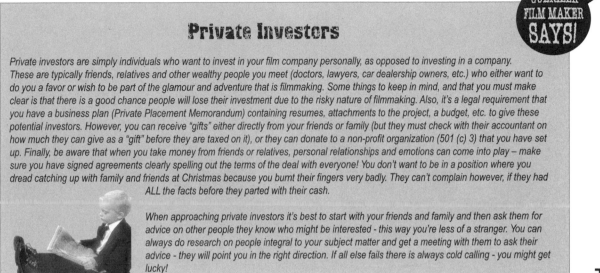

When approaching private investors it's best to start with your friends and family and then ask them for advice on other people they know who might be interested - this way you're less of a stranger. You can always do research on people integral to your subject matter and get a meeting with them to ask their advice - they will point you in the right direction. If all else fails there is always cold calling - you might get lucky!

NEA

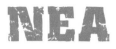

Q – What is the NEA and how does it differ from the NEH?

Ted – Both of the organizations were created by the same act of Congress in 1965, but have developed into separate agencies and have adopted different ways of working. They are both the main bodies of government funding in their respective areas – arts and humanities. The National Endowment for the Arts has developed a series of programs that are discipline oriented, such as music and opera, music theater, dance, visual arts, museums, media arts (including a special leadership initiative called Arts on Radio and Television), and literature. The NEH is concerned more with funding programs with a historical perspective on the humanities. The NEH do, however award a great deal more money when it makes its grants for documentaries than we are able to. Documentaries are the main thrust of their interest, whereas they are just one part of the media arts that we must cover. A lot of what we cover is ongoing series on television and radio.

Q – How would documentary filmmaking fit into NEA grants?

Ted – Documentary film is one style of filmmaking that is considered an art. Since about the early 1990's the Agency has been able to award grants only to organizations—and only to organizations with 501 (c) 3 status. There are a few exceptions to that provision and most of those are found in literature where there are some fellowships for translation and poetry. We support documentaries through grants to organizations that create documentary film or that arrange for documentaries to be made. If there's a non-profit organization in the business of doing that, or if a filmmaker or consortium have non-profit status, then they can apply for support directly. But in filmmaking, it's very often an individual activity. A filmmaker will work on a project and will associate with other individuals and then go onto another project with different people. So what happens in those cases is that an organization that does have 501 (c) 3 status will come to the agency for that project and work contractually with a filmmaker. We support the making of documentaries both in the media arts program and arts on radio and television for those films that might get national broadcast distribution. These grants typically can be for any aspect of the process from R&D up through completion and distribution. It has happened that some projects have received funding several different times in their life spans.

Q – What are the type of grants available to documentary filmmakers at the NEA and what are their amounts?

Ted – The general grant amounts will range from $10,000 up to as much as $50,000 in media arts and maybe a little more than that in Arts on Radio and Television for documentaries. It really depends on the size of the project itself and the amount that is asked for. All of the grants need to be matched one to one at least. Usually you will not request more than you can match, and you are likely to get less in any case because that's the way things go here. We hardly ever fund a project at the amount requested in the application, in any discipline. We don't divide up our grants as the NEH does in so far as having a grant for writing and one for production and so on. We say that support is available for any phase of the project. You just come in and tell us what you want the money for. If you're doing R&D, then you tell us so. If it's for production, then you tell us that. Budgets are supplied with the application along with a narrative of the project and the work that would be done with our grant. You also have to have a time frame that you're going to be doing it in.

Q – How does someone apply for an NEA grant?

Ted – Our website (www.nea.gov) has what grants are offered and supplies the guidelines and information about the deadlines. A documentary would most likely go to Arts on Radio and Television if it were a project about the arts destined for television distribution. Not all documentaries are, and those that aren't would go to Media Arts. Also there are other areas where one might wish to submit an application for a documentary film. For instance, if your subject has to do with folk arts, you could apply under that discipline. We increasingly want to see the documentaries we support focusing on the arts rather than on historical or social issues. The latter, again, is more the thrust of the NEH.

Q – What does the application require and what do you like to see in it?

Ted – The application will require necessary information about the applicant organization. What it is and how it can be reached. It'll need to include the IRS letter that states it has 501 (c) 3 status. It will include a project description stating what will be accomplished under this project or grant. It'll include a list of the principal participants like the filmmaker, the editor, the main members of the organization, etc. It'll include a budget, and that will show if any other funding has been secured and how much, or what the plans for other funding are, as we need to have a match. We realize that at the time an applicant comes to us, the funding may not be secured, but we like to see that they're applying and to whom and for how much. Very shortly all applications for our area will be made electronically through www.grants.gov, which is a requirement of the federal government.

Q – Can an applicant send in samples of their work?

Ted – Absolutely. That's a requirement for applications. We like to see samples of previous work or of the work-in-progress. If a filmmaker can send footage from what they're working on, that's very helpful. Now obviously, nobody is at the point yet where they can submit that stuff electronically. The bandwidth doesn't exist and it may never be possible to accurately convey film. So the work samples are sent separately from the paper part. The work samples are important—as important as having a strong project, a plausible budget and a track record. What I often say to people is that a strong application with weak work samples doesn't get anywhere. But a weak application with strong samples can. So in other words, if the narrative is written beautifully and the samples are weak, it's curtains. Make sure you state the relevance and significance of it to the project. They might say it shows their ability to work with black and white photography or outdoor scenes that might be required for the project. If there are teams of people involved, a cinematographer, a director, a writer, and you have different things to show their various skills that is fine. And having a work-in-progress is fine, too. It often is the most interesting because it's a clear demonstration of what is taking shape. But make sure you put your best work forward. And don't send in a dozen things for the panels look at. It's good to have choices, but the panels don't have time to look through everything.

Q – How can a first time filmmaker increase their chances?

Ted – Well, if they had anything they made as a student filmmaker that would help. The panel would want to see that. Or they could team up with a more experienced filmmaker and use that person's samples. But if they've worked with other people, it must be clear what their role was in order for it to be useful.

Q – Who is on the panels?

Ted – Top practitioners with tremendous depth of knowledge and experience. Once we have the applications, we start casting around to find the best panelists we can for that particular group of applications, based on what is in it. The panels score these applications on the basis of two considerations: artistic merit and artistic excellence.The entire process—from the meeting of the panel, to the staff's review of its recommendations, to submission of those recommendations to the National Council on the Arts and the Chairman of the NEA—takes about eight months. The panels themselves last three or four days. We go through 50 to 70 or 80 applications in that time.

Q – Is there any art form that you particularly like to fund?

Ted – No. There is no specific thing within the arts that we fund more than any other. Not even American versus international subject matter. There is just now an increasing need to fund documentaries that focus on the arts or an artist.

Q – Do you have to be an American citizen or organization to get funding?

Ted – Yes. We can't fund overseas applications. Even if it's an American subject, we can't do it.

Q – If the documentary wanted to have a theatrical release, could it?

Ted – Sure. It's just that if it's destined for television, then the application goes to the Arts on Radio and Television program. Otherwise, say for theatrical release, it should go to the Media Arts program. There are two application rounds for Media Arts. One has a deadline in March and one has an August deadline. The March deadline is mainly for festivals, curated series and distribution projects. And the August one is for services to the field and production. Check the website and determine which one is right for you.

Q – Are there any requirements if the NEA funds a film?

Ted – We expect credit when things are broadcast on a series we support, such as *American Masters* or *POV*. But there's no specific requirement that it carry an acknowledgement, although it's a good idea for filmmakers to credit Endowment support because part of the point of having a grant from the NEA is that it's kind of a stamp of approval. Your work has been judged by a formidable panel in the field and deemed worthy. As far as rights are concerned, the only thing we might want is to show the film or parts of it at conferences or presentations to various groups where our purpose is to demonstrate what we have funded.

Q – How many times can one apply per cycle?

Ted – Once per cycle. For most Endowment programs there is a limit to the number of applications an organization can make in a given round. But check the website, because in the Arts on Radio and Television, applicants can submit more than one application.

Q – Can applicants call you to discuss how to make their applications better or even to find out if their project fits within your guidelines?

Ted – Always. We're always happy to speak to applicants. It's our job and we enjoy it. If there're questions about any aspect of the application, they can call us or e-mail us. They can also get those details right on our website.

Q – What are the common mistakes that you see filmmakers make when applying for NEA grants?

Ted – If someone's project is off base as far as something we fund, we contact them and let them know. One common mistake used to be incomplete applications, but it is very clear to everybody that if an application is incomplete it won't be considered. Therefore, people aren't making that mistake any more.

Q – What advice would you give a documentary filmmaker?

Ted – Preserve your very best work so that you can submit it as a sample. Have access to it and keep it in good shape. Think critically of your own strengths as a filmmaker when you're preparing an application because it's those strengths that you want to put forward. And for younger filmmakers, take part in workshops or work on other people's projects so that you have samples to put forward until you have something of your own to show.

ANATOMY OF A DOCUMENTARY SECTION 7

BROADCASTERS

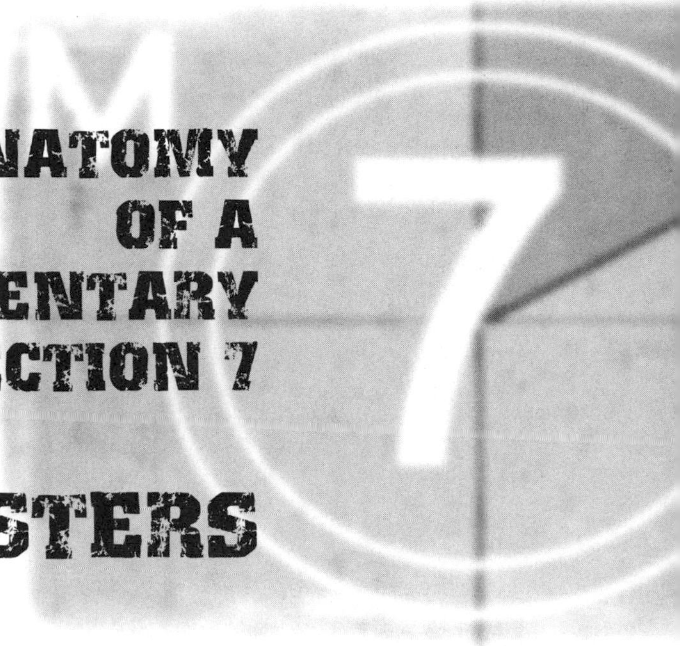

Denise Diianni
Exec. Producer

WGBH

Q – What is your job?

Denise – I'm in charge for Boston Media Productions, which is a production unit of WGBH-TV. These days, our content is sometimes distributed nationally through PBS, through public syndication services and via the Web. And we're doing more and more work to provide content for new media outlets. I'm also founding director of the WGBH Lab, which is exploring innovative approaches to story telling and finding ways to work with emerging documentary makers.

Q – What kind of productions do you get involved in?

Denise – We do a fair amount of standard TV fare that runs the gamut. We do more than 200 programs a year – most of that comes out of our daily news and public affairs show, Greater Boston. We have *Basic Black*, the longest running African American show in the system at 40 years; *La Plaza*, the longest running Latino show at 30 years of production. We also do *Eye On Education*, which we launched six years ago. It's a multimedia journalistic exploration of the state of education in Massachusetts with a focus on Boston. Initially I created *Eye on Education* because I wanted an opportunity for all our teams to work together on one content area - to shed a multi faceted journalistic spotlight. Also, TV, radio and the web were converging and I wanted our teams producing content for all these platforms. In its early years, *Eye on Education* enabled our documentary units to follow issues in education and to compare and contrast documentary stories. For example, *La Plaza* followed a few high school students from freshman year through graduation. These were low budget programs but they were really fine documentaries made by very talented producers. We also developed a documentary called *Day in the Life*; six very accomplished documentary makers and film crews focused on one school for just one day to capture different realities – sort of Rashomon style.

Q – How does WGBH work in the PBS system?

Denise – Primarily PBS is a syndicator of the Corporation for Public Broadcasting – an umbrella under which about 350 independently owned local stations reside. WGBH is often referred to as a leader in the PBS system because it produces about 30% of the primetime lineup, including *NOVA, Frontline, American Experience, Mystery! and Masterpiece Theatre* and many of the finest children's programs in the system. You can think of WGBH as one of the half a dozen or so major national producers, PBS as the aggregator of content, and the smaller local stations as the distributors of content.

Q – What is the Lab and to whom is it available?

Denise – The Lab stands on the shoulders of the New Television Workshop, and a remarkable generation of innovators from 20 and 30 years ago. It was a time when there was more money for experimentation at WGBH. The New Television Workshop brought in artists and video artists and choreographers to work along side producers. Then funding dried up and the world became very complicated. I decided that there was now an opportunity here to reassert WGBH's regional leadership in innovation, and the Lab seemed to be one way to do that with minimal investments. We wanted to reach out to emerging filmmakers and to say - we want you to help us. It was not, *"Here do it this way,"* it was, *"We think you have something to offer us."* At first, the Lab was conceptual and virtual, but now it is a workspace with an editing room, and access to a compression room, a conference room, screening rooms. It's a place where we invite filmmakers to come for six to nine month's residency to work on site with independently financed projects. The documentary makers receive access to an editorial consultant and a critical mass of creative energy here. We offer a modest honorarium that comes from an outside funder, LEF. We've had a range of filmmakers-in-residence. Currently, we have people who are very experienced in the business such as noted film critic, Gerry Peary, who's making his first film about film criticism, which is very brave because he's been reviewing other people's films for 20 years! We try to find ways for our standing staff to interact with these filmmakers. We have lunches and invite people throughout the foundation, not just in our small area, but people in radio, web, sometimes business and marketing colleagues – and we all sit around the table taking about documentary work. We talk about why a film works and why it doesn't work. We will also discuss other craft oriented topics. We try to push the approaches to factual story telling.

Q – What is 6:55?

Denise – The 6:55 Open Call is a call for proposals or pitches for short video content, with a focus on documentary storytelling. It gets it's name from shorts usually being under 7 minutes long. Each year a number of proposals are selected and WGBH then supports the production of these shorts. The shorts then premiere online and via our regional broadcast services. This year we're scaling the call via a new partnership with Open Media Network (OMN.org). OMN also allows us to involve an on-line community in the selection of the pitches we support. If audiences are using media in new ways, visual storytellers need to keep up with that. So 6:55 is a call for entries to the larger community of independent producers; it's a creative challenge to emerging and independent producers. We're trying to attract filmmakers, students, and animators, even advertisers. I think the most incredible visual short stories are the well-crafted 30 to 60 second commercials. We want to engage communities of interest and new content producers.

One demand of new media storytelling has to do with duration. Most people would prefer to watch short content – at least in many new media settings. The other thing to look at is the size of the screen. If you are making a theatrical release, you're probably going to make different visual decisions than if you're creating content to watch on a cell phone. We started a series a few years ago called *Storybreaks*. It was a very low budget real-life serialized soap opera – documentary stories that were told in extremely short segments. They're each four to seven minutes long, and each segment ends with a real life cliffhanger. We wanted to experiment with offering modular stories in the broadcast context that would pop up unexpectedly and hook your interest – like the best commercial breaks. It is just one example of the type of work we do at the Lab and with 6:55. To learn more about the 6:55 Call for Entries, the filmmakers-in-residence and the Lab, visit our site at wgbh.org/producingforwgbh.

Q – How do you choose the filmmakers who come to the Labs?

Denise – We have a review panel of 3-5 people from the filmmaking community. We look at applications and lots of supporting materials including past work, letters of recommendations, etc. Then we make selections based on how feasible we think the project is, and whether we think we can assist the filmmaker. If someone comes in and says they need to raise $3 million, then we're probably not a good match. But if someone comes in and says that they have to work on their sales reel and they want to do it in three months – that's more the scale of what we can help with. We wish we could provide more. Most of the projects we review are worthy and deserve support; we are trying to make the best match with what we can offer.

Q – How many filmmakers do you take on?

Denise – We usually take three. It's very rewarding. These are people who are so excited to be at WGBH. They are energetic and come from different ranges of experience and backgrounds. We do look for diversity of all kinds – age, gender, ethnicity, sexual orientation, and point of view. We want to shake things up. I know what I think about telling stories; I want to understand what people outside of WGBH think.

Q – What is the central focus of NOVA?

Denise – The *NOVA Science Unit* is headed by a very dynamic and talented Senior Executive Producer, Paula Apsell. *NOVA* is a single subject, hour-long science documentary series. They also produce a magazine show called *NOVA Science Now* and a number of groundbreaking limited series. They are very ambitious in what they cover and what they take on.

Q – Do you ever work with outside production houses?

Denise – Increasingly the WGBH big, signature series rely on outside producers regionally, nationally and even internationally. We have done a lot of business with international co-producers.

Q – How would someone go about approaching WGBH about a show and would you consider a first time filmmaker?

Denise – One of the reasons that I started the Lab was to support emerging filmmakers. We can do that here but it would be hard for a place like *NOVA* to say to an inexperienced filmmaker,*"Sure. Here's a full film budget – show us what you can do."* I want to make it easier for independent makers in the region to approach WGBH. That's why we created our Web site, wgbh.org/producingforwgbh. If you have an idea and it's relatively small or you are self-funded or you need editorial guidance and not a lot of cash, we may be able to help. In terms of people wanting to make *NOVA* programs or other national programs, the reality is that it's up to the executive producers of each series. And those signature shows tend to have a stable of highly accomplished outside producers with whom they like to work. But because these series have very good, dynamic leadership they keep reconfiguring their teams and are open to emerging talent with some track record. A first time maker with a great idea or entry into a great story could team up with an experienced producer and then become part of the production team.

Q – So if you had a finished film you could approach them for acquisitions?

Denise – Yes. It used to be that *NOVA* did lots of in-house production, but the financing of that has changed and now they frequently work with co-producers or commissioned projects and acquisitions. If someone has a science and technology program, they should absolutely approach *NOVA*. They are organized to consider proposals. But remember, *NOVA* doesn't look for small, quirky independent films.

Q – What kind of documentary project would get you excited?

Denise – Either something that I know has worked and has reason to believe will work again or something that I have never seen before. We have been talking about WGBH's main series, but in addition to those brands we have miniseries. So if there was something that we know has succeeded with our viewer ship, then I would take that seriously. The Lab is more about projects on the edges - smaller projects, independent projects that don't really have an obvious place to go, at least not in the broadcast context.

Q – Is there anything that you wouldn't do?

Denise – I wouldn't do anything that undermines the WGBH mission. Our mission is concrete: to inform, to educate, and to inspire, to serve the community, to present diversity of opinion, to embrace independent voices. We get opportunities to take on commercial stories and I usually say no if it doesn't adhere to the mission. If we're going cover the pornography industry, as *Frontline* has done, it will be in an investigative way, not a salacious way. If we're going to do comedy, it will have a social or political observation component to it. That's not to say there's a certain topic that we wouldn't do, but it must be approached in a way that aligns with the underlying values of our mission. Now the mission does grow, it's not static. It evolves over time. But if it doesn't serve the public and public discourse, we won't do it. It has to have some merit to it, which may be as simple as a worthy project that's not available elsewhere. Most of our programming is counter-programming.

Q – Have you noticed since 9/11 that the US market and Americans have opened up to more international stories?

Denise – I think and hope that is true. It's certainly true at WGBH in terms of *The World*, an international radio program that has grown in the wake of 9/11. It's a co-production between WGBH the BBC and Public Radio International. *Frontline* has always been committed to international coverage. *Frontline World* is a spin off of *Frontline* and that has also grown since 9/11. It's WGBH's way of embracing young journalists around the world - give them modest funds, a camera or a plane ticket and tell them to go make a story.

Q – What are the common mistakes that you see documentary filmmakers make?

Denise – One mistake filmmakers make is not knowing what their story is. You have to be able to describe your story in a one-sentence tag line or a one-paragraph pitch. Many passionate people who have all the talent, craft and technology don't know what their story is. They bring back this unwieldy material. Now sometimes, you want a true verité story, and it has to found in the edit room – but very few filmmakers today have that luxury. And less is more; for me it's better to tell a smaller story deeply and authentically and get your multiple complex messages going in this finite story frame, rather than trying to tell everything about a topic or a person. Another common mistake is not having the distance to understand what their film is really saying to the audience. Mentors are good for this because no matter how much of a guerilla, one-man band you want to be, you're going to need other people to help you see if you are communicating what you think you are communicating to someone at a distance from your vision.

Q – What advice would you give new filmmakers?

Denise – I think on one hand this is the best of times because no one is going to get cut out of the work due to the cost of the means of production. My kids are cutting movies on the kitchen table - and they're good. When I was coming up, very few people had enough access to the production technologies so some unique voices with messages and stories to tell were lost. Thankfully, this happens much less frequently now. The bad news is that technology allows people into the game who might not be passionately committed to filmmaking, so there is more clutter, in my opinion. I think many people can make films, but I don't think everyone can. Also, I think it's really important to know what motivates you to make documentaries. If you're in it for fame and success, this is probably the wrong business. I advise people to not be swayed by the recent stunning success of a few documentaries – this is good for documentary making – and documentary watching – but most documentary makers still have be very single-minded to keep doing what they are doing. It's hard to make a go of it. Finally, it is very important to find mentors. I wouldn't have made it in the business if I hadn't had talented mentors. And this is a cliché, but it is true, if you really want to do this work, find people whose films you admire and if possible, hook up with them.

Nancy Abraham
VP: Original Programming

HBO

Q – What is your job?

Nancy – My title is Vice-President, Documentary Programming and I develop new ideas for HBO to produce as documentaries. I also acquire documentaries. For a certain number of the shows that HBO is producing or commissioning, I'm the supervising producer. I'm responsible for overseeing all the day-to-day operations and editorial direction of those productions.

Q – Why has HBO made documentaries such an integral part of their programming?

Nancy – I think Sheila Nevins who's the founder and the President of the division here at HBO always felt that non-fiction could stand on a par with big Hollywood entertainment and the others kinds of original programming that HBO was offering. She had a passion and conviction about non-fiction programming. Many of our documentaries aren't shows that the audience think of as documentaries per se. They're just programs that interest people or touch people.

Q – What kind of documentary films does HBO look for?

Nancy – Our main flagship anthology series is something called *America Undercover* and for that we're mainly looking for documentaries that deal with contemporary social issues in the United States. The hallmark is that they're generally films with a present-tense storyline and are verité in style. They tend to be strong, character-driven narratives and usually have visceral or gritty subject matter. We also have for the last ten years now been running a series on our sister channel, Cinemax called Cinemax *Reel Life* and that's really a showcase for independent documentaries from around the world. It's more eclectic in terms of subject and style and we have a variety of feature docs in that series.

Q – Are the docs on Reel Life ones that you generally acquire and does your department oversee them?

Nancy – Yes. We're in charge of that series even though they are on Cinemax. We generally don't produce them or even co-produce them. We generally get involved when there's something we can see, like a rough cut. If we're interested at that point we'll put in completion funds. Some are straight acquisitions of completed films. And sometimes we have suggestions even when they are completed films, that the filmmaker can embrace and decide if they want to do or not.

Q – What kind of film proposal would get you excited?

Nancy – There are very few that do, honestly! In terms of a written idea, without any footage to back it up, it would have to be very persuasive. And by that I mean it shouldn't seem familiar, it shouldn't feel like you've seen it before, it shouldn't seem like something that would appropriately be on another channel because of its genre or subject matter. For our purposes, it should be a story that's really character-based or access-based, that's following a present tense, unfolding story, not something that has happened primarily in the past. So, if the action is yet to come, how do you write a proposal about that? It mostly depends on the characters. Why are they compelling? What's going on with their lives? What's going to happen to them -- something that we are going to follow? The obvious scenarios include competitions or criminal trials, where there is a distinct beginning, middle and end. But it doesn't have to be those scenarios, and it shouldn't be just those scenarios, because God knows there are enough competition films and trial films. But if we can have a sense of why and how the story line relates to a bigger social issue, that's relevant and important, then we will pursue it.

Q – So you would like to see some footage or a rough assembly preferably, before getting involved with a film?

Nancy – Yes. If it's a subject matter that does not fit into *America Undercover,* and does not have to do with contemporary America and the social issues of the day, then we would need to see a rough cut because we'd be considering it for Cinemax *Reel Life.* If it's something that could fit in with *America Undercover*, it still needs to be suitable to a verité treatment, not something that is told solely via interviews. We will consider and we have developed things from written proposals, but it helps to have at least a few minutes of footage. If it's a character-driven piece, then a few minutes with the main character is helpful. If it's access-driven, then a few minutes of the institution or whatever it is.

Q – Do you work with first time filmmakers and if so how can one improve their odds of attracting HBO as a distributor?

Nancy – Yes, we do work with first-time filmmakers. For a first time filmmaker it's helpful to supply some footage with your proposal. And then, on top of that, one should be open to the possibility of working with another qualified person, an established producer perhaps. We've often made those marriages, and many of them have been very successful collaborations.

Q – Does HBO prefer one off documentaries or series?

Nancy – Our hallmark is the one off documentary, often feature length. So that's what we look for. Partly because we don't have the scheduling slots to do many series. If we did a series, it would take up half our schedule! But there are a few exceptions. We've done some late-night series, like *Cathouse*. And we recently did a 10-part series called *Family Bonds.*

Q – Do you generate any of your programming ideas in-house or do they come from outside producers?

Nancy – It's about half and half.

Q – What kind of budgets do you like to work within?

Nancy – If it's something we're commissioning, then whatever it takes to do it properly. If it's something we've developed for *America Undercover*, we'll make sure there is an ample budget. A lot of our projects take over a year to produce, so without naming numbers, I'd say they're generous budgets that you would need to pursue a verité story in which you don't have a script in advance. We allow as many days as are needed to tell the story. And if something happens, like we need to wait three months or go back and shoot for five more days, we can usually cover it. Our editing time is generally more generous than other networks, who are turning around films much more quickly. Again, a film, which has more of a script in advance, is more straightforward to edit. Our films' stories often come together in the edit room, so you need a lot of time to explore the options.

Q – Does HBO have on site editing facilities that filmmakers can use?

Nancy – Yes. But our producers usually go to outside facilities or they have their own. We only do a few shows in-house.

Q – When you acquire a film, what kind of deliverables do they need to bring you?

Nancy - They're extensive and are outlined in the contract that you sign. I wouldn't want to begin to describe it myself! We have a great post-production department here that handles all that.

Q – Do you allow your films to have a theatrical release prior to airing on HBO?

Nancy – It depends. It's really on a case-by-case basis. Most of our documentaries premiere on HBO prior to a theatrical release, excluding festival exposure and special screenings. But we're always open to the possibility of a different arrangement. There're very few projects that would actually get a broad commercial release. On the other hand, there're some documentaries that we come to at a later stage, after the theatrical release is already underway, that we then acquire. It just depends on the film and how it fits into our overall picture.

Q – For your late night programming, what are your philosophies there and how would a filmmaker approach you with that type of programming?

Nancy – *Real Sex* is our longest-running, late-night show. It's a magazine-style program that covers the broad range of human sexuality. It's fun, sometime funny, titillating. From the beginning we made a deliberate choice to produce it at a very high level – hiring the best DPs, editors and directors in the documentary business.

Q – For Real Sex, did the various segment directors pitch you those ideas or were they your own?

Nancy – Both. Many ideas were generated by the series producer, Patti Kaplan, who had previously worked at Children's Television Workshop - which was definitely casting against type! Otherwise, outside producers, if they do have an idea for a segment can send it in like any other proposal.

Q – What's your process for evaluating material and deciding what gets acquired?

Nancy – For cold, unsolicited submissions that come in, one person will look at it and write coverage initially. If it's favorable, it'll get passed on to me or one of the other supervising producers. If I really like it, I would bring it to Sheila, who has the final say. But along the way, we all share things with our colleagues. *"What do you think of this?"* It's not always black and white. But, because we don't have a huge number of slots, we are looking for something that really jumps at you. Sometimes you'll see a rough cut that has potential – a germ of an idea worth exploring. We would then work with the filmmaker to do that.

Q – How hands on is HBO either in the production or editing stages of your films?

Nancy – We're pretty hands on compared to most places, I think. Partly because we're not dealing with hundreds of shows per year although in the production stage, we're pretty much hands-off. An idea is developed and we all have to feel good about it going in, but during the whole shooting process we're hands-off. It's a very intimate process between the filmmaking team and the subjects. Where we do get very involved is in the editing phases. We spend a lot of time at that point and are very hands on. No matter how good a show is, we're seeing it at a stage when it could be better. And because these are often verité films, there are a lot of different ways the story can be put together, and different things need to be tried. There's not necessarily a clear roadmap, so to get the best film you have to pull it and push it in different ways. We often have all day screenings with filmmakers to go through the film frame by frame. So it isn't like we're just e-mailing notes. It's more collaborative. A lot of the time you don't know what's wrong, you just know something is. So we sit together and try to figure it out. It's not as simple as lopping off a scene. It's more like, *"It's faltering here. How can we shore up the pacing in this section?"* That's something you need to discuss. It's intense, but that's the most fun part of the job.

Q – What do you see as the future of documentary filmmaking?

Nancy – I think the future is very bright for non-fiction. It only seems to be getting more exciting and more broadly defined. There's a bigger and bigger audience acceptance of non-fiction. From a programmer's perspective, the whole accessibility of technology to make a documentary is both a blessing and a burden. There's a lot more out there to wade through in order to find something good. But there's also a lot more good material. The reality is that, unlike a scripted narrative film, you can get your documentary film off the ground rather cheaply and on your own. So that's exciting. I think all these things go through cycles and we're in an upswing right now. But I don't think we're going to slide back too much.

Q – What common mistakes do you see filmmakers make?

Nancy – In terms of pitching, the classic one that happens all the time, is that people don't have a sense of what your channel is and what types of documentaries you do – even when the information is readily available. I know we're a pay TV channel, but we do have a website. I can't tell you how many people blindly pitch, and that is a waste of everyone's time. In addition to that, people should have a sense of the general documentary landscape around them. I think to be a really good documentary filmmaker you have to love documentaries and be a student of them. You have to learn from other films, seek them out and watch them. Just like narrative film students or filmmakers would. Some people operate in a bubble and will pitch something that there have already been a million films on. The internet is a great tool. Look at all the major film festivals and see what films are coming out and get descriptions of them. Look at what television channels are doing. Join organizations like AIVF or IFP. Get into the filmmaking community and get advice that way. If you're doing a verité film, you have to provide as much information as you can to explain why you think your characters are worth following. And that no matter what the outcome, it will be interesting. If you have a scripted documentary, you have to clearly illustrate why it should be a movie and not an article or a radio program. If it's just interviews on a subject, then you have to convince someone that interviews only on this subject will be compelling enough. There certainly have been films like that.

Q – What advice would you give a filmmaker?

Nancy – To have a healthy sense of self-criticism. Sometimes people get enthralled by the worthiness of their subject. They become lax editorially, in the telling of their story. Yes, the issues that documentaries focus on are important and deserve to get out there, but it is your responsibility to make a good piece of visual entertainment or art. Be creative. Have high standards. And of course, think in advance about releases, clearances, good sound, etc. Get advice from peers from the documentary community. Learn from other people's work and get them to help you with yours.

GUERILLA FILM MAKER SAYS!

Your Master Tapes

All your efforts as a filmmaker are sealed in the master tapes (unless you're really lucky and shooting film, then it's your neg). It's therefore a good idea to treat your masters as through they were gold dust.

1. Your master tapes are just that – masters. Consider making clones and use those as your work tapes for digitizing footage or logging. Ensure the correct time codes are transferred at the time of making the clones.

2. Minimize wear and tear on your tapes. Don't keep rewinding and fast forwarding just to watch your favorite shot.

3. Always completely rewind tapes before storage. This will avoid kinks in the tape forming over long-term storage.

4. Tapes should be fast forwarded and rewound every 5 years.

5. In due course, you may consider cloning your tapes to a future technology, such as DVDs or hard disk.

6. Your sound masters are important, too. If you used any DATs, treat them as you would your video masters.

7. Buy a fire proof safe and put the masters of your current project in there. Disasters DO happen.

8. Keep your masters away from anything magnetized or with electrical current running through them – that's the fastest way to erase them.

DISCOVERY NETWORKS

Q – What is your job?

Abby – I'm head of programming and development at Discovery Channel. What that entails is basically to come up with the programming strategy for the network such as working with the development team to come up with great shows and figure out how they are to be scheduled. Also, I work on figuring out what are we going to pay for our shows, managing the programming budget and working with marketing, research and ad sales to figure out how we package and talk about the network.

Q – What kind of programming is Discovery Channel looking for?

Abby – We're a non-fiction network so we're looking for any and all kind of real world stories. But the key there is that we're looking for new ways to extend the power of the Discovery brand into programming that deals with the real world, in compelling new ways. We want stories that are immersive, captivating, and increasingly looking for series – long running series ideas. The ones that have been successful I think are the ones that combine great personalities, which is different from hosts – these are people who are the real deal. They're naturally passionate knowledgeable people who're embedded in some kind of world we think our viewers would be interested in. Whether it's a show that has to do with science, building motorcycles or cars or incredible structures, they get a window into their passion. Also we want a cleverness in a story that makes it feel distinctive from reality TV or on the other hand, scripted drama.

Q – When you see a project come in, what makes you distinguish a series idea from a one or two hour one-off documentary idea?

Abby – Mainly a series is something that needs to be on the schedule week in and week out. So there has to be something about the format or the way the series is conceived itself, just like any great drama has kind of classic beats in the story. *Law and Order* is a classic that has those format parts and you will watch that show an infinite number of times because there's always a problem, a mystery and a resolution. So a great series concept has to have built in format beats to it. It also needs, if not a great character at the core, someone or something that's going to be interesting to bring people back week in and week out. Specials are really a kind of different animal for us and increasingly we're looking less at specials and more at event programming. So as opposed to doing one off documentaries that air sort of in a vacuum, we're increasingly looking for big projects that almost extend beyond the television screen. So they might be things that engage viewers in a different way whether it's getting them to vote or getting them to engage in a television program. And increasingly we're moving from a kind of one-off documentary model to ideas that will last over multiple days or weeks. Those things almost self identify themselves – when they come up, they're so big and they're so high concept that as a programmer you say *"I get it"* and that can be huge. Those are kind of specials we look for. They are very different from the kind of programming that you'd watch week and week out that have at their core great format points, high quality and characters that touch on what all of Discovery is about.

Q – How does a producer or filmmaker approach Discovery Channel with a show idea and how much is acquired versions created in house?

Abby – Discovery produces very little in house. Most of what we do is partnering with outside production companies from all over the world. However, we do a lot development in house. So in a lot of cases we may come up with the kernel of an idea or in some cases the bones of a format of a series and partner with one of many producers or production companies to flesh that out. That's one model. The other model is where someone brings us an idea. The most successful way in which people do that, rather than bringing 100 ideas is for someone to bring the one idea that they really thought through that they are passionate about and say, *"I have one great idea and here is what it is."* Because from a development perspective it's much more valuable for someone to bring an idea that they're truly passionate about rather than what I call the machine gun approach where they just come with fifteen titles and let me throw them out and maybe one of them will stick. Also, as a person within a network, you really want to know that this producer knows your network so they have a sense of what is on your air, what's working. We don't want *British Chopper* or *American Chopper in Australia*. Those ideas are not distinctive enough. We're always looking for what is the next big idea.

Q – What are some tips on pitching ideas to you?

Abby – The most compelling method of pitching is to have a tape or if it's a character driven concept, have footage of the character. Nothing will get a development or programming person more excited than seeing a tape, even if it's very cheaply done. The execution of it doesn't matter so much, because someone who has been a producer themselves knows all of that can come with a good budget. What's the core idea? What are the format points of the show and who's that personality that I'm going to be engaged in? The other way that we might work is often if we think that there's a kernel of a good idea, we may pay for someone to create a taster tape for not a whole lot of money. But just enough to showcase what format is, what's the core proposition for this idea in the same way if we're going to market it to a viewer, you have to get it across in one line. The best ideas are simple so even if the architecture of the show is incredibly complicated, you want to have that one liner in the same way a viewer will read it in a listing . So the producer needs to think through what the show is and how it will be made, but also what is that one line hook that the programmer who is always thinking about the viewer can say, *"I get it, that is so simple." Mythbusters* – A show where the hosts tackle popular myths to see if they are fact or fiction. I get it. It's almost like a producer thinking like a marketer and like a promo producer and if you can distill an idea down to its essence, they tend to be the strongest ideas. A combination of the hook, or a tape or paper document that demonstrates how the show will be made and what it will look like, the tone - those are the most important things and then proving that you have the talent side to execute. You could have the most brilliant idea in the world and not have the production experience or expertise to execute which is sort of the third piece. So we'll look for someone to have a proven track record doing or partnering with someone who has.

Q – Do you work with first time producers or filmmakers?

Abby – Yes, but we'd partner them up with a more experienced producer. And to be honest a lot of times it's absolutely more difficult for a first time producer to make that case, so partnering with someone who has worked with us before or coming through a production company – actually working for a production company and developing an idea and then bringing it to Discovery so you are under the umbrella of a production company works best. The other thing that Discovery has is an initiative called Discovery Docs, which is explicitly designed with developing first time filmmakers and we have a partnership with the AFI annual documentary film festival. These projects are an opportunity for us to both work with and find out about and cultivate first time filmmakers. In some cases, like one of the films shown at this years' festival was *Control Room*, which was not a first time filmmaker, but she was a young filmmaker who has had a very early successful career who brought other people into her production team who are first time filmmakers.

Q – What kind of deal would a producer be looking at for a project and what kind of budget could they expect?

Abby – Totally depends on the project. Discovery is a global company so we have Discovery Channels around the world so depending on the content of the show it may be something we can fully fund and run on all of our networks around the world or it might be something that is just a domestic oriented program in which we buy in for a partial sum of the budget for partial rights. It really depends on the project. I couldn't give you a definitive dollar or deal structure answer. What I will say is that we look for great ideas first. And then we start figuring out what is the budget and the deal. So we start with the great

GUERILLA FILM MAKER SAYS!

Co-productions

A big change in the way broadcasters fund documentaries these days is that instead of giving you all of your budget, they will give you a percentage and then it is up to you to find the rest. This is especially true of broadcasters outside the US where co-productions have become the norm. Co-productions not only allow broadcasters to split the risk of production costs, but it also allows them to take advantage of certain tax breaks on labor, production and post costs (though these schemes usually bring bigger benefits to narrative features with larger budgets). While most prevalent in Europe, Canada and Australia, American producers can still take advantage of these schemes by teaming up with several foreign broadcasters and then bringing in someone like Discovery Networks for a portion of the pie – usually less than 30%. Co-productions can be complicated contractually, so make sure you have a good lawyer looking after your interests.

Most first time filmmakers probably won't be at the budget level where they will need to deal with co-productions and we'll be getting most of their money from grants, credit cards and private investors. But it's good to think ahead and start making relationships with commissioning executives from these places or producer/filmmakers from other countries when you are out on the festival circuit! Check out our Global Perspective chapter for broadcasters to team up with.

idea and then figure a way for the deal to work. Is it an international project? A domestic project? What is the budget?

Q – Do you ever see a project come through that can't be done due to difficulty, expense or too dangerous?

Abby – There are always projects that you can't do because they're simply too expensive. I will say that one thing Discovery has as an advantage is its global presence so we are able to finance projects either by partnering with our international channels or often we will encourage a producer to hook up with a terrestrial channel elsewhere in the world to help fund a project.

Q – Do you shoot on any specific format?

Abby – Depends on the project. Some on film, some on HD, some on Beta. We are increasingly shooting more of our big events specials on HD. It also depends on what creatively needs to be done do get it shot.

Q – What are the common mistakes that you see documentary filmmakers make?

Abby – Pitching too many programs, and not focusing on the one or two that someone's most passionate about.

Q – What advice would you give a new documentary filmmaker?

Abby – My advice would be to watch a lot of films and television to see what's out there, but don't be afraid to do something completely different. The best ideas are unique.

World Distribution Of The Three Major TV Standards

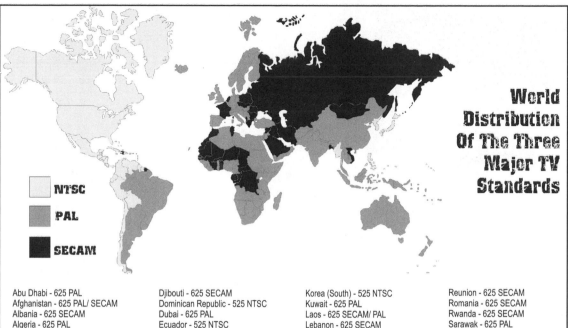

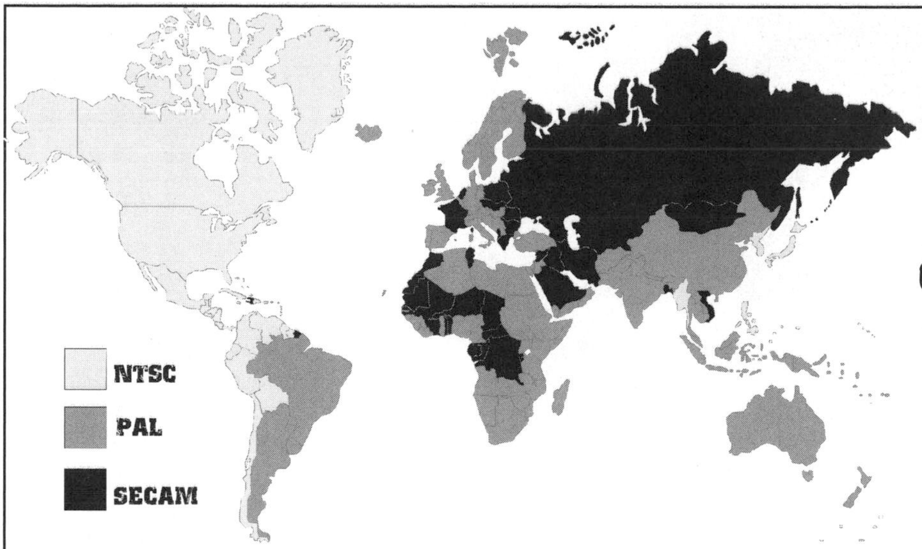

Abu Dhabi - 625 PAL
Afghanistan - 625 PAL/ SECAM
Albania - 625 SECAM
Algeria - 625 PAL
Andorra - 625 PAL
Angola - 625 PAL
Antigua - 525 NTSC
Argentina - 625 PAL N
Australia - 625 PAL
Austria - 625 PAL
The Azores - 625 PAL
Bahamas - 525 NTSC
Bahrain - 625 PAL
Bangladesh - 625 PAL
Barbados - 525 NTSC
Belgium - 625 PAL
Belize - 525 NTSC
Benin - 625 SECAM
Bermuda - 525 NTSC
Bolivia - 525 NTSC
Bophuthatswana - 625 PAL
Bosnia/Herzegovina - 625 PAL
Botswana - 625 PAL
Brazil - 525 PAL M
British Virgin Isles - 525 NTSC
Brunei - 625 PAL
Bulgaria - 625 SECAM
Bukina Faso - 625 SECAM
Burma - 525 NTSC
Burundi - 625 SECAM
Cameroon - 625 PAL
Canada - 525 NTSC
Canary Islands - 625 PAL
Central African Republic - 625 SECAM
Chad - 625 SECAM
Chile - 525 NTSC
China - 625 PAL
Colombia - 525 NTSC
Congo - 625 SECAM
Cook Islands - 625 PAL
Croatia - 625 PAL
Cuba - 525 NTSC
Curacao - 525 NTSC
Cyprus - 625 PAL/ SECAM
Czechoslovakia - 625 SECAM
Denmark - 625 PAL
Djibouti - 625 SECAM
Dominican Republic - 525 NTSC
Dubai - 625 PAL
Ecuador - 525 NTSC
Eire - 625 PAL
Eqypt - 625 PAL/ SECAM
El Salvador - 525 NTSC
Equatorial Guinea - 625 SECAM
Ethiopia - 625 PAL
Faeroe Islands - 625 PAL
Fiji - 625 PAL
Finland - 625 PAL
France - 625 SECAM
French Polynesia - 625 SECAM
Gabon - 625 SECAM
Galapagos Isles - 525 NTSC
Germany - 625 PAL
Ghana - 625 PAL
Gibraltar - 625 PAL
Greece - 625 SECAM
Greenland - 625 PAL
Grenada - 525 NTSC
Guadalope - 625 SECAM
Guam - 525 NTSC
Guatemala - 525 NTSC
Guinea (French) - 625 SECAM
Guinea - 625 SECAM
Guyana Republic - 625 SECAM
Haiti - 625 SECAM
Honduras - 525 NTSC
Hong Kong - 625 PAL
Hungary - 625 SECAM/ PAL
Iceland - 625 PAL
India - 625 PAL
Indonesia - 625 PAL
Iran - 625 SECAM/ PAL
Iraq - 625 SECAM
Israel - 625 PAL
Italy - 625 PAL
Ivory Coast - 625 SECAM
Jamaica - 525 NTSC
Japan - 525 NTSC
Jordan - 625 PAL
Kampuchea - 525 NTSC
Kenya - 625 PAL
Korea (North) - 625 SECAM/ 525 NTSC
Korea (South) - 525 NTSC
Kuwait - 625 PAL
Laos - 625 SECAM/ PAL
Lebanon - 625 SECAM
Leeward Isles - 525 NTSC
Lesotho - 625 PAL
Liberia - 625 PAL
Libya - 625 SECAM
Luxembourg - 625 SECAM/ PAL
Macedonia - 625 PAL
Madagascar - 625 SECAM
Madeira - 625 PAL
Malawi - 625 PAL
Malaysia - 625 PAL
Maldives - 625 PAL
Mali - 625 SECAM
Malta - 625 PAL
Martinique - 625 SECAM
Mauritius - 625 SECAM
Mexico - 525 NTSC
Monaco - 625 PAL/SECAM
Mongolia - 625 SECAM
Morocco - 625 SECAM
Mozambique - 625 PAL
Namibia - 625 PAL
Nepal - 625 PAL
Netherlands - 625 PAL
Netherlands Antilles - 525 NTSC
New Caledonia - 625 SECAM
New Zealand - 625 PAL
Nicaragua - 525 NTSC
Niger - 625 SECAM
Nigeria - 625 PAL
Norway - 625 PAL
Oman - 625 PAL
Pakistan - 625 PAL
Panama - 525 NTSC
Papua New Guinea - 625 PAL
Paraguay - 625 PAL M
Peru - 525 NTSC
Philippines - 525 NTSC
Poland - 625 SECAM
Polynesia - 625 SECAM
Portugual - 625 PAL
Puerto Rico - 525 NTSC
Qatar - 625 PAL
Reunion - 625 SECAM
Romania - 625 SECAM
Rwanda - 625 SECAM
Sarawak - 625 PAL
Samoa (Eastern) - 525 NTSC
San Marino - 625 PAL
Saudi Arabia - 625 SECAM
Senegal - 625 SECAM
Seychelles - 625 PAL
Sierra Leone - 625 PAL
Singapore - 625 PAL
South Africa - 625 PAL
South West Africa - 625 PAL
Spain - 625 PAL
Sri Lanka - 625 PAL
St. Kitts & Nevis - 525 NTSC
Sudan - 625 PAL
Surinam - 525 NTSC
Swaziland - 625 PAL
Sweden - 625 PAL
Switzerland - 625 PAL
Syria - 625 SECAM
Tahiti - 625 SECAM
Taiwan - 525 NTSC
Thailand - 625 PAL
Togo - 625 SECAM
Trinidad & Tobago - 525 NTSC
Tunisia - 625 SECAM
Turkey - 625 PAL
Uganda - 625 PAL
United Arab Emirates - 625 PAL
United Kingdom - 625 PAL
Uruguay - 625 PAL M
USA - 525 NTSC
Former USSR - 625 SECAM
Vatican City - 625 PAL
Venezuala - 525 NTSC
Vietnam - 625 SECAM/ NTSC
Virgin Isles - 525 NTSC
Yemen - 625 PAL/ SECAM
Former Yugoslavia - 625 PAL
Zaire - 625 SECAM
Zambia - 625 PAL
Zanzibar (Tanzania) - 625 PAL
Zimbabwe - 625 PAL

BROADCASTERS

PBS

Q – Generally, what kind of documentary is PBS looking for?

Coby – We're a variety service so we don't have a narrow focus. In all of the research that we have done, our viewers really appreciate the fact that they can see a dance performance one night, a great science series like *NOVA* another night, and a Ken Burns history series on another night. What distinguishes PBS is that we have a very definite mission, which is not a commercial one. Our mission is to engage, educate and inspire our viewers across all genres, and we take that very seriously. We look for definitive work in subjects, like what Ken Burns has done. Or we look for a personal way of telling the story that engages people by telling them something they wouldn't have known any other way. We just aired an amazing film series by David Sutherland called *Country Boys*, where he spent three or four years focusing on two young men in Appalachia and what their lives, aspirations and goals were. So we look for that kind of in-depth programming that really get you into a story. We try to be really open to great storytelling.

Q – What's something that you would never program?

Coby – If it doesn't have any educational benefit to it and that doesn't mean that it always has to be heavy lifting or like a graduate course at Harvard. *Antiques Roadshow* doesn't seem so intense and educational, but you do learn from it. Then again, we're in the process of running *Monty Python* again, so can I say always? Mostly always. So something like *My Date With Drew* is something that we wouldn't program, but *Mad Hot Ballroom* we would.

Q – How do PBS proper, the various stations and production companies like POV work together or separately at making the shows for programming?

Coby – It works differently for different programs. One of the things we have on the air is our icon series. Those are things like *American Experience* through WGBH or *American Masters* through WNET. They're made with the executive producers at those stations making the decisions about what content they want to develop and produce. They consult with us, but they do pretty much what they think is right for the series. Very rarely do we at "headquarters" say to Mark Samels at *American Experience*, *"Oh, don't do that."* We might say to him that we have seen documentaries on that subject a lot and then he'll tell us why we need to do it and then usually we'll get it. PBS has a long history of being producer-oriented. Producers have the control over their series. However, we have a lot of programs that come directly to PBS that do not come from producing stations. They'll be pitched directly to us and we'll say "*yes*" or *"no"* to them. And while we don't produce, we'll be more involved with them than programs that come to us through our producing stations. With our icon series, PBS puts in a significant amount of money into the production of those programs. However, the producing station has to often find as much as 50% of the production dollars from other places. We very rarely fully fund a series. One exception to that would be *Frontline*, which occasionally gets some foundation money, but has never really been able to find corporate underwriting dollars. Not because it isn't excellent, but because it often tackles subjects that make people uncomfortable. They take on hard stories. So we fund that to 80%-90%.

Q – Where do your stations find the rest of the money?

Coby – A lot of it can come from international co-productions with the BBC and Channel 4 in the UK. And then producers get foundation money. *NOVA* gets money from The Alfred P. Sloan Foundation. It's such an uphill battle and I have such respect for the hard work that our producers have to do to get their films into production. When I was at Turner Broadcasting, it was very hard to get the higher-ups to OK a production, but once we got a yes, we got a check for 100% of the costs of the production. With us, it's easier to get a yes, but it doesn't come with a check for 100%.

Q – If a producer comes to you, do you let them go off and do the production by themselves or do you team them up with a local PBS station in their area?

Coby – We talk them through the options. There always is an advantage working with a local station because they understand the system so well. They understand the deliverables. They understand our audience. But we never want to say they must do that. There are two ways a producer can work with a station. They can work very closely as a co-production with a station like WGBH, or, you can go to the station and say, *"Look, I've got the money and I am going to approach the film this way. Do you want to be the presenting station?"* What that means is they help with promotion and station relations, but they don't have the strong editorial control they would if they were producing. We give producers all the options so they can make a decision based on what's best for their work.

Q – Do you talk to the stations and the production companies? Especially when it comes to sharing projects?

Coby – We always talk to one another. Although, it's very rare when you can say to Mark Samels at *American Experience* that we have just seen a great treatment for X – please consider it. Of course, I will do that, but he has his own projects that he has developed. It is a long shot. They are always open to it. And they do listen if we find something and say to them that we will put significant dollars into it, but it would nest best under one of our icon series.

Q – Does PBS prefer series or one off documentaries?

Coby – It doesn't so much matter to us. The truth is we're really looking for fantastic things. What we're not so keen on is somebody coming in stating they want to do eight hours on something. It's very hard these days to hold an audience over multiple weeks with a limited series. Obviously, Ken Burns does it brilliantly, but he is the exception rather than the rule. What works best for us is two nights or maybe two hours or four hours that would play over two weeks. That said, if there's a great one-shot film that we want, we also take those. But *POV* and *Independent Lens* have a year round presence on our schedule. They're the home for a lot of independent, personal films that otherwise get lost in the system.

Q – Do you do shorts at all?

Coby – The only place is on *Independent Lens*. Usually the shortest thing we do is half an hour. We're interested in looking at shorts for the internet and we're about to launch a non-fiction digital service called World Public Square. There will be more opportunities there for shorts and things that don't really fit in an hour or 90 minute time frame.

Q – How does a filmmaker go about proposing a project to PBS?

Coby – The first thing is to go to www.pbs.org and go to the section "Producing For PBS." It will walk you through everything – from how to submit a project to our specs for delivering projects. So you submit a proposal or a finished film to us, and it will get to the content team that report to John Wilson, my East Coast counterpart, and me and they make their recommendations. Then, he and I make the final decisions on what makes sense for us.

Q – In the PBS model, what is the most important part of the proposal?

Coby – There're a few things that are equally important. The idea is certainly important, just the basic concept of what you plan to do. Then how are you going to execute it? The third part is if you are a new filmmaker to us, can you submit something that will tell us that we should have the confidence that you can deliver what you say you can deliver? This is where *POV* and *Independent Lens* can be helpful. Both groups and ITVS are really used to working with first time filmmakers and can really help them navigate every aspect of production – particularly ITVS. They're set up to really be the representative for independent filmmakers and help them get their work to where it would be appropriate for the national schedule.

Q – So the path to greatest success at PBS is for a filmmaker, especially a newer one, to go to one of these entities, get them on board and then come to you?

Coby – Yes. At the same time, what happens with the content team is that we'll see some work that's really promising and we'll say that it seems right for *Independent Lens* and we'd get it to them. But everyone must bear in mind that there are only 3 hours of primetime a night; so it's very competitive and so there will be many more "no's" than there will be "yes's".

Q – What kind of license fee can one expect for a finished film?

Coby – It varies completely. It can be not a lot of money to a decent amount of money. We are never in the ballpark of HBO. They have a lot more money to back a film than we do. That's why we could never compete to get a *Mad Hot Ballroom.* And it can vary what kind of rights we can get. We might want the right to broadcast it four times over two years or we'd want home video rights.

Q – Would you allow one of your films to get a theatrical run if it were warranted?

Coby – Absolutely and it has happened with us. There is a wonderful Sydney Pollack film coming from *American Masters* on the American architect Frank Gehry. We've moved our broadcast date several times to accommodate a theatrical release. We're happy to do that. We would never stop that because of a prior broadcast commitment. We'll always work with the filmmaker on that.

Q – Does it matter to PBS what format a film is shot on?

Coby – No. We have all these technical specs that have to match and if it passes muster, it's fine. A lot of people are shooting HD and we're very interested in that right now. But I wouldn't want to give the impression to young or newer filmmakers that if you're going to do a film about your remarkable grandmother that it has to be shot on HD.

Q – I noticed that American Experience wants to do some podcasting?

Coby – We are doing podcasting for most of our news series because they're easier to broadcast due to hardly any rights issues involved. We want to make available as many of our programs as possible for podcasting, but as you know a lot of this is tied up in some very complicated rights that quite honestly a lot of very smart lawyers in the world are looking at and can't figure out.

Q – Have you seen any trends in documentary filmmaking over the last few years?

Coby – There was a point where everyone fell in love with recreations. I think because they're hard to do very well and now whenever we see anything that calls for lots of recreation, we kind of groan a little. We have been seeing a lot of political documentaries lately and that's a good thing. Point-of-view documentaries are a big part of what we do. I think we're in an interesting period where technology has made it pretty easy to tell the stories people want to tell. However, even though everyone has a pencil and a piece of paper, it doesn't mean everyone can be a good writer. So just because cameras are light and cheap, and digital editing is easy doesn't mean that everyone knows how to tell a good story.

Q – Do you have to be an American citizen to do something at PBS?

Coby – Absolutely not. We work with international filmmakers all the time. Usually they are co-productions instead of getting calls directly from a French filmmaker, for example. If we did and we liked it, we would air it. If you're an international filmmaker without much of a track record, you can come to us through a co-production, one of our icon series or directly to us. But if you're well known, you probably know one of us already as we have meetings all the time with filmmakers. We do a lot of work with British filmmakers because their sensibilities are similar to ours.

Q – Does the US government provide any of PBS' funding?

Coby – Only a small, but crucial amount. We get most of our funding from corporations, funders and our members – the viewers.

Q – What are the common mistakes that you see documentary filmmakers make?

Coby – Not understanding who you submitted your project to. We don't see this too much anymore, but we would get something in and wonder if they watched PBS at all. It usually happens more with a proposal than a finished film. They send it everywhere and to us too and it would not be appropriate for us. I would tell any filmmaker to watch PBS for a while to see what the place they're going to send it to is like. The other mistake, maybe, is a misjudgment on how daunting it is to find the rest of your production money. It can take years.

Q – What advice would you give a new documentary filmmaker?

Coby – Get a thick skin and learn tenacity because you're going to hear "no" more than you are going to hear "yes." And you have to believe in yourself.

GUERILLA FILM MAKER SAYS!

US Broadcasters & Cable Networks

Most of the documentaries shown in the US come through public TV (PBS) or the cable stations. Most of them have "producing for" sections that list their project submission process. As for the major networks (ABC, NBC), they usually want you to come to them via a production company, manager or agent.

Broadcasters

ABC
www.abc.go.com

CW
www.cw.com

CBS
www.cbs.com

Fox
www.fox.com

NBC
www.nbc.com

PBS
www.pbs.org

Cable

A&E
www.aetv.com

Animal Planet
www.animal.dsicovery.com

Bravo
www.bravo.com

Cinemax
www.cinemax.com

CNN
www.cnn.com

Court TV
www.courttv.com

Discovery Channel
www.discovery.com

Documentary Channel (DOC)
www.documentarychannel.com

ESPN
www.espn.go.com

HBO
www.hbo.com

History Channel
www.historychannel.com

Home & Garden TV
www.hgtv.com

Military Channel
www,militarychannel.com

MTV
www.mtv.com

National Geographic Channel
www.channel.nationalgeographic.com

The Learning Channel
www.tlc.dicovery.com

The Science Channel
www.science.discovery.com

Showtime
www.sho.com

The Travel Channel
www.travel.discovery.com

VH-1
www.vh1.com

Heather Moran
VP: Programming, Development

NATIONAL GEOGRAPHIC CHANNEL

Q – What kind of documentaries does National Geographic Channel want?

Heather – While I don't want to recite a marketing tagline for you, it really does fit in this case – National Geographic Channel is the channel for viewers who dare to explore. And that's what we look for in our programming – we explore anything and everything – from natural history to moments of great historical importance to new discoveries like *The Gospel of Judas*. We always want to amaze viewers and provide a deeper understanding of our world and everything that's in it.

Q – It seems that your shows have a thrilling aspect to them.

Heather – We always use the word "amazing" with our producers because when you look at our world you sometimes forget how amazing it is. We're looking for that awe inspiring stuff. We typically look within a couple of genres and those are science, engineering and technology, natural history – a natural extension of the Nat Geo brand. We like history both contemporary and ancient and exploration. And then we have some shows that fall under human behavior.

Q – Do you do reenactments?

Heather – Reenactments are a necessary part of documentary storytelling. Many of the subjects we tackle happened years ago – some thousands and thousands of years ago. Obviously there was no video at the time, so reenactments help tell the story in a visually compelling manner. With large-scale reenactments, increased budgets and CGI, we can show viewers things that you would never have been able to see before.

Q – Do you prefer series or one-off documentaries?

Heather – We have a healthy mix of both.

Q – What type of series would excite you?

Heather – It needs to be sustainable. We hear a lot of really great ideas, but when you really drill down on the concept, it's only a 4-6 part idea. When we're looking at a series we want them in groups of 13, but then we want to know what episode 27 would look like and episode 57, etc. The best series have a tight format to them so the viewers know what to expect from them when they're watching. You can have a series in any one of the genres I talked about.

Q – How does a producer or filmmaker approach you with a program?

Heather – You go to our website – www.ngcideas.com. And a lot of people don't believe that we actually look at the website, but we have people reviewing every proposal that comes in. Our process is producer friendly, and we really pride ourselves on that. Producers are the lifeblood of our channel, and our website and our application is really easy to fill out, we accept ideas in any format all in the interest of receiving as many ideas as possible.

Q – What in that proposal would excite you?

Heather – I think it depends on what you are pitching whether it's a special or a series or a one off. It also depends if it's someone that we've worked with before. It's always tough for the new producers, which is the worst kind of Catch-22. But generally, we want a paragraph giving us an overall concept of the program and some kind of sense of style. How you visualize it and what are we going to see. Let's say it's a three pack, we'd want an episodic breakdown with different episode ideas and an act break down of the first episode.

Q – Is there anything a first time filmmaker can do to increase their chances?

Heather – If it's their very first time and they haven't done anything, it's very hard. If they have unique access to a story, that's always helpful because we really want to get inside and deliver an immersive experience to our viewers. So if that access in inextricably linked to you as the producer that can open our eyes. It also depends on what you mean by a first time filmmaker, too. If you worked with another company at one point, that's good. What kind of shows did you work on? Are they shows that we know? It always helps to show sample reels. But it's very difficult for a brand new filmmaker to get a deal with this channel from the development stage. But not impossible. We had a very successful premiere last year called *Bounty Hunters* from a first time filmmaker, and just aired a second project from him. We'll acquire a first time film as the risk is a lot lower when you see what you're getting.

Q – How much of your programming is acquired versus in-house?

Heather – A pretty small percentage of it. Most of what we do is original production. And of that larger percentage, the majority of that is co-produced. We really like sharing the risk because we do shows that are pretty high budget. We usually come in at a healthy percentage of the budget and we are often the majority funder. That's another thing that's really tough on first time filmmakers as many times they need an original commission, which is a pretty risky endeavor so it always helps to have some financing.

Q – What's the process once you read an idea that you like?

Heather – It will probably take numerous conversations before we get to the greenlight. More often or not we'll like an idea, give the producer a call and ask them about their access and the story. We might have something like that in the inventory so it's a bit of a back and forth process. When we decide to go forward with it, the first step is negotiating the deal. Since we do a lot of co-financing and we're not commissioning everything straight out, we are pretty easy to work with in terms of not taking all of the rights. There are a lot of broadcasters out there who want to commission everything and own everything in perpetuity.

Q – Once you greenlight something, what does the producer have to do?

Heather – We don't greenlight without a treatment and what you submit to us online initially is considered the treatment. So if it were a three hour show, we might greenlight it after just seeing an act break out for episode one and just good detailed paragraphs about episodes two and three. And then we would need to see a budget and a schedule before we green light it.

Q – Do the budget and the schedule fall to the producer to generate or does National Geographic have a line producer they work with?

Heather – Totally falls to the producer. We have a production management team that vets the budget and says that they're spending too much money here or there. But we don't put the budgets together for people.

Q – Do you have facilities that filmmakers can use for production and post?

Heather – Generally, no. But we shoot everything and broadcast in HD. The Channel launched an HD network this past January to celebrate its fifth anniversary, and by the end of this year 100% of our primetime will be in HD. That can be tough for some producers, so in order to assist them with that, we do have a certain number of HD camera packages that we will loan out to production companies. But we don't have a lot of them and it's something we would negotiate as we go along. It's rare that we share our production resources mainly because we are in DC and most of our producers aren't. So they usually own it or rent it where they are.

Q – Do you allow anyone to shoot film still?

Heather – You have to have a really good reason to shoot film. We are simulcast in HD so it's really important that we have a really clear HD signal.

Q – How hands on or off are you during the production and editing stages?

Heather – Depends on the filmmaker. If it's someone that we have worked with a lot, it's easier to not get involved. But we always have an executive producer that's on our staff that is assigned to the projects. So you have a little team assigned to you. An executive producer, a production manager and a unit manager that will make sure you deliver on time. Then the EP will be in the editorial with you.

Q – Do you do IMAX at all?

Heather – To my knowledge, we've never greenlit anything in IMAX, but we have acquired IMAX films.

Q – We understand getting your facts straight is of paramount importance to you.

Heather – Yes. Because the brand has been around for so long and we value it as much as we do, we have very aggressive standards and practices procedures. So you're also assigned a contact in Standards & Practices who works with you through every stage of the process. When you deliver scripts, they have to be annotated with your source material and we fact-check all in-show interviews. If it's a controversial topic we take pride in working to incorporate all sides of an issue. It's hardcore.

Q – If someone wants to approach you on a show about animals, is there anything they should be thinking about?

Heather – It's hard to be a natural history filmmaker. To do these shows the right way, you have to spend a lot of time in the field. You need to have a lot of access. And depending on what you're shooting, sometimes you're there for 12 months trying to get the full story on a wildebeest migration. So there obviously needs to be a big commitment and you need to have that kind of experience. For example, we're doing a show called *Africa's Deadly Dozen* about the deadliest snakes in Africa. If you came to us and said you had this great idea to do a show about snakes, I'd say when could I have it. And you say, *"Oh, I could have it in four months."* Well, can you really do it in four months? Maybe the snakes don't come out until May. So you have to make sure that they're really entrenched in whatever the subject is.

Q – What are the common mistakes that documentary filmmakers make?

Heather – They fall in love with their idea and don't think about whether there's an audience out there for that kind of programming. They also pitch us without taking time to understand our audience.

Q – What advice would you give a new documentary filmmakers?

Heather – They have to pitch the show differently depending on where they're pitching it. They really need to have an understanding of the person they're trying to sell their idea to in terms of what their needs are as a programmer. There are a lot of great ideas out there, but they don't necessarily make sense for me here at National Geographic. And when a filmmaker takes the time to watch what's on our air and figure out what we're looking for, that's when we have some of the best meetings.

GUERILLA FILM MAKER SAYS!

The Technological Mine Field – What Route To Choose?

Gone are the days of a single tried and tested film post production route. It's now digital technology throughout, HD, editing on computers, mixing formats, home editing, multiple shooting formats etc…the list is endless, the combinations seemingly infinite. So how do you chose the right post production route for your film?

1. There is no right route, but there is the best route for your doc. That should be the balance of artistic aspiration (what do you want it to look like), technical excellence (what's the best equipment you can get and the best crew to use it) and budget (what can I get for what I have).

2. Plan your post before you shoot! Make sure it all works. Make sure your editor (or you if you're the editor) understands it all. Make sure YOU understand it in concept. Ask lots of questions. Draw a flow chart for your project, not a generic project flowchart you are going to copy, and make sure everything is covered. Don't forget sound.

3. Talk to your Digital Lab beforehand to again go through the process and make sure that there will be no hidden surprises later on down the line.

4. Make the distinction between the shooting format and the distribution format. You can shoot on any format and end up on any format. Shoot HD, end up on HD, shoot HD, end up on film, shoot DV, end up on HD…Any combination works. Generally though, whatever you shoot on, you will in the first instance, need an HD Universal master (current favorite is D5 HD). Film out for a theatrical release may soon become redundant as we switch to 100 % digital distribution but always check with your distributor.

5. Chose your shooting format based on what best serves your doc. Do not discount film as either too expensive, too difficult or old hat. Film still has the 'look' and it has immense exposure latitude. Shooting a nature documentary in Antarctica or a gritty looking sports doc might be the perfect format for film.

6. Do not confuse top end HD formats, such as HDCam, with low-end formats like HDV. They are not the same and when shown side by side, the difference is staggering. It's not just about frame size, but about the technology inside the camera. Often low-end formats end up looking like hi-res home movies.

7. There is no doubt that HD is here. Just ensure that when you say HD, you know what specific technology you're referring to.

8. Remember if shooting DV, you'll spend a significantly increased time in the post production facility in order to maximize the visual image.

9. If shooting HD, you may need more hardware and almost will certainly need more storage than you think.

10. Keep in mind that there's going to be more distribution outlets than TV, DVD and theaters in the near future. Do research on new media like Ipods and Cell phones to see what their technology needs are that you should take into account when you start.

MTV

Q – What makes a good documentary?

Lauren – Compelling storytelling is first and foremost. Strong characters. Pure entertainment value. Finding that nexus between entertaining and enlightening. Documentary films are films so they need to be visually enjoyable. And you should really feel like the film is taking you somewhere, and that you're someplace different at the end of it.

Q – MTV started a trend in the United States of bringing documentary type shows to TV with things like The Real World.

Lauren – I formed the documentary division of MTV News many years ago – even before *The Real World* was even created. *The Real World* was never conceived of as a documentary. It was always thought of as a real life soap opera and it was very separate from our documentary division. What we did in the news division was very different. Our shows were always very entertaining, but they were a lot closer to traditional documentaries than people who don't watch the channel would guess. I think what we tried to do is closer to what HBO does now. One third of our documentaries were entertainment shows like *Cribs*. Another third were more traditional verite films like *True Life*. And the last third were pro-social like anything under our *Think* campaign or *Choose or Lose* where we addressed hard news topics in a long form format. So documentary has meant a mix of things at MTV, but it's always about truth. It's always real. And it's always programming that reflects some aspect of our viewers' lives or interests.

Q – Your shows seem to be at the nexus of reality television and pure documentaries.

Lauren –The thing I love about documentaries is that the form is so fluid. There are so many kinds of filmmaking that can be classified under "documentary films". That's what I love about the art form – it's really open. Our viewers are more open-minded than some filmmakers may think. They'll accept any premise that you throw out to them as long as you set it up very clearly and honestly in the beginning. You know: *"These are actors, these are not". "We paid these people to do this". "These people were not paid"*. If you lay out very clearly, they'll go along for the ride.

Q – Do you tend to look for more series shows or one-off documentaries?

Lauren – I'd say the trend now is more toward series. There're still some anthology series where independent filmmakers can make one film that fits into that anthology, but for the most part executives are looking for series because the production dollars can be maximized. Certainly, we'll do one off specials under some of our campaigns like *Think*.

Q – Do you use first time filmmakers or do you like to use people that you've worked with before?

Lauren – There are some people on staff at MTV Networks that make shows. Then there are a lot of freelancers that come right out of college. We kind of run a mini film school, not officially, of course. But we do train them how to make good TV documentaries and in a couple of years the good "trainees" are producing on their own. I'd say most people are freelance, but they work on a pretty consistent basis. A lot of people who are more experienced now have their own production companies and we will farm stuff out to them. But sometimes very experienced filmmakers will come to us with an idea that they have and it fits perfectly with one of the channels and we'll work with them if we can get a budget that works. So we work with a whole range of people. I'll say that if someone is really inexperienced, they need to make up for it in enthusiasm and working long hours.

Q – What if they had unique access to something? Would that be helpful?

Lauren – Yes. I'd probably pair them with a more seasoned filmmaker to work as a team.

Q – Do you find these filmmakers from around the world?

Lauren – I don't really recruit. They usually find us. A lot of the people I work with originally came from our intern pool. Many of the best of those go on to become PA's and then AP's and then producers.

Q – If someone had an idea that they wanted to approach you with, how would they go about doing that?

Lauren – They would fill out a proposal submission form and send their pitch in. Increasingly, executives do like to get pitches from agents and managers. I don't care for unsolicited pitches so it really helps if they have a contact. A lot of times I'll go to film festivals like Sundance or Full Frame and I'll see films that I like and I'll ask the filmmaker if they have any ideas to please come pitch to us. That film might not be right for MTV Networks, but I could see that they have the talent and it would be really great to work with them.

Q – If you like someone's pitch, what are the stages the filmmaker goes through on the way to production?

Lauren – In general, there's a little bit of money for development where ideas are fleshed out on paper and then after that a budget for the project is created. After that there is a "casting" process where we find characters for the documentary and then there is ultimately a greenlight for production. But there's not one set way that these things go. All the series are different.

Q – Do you get your crews from local places or do you send them out from New York or Los Angeles?

Lauren – More and more people are shooting their own material. They're their own cameramen and editors. That's definitely the trend as then filmmakers can keep more of the production dollars. We do hire production companies that are usually New York or LA based. We will pick up local crews for some projects. We'll fly in some for others. When I directed *Tupac: Resurrection*, I flew my cameraman everywhere I went. For something like a news piece we will use a local crew and after a while you find crews in different cities that you like.

Q – Does anyone still shoot film?

Lauren – I love the look of film and you can make deals with Kodak so that it's not so cost prohibitive, but in general formats change every few months and right now pretty much everyone is shooting on 24p. I'd say editing and shooting formats have changed maybe 50 times since I started filmmaking. I always tell the college kids and PA's to not waste their college years and film school years majoring in television. Don't waste a dollar of your tuition on learning equipment. It's all going to change as soon as you get out in the real world. Spend your time learning storytelling. Learn how to read critically, think analytically and have stories to tell. The equipment you will learn later.

Q – Any tips on storytelling that you would like to pass along?

Lauren – Find what interests you. People spend a lot of time pitching ideas that I don't even know if they're interested in. It kind of starts internally. You have to have a story and an idea that really excites you. I think you need to think dramatically as executives aren't really doing profile pieces much anymore. They want to see a character go through a change and a story to have a beginning, middle and an end. Think about what is filmable. A lot of very smart people pitch shows about things that are essentially not visual and that is not TV or film. You have to be able to see it. And you have to have access.

Don't pitch topics if you don't know if you can get access to it.

Q – Any tips on pitching?

Lauren - Do a lot of research and watch the channels that you're going to pitch to. A lot of people come and pitch randomly to as many networks as they can get a name. More and more, especially with cable, the channels are becoming more niche and have very specific kind of documentary that they program. If you watch the channel, you can get into the mindset of that universe. I'd also say before pitching anyone, try to watch something that the executive that you're meeting with had a hand in making. Nothing impresses someone more than when you come into their office and say that you saw one of their shows. That way you can have a more meaningful dialogue.

Q – Is MTV more hands on or hands off in the editing process of the shows?

Lauren – We don't have editors on staff here. Everyone is freelance. There are a lot of filmmakers who edit their own material. When it comes to editing, I'm a big believer in scripting first. When it comes to my own projects, I always script everything out before walking into the edit room. And I pretty much insist upon that with all my filmmakers including verite filmmakers. A lot of verité filmmakers like to do their scripting in the edit room, but I think it's better and cheaper to watch your material and get a really good sense of it and at least have a very detailed outline before editing. It doesn't mean that your film doesn't change once you get into the edit room. I always tell the filmmakers I work with that there are three films. There's the film that you have in your head before you go out to shoot. Then you go and shoot and you bring home the second film. Then you script that all out and go into the edit room and there you make your third film. A film is a living organism that continually changes along the way, but I don't think preplanning kills that.

Q – Do you think it's wise to be editing in your head while you're shooting or should they just go with the flow and edit later once they have all their footage?

Lauren – There really is no "going with the flow" in documentary filmmaking. Audiences feel there is because when they are watching a great documentary they feel like they are "going with the flow", but great documentarians plan and plan and plan. They plan for what they want to get and they plan for what happens when they don't get what they want to get. They create opportunities for themselves continually. They go with the flow with what's unfolding in front of the camera, but believe me, they are thinking of camera angles and storytelling and how this is all going to fit into the larger picture of the story they want to tell. The best filmmakers that I know are tremendously organized thinkers. But that doesn't mean that you can't put your plans aside when something exciting happens. You need to capture something as it avails, but you'll capture it better if you have an idea of what you're doing.

Q – What things should the filmmaker think about from a business standpoint in the editing process?

Lauren – Well, there are usually a few rounds of notes before a project makes the air that come from my bosses and me. And after those have been addressed, the standards department will weigh in and then the rights and clearances department gets involved. Every network has their own internal vetting process and a filmmaker should be prepared for that. They need to be buttoned up as far as location and personal releases are concerned. Then every network has their own requirements as far as the format you need to deliver the project on and you need to know what it is so you can budget accordingly.

Q – Do you have any special deals with licensing music since you are MTV?

Lauren – Our licensing deals with the record companies have changed over the years. There are now several stock music libraries that we work with where people can use music from those places for free for our shows. Obviously, if you are doing a piece on a specific musician, you want to use their music and that's a whole different licensing arrangement. One thing I should say is that the music editors we work with are usually excellent music editors. And we do some scoring as well.

Q – What tips would you give on casting a documentary?

Lauren – I think you have to know what the laws are if you're doing a "call out" on the internet or that kind of thing. I think the more specific you can be about what you're looking for the better. And try not to rely 100% on the internet for casting because it can be kind of limiting. Diversity of experience is important in TV documentaries. In the end, there's a lot of phone calling, reference checking and being able to think out of the box about how to find somebody unique. And it's really important to be honest about what your film is about and what you want them to do. You're asking people to give up their privacy and part of their life. It's a real privilege to be allowed into someone's life and you have to respect that first and foremost. A lot of filmmakers get caught up with what they want from a subject and if they are sharing something with you it's because they trust you. And you need to earn that trust every single day of shooting and editing.

Q – Are there any things to consider when interviewing a celebrity as opposed to a regular person?

Lauren – You will be dealing with a lot more people like their managers, their publicists and maybe their families. You need to understand and get along with a lot of different kinds of people who have different kinds of expectations for that artist. You have to make sure that your schedule is flexible enough to accommodate someone who is really busy. For myself, whenever I worked with a celebrity or a professional it's because they wanted something out of the film as well, so really it's a collaboration. But it's always a collaboration. The art of documentary is the art of collaboration. You have to be able to motivate your team, your executives and your subjects. You need to have a vision and stay true to it from the get go and include everyone. I spend a lot of time speaking to the finance people who sign the checks because guess what, they are part of your team. Things go a lot smoother if you can get them excited about your vision for your project.

Q – What if you can't motivate people and trouble within the cast or crew arises?

Lauren – If you're having problems with people that you're shooting, I think you have to stop shooting. You need to deflate the situation and take a step back. If they feel you have overstepped a trust you need to be able to put down your work and talk it through with them. Most problems I have had are technical problems and you just have to know that's par for the course. You have to know that one day you are going to come back from a shoot and there's going to be no sound. You should have checked it and you didn't. When that happens to you, you really have to learn from that experience.

Q – Do you do acquisitions?

Lauren – Yes. We are more open to co-productions, though.

Q – What are the common mistakes that you see filmmaker make?

Lauren – The most common problem is that people go over time and over budget and I'd say that the earlier you can tell your executive and give them a heads up on that, the better. Most executives are very understanding of the documentary filmmaking process. Some topics are just harder to crack than others and they know that.

Q – What advice would you give a documentary filmmaker?

Lauren – See a lot of films and try to meet the people who made them. By and large, documentary filmmakers are very accessible and interesting people. Most production companies are pretty lean and mean and there are a lot of opportunities for students getting out of college who want to get into filmmaking. You can usually get PA work pretty quickly and when you get that opportunity, work really hard even if it's a small, menial task like logging footage. Most documentary crews are really small, so every job is important and if you work hard, you will move up the food chain quickly. The key thing is to do your part really well and you'll be noticed.

Christian Vesper
VP, Acquistions

SUNDANCE CHANNEL

Q – When you look to program a documentary film, what subject matter excites you?

Christian – We're open to any subject matter to be perfectly honest. What's important to us is the story told. Is it a good story? Is it interesting? Is it compelling or dramatic or is it entertaining and funny? I think that because of who we are - part of the Sundance family, what's important to us is the quality of filmmaking. So an interesting story, well told by a skilled filmmaker is what we look for. We do try to find great stories about unusual subjects, but when we first started Doc Day it was really hard to figure out what we were looking for. Then we went out into the marketplace and the easy way to describe it to domestic and foreign sales agents is that we're looking for author driven films. Sundance and the Channel have always been about the filmmaker. Not about the filmmaker in the way that IFC focuses on the process, but literally what's the filmmaker's vision and how we can we best bring that to the network. As the network has grown, the focus has broadened beyond just the filmmaker, but I think what we're really looking at in a broader sense is independent voices.

Q – Is there any particular style of documentary film or storytelling that you prefer? Say verité over archival footage dominated films?

Christian – I wouldn't say one is better than the other. If it's between verité and a heavily narrated film, our taste would lean toward the verité project. Because it is style that reflects a strength in storytelling and filmmaking. But you can make a great film using lots of archive footage. In those films, you're talking more about the editing. So if you have too much narration, it means in our opinion that you probably haven't told the story well enough in your filmmaking.

Q – Where do you find the films that you program?

Christian – I have an acquisitions director that works for me as well as two program managers and between the four of us we go to major film festivals and TV markets and documentary markets. We obviously go to Sundance. We bought between 10-20 projects out of the 2005 Sundance Film Festival. We go to Berlin. We go to MIP-TV and MIP-COM, which are the two markets in Cannes. We go to Tribeca and the market in Marseilles in June. We go to IDFA in the fall and Toronto. A lot of the smaller or territory-based markets will fly us out, we can't afford to go to everything, but if it's over a weekend and we're invited as guests, we try to hit a lot of the smaller ones. You never know what you're going to find.

Q – Do you solely do acquisitions or do you create projects in-house?

Christian – We generally have been an acquisitions based channel, but recently we have gotten involved in creating one-off documentaries. Now this is all changing and fluid so by the time this book is published or someone reads this, we might be fully financing documentaries. This subject is constantly evolving. But the philosophy now is that we're last in for North American rights and it would never be for more than 20% of the overall budget. Beyond that, we are doing development and production of non-fiction series, but that's out of our original programming department. Those are done through experienced producers and their productions companies.

Q – With those pre-buys, would you consider a first time filmmaker?

Christian – We don't want to discourage anyone from bringing us a project, and this goes for first time filmmakers with completed films as well. If you really are a young filmmaker, you should really seek out an experienced producer or sales agent or in the case of a series, start with production companies because they are going to have the access. I deal with acquisition side where we try to see everything that is submitted to us, but what we watch first are films that come to us through sales agents that we have relationships with. I trust that a good sales agent will know my and my network's taste and that they know what we pay for films. And when and if we decide to do a deal, it's hard with first time filmmakers because there are a lot of moving parts that have to be explained in terms of delivery, clearances, insurance and masters that I'd rather have the sales agent dealing with the producer on that, then having my or my staff spending a couple hours a day for a few weeks on the phone with the producer or sales agent to make sure that the film is deliverable. It's just a time issue. We buy 200 films a year and we can't work on explaining delivery to someone.

Q – What do you think filmmakers should be looking for in a sales agent from your perspective?

Christian – My advice would be to find a sales agent who represents films of a similar size and style to yours. You don't want to go with a sales agent where you're a tiny documentary on a slate of several medium independent features with talent because you're not going to be their priority. There are a few sales agents that focus exclusively on docs. Try to find them and ask other filmmakers who used them how did they do. Did they return your calls? Did they make a lot of sales? With the representations that they made to you, have they tried to live up to them?

Q – How much interface do you have with the Sundance Labs and The Doc Institute?

Christian – We are sort of the end game. Films that come through the labs, they don't want to hear from us right away because usually I think the filmmakers that get that far have an ideal of getting a theatrical release or some sort of big festival attention. They don't want to jump to the end of the story and sell it to TV right away. Some people understand that their film is a really great TV documentary; I'm going to try and fund it through various TV networks in Europe and North America. But the lab people want the freedom to shop it around. That said, we're very supportive. When a film comes out of the Labs or Sundance we try to see all of them and if something fits our programming model then we will do our best to support them and get it on the air. And if someone from the festival or the Labs call us to tell us about a film, we take their world very seriously.

Q – What is Doc Day?

Christian – A few years ago, we wanted to test the waters, the appetite of the premium cable audience for documentary films so we focused one day of programming on documentaries. And it worked really well. People were very excited. It was very unusual for us to devote a whole day to one type of programming, but it has become a touchstone of the network – something that people tune in for. We premiere a new doc from the US or the world every Monday at 9pm. It gives us 52 opportunities a year to show something really interesting.

Q – Do you have much to do with your online Doc Day Discussions?

Christian – I personally don't have a lot to do with that, but it does sort of fit into our original voice idea. We want to hear from our viewers. So they can go to our website and give comments in forums about our documentaries that we program. The documentaries that we show are provocative in the very basic sense of the word. They are thought provoking and we have found that our audience wants to talk about them.

Q – What is Iconoclasts?

Christian – That falls under the Original Programming department. They developed that with Conde Nast and Grey Goose Entertainment. It's a non-fiction six part series, where two people in their respective fields who have achieved something of note, forged their own path or made a special contribution or impact and have them interview each other. It's a way to invigorate the biography/interview format.

Q – What kind of things should a filmmaker be thinking about when a deal is struck and a contract comes in?

Christian – Number one, and I hate to be negative and I know that documentaries have gotten a lot of attention in the last few years, but I think you have to look at how many documentaries that did well in festivals got real theatrical releases and made any money. At this stage of the game, documentary filmmakers really need to temper their expectations because there are only a small handful of documentaries that may have any impact theatrically at all. I wish more would, but the market forces don't work that way. And because of that TV in both the US and internationally as well as home video is really where you can make back your money, if you can. You shouldn't go into documentaries to make money. Anyone is lucky if they break even. Having a good sales agent can help you navigate those pitfalls. Another thing is clearances. We are not going to pay your clearances. Broadcasters don't do that. I run into situations all the time where people are counting on my money to pay their clearances, but I for one, at this network, I can't pay until a film is delivered. So that theory doesn't work. But every network's policy is different. Insurance is something that is expensive and something that people don't want to deal with, but I cannot air a film without it. And networks don't usually provide that for filmmakers – it's part of delivery. Those are the two things that hang up deals the most with us. Format you can always get around. Usually we like to get a NTSC Digibeta or a D5 is great.

Q – Do you see your network dealing more with Hi Def in the future?

Christian – Yes. We are definitely happy to have the option. The more of them that are available on Hi-Def the better.

Q – Do you handle a deal differently if you're considered a foreign distributor?

Christian – Not really. The same issues come up that do with domestic films. We buy up to 50%, maybe even 60%, if not more of our documentaries and fiction from foreign. We still need things to be cleared and we still need E&O insurance. We do our best to help foreign producers find E&O insurance. It has always been a big deal for them because it's not something that's required in foreign territories. It has taken years for us to convince them that's what we need. Also it's difficult to get a NTSC tape from foreign producers – it's usually PAL. But we will figure out a way to get it converted. We will work with them because we have to. We want to represent voices from everywhere.

Q – Do you program documentary shorts?

Christian – Yes we do. Ian Brick who works in my programming group oversees all the acquisitions of shorts. We buy a lot some years and not so many others. It all depends on how we can use them. But they are an important part of the mix. Sometimes we do shorts blocks and sometimes and interstitials.

Q – What are the common mistakes that you see?

Christian – The only other thing other than insurance and clearances, and this goes to managing expectations, is it has happened a couple of times where films have come in that we have liked and the filmmaker will put us and other networks off in hopes of a big theatrical or festival release. Then it doesn't come to fruition because it's very rare and then they see interest from TV go away. You need to be very clear about what the realistic opportunities for distribution are.

Q – What advice would you give a new documentary filmmaker?

Christian – Partner with a good producer because the business side and the paperwork can always come back to haunt you.

GUERILLA FILM MAKER SAYS!

The Business Plan

You've gone down the grant making route and you don't seem to be getting anywhere, so now you've turned towards raising your budget through private investors – in which case the first question they will ask is, "Do you have any paperwork I can study – I need details!" You might think it's easy to put a prospectus together but – it is illegal in the US under the Blue Sky Laws to offer advertisement to potential investors, without having presented them with your business plan (or private placement offering memorandum). This must list all the risks for the potential investor, and must also include all legal disclaimers by the owners/managers of the production company. It's adviseable to talk this through with your lawyer as these private placement offering memorandums can cost a LOT of money to put together. So here is an idea of what is actually legally required to be in this document:

1. The *main disclaimer* that must be listed on the front page: This document is for informational purposes only. It is not a prospectus. It does not constitute a legal contract or offer information beyond the scope, such as tax advice or partnership documents. This document does not constitute an offer to sell or solicitation of an offer to buy any security. Neither does this document nor any other of the proprietary information herein be published, reproduced, copied, disclosed, or used for any purpose without the prior written consent of (name of company). Filmmaking is a high risk business, and no guarantees are offered that investors will recoup any or all of their investment.

2. *The Executive Summary* which will include:

A) An *overview* of what the production company's intention is i.e the film they intend to produce and distribute;

B) *The production team; the product* – i.e. a brief synopsis of the doc;

C) *The industry* – a brief of the present industry & the particular genre that this film relates to;

D) *The market* i.e. of documentary films, their successes and if cost effective;

E) *Distribution* – whether a distributor is presently interested or attached, or list the ways of attracting potential distributors;

F) *The investment opportunity* i.e. the budget of the film, how it will be raised i.e. through 50 equity interests of $15k each, and when the investors should recoup their investment i.e. after distribution fees, expenses, repayment of any borrowed or advanced funds. Once investors have recouped 100% of their investment, any and all deferred payment compensation to cast and crew, and (if any) talent residuals have been paid – the investors shall receive 50% and the Company shall receive 50% of any and all subsequent revenues.

3. *The Company*: When established, what type of company, the directors & managers: management and organization.

4. *The Film*: Who is the target audience, when you plan to shoot, story synopsis.

5. *Industry Overview*: Explanation of documentary filmmaking production and it's different phases, theatrical exhibition, non theatrical, dvd/ video and ancillary including overseas distribution.

6. *The Independent Market*: A view on the present documentary film market.

7. *Distribution*: Looking at the Distribution of your project.

8. *The Investment:* The budget of the film, the equity opportunity offered, when the company may commence production of the film.

9. *Risk Factors:* Before the investor makes a decision to purchase the interests offered, prospective investors should consider the following factors, among the others set forth in the informational memorandum.

A) *Risk of motion picture financing* – explain the high risk and that it's only suitable for investors who are prepared to lose their entire investment;

B) *Risk of production* – explain that it's possible that the investor contributions may be expended without the completion of the motion picture and includes indemnities etc. i.e. the managers can't and don't guarantee that any of the key actors or production crew will fulfill their obligations under any contracts that they might have now or in the future – and that if certain key personnel cease to be associated with the project, it may be necessary to terminate the production;

C) *Risk of Distribution* – explain that there's no guarantee that the either contracted or not contracted distributors will undertake to distribute the film. And even if they do distribute, there's no guarantee that the marketing of the film will result in any financial returns.

D) *Lack of liquidity* – No such transfer of investor's interests will be transferred w/o the consent of the managers. Holders of the interests may not be able to liquidate their investments.

E) *Tax Risks* – All tax risks depend on each individual investor's situation and prospective investors are advised to consult their own advisors as to all tax and legal consequences of an investment in a company. The managers cannot and do not make any representations, nor warranties, with regard to the tax treatment of any investment in the company.

F) *Lack of operating history* – The company is in the organizational stage and will not be formed until the capitalization of the Company occurs. As such, the Company is subject to all the risks incident to the creation and development of a new business, including the absence of a history of operations.

CONTINUED...

CBC

Q – What kind of documentaries does the Canadian Broadcasting Corporation look for?

Jerry – CBC Television seeks documentaries that will have an impact on public perception by engaging large numbers of Canadians, about 800,000 per episode, with the significant issues of our time. We're pursuing a strategy of "big ticket" specials, limited episode documentary series, and feature-length theatrical documentaries. At the same time as CBC Television is pursuing a strategy of "fewer, bigger" titles, our cable news channel CBC Newsworld remains committed to "auteur driven" single documentaries within the anthology strands *The Lens* and *The Passionate Eye*. This creates engaging, diverse and a compelling range of documentaries from Canada's independent production community.

Q – Do you only commission Canadian filmmakers?

Jerry – We primarily commission Canadian filmmakers but on occasion we pre-license or co-produce with international partners. We also prefer to work with teams with appropriate levels of previous experience.

Q – As a broadcaster, do ratings dictate what kind of topics you commission?

Jerry – Yes. They matter a great deal.

Q – How should documentary filmmakers pitch their ideas to you and what makes a proposal stand out?

Jerry – An email or brief, 2-3-page, written pitch document is best. We like strong narratives built around compelling central characters that echo the structure of successful dramatic programs. We find this draws audiences into a more personal experience of the story. Active, experiential narrative devices are essential, showing audiences - not telling them what to think. Simplicity of narrative construction combined with relevance to our audiences' lives enables us to connect more intimately and with greater impact. Emotional, real experiences are vital. We like when ideas demonstrate that there's risk in the lives of the central characters. We want our audiences to experience the "raw" emotion of the subject. A sense of adventure or romance works, too, as it provides inspiring connections to the exotic aspect of documentaries. And it allows them to escape their everyday lives. Finally, our documentaries must include a sense of revelation, delivering on the promise of public television as a source of illumination for society.

Q – Do you fully fund productions and what are the budgets that you work with?

Jerry – We rely on the funding formulas that apply to Canadian independent productions that qualify for the Canadian Television Fund. Budgets range from $250K CDN to $1 Million CDN per hour.

Q – Do you do acquisitions?

Jerry – We acquire a substantial number of hours of documentaries for *The Passionate Eye* strand on our cable news channel CBC Newsworld.

Q – More in general, how are most Canadian documentary films funded?

Jerry – Canadian documentaries are usually funded through a combination of sources. Broadcast licenses from places like ourselves is one place. And the Canadian Television Fund is another. Then there are a lot of tax-credits/relief schemes at the federal and provincial level filmmakers can take advantage of. And of course, there's always private foundations and international co-productions.

Q – Does the indigenous population of Canada have any kind of separate funding that they can take advantage of?

Jerry – Yes, there are funds set aside by the Canadian Television Fund to support aboriginal programming.

Q – What common mistakes do you see with new documentary filmmakers that could be avoided?

Jerry – Proposing stories that are issue based rather than narrative or character based.

Q – What advice would you give a new documentary filmmaker?

Jerry – Go make your documentary and show it to anyone who's willing to look at it.

GUERILLA FILM MAKER SAYS!

The Business Plan cont.

G) *Liability* – An investor's personal liability for obligations of the Company is limited to the loss of their original capital contribution and to any undistributed assets of the Company. The Managers shall only be liable to the Company or investors for losses, judgments, liabilities and expenses that result out of gross negligence, willful misconduct, or fraud. The managers will not be liable to the Company or the investors for alleged errors or omissions. The Company will indemnify the managers for losses, judgments, liabilities, expenses and amounts paid in settlement of any claims sustained by it in connection with the Company other than those resulting from the Manager's gross negligence, willful misconduct, or fraud. Any indemnification payment could deplete the Company's cash available for investment in the motion picture or distribution to the investors.

H) *Loss on Dissolution* - Upon dissolution of the Company, the proceeds realized from the liquidation of assets, if any, will be distributed to the Investors only after the satisfaction of the claims of the Company, creditors, and the establishment of any reserves that the managers deem necessary for any contingent or unforeseen liabilities or obligations to the Company. Accordingly the ability of an Investment Partner to recover all or any portion of his investment under such circumstances will depend upon the amount of funds so realized and claims to be satisfied.

10. *Schedules: Schedule A*: The Production Budget cover sheet and notes. Schedule B: A list of recently independently produced doc features with reported budget and domestic box office returns.

11. *Biographies of the Managers.*

12. *Confidentiality Statement:* This Memorandum has been prepared by – Pictures, in regards to the production of the motion picture entitled (name of film). While the information herein is believed to be accurate, the Managers expressly disclaim any and all liability for representatives or warranties, express or implied, contained in, or for omissions from, this memorandum or any other written or oral information provided or made available by the Managers. Estimates and projections contained herein shall not be relied upon as a promise or representation as to future results. This memorandum is intended solely for the persons receiving it in connection with this offering and is not authorized for any reproduction or distribution to others whatsoever. The memorandum and other information provided to the persons receiving this memorandum shall be disclosed only to such employees, agents or other representatives of the recipient who shall reasonably need to know the same in connection with their evaluation of an investment in the Company. All copies of the memorandum and any other information given to persons receiving the memorandum shall be returned to the Company upon request if a transaction with the Company is not consummated. The information contained herein is proprietary, non-public information which may not be used other than for the purpose of evaluating this offering and must be kept strictly confidential. The recipient of this memorandum acknowledges compliance with the above.

For more informaton on contracts and dealmaking check out Mark Litwak's series of books - *Dealmaking for the Film and Television Industry: From Negotiations through Final Contract (right), Contracts for the Film and Television Industry, Movie Magic Contracts: Automated Contracts for the Film and Television Industry* and *Reel Power: The Struggle for Influence and Success in the New Hollywood.*

THE DOCUMENTARY CHANNEL

Q – What is your job?

Michael – I'm the director of programming for The Documentary Channel, Canada, which means I make decisions that relate to all the content on the channel.

Q – What kind of films does The Documentary Channel like to program?

Michael – We're a movie channel. We program solely feature length, hopefully theatrical films. We care less about the topic than others. We are more director driven. We like films that celebrate the craft of filmmaking.

Q – Do you go to film festivals to find your content?

Michael – I do go to them, but mostly to take the temperature of what's going on. So I'll go to Sundance, Berlin, IDFA and South By Southwest when they come around. But whether I'll buy anything, especially in this era of documentary filmmakers excited by theatrical distribution is unclear. It has happened, but it's rare. But I become sensitized to what people are excited about. Some of the things I see at Sundance will eventually be programmed on The Documentary Channel, just not right away.

Q – Do you see an attitude in documentary filmmakers recently where they expect their film will get a theatrical release?

Michael – That has been the big change in the last couple of years. This channel started around 2002 and at that time it was rare for people to get theatrical deals. I'd make deals at Sundance, South By Southwest and IDFA for sure, but now filmmakers are happy to know that I'm interested but are gunning for a theatrical deal. On the other hand, some of the films at these festivals have already Documentary Channel licenses. We don't only license finished films. We license things as concepts and things as co-productions. We may even commission something ourselves.

Q – How would a filmmaker go about getting a film commissioned by The Documentary Channel?

Michael – There's no set way, but my preference is to either know the person or their work. In that case, a couple of paragraphs will do the trick. On the other hand, it's very difficult to commit to a feature doc that you're looking to have in theaters and play in festivals from a first time director. Not that it hasn't happened and not that it hasn't happened from this channel or some other channel that I wasn't involved in. But if you're excited about director driven films, then not knowing the director or his/work is challenging.

Q – Is there a way a less experienced filmmaker could improve their chances? Maybe team up with a well known producer?

Michael – I can't think of a producer who would change a "no" to a "yes", but I can imagine a pre-existing license from people that I like or people that work well with our channel would have at least a positive impact. For instance, we in general don't work well with PBS or ITVS because of the kinds of films they tend to like. They are less about craft and more about topical stuff. But the other part of it is PBS is available to 90% of Canadians by cable television and border stations. We are a subscription service – you have to pay for us – so we can't easily show things that are available elsewhere for free. So A&E, which is also available on basic cable and the broadcast networks isn't a good match for us. On the other hand, HBO for whom we're the output channel for documentaries in Canada and The Sundance Channel and to the lesser extent IFC, those are much better partners. And that is more meaningful to us. So if someone comes in with a good HBO or Sundance license, our ears perk up.

Q – Sometimes when people talk about territories for sales, they consider the United States and Canada one unit. Is that common?

Michael – The answer is a complicated one. Up until about twenty years ago, North America was a single theatrical film market. The studios dealt with a theater in Winnipeg the same way they dealt with a theater in Denver. It'd be serviced with a branch office that would take care of the one sheets and things like that. Then the Canadian government began to think that wasn't right. They instituted a policy where only the big studios, who were already active in Canada, to sell directly into Canada. So Miramax would have to work through Alliance, which is a big distributor in Canada. Sony Classics works through Mongrel Media. In most cases the smaller films do not have North American markets, they have separate markets for both the US and Canada. Now these deals between Sony Classics and Mongrel or New Line and Alliance are really just service deals. The one sheets and the campaign are the same and they are placed in more or the less the same way. I just will deal with the Canadian entity. But if I want to buy *March Of The Penguins* I have to buy that directly from Warner Brothers.

Q – Do you have production facilities that filmmakers can use?

Michael – We do, but we don't include them in deals unless there is a specific reason to use them. We are owned by a conglomerate called Corus Entertainment, which owns numerous other TV stations, radio station and production facilities that deal particularly with animation. So we have studios, cameras and all the things you would want, but what we really do is license, commission and co-produce with independent producers who can make their own deals wherever they want.

Q – Do you have to have a certain percentage of your programming be Canadian and because of that do you look first for Canadian films to acquire?

Michael – Yes, by condition of license we have to be predominantly Canadian in prime time and in the broadcast day, which is between 6am and midnight. Between midnight and 6am, there are no regulations. And this is Eastern time. Both the Canadian Broadcasting Corporation and the NFB, the National Film Board of Canada, own small equity pieces in the channel in exchange for library material. So between 6pm and 8pm every night, we show library material from their archives, which are voluminous. And then between 8pm and midnight we show two feature docs, which are acquired separately. And then after midnight, we program much of HBO's late night programming including *America Undercover.*

Q – Do you have any kind of on going series programming?

Michael – We have what we call "strands" that aren't expressed as series. At midnight, we have something called *Exposure* that shows harder nosed, racier stuff. At 8pm and 10pm, we have a strand called *The Film You About To See*, which are feature docs like those you might see on Sundance Channel.

Q – Do you have any in-house producers or do you handle the development process?

Michael – Me. I do it!

Q – Is your process of making a film that you commission the same as a narrative feature?

Michael – Yes, same thing. You pitch it, then write a treatment, then rewrite it until we are happy with it and then go to production. In fact, I used to be a producer of dramatic films here and in Los Angeles and the process is exactly the same. The same in how you choose material and how the films are made. They are obviously smaller and the budgets are lower but the decisions and the things that I liked and the movies that I produced were those moments that told you were there. Documentary moments. *"Where can I take you that you haven't been,"* were the movies that I produced. I didn't do Hollywood, big popcorn films. The decision-making is exactly the same.

Q – Do you have a standard license fee that you give or is it on a case-by-case basis?

Michael – Case by case.

Canadian Broadcasters & Cable Networks

Terrestrial
CBC
www.cbc.ca

ITV
www.itv.ca

CTV
www.ctv.ca

Saskatchewan Communications Network
www.scn.ca

TVOntario
www.tvo.org

Cable
Bravo! TV
www.bravo.ca

Discovery Channel
www.discovery.ca

The Documentary Channel
www.documentary channel.ca

History Television
www.history.ca

Life Network
www.lifenetwork.ca

TV-5
www.tv5.ca

Télé-Québec
www.telequebec.qc.ca

Q – What format do you like the movie to be delivered on?

Michael – Our favorite is a Digibeta or Beta SP tape that is letterboxed 16x9 because we like theatrical-looking films. But we also have a video on demand service that is on the verge of Hi-Def.

Q – What are your requirements as far as E&O insurance?

Michael – We have to have it. This is a big company with deep pockets so we need active E&O. It's never killed a deal, though. In one case, there was a film that we wanted, but their E&O policy was only for one year and it had expired. To renew it would be a big deal. So we found a third party who could act as a distributor for a small fee and with the distributor the E&O became automatic. I don't think we should ever let that get in the way.

Q – Do you notice a specific tone, mood or artistic style to documentary films that might be different from other film cultures?

Michael – The one major trend that I see now is that the world of documentaries has become similar to art house or independent fiction films in that there are a whole bunch of films that are made for television. They play on television and they have foreign sales and they go away. They're successful if they get ratings. But they are made for a price and the price is based on what the prospects for return are. On the other hand, there are films like *Lost In Translation*, which are made for a price much cheaper than *The Chronicles Of Narnia*, and they have stars of lesser caliber who get less money. But if those films end up being good and they play well on TV and the DVD market, but don't get theatrical releases, they are flops. They're straight to video titles. That same model seems to be at work in the world of documentaries. So with feature docs, a number of them will show at Sundance and even if they're good and sell well in foreign markets and the DVD is well received and the TV sales good, but they don't get theatrical releases, they're flops. That's the kind of film that we commission, co-produce or pre-buy, or acquire – hopefully prior to getting a theatrical release. Our channel is a pay channel so we want to say to people that they heard about a film at a film festival and the reviews are good when it was released. If you want to see it, you better get the channel. We're always looking for new subscriptions.

Q – That goes back to what you were saying about the shift in filmmaker expectations for their projects.

Michael – Yes. You can talk about Michael Moore all you want, but I think it was *Spellbound* that changed everyone's minds. It didn't make that much money, but it told people that you could put a film out there and if the word of mouth was really strong, you couldn't keep people away. Now I think documentaries have access to the theatrical market, but when someone sits at home and is thinking about what he wants to see when he goes to the movies that night, he just sees an ad in the paper. He might not know that it's a documentary, if he even knows what a documentary is. He has read the reviews, heard the word of mouth and then goes buy to a ticket. So with *March Of The Penguins*, I think a huge percentage of the people that went to see it didn't get the sense that they were going to see a documentary – just an entertainment.

Q – Do you think documentary films will ever be seen as a viable business so that even the large US studios might have a separate documentary label?

Michael – Yes. No question. Now that documentaries have access to the theatrical market in North America which opens the DVD market, the VOD market, the PayTV market, and of course the TV market, I think they are terrific investments. You can make two or three for the price of one dramatic film and they now have the same revenue potential. *March of the Penguins* did $80 million and shipped 4 million DVDs. I sure don't know of a better film investment this year.

Q – What are the common mistakes that you see filmmakers make in their films?

Michael – One thing is that you have to be very, very good for a film to play any longer than it has to be. What I look for are ways in post-production for films to be shorter. It isn't always easy, but it's important. It's your bond with the audience that you aren't going to make them watch something longer than it has to be.

Q – What advice would you give a new documentary filmmaker?

Michael – Make a film. Make a bunch of films. The equipment is such that, it may not be the best quality, but I need to assess the filmmaking abilities of someone who brings me a project. And no matter how small or under-funded it is, one can see filmmaking talent and that ' a very crucial thing in the films that this channel makes. We co-produced a film with France-2 about the Monarch butterfly. The French broadcast executive was Yves Jeanneau and the French press was on him because there were no French elements in the film. The butterfly goes from Canada to Mexico and back. It dies and is reborn 4 times on the way. It's an amazing trip. Anyway, he said we love Monarchs and it's all about the director anyway. It's not the topic or where it is. A guy from the French press said, *"What if a guy comes in and wants to make a film about his brother with a bad leg?"* And Yves said, *"If it's Martin Scorsese, I say where do I sign?"* It's all about the director. So make a film or three films so we know how good you are. If we like your work, then it's simply about finding something to do together.

Canadian Film Commissions

National
Canadian Federal Tax Credit
www.pch.gc.ca/cavco

National Film Board of Canada
www.nfb.ca

Telefilm Canada
www.telefilm.gc.ca

Regional
Alberta Film Commission
www.albertafilm.ca

Alberta Motion Picture Industries Association
www.ampia.org

BC Film Commission
www.bcfilmcommission.com

British Colombia Tax Credits
www.bcfilm.bc.ca

Calgary Film Commission
www.moviemakersguide.com/data/c/calfo0521a.htm

Edmonton Film Office
www.filminedmonton.com

Edmonton Motion Picture & TV Bureau
(800) 661-6965

Alberni Clayoquot Regional Film Commission
www.acrd.bc.ca

Arrowsmith Film Commission
lsolecki@shaw.ca

British Columbia Film Commission
www.bcfilmcommission.com

Burnaby Film Office
www.city.burnaby.bc.ca

Comox Valley Film Commission
www.filmlocations.ca

Cowichan Motion Picture Association
duncan@cow-net.com

Greater Victoria Film Commission
www.filmvictoria.com

Island North Film Commission
www.infilm.ca

Town of Ladysmith
info@town.ladysmith.bc.ca

Nanaimo and Mid-Island Film and Video Commission
www.city.nanaimo.bc.ca/film

Okanagan-Similkameen Film Commission
www.nocdc.bc.ca/projects/film.htm

Powell River Regional Film Commission
www.prfilm.ca

Sooke Film Commission
www.film.bc.ca/film

Manitoba Film & Sound
www.mbfilmsound.mb.ca

Newfoundland Film Commission
Ph: 709 729-5632

Northwest Territories
Ph: 403 873-5772

Nova Scotia Film Commission
www.film.ns.ca

South West Shore Film Commission
www.yarmouth.org/swsfc

Ontario Media Development Corporation
www.omdc.on.ca

Toronto Film and Television Office
www.toronto.ca/tfto

Prince Edward Island
www.gov.pe.ca

Province of Québec Film & TV Office
www.filminquebec.com

Montreal Film & Television Commission
www.montrealfilm.com

Quebec City Film Bureau
Ph: 418 692-5338

Saskatchewan: SaskFILM
www.saskfilm.com

City of Regina
Regina, Saskatchewan.
Ph: 306 777-7486

Yukon Film Commission
www.reelyukon.com

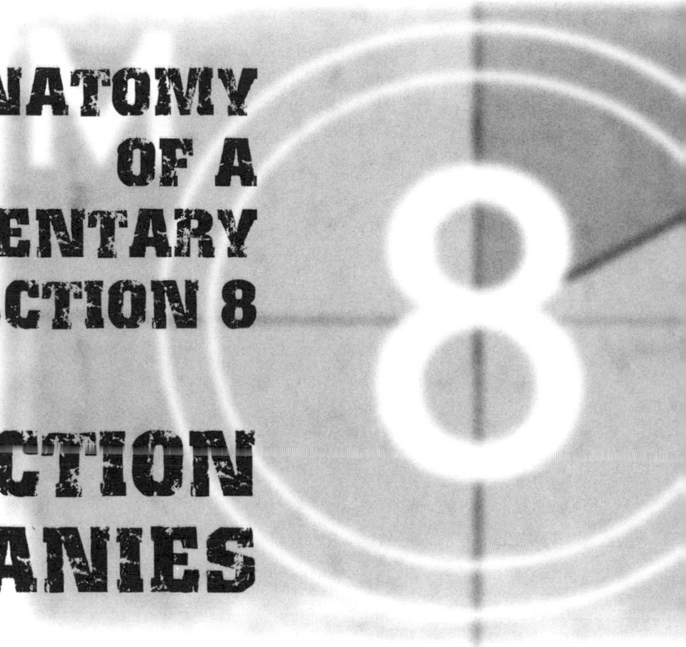

ANATOMY OF A DOCUMENTARY SECTION 8

PRODUCTION COMPANIES

Adam Leipzig
President, NGFF

NATIONAL GEOGRAPHIC FEATURE FILMS

Q – What subjects does National Geographic Films cover?

Adam – We have a very big tent. We're trying to expand the tent all the time in just the right ways to fit the brand. Any story that is about human aspiration, a desire adventure and explore in the world, whether that world is as the top of a mountain, the bottom of the ocean or across the street, could conceivably fit our brand. Any historic story of great human achievement or contemporary human achievement fit into what National Geographic is all about – which is exciting people to explore their world. I think there's an underlying sense of optimism and hopefulness in the kind of movies that we do. We want to make films that inspire people, have a long shelf life and that are very high quality, both in front of the camera and behind.

Q – You said human achievement, are our animal friends still part of the National Geographic brand?

Adam – Absolutely. Anything that is in the world. And maybe some things that are in space would fit what we're trying to do.

Q – What excites you and National Geographic about a documentary film?

Adam – First it has to have a great story. It has to be really emotional. It has to get me involved. It has to make me laugh or cry and deeply care. It has to take me to a world that I have never been before or let me see the world that I think I know in a completely different way. It has to be marketable. By which I mean in the documentary world, very publicity friendly. I have to be able to get ink on it as opposed to just buying ads. I have to feel that it can achieve in the commercial marketplace.

Q – Is there anything that you wouldn't do?

Adam – We wouldn't have made *The Aristocrats*.

Q – Do you or the National Geographic Channel do short films?

Adam – Shorts are a great from, but they have no commercial value.

Q – Do you generate most of your projects in house or acquire them?

Adam – Both. Filmmakers come to us all the time and we're always coming up with ideas ourselves for movies; constantly mining the incredibly rich treasure trove of National Geographic. There're over 300 scientific expeditions and explorations that National Geographic finances. Every year we publish 5 different magazines in 28 different languages in 144 countries. Historically, there are stories going back to when the Society was founded 119 years ago, so there is a rich portfolio for us to draw from. So normally a filmmaker that we like would pitch something to us or we'd give them one of these stories.

Q – Do you ever consider using first time filmmakers?

Adam – We haven't yet. It's unlikely, but you notice that I'm not saying never. We aren't going to get involved in a lot of feature documentaries. And because of that we're going to take very careful shots.

Q – What would increase the chances that they could get their project through?

Adam – I can't think of anything that would. Coming in with an established producer or production company wouldn't make a difference because I think of us as an established production company. We're all about partnership, but the level of expertise of production is not something that we to have brought to the table. We can do it ourselves. I suppose they would have to convince us that they could make a great movie. Not good, great. How are they going to do that if they haven't made one before? I guess it's about being inventive.

Q – Would having support footage or one documentary under their belt help?

Adam – Yes. I'd probably see their whole reel. If we were considering going down the road with somebody on something, I'd see all of their work. I wouldn't just rely on clips.

Q – Do you have any pitching tips when producers come in?

Adam – Don't pitch. We're very content driven. We do a very small number of projects, especially of feature film documentaries. We support them, but we have to believe that whatever we make can achieve feature film distribution and sustain it in the US marketplace are. Do you know what the odds of that are? So we are going to be very selective. If we're involved in one or two feature docs every year, we'll be doing well.

Q – Do you get involved in the editing process at all?

Adam – Sure. The intention is to support filmmakers and their work. And the intention is to create an environment where there are sufficient resources where filmmakers can make their best work. The least important of all those resources is money. The most important is collaboration, trust, resources, smart people and good team members. That's what makes the difference. At the same time, we have a legacy brand and if a documentary comes out bearing the National Geographic name that means something to the audience so we have to have a certain level of quality to uphold. So we will be present to ensure that level of quality.

Q – How did March Of The Penguins first come to you?

Adam – We were aware of the film being made in Antarctica and we saw some of the footage coming out of the lab in Paris. We knew we wanted to be involved at that point because it's a great story and he did a great job. Our opportunity to be involved happened when the film screened at Sundance and we partnered with Warner Independent Pictures to acquire the film and had an extraordinarily good collaborate relationship with Warner Independent Pictures. They did a phenomenal job distributing the film. A textbook job. The best release of any movie that year.

Q – Do you have production facilities that filmmakers can use?

Adam – Yes and for a feature doc we would rent them as needed. At our headquarters in DC, where they make hundreds of hours of television programming and specials and documentaries a year, they have a massive production facility. But here in LA, we put together the team and the facility, as we need it.

Q – What is the All Roads Film Program?

Adam – It's a film festival that National Geographic sponsors each year in LA and DC. It will be in other cities soon. The purpose of this festival is to give screenings to indigenous filmmakers from around the world. It's curated out of our headquarters in Washington who seek out films for the festival and also put out a call for films through their various members of the indigenous community who are on the advisory board of All Roads. All Roads has some exciting filmmaking going on from indigenous populations in Australia and New Zealand, Asia, Europe, Africa, North and South America. I'd invite people to come to the festival. It's done at the Egyptian theater in Los Angeles over a three-day weekend and it's great. Forty movies that will alas never get theatrical distribution because they are not good vehicles for that, but very interesting nonetheless. And we hope to work with some of them in the future on other projects.

Q – You give seed grants for some films. What is that?

Adam – A seed grant is a small amount of money to get a film going. It could be for indigenous filmmakers who are trying to incubate projects, which the program decides it wants to support.

Q – Do you do IMAX films?

Adam – We do have a giant screen division that does make giant screen movies. We have *Forces of Nature* out now and *Mysteries of Egypt*, which is one of the highest grossing IMAX films of all time. We do them out of the DC office. IMAX films are a different creature. They're a different format, a different length, different structure, different storytelling, different economic model.

Q – Do you do any distribution?

Adam – We partner for distribution. We are very involved in it, but we do not do it.

Q – What common mistakes do you see from filmmakers?

Adam – Don't take this the wrong way, but believing that people care. By which I mean, these are people who want to make theatrical feature docs, so I would ask the feature documentarian to put himself or herself in the mind of the audience. Someone is on the phone to her friend and it is Friday at 4pm. And they say, *"What should we do tonight?"* Well, they could go out and see some friends. They could have dinner together. One could go over to the other's house and play poker. They could go to a movie. They open the paper and they see a movie starring Tom Cruise, another with Russell Crowe, one with Brad Pitt, and one with Nicole Kidman. They could go to a concert. They could watching something they TiVo'ed last week. Unless your movie is going to be something they both agree on and do instead of all of those other things, why do you think that your movie is going to have a theatrical release? All distributors ask themselves that.

Q – What advice would you give a new filmmaker?

Adam – It's ridiculous to want to be a filmmaker in today's world. You should embrace that ridiculousness and go make your movie. But there's something I would want documentarians to know. I want to diffuse people of the notion that despite movies like *March Of The Penguins, Super Size Me* or *Bowling for Columbine*, that documentaries are a business. Guys, they aren't. It doesn't mean you shouldn't make them, but it doesn't mean that we should work on them with you. But we have to do it in a way that is financially prudent so we can still pay our rent. In the past decade there have been 445 feature docs that were released without NC-17 or R ratings. If you take out the IMAX movies, there are only 28 that grossed over $1 million. That means that the average gross of all 445 films, including those 28, is about $400,000. Therefore, be prudent.

Q – So is there is a point to making a theatrical documentary?

Adam – There is a point and I think they are really important to make. I think feature docs will be the recipient of new technologies and distribution models that we are going to see in the next few years. And we will be aggressively pursuing them.

GUERILLA FILM MAKER SAYS!

Keeping Track of Your Petty Cash

All receipts MUST HAVE the vendor's name, address, telephone number either stamped or attached with a business card. If you spend petty cash on items where there are no receipts (i.e gratuities, parking meters, pay phones) – you must make up a receipt, listing the expense and the date. Wherever possible, try and use checks as this creates an accountable paper trail. Here's an idea of where petty cash may come in handy:

1. Interviewing subjects on the fly: Cash may be needed for a spur of the moment interview. If so, make sure you have their signature of receipt and that they've signed a release form stating that they've been paid for their contribution.

2. Location receipts: There may often be last minute location expenses needed to be made, whether you're overseas or not. If overseas, having a few separate bills on you, may very well come in handy to help facilitate your production needs – bribes etc. If no receipts are available, make up a receipt listing the expense and the date.

3. Cell phones: Cell phones are always needed when filming, and if you as the production company have agreed to reimburse the use of your crew's cell phones, it can get horribly out of control and you could find yourself with huge bills to pay. Try and avoid doing this, unless however you're working on a big budget doc and can include it within the budget. If so, then try and restrict cell phone use to certain crew members and cap the usage. Request that the crew members submit their bills containing all work related calls (circled) to the production office, in order for reimbursement.

4. Mileage/Gas reimbursement: This can be done either through reimbursement of gas receipts or paying an agreed rate per mile (i.e. 32 cents per mile), BUT NOT BOTH. Drive To's can be arranged for rural locations where mileage is determined by calculating the mileage from the production office to the location and back, and multiplied by 32 c per mile. The IRS has a set allowance and if the reimbursement exceeds, anything over is considered taxable income.

5. Restaurant meals: The INS require charges over $25 to be submitted on credit card receipts along with what was ordered from the menu and a list of all crew who ate with you. If you paid by another method other than credit card, then you must have an itemized receipt with a business card of the establishment.

6. Kit/Box Rental: Certain crew members may have negotiated kit rental with the production rather than including it in their flat fee i.e. a sound guy may include his/her equipment under kit/box rental. This is considered taxable income, in which case would be declared in a 1099 at the end of the year. Try and get the kit included with the crew member.

7. Supplies: Batteries, tapestock – last minute requirements where you need to pick up that extra battery. Again make sure you have a fully itemized receipt, with date and name of vendor.

8. On set Food: Bottled water, tea, coffee, milk, snacks: Remember a valued crew is a happy crew and the best way to keep them happy is to have food and drink available at all times. Make sure all small receipts for the odd occasional item is always kept and if not already itemized, write on it what it is.

Cara Mertes

POV

Q – What is POV?

Cara – *POV* is a full service broadcast platform for contemporary issue documentary. That's a lot of fancy words for what we do – we identify, we co-produce often, we present and we platform your project for really long use. These films are what we consider to be the best in social issue documentary of that year. We get 1,000 plus inquiries, we go through them, we choose 15-20 new projects to include in the series. The lynchpin is of our activity is a broadcast on public television, but increasingly we see our activities towards a '10 for 10' model, i.e. if it takes you 10 years to make your film, we want to make sure that people are using your film for 10 more years. At *POV*, we create tools so it can be used educationally, in community settings, with faith-based groups, and other groups that are already invested in the issues. Your film will further a dialogue or a discussion or a local problem solving around that issue.

Q – What makes your films stand out?

Cara – There are five criteria that the films meet. The films have to have a strong *POV*, which can be an artistic imprint. So stylistically it has to stand out. Alan Berliner is an excellent example – four of his films have been on *POV* because he has a very strong aesthetic. Ross McElwee is another example of a very personal stamp. Another kind of *POV* if it's not the filmmaker telling the story, is that it's from the point of view of a community or a particular character. We see increasingly over the last few years people choosing characters as opposed to self-narration to carry their stories. Then, the films are typically about contemporary issues that are already in discussion around the country. While we focus on American audiences, we do take international films, but they're international films that would be of interest to an American audience. We're broadcast on PBS, which reaches the most people in the country. So we're looking for films that are going to be of interest from Oregon to Florida. The third criteria is that we look for high quality storytelling. We want to make sure that the films we show are very well put together. They're very highly produced and well structured. I don't mean that they are all shot on PAL HD – I mean that there's a really strong emphasis on the way that the story is told. *POV* doesn't necessarily look for objectivity and balance; we look for fairness and accuracy. So for instance, if you're doing something about an issue that's playing out in a community we want to either see that you've achieved an interview with the other side and have in some way represented their argument. And we want to make sure that every fact that you have in your film is accurate so we do fact checking. Those are PBS standards for everything that airs on PBS. There's also a funding test. There can't be perception of conflict of interest in funding. Access is the fifth thing. Unique access into a topic that we wouldn't ordinarily see. Whether this is an underserved community, a story that isn't told very often or it's a perspective that you never see about a story that's very common. We are always looking for that twist.

Q – If you see that a fact is wrong, do you tell the filmmaker to put in a title with the correct information?

Cara – POV doesn't take editorial control of the films. In other words, we don't have final cut, but we can keep talking to you about where and how the film isn't working as well as it could. We don't tell you how to solve every problem specifically, but we do tell you what to address. I do give notes to a filmmaker and that can consist of anything from several bullet points to an annotated script to sitting in the edit room with them and working through issues. And hopefully we'll create a kind of dialectic where my solution won't necessarily be the solution, their solution won't necessarily be the solution, but through a meeting of the minds we come up with a new direction or a new way of addressing whatever the issue is. That seems to be very successful with the filmmakers that we work with and it's a great process.

Q – What's the process of choosing your films?

Cara – We get 1,000 plus projects a year. We have about 20-30 pre-screeners who are media professionals who look at films. Every film has two people on staff and two people not on staff reviewing it. I'll generally look at between 200 - 300 of the films just to make sure things aren't falling through the cracks. Of particular interest are films that inspire an extreme reaction—often they get lost, because when notes are 'averaged,' someone who really doesn't appreciate a film can bury it. I find it of particular interest when a film inspires and kind of love/hate reaction—it might be very interesting, so I check for that. Then we'll take about 40 or 50 of our top films to an editorial committee meeting, which happens once a year. We bring in station programmers from around the country – public TV station programmers and independent media professionals – curators, directors, writers, etc. to sit and discuss these top films. Should this be a POV? What is PBS' responsibility for airing this? Is this a topic that needs to be seen right now? How good is the craft of the filmmaking? They come back to me with a ranked list and that's what I work with to curate the series. It's very fair. It's very wide ranging.

Q – Are there any budgetary restraints?

Cara – We have an acquisition fee, which is published at $525/minute for acquisition only and we go from there based on the needs of the filmmaker. Do they need completion money? We're more and more capable of entering into co-productions with filmmakers but those are all individual discussions. And the budget can be anything. We have aired $2 million films and we've aired $30,000 films.

Q – What format does it have to be?

Cara – Any as long as it passes technical standards for PBS. Increasingly that's not a problem because things can be transferred fairly easily. I don't know that we've aired Pixel, but we've aired VHS, original material. 8mm. Of course it's corrected in post and has to meet basic standards. So, if you have stuff you can't hear or the visual quality is just so bad that it's going to break receivers then obviously it is not going to pass muster.

Q – Does POV ever commission work?

Cara – No, but I'm in conversation as filmmakers are having ideas and there are times when we could do very small amount of seed funding for a first look option and then come back and do completion funding at the other side. *Family Fundamentals* is a film that Arthur Dong did and we gave him his first grant and his last grant on that film. I wanted it for *POV* and it all came out of his discussions and he sent me some raw footage and explained what he wanted to do.

Q – What kind of minimal funding can you do up front?

Cara – $5-10K. That enables a filmmaker to investigate the story and perhaps produce a small trailer.

Q – In terms of post, do you have your own equipment?

Cara – We do. There are times where we've had filmmakers use our Avid but that tends to be local filmmakers. Very often we find that filmmakers can get better deals than we can. But we help to get the budget down to a manageable size.

Q – I understand you have a distribution deal with Docurama and Netflix. What's the relationship there?

Cara – We have pre-negotiated a contract. Anything that gets into *POV* automatically gets an offer of this contract with Netflix and Docurama. It's up to the filmmaker to decide if they want or can take it and I say that because sometimes rights are already taken away that preclude them signing on to this contract. If you accept the Netflix deal, your film is offered the day of broadcast on Netflix indefinitely. 60 days later you pick up the Docurama home video purchase deal on top of that.

It's a step deal so that if you take all three you go *POV*, Netflix, Docurama and you have a guaranteed distribution chain. People don't have to take this deal at all, but we wanted to provide another service and pre-negotiate agreements and take off three months of a filmmaker's work. These are industry rates, so it's not like you get a lot less money because you do this deal. It's about what filmmakers would get if they negotiated it themselves, but they get the *POV* brand name, they get original materials on the DVD and the deal is already done for them. There's some negotiation room, but not much.

Q – Does POV negotiate for a theatrical release?

Cara – We don't negotiate theatrical releases but we'll allow theatrical releases. That's a conversation that takes place on a case-by-case basis. If PBS has funded the project through such as via ITVS, POV, and the Minority Consortium – if there's public TV money in a project, public television holds rights approval over any distribution deal. So we want to work out something that retains public television investment in the film but at the same time allows the filmmaker to get out there and get their film into theaters and do an Academy run if they want to or can. Netflix makes an offer up front to them that's an advance and it depends on the amount of business Netflix calculates that it will do on a particular film. So the advances vary slightly and *POV* takes a small percentage for overhead and managing the payments and tracking the rights. The ranges are industry rates for DVD – anywhere between $3K-10K. And that is this year. Next year it might be different. As for the international rights, we don't reserve anything there.

Q – Is your web series still going?

Cara – Yes. We needed to experiment with non-fiction content on the internet. So we've had enormous success with a web only showcase for non-fiction media on the internet called *POV's Borders*. We did a prototype and we now have done a first episode, which has won all kinds of awards. Essentially it's our exploration of interactive non-fiction storytelling online. I think in three to five years when people are really getting a lot of content from online and skipping broadcast all together that this is going to be a showcase that's really going to rise in prominence, even as broadcast becomes more fragmented.

Q – Does POV fund this from the beginning?

Cara – Yes, that we commission and produce ourselves. It's a very fluid environment. It's very general themes but at the same time, very specific so that we can get a lot of different kinds of media and play with them online and see what really works. As we are with broadcast, we're very interested in the community-building aspect of our media and films. So we're looking at how people come together, how they create communities and action around the specific forms of media.

Q – Do the filmmakers you deal with have to be established filmmakers?

Cara – No not at all for either series – broadcast or the online. We work with beginners and Academy Award winners. And oddly enough there is a funny phenomenon where Hollywood directors are looking at doing documentaries that they are funding because they can afford to. But, they want to give something back. Jonathan Demme produced documentaries in between his narratives. There are those people that want to exercise those documentary muscles in the service of their larger filmmaking experience.

Q – Have you seen an impact on your submissions since 9/11 that maybe look at things on a global scale?

Cara – No. What I've noticed is a demand on the part of audiences to see international perspectives, so I've really tried to get international films to speak to that. The two films that I have done that are international are oddly enough about the Middle East. One was a co-production about *Afghanistan: Year 1380*, which was six months in Afghanistan after the fall of the Taliban. The second film was *War Feels Like War,* which was a verité piece about non-embedded journalists on the eve of the invasion of Baghdad trying to get the story. Both are European productions and they represent viewpoints that we simply don't see in American media. This is a story that nobody's covering in the States. But I wouldn't say that American producers are becoming more international by in large in terms of their interests. Though I think we're going to see in the next couple of years bigger projects that are looking at the American role in this global enterprise that we have, but those are taking a few years to produce so they are not the first ones off the presses.

Q – Does POV help getting screenings out in the community?

Cara – One of the things makes *POV* really distinctive in terms of any other broadcaster inside or outside of PBS is the amount of support services that we offer for a film. We believe that a film needs to be used. It's not done until people are sitting there watching it, talking about it and doing something about it. In order to see that happen, every single film that comes into *POV* gets a website for the film and we underwrite some community activities which we call Community Engagement. We do a national press and promotion campaign – we don't have money for advertising, but we find all kinds of ways to get the film into the public eye into a dialogue through print, radio and television. And we provide educational materials. We do a discussion guide that's for general audience use and we do lesson plans. So we really want to see these films move into classrooms really quickly so that teachers can use them particularly in the high school and even in the middle school, but at the high school and college levels to talk about various issues. They are available on the website, in perpetuity it makes it very easy for a teacher to come to our website and type in women's issues and five films come up that they can use. They can download the lesson plans and they can go to the website that has a whole extension of the themes and very often has a discussion and perhaps a panel that we have put together. Or some original essays or a game that we have invented that helps you understand the issue better. It's great for a filmmaker to have an Arts & Leisure feature in *The New York Times*, but that's not the thing that is going to last.

Q – What is the Youth Views Institute?

Cara – There are a lot of young people that are very invested and actually see this heavy burden of inheritance that they have to immediately need to work on as soon they become aware of environment degradation. They think, *"It's over in my generation if I don't do something."* There's a lot of urgency around the work that young people are doing and our films help people do that. Particularly for young people who aren't so articulate about the issues, they aren't so sure about their identities their place in the world – a film will allow them to create a sort of safe area for discussion. They don't have to talk about their own personal experience, but they can talk about somebody else's via the film and it opens up discussion to help them figure out what their views are. We think that they're a really great introduction because it is one person telling another person a story. It's not a report – it's not meant to be objective. That works really well for young people to sort of open them to say, *"Here's what I think about this experience."* It works in two fronts – we generate events and we offer our films for screenings across the country with youth serving organizations and help them organize those, provide the films and materials. The second thing we do is have a local New York City Youth Views Institute where we get 20 people, mostly from the region but we've had people apply from around the country. They come for a weekend and get training in critical thinking skills, facilitation skills, organizing skills and get introduced to the power of this media. We have trained about 90 students over three years and we hope to expand it next year. We're now working with the Human Rights Watch – the international film festival, which has brought in educators who are interested with young people and human rights media.

Q – Any mistakes that could be avoided by filmmakers?

Cara – Yes. If they don't do their research to make sure that their project is POV type of film. The second mistake is sending a trailer in when what you really need to do is send in a work in progress. I'm not a big believer in trailers because they don't really represent what the film is meant to do, what the style is meant to be. They're meant to sell the concept of the film and I don't necessarily need that. I'm much more interested in a five minute scene than a five minute trailer.

Q – What advice would you give a new filmmaker?

Cara – Do your research. Persevere. Find a topic that you love because if you don't love it you are going to get a divorce.

AUTHOR NOTE: As of the publishing of this book, Cara Mertes left POV to work as the director of the Sundance Institute Documentary Film Program.

Lois Vossen
Series Programmer, Co-curator

INDEPENDENT LENS

Q – What is Independent Lens and how does it differ from POV?

Lois – It's a nine-month, anthology series. We're different from *POV* because by its very name it's about point of view documentaries. *Independent Lens* looks at and broadcasts the entire range of what independents are doing. So we have a limited amount of dramas. Every year we have some animation. We do a special episode of all shorts. I try to sprinkle in shorts with feature length docs. And we have a lot of international work. We share a time slot with *POV*, which is on the other three months of the year so there's this year round footprint on PBS for independent filmmakers.

Q – What is your affiliation with ITVS?

Lois – *Independent Lens* is a program of ITVS, is funded primarily by ITVS and I work for ITVS. For years, we were sending our tapes to PBS and they didn't really have slots for a lot of our work. A large number of them got on *POV*, but the rest of them didn't have a place to go. And we had a lot of conversations with PBS about creating this year round footprint for independents. When Pat Mitchell came on board at PBS, she, Coby Atlas and John Wilson agreed that it seemed like a good idea. So they asked ITVS to host and present Independent Lens.

Q – What percentage of films that ITVS funds make it to Independent Lens?

Lois – There's no one-time answer. The first season it was 42%. The next season it jumped to 50%. For the new season that we're about to announce, it looks like it will be 65-75%. So it varies. Our goal is to continue to be the best independent film series on television so every film has to compete for a slot and it doesn't matter if it's ITVS funded, or it came in as a submission or I saw it at a festival. There's no guarantee that if you're funded by ITVS that you'll get on *Independent Lens* or *POV*. I should say that we also place ITVS films on *Frontline, American Experience* and *Wide Angle* and other PBS strands.

Q – What kind of documentary films are you looking for?

Lois – I'm looking for stories that haven't been told before. For example, we had a great series on this year about pediatric cancer. Now I'm probably not going to acquire another film about kids with cancer. That's not what I'm looking for. We've tackled that issue. If you're going to pick a topic that's more universal like juvenile justice or capital punishment, you have to have a new take on it. We're also specifically interested in minorities and underrepresented audiences because that's the mission of ITVS. So a large portion of our films have Native American content, African American content, Latino content, disabled, the elderly – groups that really are underrepresented in the media.

Q – What would you never take?

Lois – We wouldn't take something that the other PBS series do. For example, since *NOVA* is all about science, we don't do science films per se. We don't do nature shows if it was about a safari or the extinction of the bald eagle. *American*

Experience tackles American history. However, if somebody came to us and said here is a great film about the sit-ins at Woolworth counters that were lead by four young African American college students that sparked the Civil Rights movement that is American history, but no one had done a comprehensive documentary on that before. We'd be thrilled and happy to have a film like that. In fact we did. It was *February One*. But other than that, there's no topic that would be off limits. We're interested in the left, the right and countries that are going through political change. We're interested in personal stories. The other hallmark of *Independent Lens* is that our programs are about people. *Almost Home*, has the topic of a nursing home but at the end of the day the film is about three or four characters that live in the home and are revolutionizing elder care. And through those people we see an issue.

Q – What about entertainment based docs like My Date With Drew?

Lois – We're a one-hour show, so we wouldn't curate a feature length doc like that and we probably don't have the money to license it. We do have a film on this season called *The League Of Ordinary Gentleman* – probably not a huge social issue, bowling, but it's entertaining and it does look at lives that are outside the mainstream. We aren't purists where everything has to be about grinding social issues. I think films like *End Of The Century: The Ramones* or *Double Dare* are very mainstream in their appeal, but they're by independent filmmakers who have unique takes on that subject matter.

Q – If someone has a film longer than an hour, will you edit it down or take it as is?

Lois – I either have the filmmaker do it completely or I work with the filmmaker. Sometimes we get things that are 58 minutes or 62 minutes and they have to be brought down. Almost every filmmaker has to do a little trimming. A good example is *The Real Dirt On Farmer John* – ITVS funded it as a one-hour version, the filmmaker made a longer version and had a limited theatrical release. Then there are some exceptions because some stories cannot be told in an hour. So I work with PBS every year to get 7 to 9 slots for those shows that need that extra time. Sometimes the film should be 72-75 minutes and then I round out the broadcast time with shorts. It's an interesting thing. Most filmmakers want it longer and most viewers want it shorter.

Q – How does one submit a film to Independent Lens?

Lois – We have an annual deadline that is around September 15th and people just have to send in two copies of their film on VHS or DVD. We get around 500 submissions and my colleague Claire Aguilar and I go out to a lot of festivals and probably bring back about 100-125 films. So it takes us about six months to get through all those tapes and we have our decisions made by the end of April. Then we notify everyone who submitted a film whether their film was accepted the first week of May.

Q – What's the deal they sign?

Lois – The license period is three years and so that is the deal we make. The stations can show the films four times over three years. And that deal is for all TV in the US. So cable and the other broadcasters cannot run it.

Q – What kind of license fee can they expect?

Lois – Our standard license fee is $30,000 for one hour. I might go up a little more if the market pressure bears it. If I'm buying a short it's going to be less.

Q – How can a filmmaker make their film stand out in that stack of 625 films?

Lois – If they grab the viewer's attention in the first five minutes that helps. That's critical in TV. And some films that work great in festivals and theatrical screenings don't work on TV. The audience has plunked down their money, they've gotten the babysitter and bought a bag of popcorn. They're going to sit and watch it. In TV, they've a clicker and either 7 or 700 other options. So if you don't grab their interest in the first five minutes, chances are they're gone. The question is what does it take to grab a viewer's attention? That varies from show to show. An example would be that we had a film called *Sentencing the Victim* – a film about a woman who was gang raped. She wasn't a filmmaker, but at that time she started recording herself talking about the incident, the trial and then subsequent having to go to the parole board and restate what happened to her five times a year since there were five men that did this it to her. So it wasn't only about the crime, the ordeal and the aftermath, but it was also about the justice system. When I popped that into my VCR the quality of the filmmaking wasn't exceptional, but she was so riveting as a character. I couldn't turn it off. So in that case it didn't matter that it was beautiful or that they got to a great moment within the first few minutes. What mattered was that you immediately identified with this character. For other films, it's different because you have to set it up first before you go in. Films about certain issues like a rare illness, you need to unfold it. It's about giving the viewer something in those first few minutes that makes them so curious they don't want to turn the channel. So I'm interested in new things and I want people to share their views with me, but I don't want them getting shoved down my throat. The strongest films are the ones that allow the viewers to draw their own conclusions.

Q – Does it matter what format the film is shot on?

Lois – No. It's all about content. But we don't want to encourage sloppy filmmaking. PBS has the highest standards of any broadcaster. If you can make it through our very rigid technical specs, you can make a film for anybody. And that can be an issue for some independent filmmaker who might be catching an interview on the side with a hand held camera. So over the years, we have spent a lot of time helping films look better with color correction and the like.

Q – Do you require E&O insurance?

Lois – PBS requires E&O insurance for anything that is over 10 minutes.

Q – If a doc can live beyond the box and be used for community outreach, does that help its chances?

Lois – We won't choose a film just because it has great outreach. And we won't turn down a film because it doesn't. But if we have a great film that we love and it has outreach potential, then there's a great opportunity to bring those two things together. And most documentary filmmakers make their films because they want to change the world. There's some issue that they want to bring forth. Unfortunately, our small staff cannot do an outreach campaign every week over nine months. So we end up choosing 9 or 10 shows and giving them an outreach campaign, which is community screenings in our *Independent Lens Community Cinema* in 14 cities around the country. They show it a month before the film is broadcast. Then there are viewers and teachers guides. For *A Lion In The House*, the film on pediatric cancer, we have been working with the Lance Armstrong Foundation, the Center for Disease Control, and about 2500 cancer organizations. They're hungry for a show that talks about this issue. Since we are publicly funded, we take that really seriously. We want the films to live longer than their broadcast. We want them available 24/7. The outreach is about putting the films in the hands of organizations that will educate citizens about various topics. And that is why we make websites for all the films so that people in these organizations and all viewers can have access to the content.

Q – What kind of fee does the filmmaker get if the film is used by an organization?

Lois – We try to work closely with the distributors whether it is California Newsreel, Women Make Movies or Films Transit, etc. to not duplicate their efforts and not take away any income that may go to an independent filmmaker. Our outreach is all non-profit free. We provide information on how they can buy the DVD or send people to the broadcast of the film.

Q – What is the Independent Lens Online Shorts Film Festival?

Lois – We wanted to reach younger filmmakers and a lot of filmmakers start by making a short. And since we have shown shorts since we opened our doors, it seemed like a good marriage of the two ideas. The winner is broadcast on *Independent Lens* and they get a cash prize of $2,500. The other ten finalists get $1,000 and their films will premier on online. The PBS website is one of the mostly highly trafficked website in the world so this is no small potatoes. I know that four of the shorts filmmakers that have been broadcast on *Independent Lens* used it to leverage their next deal. So anything we can do to help their careers is great. Plus we get some great content and awareness of PBS, ITVS and *Independent Lens.* We want great filmmakers to come to us.

Q – What are the common mistakes that you see documentary filmmaker make?

Lois – I'd have to go back to my earlier comment about having to tell the viewer what to think. People want their intelligence to be valued and they're tuning into a documentary because they want to learn about something and they are smart people. They have their own life experiences and they will draw their own conclusions. I feel very strongly that some filmmakers try way too hard to convince people of their point of view and are afraid to give people information that would give the viewer a better understanding of the situation. The other thing is length. There's a big misconception that you have to have a feature length doc to get into Sundance. Forty-three ITVS funded documentaries have premiered at Sundance and 90% of them of them were under an hour. I'm not saying that everything needs to be chopped up and made shorter – we accept that some things need more time. But after watching over 600 films a year, I am convinced that more filmmakers need to be friendlier with the edit. They need to welcome a good, strong editor. In most instances, making a one-hour documentary will attract more viewers. Then the last thing I would say is a very delicate topic. I think there's a bit of a myth that the marketplace is clamoring for documentaries to go into cinemas. Based on my experience, the marketplace wants a few docs. And those docs have to have some broader appeal. Don't think only theatrically and consider TV that thing you do at the end. The reality is that more people will see your film on TV than in the cinema. By only going theatrical, they will exhaust all many publicity opportunities. They'll get a local writer to write about the theatrical screening, and 9 times out of 10 that journalist will not write about it when it is on TV three weeks later. In fact, you should strategize with your film and TV release so you can maximize press. Our *Independent Lens* publicity staff is very good at that because many of them came from the theatrical world and are aware of how it works.

Minority Filmmaking Sites

AFRICAN AMERICAN
www.uafw.org
www.dvrepublic.com
www.blackfilmmakers.net
www.blacktalentnews.com
www.blackfilm.com
www.blackflix.com

ASIAN
www.naatanet.org
www.asianamericanfilm.com
www.asianamericanfilm.com
www.theworkshop.org
www.asiancinevision.org
www.capeusa.org

LATINO
www.lasculturas.com
www.nalip.com
www.latinofilmnetwork.com
www.clnet.ucr.edu/community/nlcc
www.premiereweekend.org
www.golemi.org

NATIVE AMERICAN
www.nativenetworks.si.edu
www.nativetelecom.org
www.ableza.org
www.aifisf.com
www.piccom.org

Q – What advice would you give a new documentary filmmaker?

Lois – What filmmakers often say to each other is that you have to have a passion. If you don't it will break your bank and your heart. What I would say is that if you have the passion, then the world "no" is just someone who hasn't said yes yet. You have to develop a thick skin and keep going. You have to follow your dream and go for it.

CACTUS 3

Q – What is Cactus 3?

Julie – We secure financing and act as executive producers and creative executive producers on projects. We like to be involved as soon as possible; from the stage of having a proposal and then work with the production team and the filmmakers to develop the project, find financing mainly through co-production deals and then to position the film for theatrical, film festivals and international.

Q – What kind of projects are you looking for and what projects get you excited?

Caroline – We aren't looking for a specific topic. It's about our passion for a project, but we tend to like socio-cultural films that have a unique voice or a unique take on a story. You figure that we have to live with these films for a while, so we look for projects that will stay interesting as they progress.

Q – Can a filmmaker approach you at the idea stage?

Krysanne – We get approached at all stages. Sometimes they come to us with an idea or a magazine article or a book they want to option. Others have very well developed treatments. Some have already shot 500 hours or have a broadcaster attached. Other times we're overseeing production for a broadcaster trying to keep it on budget. Other times, we're positioning it for film festivals and selling it.

Q – Do you have a discretionary fund so you can option underlying material and does that affect your role in a film?

Caroline – Yes. We're putting that together now. The earlier we come in, if we're putting finance in, then we have a bigger role in the film. We also have some access to deficit financing.

Q – Most of the films you, do have well-established filmmakers behind them. Would you work with a first time filmmaker?

Krysanne – We definitely work with a mixture of first time filmmakers, second time filmmakers and high-end filmmakers. It is a matter of having a balance for the company and who is appropriate for the project. If we have a big budget film coming in then we want a high level team working on it. Other times we have a first time filmmaker who is making a very personal story about their family.

Julie – We often work with people that we have relationships with and we may do two or three projects with them over a period of years.

Q – Do you work with non-American filmmakers or just American filmmakers?

Julie – Both.

Q – Do you notice any specific tendencies in storytelling for non-American filmmakers?

Krysanne – There are definitely various styles, and that makes co-productions sometimes difficult. When we deal with French filmmakers and French channels they tend to be a little more esoteric than American channels. So we have to be very wary of the various stories. Sometimes you have to create more than one version. And sometimes you don't get involved because you know it won't translate.

Julie – We have been doing this long enough where we can read a treatment or see footage and know it if is going to translate. There's a smaller and smaller TV window in the United States for films. There are less and less slots so you have to be careful with what you get out there.

Q – If it won't translate to the US market, does that color your judgment of a film?

Julie – I think what we'll do is look at the international landscape and see if the film can be fully financed internationally and then try to back into a smaller deal here. We look at each film and see how it's going to have the best life and get seen by the widest possible audience.

Q – How do you like to be contacted by a filmmaker?

Krysanne – They can give us an idea of what they're thinking about by e-mail and we will respond to tell them if we're interested in not. People need to be very up front about whom they've spoken to and what broadcasters.

Caroline – And that it isn't out to four other executive producers. I think some people tend to have a hard time understanding why it's important that we're involved in mapping out the whole thing as opposed to having someone taking care of overseas and us taking domestic. It's hard to do when you only have only a portion of the plan.

Q – Have you ever been in the situation where a filmmaker has been turned down by broadcasters and because they are now with you, you have turned a no into a yes?

Caroline – We will know why they said no and figure out what they needed. Sometimes they need to bring in another person who is more seasoned. Sometimes they have to make it more international in order to get an international broadcaster involved. Sometimes they send it cold and it gets lost. We have the relationships so we can go directly to whom it needs to get to. The broadcasters need to have films for their slots. They will tell us what they're looking for or they will ask us what we're working on. There are times when broadcasters come to us with projects they can only partially finance. They'll put us together with the filmmakers because they know we can take it to another part of the world.

Q – How do you go about raising the money for a project that you like?

Caroline – It should have a treatment. Footage is always huge. So a trailer showing that you have the access to the story that nobody else has is good. If they don't have a trailer, we try to create a development deal from either our own monies or a broadcaster so that footage can be gotten and reviewed.

Julie – It would also be to see if the project could go forward. If the access that supposedly is there is really there. The other thing we like to do is get a director's statement early where the director tells us why they were drawn to this project and why they are the right person for the project. That's more typical in Europe, but it's helpful here, too. After we have all of this, we'd approach the appropriate broadcasters or distributors for financing.

Q – Do you go after private equity or grants?

Julie – Yes. Any legal way that you can think of to finance a film, we have tried!

Q – Do you act as a fiscal sponsor for grants?

Julie – No. We aren't a 501 (c) 3. But we can find one for a filmmaker.

Q – Are co-productions hard to put together and what is the state of them in the world today?

Krysanne – They're always difficult, but we pride ourselves in finding opportunities through the relationships that we've developed. We've found that the best way to pull together a co-production is by pulling together broadcasters as opposed to theatrical monies.

Caroline – It's difficult if you don't know whom to go to. People will say to go to the BBC, but there are so many people working at the BBC. Everyone is specific to different projects that people will say that they tried there and they passed. But that wasn't the right person to go to. So you have to know how to navigate those big bureaucracies.

Q – How many entities would you feel comfortable with when entering into a co-production and do they tend to be hands on or off?

Julie – Ideally we like to have two because it's the simplest way to work. You don't have a lot of needs that you're dealing with when trying to make one film. When you sell the film, you sell it as is. There are also possibilities where you get pre-sales where you don't have to tailor it in the same way as a co-production. You can line up a bunch of those if you can get them and they are less onerous.

Q – Do you try to shelter the filmmaker from those entities' opinions?

Caroline – To a certain extent. Notes have to be addressed. We might take the first punch and if we don't agree with it, try to steer it in two directions so they're left with the things that they really, really have to change or they feel strongly about as opposed to a laundry list of changes. That, we will shelter the filmmaker from.

Q – Will you handle a finished film?

Krysanne – Very occasionally we will take on a finished film as a sales agent. We're looking at creating a distribution division, but we're not there yet.

Q – Do you do the deal negotiation on your films?

Krysanne – Yes, we do that on behalf of the filmmakers.

Q – What are license fees like these days?

Krysanne – They definitely shrink depending on what is the thing of the hour. We try to be as aggressive as possible and do the best deal for our filmmakers.

Q – Do you care what format the filmmakers are shooting on?

Julie – They have to have a pretty good reason to be shooting on 35mm or Super 16mm. It has to support something very specific in the story to financially make sense. Especially since a lot of theaters are projecting digitally. HD is hugely advantageous and it's getting less expensive. If you have someone who knows how to shoot it and it looks cinematic, then there is no reason to think it should be shot on film.

Caroline – Broadcasters want HD masters more and more. Japan has been that way for a while. They don't even want to know if it's not on HD.

Q – What is your fee?

Caroline – It ranges, but it is a percentage of the monies brought in. It also depends on how early we're involved. If it's early enough, we can get a line item as executive producer in the budget plus a percentage of the money raised. Then the back end varies.

Q – What do you see as the future of documentaries in the domestic and world markets?

Krysanne – I think there has always been a place for documentaries and there will continue to be. Right now it's very healthy because all the major cable stations are producing and looking for them.

Caroline – It also helps that the Hollywood films are bereft of ideas. Occasionally you'll get a great indie film that's that way, but people like those intimate stories as they're voyeuristic. They think they're getting the real thing. That's why reality shows, God forbid, work so well. People used to make documentaries on a shoestring and they did so because they had to make it and they loved the story. Wanting to make money from a documentary is the wrong reason to do it.

Q – What are the common mistakes that you see filmmakers make?

Caroline – For long-term projects, they get way too close. Just because you've been living with these people for four years and you know them better than anyone else, doesn't mean that you shouldn't take a step back and get feedback from friends or the community. That can keep a good film from being brilliant.

Julie – Sometimes they partner with a broadcaster and they don't pay attention to what the broadcaster is showing on air. They don't realize that they're going to need commercial breaks and things like that. And the budget, they have to be realistic. To come in with a million dollar picture that will never be bought for more than $300,000 means that you'll never get your film made.

Caroline – Not every film is a theatrical film. Yes, it can have a festival run, but that's different from opening up in theaters.

Q – What advice would you give a new filmmaker?

Caroline – You've got to love what you are doing more than life itself.

Krysanne – That's the advice we give ourselves.

NFL FILMS

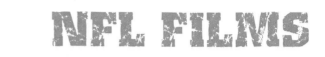

Q – How did NFL Films start?

Steve – NFL Films started with a wedding present. My father was in the overcoat business and hated it. But his hobby was home movies and as a wedding present he got from my grandmother a 16mm wind up Bell and Howell movie camera. Everything that I did, as his only son, he captured on film. My first pony ride, my first haircut, my first football game. And he filmed every football game that I played in up until I was a senior in high school. When I left to go to college in Colorado, my Dad decided that he would quit his job and try to make a living doing his hobby - making movies. In 1962, he found out that the film rights for the NFL Championship game had been sold to the highest bidder for $1500. In 1962, he doubled the bid. Pete Rozell, when looking at my Dad's application was very happy that someone would think that highly of the National Football League to pay $3000 for the film rights. But he was a little concerned about my Dad's experience when all my Dad had was filming his 14-year-old son. I remember that night I got a phone call from my father. He said, "I see by your grades that all you have been doing out there for the last four years at Colorado is playing football and going to the movies. So that makes you uniquely qualified to help me." I quit school and came back and helped him film the first championship game in 1962. Then we won the rights in 1963 and 1964. In 1965, my Dad had the entrepreneurial vision to tell the NFL, *"Why don't you start your own film company and we'll document all the games. We'll make highlight reels for you and preserve the history of the sport."* Pete Rozell thought it was a good idea and convinced the twelve owners to put up $20,000 and they bought our film company – which was called Blair Motion Pictures – named after my sister.

Q – So you didn't really have a background in filmmaking?

Steve – No I was an art major. There weren't any film schools in the late '50's and early '60's. I studied Picasso and George Braque. A lot of the classic and cubist painters and a lot of the things that I learned from them I applied to our films. So even though I had no experience making films, I had a feeling about how I wanted it to look. I always looked at the game in dramaturgical terms. To me it wasn't about the score, it was about the struggle. The way the players looked with the grease paint under their eyes. The helmets and the passage of time and the weather. To me football fascinated me because it was a game of bold gestures and grand passions and that's the kind of thing that translates into movies.

Q – What are some important things to know about interviewing athletes?

Steve – One of things that I've found is that you don't have to be very slick. I think that sometimes interviewers are more concerned about how articulate and knowledgeable they seem and sometimes they intimidate the athlete. I've found it's better to stammer and stumble along and in some ways it makes the athlete more comfortable during the interview. And since almost every interview I do is on film, I'm not really worried about myself. I can always go back and redub my questions which I do a lot of times because I'm not a concise interviewer. I know the subject, but sometimes I tend to ramble in the questions. I don't worry about that because I think when you tend to ramble, it gives the person a chance to collect their thoughts. This is all interviewing on film that can be edited afterwards – this is certainly not the kind of technique that I would advocate if someone were doing a live interview. But to me, the most important thing is to make the person feel relaxed and not worry about how knowledgeable you might sound. Also, since the most important thing is to get the most out of the subject you're interviewing, make sure that you are in a setting where you can get his attention. It's not after a practice or in a locker room. We like to do it in a hotel room or back at the player's house where you get their complete attention.

Q – When you're shooting a game – how many cameras do you use and what kind of film stock do you use?

Steve – We shoot Super 16mm with the 16x9 ratio – the wide screen. We have a formula where we have three cameras at most of the games. We have a top camera – he's called a tree. He's rooted into position and he's usually on the 40 or 50 yard line. He shoots at 32 frames and covers all the action. Then we have a mole – a ground handheld camera with a 12-240mm zoom, sometimes with an extender to make it go out to 400mm. He shoots anywhere from 48 frames to 200 frames. It's his job to give you that eyeball-to-eyeball ground level look at the game. To me when we started that was one of the philosophies. I wanted to show the game the way I experienced it as a player with the sweat flying, the snot spraying and eyeballs bulging. And that's the camera that gives that classic NFL Films look. Then we have another camera called the Weasel. His job is to shoot everything but the action. He focuses on the bench, the fans, the details, the sun coming over the stadium and the cleat marks in the mud. When I was an art major, I remember Paul Cezanne said that all art is selected detail and that is job of the Weasel is to get the little bits of artistic shots that you sprinkle in to make it more than just a highlight film. Very often the Weasel is attached to a soundman. Sometimes we put microphones on the pads of players or on coaches and we will shoot them from across the field on a telephoto lens. But a Weasel is handheld, 12-120mm lens and he shoots all the little story telling shots and very often synch sound.

Q – What about using slow motion, which you guys do a ton?

Steve – That goes back my art training. I took an approach sort of like the old Cubist painters of the 1930's – Picasso and Braque. What I try to do is take a single image and look at it from multiple perspectives and separate moments in time. So shoot at 32 frames, 48 frames, shoot at 128 frames and then be able to at it from across the field, from the end zone. So we would have two or three cameras all shooting the same thing but at different speeds and from different angles. What Picasso did with a bowl of fruit or a woman's face, in essence we were doing the same thing with a football play. We were fracturing the time and space.

Q – How much independence do your camera people have? Are they flying on their own?

Steve – I started out as a cameraman and I found it very annoying and distracting having someone telling me what to do. If I'm an artist and a cameraman, drop me in the situation and rely on my point of view and my talent. I didn't want somebody back in a truck telling me how to shoot. When I became our DP, I always used the philosophy that Teddy Roosevelt used when he charged San Juan Hill and got all the Rough Riders together and he said, *"Do what you can with what you have, where you are."* And that's what cameramen want. We have a little meeting before the game and each one is left up to their own devices. We've worked together for so long that you know each guy's style. One guy follows the ball in the air, another guy zooms down to the receiver, some guy shoots in the squatting position, other guys standing up and would rather be in the end zone. Donnie Marx who is generally accepted as the greatest sports cinematographer in the world, he is full time for us, but he also does the Olympics, baseball and basketball. Steve Andrich, Hank McElwee, guys that have been working with me for 25-30 years and you know exactly how they shoot and what they're good at and they are on their own. You never know what's going to happen. There are no retakes in this business.

Q – How do you come up with your music? Who composes it?

Steve – Music is such a big part of our lives. You get married to music, you get buried to music, you go to war to music and you make love to music. Music has always been a part of football. Every kid that's ever been to a football game can think of the thump of that base drum as the teams prepare to come out on the field. I just wanted us to have our own distinctive music. As a kid my favorite music was *Peter and the Wolf* where they used leitmotifs. A bassoon as the grandfather, the menacing French horns as the wolf, the piccolo would be Peter. So we decided to take certain melodies, old campfire melodies, that conveyed a rhythm and a storyline and re-orchestrated them with really big 60-70 piece orchestras and that became the style of NFL music. I've always felt our movies were made, not to make you think but to make you feel and nothing makes you feel more than music. Our original music was written by Sam Spence. Now it's written by Tom Hedden and Dave Robidoux. They're full time staff.

Q – What tips would you give for capturing fast moving objects?

Steve – Number one – be in the right position. Have an understanding of where they object is going to move, how fast it is going to go and to be in a position where you don't have to pan as much. Some of our best shots come from the catty corner where you don't have to swish pan and the action comes into you. Make sure that you have an eyepiece with a space around the receptacle, so you can see as much as you can. Our cameras are specially designed racecars, the motor is French, the viewing system is English, the body casing is built in America and they are balanced like sniper rifles for each one of our cameraman. Shooting football is difficult because not only do you have to follow the ball and the action but you can get hit! Guys get whacked on the sidelines.

Q – Do you have problems with breakage of equipment?

Steve – Not that much. The weather used to be a big problem, but not so much anymore.

Q – How do you handle your narration? Who writes it?

Steve – Originally football films were written in a very breezy, clever style that was like, *"Milt Plum makes a peach of a pass to become the apple of Coach George Wilson's eye."* Clever, but I wanted to write less script. I felt that the pictures and the music and the sounds of the game would convey the drama of the game. There was a newscaster in Philadelphia by the name of John Facenda who had this great oaken voice – he was the Walter Cronkite of Philadelphia. We hired him to read the scripts because we wanted to write less, not more. To me words are like medicine, if they are doled out properly they can work wonders, but an overdose can be fatal and Facenda could deliver these very terse tight sentences. When you are writing for film you don't need adjectives. My rule is that you could take any script and just take a pencil though almost every adjective and adverb and it would make the script stronger. Good scripts are good verbs, nouns and that's it because everything else you can see. The writing should add something to what the audience is seeing, not repeat or describe what the audience is seeing.

Q – How hard is it to find good writers?

Steve – The most elusive talent in our business is writing. When we hire someone that's the first thing we look for. If a person cannot write, we don't even consider them. A person that can really write well, we feel we can teach them how to edit and construct a film. When you see something in sports television that's written well, it brings you right up out of your chair.

Q – How do you find writers for NFL Films?

Steve – I have a file here of 560 applications. We get applications here at a rate of 10 a week. Then we ask for writing samples and we have an intern program. We hire people as interns for 6 months because one thing about making a film, it's an art form, but it's not like a painter who has just a brush and a canvas or a writer that's got an pencil and a piece of paper. To make a film you need an army and in order to be a good filmmaker you have to work with all the members of that army and you have to be able to get along with all the members of that army because filmmaking is such a temperamental, personal, emotional profession and you deal with people who are temperamental and emotional. And unless you can understand that and deal with people like that, you'll never be any good as a filmmaker. We have very few temperamental assholes. We weed them out. That's one thing that should be taught in all film schools is people skills. I've seen a lot people come though that have some talent, but because they are such pricks nobody wants to work with them. On the other hand, I have people with very average talents, but great people skills and everyone rallies around them and wants them to succeed. When you think our business and how many layers go into just our *Game of the Week*, which is on NFL Network. You hope it's a good game, and if it's a good game, did the cameraman have a good day? Then is the film processed properly? Then is it edited properly? Then is the script written? then is the music laid in right? Is the mix done right? Every step of the way you can screwed and that's why there are so many steps that make the business so difficult and that's why you so see so few good films because there are so many stages that a film has to go through and at each stage you need someone that is personally involved, really committed to doing the best job possible. If you have a mixer that doesn't pay attention or a music cutter that doesn't lay the music in right and that can diminish all the work of everyone that has gone on before.

Q – What tips do you have editing to make a sports documentary really exciting?

Steve – I think that you have to let the sport be the most important thing in your mind. To me sports has a beauty onto its own. The editing should be like a Fred Astaire-Ginger Rodger musical. The best shot was a head to toe with no cuts because you really got to see the teamwork, the grace and the flow. The minute you start editing, then you start adding something artificial. When we have a great play, we like to let it go from the beginning to the end. You can repeat it, but sometimes when you start editing you can over cut things because there is such a plethora of things on TV, that everybody wants to do highlights to make theirs different – cut it quick or speed it up. I hate that. To me, the beauty of what we do is that athletes are the subject, not the filmmaker. And when the filmmakers decides that he is more important and it's editing or he is going to inflict his point of view on it, you destroy the experience for millions of fans who want to watch Barry Sanders run or Dan Marino throw the ball. That is something that I have noticed creeping into more and more sports documentaries – overediting.

Q – Do you need to get releases from athletes and fans when you shoot?

Steve – No. Most fans love to be on NFL Films and if anything we have to keep them out of the camera. They are yelling and screaming and it is the opposite for us. It is hard to get some authentic shots when everyone is posturing. The thing we ran into when we started in the 60's and 70's was that the fans were actually spectators. Now fans are part of the spectacle themselves. You go to an NFL game and it looks like a Halloween party every weekend. Everyone comes in costume and they are clambering to be part of it. They expect to be part of it.

Q – Can people license footage from NFL Films?

Steve – Yes.

Q – What is the Game of the Week?

Steve – *Game of the Week* is about choices and decision. We try to explain the reasons that one course was taken instead of another. I look at a football game as a big artichoke and you peel back the layers of the game. The strategy, the tactics, the emotions, the spirit, the situations and then we rely heavily on our music and our sound and we look on each game as a story. And what makes *Game of the Week* unique is that there is no other network or sport that treats a current game with the detail and the analysis that we do. The game is played on Sunday and we come back Wednesday night with a one hour show complete with a written narration, sound, music – all the elements that go into a documentary film and we do it in 48 hours. Most shows, if you want to see something like that you go to the Classic Channel and see something that was played in 1975. We are the only show that comes back with a comprehensive, detailed account of a current game in a one-hour format. And it isn't regurgitated broadcast tapes; it's in Super 16mm film. It's the game looked at from a totally different perspective.

Q – How much footage do you shoot and how many editors?

Steve – We have about five editors that work on it and we shoot about 20 miles of film. We shoot 900 miles of film each year on football. We are Kodak's biggest client. We have three camera s each camera shoots about 15 rolls of films and each roll is 400 feet. 35 rolls on a *Game of the Week*. Each roll is 400 feet.

Q – What productions services do you offer at NFL Films?

Steve – We have a complete mixing facility. We have a lab that processes 35mm film as well as 16mm. We have telecine. We do everything here except make the film. Every element, recording studios that can handle a 72 piece orchestra. We have two sound stages. It's Hollywood on the Delaware River.

Q – Can anyone use them?

Steve – Yes. You have to call ahead because we're pretty busy, but it's a business that we run.

Q – What advice would you give a new documentary filmmaker?

Steve – It's so hard to get started in this business. I would try to get in at any level doing anything that you can. Even if you think you want to be a cameraman and there's an opening in sales – go for it. When we started NFL Films it was great combination in that my dad was the great entrepreneurial vision and I was the creative director. We were in a profession that had never been done before. That old saying by Mark Twain, *"All you need is ignorance and confidence and success is sure."* People didn't know if it was good or bad in the beginning and neither did we. Be persistent, have patience and try to get yourself in a situation where you have an opportunity what you are good at. You might think you're going to be a good cameraman but might end up being a better editor. You might think you want to be a salesman, but you have a good eye to be a cameraman. You don't want to cubbyhole yourself, but you need so many elements to make films, that it's hard to decide all of a sudden I want to be a filmmaker and pick up a camera and go out and do it.

GUERILLA FILM MAKER SAYS!

Shooting Sports

Sports documentaries have a lot going for them mainly because of the built in conflict of competition and typically larger than life personalities. Here are some tips for dealing with athletics focused docs.

1. Watch the sport so you know the rules of the game so you can build in that drama into the story.

2. Watch closely how the players, balls, pucks, equipment and officials move so you can anticipate where you need to plant cameras in order to catch the fast moving action.

3. Slow motion looks great with most sporting events – especially those that are very physical.

4. When interviewing athletes, be prepared for some very simple and cliché answers during the event or just after. They are trained to do this so they don't make their team look bad.

5. Be careful of interviewing athletes before their event as they tend to be focused and don't want any interruptions.

6. If things go well, get right in there (just be mindful of the free flowing champagne). If things go bad, give athletes some distance right after and use a long lens or zoom in.

7. Try to get cameras into the action somehow such as putting them on the bow of a boat or in the passenger side of a racecar.

8. Shoot the crowd! There is nothing more colorful and mood building that what Joe Fan is doing up in the stands whether it's painting his face or wearing some fun costume.

9. You will have to get permission from the team's officials to shoot anyone in the organization. You will also have to get permission to shoot in certain venues, but doing so will probably mean that you can shoot anything in that venue and not have to get a release.

10. Get the details. This adds color and tension such as shooting a close up a soccer player setting the ball before a penalty shot or a football player digging in before a play.

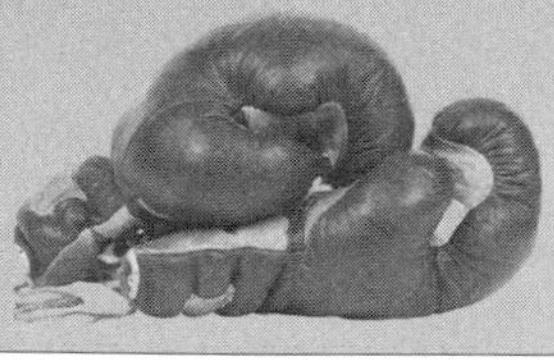

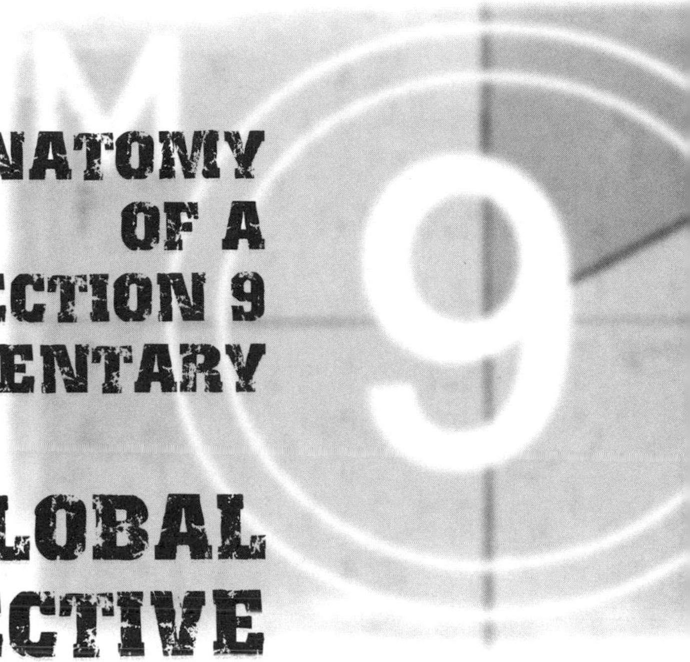

ANATOMY OF A SECTION 9 DOCUMENTARY

GLOBAL PERSPECTIVE

EUROPEAN DOCUMENTARY NETWORK

Q – What is the EDN?

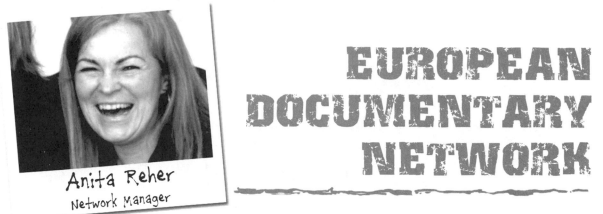

Anita – EDN is a membership organization for professionals working within documentary film and television. Its purpose is to support, stimulate and create networks within the documentary sector in Europe. One of our major focuses is to inform members about possibilities for financing, the EU MEDIA program and other funding options, development, co-production and collaboration across borders – i.e. where to take a finished film, distribution, festivals and markets, and production contacts in other countries. This is done via individual consultancy to members on documentary projects as well as activities like workshops, seminars, conferences and the two indispensable publications *DOX* magazine and The *EDN TV-Guide*. We cover all of Europe and our network is open to all countries but our knowledge is primarily European. We have more than 800 members and you can join on www.edn.dk. An annual membership is 110 Euros and runs for 12 months from the day you sign up.

Q – What is the EU Media Program and how does that help documentary filmmakers?

Anita – The EU Media Program is a support structure where EU-based doc. filmmakers can get support for their projects for production or distribution. The Media program also supports activities and promotion.

Q – What is the EDN TV-Guide?

Anita – The EDN TV-Guide is an annual guide and an essential tool for documentary filmmakers, producers, distributors and program sellers looking for financing, co-financing and sales of their projects. It provides all the insight you need to direct your proposals or finished film to the right person at the right place. It contains full information on more than 100 European TV Channels including Channel profiles, documentary profiles, documentary strands, slots, lengths and themes, commissioning editors and buyers with telephone and email contact details. It's free for members, but you can also buy it separately.

Q – What is DOX magazine?

Anita – *DOX* is an international English language film magazine dedicated entirely to cover all aspects of the documentary genre. It offers an insight into the work of doc filmmakers, reports on distribution and production possibilities, looks out for new formalistic and aesthetic developments, reviews the significant new films and presents itself as a platform for discussion. The magazine contains important information on festivals, markets and funding bodies. It contains everything from the latest news, personal POV's, festival reports, short and long reviews, special features as well as festival and market calendars. Everybody can subscribe - you don't need to be a member.

Q – Can the EDN help in finding funding & distribution?

Anita – EDN is not a producer - so we don't find the funding or the distributor for our members - but we like to call ourselves "matchmakers". We advise our members on questions regarding financing and distribution. We read projects and see finished films made by our members and share with the members our knowledge on which financiers and distributors that could be Interested in their project or film.

Q – Are all members accessible to each other on the network?

Anita – All members can find a profile of the other members on the EDN website - but members often contact us in the office for more personal information - and we frequently put members in contact with each other.

Q – What kind of events does the EDN help organize?

Anita – EDN helps organize a wide range of events - all depending on the need of a certain region or organization that is asking for our help. We organize everything from pitching sessions, co-production workshops, mini-festivals/film screenings where the filmmakers are present to talk about their films, master-classes - you name it!

Q – What are the most important documentary events in Europe that a documentary filmmaker should seriously consider attending (with or without a film)?

Anita – It would be impossible to mention ONE major event that everyone should attend - as it all depends on your focus within the business. To mention 2 major events would be IDFA in Amsterdam and Sunny Side Of The Doc in France. IDFA is the most important documentary film festival in the world and in conjunction with this is the largest co-financing FORUM. Sunny Side is the other end of the business - a film market with focus on documentaries. Beside these there are numerous smaller events during the year where you can do business in a more comfortable way. We recommend that you check the EDN activity calender on the web!

GUERILLA FILM MAKER SAYS!

Helpful European Websites

Cineuropa *(European film magazine)*
www.cineuropa.org

Film File Europe *(European film business site)*
www.filmfileeurope.com

European Film Promotion
www.efp-online.com

The Marketplace
www.marketplace-events.com

European coordination of film festivals
www.eurofilmfest.org

Holland Film
www.hollandfilm.nl

VAR Flemish Audio Visual Fund
www.vaf.be

Flanders Image
www.flanders-image.com

Film Fund Luxembourg
www.filmfund.lu

Greek Film Centre
www.gfc.gr

Danish Film Institute
www.dfi.dk

Film France
www.filmfrance.net

Commission Nationale du Film France
www.cnc.fr

Rhone-Alpes Cinema
www.rhone-alpes.fr

The German Federal Film Board
www.ffa.de

FilmForderung Hamburg
www.ffhh.de

German Film
www.german-films.de

Bavarian Film and TV Fund
www.fff-bayern.de

Berlin/Brandenburg Film Board
www.filmboard.de

North Rhein-Westphalia Film Fund
www.filmstiftung.de

Austrian Film Commission
www.afc.at

Swiss Film Center
www.swissfilms.ch

Italia Cinema
www.italiacinema.net

Irish Film Board
www.filmboard.ie

CONTINUED...

CHANNEL 4 - UK

Q – How would you define British documentary filmmaking in terms of the rest of the world?

Simon – It's very passionate. It's very driven. It's very socially and politically minded. It's popular. It's well made. It's commercial. It's amongst the very best. It's a tremendous privilege to be working in commissioning in this country. One way or the other, we've been at the forefront of innovation over the years.

Q – What kind of documentaries is Channel 4 looking for?

Simon – We have a lot of different divisions here looking for lots of different things. I specialize in human-interest documentaries like *The Boy Whose Skin Fell Off*, which won the Emmy for best doc. I've gone off to do a bunch of films in that vein. But there's a lot of different stuff going on within the Channel, whether it's documentaries or pop docs, which are designed to rate as opposed to bring us any sort of recognition. I suppose the thing that unites all of the films that we do is a tone of voice. A tone of voice that can be questioning, scurrilous, irreverent or anti-establishment. Even when we do history and science programs, we try and do them in a counter-intuitive way that presents new ways of looking at the world.

Q – Are there any documentaries that you wouldn't be interested in?

Simon – Long-winded, history, Eskimos fishing up in the frozen wasteland types. Channel 4 is a ruthlessly contemporary broadcaster that's got its finger on the pulse of young, upwardly mobile, smart, free thinking Britain. While we do international subjects, we'd do them with an eye on what they say about us. I don't think we'd go off and burrow down into the microscopic details of remote communities. We tend to leave that to the BBC where they send out explorers to hang out with them.

Q – So it must have a British angle?

Simon – No, it doesn't have to have a British angle, but we are a British broadcaster. So we're at our best either making films about Britain or looking at international stories in a way that addresses the curiosity and needs of a British audience. So, clearly, when we go to Iran or Iraq, we're addressing what we see on the ground there in a way that we think suits the people that watch us. We're trying to stimulate and get into places that other people may not choose to go. And that involves going to countries where people may not want or choose to go like in our series *Unreported World*. Or it may involve going into emotional territories with people in a way that other broadcasters may choose to avoid such as an upcoming series we have on how we deal with our parents when they get old and we have to look after them. So there's kind of a feeling that we tread into territories that other folk find less appealing. The challenge for us is to create entertaining and watchable programs around those territories.

Q – As a commercial channel, do ratings come into play?

Simon – Oh, yes. We measure everything by ratings and reputations. So if something's achieved high ratings and high reputation. And by that I mean it was so good or well known that stakeholders, politicians, the public and newspapers know

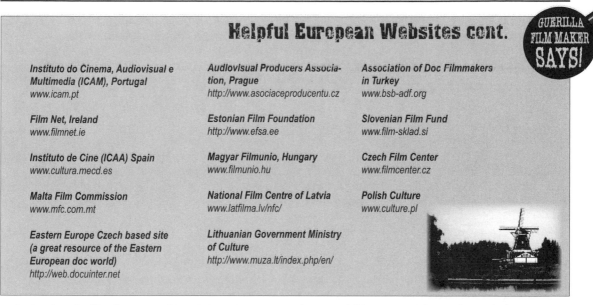

Helpful European Websites cont.

Instituto do Cinema, Audiovisual e Multimedia (ICAM), Portugal
www.icam.pt

Film Net, Ireland
www.filmnet.ie

Instituto de Cine (ICAA) Spain
www.cultura.mecd.es

Malta Film Commission
www.mfc.com.mt

Eastern Europe Czech based site (a great resource of the Eastern European doc world)
http://web.docuinter.net

Audiovisual Producers Association, Prague
http://www.asociaceproducentu.cz

Estonian Film Foundation
http://www.efsa.ee

Magyar Filmunio, Hungary
www.filmunio.hu

National Film Centre of Latvia
www.latfilma.lv/nfc/

Lithuanian Government Ministry of Culture
http://www.muza.lt/index.php/en/

Association of Doc Filmmakers in Turkey
www.bsb-adf.org

Slovenian Film Fund
www.film-sklad.si

Czech Film Center
www.filmcenter.cz

Polish Culture
www.culture.pl

and write about the film. So some achieve both and some one or the other. I think we are quite good at achieving a mix across our output. What we don't like are things that don't do either.

Q – Can an independent documentary producer approach you directly with an idea?

Simon – We recently moved away from that approach because there are so many demands on our time that evaluating such one offs is too time consuming. So we'd rather things came through an independent production company via an electronic proposal system that we've got. The truth is and I'm not unique in saying this, I get a hundred e-mails a day and sometimes they have a program idea tucked in there or someone I know is pitching an idea or saying, *"Thanks for the advice on X, would you like to do a film on Y?"* And I accept those if they come from people that are current suppliers and I know them personally. To be honest, I wouldn't be over the moon about getting a whole pile of unsolicited pitches from filmmakers around the world. I understand it's not always possible to get an independent company to sponsor your ideas, but it's a way to get a stamp of approval and to filter out the bad ideas.

Q – Does it help if the independent company has worked with you before?

Simon – It doesn't have to be that way. *The Boy Whose Skin Fell Off* was from an independent company that had never made a film for Channel 4. And it was directed by someone who had never done a long film before. I was very happy to take that because it very much felt like the right thing. But for the most part, it isn't practical to work that way because all those people that have never made films before don't have much infrastructure. They'll need huge amounts of help in order to realize their creative ambition. It's massively time consuming. We're happy to, but we can't do it on all of our shows. We have to supply an executive producer and maybe it ends up costing us a bit more because the program may overrun for any number of reasons. I always want and have a small number of people doing things for me for the first time in the mix because without that fresh input it would all get very boring.

Q – So people submit proposals via the internet?

Simon – Yes. We have a website www.4producers.co.uk. For independent filmmakers with some track record submitting, say from the States, another important person to look for within our organization is Katie Speight who's responsible for acquiring a lot of the American and international docs for our sister channel, More 4. That's a cable or satellite channel, which has a strong documentary brief. It's quite new and it's already begun to perform quite well. I spend more of my time commissioning series and then you have to look at format. Is it something that we have witnessed on BBC? I think there are different ways into different projects and people and the trick is, if you're a guerilla documentary filmmaker, try a few different ones. And bear in mind that we would love to read everything that comes in but it's not always possible.

Q – Does More 4 look at ideas as well as acquisitions?

Simon – Yes. Absolutely.

Q – Will Channel 4 fully fund a project that they commission?

Simon – We can, but not always. Sometimes we'll work with an American co-producer like Discovery. We'd buy the UK rights and they buy American rights. We'd take that for Channel 4 and More 4. So we have the terrestrial window and the satellite window. And then the independent is at liberty to sell the rest of the international rights to whomsoever they choose. They could partner up with a distributor who sells the rights to someone like Channel 4 International or RDF International.

Q – Do you get the copyright?

Simon – No, that lies with the independent producer. We just buy licenses. It's felt that we are entering into a time of positive growth in the independent TV sector and that's why big independent companies are snapping up smaller ones. There's a lot of investment interest in this sector because the balance of power in some ways has swung back to the indie.

Q – How do you work with a producer on a commissioned project? Do you act as an executive producer?

Simon – Sometimes. The best situation for me is that I get the program made by a great director with a great exec producer so I don't have to do very much. The less I have to do on the program the more time I can spend thinking about the future and look for other programs that need more help. I always am happy when someone does their job very well and I always want to work with those people again. I'm less inclined to work with people who make my job more difficult. So someone who really believes in what they're doing and is very passionate and committed is always going to get work because they build up trust with the broadcaster.

Q – How long does the process take once the project has been given the greenlight?

Simon – It depends on the story. We can go into production right away or we can delay it by several weeks in order to get the right talent.

Q – What kind of formats do you shoot on these days?

Simon – Mostly Digibeta and Sony DSRs and some DV. Some people shoot HD. Not much film anymore unless it's for a particular effect. Ultimately, it's the story that excites me, not what it's shot on.

Q – If you find a feature length doc that has commercial appeal, would you ever go theatrical with it?

Simon – It's up to the people that made it. That's fine. I'm happy for that to happen.

Q – If you commission a project, do you have final cut?

Simon – Yes, I have final approval.

Q – One of your programs, Jamie's School Dinners, created a change in UK public policy for school dinners - was that unexpected?

Channel 4 Documentary Film Foundation

Maxyne Franklin

Q – What is the Channel Four Documentary Film Foundation?

Maxyne – We're a fund that has £500,000 a year to give to filmmakers whose projects fall outside the TV system and would otherwise not get funding. The fund is open to British directors and directors based in Britain. Last year we funded a Chinese director based in Britain and a British director who lives in Shanghai. It's the director who must apply and whom we fund with a grant based on the money needed to complete their project. Once funded we offer mentorship and advice but the filmmaker retains full editorial control. We also work with the filmmaker once the film is completed to ensure a successful festival, press and distribution strategy. We have an additional £100,000 a year to ensure that the films that are made can make an international impact.

Q – How much can you provide as funds for documentary filmmakers and do you ask for anything in return?

Maxyne – In our first year of operation we gave away £350,000 to around 16 filmmakers. The grants varied from £5,000 towards a short - to £50,000 completion money on a feature. We also help filmmakers apply for other grants. Channel 4 have a £1 option on the TV rights of the films we give grants to but there is a generous festival/theatrical/DVD window. If Channel 4 pass on their option then all the rights revert to the filmmaker. The foundation takes no rights in the film at all, we just want our logo on it.

Q – How does your first look deal with Channel Four help documentary filmmakers who receive money from the fund?

Maxyne – We have a check box on our application form to see whether an idea has been pitched to TV and been rejected before coming to us. If that box in not ticked and we think that TV could potentially pick it up, we put the filmmaker in touch with commissioning editors at C4 and other places. We are looking to fund films that would not be funded within the system but also hoping that by making them an independent success, by getting them into major festivals etc we can make them ultimately more appealing to Channel 4. A film like *Super Size Me* would not have been commissioned as a feature, but because of its success it has been shown in primetime more often than other documentaries.

Q – What lengths of docs will you look at?

Maxyne – Everything! And at every stage too – development, production or completion.

Q – What are you looking for in a proposal?

Maxyne – We're looking for directors who are passionate and determined to make their film even though it's going to be very tough to do it independently.

Q – What is BRITDOC, when is it and how will it benefit a documentary filmmaker?

Maxyne – It's Britain's first major international feature documentary event and we have a lot of amazing people who come from the US and Europe. We have 12 British feature documentaries in competition, 12 International ones, an International Pitching forum hosted this year by Morgan Spurlock in front of funders from HBO, Discovery, Sundance, The Ford Foundation etc. Plus a great line up of masterclasses on financing, editing, archive and interviews with master filmmakers and more. Info on the fund and festival can be found at www.britdoc.org.

Simon – There was always an intention to make waves. I think the response was more than expected, but upon reflection was entirely justifiable given the quality of those programs. I think that changing policy and attracting attention to things that aren't being spoken about is a key Channel 4 mandate. In any given week, there's always something in the schedule that's trying to encourage people to look at the world in a different way. It's a big thing for us.

Q – Have you noticed any change in the style of documentaries in the last few years?

Simon – I think in the cinema there's more authorship and we could do with more of that on TV. I think that the technology has gotten more compact and people are using it to push their way into situations that they previously weren't in. I admire stuff like *Capturing The Friedmans* for its ability to make you feel like you were present in something that was unique. I think

Shooting People

Q - What is Shooting People and how does it benefit documentary filmmakers?

Jess - We're a smart community network that links together filmmakers so they can share what they know and get what they need for their production. We have 20,000 members in the UK and another 10,000 in New York and we have just launched in Los Angeles and San Francisco. We are an independent organization, which runs on a subscription fee but new members can take a free trial first. Our aim is to help our members make films faster, easier, cheaper and better and then help them get them seen. We send out a daily Documentary email bulletin to over 6,000 subscribers which contains news and postings from other members. So if you're looking for collaborators in your area, a recommendation for a good place to get transcripts, want to tell people your documentary is on somewhere or want to ask for help with a technical problem – we're your solution. If your film is really good, when it's finished then we do a big interview with you for the site.

We also have a book called *Get Your Documentary Funded and Distributed* (at bottom left) written by me and our documentary editor Melissa McCarthy which is a comprehensive pull together of UK and international options. The final way we help documentary filmmakers is through the Shooting People calendar (www.shootingpeople.org/calendar) which aims to be a comprehensive listing of all small independent film events, talks and screenings – the really interesting stuff that more mainstream listings usually miss. You can filter the events by documentary and get email reminders for those that interest you. It's a great place to advertise any screenings of your film.

Q - Shooting People in the US, focuses more on documentary filmmakers who live in New York, can you benefit filmmakers elsewhere in America?

Jess - We launched in New York much later than in the UK but we've grown more quickly there. The current NY Shooters team, also happen to be documentarians so the coverage of NY doc scene is very good and Morgan Spurlock is one of our patrons there. The US is too large for us to run a single service that covers the whole place like in the UK but we have now launched a West Coast branch in Los Angeles and San Francisco. American documentary filmmakers in other parts of the US will find many aspects of what we do – the discussions, interviews and Q&As very helpful but they'll still need to find other ways to find a sound recordist in their town.

documentary unlike any other medium is unique in its ability to take you into places that are real. It's sort of the Holy Grail of storytelling. It's like waking up one morning and finding out that *Jack and the Beanstalk* really happened. That's what documentary means to me.

Q – What are the common mistakes that you experience with documentary filmmakers?

Simon – The biggest mistake is not pushing hard enough and not asking the tough questions. People say to me that if they had asked certain questions they would've lost the access and that's the point when you know that your film is never going to be as good as it could have been. Getting hung up on the format, the HD or the DV and all of that rather than worrying about the story is another mistake.

Q – What advice would you give a documentary filmmaker?

Simon – Ask yourself who is going to watch the film that you're going to make. Get friends and family to be tough with you about if what you're proposing is going to be of value to people. And don't get too hung up if people express distaste for one particular thing. I know it sounds like a cliché, but you have to remain confident that if you want to tell stories about the way people live and work and how they are you have to be prepared to drop some and tell others. So having a range of projects is important. Also, watch TV. Sometimes people come in and they say they aren't interested in TV and I think why should I give you any money? I make TV and I think it takes an extra level of skill to make something in an environment where people have a remote control, a fridge, a games room, a Nintendo, a DVD player – in the cinema you have paid your money and you sit and get to the end of it. TV is not like that so some filmmakers have to drop this attitude that cinema docs are a higher art form. In some ways it's a lesser art form. The best way to describe it is that it's a different art form. I think taking time to think about how these two mediums are different and overlap in terms of speaking to the world is essential.

UK & Northern Ireland Useful Doc Funding Resources

UK Film Council
New Cinema Fund is open to documentaries.
The UK Film Council also invests in film through the Regional Screen Agencies around the country, which support filmmakers based in their area (EM. Media, Film London, Northern Film and Media, North West Vision, Screen East, Screen South, Screen West Midlands, South West Screen, Northern Ireland Film and Television Commission, Wales Screen Commission and Scottish Screen.) Check out the UK Film Council's website for the area that applies to you. ***www.ukfilmcouncil.org.uk/***

UK Film Council International Sales Support Scheme
www.ukfilmcouncil.org.uk/filmmaking/funding/ifss/

The British Council - www.britishcouncil.org

CBA-DFID Broadcast Media Scheme
2 funds available: DFID Programme Development Fund and DFID Travel Bursary Fund - ***www.cba.org.uk***

Foundations:
The Princes' Trust
The Business Programme offers funding and support for 18-30 year olds to aid them in starting up their own businesses. Group Awards are also available to help groups of young people who want to help their communities. ***www.princes-trust.co.uk***

UnLtd. Charity
Supports social entrepreneurs - people who have the ideas and the commitment to make a difference in their communities - by providing a complete package of funding and support, to help these individuals start up and run projects that deliver social benefit.
www.unltd.org.uk

The Jerwood Charity
Funds across the visual and performing arts, film, literature, conservation and other areas of human endeavour, to find ways of supporting and nurturing talented artists in the early stages of their careers. ***www.jerwood.org***

The Wellcome Trust
Funds medical, social, cultural and scientific research that improves human and animal health. ***www.wellcome.ac.uk***

The Winston Churchill Memorial Trust
The Fellowships enable men and women from all walks of life to acquire knowledge and experience abroad. In the process, they gain a better understanding of the lives and different cultures of people overseas and, on their return, their effectiveness at work and their contribution to the community is enhanced greatly.
www.wcmt.org.uk

The Channel 4 British Documentary Film Foundation
Provides development money and completion funding as well as another fund, BRITDOCART which is supported by the Institute of Contemporary Arts and Arts Council England. The fund is aimed at established artists interested in making documentaries.
www.britdoc.org

NESTA
The National Endowment for Science, Technology and the Arts
www.nesta.org.uk

Lottery Funding:
The National Lottery has transformed the landscape for audiences and artists, injecting around £2 billion into the arts. Grants can be accessed through the various Arts Councils around the UK and Northern Ireland:

Arts Council of England - www.artscouncil.org.uk

Scottish Arts Council - www.scottisharts.org.uk

Arts Council of Northern Ireland - www.artscouncil-ni.org

Northern Ireland Film and Television Commission
www.niftc.co.uk

Arts Council of Wales - www.artswales.org.uk

Sgrin Cymru Wales - www.sgrin.co.uk

Heritage Lottery Fund - www.hlf.org.uk

Awards For All - www.awardsforall.org.uk

Isle of Man Film Commission
www.gov.im/dti/iomfilm

Additional Documentary Resources in Scotland:
The Scottish Documentary Institute
www.scottishdocinstitute.com

Glasgow Film Office: www.glasgowfilm.org.uk

UK online Documentary communities:
www.shootingpeople.org
www.dfglondon.com
www.docspace.org.uk
www.dochouse.org
www.britfilms.com

For more ideas/resources for Fundraising in the UK visit www.fundraising.co.uk. www.trustfunding.org.uk or www.grantsforindividuals.org.uk

BBC STORYVILLE-UK

Q – What is Storyville?

Jo – Storyville is a strand of documentary for the BBC that focuses on international stories with distinct editorial voices. We show forty or so films each year which are created by means of shifting partnerships linking the BBC with European, North American, Asian and African broadcasters and financing bodies. We generally don't contribute more than 30% of the budget to any one film, but nor do we just buy films off the shelf at some great 'documentary deli.' When we take on a project, we will help to raise all the necessary financing. We also invest in films for theatrical distribution as we don't think of documentaries as belonging solely to TV.

Q – What are you looking for in a Storyville film and is there a particular style to a Storyville film?

Jo – We look for narrative and ambition and no we don't have any particular style. Our films are enormously diverse. We tend to avoid subject areas that are well covered by other areas of the BBC, like History and Science. Ratings don't realy matter to us. We prefer original work and ratings do not drive the choice of project.

Q – How do filmmakers pitch their ideas to Storyville and what makes it stand out?

Jo – We like to receive a one page outline and a short selection of shot and edited material, plus some background information on the filmmaking team. In total the proposal should be no more than 2 pages. We're looking for a short proposal that tells you what's going to be in the film. Background information to subjects/places etc. is always useful, but essentially we want to know what story the film is going to tell. And we always like to receive a taster tape, especially with observation films, that give an idea of look, tone, characters, pacing etc.

Q – Do you have to be British or do you welcome proposals worldwide?

Jo – No, you don't have to be British. We work with filmmakers globally. And we quite often work with first time and relatively inexperienced filmmakers. All our films are made in co-production with other broadcasters and finance bodies.

Q – Would you advise a new filmmaker to work with an experienced producer or one you've worked with before?

Jo – I think it depends on the nature of the project, the individuals concerned and their particular experience and the complexity of the co-production. For instance, we might advise a relatively new filmmaker who hasn't worked outside of their domestic market before to team up with a producer who is more experienced internationally.

Q – How long is the process of putting together finance for a film once it's got the greenlight?

Jo – I'd estimate an average of somewhere between 6 months and a year. However, sometimes it can be much longer, depending on the project.

Q – With a co-production, does the filmmaker retain any control over his or her film?

UK Tax Relief

Tax Relief is provided directly to a Film Production Company (FPC) and is not available to those whose involvement in filmmaking is restricted to providing finance; It's also available to an FPC making culturally British films, intended to be shown in cinemas, where at least 25% of the total qualifying production expenditure is incurred on filming activities which take place within the UK - irrespective of the nationality of the persons carrying out the activity.
For films that cost up to £20 million, the FCP will be able to claim an enhanced deduction of 100% with a payable cash element of 25% of UK qualifying film production expenditure. For films that cost over £20 million, the FPC will be able to claim an enhanced deduction of 80% with a payable cash element of 20% of UK qualifying film production expenditure. Tax relief is available on qualifying UK production expenditure up to a maximum of 80% of total qualifying costs.
For more information, check out the following websites:
HM Revenue and Customs at www.hmrc.gov.uk/films/
UK Film Council at www.ukfilmcouncil.org.uk/filmmaking/filmingUK/taxreliefbritfilms/
The DCMS at www.culture.gov.uk

Jo – Again, each deal is different – and the deals can be different in each territory a film is sold in depending on the level of investment. And I'd always recommend any production with three or more investors to keep a re-versioning contingency in their budget. If you've been funded by a wide range of organizations, you may find that they have very different audiences and needs so require slightly different versions. This is becoming more and more the case, but shouldn't prove to be a problem if it has been planned for within the budget and the production schedule. It's obvious to say, but always check the contract at the planning stage for deliverables for each investor. Broadcasters especially often require specific running times and formats, which if properly accounted for early on, should not cause problems later.

Q – How does Storyville work with the producers/filmmakers on projects?

Jo – We generally get involved during development and then again when the film is in the cutting room. The BBC is responsible for everything that it broadcasts, so we'll always retain editorial control. We wouldn't expect to get involved in the day to day decision making, but do expect to screen films at rough cut and fine cut stages, and be consulted over any scripts, translations etc for our version. We always have a BBC Exec Producer attached to each project.

Q – Do you collaborate in any way, with any of the European organizations, other than broadcasters?

Jo – Yes, we have been involved with the Discovery Campus Masterschool since it began where we tutor a project each year and sit on the selection committee. We also collaborate with numerous other non-broadcast organizations.

Q – Have you noticed a change in documentary filmmaking in the UK over the last few years?

Jo – The UK is a little different to what's been going on in North America. I think that the majority of audiences and producers still look to television for documentary so there has been less box office impact here than elsewhere.

Q – What advice would you offer documentary filmmakers?

Jo – Firstly, I'd really encourage filmmakers embarking on a co-production to read their contracts carefully and to always always call if they're in any doubt about anything – especially technical standards. I'd also advise anyone interested in Storyville to check out our website (bbc.co.uk/storyville) which has pages for all the films we've ever shown and gives a good idea of the kind of thing that works for us. We also publish a monthly newsletter which I'd recommend people sign up to if they're interested in what we do. And if any producers out there are thinking about submitting to the BBC, but don't know where to start, I'd advise them to have a look at the BBC's commissioning website - www.bbc.co.uk/commissioning. There's a wealth of information about who commissions what and how best to approach them. Finally I'd like to encourage anyone thinking of embarking on a project and that if they're determined and truly committed, then in my experience, they'll always find a way.

Thierry Garrel
Director, Documentary Unit

ARTE - EUROPE

Q – What is ARTE?

Thierry – ARTE is a cultural European channel and is a joint venture between France and Germany. It airs all over Europe in both French and German.

Q – What type of documentaries do you program?

Thierry – There are several strands of documentaries that we like to program. 40% of ARTE's schedule is documentaries. From the auteuristic, poetic approach to the 26 minute series on art collections to the feature length documentary.

Q – Does the subject matter relate to European audiences mostly?

Thierry – Not at all. The general aim of the channel is to have cross-cultural exchanges between European cultures. But as a cultural channel we're wide open to the world. We don't have to be French or German. And the filmmakers don't have to be only from those countries, either. One third of them are French. One third are German. And the other third would be from the rest of the world. But we have no quotas – that's just how it works out.

Q – What type of documentaries are you not interested in?

Thierry – Animals. Discoveries. Travel shows. Also we're not interested in plain reportage.

Q – Do most French documentaries come through public TV?

Thierry – Yes, most documentaries come through the public channels.

Q – What is the independent documentary industry like in France?

Thierry – There are more independent producers and directors in France these days. And their separate companies are working together as opposed to the States where most of the companies are doing both directing and producing. This is very specific as it creates a dialogue between creative people on one side and producers on the other side. There is a very rich network of companies dealing with documentaries.

Q – Do you fully fund your documentaries?

Thierry – No. We usually give between 40%-50%. We usually do co-producing and co-financing. We have no in-house production facilities. The rest of the budget would be for example 20% through the Center of Cinema, another 20% with some other broadcaster or institution like a museum. And then maybe the last 10% comes from presales or DVD exploitation.

Q – Do ratings come into play with what you decide to program?

Thierry – Yes. As a public channel we have figures to achieve on a yearly basis. And the ratings we have to achieve are different depending on each slot. For example, we have two prime time slots for documentaries one with history and the other with human sciences and archeology. On these slots, we have clear aims to achieve. But with the others, we try to combine the creativity on one hand and the need to build an audience on the other.

Q – Can new documentary filmmakers come to you with ideas?

Thierry – Yes. Every year we work with young and new filmmakers. It's very important for a public channel to take care of what tomorrow will be.

Q – How do filmmakers pitch ARTE?

Thierry – Usually through a producer. The first stage would be receiving a written project. I receive about 1,500 a year and we receive them all year long. When we find the ones we like, we may screen a filmmaker's previous work or have a special meeting with them to discuss the project. We don't have a formal pitch process.

Q – What makes a proposal stand out to you?

Thierry – Showing that there is a real strategy of how to turn an idea into a story. And a reason why the director would be committed to the film. Also, I like to see an explanation on how the directing itself would go. The author's point of view is very important to us. We're not interested in a general motive on how to make a documentary. Each project should invent its own creative way of telling things.

Q – How do you define documentaries and their role in society?

Thierry – The shortest way to share an experience about the human condition. That's what interests us. Not only the commitment of the author on this aspect of life, but that he is trying to share this experience through filmic language – which is wider than words.

Q – How do documentaries do with theatrical distribution?

Thierry – Some films are doing very well. This has a lot to do with the audience. I think ARTE has a lot to do with recreating an audience for documentaries. They almost disappeared from public TV at the beginning of the 1990's. But in the late 1990's and the last five years, there have been more documentaries in theatrical release. And many of them came from public TV. And now there are at least two or three films that get audiences of over 200,000 people in the cinema. *Darwin's Nightmare*, for example. And five or six that get 40,000-50,000 viewers, which is still very important even compared to the fiction films. But it's still not enough to build an economy for theatrical documentary films. The most ambitious are still produced through TV.

Q – What are the common mistakes that you see documentary filmmakers make?

Thierry – Some filmmakers don't seem to understand why it's important to have a dialogue with a producer. Some filmmakers believe they must express their sensibilities without other people. But I feel that they need to exchange ideas with producers and broadcasters in order to make the best films. On one hand, we believe in a TV of auteurs and on the other hand, the auteurs don't know what TV is.

Q – What advice would you give a new documentary filmmaker?

Thierry – To be strong and to be stronger again. You aren't going to rich, so your commitments to your film and other human beings needs to be firmly attached in your hearts.

TV-2 DENMARK

Q – What kind of documentaries are you looking for to program for TV-2?

Mette – We are always looking for strong narratives in most genres. We have weekly crime, current affairs and human-interest slots. In addition to this we find space in the plan for many one off prime time human-interest stories. Our feature length slot HOT DOKS runs 10 times a year. We're looking for clever, insightful stories to reach a big audience. We're not looking for history and art shows.

Q – As a broadcaster, do ratings come into play on the choice of documentary?

Mette – It's a balance, but we transmit 500-600 titles a year, so some ensure big ratings and some make sure we reflect the interest and trends of society and knowledge of what is happening in the world.

Q – How do filmmakers pitch their ideas to you?

Mette – One page is fine as the first contact, including track record and other partners involved. We welcome proposals from Denmark and worldwide. Sometimes I take proposals from new filmmakers, but they must have something they've shot behind them. Sometimes I'd suggest for a new filmmaker to team up with a more experienced producer or someone we've worked with before, but it really depends on the story and the investment etc.

Q – Do you fully fund productions and/or do you work with certain partners as a co-production?

Mette – We fully fund most Danish production and co-produce with anybody from anywhere in the world if they have a great story. In general, the filmmaker doesn't ever retain editorial control and they'll always have to please at least the big investors/co-producers/broadcasters. As an executive producer, sometimes I have final cut.

Q – How long is the process of putting together finance for a film once it's got the greenlight?

Mette – If we fully finance, it can happen very quickly. If I help getting the finance in place, it's difficult to say but it can take from one month to one year. Some broadcasters take several months just to make the contract even though the project has been editorially agreed to.

Q – Have you noticed a change in the style/form of documentary filmmaking in Denmark and Europe over the last few years?

Mette – The change has perhaps gone from more personal stories to more political journalistic films such as *Super Size Me* and Michael Moore's films etc. The downside is that everybody wants to make feature length films and not all stories and filmmakers are good enough for this.

Q – What common mistakes have you noticed with European documentary filmmakers?

Mette – I think European filmmakers should invest more time finding the right stories as they do around the world where filmmakers are not so spoiled.

Q – What advice would you give a documentary filmmaker?

Mette – Be brave and trust the instinct, research the market, know who you contact as partner. Be brave enough to say no, if the editorial style of a broadcaster does not fit your style.

European Broadcasters

Belgium
TV1
www.een.be/televisie1
Kanaal 2
www.kanaaltwee.be

Czech Republic
Ceská Televize (CT1, CT2)
www.ceskatelevize.cz

Nova TV
www.nova.cz

Prima TV
www.iprima.cz

Denmark
DR1
www.dr.dk/dr1

DR2
www.dr.dk/dr2

TV2
http://tv2.dk

Finland
YLE TV1
www.yle.fi/tv1

YLE TV2
www.yle.fi/tv2

MTV3
www.mtv3.fi/

Nelonen
www.nelonen.fi

France
Canal Plus
www.canalplus.fr

France 2
www.france2.fr

France 3
www.france3.fr

ARTE
www.arte-tv.com

TF1
www.tf1.fr

TV5
www.france5.fr

Germany
ARD
www.ard.de

ZDF
www.zdf.de

ARTE
www.arte-tv.com

Spiegel TV
www.spiegel.de/sptv

Greece
Alpha TV
www.alphatv.gr

ERT
www.ert.gr

Hungary
ATV
www.atv.hu

HIRTV
www.hirtv.hu

TV2
www.tv2.hu

Ireland
RTE
www.rte.ie

Italy
RAI
http://rai.it/

Mediaset
www.mediaset.it

Luxembourg
RTL
www.rtl.lu

The Netherlands
Omroep (NED-1, NED-2, NED-3)
http://portal.omroep.nl

AVRO
http://central.avro.nl

KRO
www.kro.nl

TROS
www.tros.nl

VARA
www.vara.nl

VPRO
www.vpro.nl

Norway
NRK-1
www.nrk.no/nrk1

NRK-2
www.nrk.no/nrk2

TV2
http://pub.tv2.no/TV2

Poland
TVP-1, TVP-2, TV-3
Regionalna
http://ww6.tvp.pl/2.dzialy

Polsat
www.polsat.com.pl

Telewizja Puls
www.pulstv.pl

TV4
www.tv4.pl

TVN
www.tvn.pl

Portugal
RTP-1, A2
http://programas.rtp.pt/EPG/epg-dia.php

SIC
http://sic.sapo.pt

TVI
http://www.tvi.iol.pt/home.php

Romania
TVR-1, TVR-2
www.tvr.ro

Antena
www.antena1.ro

Prima TV
www.primatv.ro

ProTV
www.protv.ro

Russian Federation
1TV
www.1tv.ru

Kultura Telekanal
www.tvkultura.ru

Telekanal Rossia
www.rutv.ru

Spain
TVE
www.rtve.es

Antena 3
www.antena3tv.com

Cuarto
www.cuarto.com

Telecinco
www.telecinco.es

Sweden
SVT-1, SVT-2
http://svt.se

TV4
www.tv4.se

Switzerland
SF1
www.sf.tv

TSI-1
www.rtsi.ch/prog/rtsi/welcome.cfm

TSR1
www.tsr.ch

UK
BBC
www.bbc.co.uk/commissioning
www.bbc.co.uk/storyville

Channel 4
www.4producers.co.uk

ITV
www.itv.com

Sky
www.sky.com

Other:
Discovery Network Europe
www.discovery.europe.com

The History Channel/The Biography Channel UK
www.thehistorychannel.co.uk

FINNISH FILM FOUNDATION

Q – How can the Finnish Film Foundation help documentary filmmakers?

Miia – We offer scriptwriting grants for individual filmmakers, and development support and production support for producers. The maximum grant you can receive for the screenwriting is 8,500 Euros. That's eligible for filmmakers only. The development and production support grants are for registered companies only and Production support may be granted or not, regardless of whether the project has received previous funding from the Foundation. We also support the producers' efforts to gain international financing by helping to pitch the project internationally. The Foundation makes a production consultant available to the producer and they're available for consultation regarding any aspect of production during production. The Foundation also supports the producer's efforts to reach an audience domestically and internationally, so if the film is released for theatrical distribution, the producer can apply for marketing support and distribution support. With international distribution, a grant from the Foundation may pay for a film print or other formats. Travel support is also available for the production team, to allow them to accompany their film to festivals for which it has been accepted.

Q – Do you have to be Finnish to access the foundation?

Miia – You don't have to be a Finnish citizen to have access to our grants. A filmmaker living and working in Finland qualifies. The production company does not need to be registered in Finland, but it has to own the rights of the film in Finland. There are no requirements as to the subject of the film.

Q – Do you work with co-productions?

Miia – We participate in about two or three documentary co-productions yearly. Support may be granted provided that at least one of the key artistic members of the team is Finnish and that the film has a television distribution agreement in Finland and it must be the Finnish co-producer who presents the project to the Foundation.

Q – What type of documentary films are you looking to help?

Miia – My aim as a production consultant is to support creative documentaries with a strong artistic vision as to the subject matter and cinematic expression. We're also looking to encourage a diversity of voices in documentary filmmaking.

Q – What are you looking for in a proposal?

Miia – Clarity in the way an idea is presented and in the way the filmmaker intends to turn her idea into a film. It's alright for me that the end result is somewhat hazy at the application stage as long as the filmmaker is genuinely alert for the possibility of a new turn of events and does not necessarily stick to the script if the film takes her elsewhere.

Q – Can a filmmaker come to you with works-in progress for finishing funds?

Miia – Yes, we may grant production support for films before they are completed.

Q – Is a new filmmaker with no experience behind them, likely to receive a grant?

Miia – It's important to give the new generation of documentary filmmakers opportunities to express themselves and their outlook on life and of course it's more beneficial for them to work with more experienced producers so that good ideas are not wasted because of incompetence.

Q – Must the filmmaker already have a percentage of the money in place?

Miia – No, but the producer needs to have a television distribution deal for the film.

Q – What is the state of the documentary filmmaking scene in Finland and Scandinavia compared with the rest of the world?

Miia – Financially speaking, things are not as bad in Finland as in many other countries. Luckily there are still a few good slots reserved for creative documentaries. In addition to us here at the Finnish Film Foundation, there are other sources of public funding, like the Promotion Center for Audiovisual Culture or AVEK. Over the past five years a few Finnish documentaries have been released for theatrical distribution and it seems that they have found an audience, although still a rather small one.

Q – If you receive a grant by the Finnish Film Foundation does that help to receive a broadcast deal with the Finnish broadcasting company YLE?

Miia – A grant from the Finnish Film Foundation may still be considerd as an important signal and can therefore make negotiating with YLE easier. YLE makes its decisions independently from the Foundation, however.

GUERILLA FILM MAKER SAYS!

Helpful Scandinavian Websites

Arctic
Barents Euro Arctic Film Commission
www.barentsinfo.org

Finland
Finnish Film Foundation
www.ses.fi

Promotion Center for Audiovisual Culture (AVEK)
www.kopiosto.fi

Iceland
Icelandic Film Fund
www.iff.is

Association of Icelandic Producers
www.producers.is

Norway
Norwegian Film Institute
www.nfi.no

Norwegian Film and Tv Producers Association
www.produsentforeningen.no

Norwegian Film Commission
www.norwegian-film.com.org

The North Norwegian Film Centre
www.nnfs.no

Sweden
Swedish Film Institute
www.sfi.se

Oresond Film Commission
www.oresundfilm.com

Michael Auret
CEO, Festival Director

SITHENGI AFRICA

Q – What is Sithengi and when is it?

Michael – Sithengi is a not-for-profit organization established in 1995 to promote and develop the production of, and trade in African film and television projects and products. It accomplishes this through the hosting of two events, the Sithengi Film and TV Market established in 1996 and the Cape Town World Cinema Festival established in 2002. It is also engaged with training of producers throughout the year in Zimbabwe, Nigeria, Kenya, Tanzania and South Africa during its co-production forums, which are held in the different countries. Sithengi also manages the HIVOS/Sithengi Film Fund under which we make awards to documentary filmmakers for the production of their documentaries. Sithengi operates year round but the events usually occur in November.

Q – How can Sithengi help documentary filmmakers in Africa and/or around the world?

Michael – It can help in a variety of ways. Firstly, by showing documentary films in the Cape Town World Cinema Festival and having an award for Best Documentary at the awards ceremony. Secondly, filmmakers trying to sell documentaries can place them in the Product Library of the Product Market where buyers can watch them. And finally we host a Documentary Co-production Forum as part of the Sithengi Market and we invite Commissioning Editors from all over the world to listen to documentary pitches from filmmakers over two days.

Q – What networking events are at Sithengi for filmmakers?

Michael – Generally all delegates and members of Sithengi can attend all the parties for free although some are members only. The parties and networking events are too many to mention but basically there is usually a lunch and evening function throughout the 4 days of the market and there are evening functions throughout the 10 days of the festival. As a paid up delegate or member you can have access to everything, including all seminars, workshops etc. The co-production forums are only open to members.

Q – How important is networking at a market?

Michael – The primary importance of a market is the networking exposure that you gain at the market and we normally find that a lot of business is done subsequent to the market through networking contacts made at the market.

Q – What is the Sithengi Talent Campus?

Michael – The Talent Campus provides 10 days of masterclasses from visiting directors, producers, distributors, sales agents etc. who are out here for the festival. The masterclasses are given to about 60 people who apply and submit a piece of their work to get in. It is hosted in conjunction with the Berlin Film Festival.

Q – Can documentary filmmakers screen their films at the market?

Michael - Filmmakers can have Market screenings which cost R 2000 ($330) and they can have their films in the Product

Library which is free for members but costs R250 ($40) for delegates. The 2005 rate for members is R1750 ($290) and delegates R1200 ($200).

Q – What is the state of documentary filmmaking in Africa?

Michael – Documentaries are a main stay of the South African industry in that now that there's a regular slot for local documentaries on SABC and we're beginning to see many new directors making documentaries for television. There are already a number of well-known directors like Khalo Matabane, Dumisani Phakati, Rehad Desai and Craig and Damon Foster who have had their work shown all over the world at international festivals.There are many festivals catering to documentary including The Encounters Documentary Festival, the Three Continents Festival and the Wildtalk Festival. There's a very lucrative and successful wildlife documentary community in South Africa. Outside of South Africa, filmmakers suffer from a lack of funding to make documentaries and also a lack of commissioning and buying of local programs by local broadcasters. Therefore there are very few documentaries coming out from the rest of Africa and most of them are made with some social message and are funded by donors.

Q – Are there any particular African countries that are faring better than others towards documentaries?

Michael – As far as I know only South Africa has significant documentary production and has documentaries that you would find at the international documentary festivals like IDFA and Hot Docs.

Q – Are there many government-funding schemes or grant organizations within Africa that documentary filmmakers can apply to?

Michael – In South Africa filmmakers can apply to the National Film and Video Foundation. All Africans can apply to the Jan Vrijman Fund attached to IDFA, the Soros Documentary Fund, which is run through Sundance and Southern Africans can apply to the HIVOS/Sithengi film fund. Other than this, all donors in Africa are open to funding documentaries if they communicate the right message. As far as I know all the doc funds cover all genres but obviously donor

GUERILLA FILM MAKER SAYS!

Traveling In Underdeveloped Countries

1. Find out about the appropriate clothing requirements of the country you're visiting, i.e. do women have to cover up, wear long dresses, long sleeved arms etc.?

2. If visiting hot countries, pack cheap clothes that can be left behind when you leave.

3. Learn the customs of the country you're visiting so you don't do something to offend anyone when you greet them, i.e. in West Africa when you shake hands with someone, hold your right forearm with your left hand as a sign of respect.

4. Make sure you've checked the legal requirements for filming before you visit the country.

5. Get all your shots that are required before you go, i.e. malaria tablets etc.

6. Take a cell phone that works internationally and double check that it covers that particular country.

7. Have on you at all times, a list of contacts that could help you if any problems arise, depending on your subject matter and where you're going, i.e the number for the nearest U.S. Embassy, the head of the organization that corresponds with your subject matter and the local peace corps workers etc.

8. If your project is charitable, you may be able to request several months in advance a complementary high clearance rental car from rental companies such as Avis.

9. Pack mosquito spray/coils/nets, First Aid kit including Pepto Bismol, water tablets and candy.

10. Take a quick course in the language of the country you're visiting and a basic first aid course.

11. Cash. Take bills large and small. Large for better exchange rates and small for facilitating an easier stay.

12. Make sure you have all your official documents on you including letters of any high up officials in that particular country.

Helpful African Websites

Abuja International Film and Video Festival
www.nffo.org

Africa Film and TV Directory
www.africafilmtv.com

African Film Commission (USA)
www.africanfilmcommission.org

Cape Tourism
www.capeinfo.com

Cape Town Film Commission
www.capefilmcommission.co.za

Durban Film Office
www.durbanfilmoffice.com

FESPACO
www.fespaco.bf

Film Resource Unit
www.fru.co.za

Filmmaker South Africa Resource
http://filmmaker.co.za

French Institute
www.ifas.org.za

Gauteng Film Office
www.gfo.co.za

Kenya Film Production Department
254-20-650120
fpd@skyweb.co.ke

Tangier Film (Morocco)
www.tangierfilm.com

Namibian Film Commission
264 61 256051/3
nfc@mib.gov.na

National Arts Council
www.nfvf.co.za

Nigerian Film Corp
Tel: 73 463519

Pan African Arts Organization
www.panafricanarts.org.dpaff.htm

Screen Africa Magazine
www.screenafrica.com

Sithengi Film & TV Market
www.sithengi.co.za

Cape Town World Cinema Festival
www.sithengi.co.za

HIVOS/Sithengi Film Fund
www.sithengi.co.za

South African Film Web
www.safilmweb.com

South African International Documentary Festival
www.encounters.co.za

South Africa Development Fund
www.southafrica-newyork.net/sadf.htm

South African National Film and Video Foundation
www.nfvf.co.za

Southern Africa Communications for Development
www.sacod.org.za

SABC
www.sabc.co.za

Zanzibar Film Festival
www.ziff.or.tz

Zimbabwe
Ministry of Information
Tel: 4 703891

funds are message dependent.

Q – Since the end of Apartheid, has there been a big difference in documentary filmmaking in South Africa?

Michael – Obviously there are now many more black filmmakers and also more women. There are more documentaries being made in general because of the slots opening up on SABC. Again obviously there have been and still are many documentaries focusing on Apartheid and the struggle against it and also the telling of stories previously untold.

Q – What is distribution like for documentaries in Africa?

Michael – In Africa, outside of South Africa, there is hardly any distribution – there are very few countries with cinemas and very few countries that commission or buy local documentaries and so I do not believe that there is much going on elsewhere in Africa. In South Africa we have had *Sophiatown*, *Amandla! A Revolution In Three Part Harmony, Cosmic Africa* and *Born Into Struggle* released theatrically. The majority of docs are shown on TV and only some get DVD releases, normally those that have a theatrical run.

Q – What advice would you offer a documentary filmmaker attending a market like Sithengi?

Michael – To prepare to pitch their project to the invited commissioning editors by researching the commissioning editors and their broadcasters on the net to ensure that the project fits with the remit of the broadcasters. Then to make the project as tight as possible on paper and prepare a great pitch. Then enter the co-production forum and pitch the project. If a filmmaker does not get into the forum to make a formal pitch, he or she should make contact with the commissioning editors independently and set up meetings during the market to pitch their project.

Q – What is the biggest problem or challenges facing African documentary filmmakers today?

Michael – Outside of South Africa and possibly North Africa, there are no funds to make documentaries and no broadcasters who commission documentaries or pay good rates for acquisitions. Thus there is no money to produce documentaries in Africa outside of South Africa. There's a small amount from international funds but they're usually never enough to cover the production and usually require the local broadcaster to be involved which is nearly always impossible. The lack of broadcasters showing documentaries outside of South Africa is a major challenge.

Q – What advice would you offer a new documentary filmmaker?

Michael – If they were outside South Africa I would say if you want to make a living don't try and make documentaries unless it is for the NGO (non-governmental organization) community backed by donors. But generally I would say make sure you know who you're going to sell to and what time slots they buy or commission for, in which genre and format. Then, find subjects that will allow you to get commissions or pre-sales which can be topped up with money from the funds. Don't come up with documentary ideas for the hell of it without looking at what broadcasters are looking for.

GUERILLA FILM MAKER SAYS!

Networking

Making your first doc, is about just 'doing it' with the available resources. But once you've completed it and are now attending festivals and markets all around the world, making contacts and forming new relationships is ever more important. These tips may seem a little predatory or sleazy but it's basic business in the film world!

1. Form as many contacts as possible. This can be people you do business with daily or through social events. People do favors for those that they know.

2. Get on the phone and stay on the phone. Find out the latest news about projects and the needs of production companies/ broadcasters/funders. The more in the know you are, the better game you can talk.

3. Set breakfasts, lunches and drinks and dinners with people you want to meet. Pick fun places to go so that you are associated with an upbeat, friendly feeling.

4. Research the person that you want to talk to and their company/clients and try to fit their strengths to your needs.

5. Have a plan when you talk to people. Know what you want to get out of a meeting or phone call so that the other person does not feel like you're wasting their time.

6. Use connections that you have already made to get introductions to new people. A phone call placed on your behalf can make a stranger more open to listening to you.

7. Meet other documentary filmmakers as they may be able to help you, give advice and put you in contact with other people from new organizations/foundations/production companies/networks/ distributors etc.

8. Do activities outside of work with your contacts (some of which may even become your friends), such as going to sporting events, movies and parties. It gives you shared memories and you have something to bond over.

9. Create customer loyalty by using the same rental companies over and over again. They are more likely to cut deals with people that they know personally.

10. Join organizations and documentary online communities in your own country but also overseas, for networking.

11. Be respectful to assistants. They have lousy jobs and low pay, but they are the gatekeepers to their bosses. Further, they may soon be the next person in power that can help you.

THE MIDDLE EAST

Q – What is Arab Film Distribution ?

John – In 1990, we produced the first Arab Film Festival in Seattle and after the festival, we had five 35mm prints with no forwarding destination. So the organizer at the time decided to rent them out to universities and colleges. She made deals with the filmmakers to rent the prints and that is how Arab Film Distribution started. The distribution business later evolved into selling copies on home video and DVD and, more recently, we started releasing films theatrically as well as for broadcast. Today we represent about 300 films from and about the Arab world. We focus mostly on the US and Canadian territories.

Q – Where do you find most of your films?

John – I try to go to festivals and we produce our own Seattle Arab and Iranian Film Festival (www.saiff.com). But we're such a niche player that many Arab filmmakers already know about us. We also keep a close eye on what's going on with Arab cinema. It's not like there are hundreds of films that are coming out every year.

Q – What kind of distribution deal do you offer the filmmakers?

John – We offer different percentages for TV, theatrical, home video and educational. We absorb all the marketing costs from our percentage so our deductions are low. But as far as specific percentages, it varies, but it's usually 50/50.

Q – How do Arab films fare here in the US?

John – Even though Iranian cinema has gotten some well-deserved recognition on the international film scene, Arab cinema is still probably one of the least recognized cinemas in the world. Before 9/11 there was very limited interest and knowledge about the Arab world. 9/11 galvanized a lot of people's attention and focus on the area. Every now and then a film from the Arab world breaks into more mainstream distribution, like the recent Palestinian film that was nominated for an Oscar, *Paradise Now*. I distribute Arab films because I believe in the importance of having a two-way flow of communication as opposed to just one-way from here to there. Also, the quality of films has been steadily improving.

Q – How do you find American film portrays Arab people?

John – After 9/11, people in the US were wondering why Arabs hated America. But Arabs have been wondering why Americans hate Arabs for years. When Arabs watch Hollywood movies, they're usually seeing themselves being slaughtered on the screen by well-armed white Americans. The stereotypical images that were channeled by politicians to sell the wars in Iraq and Afghanistan were the same images that Hollywood had manufactured and enforced for years. So instead of looking at the Arab world as an area inhabited by 300 million different people and the Muslim world by 1.5 billion people, we end up looking at the area only as the origin of 17 terrorists – i.e. as pure evil. The discussion of the war on terror quickly degenerated into a good-versus-evil debate that matches the simplistic Hollywood filmmaking paradigm.

Q – Have you noticed that documentaries are more in demand in the US since 9/11?

John – Documentaries are definitely more in demand nowadays. 9/11 made people realize that they're missing a good part of the informational equation. People had questions that they wanted answered and, since a lot of people don't read, documentaries became a good way to catch up on some of this missing information. The other thing is that the reality phenomenon that started on TV opened up the idea that real images could be entertaining. Having said that, I'm not as optimistic as many other people because the films that are doing well are the escapist documentaries like *Super Size Me* and *March Of The Penguins*. Films like *Fahrenheit 9/11*, I have issues with them being called documentaries. I feel a better category for them would be political film essays. *Fahrenheit 9/11* was fun to watch and really tapped into an audience that was hoping to defeat George Bush. But I was at Sundance this year and most of the documentaries that sold were of a very light nature. There was one about the New York Times' crossword puzzle. But our documentary, *Iraq In Fragments*, which won three awards at Sundance still doesn't have a solid distribution offer. Because of the sheer number of documentaries being made, broadcasting them is becoming more of a privilege; i.e. you should just be happy that your film is being shown. PBS is a case in point. You would be lucky if they pay $1,000 - $2000 to broadcast your film in any city.

Q – Do you think that has to do with the fact that it's an Arab film?

John – No. Part of it is that the Arab point of view is not the mainstream point of view. Anyone who offers it is taking a risk. US institutions, whether public or private, are very a-political and risk-averse. It's just supply and demand.

Q – Weren't your offices attacked at one point?

John – We were, a few years ago around the 9/11 anniversary. We still don't know why. We came to the office one day and found that the front window had been smashed and the floor was covered with glass.

Q – Have you experienced any prejudice with your film or your film festival?

John – Nothing major yet. But every year I wonder if this is the year that we are going to need external security for the festival. Things are certainly not going in the right direction.

Q – Do you have problems bringing in any filmmakers when you screen their films?

John – Yes. Visas are always a problem. I understand that Homeland Security needs to be proactive when looking at who and what goes in and out of the country, however, we no longer put Arab Film Distribution as the source on shipping cases because it might delay things at the borders. If you go to our website right now, you won't even find the company address online. That's the reality of the age we live in.

Q – How are documentaries generally funded in the Middle East and Northern Africa?

John – There are a lot of co-productions. Most Arab documentary filmmakers look for money outside the Arab world. European television companies often provide funds for Arab cinema. The film market is very difficult because there really isn't a reliable theatrical system for movies in the Arab world. Some countries have a very basic one, but most don't. When the satellite revolution happened in the Arab world in the late 1980s with Al Jazeera and a whole bunch of stations, there was a boom in terms of providing people with avenues to show things to people on a pan-Arab basis. It got people excited and now there are a lot of independent documentaries being made. There's a new wave of filmmaker-based shows and documentaries. But having said that, getting Al Jazeera or Al Arabiya to show your film won't be enough to recover your investment. But there are some companies that distribute documentaries on DVD in the Arab world.

Q – Is there one genre of documentary that is more popular in the Arab world?

John – There's a lot of political filmmaking, that's for sure. Politics is a primary concern and a lot of people are motivated by expressing themselves politically through film. Programs produced for TV are of the standard documentary type; talking heads, etc. A lot of the productions that are being produced by individuals, for example in Lebanon, tend to be more quirky and experimental. Traditionally, the documentaries from the Middle East have been very didactic. Nowadays we're seeing more intelligent and innovative films coming from the Middle East, films that are more accessible to Western audiences.

Q – What are you looking for when you take on a film?

John – I try to determine how well the film is going to translate to a Western audience – especially in the US, as there are limitations as to what you can show here. Production quality is number two. Also, does it have value in the educational market? Is this something that can air on TV or is it going to be completely dismissed as being propaganda by television programmers? These are some of the things I think about.

Q – What is censorship like in the Middle East?

John – Censorship in the Middle East is alive and well, especially in the traditional state-sponsored media. For example, I just got a request from the "Director of Programming and Censorship" of a major TV station to broadcast one of the films that we distribute. Those two jobs are combined for that broadcaster! Why waste money by hiring two different people? But the thing is they don't look at censorship the same way we do in the West. The primary focus of censorship there is to protect the morals of the viewer. For example, we have a film that features Muslim lesbians talking about what Islam means to them. That will be very difficult for TV stations in the Arab world to air. But Al Jazeera has opened up so many issues that were previously taboo. So from that standpoint there's less censorship. And now that you can make a film on your own, people are taking more risks. And the internet has opened the door for a lot of questioning.

Q – What are most documentaries shot on there?

John – DV or Mini DV. Unless you're dealing with the large stations then you're probably using Digi-Beta or HD. Mini-DV to DVD is a friendly road. We master the film on Beta and that is what is broadcast.

Q – How rampant is piracy in the Middle East and how does that affect your job?

GUERILLA FILM MAKER SAYS!

What To Do If Arrested Overseas

1. Stay cool! Don't get angry with the situation – always try to smile and appear friendly.

2. Ask the authorities to notify the nearest US Embassy or consulate. Under international agreements, you DO have the right to talk to an official from the US Embassy promptly. If, for whatever reason you are denied this right, be persistent and try to get someone to get in touch with them for you.

3. Once they're informed, U.S. officials should visit you and advise you of your rights according to the local laws, and help get in touch with family and friends.

4. The U.S. official will help you find legal representation, but there is little else they can do, apart from monitoring that there is no abuse and breach of international law regarding the treatment of prisoners and that if you go to trial they will monitor the case to ensure that proceedings are lawful, transparent and fair.

5. Remember, you are subject to foreign laws overseas and have no US constitutional rights. Trials are conducted in the language of that country.

6. Some under developed countries might have certain officials who will expect bribery, but remember one 'gratuity' can lead to many more, and this is dangerous territory.

7. Showing official looking documents can help but be sure not to push these in front of any anti-government 'terrorist' types.

8. BEFORE you go to a specific country to film, contact that country's local Embassy in the US or their tourist office to find information on whether they have any filming restrictions or not. Once abroad, you should also check with the nearest U.S. Embassy.

9. Also remember that certain things we take for granted are not so in foreign countries. For instance, you could be held without bail for 28 days or even more before you're brought before a judge.

10. Certain prescription drugs in the U.S. may not be considered as prescription drugs elsewhere and you could find yourself with a serious problem that carries a life sentence or a death penalty. If you're carrying medicines, ALWAYS, check with the embassies of the countries you'll be visiting before you leave the US.

John – Piracy is pretty rampant. In the US it's less of an issue, but it's still a problem. For example, the popular titles like the mass-entertainment films coming out of Egypt, those films end up being sold on the streets of Brooklyn at very low prices. I've had that happen with a film I was distributing. I gave a tape to a critic who gave it to a friend who is Egyptian who gave it to another guy. We were four-walling the film in a theater in DC while it was being sold in the street for a few bucks. That destroyed the film's theatrical potential. But most of the films I distribute tend to be on the artistic side and piracy is a lesser issue with those.

Q – What are the biggest problems facing Arab documentary filmmakers?

John – Probably funding problems that then lead to identity problems for the film. The funding comes from outside the Arab world and because of that, the films tend to cater to a Western sensibility. They tend to be much more liberal than what the audience can accept in the Arab world. Arab audiences question the validity of the films because of where these filmmakers received their funding. So the filmmaker is caught between these two worlds: the financier and the viewer. To this date there is no entity that finances films on a regular basis in the Arab world. There are some governments, like in Syria and Algeria, that have some financing, but they produce only four or five films a year.

Q – What are the big documentary filmmaking events in the Middle East?

John – There's a famous documentary festival in Alexandria, Egypt, called The Alexandria Film Festival that's been going on for years. There's one in Lebanon called Doc Days that's fairly new. And there's the Carthage Film Festival in Tunisia every other year that shows all kinds of films, including some documentaries. The Arab World Institute in Paris has a festival every other year and they show a lot of documentary films. And in the US, believe it or not, more film festivals are cropping up every year. People realize the need to have a symbolic showcase of what's happening in the Middle East. There's one in Seattle, Chicago, New York and a big one in San Francisco.

Q – What common mistakes do you see documentary filmmakers make?

John – Filmmakers tend to forget that they need high-resolution stills to promote the film. And if they do have stills, they tend to be of talking heads. Every film needs an iconic still that is going to get people to watch it. When people go to a festival and they look at a program, they only have that one image to get them interested in the film. The other thing would be that documentaries should be more innovative in terms of the way the way they approach their subjects. The standard ways of people talking to the camera and narration are okay if the subject is groundbreaking or rare, but if you have a subject like Iraq, you have to do something that hasn't been done before. It has to be fresh. Production quality still counts. Good sound and cinematography still count.

Q – What advice would you give a new documentary filmmaker?

John – Documentaries that don't challenge the viewer are already being produced and paid for with a lot of money by the History and Discovery Channel. If you want to make money, work for a satellite or cable channel. If you want to make a difference, make documentaries that challenge and question in a big way. We live in very difficult times. If you are going to spend time and money making a documentary, make it count. Don't make a film that mimics what is being shown on satellite and cable 24 hours a day.

ISRAEL & PALESTINE

Q – What is your job?

Philippa – I own and run Cinephil, which is a sales agency and we do distribution and co-productions around the world of predominantly documentaries from the Middle East. If we co-produce we help filmmakers either raise finance or put them in contact with someone who can. And then we don't vanish; we follow through till the completion of production, which is when we'll distribute the documentary around the world.

Q – Being an Israeli comapny, can you distribute to the Muslim countries easily?

Philippa – Not directly. If we want to distribute to Lebanon, Syria, etc, then we get assistance there.

Q – Do you work with Palestinian filmmakers?

Philippa – We try and do work with some Palestinian filmmakers and assist them even if we don't work with them. We try to have an open door policy to any Palestinian.

Q – Is a Palestinian film considered foreign or domestic if they come to you?

Philippa – If they're a Palestinian living in Israel, then it's domestic. If they live in the West Bank or Palestine, they're foreign. Though it doesn't matter to us when we sell it around the world – to us the filmmaker is Palestinian. It doesn't matter how their film is funded – it's a Palestinian film. If a Palestinian lives within Israel and has an Israeli passport, then they're entitled to all the funding and the privileges that we are entitled to. That means an Israeli broadcaster can finance them. If they are from Ramallah, then they aren't because they're citizens of what is or is about to be Palestine. But really, I don't sell it as an Israeli film or a Palestinian film. I sell it as a film that's relevant.

Q – What kind of films are you looking for?

Philippa – I like films that touch me that I can relate to what they're trying to say, especially if the statement isn't explicit. I like smart films, funny films and films that make me cry. Films that say something important like *Trembling Before G-d, Five Days,* which is about the disengagement, or *Badal*, Palestinian culture within Israel about arranged marriages – a brother and sister of one family marry the brother and sister of another family. According to the customs of society they are interlocked together so a divorce on one side will lead to a divorce on the other side. That's such a terrible thing! The filmmaker follows her aunt who married ten of her kids that way. Or even a film like *Watermarks.* It looks at remembrance and breaks the conception that Jews are only scholarly. Jews are also sports people – and it's women sports. The strongest swimmers in pre-Nazi Austria were Jews.

Q – What are the types of documentaries that sell well around the world?

Philippa – Current affairs - with an edge, good stories, great filmmaking, scoops. Jewish champion women swimmers in the 1930's makes everyone's eye's light up. The film started in Israel with money from the film foundation and then received backing from Israeli broadcasters. The film is a co-production with Paris based Zadig Productions who brought ARTE and the ORF on board. Then several foundations in the UK, France and the US came on board. Once the film was in the rough cut stage we introduced it to HBO and they came on board. Then we got the film into important festivals around the world. And we had theatrical distribution in the US, Canada and several other countries.

Q – Is cobbling together lots of different funders the common way documentaries are financed in Israel?

Philippa – The most common way is to get money from TV. And TV is obliged by the state regulator to put up significant funds. They have quotas that they have to meet for local filmmaking. An Israeli filmmaker can get about $50,000 from an Israeli broadcaster. Then they get money from the Film Council, which is funded by the government. So we have those two big funders and a bunch of smaller ones and then the filmmaker goes shopping. Filmmakers can also raise financing from film funds which are predominantly funded by the Israeli Film Council, which is mainly funded by the government. You can get up to $50,000 from these funds usually. So that's $100,000 to make a film and that's a reasonable amount in Israel. Palestine has some projects now to try and arrange funds like these, but at the moment they don't have the infrastructure we do. And again the Israeli funds are open to Palestinians with an Israeli identification card – not those who live in the West Bank or Gaza.

Q – What would you never do?

Philippa – I try not to take documentaries that will only play locally or only in London, Paris and Berlin. I like it when it can transcend all borders. That said, the slots for creative documentaries are often limited and sometimes docs have great topics or are too slow or hard to comprehend. These may do better in film festivals than on TV. The other way around, we may have a film that is good for TV that isn't sophisticated enough in the eyes of the festival programmers. And some do both like *No. 17*. There was a bus that was bombed on the way to Tiberius and 17 people were killed. Israel is so small that usually all bodies get identified. Well, for the first time one wasn't and they gave up after a few weeks. A filmmaker read that and thought no matter whom it is, their family needs to know their loved one was killed. So he and the producer set out to find number 17 and they did six months later. It went into a lot of film festivals and we sold it everywhere on TV, but it didn't go theatrical. That's OK, not all films have to go into the cinema.

Q – What are most films that you see shot on?

Philippa – Video. *Five Days* was shot on high-end DV cameras with great resolution. The filmmaker Yoav Shamir is someone who cares about cinematography. So although they are small cameras, not Betacam, but good cameras, we had no complaints from any of the channels. We spend a lot of money in the online session. We did have to transfer it to HD for the Sundance Film Festival. And now festivals have the option to show it on HD or Digibeta. It also depends on the subject of the film. If you need to get close with your subject, you cannot have this mega-machine. More importantly for filmmakers is to know what the technical aspects of the deliverables are. Are they going to shoot 4:3 or 16:9 anamorphic? All of this technical stuff may sound Chinese to some filmmakers, but it's crucial for delivery to broadcasters.

Q – Does it matter to you if the primary language of the film is English, Hebrew, Arabic or some other?

Philippa – It doesn't matter to me at all. Most of my films are not English speaking films. Even the US broadcasters are happy to show films that don't speak English. It's easier if they do, but I think it's terrible to force someone to speak a language they don't feel comfortable in and then it comes out so artificial.

Q – How is the documentary industry fairing in Israel these days?

Philippa – It's flourishing. There's a Forum for co-productions in Tel Aviv similar to that in Amsterdam/IDFA and Toronto/TDF that brings together filmmakers and broadcasters. Leading broadcasters from around the world attend: BBC, ITVS, Sundance Channel, VPRO/Netherlands, TV-2 Denmark and many others.

Q – Have you come across any censorship in your part of the world?

Philippa – There's an important Palestinian artist who lives here called Muhammad Bakri who made a film titled: *Jenin, Jenin* that was censored. Bakri is like the John Wayne of the Middle East and he made a film about the massacre that happened in Jenin. The film wasn't well received by the Israelis. Now he has made a film called *Since You've Been Gone*, which talks about his experiences with *Jenin* and the censorship he endured. It was a dark moment in our culture.

Q – Why was it censored?

Philippa – The government thought that he wasn't accurate about what happened in Jenin. And most Israelis believe that there was no massacre there. He was implying there was one. Finally, it was allowed to be shown in the cinematechs in Israel, who supported him all along regardless of anything.

Q – Do you or your filmmakers have problems producing and selling some of your more politically charged films?

Philippa – I haven't come across anyone who wouldn't take a film because its of a certain topic or content. I have come across people saying that they have too many films from the Middle East. There is certainly Holocaust fatigue. Also my personal understanding of the political situation is often the same as many of the Europeans I work with - which makes everything much simpler.

Q – What kind of deal can a filmmaker expect from Cinephil?

Philippa – If you come to me with an idea on a piece of paper, and if I fall for the project, the first thing I'll want to know is your wish list. I want to know your goals. Are you in for the fame and the money, or do you want to make a difference in the world with the film? One such filmmaker is Sandi Dubowski. Sandi had a dream to get the whole world to see and discuss *Trembling Before G-d*. That was the priority - and that determined the distribution strategy. Generally speaking, we work on percentage so if we don't succeed, we don't make any money. Cinephil takes less of a percentage for a development project, and more if the film is complete. This is because we get larger sums of money for projects than we do for completed films. Also, the funds for the projects are for the actual production of the films. The money for completed films is usually profits. In Europe the earlier the broadcasters join a project, the larger their contribution of funding is going to be. The idea behind this is two fold - first, the feeling is that at this stage the broadcaster will be able to influence the film, and in effect get a film which suits its needs best. Second, some broadcasters are interested in a backend in return for the larger investment - or a small section of the films equity. Sales agent rates for a completed film are the standard 70/30% split. We don't give advances or money guarantees.

Q – What would you consider a big budget documentary co-production?

Philippa – About $500,000 to $1 million.

Q – What is the theatrical distribution landscape in Israel like?

Philippa – It's an unhealthy environment where two or three companies own, distribute (and sometimes produce) the films. They own approximately 80% of the market place. This vertical integration works against the smaller films, and as a result there are very few independent distributors in Israel.

Q – How about the other Middle Eastern countries?

Philippa – Egypt has a great cinema culture. We used to get Egyptian films on TV when I was growing up when we only had one channel. But I am not sure how the cinema system works there. It's hard for us to work with Egyptians. I know that the Royal Jordanian Commission is doing their best to develop cinema there and in the region. We will work with anyone in the Middle East because we have to transcend politics.

Middle East Helpful Websites

GUERILLA FILM MAKER SAYS!

There is not a lot of infrastructure as far as commissions are concerned in the Middle East. There are many film festivals and some productuion companies, so if you end up travelling there check those out as well as sites like mandy.com.

Jordan
Royal Film Commission
www.film.jo

Iran
Assoc. of Iranian Doc Film Producers
www.iranshad.com/irandoc

Israel
Jerusalem Film Cinematheque
www.jer-cin.org.il

Doc Aviv
www.docaviv.co.il

The Israel Forum for International Documentary Co-Productions
www.copro.co.il

The New Foundation For Cinema & TV
www.nfct.org.il/

Al Jazeera
http://english.aljazeera.net

Alamanar TV
www.almanar.com.lb

Citruss
http://citruss.com

Infinitity
www.infinitytv.tv

Al Arabiya
www.alarabiya.net

Q – Are you finding that the Muslim countries are a little more open to co-productions with Israel?

Philippa – No, with the exception of Jordan. However, on a personal level things are very different - and there's much curiosity on all sides, and great friendships.

Q – The documentary, Ford Transit raised some questions at festivals because it had some actors in it. What happened there?

Philippa – The broadcasters had problems because they have programming slots that are for documentaries and they thought it wasn't one. It's a hybrid with some scripted material.

Q – What are the important film festivals and markets in the Middle East?

Philippa – In Israel, there is only one festival that's 100% documentary and that is Doc Aviv in Tel Aviv in April. Then there are two big film festivals in Jerusalem in July and one in Haifa. The Haifa Film Festival is very open to our neighbors. Films from the whole region including North Africa are shown there. The Jerusalem Film Festival has an open door for anyone, especially Palestinians. They promote human rights a lot. There's a great film festival in Beirut. I don't think there's one in Jordan. In Palestine, there will be one in Rummalah. Cairo has a big one. The North African countries have great festivals.

Q – What are the common mistakes that you see documentary filmmakers make?

Philippa – Many filmmakers don't think about the distribution of their film when they start making it. They should be asking themselves why and for whom are they making the film? Then they should gear their film in the best direction.Think about using websites and other grass roots efforts to get your film out into the world. Take the trouble to take stills - so simple, very rare! If there are no stills how are you going to promote the film when the day comes and you want to get it out into the world? Clear music rights - before you leave the editing suite - see if you can afford them. Sales agents and distributors need your assistance to succeed for you.

Q – What advice would you give a new documentary filmmakers?

Philippa – Making good documentaries requires commitment - full time, all the time every day. If you aren't truly passionate about your subject, I'd think again before diving into the adventure of making a documentary film. But, if you are, and you do make one of these wonderful films about a small town somewhere, telling a great story, with outstanding characters, unbelievable access, great photography, and moving moments – there's so much gratification on so many levels on its way. It will be you who open people's minds and hearts. It will be you who can make a difference, informing and entertaining simultaneously.

THAILAND

Q - What is the state of documentary filmmaking in Thailand?

Thunska –Thai documentary used to be about traveling, environment conservation, antiques or celebrities but nowadays they're about the history of the big guns (of the Royal Thai Air Force), environmental concern, and bitter and sorrowful lives of the poor. In 2004, a TV program was launched, *Kon-Kon-Kon (People & People)*, which told sorrowful stories of ordinary people. Also, there was *Tum-Pid-Yah-Pler (You Better Watch Out)* that presented social problems like school kids' fighting and gay prostitutes. Recently there's been a breakout of reality TV, with programs like *Academy Fantasia*, but these shows have all been designed as a brand-new form of entertainment just for businesses. However there was a really interesting documentary made in 1975, *Kum-Ma-Korn-Ying-Ha-Ra (Female Laborers of Hara)*, directed by Jon Ungphakorn, which was about a group of female laborers in Hara's jeans factory who usurped the factory because their wage was depreciated. Since then, there hasn't been anything powerful like it.

Q – How does this compare with the rest of your neighboring Southeast Asian countries?

Thunska – Documentaries in my neighboring countries have much more variety. In Cambodia, Rithee Pahn made a documentary called *The Land of Wondering Soul*, which is about laborers who set underground fiber optics cable for communication networks such as TV channels or the internet while there are still bombs buried in some areas. That country is really not yet ready for that technology because it has just recovered from war. In Singapore, there is *Moving House* by Tan Pin Pin, which tells a story of cemeteries surrendered to the government because of excessive population. This reflects a Singapore policy that seems to be able to handle any issues on the surface, but never anything deeper that will really have an affect on the people. So in these countries, documentaries are driven by the filmmaker's personal interest in certain issues, rather than doing it just for money.

Q – How are most Thai documentaries funded and what are their budgets?

Thunska – It depends on the kind of documentary. If it's a documentary for TV broadcast, or for education in organizations, the fund is either from that organization or the company or TV station will sponsor it. If not, it's often personal funding. My first feature documentary, *Voodoo Girls* (2002), was made with my own money. When it was shown in America, Modern Films contacted me and offered finance for *Happy Berry* (2004), and also some monies for my next documentary, *Futon*. But more than 80% is financed by myself and almost 15% is from Office of Contemporary Art and Culture, Ministry of Culture. It's interesting because this is the first film that the Ministry of Culture has approved for funding.

Q – Are co-productions big in Thailand?

Thunska – Not many people care to fund independent documentary. In fact I'd say, almost none.

Q – Is there a particular type of subject matter that is more successful than others in Thailand?

Thunska – Successful documentary has not yet been found in Thailand. Last year (2005), there was a documentary called *Innocent* that got theatrical runs, but the tickets were sold for charity. The film is about taking poor students from the north to the sea. It stirred up the trend of going to see this film as a benevolent activity. But whenever "documentary" is mentioned, people find it boring, rather than a film for entertainment, so they don't pay much attention.

Q – Do all docs get theatrical runs in Thailand?

Thunska – Including *Innocent*, there have been only three documentaries that have come out theatrically. One was *Crying Tiger* which is about hard lives of people from northeastern region who have to go and work in Bangkok. This film was not as successful as it should have been. It's earnings were so slight that the company never considered investing in documentary ever again.

Q – How important is the DVD market? Is piracy a big problem?

Thunska – It's a problem and also it's not. Film companies think people don't go to the cinema because of piracy. Actually no one pirates Thai films, and still Thai films have few audiences. Nowadays DVD piracy offers more variety than theatrical cinemas. Films on big screens that become copyright DVDs later are always movies for entertainment, while piracy DVDs offer more choices. So new film viewers who want to see different things like documentaries tend to prefer piracy DVDs more than the Hollywood or Thai films that are copying the Hollywood style.

Q – Are there any film organizations where people who want to shoot in Thailand can go to get advice?

Thunska – No, there aren't any organizations like that. Although, the Tourism Authority of Thailand is trying, with a commercial objective - to bring foreign movie units to Thailand. That causes a new problem. Whenever a foreign movie unit comes here - Thai crew and companies such as lights, cameras etc. would flourish, because they're offered better wages. Sometimes Thai movie units have to go on hold because everyone mobilizes to reinforce the foreign movie unit on the scene at that time.

Q – What are the important documentary events in Thailand?

Thunska – We don't have anything like that. Since documentary in Thailand is considered boring, no one pays attention and they don't feel there's a need.

Q – Does censorship appear in Thailand?

Thunska – Thailand is quite unique. We operate everything under a moral frame. This means anything that doesn't fit within our culture, would not be accepted by society. Some things that seem to be strict are actually loose, while some things that seem to be loose are strict and not allowed. For example, we have TV campaigns against women wearing spaghetti-strapped tops but they're all wearing them. We don't support prostitute legalization, but it is widely known that prostitutes populate here more than anywhere else in Asia. It affects our censorship policy. On TV, we don't use vulgarism, we don't kiss, and we don't drink or smoke. Whenever we do, there will be a mosaic screen on those alcohol bottles. Even when we put our feet on a table, it is against our gracious culture, so there will be a mosaic screen on those feet too. This also happens in cinemas. Sexual images like nudity in Thai films would be censored while it is ok in foreign films. We are highly sensitive in sexual issues more than violence. Films with gunshots, head explosions, blood splashes are not censored. They are however most watchful on sex. Once, I made a short film, *Sigh*, which has male nudity. It was shown in a short film competition in The 3rd Bangkok Film Festival. A year later, this same film was asked to screen in a Thai Film Festival in Hong Kong, but it was banned by the Thai embassy there. And another year later, *Voodoo Girls* was banned by the Bangkok International Film Festival because of nudity and vulgarism used by women in the film. They said it would build a bad image of Thai women.

Q – What does documentary filmmaking mean to you?

Thunska – For me, documentary filmmaking should be for the filmmaker's interest, rather than other reasons, and it should present the social situation beyond the concept under society obligations. It should not be for profit or popularity, but made

GUERILLA FILM MAKER SAYS!

Helpful Asian Websites

Asian Film Commission Network (AFCNet)
www.afcnet.org

Cambodia
Ministry of Culture and Fine Arts,
Cinema and Cultural Diffusion Department
Tel:: +85 5 12 619 012

China
Western Movie Group Corp.
TEL: 86-29-85528622

Changchun Film Studio
www.cyyy.com.cn

Eastern Russia
Vladivostok Film Commission
www.vladfc.ru

Fiji
Fiji Island Film Commission
www.Bulafiji.com

Hong Kong
Hong Kong Film Services Office. TELA
www.fso-tela.gov.hk

India
National Film Development Corporation – NFDC
www.nfdcindia.com

Indian Motion Pictures
www.indianmotionpictures.com

The Film and Television Producers Guild of India
www.filmtvguild.in

Indonesia
Bali Film Commission
www.balifilm.com

Japan
Japanese Film Commission
www.film-com.jp

Sapporo Film Commission
www.plaza-sapporo.or.jp/fc

Sendai Miyagi Film Commission
www.sendaimiyagi-fc.jp

Tokyo Location Box
www.seikatubunka.metro.tokyo.jp/tlb/index.html

Yokohama Film Commission
www.welcome.city.yokohama.jp/tourism

Nagoya Location Navi
www.ncvb.or.jp/location

Osaka Film Council
ww.osaka-fc.jp

Kobe Film Office
www.kobefilm.jp

Himeji Film Commision
www.city.himeji.hyogo.jp/fc

Hiroshima Film Commission
www.fc.hcvb.city.hiroshima.jp

Fukuoka Film Commision
www.fukuoka-film.com

Nagasaki Film & Media Commission
www.ngs-kenkanren.com/fc

Okinawa Film Office
filmoffice.ocvb.or.jp

Malaysia
Multimedia Development Corporation
www.mdc.com.my

North Korea
The Korean Film Export and Import Corporation
www.kcckp.net/en

South Korea
Busan Film Commission
www.bfc.or.kr

Namdo Film Commission
www.ndfc.or.kr

Seoul Film Commission
www.seoulfc.or.kr

Singapore
Singapore Film Commission
www.sfc.org.sg

Thailand
Thailand Film Office
www.thailandfilmoffice.org

Thailand Film Foundation
www.thaifilm.com

Tourism Authority Of Thailand
www.tourismthailand.org

by the genuine interest of filmmakers. For example, I'm interested in Bangkok teenagers. Most films are made to please adults, no rude words, no love in school, while teenagers in our current society are not following the old life frames. I focus on presenting state of affairs, rather than judging their behavior whether they are right or wrong.

Q – What are the common mistakes that you see documentary filmmakers make?

Thunska – Uniformity and being too strict under social obligations.

Q – What advice would you give a new documentary filmmaker?

Thunska – Thai filmmakers these days often premeditate about rewards, like how to make films that get awards or how to attract many viewers. For me, I'm interested only in what I'm interested in! You have to ask yourself about the message you want to deliver, how you're interested in that issue, rather than worry whether you will get an audience or an award or not.

GUERILLA FILM MAKER SAYS!

HD vs DV

The DV format has arguably had its day and is beginning to be replaced by HD technology as broadcasters continue to move that way. However, this does not mean that DV is not a viable format for the seriously broke new documentary maker who's ready to jump into the story before funds become available. In fact, in much of the world, DV is still a viable acquisition standard. And of course, it is very easy to get DV onto DVDs. Here are some points to bear in mind:

1. HD has 6 times more lines of resolution than DV, and therefore is MUCH sharper.

2. Hiring quality DPs are more important when shooting HD because the cameras can 'see more'. While good lighting can always help any shoot, low-end DV cameras lenses are harder to focus and the white balance capabilities are less precise. You will end up wasting time trying to get a perfect picture with a device that really cannot give you something superior.

3. If your doc is accepted into a film festival, the DV image generally falls apart when bumped up to HD for projection. HD can be very successfully projected in a large theater.

4. The cost of transferring a film from HD or DV to 35mm is about the same.

5. DV has poor audio functions (often no manual levels or poor metering), so frequently you will end up renting a DAT recorder and pay more for synchronization in post. With HD, this is not such a problem.

6. Lower end miniDV cameras don't have the ability to record continuous time code if the camera is stopped and the video reviewed. This is essential for editing because there can be errors introduced in the EDL (Edit Decision List) that may not show up until the final conform, and that by this stage, any corrections will be time consuming and probably expensive. Some DV cameras might also reset the timecode to zero when changing batteries, causing more editor nightmares. HD cameras do not have these problems.

7. Distributors know that HD24p is a good alternative to 35mm (HD24p has a shutter of 1/48" sec, which gives similar motion artifacts as shooting film).

8. The novelty of shooting DV has worn off and distributors are now more critical of quality issues.

9. DV cameras and tape stock cost significantly less to rent and buy than HD cameras and tape stock. There are also more DV cameras readily available to buy and rent, and more technical people with enough experience to help you troubleshoot when things go wrong.

10. Shooting PAL DV is MUCH better than NTSC, as it's frame rate can be converted to 24fps without having to perform an image manipulation (aside from de-interlacing if you did not shoot with a progressive camera). PAL is also higher resolution than NTSC.

11. The major advantage to DV is that for a modest investment you can set up with a camera and edit suite and complete your doc in your bedroom.

12. Due to it's lower costs, shooting on DV allows you to do longer tapes. An advantage in the right hands, and disadvantage in the wrong (as post costs can spiral).

13. Playing around with the HD camera set up menus can take some time. However, these can be preset.

14. Special HD film setup cards can be inserted into the camera to duplicate the look of film stocks.

15. Arguably, audiences do not see the difference between HD, 35mm or DV – as long as the content is gripping. If you've got that, you're as good as gold!

Elena Fortes
Ambulante

MEXICO

Q – What is the Travelling Documentary Festival, Ambulante and how can it help documentary filmmakers in Mexico?

Elena – Ambulante is a project set up by the production house, CANANA, which is headed by actors Gael García Bernal, Diego Luna, (*Y Tu Mama Tambien*) and producer Pablo Cruz. It lasts for two months beginning in February and it travels through 15 cities - Mexico City, Guadalajara, Metepec, Puebla, Monterrey, Veracruz, Cd. Juárez, Villahermosa, Tijuana, Cancún, Morelia, Oaxaca, León, Mérida and Cuernavaca - offering a selection of 19 documentaries which are each exhibited during one week in each city. Ambulante was inspired by Eugenio Polgovsky's documentary *Trópico de cancer* (Tropic of cancer) about the life of families in the desert of San Luis Potosí, who hunt wild animals and sell them on the freeway in order to survive. After watching the documentary, Gael and Diego began to question the state of documentary film in Mexico, particularly why documentaries such as *Tropic of Cancer* are rarely seen, and are limited to certain cities and art-house circuits. They came up with the idea of the traveling festival in order to confront the current encapsulation of the genre, and to allow documentaries to begin to acquire their own space in theaters, and to reclaim their value and place within Mexico's cinematographic culture. CANANA teamed up with Cinepolis which is a leading movie theater chain in Mexico, and the Morelia International Film Festival (which focuses on documentaries) which helped provide the infrastructure and support for Ambulante.

Ambulante is meant to assist primarily in the exhibition and distribution of documentaries, as well as to inspire their production. Ticket sale shares are meant to finance documentary projects, and we're planning a traveling documentary workshop to go along with the festival. Along its way, Ambulante hopes to raise debate around the films across the country, and thus serve as an important channel of expression. By bringing directors to different cities, we hope to encourage a direct dialogue between documentary makers and audiences, hoping to build a nation-wide culture for documentaries, to mobilize public opinion, and to strengthen ties with audiences at a more intimate level. Hopefully in the future, Ambulante will be able to reach the most remote places in Mexico, and extend to Central and South America.

Q – Are all the films you include from Mexico?

Elena - The majority are Mexican (12 out of 19), since we are particularly interested in motivating production and distribution of Mexican documentaries, and to begin breaking with stereotypes and misconceptions of the documentary genre in Mexico - for instance, documentaries are usually confused with instructional films, travelogues, etc. The rest of the films are from abroad. We also include the past winners within the documentary category of the Morelia International Film Festival. Most of the selected films center on social issues, although we try to make a selection that offers films that stretch the boundaries of the genre, in terms of form and content, in order to present a fairly representative spectrum of documentary.

Q – What is the documentary filmmaking scene like in Mexico?

Elena – The documentary scene is just beginning to regain ground in Mexico, though it's still far from being comparable to the one in Europe or North America. During the 60s and 70s it flourished with documentary filmmakers such as Nicolas Echevarría, Paul Leduc and Eduardo Maldonado and then slumped through the 80's and early 90s. There has been a growing interest in documentary filmmaking over the past years, particularly by the younger generations but unfortunately, this increased enthusiasm for filmmaking has not found adequate institutional support. There's no solid infrastructure or system for funding and distribution. Unlike the United States, documentary filmmakers here cannot count on an educational market. As long as this infrastructure for distribution and potential sources for funding are lacking, documentary makers will continue to face challenges in Mexico.

From a global perspective, I believe more and more people are turning to documentaries for reliable or at least alternative sources of information, given the rising controversy regarding media manipulation, and government control of information. This makes it all the more pressing to support the effort of filmmakers wishing to document the problems we are facing, and reach out to audiences who might otherwise be only exposed to the most vulnerable (to manipulation) media sources. Documentaries dealing with controversial political and social issues have recently become popular in Mexico and Latin America, as a result of the political and economic changes that we've been undergoing recently, and political scandals incited by issues related to migration, corruption, human rights violations, and the possible privatization of certain natural resources.

Q – Are there many government-funding schemes or grant organizations within Mexico that documentary filmmakers can apply to?

Elena – There are few government-funding schemes and grant organizations within Mexico that documentary filmmakers can apply to. Part of the reason for this lack of funding has to do with Mexico's cultural policies, which pay little attention to the cinematographic community. IMCINE (Mexican Institute of Cinematography) and FONCA (National Fund for Arts and Culture) offer a few, although they are not exclusively directed to documentary projects, so it's difficult to assess the specific amounts allocated to fiction and to documentaries. IMCINE, however, has very recently launched a new initiative along with Channel 22 and CAACI (Latin American Conference of Audiovisual and Cinematographic Authorities) in Mexico and Latin America (DOCTV), specifically directed to documentary projects, which offers $100,000 to selected projects and inclusion in TV programming. Some TV channels offer funding as well, such as TVUNAM C22, C11, CLIO, however they usually seek traditional documentaries, or instructional didactic films (like historical, nature, and art) rather than personal documentaries or documentaries that deal with highly controversial social and political issues.

Documentary filmmakers here in Mexico can also apply to foundations in the US and Europe, such as The MacArthur Foundation, Rockefeller, and Hubert Bals. A few of the major festivals offer funding as well (Morelia International Film Festival-FICM, Guadalajara International Film Festival-FICG, Mexico City International Film Festival-FICCO), usually through partner organizations outside of Mexico. Overall, however, there is a pressure to produce content that can be exported and exhibited internationally, and this affects the criteria for developing treatments for documentaries. Both IMCINE, FONCA, and particularly the film schools such as CCC and CUEC, are more open to experimental and personal documentary project proposals than the TV channels.

Q – What is distribution like for documentaries in Mexico?

Elena – Distribution for documentaries in Mexico is very limited, since it's considered a precarious business. There's no market infrastructure for documentaries in Mexico and Latin America, just as there's no market infrastructure for independent film in general. Distribution is limited to certain large cities, and to art house and cultural circuits. There's no educational market in which universities and schools can acquire the documentaries and distribute them within the academic circles. Only certain documentaries are transmitted on TV which are usually paid for by the same TV channel. At the commercial theater level, only those international documentaries that have been successful elsewhere which have been bought by large distributors, reach the major theaters. For instance, *March Of The Penguins*, Michael Moore's films etc. But they face severe competition from large Hollywood productions, which basically dominate the screens, particularly outside the major cities.

The life of independent films and documentaries is basically sustained by festivals within Mexico (FICM, FICG, FICCO and Voices Against Silence, a documentary festival centered on human rights). Some of the larger festivals have also begun to incorporate a market structure for independent film. There are few documentaries that have made it to the DVD market, and recently small distributors have been popping up, such as Tarantula Films, that are focusing on distributing

GUERILLA FILM MAKER SAYS!

Mexico, Central & South American Film Websites

Mexico

Instituto Mexicano de Cinematografia (IMCINE)
www.imcine.gob.mx

Comision Nacional de Filmaciones (National Film Commission)
www.conafilm.org.mx

The National Fund For Arts and Culture (FONCA)
http://fonca.conaculta.gob.mx/index.html

TV UNAM (Channel 22)
www.tvunam.unam.mx

Canal Once (Channel 11)
http://oncetv-ipn.net/index.php

TV Azteca
www.tvazteca.com

Morelia International Film Festival
www.moreliafilmfest.com

Guadalajara International Film Festival & Market
www.guadalajaracinemafest.com

Mexico City Contemporary International Film Festival
www.ficco.com.mx

Costa Rica
Costa Rica Production Services
www.costaricaproductionservices.com

Guatemala
www.visitguatemala.com

Argentina
Cine Ojo Films & Video
www.cineojo.com.ar/

Argentina Film Commission
www.filmcom.arg.ar

Mendoza Film Commission
www.filmcomm.gov.ar

Comision Argentina de Filmaciones
www.caf.gov.ar

Bolivia
Apoyo Para el Campesino Indígena del Oriente Boliviano (APCOB)
www.apcob.org.bo/videos.htm_APCOB

Producciones Nicobis
http://www.utopos.org/Cine/Produc/Nicobis.htm

Brazil
Amazon Film Commission
www.amazonasfilm.com.br

Brazil Film Commission
www.minasfilmcommission.com

Minas Gerais
www.cultura.mg.gov.br

Bureau De Cinema Do Ceara Tel:
Tel: 55-85-244-4549 or +55-85-268-3199

The International Documentary Conference @
It's All True International Documentary Festival
www.itsalltrue.com.br

Chile
ChileCine: Una Ventana al Mundo Audiovisual Chileno
www.chilecine.cl/espanol/index.php_ProChile

Planet Vivo
www.planetavivo.org

Colombia
Ministry of Culture, Film Office
www.mincultura.gov.co

Bogota Film Festival
www.bogocine.com

Peru
Chirapaq: Centro de Culturas Indias
www.chirapaq.org.pe/_Chirapaq

Uruguay
Film Services Office Uruguay
Tel: 915-7469

Venezuela
Venezuela Film Commission
www.diatriba.net/
venezuelafilmcommission

General Latin American Resources

Latin American Conference of Audiovisual and Cinematographic Authorities (CAACI)
www.cinecaaci.com

DOC TV-IB
www.lacult.org

documentaries. Also, some major theater chains have recently begun to open a space within their programming for independent film. CANANA will acquire the rights of some of the documentaries in Ambulante in order to distribute them in TV and DVD markets in Mexico.

Based on our experience, we've had a considerable turn-out along the festival, and a magnificent response from a wide variety of audiences across the country. For us, the sustainability of a documentary culture is not a question of a lack of audience for documentaries, nor of a lack of production, but rather, a question of a lack of distribution and exhibition.

Q – What is the biggest problem for documentaries in Mexico?

Elena – The biggest problem is distribution, and perhaps to a lesser degree, funding. However, given the recent technological advances, it has become relatively cheaper to make documentaries. Tin Dirdamal's documentary *De nadie*, for example, recently received the Sundance Audience Award, and required minimum funding. The same occurred with *Tropic of Cancer*. Regarding distribution, there are reasons to remain optimistic. Major theaters, independent distributors and cultural institutions are slowly shifting their attention towards documentaries.

Q – What is the biggest problem or challenges facing Mexican/Latin American documentary filmmakers today?

Elena – The biggest problem is that it is almost impossible to make a living out of documentaries, precisely due to the lack of a market infrastructure. There are currently no economic incentives for documentaries, so filmmakers that venture into it, do so solely as a result of personal conviction or passion. One of the documentaries we included in Ambulante, was financed through the selling of artworks. A friend of the filmmaker happened to be a well known painter who decided to give him a couple of his works so that he could sell them and get the money for his project.

Q – What advice would you offer a new documentary filmmaker?

Elena – I would say timing is key. I would advise filmmakers to be conscious of the issues that affect their current surroundings - to be aware of the kind of audiences they want to reach out to, and when selecting a subject for their documentary, to ask themselves why they want to make this film and why their selected subject is important at that point in time - who they are making this film for, etc. I would also recommend them to take advantage of all available resources, and to plan ahead, develop a strategy before applying to festivals. Finally, I would advise them not to be afraid of making more personal and experimental documentaries, and at the risk of sounding cliché I would say, be creative and experiment, grab a camera, get out there.

Essential Television Statistics (ETS)

It's scary when you hand your doc off to your sales agent and they sell it to a distributor – how can you know when and where it plays? One way is to contact ETS who track 144 channels in 20 countries looking for when TV shows and feature films air. It's important because your distribution contract usually gives a distributor a limited number of runs or plays of your doc over the course of a certain amount of time. Once they go over that, they HAVE to renegotiate with you. And of course, they will not volunteer this info maybe hoping to get an extra showing or two for free! Go to www.etstv.com to find out more information.

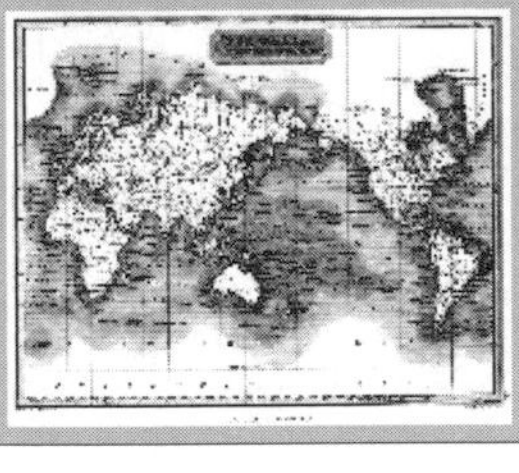

Amir Labaki
Its All True Int. Doc. Festival

SOUTH AMERICA

Q – What is the It's All True International Documentary Film Festival and how can it help documentary filmmakers in South America?

Amir – It´s All True is the leading film festival devoted exclusively to documentaries in South America. The festival takes place simultaneously in São Paulo and Rio de Janeiro late March-early April every year. I started it wishing to develop the documentary culture and market in Brazil through the opening of a special yearly window for non-fictional film and video.

Q – Are all the films you include from South America? Must they be Latin American filmmakers?

Amir – No and no. The festival has an international competition with around 15 titles from all the over the world, two Brazilian competitions (features and shorts), an informative section for Latin American and Caribbean docs, another for international productions (*State of Things*), one more for experimental docs (*Horizon*), and two retrospectives. The festival organizes also with Cinusp, the movie theater that belongs to Universidade de São Paulo, the International Documentary Conference – its seventh edition will take place next year. We are also putting together the first edition of the Visible Evidence conference in Latin America.

Q – What is the documentary filmmaking scene like in Brazil and South America?

Amir – The documentary scene seems to have improved a lot in the last few years in countries such as Argentina, Chile and Equador, with small but alive doc festivals and a marginal but growing market for docs in theaters and on DVDs. In Brazil we are facing the best time for documentaries in a long time. The digital age enhanced the definition of the documentary maker in Brazil in the '80s and '90s when video-artists started producing music portraits and in doing so established the most original school of Brazilian documentary in the last decade. Brazilian documentaries are now no longer rooted just in social compromises or political responsibilities. Some degree of esthetical autonomy has been finally achieved. Misery, violence, historical figures, natural or cultural treasures are no more the leading subjects. Autobiography, daily life, private experiences, silly pleasures legitimate themselves are themes. The old model, Grierson´s didacticism, is gone. A doc is a doc is a doc.

The Brazilian documentary exists economically thanks to favors from the State and the producer's voluntarism. The increase market in film theaters is just a beginning, as the releases in DVD format are now real but still largely incipient. The partnership with TV, essential all over the world, does not exist or at best is marginal. DocTV, a project backed by the Ministry of Culture, the public TV system and the national association of documentary-makers, is the leading exception. From an industrial point of view, it´s a no-win game. No documentary recovers its costs, no production house accumulates any capital. Each doc is a new journey with the same no return end. In such a precarious scenario, this peak will not last long.

Q – How do docs fare at the movie theater?

Amir – The presence of Brazilian documentaries at movie theatres is living an ascendant curve. Two documentaries were released in 1998; four in 1999; six in 2000; eight in 2001; eleven in 2002; five in 2003 (15% of the total national movies being shown); until reaching the impressive mark of 17 documentaries on the big screen last year, nothing less than 1/3 of the total of national titles that achieved a theatrical distribution. The performance of each title is the Achilles´ heel, with an average of 15,000 to 20,000 spectators.

Q – Are there many government-funding schemes or grant organizations within Brazil & South America that documentary filmmakers can apply to?

Amir – There are government-funding schemes in Brazil and Chile, for sure. In Brazil there are a few grants available. They are quite open for all kinds of documentaries. I think the greatest challenge for doc production in South America is the divorce between the TVs and the independent doc production. It is really tough to produce films that demand higher budgets, let´s say, from US$ 100,000.

Q – What is distribution like for documentaries in Brazil ?

Amir – One third (13 titles) of the Brazilian films that got a theatrical release in the last two years in Brazil were documentaries. That´s the good news. The bad. first, the standard audience is seldom larger than 30,000 viewers in the theaters. One title succeed in selling 250,000 tickets last year –a record for Brazilian docs since 1983! Secondly, the TV market is almost close but the DVD distribution is starting to be relevant.

Q – What is the biggest problem for documentaries in Brazil and South America?

Amir – The fact that the TV market, open or pay channels which, is still overseeing the potential for documentaries, almost never buy or co-produce them. An exception in Brazil is a project called DocTV, started by the Ministry of Culture and the public channels, it producing around 30 titles a year since 2005.

Q – What are the biggest problems or challenges facing South American/Latin American documentary filmmakers today?

Amir – Developing a real market. Making available much more national and international titles. Opening a new relationship with TV, as in Europe.

Q – What advice would you offer a new documentary filmmaker?

Amir – Study the tradition. Make it new. Make it personal. Break the rules. Be bold. And send your doc to It´s All True!

AUSTRALIA

Q – What kind of documentaries does SBS look for?

Trevor – I principally commission for two strands called *Storyline Australia* and *Inside Australia*. And as those titles suggest these are largely Australian stories that focus on strong character based, strong narrative type stories. Having said that, especially for Storyline Australia, there's what I'd call international stories that play within that strand. But they're about other Australians working internationally or the story has some strong connection to Australia. For instance, I'm about to commission a project on the Santa Cruz massacre, which happened in East Timor in 1991. The story is about a team of Australian and Argentinean forensic archeologists who are going to unearth the mass grave and find out the specifics of how they died. Occasionally, I commission purely international stories. For instance, I've commissioned a three-part science story that's a co-production between Australia and France. The documentaries should also have an entertaining element, no matter how serious the subject is. We are not interested in lifestyle and wildlife docs at all.

Q – Do you only commission Australian filmmakers?

Trevor – We legally can only contract with Australian filmmakers, but that doesn't stop them from having international partners with foreign co-producers.

Q – As a broadcaster, do ratings dictate what kind of topics you commission?

Trevor – Ratings come into play with all our decisions, but I approach it from another angle which is we are trying to get the maximum audiences to watch the documentaries that we commission. Constantly I speak to filmmakers about the accessibility of their story and the need to draw in as large an audience as possible. Having said that, we'll tackle really hard and difficult subject matters that aren't populist in approach. We're trying to find a balance between what is populist and what is difficult.

Q – How do filmmakers pitch their ideas to you?

Trevor – They can ring up and make an appointment and come in and pitch me in person. They can pitch me over the phone. They can send things via the mail. I discourage people from sending things via e-mail because it just creates a bigger workload.

Q – Do you take proposals from new documentary filmmakers or must they have to have a certain amount of experience behind them?

Trevor – A first time director I probably will not deal with unless they are attached to an experienced producer. And for an inexperienced producer, I would want them to have a mentor producer on their team as well as an experienced director. The door is open, but under certain conditions.

Q – What makes a proposal stand out to you?

Trevor – I'm looking for strong characters and stories, so when a proposal speaks to me on that level I get instantly engaged. And there should be some major, universal themes informing those stories. That can happen in two pages or twenty pages and sometimes I read things that are 40-50 pages long that are more like a fully developed script. At that stage, it had better be really, really good.

Q – Do you welcome trailers or samples of work as part of a proposal?

Trevor – All the time. But my attitude is that trailers are a bit like when you see a trailer for a dramatic feature film. They can be a really good tease and then when you go see the film, it can be disappointing. That's why I like to see it on paper. And I also want to talk about the film to feel confident that people are taking it in a direction that I want.

Q – What is the SBS-FFC accord and how does that help documentaries?

Trevor – They don't have an accord at the moment and the rules are about to change, but in a broad sense there's a two-door approach to the funding of documentaries between SBS and The Film Finance Corporation. With both doors, there has to be a broadcast license agreement, which we put up, for it to qualify to go to the FFC. If the project has other significant international money attached to it, either through another international broadcaster or a distribution advance, then the filmmaker can go to the FFC. With our license agreement, the FFC will consider it under what it calls its marketplace evaluation. It's purely a financial deal they're looking at. It has to have international money and Australian money. That usually applies to stories that are kind of international. There's another form of funding that applies to purely Australian based stories. They have to have a license agreement with us as well and the FFC is developing a proposed system where they make an evaluation of the creative potential of a program. Under that system, you are only ever going to be able to ask for up to 65% of the budget from the FFC. So they will be programs that are more restrictive in international potential and more Australian based stories.

Q – Do you fully fund productions?

Trevor – We usually do that for half hour series more than one off documentaries. It's more attractive to us if the filmmaker comes in with some of the money already in place.

Q – Do you offer pre-sales for license?

Trevor – Yes. We mostly offer a license agreement in the form of a pre-sale. Sometimes we'll offer a license agreement and some investment for things of a larger budget and we want to have a slice of the action in terms of potential returns. Frequently, SBS sales will give some money for DVD rights. Our license agreements usually last for 3 runs over 5 years.

Q – What are the kind of budgets that you work with?

Trevor – I can give you an instance of when something was already shot where we offered a license agreement of $60,000AUS and that allowed the program to be finished. That's at the cheaper end of the scale. So from as little as $60,000AUS to $3.2 million AUS (total budget, not pre-sale) for that three-part science program I was taking about. So it depends on the scale of the program and if it has international finance attached. International projects tend to be around $500,000AUS, or more, and for smaller domestic programs, we're looking at budgets around $250,000-$350,000AUS.

Q – Do you do acquisitions?

Trevor – SBS does a lot of that. SBS's mandate is to reflect the diversity of Australian culture and life and the great patchwork that is Australian society. One way it does that as a network, is to buy films, documentaries, TV series from all over the world and broadcast them in their own language. We're probably the only broadcaster in the world that embraces subtitling. So we acquire a large amount of documentaries and they don't have to have Australian content. We broadcast about 800 hours of documentary a year and our local programming is a small portion of that. We have deals with PBS and

Helfpul Australian & New Zealand Websites

AUSTRALIA

Australian Film Commission
National film funding and production resource www.afc.gov.au

Australian Documentary Forum
www.ozdox.org

Australian International Documentary Conference
Market component includes Australian DOCUmart, a day long pitching forum
www.aidc.com.au

ASDA - Australian Screen Directors Association www.asdafilm.org.au

ABC TV Documentaries
www.abc.net.au/tv/documentaries

AFC – ABC Documentary online
http://abc.net.au/documentaryonline/default.htm

Film Australia
Commissioning & funding films in the national interest www.filmaust.com.au

Film Finance Corporation
www.ffc.gov.au

Metro Magazine
Academic articles on documentary (canresearch back issues)
www.metromagazine.com.au

SBS Broadcasting and SBS Independent (SBSi)
www.sbs.com.au

Screen hub
Daily email service for film professionals
www.screenhub.com.au

Screen Network Australia
www.screennetwork.com.au

SPAA - Screen Producers Association of Australia
www.spaa.org.au

State Agencies:
Northern Territory Film Office –www.nt.gov.au/nreta/arts/ntfo/grants
Screen West – www.screenwest.com.au/
Film Victoria – www.film.vic.gov.au/
South Australian Film Corporation - www.safilm.com.au/
Pacific Film and Television Commission - www.pftc.com.au

Training:
AFTRS (Australian Film Television and Radio School) www.aftrs.edu.au

Summer Film School, Melbourne University www.summerfilmschool.com

NEW ZEALAND

The New Zealand Documentary Conference
www.docnzfestival.com

Film New Zealand
www.filmnz.co.nz

Maori in Film, Video and TV
www.ngaahowhakaari.co.nz

Film South New Zealand
www.filmsouth.com

Film Wellington
www.filmwellington.com

TVNZ
http://tvnz.co.nz

Sky TV
www.skytv.co.nz

Triangle TV
www.tritv.co.nz

NZ On Air
www.nzonair.govt.nz

Signature TV
www.thefilm.co.nz

NZ Film Archive
www.filmarchive.org.nz/

Screen Directors Guild of NZ
www.sdgnz.co.nz

Screen Production and Development Association (SPADA)
www.spada.co.nz

Asia New Zealand Film Foundation Trust
www.anzfft.org.nz

Open Door
www.opendoor.net.nz.

New Zealand Writers Guild
www.nzwritersguild.org.nz

Training:
The New Zealand Film and Television School
www.filmschool.org.nz

New Zealand Film Academy
www.nzfilmacademy.com

an output deal with the BBC.

Q – Can an independent producer approach you with a finished program?

Trevor – Sure, but I pass the information onto our acquisitions department.

Q – What is The Indigenous Protocol?

Trevor – With the Australian context, we have as part of our mandate to support indigenous filmmakers because indigenous filmmakers are a very important part of our makeup as a network. We're currently doing a nine-hour series called *First Nations*, which is a view of Australian history from the time of colonization by Europeans through to the present day. We are working with Claire Aguilar at ITVS on that one. The Indigenous Protocols are how we engage with filmmakers and how filmmakers engage with indigenous communities. It's just a set of protocols to ensure that indigenous culture is being honored and the stories are being told in a way that is suitable for that community. So in other words, so people's rights are not being trampled on.

Q – How long does the process take to put the finance together once you greenlight it?

Trevor – That's on a case-by-case basis. Sometimes it can take 4-6 weeks to decide on a project. And others can come in and they just leap off the page and we make a decision in one or two days. We give our letters of offer to the producer and then they go talk to the FFC. The way it works in Australia is that we give a license and then the filmmaker has to go find the rest of the money. Sometimes we provide a third or less of the money. That can be quick and take two or three months. Sometimes it might take six months.

Q – Have you noticed any changes in documentaries since the advent of the new digital technologies?

Trevor – There does seem to be more and more people going out and taking a punt and shooting X amount of footage before they approach a broadcaster. That's simply because of Mini-DV cameras, Final Cut Pro and Avid Xpress. But I also think that tends to be at that lower end of the production scale and people who are ambitious about doing a big international co-production might just shoot enough to show a trailer, but they aren't going to shoot more than that.

Q – Do you do feature length documentaries?

Trevor – I get a fair amount of proposals where producers want to make a feature length version of the film. We make an evaluation on that as to whether we think the material justifies 85-90 minutes. If we decide it has legs then we say we want two versions – an 85-minute version to run on first broadcast and then a 52-minute version for second broadcast. To run a feature doc, it has to be really good because we have to shift our programming around to accommodate that such as the evening news. People don't like that. So we rarely take feature length for commissioning.

Q – Are documentaries playing in the cinema more and more in Australia?

Trevor – Michael Moore's films have done very well in Australia. They've created a buzz amongst producers to try to create feature length films as well. But my attitude on this is very skeptical. I think the Michael Moore films are very good and there're a spate of half a dozen films that have done well in Australia like *Touching The Void*. It had a huge production budget by Australian standards – almost like a drama. I think Australian producers are scratching to tell stories of that significance and reach a theatrical audience. I think it's a harder call here for a locally made feature film because there are less bums on seats. Michael Moore can recoup his budget in America easily and what he makes in Australia is pocket money. It's like Hollywood films. People go see them because they're popular. Michael Moore's films are funny, about America, often about George Bush and people like to go and laugh. So there's a reason why they work.

Q – What common mistakes do you see documentary filmmaker make?

Trevor – The biggest issue I face is that filmmakers are so passionate about telling a story that they can't tell when a story isn't really engaging. The stories are terrific, but the methodology is hampered because they can't see the woods through the trees. Filmmakers have to think about audience. That's why Michael Moore works so well. Strong comedic stories with a strong character it in it – him.

Q – What piece of advice would you give a new documentary filmmaker?

Trevor – Be persistent and strong. Keep on going until you get your film made if you really believe in the story.

Useful Books

You can never have too much information. So go out and read all of the books on this page so you will have a really deep understanding of the documentary genre. Who knows, the idea for your next project or the tip that gets you through your technical or financial nightmare may be just fingertips away!

Cross-Cultural Filmmaking: A Handbook for Making Documentary and Ethnographic Films
By Ilisa Barbash & Lucien Taylor
Inspired by concerns that anthopolgists had on how subjects were covered in the field, this book focuses on the practical, technical, and theoretical aspects of filming from fundraising to exhibition.

Documentary Storytelling for Video and Filmmakers
By Sheila Curran Bernard
A common sense approach to making documentary films. Good for first timers and students.

Directing The Documentary
By Michael Rabiger
A well established documentarian gives neophytes lots of valuable info in practical terms through graphs, pictures and drawings.

Writing, Directing, and Producing Documentary Films and Videos
By Alan Rosenthal
Perhaps the most respected book on documentary filmmaking. It has been around for a long time and is still used by just about every film school. Says a lot right there.

Cinematography
By Kris Malkiewicz & M. David Mullen
Deals with the various aspects of cinematography in a non-technical way, so that those unfamilair can have a working knowledge of the terms and principles of shooting film. In addition, there are sections on shooting digitally, which will be very helpful for documentary filmmakers.

The Complete Film Production Handbook
By Eve Light Honthener
Focuses on the day-by-day details of film production. Includes information on pre-production tasks, establishing company policy, insurance, dealing with talent, music clearance, visas and customs, and much more.

The Guerilla Film Makers Handbook - US (yellow) & UK (green) versions & The Guerilla Film Makers Movie Blue Print (blue)
OK, so it's a little cheeky putting our sister books in here, but as Chris Gore says, "Your book is the greatest resource, filmmaking tool to come along in the last decade. Hell, I would put it up there with any of the technological advances in the industry, yes, it's that good." So who are we to argue?! The US and UK books are jam packed with over 150 interviews each with leading industry experts and in-depth case studies that look at not only low budget movies, but the ins and outs of the Hollywood system. The Blueprint book, although slanted towards the UK, takes you thorugh a step-by-step process of making your film.

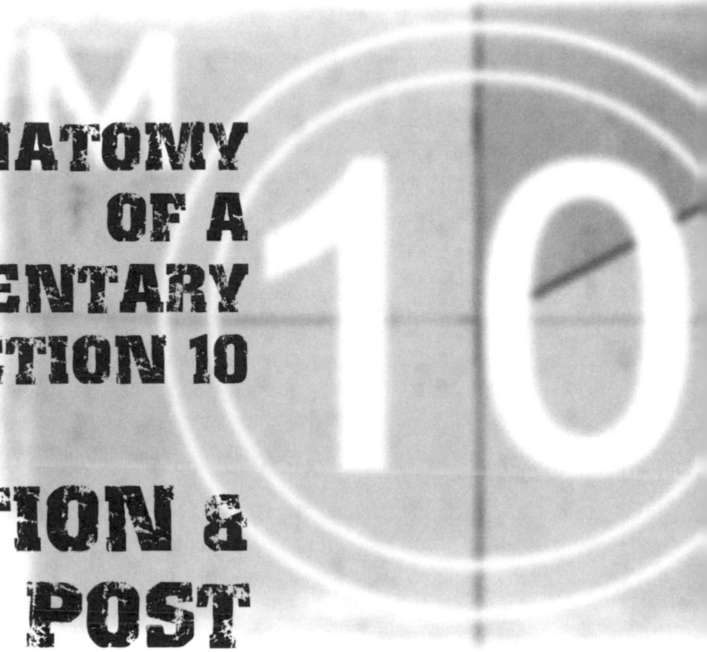

ANATOMY OF A DOCUMENTARY SECTION 10

PRODUCTION & POST

THE PRODUCER

Q – Did you always produce documentaries?

Agi – I didn't do any documentaries. I started as a sales rep bringing French films to the US. Then I started producing my own feature films, but was having trouble getting them made. One night, I met Stacy Peralta at a party. I didn't know much about him other than he had been a famous skater. But then I saw the *Spin* magazine article about Dogtown and the Z-Boys. I knew the Vans people because I had a snowboarding feature project in development and I was trying to get them to put money into it. I called Vans and asked them if they wanted to invest in a documentary. I had another company who said they were interested and they had similar demographics, but they fell out. Vans said they would finance the whole thing in order to help me out because they had seen me work hard. If you're passionate and work hard people are going to want to work with and help you. They didn't give us a lot of money, but they gave us total creative control. Jay Wilson, the head of Vans didn't even look at a cut. I said, *"Jay, you have to come in and take a look."* He got there and said, *"You look tired. I'm taking you to lunch."* And he still never saw the cut. He totally trusted us.

Q – Was it easier to get things going after Dogtown & Z-Boys?

Agi – People started calling me back. It really was a calling card. I'd get a call a week with someone saying they had a project just like *Dogtown & Z-Boys*. So I would ask them what the story was and they didn't have one. They didn't understand that concept wasn't enough. I'd explain that skateboarding has a core audience, but beyond that no one really knows about it. I didn't know skating, but I know that Madison Avenue designers were designing skate clothing. When you have a wider audience you need to stay true to the core, but you try to find a way to make it appealing cross-culturally. Skating, snowboarding and surfing appeal to people who don't do it. So really do your homework. When we were doing press, some of the journalists had never seen the film. How can you ask questions that way? It is the same thing with producing. You have to know whom you're talking to and ask intelligent questions if you want them to help you.

Q – What are you looking for when you're coming up with a new documentary film idea?

Agi – A documentary is much harder than a feature. For investors, I do warn them – we have idea, a concept and a vision, but until you do your interviews, you really don't know what will happen. We thought one person would be the main story, but they weren't. But you have an idea and you have to write a treatment. A documentary is always made up of people who have interesting stories and then you have to know how to tell it. So your interviews are crucial and because we shoot film, not tape, you have to lead them into what you want. They cannot go on and on. You have to find the sound bites.

Q – Do you transcribe your footage?

Agi – Yes. We hire people to do that. Then Stacy makes a notebook out of the transcripts. and he writes the scripts. And while he's doing all of that, my job is to do research and bring in the visuals that Paul Crowder, our editor, needs. Then Stacy and Paul find a real interesting way to tell the story. I think that's why our films have been so successful. I had a project with Steven Spielberg and he was in two or three of our meetings. He said, *"You want to make sure that anything the audience sees, they haven't seen before. If they have, they will click off."* I think that's a problem for a lot of documentary filmmakers. Sometimes we'll do a whole act and if it doesn't work, we have to start all over again.

Q – Do you deal with any of the nuts and bolts of the business side of the filmmaking?

Agi – Yes. I like to write the checks. I guess I'm an entrepreneur at heart. I don't use payroll as I like to keep as much money in the coffer and on the screen. One reason to use payroll is that they include worker's comp. Instead, you can go to the state, which isn't that bureaucratic, and fill out the paperwork. You can call them on the phone for help. It's not expensive and you get money back at the end if you've gone the whole year and not filed enough claims to use it all. Then you need to have E&O insurance, which is expensive. It used to be $10,000 and now it may be more like $15,000. You need it. You can't get a distribution deal without it.

Q – Do you have to get E&O for each individual show or can you run several productions one policy?

Agi – You can do that for TV shows, but you can't for documentaries. So for each one, add $15,000 to the budget. They have different polices that are 1 year, 3 years and 5 years and it doesn't start until you have your first showing. So if you think you're going to get into Sundance, then you'll prepare your insurance agent to start on a certain date in January. That means you will have to have a financial backer ready to pay that $15,000. You don't need to clear your music for festival screenings and I try to clear all the stock footage or at least let them know you are going to be working with them. But it's always best to not show it in public without insurance.

Q – Is that something you can get once you have a deal?

Agi – Yes. But you have to have it in your budget from the outset.

Q – What are some of the tricky parts of clearing footage?

Agi – Well, with festivals you're always cutting until the last minute. For Sundance, you find out around Thanksgiving and it has to be done by late January. You try to get at least an online so you have to find people who are willing to work late hours around Christmas and New Years. So we don't clear all the stock footage, but we try to make sure that no one is going to have a problem with us using it. After the festival, we like to have a public screening of what is not the final cut and through audience reaction at various screenings to see what needs to be tweaked. If a distributor wants it right there and then, and they want you to make all sorts of cuts that you don't want to make you can tell them no. But you make the cuts you want to make.

Q – What should documentary producers think about when doing interviews?

Agi – You have to do your research and as the producer you want to facilitate that by getting all the information. You want to meet the person, but don't have them start telling you stories because you want it fresh.

Q – Do you get your interviewees to sign releases?

Agi – Yes. You try and get it before the interview, but sometimes it doesn't happen until after. If you're shooting in a public place or a nightclub or something, then you want to put a sign on a door saying, *"Anyone entering here can be filmed."* Then you put the date and the name of the project and you have your cameraman shoot it because you won't be able to get everyone to sign that release. And then you have to get permission from the owner of the place – a location release. Unfortunately, we have trusted people we knew like in *Dogtown* where we had someone say they would sign a release after an interview and then they started getting funny. *"I'll get my lawyer to look at it. Oh, I lost it. I'll meet you for lunch and then I'll sign it."* Then he stood us up. Never signed it, although he gave us two interviews and then he sued. E&O covers it, but it's an expense you don't want your financial backer to have.

Q – If they've agreed to be interviewed and you film it, isn't that good enough?

Agi – Not unless they say so on camera. It's a delicate balance when you have known a person all your life. I wouldn't do that again. I might interview them, but until they sign, I might prepare everybody to not use the interview. Usually they are playing a game with you so you have to be wary of it and have a game plan.

Q – Are they usually asking for money?

Agi – Oh, it's all sorts of weird dysfunctional psychology. Dysfunctional people. And there are a lot of them around. And sometimes they make the most interesting characters. Usually money does not pass hands for interviews in documentaries. But we do like to pay whatever we can out of the budget. It's good will. And there's no set rate.

Q – What if you film on a beach, do you still have to put notices up?

Agi – You are supposed to get location permits. We try to avoid public places. We would shoot at someone's house, so it's their beach. But if you're a student filmmaker or you say you are, you can take that risk.

Q – Do you make a schedule?

Agi – Yes. I do the shooting and post-production schedules. You don't want to do more than two interviews a day because it's exhausting mentally for the director. You want to scout the locations as much as possible. Maybe scout in the morning and shoot in the afternoon. The way we do our meals is that I go out and buy it. I rent a van for transportation. I have worked on big commercials and they have trailers and all of that – that's not for me. That's all so time consuming, just like payroll. But know whom you're going to interview and they will co-operate. You will have your "A" interviews and your "B" interviews. Our documentaries are complicated because we have so many different elements – we use Super 16mm film to shoot and the stock footage comes in on all sorts of video formats and Super 8mm. So our post-production budget is always high. If you're planning on going to film-out, then you have to prepare to go to 24 fps instead of 30 fps. So you have to consider all that technology. Then you have to consider going to be HD in the lab. So if you're shooting on Beta, which is 30 fps, then you're going to have to go to 24fps HD so you have to have people who understand that.

Q – Do you like to shoot PAL?

Agi – We don't have to worry about that because we shoot film. But our stock footage on *Once In A Lifetime*, we like to get on PAL. And because a lot of it was from the BBC, we were able to do that. There's a process called Slow PAL, which is a process that takes the 25fps to 24fps, but not everybody does that. They slow it down 4% and it's so much better.

Q – Is there anything to know about working with labs or other technological aspects?

Agi – It's really important to get people who understand what you are doing. I work with different companies and they're so big and you need to establish a relationship with someone in tech. Don't just talk to your salesperson. Go over to the company and meet the tech and see if they have some sort of interest in your project.

Q – How much time do you schedule for filming an interview?

Agi – An hour. then we always budget for a second and maybe a third interview. So we do the first interview and Paul will start cutting. We might get two thirds of the way done with the film and realize that we've taken a different turn. So we might need another interview. We never set aside a week to interview people. If you have ten people that you need to interview and some live in Hawaii or Oregon, you try to group them together in one place. You try to get deals with airlines, though that's tough to get. If you go business class you can take more bags and it's worth it because it's like $150 to upgrade and you get to take twice as many bags. If you don't, you might pay $150 for every extra bag! Just make sure that they're an airline that does upgrades. The other thing that you can do with the airlines is ask them to waive their requirements.

Q – What's the standard crew that you use?

Agi – It's very small because we want people to be comfortable. We didn't use grips and gaffers in *Dogtown* but we did in *Riding Giants* and subsequent films. So one grip, one gaffer, one camera assistant, sound and a sound assistant, I get an assistant if it is local, the director and me. That's it.

Q – What makes a good documentary crew?

Agi – We want them to co-operate and not say, *"Oh, I am the grip, I can't be a gaffer. I am a sound assistant, I can't pick that up."* That's why we like to buy a lot of good will. We like to get people who are into the subject as they will work for less money. We give them a per diem. We mostly shoot non-union. Or I should say, the crew is DGA, but we can get waivers because it's lower budget. You don't need to have an AD and we couldn't because that would be too many people. And all the guilds do want indie and doc members so they have these low budget agreements to work with them.

Q – Do you make contracts with your crew?

Agi – No. It's usually just a day hire. Although, on this last film with Studio Canal, they informed us when we were turning in our deliverables that they needed a "work for hire" on everybody, which I never used. That says that you were hired to do this job and you have no rights to it so you won't sue. Most people don't use it because if they did get a part of the film, they would have a contract stipulating so. It kind of pissed our crew off to go back and ask them to sign it. And it pissed us off because it took a lot of time. I was working with executive producers who had no experience and were very difficult. If you are working for a company or studio, you should ask to see the delivery requirements when you do your budget.

Q – Any tips on paying people?

Agi – Pay them right away. That's a great thing to negotiate rates with because a lot of people have to turn in an invoice or go through payroll and it takes awhile. I like to pay them on the day or the next day.

Q – Any tips when putting together a budget?

Agi – We don't use PA's, but we do use messengers so I like to budget a lot for that. I like to put meals in as that's good will. I like to put entertainment in as well. So you pad it a little bit and that's where you can go when you need extra money for something. Post-production, you always need to budget more because things come up. Also I know how much of a budget my funder is willing to give and so I make my budget for what I think I can do it for, then pad a little bit and see where I am. In our films, we put in a lot in for music and stock footage – especially for stock footage expenses like ordering tapes. For music, people forget that you have to go out and buy CDs. You should put a little more in for transfers. We have our own decks for duplication, so we still put in for bays and since we don't have to actually charge then I can pad there a little bit. We put in a lot for graphics and titles because they make a difference.

Q – How do you find out how much things cost?

Agi – I just go back to my previous budgets and see how much I really spent. So you could look at a friend's budget on a comparable film and do the same. Then there's the old stand by of calling around and getting quotes from vendors. Sometimes you can calculate things fairly easily. For example, if you have ten one hour interviews and you are shooting Super 16mm film and each roll is 11 minutes long, you can figure that price out. Tape is the same way. And don't forget to add in tapes for the post process.

Q – How do you get deals from rental houses and vendors?

Agi – Most of my crew owns their equipment. But once again, you take whatever your subject is and look at the vendors. The sound facility that just won an Academy Award, they have a guy who they are mentoring who is a skater! So they're

Budget Tips

GUERILLA FILM MAKER SAYS!

Every funder is going to want to see a budget. If you can't afford Movie Magic software, Excel works just as well.

1. Always budget a fee for yourself.

2. Don't put in overhead or contingency. Most funders don't know what that is.

3. Never list anything or anyone as deferred. Budget things as they cost.

4. Do not overbudget or you might scare people away, but don't underbudget or you may be held to those numbers if you get the money.

5. Make sure to budget for publicity materials like a publicist, production stills, posters, flyers, a website, festival expenses, etc.

6. Make sure to budget for festival fees and related expenses.

7. If you have any special equipment or locations that you plan to use or shoot, write a page of notes explaining this to potential funders.

8. To find out rates, call around to local vendors and ask them. If you are a low budget production, tell them and they will work with you on the price.

9. Even if you own your own equipment, put it as a line item in the budget. It's an expense and it is being used. If you want to give a discount, that's fine, but say so in the "notes" section.

10. Remember the little things: tape stock for production and post, food, postage, gas, office supplies, batteries, etc. It'll bite you in the ass if you don't budget for it.

11. The easiest way to reduce your budget is to get rid of people.

12. If you can afford it, have an experienced line producer review your budget to make sure it's reasonable.

going to want to work with me. Always try to get to the top person and try to get them to help you out. With our sound we worked with Dane Tracks who just won an Academy Award for *The Matrix*. They asked us how much we had in the budget for post sound and we had nothing. So we made a deal – if we get a distributor then we'll pay you what you should get, which I did negotiate down a bit. And I did pay. They sent me a letter saying I was the first person who ever paid. So when I went to them with my next film, they worked with us. So be really direct and open. You are dealing with businesses and they need to, not necessarily make money on you, but if you can bring them something that covers their overhead and helps people they are mentoring, that's a way to do it. And if you think you're going to be high profile and are going to be interviewed by the news or magazines, you can say that we will always mention them.

Q – Is it hard to do if you don't have a track record like you did with Dogtown?

Agi – No. On *Dogtown*, I called the Jimi Hendrix people and nobody knew who we were. We said that we didn't have any money, but we could send them Vans shoes. And they said OK. They wanted shoes! The richer people are, the more into it they are. So if you really believe in what you're doing and you're not bullshitting people, they'll respond.

Q – How do you go about raising money?

Agi – Well, with *Dogtown* it was a niche market and Vans was right in there. They had the first skate shoe and when I called and said Stacy Peralta was the director – they said, *"Stacy was our first sponsored skater. He was responsible at 16."* And when I told them he had been directing TV for ten years they were in. The whole cost of the film was less than what they would spend on one commercial. They got a lot of bang for their buck, but I was dealing with a very creative person in Jay Wilson. And what I've found in my whole career is that if you go to the top, they're not afraid to spend money. They're not going to say no because they're afraid of losing their jobs if they say yes. I had to talk Jay into taking a producer's credit – that's the kind of person you want. And if you aren't dealing with the top person and you're not getting anywhere, as long as it's not stepping on toes, you can try calling someone else there and find a rapport. My agent told me this a long time ago, *"When you go into pitch, find out what they want and what they are about and don't pitch them something that they are not going to be interested in. Because the next time you call they're not going to be as open."* Also, you don't want to waste their time. Make sure to be nice to the assistant because that person may be an executive some day. And they may be able to give you an insight into whom to call.

Q – What is important to put into a proposal?

Agi – It depends on the project, but try not to send too much. Try and get into the room and don't leave anything behind. They could show it to someone else and misrepresent it. If they have to show their boss, just say that you will come back and show it to them. Get them to call your representation if you have some. And if someone isn't interested, then don't push things.

Q – Any tips on dealing with distributors?

Agi – You want to make sure that the trailer is representative of your film. Same goes for artwork. Get them to send you mock ups and if you don't think that it's right, see if you can get some money to do it yourself. We are very fortunate because our genre is something that we know more about than they do and they want us on their side.

Q – How about advice on dealing with lawyers?

Agi – Get a good one and get all your contracts and releases airtight. Try to establish a relationship with one to the point of being a friend so you can call them at midnight if things go horribly wrong.

Q – What are things to think about should things go wrong during production?

Agi – I always try to have a personal rapport with crew and the subjects so I can explain what we're doing from the start. With crew, I say that there are only three of us and if they're going to be difficult, don't hire them if they can't work the way you are working. Be open. Also if the police come and you don't have a permit, be very apologetic and plead ignorance. It's a lot easier to do when you don't have big cameras. Be aware that they can confiscate your equipment. I'm not sure about your footage.

Q – What are the most common mistakes that documentary filmmakers make?

Agi – They don't choose good interview subjects and they don't realize how important it is. Interviews should be intimate. And you don't want it to be all over the place. It's OK to get different backgrounds, but you want to pick that intimate angle so it doesn't get too busy. We don't do cinema verite because we find it distracting and you don't get that intimacy. You don't get their eyes. If it's an action film then you don't want too much of the sport or else it becomes sport porn. You need to have story, feeling and drama.

Q – What advice would you give a new documentary filmmaker?

Agi – Develop relationships with people and bring the right project to the right person and don't bug them. Make them want to talk to you. And also asking people for advice makes them want to help you.

INSURANCE

Q – What is your job?

Kent – I'm an insurance broker for the entertainment business. A broker, unlike an insurance agent, serves the producer not the insurance company and finds the most appropriate insurance for what the producer is doing. New producers always think insurance is a waste of money and they don't want to deal with it. But for the more experienced producer, we are their first call. It's important and it matters who you have on your side.

Q – Without insurance, what problems could befall a filmmaker or producer?

Kent – You always worry about liability. Liability is injury or damage to the pubic. Usually, the minimum requirement is $1 million. For example, you're driving and you kill somebody – that's auto liability. Or somebody trips over one of your wires or you bump into an old lady and break her arm – the law will hold you responsible. Without insurance, those people can file a claim against you and, if the claim is valid, you'll have to pay for their injury. They can attack the value of your company and even the value of your film. That's why insurance was invented. Insurance takes your individual risk, quantifies a premium for it, pools that premium with others and then pays for your loss, if and when it happens. For instance, one of the people on your crew kills someone with a car by accident. Instead of that family being awarded a million dollars against your movie company and perhaps either closing down your company or taking all or most of the profits from your film, the relatively small amount of money you pay the insurance company for non owned auto cover makes the insurance company, not you, responsible for paying that loss.

Q – Is this why all equipment rental houses require insurance?

Kent – Yes. And they not only require that you have equipment coverage, but they also want liability. What if you drop their camera on somebody? That covers them for your activities with their camera. That's why they want to be named additional insured to your insurance policy.

Q - How much money should a producer set aside for insurance?

Kent – It's impossible to say without knowing what the budget is and knowing what the needs are. One movie may be worth $20 million and another may be worth $100,000. The insurance is related to the value of the budget that it needs to protect. It also matters what country you're shooting in. A film shooting in a third world country is usually deemed more risky then one shot in Los Angeles. You need to take your production to a professional broker who can analyze the needs that you have. There're a series of polices that you usually need. There's a producer's policy that covers your negative or tape, and liability and worker's compensation. Workers compensation covers injury to the people working for you.

Q – Say you have a documentary at $100,000 with a two-person crew that is going to be shot entirely in US and in no dangerous or bizarre situations.

Kent – There's still many things that would need to be known. Let's suppose your shoot is less than 10 days and has no stunts or pyros. In that case you might qualify for a short- term policy that could cost you about half of what a regular policy would cost.

Q – When should a producer approach you and what should they give you?

Kent – They should contact us at least four weeks ahead of production, preferably more. This is because the carriers sometimes react slowly and also with extra time we can guide people to a better way of insuring their project. Like going for short-term over a long-term policy. Or, if they're doing many productions, there may be a way to combine them all under one long policy. In the long run a long-term policy could be a lot less expensive for a group of policies then a several short-term policies. This is a business of specifics and that's why we don't like to generalize. A broker needs a synopsis, some idea of the schedule of the shoot and a full budget.

Q – What are the lengths of short-term and long-term policies?

Kent – You can get as short as three days for a weekend. It'll have very limited coverage - negative and faulty. You may not get coverage for the full value of the film. You might have $25,000 in negative and faulty cover, but that isn't going to help you a lot if you have a $100,000 film loss. The long term would be a yearlong policy. You can renew it every year if your production continues.

Q – What are the main differences between what a documentary filmmaker and a narrative filmmaker might need for insurance?

Kent – One of the things is cast insurance. Unlike a feature film documentaries usually don't have a group of actors that are instrumental to the film. Some do if they're recreations or if there's a certain host or director who is of some importance. The problem comes that documentaries are shot over a long period of time and cast insurance for movies usually only lasts 2-10 weeks. It's expensive to cover someone for cast cover for a long time because there is a greater chance that the person may get sick or die and therefore the insurance company is on for a greater risk. I'm quoting a documentary right now where they have to have it because they have an expert in a particular field that they need covered.

Q – How does general liability work?

Kent – That again is injury or damage to the public. If someone in the public gets hurt because of your activities that's what it covers. That should include auto. One coverage that you should never go without is non-owned auto. You can go without auto physical damage, especially if you're a small production and you're only renting a car for a few days. You can get that from a car rental company. But with non-owned, it covers if someone you hire is running an errand for you and kills somebody, it protects the company. It doesn't protect the individual. But they're going to go after the individual and then they're going to come after your company. Every once in awhile, I see someone trying to save money and not get it. They're insane. $550 protects you from a big loss. It doesn't happen very often, but if it does you're in big trouble.

Q – What other kinds of insurance would be good to have for a documentary film?

Kent – Worker's comp. It's required by law. You have to protect all the people that you hire and your independent contractors. It's a myth that they're independent contractors. In our industry, if someone is working under your direction, you're responsible for them unless they can provide you with their own worker's comp. If they get injured, they or their family or lawyer are coming after you. What's really bad about worker's comp if you don't have it – the state goes after you. And OSHA (Occupational Safety and Health Administration) comes after you. If somebody gets hurt, you're going to have to pay for their claim and pay a fine to the state of California or whatever state you're in. It's not a good idea to mess with worker's comp because there's a moral obligation to take care of the people working for you. Some insurance companies will pick up your worker's comp for you, or you can go through a payroll company or through the state fund to get your coverages. The other major policy is the producer's policy. That covers your negative, which also applies to tape and computer work – whatever you get your image on and go to post with. The faulty portion is if the lab screws up or somehow the machinery gets all messed up and ruins the film. Then you have your equipment. You have props, sets and wardrobe cover for that. You have something called extra expense that if any of your equipment fails you like your generator goes out or your camera fails and you are down – that helps you get money back to redo the shoot. Then there's office contents. A really important one is third party property damage. Let's say you are shooting in a restaurant. You've made a contract with the owner, so it is not the public. So say you damage the bar or a table, third party is for those contractual situations that you make for locations. If you're going foreign, you need foreign liability and foreign worker's comp. And errors and omissions is coverage if you libel or slander someone and many distributors won't touch your film without it. The requirements for that usually come from the distributor. Usually it's three years at $3 million with a $10,000-$25,000 deductible.

Q – When should you get E&O insurance?

Kent – Tricky question. If you're making a movie and it's bonded or banked, they're going to require it at the start of principle photography. There's risk right away. Someone reads about the film in the newspaper or believes somehow that you stole their idea and can file a claim. They can get an injunction issued that could stop you from shooting. But the reality is that most documentaries, don't get the cover when you make your deal with the distributor. It's expensive. It can cost $5,000-$15,000 easy. And it depends on how many distributors you're going to have and their requirements. If you only have one distributor, you can get a one-year policy that lasts the length of your contract. That is called a Rights Period Endorsement. If you're going to have a lot of people, that isn't going to work. You want a broader policy then.

Q – Does E&O cover music clearance and licensing problems?

Kent – That's what it's all about. Script, music, film clips – all those things have to be cleared and most distributors will require a lawyer to review it. I've seen many movies get made and sadly they cannot get distribution because they didn't do the right clearance work. For instance they shoot underage kids in weird situations – that might make a great movie, but they are minors and you need a sophisticated lawyer to help you from the get go to get the proper releases.

Q – Are there any tips for reducing risk so that you don't cause damages?

Kent – Common sense should prevail. If you are a low budget producer and you're going to shoot in a mansion, don't park in the driveway if your cars leak oil or fluids. We've replaced half the driveways in Hollywood. Look at an environment, walk through it and think how can I not damage it. If you're moving a lot of equipment and the house has a brick steps, have your carpenters put some wood over it or find a different route. Put matting on nice floors. Fence off areas and don't walk across grass. You destroy a fancy guy's grass, he's going to have you pay to have put it back in. And it may be a lot more than your deductible. One of the worst things that can happen are automobile issues. Documentaries are many times done by inexperienced people working under strain and duress. They work long hours, they're tired and they back up a truck or car into someone. One rule you can do is always have a second person there to watch that.

Q – Is there anything else about worker's comp we should know?

Kent – The only person who can legally exclude themselves from cover is an owner of a production company. That can save you some money to exclude yourself because it can get expensive, as there are minimums and maximums for owners.

Q – What if you buy a car for a production?

Kent – It needs to be covered separately than if you're going to rent a car. Usually it's not great to buy a car if you can rent it instead. It's a lot more expensive.

Q – What's a deductible?

Kent – When you get a policy, you go into business with the insurance company and the first hit, the first money paid is yours. They want you to pay attention and not have losses. They want you to know that this hurts – it hurts them and you.

So you have to pay a certain amount out before your policy kicks in – that's a deductible.

Q – How does one submit a claim and what is the process after that?

Kent – You just call up and file the claim. We have a claims adjuster who is very good and she files the paperwork. She gives it to the insurance company and monitors them to make sure they are doing their job and you are getting responses. When you get a claim, it's a terrible thing because you're afraid you're going to lose money, not finish your project or claimants will come after you personally. Co-operate and tell the truth because professional investigators will find it out eventually. They've seen it all before. Their job is to help you. And if it's a large claim, they tend to hire professionals that don't work for the insurance company who's job it is to solely document and then make an opinion of the loss and give it to the insurance company. What happens is you get filmmakers who are very busy and overworked. Compiling the accounting is difficult and tedious and then they get mad at the insurance company for not paying. Well, they don't pay unless you have the right documentation. Hiring an experienced accountant helps solve this. If it's part of the policy that you have to make a good case for your loss. If you make a good case and it is covered under the policy, you will get paid. That is the law.

Q – How long does it take to turn around a claim?

Kent – It takes as long as reporting the claim and providing the correct documentation, which is often up to

Insurance Types

GUERILLA FILM MAKER SAYS!

NEGATIVE FILM AND VIDEOTAPE
Direct physical loss, damage or destruction of raw film or tape stock, exposed film (devel. or undevel.), recorded videotape, soundtracks and tapes and software used to generate computer images, up to the amount of insured production costs.

FAULTY STOCK, CAMERA AND PROCESSING
Covers loss, damage or destruction of raw film or tape stock, exposed film (developed or undeveloped), recorded videotapes, soundtracks and tapes, caused by or resulting from fogging or the use of faulty materials (including cameras and videotape recorders); faulty sound equipment; faulty developing: faulty editing or faulty processing; and accidental erasure of videotape recordings.

MISCELLANEOUS EQUIPMENT
Covers against risks of direct physical loss, damage or destruction to cameras, camera equipment, sound, lighting (including breakage of globes) and grip equipment, owned by or rented to the production company.

PROPERTY DAMAGE LIABILITY
Pays for damage or destruction of property of others (including loss of use of the property) while the property is in the care, custody or control of the production company and is used or to be used in an insured production.

ERRORS AND OMISSIONS
Covers legal liability and defense for the production company against lawsuits alleging unauthorized use of title, format, ideas, characters, plots, plagiarism, unfair competition or piracy. Also protects for alleged libel, slander, defamation of character or invasion of privacy. This coverage will usually be required by a distributor prior to release of any theatrical or television production.

WORKERS' COMPENSATION
This coverage is required to be carried by State law and applies to all temporary or permanent cast or production crew members. Coverage provides medical, disability or death benefits to any cast or crew member who becomes injured in the course of their employment. Coverage usually applies on a 24 hour per day basis whenever employees are on location away from their homes.

Even though a production company may be using a payroll service, which usually provides Workers' Compensation insurance to all payrolled employees, the company should always consider carrying a "back-up" policy of their own. This will protect the production company for any unpaid interns or others who may not be payrolled.

COMMERCIAL GENERAL LIABILITY
Protects the production company against claims for Bodily Injury or Property Damage Liability arising out of operations in connection with filming activity. This coverage will be required prior to filming on any city or state roadways, or any location sites requiring filming permits.

BUSINESS AUTO POLICY
Protects the production company against claims for Bodily Injury or Property Damage Liability for use of all non-owned and hired vehicles. This coverage includes picture cars and all production vehicles.

Courtesy of Truman Van Dyke Company

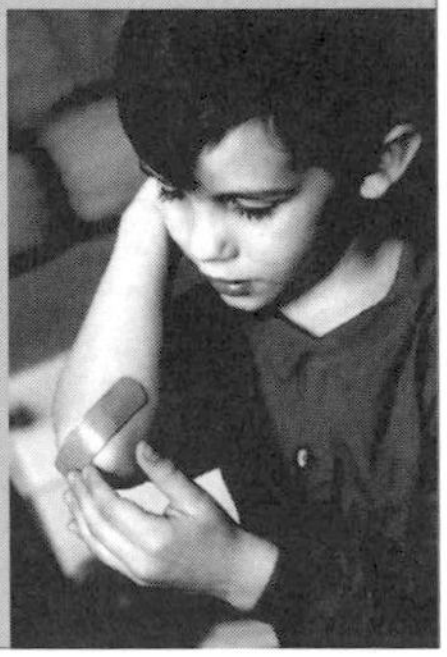

the producer. So if they get everything in the correct way, it should take a couple of weeks. One thing that's important is to report the claim as soon as it happens. Production people get busy because they're moving fast and the guy who had the accident may be on another show in three days. Once he's in North Carolina or wherever, it's going to be harder to get his statement and that will slow down the claim. It looks bad if you had a claim and you don't report it for three weeks. Cast coverage is immediate. They need to have a doctor there and maybe even a lab person.

Q – Is there anything that you won't cover?

Kent – Some things are not insurable. Such as whether you make a profit or not . Weather insurance. And we won't cover fraud or you lying.

Q – What if you're shooting wild animals, underwater or in dangerous parts of the world?

Kent – Every issue affects the policy. Let's take the most important part – the people. Worker's comp is related to what country you're in and for how long. Each country has a rating and some countries like Cuba they won't cover because of treaties. Some countries are at war and they won't cover anything save for special polices for news people. A good broker will ask you where are you going and for how long. That will be the basis for what you're charged. Then they'll ask you what you're doing. If you're doing something dangerous, the company wants more premium because your chances of someone getting hurt are greater. If you're working with a lion or something like that, you have to let the insurance company know. You may need animal mortality as the lion trainer may require that you cover the lion should it die. And liability – if the lion eats someone's face off, the insurance company needs to evaluate that risk. Anything out of the normal, you have to discuss with your broker.

Q – Is there anything people from other countries need to know about if they are coming to the United States to shoot?

Kent – Say you're in London and you're coming here. Your policy in the UK may extend. Generally, they won't accept your liability portion if they know you're coming from abroad. You have to check if it does.

Permits

GUERILLA FILM MAKER SAYS!

1. If you're shooting at a public institution (school, hospital, etc.), you're going to have to get permission.

2. You probably don't need permission to shoot your friend getting stitches at a hospital. You just need it from your friend.

3. Every city and state has some sort of council or office that handles filming permits like the EIDC in Los Angles and the MOFTB in New York. Give them a call to find out if you need any special permits for what you are doing.

4. Permits come from bureaucratic places – factor in the time to clear the red tape into your shooting schedule.

5. Public places like beaches and restaurants can be a pain because not only may they require permits, you could get random people in your shot and have to get them to sign releases. Try to avoid these places if possible.

6. Though rare, some fees are reimbursable once you finish production. These tend to be at certain governmental landmarks.

7. Always keep your permits handy when shooting. Police and officials will be around to check on you.

8. If you can't afford the permit, make a deal with the owners for publicity or a special thanks in the credits.

9. Certain states require permits for shooting with small, hand held cameras and some don't. Again, check with the film commission to see.

10. If you decide to shoot guerilla style, be careful with what you're shooting and how you're shooting it. Looking suspicious and nervous while shooting at The Empire State Building might land you in the FBI's custody.

11. If you go overseas, some countries require that you get a permit to practice journalism. Check with that country's consulate to be sure.

12. Permits are not always fool proof. People can go back on their word and it may come down to a bribe to keep shooting.

Usually what happens is that people coming here get an American liability policy at least and definitely worker's comp for the Americans. Some people from foreign countries don't have a concept of insurance – it's not in their vocabularies. That needs to be driven home. If you're an American and you are hired by an Asian company, they often don't think about worker's comp. Be sure to protect yourself.

Q – Any other tips for saving money on insurance and still being properly covered?

Kent – There are some organizations that set up insurance deals for documentaries. Some of these are quite legitimate, others aren't. Some of these illegal companies are quite attractive because they are cheap. You want to buy insurance from a licensed insurer and you want to be the named insured. That's important. You can't rent insurance. You can't generally get on someone else's policy unless they are truly involved in your production and it's a co-venture. Otherwise, it can be an illusion. You may find out that you don't have coverage. Sometimes you may join an organization and they supposedly have some coverage, they may not cover you as a named insured – they may just cover themselves. It's best to stay away from them. The other trick is that someone may say they have a cheap E&O policy for you. But all it covers is the distributor – you are not a named insured. Many producers are young and they see insurance as a hurdle to overcome so any way to get over it is fine with them – and they get burned. E&O claims don't come in very often, but when they do, just to defend a claim comes in at $40,000-$60,000.

Q – What common mistakes do you see documentary filmmakers make?

Kent – Not taking insurance seriously. Seeing it as an obstacle, not as help. Your insurance broker is there to help you if you get into trouble. We are your armor. But you need to understand your policies and the limits of them.

Q – What advice would you give a new documentary filmmaker?

Kent – Focus on two aspects – the creative aspects of course, but also the reality aspects like insurance. It is hard dealing with individuals that are very scattered. You have to focus on what you're doing both creatively and in the real world in order to sustain your vision. You have to use your right brain and your left brain.

GUERILLA FILM MAKER SAYS!

Production Binders

The key to saving time and money is to be organized. A production binder will help you find important information quickly when the heat is on full blast. Get yourself a 3-inch D-ring binder from an office supply store along with some dividers that can be labeled. Label the dividers into sections relevant to your film. Here are some suggestions:

Releases
Legal/Deal points
Interview Questions and notes
Crew list and contacts
Subject list and contacts
Funder contacts
Location information and contacts
Correspondence
Production Schedule *if possible*
Film safety and security *– local hospital, police, etc.*
Delivery Requirements
Editing notes/Footage log
Archival footage needs and contacts
Voice over drafts
Insurance premium information

DOCU-DRAMA PRODUCER

Q – Is there a big demand from broadcasters for docu-dramas?

Lisa – I think it's a new format that's really developed in the last four or five years especially after the major American broadcasters did them. At its best, it's a way of dramatizing history so that the emotion of the storytelling passes through. It can tell a story in a much more dramatic fashion than a straight documentary can.For anything that's outside a normal timeline, drama-docs work really well.

Q – Does Discovery Channel do a lot of these?

Lisa – Yes. Discovery and National Geographic. The BBC and Channel 5 have been doing it for some time in England. It's hybrid storytelling. *Touching The Void* is a good example of that. It's retrospective, but it uses drama to make you feel it emotionally. If they didn't use drama in that part of the film, the interviews with the three guys would've been dryer and less interesting.

Q – Do you use archival footage mixed in with the interviews and recreations?

Lisa – It's a combination of all things. There are two distinctions for drama-docs. There's a dialogue drama-doc, which is a scripted doc almost like a drama. You script the drama and the expert interviews. And then there are the non-scripted ones where you use just drama-recon. And that's in place of archive. You do that if you're doing something before archival footage was available – so anything over 150 years ago. There's no sound shot with these. It's just images to explain the narrative voice-over.

Q – Have you noticed archival houses not giving in perpetuity licenses for their footage? And will that push people to recreate things more?

Lisa – Definitely. Archive footage can be extremely expensive. Sometimes it's free and some you just pay a small fee per minute that you use. I used to make a lot of archival films in the past and that was never an issue. Now it means the shelf life of a film is just for a couple of years. That's a problem with documentaries. The good ones reappear, but most die off. Then again, if you draw up a budget on shooting a drama-doc it is about £10,000 ($17,500) a day or something like that and that will give your three to four minutes of screen time. If the archive is more than that, then it makes more sense to do a drama-doc. But archive is priceless in the right way. If you're making a film about WWII, you need archive.

Q – How do get a sense of large scale grandeur on these films?

Lisa – Well, generally speaking, I can do the sacking of Alexandria with just 10 extras in historically accurate costumes. You have to be careful of lighting and clever with camera angles so you can kind of make it look like there are much more people than there are. It's true guerilla filmmaking. A friend of mine has a good example. In Morocco, there's a set that was built by Ridley Scott for *Gladiator* where they were shooting all day for just three minutes of screen time. My friend was over there doing a film on Egypt and they did the building of the pyramids in the morning, the Sphinx in the afternoon and the killing of King Tut in the evening. A huge monumental piece of history in a few hours time. That's what it's like. You don't have anywhere near the budgets that you would need to do it properly. You have to get creative because you have to represent the idea of it and pass what it means through the script. But at the same time, it shouldn't be silly.

Q – Do you do a lot of CGI?

Lisa – Yes. It plays a large part. When you cut back to a wide shot, what a feature film director would have is a lot of money to put a lot of extras in. You have £5,000-£10,000 ($8,750-$17,500) to make a special effects shot. You double up your crowd by using CGI. So it ends up looking like 1,000 people are there instead of five. They can get expensive so you really have to plan each shot well.

Q – What are the budgets generally for these films?

Lisa – If you do a co-production with an American broadcaster like Discovery, they can be fairly generous. If you are making a straight documentary for Channel 4 in the UK, you are getting £100,000-£150,000 ($175,000-$225,000) for an hour. For a drama-doc, you normally get between £300,000-£400,000 ($525,000-$700,000). At the moment, I'm making a 90-minute movie and I have a budget of about £380,000 ($650,000). That's really low. Most of it does end up on the screen, though.

Q – What is at the forefront of your mind when you're directing one of these films?

Lisa – You've got two hats – your drama hat and your documentary hat. One is always aware of the other. I think drama-docs are a good way to practice for drama because you have these little self-inclusive vignettes that illustrate a point in the script. So within those bounds it's quite creative. From the documentary point of view, you are always looking for ways to illustrate what you're trying to say. You're driven by the words where as in a drama you are driven by the pictures. It fits into this really weird area.

Q – Do you schedule the interviews together and the drama portions separately?

Lisa – Yes. Exactly. *Da Vinci's Lost Code*, which is what I am working on now is a classic example of what you shouldn't do, but I am under pressure from the broadcasters to deliver by a certain date. We had to shoot the drama in the middle of the documentary shoot, which is not what you want to do. You really want to shoot the documentary part first as it will tell you want you need to shoot for the drama. Your story develops as you talk to the experts. But in this case, I was forced to shoot the drama first due to the nature of it. There was a lot of science being done on a painting, so we had to follow the length of how long it took them from beginning to end to do the work. So we had to go off and shoot the drama. Ideally, we'd have waited until the scientists reached a conclusion.

Q – If you do that, presumably you may have to go back and do some re-shoots?

Lisa – Exactly. And there's never enough money to do that. So you have to shoot much more generally in this specific situation. *The Thin Blue Line* is a good example of that. There are very specific story points all the way along. But you can only do that after you know what has happened. In this case, you can't be specific because I don't know what is going to happen and I am going to have to do re-shoots.

Q – Are the crews you use the same for both parts?

Lisa – Not generally. I would get a documentary crew for that side and a drama crew for the other side. The documentary side is three or four people max and up to 50 on the drama side including extras. The director remains constant.

Q – Is a lot of the story made in the cutting room much like a traditional documentary?

Crew Websites

www.craigslist.com
www.crew.net
www.crew-list.net
www.debbiesbook.com
www.filmstaff.com
www.indieclub.com
www.mandy.com
www.media-match.com
www.nowbeyond.com
www.panix.com
www.reelcontact.com
www.shootingpeople.co.uk

GUERILLA FILM MAKER SAYS!

25 Things To Think About When Shooting Overseas

1. Investigate the country and it's individual region's relevant tax incentives/tax relief.

2. Talk to the relevant film commissions who can supply you with free photos, brochures, maps, contacts (i.e. hotels, extra casting agencies if shooting a docu-drama, equipment etc.) and any necessary resource guides.

3. Research other productions that have filmed in that country so to be aware of any problems.

4. Contact the country's immigration departments to find out the policies for bringing your crew into the country and if there are any filming restrictions.

5. Hire production managers or fixers who've shot there before. Make sure they speak your native tongue.

6. Check whether you or your crew will need any immunizations or vaccines before they visit the country.

7. Make sure everyone has a current passport and that it will not expire during the production (check also that it will also not expire within 6 months even if your shoot is for one month).

8. Find out about the local country's unions and work with them to ensure their support. You may have to hire local crew.

9. Meet with local authorities to find out if permits are required.

10. Find a good freight company that specializes in the entertainment industry to handle all your shipping including necessary carnets etc. depending on the size of your film.

11. Find out if the country of production accepts carnets or if like Taiwan it accepts a different type of carnet.

12. Inform your own insurers of your filming activities that take place out of the country making sure that you have proper coverage.

13. Being in a foreign country, you will need to get local insurance. Make sure you're fully covered. To find local insurance companies, check first with your insurance broker who may have relationships with companies in that country. Bear in mind that in certain countries, if you're not fully covered you can face different procedures e.g. in Spain, you must have the correct driving insurance as otherwise if you're pulled over for whatever reason, you could find yourself staying in jail until it's resolved.

14. Find out what the local laws are in the country of your production and the procedures if you're pulled over for either speeding or drunk driving.

15. Find out what the emergency medical procedures are (i.e. such as calling the country's equivalent of 911 or 999) and find out where the local emergency medical facilities are.

16. Find a local doctor/dentist that speaks your language.

17. Depending on where you're shooting, you need to inform your crew about what they can and can't take into the country.

18. Calculate the local currency conversion and find out where the best bureaus of exchange are for your cast and crew.

19. Find out if the country is NTSC or PAL – for either your own playback equipment or to recommend your crew to bring their own necessary converters with them.

20. Set up the equivalent of a Fed Ex/UPS/DHL account.

21. Check to see whether you have to form a separate company in that country in order to operate.

22. Set up bank accounts with the local bank in order to pay your local crew.

23. Always have some petty cash on hand for bribes and last minute fixes.

24. Make sure you follow the local customs. For example, shooting a pan shot of the North Korean president from the feet up is a sign of disrepect!

25. Check the weather reports!!!

Lisa – Yes. It's just like a regular documentary in that sense because you don't know what you're going to get until you shoot it. The difference is that the director should always get two weeks to a month to write the script before you shoot, so that you can have a planned shoot and edit. That way it's more like storytelling and not just watching the rushes and finding good bits and sticking them in. You're constructing things that pass a certain flavor, feeling or emotion to the audience.

Q – Do you follow a three-act structure like you do in a narrative film?

Lisa – You do. In this case, I'm making a film about a painting – is it a Leonardo or isn't it? So the first act is who are the people, why are we watching them and why it is important. The second act is watching it unfold – the puzzle of the investigation. And the third act is the conclusion - what happens to them and why. The problem with the Discovery Channel is that they repeat everything four times. You have this awful situation where you have to tease everything before and after every commercial break. So you spend a lot of your screen time telling them what you have already told them.

Q – Is that just Discovery?

Lisa – It's definitely Discovery. It's a very American thing to patronize your audience. But at the same time, it's catching on over here in the UK as well. The audience is God and even Discovery is screen-testing drama-docs like you would a feature film. That's unprecedented. And if they don't like it, I'm going to have to go back and re-edit it. And because the audience is God, the truth gets lost in the middle. So you're making a documentary, which is meant to be factually accurate, but often isn't because the audience doesn't like the facts. That's a big worry because you become part of the Ministry of Disinformation. That's where the grey area is for drama-docs because you generalize to the point of it being meaningless.

Q – So all they care about are the ratings and not necessarily the facts?

Lisa –Years ago they would've been concerned with the quality of filmmaking in terms of are we doing something interesting and important that's going to help define ourselves as a nation and a culture. That's out the window and it is all about the popcorn.

Q – Isn't there a governing body in the UK that checks these programs out to make sure they are accurate?

Lisa – Yes. I think it is called the IAC. People can complain to them and they can shut broadcasters down. It's scary because documentaries are supposed to reflect some level of truth and if you are propagandizing it from day one by making it much more interesting, exciting or bigger than it generally is, then the real thing gets lost. America doesn't seen to have much of an ethical stance on these things. It doesn't matter as long as they get ratings.

Q – So where do you get your truth?

Lisa – It comes down to the individual filmmaker. I get asked to blur the lines a bit and I say no because the expert will be very unhappy if we said that. And they say, *"We're paying for it. We don't care."* So there's a real arrogance in terms of that. You have to fight back subtly and say you won't do things that are wrong. This is a classic example. They all wanted this film to be about a new painting by Leonardo DiVinci that was discovered. When it turned out to not be the case, they kind of turned their back on it. If there had any been any doubt about it, a gray area, they would have said it could have been by Leonardo but the expert said it isn't. They don't want to hear a movie about a guy who bought a painting for £1,000 twenty to thirty years ago and now he's spent all this time and money trying to find out and then an expert says no – it's a true reflection of society. They want a happy ending, but this is a documentary not a drama.

Q – What are some of the biggest challenges and problems of producing these programs?

Lisa – Usually not having enough time to research it properly and put it together. So you end up saying, *"Oh, that'll do."* Things are commissioned late so you hit the ground running. If they give you a bit more time, you could spend the money more wisely. The money usually goes out the window because you're trying to solve problems. Normally, you want to do a month or two of research. Then you'd film all the documentary and then break for a few weeks to plan the drama. Then you storyboard and script the drama. Then you'd go and shoot that. Then you'd spend a week or two writing the script and then you'd go into the edit room. Instead, you do it all at once – a documentary day one day, a drama day the next.

Q – Do you ever shoot a drama day if you happen to find a nice location near a documentary shoot?

Lisa – You consider that. Is Israel a good place to shoot the drama? Do the actors look right? Yes, they do. OK. In Europe you go to Tunisia or Morocco because you get more for your money. They also look right for many historical stories.

Q – Do you take equipment with you or hire it at location?

Lisa – For the documentary shoot, you have a minimal amount of kit. You take the camera with you on the plane. The lights and the rest go get locally. The drama part is a bigger palava. You tend to hire a local production company who sorts out the equipment. You take costumes, make up, all the art department stuff and props. You ship a lot of things. There are a lot of problems with carnets and other documents. If you don't sign the right document in the right way, it might be impossible to get it back. Equipment can get lost and stuck in customs. And if you don't get it, you have to do with out it.

Q – What do you shoot on?

Lisa – Hi Def for the documentary. The standard Sony Hi-Def cameras. With the drama footage I normally shoot Super 16mm, unless the budget is too low and then it's Hi-Def. I chose the Panasonic Varispeed camera because I wanted to shoot a lot of slow motion. You can get away with a lot by slowing everything down. And you can play with the focus. A trick is to keep the depth of field as close to the camera as possible and blur the background and then you can't see that there are only five people as extras.

Q – How good is that Panasonic camera?

Lisa – It's pretty good. It has an interchangeable lens and prime lenses as well. I don't like video ultimately as a format yet. It's still has that very clinical quality that film doesn't have. Film feels rich and emotive. HD doesn't unless you grade the hell out of it. Take all the brightness out of it. It's almost too perfect and it's hard to make people look attractive. It's got a lot of contrast. If you have a really ugly person that you're shooting, HD will bring out all the flaws. You have to get really creative with the lighting. The only problem is that if you pull out all the lighting with HD and make it all moody, it won't pass many of the broadcasters' specs. And you want that kind of look when you go back in time. You want it to appear as if we're in a different time.

Q – What are some of the challenges of shooting in a foreign country?

Lisa – If you are dealing with North Africa, you have to watch the local production company because you might end up paying off a lot of people that have nothing to do with what you're doing. And if you're

GUERILLA FILM MAKER SAYS!

Keep Your Receipts!

As a filmmaker, you can claim deductions on your taxes that others can't. The safest bet to know what you can do is to consult an experienced accountant, but here is a list of some things you can claim to reduce your tax burden.

Research – *this includes film tickets (checking out other docs or subject matter), DVD/VHS/CD rental or purchase, magazine and newspaper subscriptions (for story ideas),*

Equipment – *TV/VCR/DVD/computer anything can be claimed. Camera equipment, lighting equipment, production insurance and basically anything that can be used for your filmmaking business can be deducted. Clothing can only be deducted if it was used as wardrobe or relevant to your story.*

Vehicle – *you can deduct a portion (based on the percentage you use it for work or personal reasons) of your car or truck expenses, which includes maintenance, fees, gas, and registration. Sorry, you can't deduct moving violations or parking tickets!*

Office – *if you have office space, your rent and utilities can be deducted. If you have a home office, the percentage of the whole house that your office takes up is the percentage of your rent, utilities and insurance you can claim. Of course, any fax, telephone, internet provider or cell phone charges can be claimed as long as they are for business purposes.*

Health insurance – *if you pay for your health insurance or a portion of it, then a portion of it can be claimed.*

Travel – *hotels, airplane fares, rental cars, business meals and other location expenses can be claimed as well as long as you are not being reimbursed by someone.*

producing that is really annoying. Money is really tight so why am I paying for all these people? It's the way it works in those countries and you can't stop it. Everyone pays each other off and does each other favors. When I was in Egypt last year, my fixer had a wad in his pocket, which was the size of a football. He would just peel off notes and hand them out left, right and center and everyone would just disappear off in different directions and things are just done. You don't get receipts, which worries production managers immensely. They do rip you off a lot, but then again you're going there because it's cheap. So you're ripping them off as well. Directing extras in a foreign language is difficult because you give them direction and then it has to be translated. It can get mistranslated and then you turn the camera on and nothing happens. Same thing happens with the crew. Make sure everyone speaks English.

Q – How hard is it to find crew?

Lisa – You just have to trust. Tunisia has a lot of pretty good crew – especially the grips and the gaffers. They were all pretty spot on. They all spoke French, but we worked it out.

Q – Are most drama-docs commissioned or are they in-house ideas of the broadcasters?

Lisa – I have pitched specific ideas. I would take it to a production company and they would try to get it commissioned for me. If they do, then a year down the track, I'd do it. Me, as a freelance gun, I couldn't get it done alone. There are only a handful of companies that do this in the world. The best way to get into this kind of filmmaking is to find one of these companies and work for them as a researcher. And the best degree to get is a history degree since that is what most of the drama-docs are about.

Q – Do you write the voice over?

Lisa – I write it and then I get someone else to come in polish it. Maybe you'll bring in someone to come in and Americanize it for that audience. Then we get an actor to come in and read it. Sometimes we can get a big name actor to do it and they get paid a lot of money for three to four hours of reading.

Q – What are the common mistakes that you see documentary filmmakers make?

Lisa – With all of this stuff that we have been discussing about the filmmaker being less important than the ratings, what has ended up happening is that you get different directors doing different parts. A documentary director doing that part and a drama director doing the other. So the notion of storytelling as auteur-ship has dissolved. I would urge more executive producers to let people tell the story instead of creating a product with marketing bits that they hope will string together. Without that over-arching vision for the entire film, you end up making a lot of mistakes.

Q – What advice would you give a new documentary filmmaker?

Lisa – Try to have as much intellectual independence as possible. If you're making your film, place yourself in a position where you can make it without too much input. The best way to do that is make it first and then sell it. As soon as you get into commission territory, you have more people on the edit end messing with your film and your vision.

Production Budget

Below is the production budget for the documentary film, Backyard Racers. The budget is broken up into two sections. The first is called the Top Sheet and is a summary of how much money is allotted for each major section of making the film such as story, research, camera, sound and visual effects. These are then subtotaled into pre-production, production and post-production lines and a final negative cost is listed. The second part of the budget is a detailed line item account of everything you will need to make the film, the rate, the length of time needed for each item and the cost (shown here). Programs like Movie Magic Budgeting can keep all of this straight and even calculate union needs like overtime and meal penalties if you happen to be working that way (most docs aren't union). But, if you don't want to spend the cash, you can do what we did and use an Excel spreadsheet – takes a bit of time to set up the formulas, but worth it in the end. Alternatively, there is Budget from Movie Tools, which we developed for low budget films (www.movietools.com).

AC#	ACCOUNT NAME	UNITS	TYPE	RATE	TOTAL
1000	STORY - RIGHTS AND EXPENSES				$0
	TOTAL 1000				**$0**
1100	CONTINUITY AND TREATMENT				
1	WRITERS				$0
	TOTAL 1100				**$0**
1200	PRODUCERS UNIT				
1	PRODUCERS				$0
	TOTAL 1200				**$0**
1300	DIRECTORS UNIT				
1	DIRECTORS				$0
	TOTAL 1300				**$0**
	TOTAL ABOVE THE LINE: PREPRODUCTION				**$0**
1100	CONTINUITY AND TREATMENT				
1	WRITERS				$5,000
3	RESEARCH				$8,000
4	STORY EDITORS & CONSULTANTS				$0
	TOTAL 1100d				**$13,000**
1200	PRODUCERS UNIT				
1	PRODUCERS				$20,000
2	EXECUTIVE PRODUCERS				$0
3	ASSOCIATE PRODUCERS				$0
4	CO-PRODUCERS				$0
	TOTAL 1200				**$20,000**
1300	DIRECTORS UNIT				
1	DIRECTORS				$25,000
2	SECOND UNIT				$0
4	DIALOGUE DIRECTORS				$0
6	CASTING DIRECTOR				$0
	OTHER CHARGES				$0
	TOTAL 1300				**$25,000**
	TOTAL ABOVE THE LINE: PRODUCTION				**$58,000**

2000	PRODUCTION STAFF				
1	PRODUCTION MANAGER				$0
2	FIRST ASSISTANT DIRECTORS				$0
3	SECOND ASSISTANT DIRECTORS				$0
4	FIXER				$0
5	SCRIPT SUPERVISORS				$0
6	LOCATION AUDITOR				$0
7	TIMEKEEPER				$0
8	PAYROLL SERVICING ORGANIZATION				$0
9	LOCAL HIRE				$0
10	TECHNICAL ADVISORS				$1,000
11	SECRETARIES				$0
12	PRODUCTION SECRETARY				$0
13	ADDITIONAL HIRE				$0
14	OTHER CHARGES				$1,000
	TOTAL 2000				**$2,000**
2100	TALENT/INTERVIEWEES				
1	EXTRA TALENT				$0
2	**HOSTS**				**$0**
	TOTAL 2100				**$0**
2200	SET OPERATIONS				
1	OPERATIONS - SHOOTING COMPANY				$0
	OTHER CHARGES				$0
	TOTAL 2200				**$0**
2300	MAKEUP & HAIRDRESSING				$250
	TOTAL 2300				**$250**
2400	GRIP/LIGHTING				
1	LIGHTING	allow			$2,000
	OTHER CHARGES				$0
	TOTAL 2400				**$2,000**
2500	CAMERA				
1	CAMERA	allow			$5,000
2	DIRECTOR OF PHOTOGRAPHY				$0
3	CAMERA SHOOTING CREW				$0
4	CAMERA OPERATOR				$0
5	1ST ASSISTANT CAMERAMAN				$0
6	2ND ASSISTANT CAMERAMAN				$0
7	EXTRA OPERATORS				$0
8	EXTRA ASSISTANT CAMERAMEN				$0
9	STILLMAN				$0
10	DV CAMERAS	allow			$2,000
11	DV CAMERA RENTALS	allow			$3,000
12	HDTV CAMERA PACKAGE				$0
13	CAMERA CRANE				$0
14	CAMERA CAR				$0
15	CAMERA DOLLIES				$0
16	SPECIAL EQUIPMENT				$2,000
17	BOX RENTALS				$0
18	STILL EQUIPMENT				$500
19	MONITOR/CAMERA ACCESSORIES				$0
	OTHER CHARGES				$0
	TOTAL 2500				**$12,500**
2600	SOUND				
1	SOUND RENTAL	allow			$2,000
2	SOUND MIXER				$0
3	BOOM MAN				$0
4	CABLEMAN				$0
5	PLAYBACK OPERATOR				$0
6	PURCHASES				$800
7	AUDIO STOCK	15	tapes	10	$150
8	RENTALS				$0
9	SOUND CHANNEL				$0
10	WALKIE TALKIES				$500
11	SPECIAL EQUIPMENT				$0
12	PLAYBACK				$0
13	EQUIPMENT REPAIRS				$300
14	CELL PHONES				$600
	OTHER CHARGES				$0
	TOTAL 2600				**$4,350**
2700	TRANSPORTATION				
1	DRIVERS				$0
2	TRANSPORTATION COORDINATOR				$0
3	DRIVER CAPTAIN				$0
4	DRIVER CO-CAPTAIN				$0
5	DRIVERS				$0
6	VEHICLE RENTAL	2	weeks	225	$450

7	DRESSING ROOM RENTALS				$0
8	REPAIRS AND MAINTENANCE	allow			$400
9	FUEL	allow			$1,000
10	TRANSPORTATION TAXES AND PERMITS				$0
11	MILEAGE ALLOWANCE				$0
12	SPECIAL EQUIPMENT PURCHASES AND RENTALS				$0
	OTHER CHARGES				$0
	TOTAL 2700				**$1,850**

2800	LOCATION EXPENSES				
1	LOCATION				$0
2	TRANSPORTATION FARES	allow			$500
3	HOTELS, MOTELS, ETC.	allow			$3,000
4	MEALS	allow			$3,000
5	MEALS SERVED ON LOCATION				$0
6	SITE RENTALS				$0
7	OFFICE EQUIPMENT RENTALS				$0
8	TELEPHONE				$0
9	SHIPPING STATIONARY POSTAGE				$0
10	COURTESY PAYMENTS				$0
11	CUSTOM FEES, DUTIES, ETC.				$0
12	EXPORT TAXES				$0
13	FILM SHIPMENT	allow			$1,200
14	PERMITS				$0
15	FOREIGN TRAVEL PERMITS				$0
16	FLIGHT INSURANCE				$0
17	LOCATION SCOUTING				$0
18	SECRETARIES & TYPISTS				$0
19	LOCATION CONTACT				$0
20	POLICEMEN, WATCHMEN, FIREMEN				$0
	OTHER CHARGES				$0
	TOTAL 2800				**$7,700**

2850	TRAVEL AND LIVING EXPENSES				
1	AIR FARES	allow			$2,500
2	HOUSING				$0
3	TRAIN/BUS/TAXI				$0
4	PRODUCTION VEHICLE				$0
	TOTAL 2850				**$2,500**

2900	TAPE/TRANSFER				
1	PRODUCTION SUPER 16mm FILM	25	rolls	120	$3,000
2	PRODUCTION SUPER 8mm FILM	8	rolls	15	$120
3	PROCESSING: SUPER 8mm	allow			$500
4	VIDEO TAPE STOCK DV/HD	300	tapes	7	$2,100
5	NORMAL DEVELOPING: S-16mm	10000	Ft.	0.115	$1,150
6	FORCED DEVELOPING				$0
7	1 LIGHT DAILIES				$0
8	TIMED DAILIES	6	hours	85	$510
9	VIDEO TAPE STOCK BETA SP	5	tapes	42	$210
10	SPECIAL LABORATORY WORK				$0
11	STILLS - NEGATIVE & LABORATORY				$500
12	SOUND TRANSFERS DAILIES				$0
13	LABOR				$0
14	HD TO 35MM BLOWUP				$0
15	HD UNIVERSAL MASTER				$700
15	HD TO NTSC DOWNCONVERSION				$0
16	OTHER CHARGES				$0
	TOTAL 2900				**$8,090**

	TOTAL PRODUCTION	**$41,940**

3000	EDITORIAL				
1	EDITOR	12	weeks	2000	$24,000
2	ASSISTANT EDITOR				$0
3	APPRENTICE EDITOR				$0
4	ADDITIONAL HIRE				$0
5	ADR EDITOR				$0
6	SOUND EFFECTS EDITOR/FOLEY				$0
7	MUSIC EDITOR	allow			$2,500
8	MIX	allow			$7,500
9	PROJECTION (PRODUCTION & EDITING)				$0
11	FILM MESSENGER				$0
12	CUTTING ROOMS				$3,000
13	EQUIPMENT RENTALS				$3,000
14	PURCHASES				$0
15	VIDEO TRANSFERS				$4,000
16	PREVIEW EXPENSES				$0
17	DUBS				$600
18	OFF-LINE EDITING SYSTEM				$3,000
19	HDTV ON-LINE				$700
20	COLOR CORRECTION				$0
	OTHER CHARGES				$0
	TOTAL 3000				**$48,300**

3100	MUSIC				
1	MUSIC SUPERVISOR				$8,000
2	COMPOSER/CONDUCTOR				$4,500
3	MUSICIANS				$0
4	ARRANGERS				$0
5	COPYISTS				$0
6	SINGERS, CHORUS				$0
7	LABOR, MOVING INSTRUMENTS				$0
8	SYNCHRONIZATION LICENSE (FROM PUBLISHER)				$5,000
9	RECORDING RIGHTS				$5,000
10	MUSIC REUSE FEES				$5,000
11	SPECIAL INSTRUMENT RENTAL				$0
12	OTHER CHARGES				$0
	TOTAL 3100				**$27,500**

3200	**POST PRODUCTION SOUND**				
1	COMPLETE SOUND PACKAGE	allow			$7,800
	TOTAL 3200				**$7,800**

3300	**TITLES & GRAPHICS**				
1	MOTION GRAPHIC DESIGN	allow			$10,000
	TOTAL 3300				**$10,000**

3400	PUBLICITY				
1	PUBLICITY FIRM FEE				$5,000
2	NEGATIVES, PRINTS, SUPPLIES				$0
3	PRODUCTION PUBLICITY COSTS				$0
4	OTHER CHARGES				$0
	TOTAL 3400				**$5,000**

3500	INSURANCE				
1	ERRORS AND OMISSIONS				$5,000
2	LIABILITY				$0
3	WORKMEN'S COMPENSATION				$0
4	LOCAL INSURANCE REQUIREMENTS				$0
5	MISCELLANEOUS EQUIPMENT				$0
6	COMPREHENSIVE LIABILITY				$0
7	PROPERTY DAMAGE LIABILITY				$0
8	PRODUCER'S ENTERTAINMENT PKG.				$2,000
9	AUTO INSURANCE				$0
9	OTHER CHARGES				$0
	TOTAL 3500				**$4,400**

3600	GENERAL & ADMINISTRATIVE				
1	MISCELLANEOUS				$0
2	TELEPHONE AND TELEGRAPH				$2,000
3	PRINTING AND XEROXING				$400
4	LOCAL MEALS				$0
5	MPAA RATING FEE				$0
6	DIALOGUE CONTINUITIES				$0
7	ENTERTAINMENT				$0
8	OFFICE SUPPLIES	allow			$1,000
9	PRODUCTION SERVICING ORGANIZATION				$0
10	FEES & CHARGES	allow			$1,000
11	ACCOUNTING FEE				$3,500
12	LEGAL FEE				$7,500
13	OFFICE SPACE RENTAL				$5,000
14	TRANSCRIPTION				$0
15	HOSPITALITY				$0
	OTHER CHARGES				$0
	TOTAL 3600				**$20,400**

3700	FESTIVALS & SCREENINGS				
1	FEES & CHARGES				$1,000
2	FESTIVAL FEES/PASSES				$1,000
3	TRAVEL/LODGING				$2,000
4	PROMOTIONAL MATERIALS				$2,000
5	TRANSFER/DUBS				$1,000
	TOTAL 3700				**$7,000**

3800	INTERNET RE-PURPOSING				
1	WEB SITE DESIGN				$2,000
	TOTAL 3800				**$2,000**

TOTAL POST-PRODUCTION	**$135,700**
TOTAL ABOVE/BELOW THE LINE	**$234,940**

THE DP

Q – As a camerawoman, do you find the advent of high-end digital cameras a good thing or a bad thing?

Joan – It's a very exciting time right now because of the technology. It makes it easier to make documentaries technically and financially. For me, it's a complete revolution because I started out with big film cameras. I'm left eyed, so I'd have a camera on my shoulder and the eyepiece goes across my right eye to my left eye – so I'm just a big glass eye to people. I couldn't connect or talk to people. By having these little cameras that you don't have to hold to your eye, you become a human being. It's very interactive. It changes the whole form as well. We started out with *Nanook Of The North* where everything was very staged. With the lightweight cameras, the cinema verité guys could do their thing. And now we've got really cheap equipment that's broadcast quality and one person can go out and make the most amazing film. Or... one person can go out and make a lot of crap. But look at Sean McAllister's film *The Liberace of Baghdad* or Hubert Sauper's *Darwin's Nightmare*. They're wonderful, personal portraits that those filmmakers did basically on their own.

Q – What are your feelings on the discipline of shooting film in relation to shooting tape?

Joan – I grew up shooting film and you really had to think about what you were doing. It was expensive. I remember the figure $114 to buy a roll of film. That's 10 or 11 minutes of footage. I made a whole series of films with Nick Broomfield where it was just the two of us shooting women in the army or people in prison and we had four magazines. Nick would carry three of them in a backpack and I would have one on the camera. We would go into a situation knowing that if we didn't get a scene with all four magazines that we would never get the scene. I think the fact that you can stop and change a magazine, gives everybody a break. It can give you a moment to rejig how you want the interview to go because you have this little break. You have to choose carefully when you are going to start rolling. I feel that once that moment happens, I'm going to shoot my wad. I have ten minutes. But if nothing is happening, I will hold back. We're very abusive now with interviews because tape is cheap. The other thing about shooting with film is that it's a double system with the audio recorder rolling independently of the camera. The quarter inch tape was a lot cheaper than the film, so the sound person could roll much more that the film person. That way you could get the beginning of something on sound and then the camera could turn on. With tape, you are only laying down the sound when you roll camera so you have to roll more, or else you might miss something.

Q – On Nick Broomfield's films, you go into interviews with the cameras rolling. It doesn't feel over-prepared.

Joan – Nick is always prepared. He always knows what he is going for. He appears to be this kind of bumbling person, and in some senses he is because he isn't a technician, so he's struggling with the tape recorder. I don't like to do interviews at all because I think people become very presentational. They present themselves in manner that they want themselves to be seen. I think Nick doesn't want them to be prepared. He wants to catch them off guard. That way you get a real sense of what people are like. And that's why he rolls as he goes in. People expect that you will invite the crew in, have a chat and then go over and do the interview behind a desk with a flag and a plant.

Q – Do you lose that spontaneity when you change a magazine?

Joan – It takes very little time to change a mag. And if they kick us out, we'd shoot it! What's interesting is when they realize that you're shooting everything. They better figure out how they want to present themselves because it's all going to be used.

Q – What do you think makes a good documentary image?

Joan – Content. I don't care about the image so much – especially with small cameras. When I first started shooting with them I was concerned because it was hard to keep them level or move smoothly. You're always looking up people's noses. Then I threw that out the window and said it is what it is. It's completely different. It's not film. I'll use *Darwin's Nightmare* as an example. He shot a lot of that with a Sony 100A and it's completely riveting because of the content. If what you're shooting is interesting, your subjects are articulate and the camera loves them, that is what's important. I have been shooting the Dixie Chicks a lot recently. I can use the small camera and stay in the corner and not be noticed. I do it because I'm dealing with people who aren't actors and also it doesn't call attention to the filmmaking process. The small camera makes you look less of a technician and more like a human being so your subjects can connect to you.

Q – What filmmaking muscles does the documentary DP exercise?

Joan – The listening muscles, which are the most important things. In order to be a documentary filmmaker you have to be really interested in people. That comes over and people sense and respond to that. You have to listen and anticipate what is going to happen. I always say that I try to use a camera the way I'd use my eyes. If I'm interested in shooting two people having a conversation and I'm interested in looking at the reaction one person is having, that's where the camera goes. If I'm interested in the person talking, that's where the camera goes. It's not intellectual at all. It's kind of being in the moment and being part of the circle. You aren't standing outside at the end of a long lens – you are a participant. And you have to work at earning your place in that circle.

Q – Is it easier to gain people's trust with the smaller camera?

Joan – You're more able to react. People can see you better and I feel more comfortable interacting while shooting. But even with the big cameras, in the months that you shoot subjects you become part of their subculture. And you are undergoing the same thing they are experiencing. When Nick and I were shooting *Soldier Girls* we spent three and a half months going through basic training with the new recruits. Going on all the road marches, getting up at the same hour and eating with them. The same was true with *Residents*, which Alan Barker and I did through R.J. Cutler's Actual Reality company. We spent 53 weeks going through what it's like to be a medical intern. After a while, we were their buds. We all went through the anguish of watching patients, whom we had all become attached to, die.

Q – What if you aren't with someone for a long period of time, and you're doing a quick interview. Are there any tips to try and relax the interviewee?

Joan – If I'm shooting an interview, it's someone else's film and that is their job! But I keep going back to being as non-technical as possible and just being a person. As a documentary filmmaker, you're in a very privileged position where people have already agreed that it's OK to participate in the documentary. Usually it's because they have some message they want to get out to the world. You dispense with the social bullshit that you normally go through to get to know people, so you can cut to the chase. So you have incredibly intense experiences with people without knowing them intimately. I have to say because of Jerry Springer and other trashy TV shows - and we noticed this on another show we did with R.J. called *American High* - all these kids in the first week were telling us everything and more, people feel free to spill their guts out in front of a camera. *"I'm gay, but I'm in the closet. I can't let my family know because it would kill my grandmother."* Verbal diarrhea. We weren't asking for it, either. And then there was this reaction of like, *"Are you guys still here? I've already told you everything."* That was the reaction, especially amongst the parents because they began to realize that we weren't going away and would be there month after month after month. It began to percolate down, the significance of our being there for the whole year.

Q – When you're shooting a documentary are you thinking in terms of establishing shots, wide shots, medium

GUERILLA FILM MAKER SAYS!

Location Tips

Whether it's a set up interview or following lions on the Serengeti, there are some basic things you should bear in mind when going on your shoot.

1. Remember that you are a guest in anyone's home or office and you and your crew must act like guests. Be courteous and clean up after yourselves.

2. Be aware of sound issues like running refrigerators, air conditioners, airplane flight paths, traffic, etc. Try to scout out the location on the same day of the week at the same time of your location shoot to get a feel for the place.

3. Check out any lighting issues that may come up – or lack of lighting issues.

4. Many docs are shot outside, so check the weather forecast and then protect the equipment and yourself (that means sunscreen, too!).

5. Try to avoid places that require permits to shoot in like beaches. If you want the beach in the background, try to shoot at a place that looks out onto a beach.

6. Cell phone coverage. Is there access? Could come in handy.

7. Insurance. If you are going someplace dangerous or exotic, you need to let your insurance agent know about it.

8. Check to see if there is power at the location for recharging batteries, etc.

9. Aesthetics – does the location work visually for your film?

10. Accessibility – do you need a car? A four-wheel drive truck? Donkey? What's the parking and power situation like? Knowing this will affect what equipment you can take.

11. Make sure your crew knows how to get to and from the location. It's a good idea to let them know about local amenities like restaurants, ATMs and gas stations.

12. If you are in a foreign country, have someone with you who speaks the local language and knows the culture. It will save you endless headaches.

shots and close ups or does that not matter so much?

Joan – It's so engrained in me that I do it and I tell my students to do that. You want to see where you are – an establishing shot. You might want to hone it down so you might have to change angles or you have to go in tight. I try to make it all work as one continuous shot so that it can all be used as one shot. When I'm working with Nick, that's the way he works. He uses long shots and no cutaways. That's how I prefer shooting, but I make sure that it can be edited. So yes, if there are two people, make sure I get both of them. If time is an issue, I shoot a clock. But I do it as part of the continuous shot. It drives me nuts when I see camera people who think in terms of shots. They aren't thinking in terms in content. They aren't listening. They make moves just to change the angle because they figure it's time to change the angle. Sometimes it isn't appropriate to move because the situation is so tense. The first film Nick and I did called *Juvenile Liaison* was banned by the British Film Institute. It's about a program where police were sent into schools to terrorize kids who maybe had stolen an apple. They'd take them down to the prison cells and scare them. I felt really uncomfortable because I felt that I had added to the horribleness of one child's experience. I made some physical moves that I would never do now. If I had stayed in one place, maybe I could have disappeared.

Q – If it's an emotional moment, will you go in tight to capture that?

Joan – I don't intellectualize it. I just do what feels right. With Aileen Wournos, I was sucked into that face. I look at it now and it's way too tight. Especially when it's projected theatrically.

Q – What are some good things to talk about with the director before you go into a situation so that you're on the same page?

Joan – I'm really lucky because I get hired due to the type of shooter I am – that is handheld, verité shooting. Most of the time, they just turn me loose and let me get on with it. Those were my instructions from Barbara Kopple when I started working on this Dixie Chicks film. She said *"just do your thing."* But generally, you need to find out what their vision is and see what you can do to visually to augment that. A lot of people are graphically designed so they want a kind of stylized look to things. I do ask in interviews if people want me to zoom or stay at a fixed focal length if they want dissolves or do jump cuts. Other people want wide, medium, tight. Again, I don't like shooting cutaways per se, but I'll do them organically while shooting, so that's something to ask about, too.

Q – Why do you like verité filmmaking?

Joan – Well, it's fun. You learn a lot and it's a great adventure. People always ask me if I want to move into narrative shooting and I always say, *"Absolutely not."* When I walk onto a set, I get bored to tears. I'm not interested in doing something over and over again 50 times. My skills are not lighting or any of that. I'm interested in people and want to know what makes them tick. I like going all over the world, having these incredible experiences and not being a tourist. I'm let into people's lives. It's physical and I like being active. And I also grew up on it. I went to UCLA film school and Colin Young, who was the dean at the time, brought in all these different verité filmmakers who would spend a semester or a week or a day with us. When I started at film school they had just gotten an Éclair NPR. So everyone was thrilled with the possibilities. And then later you were able to shoot without a sync cable between you and the sound person. It was another one of those revolutionary changes.

Q – What kind of communication do you do with the sound person?

Joan – I have to think when was the last time I spoke to my sound person. I married all my sound people! Actually, in fact, I've been working recently with a sound person whom I think is a lump. We had this situation where someone important to the story is about to walk through a door, so I tell the sound person it's really important to get the guy walking in. So this sound person places himself between me and the door. No!! So I move him over to the other side and he thinks because I moved him over there that he should stay there. You have to really be thinking about, and anticipating what the action will be. I'm so spoiled by Alan Barker who I am told does all these great dances around me. I'm not aware of what he's doing because I'm concentrating on what I'm doing. But I'd also want the sound person to be listening and thinking about what it is we need, so that he or she is ready to go the instant we need to roll. I really don't like people who do sound by holding a great big boom overhead because it's very intimidating. It makes people feel like they're in a movie. Alan developed a simple I-bolt boom pole which you can buy in any hardware store for *Residents* because there was all this trauma and drama going on in these small rooms. Again, being in the circle, you want to be welcomed, so I wanted my sound person to hold the mic down low, although there are times when it's important to come from above. Just make sure you watch for boom shadows on peoples' faces.

Q – Have you ever found yourself in an ethical situation where you've had to turn off the camera?

Joan – Yes. I certainly felt that way looking at *Juvenile Liaison* again. You have to feel good about the relationship you have with people and you don't want to betray that trust that you have built up. You have to ask yourself this question: if you're shooting something that's happening and you think it's more important to be making a record of it because it will be seen and changes will come because of that, then keep shooting. The first film Nick and I made was banned because the police didn't like it, but it got shown in the UK Parliament and a white paper was issued. It made a difference and that's how I can live with myself. I don't believe any longer that by making a documentary you are going to change the world, but I think you can get people to ask the hard questions.

Q – Have you come across any technical issues with cameras that new DPs should be aware of?

Joan – One thing that you have to be careful of is listening to the sound being laid down by the camera. You are the one that's actually listening to what's going on that tape. I don't like wearing big headphones because I think I look like a geek or a technician, so I will wear these little ear buds. This person that I have been talking about on the Dixie Chicks, the last time we shot, there was this horrible pumping sound in the background every time someone stopped speaking. I just knew something was wrong. I had to say something three times before it got rectified and I wish I had been more adamant about it. The first time he said it was the freeway, then second time he said he couldn't judge sound with the ear buds. He put his big cans on and said it sounded fine. I should've insisted. Sound is so important in documentaries. You can cut around lack of picture, but you cannot cut around lack of sound.

Q – What type of cameras would you recommend a new filmmaker use?

Joan – It depends. You need to tailor the camera to the film. I hate these new cameras they have now – Panasonic 100A and the Sony Z-1 because I think they aren't user friendly. They're very awkward to handhold and find the right button to push...there are so many in such weird places. You must switch from manual to servo zoom. It isn't an either/or option. The button to make that switch is located in an awkward place and you generally ruin the shot when switching over. And if you didn't ruin it that way, the Z-1's got circuitry built into it so that it remembers where it was the last time you were on that function, and crash zooms to that same position. Maddening, especially as I'm always going between holding the camera up to eye level in which case you must use servo zoom, and holding it waist level which I do when shooting seated people so I can make moves smoothly and be eye level. And in that position I always prefer to manually zoom. You can't go between different color temperatures smoothly. You cannot use the push auto function to focus. Both of these were seamless on the PD-150. All your moves are delayed because you have to think about the technology. I loved the PD-150, but it's now outmoded. But both the Z-1 and the 100A do look beautiful. The HD camera (the Z1) is great in contrasty situations. We were in South Africa and we had someone in the shade in the foreground and bright, bright backgrounds and you could see everything. And the 100A in the progressive mode looks like film. But neither is anywhere near as good in low light as the PD-150.

Q – Would you advise shooting PAL?

Joan – I always shoot PAL whenever we know we are going end up on film. And I shoot a lot for British broadcasters.

Q - Would you shoot PAL even for an American broadcaster?

Joan – That's a production company decision. HD is making that work path obsolete because it's better to master in HD and then download it to either PAL or NTSC.

Q – How important is the relationship with the lab or the digital lab?

Joan – Very. They can tell you when things need to be adjusted and you can make sure they're processing things to your specs.

Q – How do you work with the editor?

Joan – I don't leave it to an editor to cut the film. I'm there the whole time.

Q – When shooting tape, do you copy your master tapes so you can use them as dailies or for offline logging?

Joan – I always make clones of the masters.

Q – What kind of lights would you recommend for doing interviews?

Joan – A very cheap and portable way to provide a beautiful soft light is to use a China ball - in reality a Japanese lantern. They're particularly good for people wearing glasses since you can position it directly above your frame and a little in front of the head to avoid reflection of the light. It's particularly forgiving and therefore good for shooters who aren't very experienced with lighting. And you can use them in the shot and they look like they belong there. That's how I've been lighting the Dixie Chicks in the recording studio. They have these big mic stands on wheels with long boom arms so I just hang the lanterns from this and raise it up. I can also move them around quickly depending on what I'm trying to light. But basically with video you don't have to light if you've got daylight coming through a window where you can set your subject up so they're lit by the daylight. Just be careful not to mix color temperatures if you are using a tungsten light as well as daylight. You have to use a blue gel on the tungsten light.

Q – Do you typically shoot with your own equipment or do you rent it?

Joan – Many productions if they're shooting over a period of time, figure it's cheaper to buy one of the small format cameras. I've finally sold my Aaton Xtrprod and most of my prime lenses. I was really sorry to see the Canon 8-64mm go. It was such a great handheld lens. And we've sold the Digibetas and now are just crawling with small format cameras: both PAL and NTSC PD-150's, the 100A and we're about to buy the Z-1. When they're using the larger cameras like the Varicams or the 900's, they come from rental houses.

Q – Do you ever use prime lenses anymore?

Joan – Not really. But when I was shooting film I had a kit of Aaton prime lenses. I think there were a 9.5, 12, 16, 25 and 50mm. I generally used the 9.5 for handheld work. And sometimes the 12mm. But really only used them when I needed the stop otherwise I prefer the flexibility of the zooms.

Q – What are the common mistakes that you see with documentary filmmakers that could be avoided?

Joan – Endless interviews. Endless shooting. People have this attitude that tape is cheap so let's shoot everything that moves. Not getting it right technically. It is frustrating looking at something that is shot poorly with terrible sound. So get your chops together. Do not ever use auto-focus.

Q – What advice would you give a new documentary filmmaker?

Joan – If you don't love people, don't do it. It's a hard life. It's hard to make a living. You have to be the kind of person who doesn't mind where they're their next check is coming form. You have to completely go with the flow. You can't make a plan because you never know when you are going to have to hop on a plane.

Working From Home

GUERILLA FILM MAKER SAYS!

1. Working from home can reduce your overheads and maximize your time. You won't have to rent offices and you can start work the moment you get out of bed (no freeway jams or the subway) and work late into the night.

2. Working from home can decrease your work time – it's all too easy to sleep in or get distracted into fixing the kitchen sink, etc. It's difficult to separate business from pleasure.

3. That said, do have one or two people around to keep yourself from getting bored or lonely. It happens and it sucks.

4. Try to keep a normal work schedule during the day. Elmore Leonard states once that he goes to his downstairs office and writes from 9am to noon or so, takes an hour lunch break and then goes back to the office and writes until 5-6pm. How many novels does he have?

5. Get DSL or a cable modem if you can. Makes research and file sharing more efficient. You can sometimes get cheaper rates through package deals with your phone, cable or satellite TV provider.

6. It may seem very LA, but exercise can wake you up when you feel burnt out.

7. Have a very safe and dry place to store your footage (tape or film) - get a fireproof safe for your current projects footage.

8. Set up an editing system (offline) separate from your main workstation in your house. This way you can reduce the cost of hiring a room and also you can rent it out to make some extra cash.

9. Make sure your workspace is a separate room from the rest of your place. This way you can have investors or subjects over for meetings in a more professional setting. Also some tax laws require that you have a distinct separate area as an office in order to claim things like rent and utilties on your taxes.

10. People or friends might assume that because you work from home you are free anytime - not true! You end up working longer and on weekends so set them straight!

Greg MacGillivray

THE IMAX DP

Q – What is the IMAX format and how does it work?

Greg – In IMAX filmmaking you shoot 70mm film where the frame is10 times larger than 35mm. That big frame is then projected with a million dollar projector onto a gigantic screen 80 feet tall and 100 feet wide that the audience sits very close to. The reason that these films are so engaging and fun is that the images give you a sense of being there. The IMAX projector is so amazing. Every film frame is pin registered and the celluloid is blown flat against a piece of glass so that you have absolute perfect sharpness edge to edge and in the center. No 35mm projector comes even close to that. So when you're sitting really close, you get a completely filled peripheral view. The effect is stunning. I saw my first IMAX theater film in 1974 at the World's Fair in Spokane, and I'm still mesmerized and awestruck by the experience today. In fact, what's interesting is that an IMAX theater audience doesn't really equate the IMAX experience with other films. They equate it more with other real experiences like a roller coaster ride or a trip to the edge of the Grand Canyon. That's why the most popular of the films have been the true-life adventures. They have grossed lots of money. The most attended IMAX theater film was our first film called *To Fly*, which has been seen by over 100 million people. But our film *Everest* is the highest grossing IMAX theater film to date with a worldwide box office gross of more than $130 million. When I made my first film there were only four IMAX theaters and today there are more than 300 theaters.

Q – How is making an IMAX theater documentary different from a regular documentary?

Greg – It's more expensive. You use different ways of writing, directing and shooting. And the result is different. You have a different audience. The films are shorter – usually 40-50 minutes in length. My company owns four cameras, all of our lenses, dollies, cranes, helicopter mounts, etc, so we are able to go out into the field with our team and make one of these specialized films efficiently. We try not to repeat the same mistake twice. We've learned how to test our limits – even though we try to test the limits creatively. We try to utilize advanced technology. For example, our film *Greece: Secrets Of The Past* has the most extensive single CGI sequence that's ever been done in a large format film. One shot over four minutes in length required two years of work.

Q – IMAX theater films seem to go places other documentaries cannot in order to get that visceral experience.

Greg – That's really important. Obviously, we're running out of some of those places since so many IMAX theater films have been done. So we do a lot of research. I do a lot of reading and subscribe to about 40 different magazines. I'm continually looking for new locations, subject matter and things that I think the audience would be interested in and would work well artistically in a large format. With these films, you don't want to do just a conventional drama like *Brokeback Mountain* or *Crash*. It wouldn't benefit that much from the format. In fact, it might even subtract from it. They're compelling on a different level. Our films are compelling on a visceral, visual and emotional level. What we have been trying to do since *To The Limit* was released in 1989 is to engage more with our characters. Develop more richly etched character stories. And we did well with that film and *The Living Sea, Storm Chasers* and *Everest*. And the films of this decade, *Dolphins, Coral Reef Adventure* and the like, all engage with stories that are wrapped around very interesting people. With *Everest*, it was very compelling because it was a life and death struggle. The same thing is true with a film we are working on now called *Hurricane on the Bayou*. It's about Hurricane Katrina and has four characters in New Orleans. It's very emotional as it's a story of perseverance, redemption, music and the richness of culture.

Q – With the personal approach, has the length of the IMAX theater film gotten longer?

Greg – I'd love to make a film that's even longer. Artistically, it would allow me to do more character development and story telling. But the IMAX theaters need a film that's less than 45 minutes in length so they can show it every hour on the hour. They want 10-13 shows a day. The theater owners tell me that if I make a film that's longer, they'll be less apt to run it. It's harder to do, but you can tell a pretty compelling story in 45 minutes. Winston Churchill said, *"If you want me to make a minute and half speech, it will take two weeks to prepare. If I do a speech that is half an hour long, I could do it right now."* And that's the way I always feel. You have to choose every word, image, piece of music carefully. You don't have a lot of time to mess around and take side journeys.

Q – How different is the structure to a regular documentary?

Greg – The conventional beginning, middle and end structure is pretty much what you have to grasp in an IMAX theater film. But you can go in different directions. You just don't have a lot of time to go in different directions. Sometimes we start with flashbacks, historical elements, change tenses. We can even do fantasy sequences.

Q – What kinds of documentaries is an IMAX theater film best suited to?

Greg – True-life adventures are the best. People want to visit someplace and experience something that they perhaps can't get to. Films that are fiction, even if they're really good fiction, aren't as interesting because you lose the component of truth. When an audience comes to an IMAX theater film, they think they're going to see something that's completely factual and truthful and has been vetted by ten different experts. In a fictional film, the audience has to suspend their disbelief and get into the story. So the fictional films, the most expensive of which done in our format was *Wings Of Courage*, directed by Jean Jacques Arnaud, wasn't popular with the public partly because it was fiction. They'd say, *"It was a pretty good story, but it wasn't as good as The Bear."* That was another of his films. They compare it to another fiction film, not an IMAX theater film. Certainly, if we were to do our New Orleans film as a fictional film, I can assure you it wouldn't be as good as a film like *Crash*. You don't want to compete with something that has ten times the budget and expertise behind it. Our films are in the $5 million budget range, so it's difficult to compete with films with higher budgets.

Q – I've read that the experience is so visceral with an IMAX theater film that when people watched The Coral Reef Adventure, their body temperatures actually dropped.

Greg – There have been those reactions. People sometimes feel nausea with films that involve flying. The vertigo reaction is common when you do a shot at the edge of a cliff. So it's true that the experience is different than seeing a conventional movie. You have to understand how the audience appreciates the medium in order to make a good IMAX theater film. It's rare for a first time director to understand it well enough to make a good film.

Q – IMAX films also tend to go to dangerous places and situations.

Greg – True. I've almost been killed a couple of times. One time was in Palau when I was shooting from a small airplane and one was in an underwater scene that I was filming for a surfing sequence. Danger is something that you manage. Proper filmmaking technique, no matter what format you are working in, requires that you manage safety issues. I lost my partner in a helicopter crash during the filming of a TV commercial 30 years ago. So the way that we manage safety issues is very carefully. We rarely get a scratch on our sets. We always go slowly when there's an exposure of risk. Going too fast or being so budget driven that you are doing things foolishly or cheaply or unsafely is just something we would never do.

Q – What are the challenges of shooting with an IMAX camera?

Greg – The challenges are akin to shooting the first Technicolor films which were done with a three strip camera - they weighed a huge amount. Or to shooting the first sound images with the cameras in 1929. The cameras are big and bulky.

Add sound dampening and they become even bigger. Put them on a crane and they are even more giant. So it's lugging equipment, planning ahead even more so than a 35mm shoot. Our heaviest cameras weigh about 200 lbs. It's a specialized camera that shoots high-speed slow motion – 100 fps. Our lightest camera is 25 lbs., it only shoots a minute and half of film, but you can mount it on a hang glider, a kayak, a Steadicam or you can hold it. Our customary sound camera that we use is about 100 lbs. and it runs almost silently so we can run sync sound very easily. The real trick with IMAX filmmaking is that you want to shoot wider than you would in any other format. Far wider. 100% wider and sometimes 200% wider. And you want each shot to last longer so that the audiences can orient themselves. Then their own vision zooms into the subjects and gets captivated by the environment. Moving the camera is a very important thing. You don't want to move the camera sideways too much with a standard dolly. You want to move it forward and backward so that you feel in the space. Try walking and then look sideways as you are walking. You're continually compelled to look forward. Same thing in IMAX. You want to look forward. It took us a long time to understand that. It's harder to do sound work and do the directing work with IMAX simply because the director has to be further away from the subject. There's a lot more space around the subject so you can't cheat things and you can't cut from one character to the other like you can with a normal feature film. You can't film a conversation with over the shoulder shots and cut between them. In IMAX, that would drive you nuts. You have to shoot a conversation in a two shot and you cut your chances of getting a good performance 50%. The struggles are all worth it, though, because if you make a good IMAX theater film, the audience will show up in big numbers and love the experience. It's not feature filmmaking or really documentary filmmaking. It's something completely different. I see myself in this very strange branch of filmmaking doing these highly technical motion pictures on a limited budget.

Q – Who finances your films?

Greg – Well, believe it or not we are true guerilla filmmakers as most of our films have been financed by our own company. We're completely independent of Hollywood or any other groups or companies. I solely own this company, which has been in operation for 40 years now. We decide what subjects to do and hire writers to get the scripts correct. We do our own marketing, publicity and distribution and essentially try to be a mini, mini, studio in Laguna Beach, CA. We release a film a year and we're always working on at least three or four films at a time. Business people like it because with only 300 IMAX theaters it's something that you can get your arms around and understand and get to know the people in it really well. You form all these great friendships because we are supplying films to these theaters every year. And they're great to work with because most of them are directors of museums and have a doctorate in geology, astronomy or physics and then they run a museum – wow, what a fascinating person to talk to.

Q – How does the sound camera work?

Greg – We have one sound camera that runs quiet perfectly in sync with the recorders. We record to either a digital recorder or a Nagra running in sync with the camera.

Q – Do you light many of your films?

Greg – Oh, yes. We have tons of lights. Huge HMI packages that we take on location. You need high contrast with IMAX so it looks super crisp, Sometimes we have trouble getting the lights in places. When we were in Russia shooting the Bolshoi Ballet, we made arrangements to work through Gorky Film Studio and utilize all their lighting. It was all at least 40 years old. We had to eventually bring over one light of our own. But the classic thing was working with all their technicians who were true pros, but had been working with antiquated equipment. They knew all the quirks of the lights. They knew which ones had to be jiggled a certain way. It was so much fun to work with them. On that shoot, we must have had 100 lights working to light that big stage. They were performing *Giselle* with 30 dancers in these beautiful white flowing costumes through smoke. It just looked beautiful. But we had to get a lot of light on the stage because we shot most of it in slow motion. You plan all these things out like you would a conventional Hollywood film.

Q – How difficult was it to film on Everest?

Greg – On *Everest*, we had a base camp and all we used were small lights. Then, battery operated lights on the mountain.

The more character oriented shots I did later on in cold climates so that I could recreate the moment but have more control over the lighting.

Q – What are some of the more unusual places that you have taken the camera?

Greg – One of the big achievements in *Coral Reef Adventure* was going 350 feet deep, which is well beyond conventional diving equipment. We did 26 dives that deep to do a sequence that lasts two and half minutes. Getting the camera to the top of Mount Everest was a challenge. It had to be lightweight and work at 40 degrees below zero. We had to hire and train a five-person Sherpa team to carry the pieces of the camera up the mountain. I have mounted the camera on jet dragsters and really strange things like the luge, a bobsled, a pair of skis, a surfboard, a hang glider, a rubber raft down a rapid, all kinds of aircraft. We have put the camera on a base jumper and a skydiver. We did this amazing sequence with a sky surfer. That took as two and a half months to plan.

Q – Presumably the cameras are very robust.

Greg – You do have calamities with the cameras. We have one that's sort of our rough and ready camera, which we are taking to the Alps. It'll be in a crash box and sit in the path of an avalanche. Essentially, that camera is triggered remotely by radio control. But then you have radio transmitters to locate the camera after the avalanche passes.

Q – How long is the production period for an IMAX theater film?

Greg –The actual shooting period is not too much different than a regular feature film, which is about two to three months. There are times we have shot nine months to a year if we wanted something like spring and winter shots. Sometimes we work with multiple crews. We shot the Greece film in eleven days because we had three crews working concurrently. We had a limited time and permits were hard to come by.

Q – How much footage is in a magazine?

Greg – The film magazines on the regular cameras are about 1,000 feet, which is about 3 minutes. And the smaller camera, is 500 feet or a minute and a half. We end up shooting about 150,000 feet on any film so our shooting ration is about 20:1. On *Coral Reef Adventure* we shot more film than anyone has ever shot for an IMAX theater film. We shot over 100 miles of film. It takes two people about a minute and a half to reload a magazine.

Q – How careful must you be to not get dirt on the lens?

Greg – Technically, you must be perfect. I was lucky to be trained by Stanley Kubrick so it comes second nature to me now. You check your lenses with columniation tests, film tests for sharpness, color and

GUERILLA FILM MAKER SAYS!

Carnets

This is a simple international customs document accepted in well over 70 participating countries to ease custom procedures when shipping your film equipment. They're valid for one year, allow unlimited exits and entries to the US and ensure that your shipment is tax free. You must list your approximate date of departure from the US and all the countries that you anticipate visiting within that year, including any in-transit countries and the number of times you expect to leave and re-enter the US There are basic processing fees to be made (up to $250), determined by the value of your shipment, and they do require a security bond which varies from country to country and again is based on the value of the goods you're shipping. This is generally around 40% of the merchandise worth, paid to the US Council for International Business (USCIB) who are the National Guaranteeing Association and who are used to cover any custom claim that might result from a misused carnet. Generally it takes 5 working days to process a carnet, however, it's recommended to do your carnet months in advance and ship your equipment with plenty of time to allow for any custom delays.
Carnets DO NOT cover: consumable goods (food and agriculture products), disposable and hazardous items, or postal traffic.
***US Council for International Business**: Carnet Headquarters, 1212 Avenue of the Americas, 18th Floor, New York, NY 10036. tel: 212 703 5078/5087 fax: 212 944 0012 www.carnetsonline.com.*
The USCIB works with two Service Providers, Roanoke Trade Services and the Corporation for International Business who also do carnets.

distortion. You have to have a carefully checked set of lenses every time you go out. The camera is checked every time you go out for steadiness and flatness, sharpness, breathing quality. You are working at the highest level of perfection – far more precise than 35mm.

Q – When it comes to editing, is it the standard editing process as on a regular film?

Greg – Pretty much. What we do that's different is that we do a lot of projection. We edit on the Avid and then we match the 35mm work prints to that Avid edit and then watch them in a projection booth on a big screen. We sit close to the screen so that we get close to the IMAX experience and then we go back and re-cut. So you continually go back and forth between the two and that has provided us with the best results.

Q – How would a new filmmaker who wants to get into IMAX filmmaking go about doing it?

Greg – It's not easy. The best thing is to learn how to make films first in cheaper formats. Start with video, then 16mm, then 35mm so that by the time you are ready to do an IMAX theatre film, you're completely aware of lighting, camera usage, editing and writing, so that you are not wasting time and money. Having said all that, you have to prove yourself as a visual filmmaker. If you're really good at drama, you probably aren't suited for an IMAX filmmaking career. But if you're good visually, and there're probably 20 people I can count off that are, then it may be for you.

Q – Is digital going to have an impact on IMAX filmmaking?

Tips On Negotiating Deals

1. Be polite. Nobody will do anything for someone they don't like. In addition, ask vendors for advice and send thank you letters or e-mail.

2. Go to vendors early so they have time to think about how they can help your situation.

3. Be realistic in what you want based on your budget. Don't give a wish list.

4. Tell them how much money you have budgeted up front so they don't feel like their time is being wasted.

5. Find out when a vendor's off season is and use them during that period. They will frequently reduce prices on equipment and services.

6. Especially in the post production phase, try using facilities after hours or in non-peak hours. In addition, see if you can hire the assistants of the main editors or telecine operators who want the opportunity to move up the ladder.

7. Go to the vendor and introduce yourself personally. People like having a face with a name.

8. Find out from friends what kind of deals they got for services and use it as a yardstick.

9. Some vendors offer accounts to customers who do a lot of business with them. Do so as it will allow you to stretch your dollar and build loyalty with that vendor.

10. Offer screen credit or product placement in exchange for various services or props to help reduce the budget. Many businesses not related to the film industry will warm to the idea of being part of a movie.

11. Be a comparative shopper. Call various places to get the best price.

12. Go into a negotiation with a top dollar amount you will pay. You can always use the car buying "walk out" ploy if the vendor cannot meet your price.

13. Paying cash up front will almost always get you a better deal.

14. If you cannot get a discount, try to get something thrown in for free.

15. Thank you gifts, such as a bottle of liquor or premiere tickets, are a good way to get good deals for your next project.

16. Take whomever you do business with out for a drink to start a personal relationship with them. People do favors for their friends.

17. Make sure you get all quotes in writing and faxed over to your office. Ask them to list the equipment or materials, the service and the dates and the exact agreed amount. This will help avoid any misunderstanding and make it harder for the company or individual to retract their offer.

Greg – It already is. We use digital all the time for special effects and titling. And in the future we will use it more for image capture. I kind of suspect that digital projection being comparable for IMAX theatre films will be a long time coming. Just because there are not enough IMAX theaters for someone to put up the R&D money to make it happen. I can see us capturing studio images digitally very soon. I have to look at it as a tool that allows me to do things that I haven't done before.

Q – What advice would you give a new filmmaker?

Greg – Never give up on your dream. If you have a desire to make IMAX theatre films, never give up on that quest. It's a sensational experience to make one of these films and see it with an audience. It's so immersive that the audience reacts to it in a wide broad way. And you can see that joy and thrill in their faces. That's the reward. Especially when I watch a bunch of children watching it. I showed a film in Chicago and a teacher came up to me afterwards and told me that taking his students to this film was one of the most rewarding experiences in his whole teaching year. He said that many of the kids will never have the joy of being in that environment or taking an airplane trip like you do in the film and seeing their world from above. Because you see it so clearly in this format, you are delivering something that half of them will never have in their lifetimes. That in terms of instruction is far more important than learning how to divide long fractions. On another note, the films, in a way, preserve the wonders of our world and teach people conservation. These kinds of rewards don't make you a lot of money, but they're the reasons I do what I do.

The Doc Crew And What They Do

Director – *The creative decision maker throughout the filmmaking process - who directs the subjects and the crew from pre to post production. Many times the director will wear more than one hat in documentary film.*

Producer – *Gets the director whatever they need to get the film done. They raise the finance for the film, and are answerable to financiers. On a low budget film, more often than not, they will be also doing the job of the line producer, such as scheduling, budgeting and research.*

Executive Producer – *Usually the person who has made the film possible in either putting together the finances and/or creative package in docs. This is usually a broadcaster or big investor.*

Production Assistants (PA) – *Assistants to the production team, where job varies from being a typist, running errands, carry equipment, etc.*

Fixer – *Usually a local from the area where you are shooting who "fixes" things with the local community. Sometimes government appointed to keep an eye on you.*

Production Sound Mixer – *Records the production sound, wild tracks, and ambience. Will either have their own kit, or will hire one from a sound house.*

Editor – *Once footage is received from the field, the editor will assemble the movie. Works closely with the director and in many ways is the screenwriter and or director of documentary filmmaking.*

Assistant Editor – *Aids editor with preparing picture and sound, synchronizing dailies if necessary, logging, maintaining good files and records and storage of all movie elements. On low budget films, not necessarily needed.*

Sound Editor – *Assembles production tracks, effects, music, recording extra effects if necessary, transferring other effects from libraries, taking control of Foley and ADR (Automatic Dialogue Replacement). Ensures all location atmospheres are covered with wild tracks. Takes film to final mix with editor and director. Should hear and approve the final optical soundtrack.*

Composer/Musician/Music Copyist – *Hired for the original score of the film and composes music in accordance with the director's wishes.*

Music Supervisor – *Hires musicians, locates and clears required additional music tracks.*

Still Photographer – *Shoots production stills for use in press kits, publicity and advertising.*

Unit Publicist – *Works with still photographer making sure the "right" shots are taken to publicize the film. Takes care of getting publicity while shooting, prepares press kits and makes sure that sufficient material is obtained during the production to publicize the film later on.*

DON'T BE SURPRISED IF YOU END UP DOING MORE THAN ONE OF THESE JOBS ON YOUR DOC!!!

PRODUCTION SOUND

Q – What makes good documentary sound?

Alan – Intelligibility. Documentary filmmaking today is mostly about verbal content. Most documentary films make no sense without the soundtrack. You could do away with the picture and not lose much of the content. It's unfortunate but most filmmakers aren't into the kind of filmmaking where images and sound go together to make something greater.

Q – Has production sound suffered with the rise of digital cameras and HD?

Alan – Not because of the equipment, but because people are working alone. You frequently see documentaries now in English with English subtitles in sections because the sound is so bad. *Super Size Me* – has just about every kind of bad sound there is. Some of that is because they were filming surreptitiously but mostly it's bad craft. However, the content is so important and presented with such great humor the bad sound doesn't stop it from becoming a successful film.

Q – Do you think using on-camera mics is a good idea?

Alan – Depends on the situation. Sometimes it's unavoidable especially if you are working alone or trying to be inconspicuous. For getting good sound, you want to get the mic off the camera and as close to the subject as you can. Shooting a sit-down interview with an on-camera mic is unforgivable. A big problem is that people tend to choose on-camera microphones that are too directional, so-called "shotgun" mics. That limits what they can shoot. If a person talking points to something in the distance, the cameraperson is hesitant to pan over to get the shot, knowing they'll lose the sound. Getting the sound dictates shot. A better option is to use a microphone on the camera that isn't so directional. I prefer cardioid microphones for on-camera use. The way Joan Churchill shoots, which is very up close and personal, I often rely on the on-camera mic as second boom mic, freeing me to boom off-camera sound.

Q – Would you recommend radio/wireless mics?

Alan – If you're shooting sit-down interviews, the best situation is to have a directional microphone overhead. I usually mount a short boom on a light stand so the microphone is pointing straight down, just out of the frame and a little in front of the subject's head. The microphone should be no more than 18 inches away from the person's mouth. That will give you a natural sound and you don't have lavaliere issues like clothing rustle or subjects touching the mic. In a professional situation, I never use a lavaliere unless I have to, say in an extremely noisy environment. If you orient the subject with their back to the noise source, their body shields a lavaliere mic from the noise. Wireless microphones have all of the problems of lavaliere microphones and wireless transmission combined. But they have become the standard and some subjects expect to have one put on them. It's laughable but many people are now so used to wireless mics they feel uncomfortable without one. Doing sound inconspicuously with a boom is becoming a lost art.

Q – Does Nick Broomfield use just a short boom?

Alan – He uses wireless lavalieres as well, often on himself since he's a character in his films. Nick is a special case.

Being somewhat bumbling as a soundman is part of his filmmaker persona. For *Aileen: Life and Death of a Serial Killer*, I set him up with an on-camera mic that he could take off and use handheld and one wireless lavaliere, no mixer. You can do that with the Sony cameras because the auto gains are so good. But the rig wasn't a good prop given the way he works the subject – he prefers to have more stuff to carry. Many equipment choices are a compromise between the best way to get the sound and the effect of the equipment on the situation.

Q – Are there any tips on not being intrusive?

Alan – It's usually best to have a wireless link between sound and camera. That way you both walk in as freestanding human beings. I try to use a very short boom pole or no pole at all. I frequently use an eight-inch metal I-bolt with a shock mount and a coil cord. I mic from below the frame. This is a lot less intrusive than an overhead pole. Of course, this only works if the shooting style is up close and engaged, the way Joan shoots. If the cameraperson shoots from a distance you have to use a boom, wireless lavs or a combination of both. Also, if someone is worried that a specific mic would intimidate people, go in and meet everybody beforehand. You become a person instead of an anonymous technician.

Q – How important is it for a sound person to keep an eye on their surroundings when shooting?

Alan – You have to be aware of your surroundings in every way. You have to listen to what people say, take it seriously and listen to the subtext. That might mean putting a wireless mic on someone is OK or it might mean stay away. You anticipate when people are going to speak. You anticipate the next camera move so you won't be in the way or have the mic in the shot. You have to be sensitive to the subject's emotional state and be respectful of it.

It's important to be at ease with your equipment so there's no fussing with it. That can quickly alienate a subject. Every time I go out on a job, I redesign my sound package for that job to make the least social impact.

Q – What happens if the sound situatlon changes or is difficult?

Alan – You have to adapt to whatever it is. A scene in Vikram Jayanti's *James Ellroy's Feast of Death* involved a table of eight police detectives eating dinner and talking with Ellroy about the Black Dahlia murder. How do you mic that many people speaking randomly? With wireless mics you would have eating noise, clothing noise and transmission issues with nine frequencies going. Booming wasn't practical because there were cameras on opposite sides of the table. I put a wireless mic on Ellroy and had the grip hang a 4'X6' sheet of clear Plexiglas over the table, just out of the shot. I put two PZM microphones on the bottom of the Plexiglas. PZM's are surface mount microphones that pick up sound very effectively from a flat surface. We used clear Plexiglas so the gaffer could light down through it.

In guerilla documentary settings, you aren't going to have that kind of rigging, so you need to be aggressive to get close enough to the person speaking. You need to be good with the boom pole and know how it works, how to feather your moves so the sound is appropriate to picture. You watch the camera and the subject and think about how the picture and sound will go together.

Q – What do you usually record on?

Alan – We usually record direct to videotape without a backup. Sometimes I will back up to DAT or fixed media of some kind, either a compact flash or hard drive recorder. You do that when you have to get every bit of the sound – even when camera is changing tapes or if you suspect a wireless link to the camera might fail.

Q – Is it the same with HD?

Alan – Yes. It's basically the same.

Q – What would be a good basic sound gear kit for a low budget documentary film?

Alan – First, a good microphone that can be used on or off the camera. That depends on which camera it is. For the Sony HVR-Z1U, PD-150, PD-170 and the Panasonic HVX-200 I prefer the Sennhieser K6-ME64. It's optimized to make speech intelligible. It has a "presence boost," which means in the 5k-8k-frequency range its response is increased to emphasize the sibilant sounds of speech. Those are the sounds that make speech intelligible. It's a harsh sounding microphone for general use but for speech it's great. The cardioid pattern, which is wider than a shotgun, gives a natural quality to off-camera sound. The K6-ME64 is not good on the Panasonic DVX-100 series cameras, there's too much motor noise. You need to use something more directional like the Audio Technica 4073A. These mics have a low-cut, also called high-pass, switch. This needs to be on for doc work. It reduces wind and handling noise. Also, it's now so easy to manipulate sound in post that as long as it's not distorted, there's a tremendous amount you can do with it.

Your second microphone would be a wireless microphone or, if you have a sound person, a more directional microphone to be used on a boom. The Sennhieser Evolution G2 wireless mics are inexpensive and pretty good. You can buy a kit that has a lavaliere mic, a body pack transmitter and a plug on transmitter that goes right into a microphone. If you have that kit, a cardioid mic and a shotgun, you have many options. There are two types of Evolution plug on transmitters. The 100 series does not have phantom power which means the mic has to be self-powered or dynamic. Right now the best inexpensive self-powered shotgun microphone is the Audio Technica AT897. It's under $300 and will work with the 100 series butt plug transmitters. The next most important piece of sound equipment is headphones or earpieces for the cameraperson. If they are not monitoring the sound, sooner or later you are going to lose something because a battery died or a connection went bad. It's too much to expect the cameraman to evaluate the quality of the sound and shoot at the same time, but they need to confirm the presence of the sound.

Q – What about wind protection devices?

Alan – Windscreens and shock mounts are essential, even indoors. On my website there's a way to modify a foam windscreen made by Shure into a very effective windscreen for the K6-ME64. I like that better than a furry windscreen because it's less conspicuous. For windy situations, you will need a furry windscreen.

Q – What can you do to reduce camera noise?

Alan – In a professional situation, you'd put something over the camera if it were on a tripod. If it's on someone's shoulder it's rare that it will make enough noise to be a problem. If you mount a microphone on the camera, you need a really good shock mount. The shock mounts on the Sony and Panasonic cameras are worthless. You need a serious shock mount on top of the camera, away from motor and handling noise.

Q – Are there any cameras that are too loud?

Alan – Not for documentary filmmaking. Usually the ambient sound is greater than the camera noise.

Q – How should the level controls on cameras be used?

Alan – Most digital cameras have a digital audio scale in which 0 dB is the loudest level you can record at without distortion. Once you hit 0 dB, the sound is trash unless the camera has a limiter – the Sony PD-150 and PD-170 have very good limiters, which are misnamed "Auto Gain." On good equipment I like to record with peaks around –12dB. With DV equipment that has more system noise, I put my peaks at about –6dB.

Q – What should you bear in mind when you go on location sound-wise?

Alan – Ambient noise if you have a choice of locations. Look out for things that might crop up later, you might be scouting at night, but will be shooting during the day. Is there a construction site next door? Are you under the flight path of an airport? The acoustics of the place – bare walls and hard surfaces make echoy recordings. The classic turning off the

GUERILLA FILM MAKER SAYS!

Getting Good Sound

1. Hire the best sound recordist you can.

2. When looking for locations, bear the sound in mind. Traffic and planes are usually the biggest culprits as are air conditioning units. Most natural sounds can be covered up and disguised in post-production.

3. Make sure to record a few minutes of "room tone" in each of your locations so your editors can cover their edits.

4. Blimps and barneys are good at filtering out most camera noise, but they will not get rid of everything.

5. A heavy atmosphere track can cover many natural sound problems.

6. Avoid using lots of wireless mics as the frequencies can interfere with one another. Also, you are relying on the fact that batteries are not going to give out.

7. Your final mix should be done in a professional studio that can shape your sound in the most dynamic ways.

8. Get the mic as close the subject as possible, maybe 12-18 inches from their mouth. For stationary interviews mic from above with a boom.

9. Anticipate where your subjects are going or coming from. Someone may come into a room while you are shooting something else – you need to be able to get that.

10. Use less directional microphones in order to capture sound from all directions.

11. Use people's bodies to shield noise.

12. Always use a windscreen when outside and a shock mount for camera mounted mics.

13. Use a mic high pass filter to get rid of handling noise.

14. Invest in a good pair of headphones so you can tell when something goes wrong!

refrigerator and the air conditioner. And there's the soundman's trick of leaving your car keys in the refrigerator so you won't forget to turn it back on. In documentaries the main problem with background noise is continuity. Halfway through an interview the refrigerator starts. The editor wants to cut from a comment without refrigerator noise to one with it. How do you smooth out the difference? That's why you record presence tracks or room tone – "atmos" in the UK. If there's something kicking in and out like an air conditioner, then you want to get a presence track with it and one without it so the editor has choices. If there are airplanes, I try to record several passes. Hopefully, the editor can patch it together.

Q – One thing about documentary sound, you can't usually get a subject to say things again if you get it wrong.

Alan – Yes, documentary sound is very interesting to do because you have to deliver the first time out and you have to adapt on the fly. The biggest problems are not getting the microphone close enough and after that, wireless problems. But, in the current film culture – if the content is good enough, the quality of the sound doesn't matter. The sound can be pretty terrible and not hurt the film too much. It's poor craft and I think people should have good craft, but content is everything.

Q – But don't distributors have certain standards for sound?

Alan – If you are making a film for HBO or PBS, they do have requirements and they do want good quality. But if there are a few problems with the audio, they are not going to turn a good film down.

Q – Do you ever do sound effects?

Alan – Not often, but if you are filming something that has interesting sounds or is more filmic project like Hubert Sauper's *Darwin's Nightmare*, then it's more common. That film was shot with a Sony PD-150 and a PD-100. If Hubert, heard an interesting sound in a scene, he would go in and get the sound again after the scene was shot, using the camera as a sound recording device. This is a simple technique that can add a lot of richness to a film.

Q – When does a sound recordist get hired and do they usually come with their own equipment?

Alan – They usually come with their own equipment unless it's a reality show. Hiring varies depends on the project. Most shows for networks or cable channels don't hire one sound person for an entire job, especially if they're traveling. They don't want to pay for airfare and hotels so they hire locally. You'll get a call anywhere a day before to a month before, and frequently the dates change. The average is a week or two before. If it's a rare job where they use a single sound person throughout, usually you're involved in the production and you consult so you know what situations you are going to be in. Those projects are rare.

It's best to get us involved as early as possible, especially if multiple wireless mics are involved. There have been numerous disasters on shows where many wireless mics have been used. They bring someone on the day of that shoot – to a new location where there may be radio interference. You need time to check out your receivers to make sure there are no interfering signals. If there are, you have to change your frequencies and chances are if you change one you will create a harmonic interference on another frequency, so you'll have to change that one as well. It takes time to get them all working properly.

Q – If a filmmaker or producer doesn't have enough money to pay your normal rate, is there anything they can do to persuade you to work for them?

Alan – Make it a very interesting project that you want to work on. But still how do you compensate a person

Music Libraries

GUERILLA FILM MAKER SAYS!

You can either order CDs from these places or download MP3/AIFF files from their websites. You must pay for licenses (sync, mechanical, performance rights) depending on what you plan to do with the music. Rough estimates can be $75 to $300 per piece of music

FirstCom Music, Inc.
Contact: Stephanie Lovick
Email: info@firstcom.com
9000 Sunset Blvd. # 300
West Hollywood CA 90069
www.firstcom.com

Global Graffiti
Contact: Skip Adams or Jacqueline Woolf
Email: ggmusic@globalgraffiti.com
22-30th Ave #A
Venice CA 90291
Phone: 310-577-8940
Fax: 310-821-1734

Killer Tracks
6534 Sunset Boulevard
Hollywood, CA 90028 USA
800.4.KILLER Toll Free
323.957.4455 International
323.957.4470 FAX
www.killertracks.com

Promusic, Inc.
Contact: Dana Ferandelli
Email: dferandelli@promusic-inc.com
11846 Ventura Blvd, Ste 304
Studio City CA 91604
United States
Phone: 888-600-8988
Fax: 818-506-8580

Sonic Licensing
Contact: Cameron Peebles
Email: Cameron@SonicLicensing.com
11301 West Olympic Blvd. Suite 336
Los Angeles CA 90064
United States
Phone: 1-866-286-9307
Fax: 1-866-286-9307

Who Did That Music Library?
Who Did That Music?
12211 West Washington Blvd. Los Angeles, CA 90066
US/Canada 1.800.400.6767
tel +1.310.572.4646
fax +1.310.572.4647

JRT Music
Post Production Services/Music Libraries
Email: jrtmusic@earthlink.net
648 Broadway
Suite 911
New York NY 10012
United States
Phone: 212-253-8908
Fax: 212-353-9317

Manhattan Production Music
355 West 52nd Street 6th Floor
New York, NY 10019
800.227.1954 Toll Free
212.333.5766 Phone
212.262.0814 Fax
Corelli-Jacobs Music & Recording
25 W. 45th St.
New York, NY 10036?4902
(212) 382-0220
Fax: (212) 382-0278

DeWolfe Music Library, Inc.
25 West 45th St.
New York, NY 10036-4902
(800) 221-6713 or (212) 382-0220
Fax: (212) 382-0278

Sound Shop
321 West 44th St.
New York, NY 10019-5818
(212) 757-5700

for working for less than what they can live on? It's hard to do. Then again, it depends on the people. If you say you have no money for crew but are spending loads on equipment, travel, etc., I'd say, *"That's nice. See you later."* But if someone calls up and explains what their project is and it's heartfelt and it has a chance of being meaningful, then I'm more inclined to work for a lower rate. My practice and the practice of some sound guys I know, is that we won't modify our rates much, but we will work for free if we love a project. I have a range of rates depending on the type of film. My rate for working on a documentary is about half of what I charge to work on a commercial. Don't worry about unions too much with docs, they almost never get involved.

Q – What are the common mistakes that filmmakers make?

Alan – Not monitoring the sound while shooting. That often ends in disaster.

Q – What advice would you give a new documentary filmmakers?

Alan – Invest in real estate. That's not a joke. I mean it. It's highly unlikely that you'll make a good living doing documentary films alone. As for filmmaking, the more meaningful life experience you have, the better your films will be. Joan and I have a saying, *"Who you are is what you get."*

Regarding small format sound, I can teach you 80% of what it takes to record sound in one day. The remaining 20% will take 10 years of experience, and you'd better have the experience if key scenes in your project rely on that 20%. Keep in mind that in verité, or "experiential" work as we like to call it, recording the sound is only part of you do as recordist.

It's important for filmmakers to be at ease with their equipment and to spend the time to have a sense of what good sound is. But the most important thing is to be present as a person that people can relate to, not just as a technician. Getting good content goes far beyond well-composed shots and clean audio tracks.

Track Laying Yourself

GUERILLA FILM MAKER SAYS!

Documentary films will often ignore the quality of the sound focusing solely on the content, which is strange because docs rely more on sound and dialogue than feature films to convey their messages. Having good soundtracks will only make your doc better. The technology is cheap and it only requires is a little know how and a lot of time consuming work. Here are some things to bear in mind in post when track laying.

Narration *– Make sure it's been recorded crisp and clean. Be careful where it comes in – you don't want it fighting a music cue.*

Audio Tracks *– Hopefully your sound recordist did his/her job and you don't have to use subtitles. In an interview, put each interviewee on a separate track so that the mixer can easily access each. However, there's many times in documentary films where you just can't stop that plane from going overhead or turn off that annoying lawnmower while you're in the middle of capturing that amazing moment – you can only hope that your mixer knows a good way to reduce the noise.*

Music *– Background or featured music. Again make sure it's not competing with your audio and narration. Think of when it's best to be silent or not.*

Sound Effects *– Though rare in docs, there may be times when you want to enhance a feeling, highlight a moment of comedy or give a little oomph to some animation/visual effects to explain a point. Sound Effects CDs are an excellent source of high quality stereo recordings of pretty much everything you could imagine. If you can't afford to buy the disks, try asking the Studio where you'll be doing your final mix and see if you can use their CD Library.*

Foley *– Recreation of all the subjects movements - rare apart from when you're doing docu-drama.*

Spot Effects *– subject and story driven sounds, so again very rare unless enhancing the sound in a shot or shooting a docu-drama.*

Ambiance *– continuous background sound/room tone that appears throughout the film. This should be recorded on set and can help your mixer cover up edit points around that annoying noise mentioned earlier.*

You can track lay the sound in your film with a number of semi-pro and domestic computer tools such as Adobe Premier, Avid Express Pro and Final Cut Pro. Using with SPDIF digital input/output and by pulling effects directly off CD, you can stay 100% digital, maintaining acoustic excellence without a silly price tag. You will need a good computer, large and quiet space, good amplifier and speakers and a high quality microphone. Best of all, both Avid Express Pro and FCP and their HD versions export OMF.

THE TRAVEL DOC HOST

Q – What was your background for becoming a TV travel presenter?

Ian – I was doing a lot of odd jobs here and there and just plodding along really in the UK. I had used video with teenagers and stuff like that so I was used to the cameras. Then I saw an advert in the paper for a presenter for *The Lonley Planet* (now *Globetrekker)* travel show and I decided to go for it. It said to send in a show reel so my friend and I thought that it would be fun to make a video around London. Like a guide, but a piss take guide. So I'd be sitting on the toilet talking about the rich foods of the country, getting beaten up and changing money on the black market. Stuff like that. It was five minutes long and done for a laugh, really. It was an excuse for me to get off my ass and do something. I didn't think anything of it. But I also new that 90% of the application forms they get are identical and this would be different. So you know there's a miniscule outside chance but you don't hold on for anything.

Q – Had you traveled before?

Ian – Yes. I had done a little bit here and there.

Q – It seems that no matter what country or culture you're in, you get really relaxed interviews.

Ian – The thing is that you have to put yourself in their shoes. Especially in the remote places that we go, most people haven't seen telly. There's that huge void between them and me. Me, too, when I saw a documentary, I thought it was just one guy with a camera. And when I tell people that there's a whole crew of five, they almost feel cheated. A good documentary or show is when you can make it look like it runs so easily. But really it's a lot of people working hard to get it to look like that.

Q – Any tips on making the interviewee feel comfortable?

Ian – Some of the stuff we do is set up and a lot of it isn't. Some of those people have never been on camera before and when you have one shoved in your face, it's intimidating and scary. You know that they're the one with the amazing story, so you want it to come over the best way it can. Usually I will chat to the person beforehand, thalking about normal things and not looking at the camera. Just pretending it isn't there. You can also relax them by telling stupid jokes and if they don't like something, they can say stop. There's no pressure. And then you chat and usually they almost forget the camera is there. I tell them to not even think about what they're going to say. Because the reason that we're talking to someone is because they have done something amazing or it's about their life. So they don't have to prepare anything. I don't need a list of questions. I'm going to plug them with question after question so they're not going to have time to think about it or worry about the camera. Also, if they feel their answer has not come over clearly enough, I tell them not to worry and we'll do it again.

Q – What are the problems with interviewees that you've faced?

Ian – Sometimes the people that you think are easy to chat to completely freeze when the camera is there. Or the funniest thing is you go to a blacksmith's and it's all rustic everywhere and rundown – like something out of *Lord Of The Rings*. And then you go down the next day to film and they've vaccuumed it, made it clean and the guy's wearing a suit. He's aware that he's showing off his place.

Q – You come across all sorts of cultures and languages. The one thing that seems to bring down all the barriers is humor. Are you conscious of using it?

Ian – Of course. Telling a joke relaxes people automatically. Humor is the best thing for that in anything like getting a point across or defusing something or just at the end of the day, getting on with people. There's no difference between that person in Mongolia and the one down at the local pub. It's just you chatting and you either get on or you don't, that's life. There's a tendency when traveling to be overpatronizing or overhumble, which is just as bad as someone who is arrogant.

Q – Are there any special qualities that a documentary travel host should have?

Ian – I think the main ability is about being honest with it because people aren't mugs and they know if you're not being honest. But then sometimes I know there are documentaries where people question and question and wait for the person to say something and say, *"Right, we got it."* The scary thing is that 80% of it is in the editing. The way I say one sentence can be cut between anything and made to be ten completely different emotions. It's frightening. Sometimes it worries me that some film crews take advantage of people who let them film them. Because, even the news has a slant to it and has been cut with a slant to it. Just because it's a documentary people think that it must be true. No. No. No. No. No. You almost have to watch them more because you forget there's hours of editing for that. For a travel program as a host, you can't do anything but be yourself. The viewers aren't stupid. They know if you lie. They know you're making it up if you say, *"That cockroach tasted lovely!"* You almost want to tap into that thing of when the viewer is sitting there, you have to think how they would feel. I'll be talking to some guy and he's a lunatic. I'll then turn to the camera and say, *"This guy is a nutter!"* And when you're sitting there you say, *"Thank God you said it because we are all thinking it."*

Q – Have you ever had a bad experience in a country when filming?

Ian – Yes. But with filming the show, if you have a really shitty day, because you're doing it for three weeks, the next day could be phenomenal. You have to remember that you're also judging a country through filming. Baja California was a nightmare because it was a textbook of everything that could go wrong with filming. We went there at the wrong time of year and the light was flat. All the cameras broke and had to be sent to Mexico City. We only went there because there was this amazing festival in La Paz, which turned out to be village fete in a parking lot. It was so barren. There's no indigenous culture or history. It was a nightmare. There was another time where I was mugged traveling in the streets of Morocco. That's the worst. You realize how vulnerable you are. But also that's why I love Morocco! Even when you're getting mugged you can haggle the price down! I swear to God that's true. The guy goes, *"Give me 100 and I'll let you go."* I said, *"I'll give you 60" "80."* Then I haggled him down to 75. Luckily I had change on me. I probably could have gotten change as well. But I never wanted to go back to Morocco again and it's a sad thing when one thing can completely screw your vision up of a country. So when I got this job, one of my first programs was bloody Morocco. I couldn't believe it! The best job in the world and now I have to go back to Morocco. But after two days, it was heaven.

Q – How do you choose your interviewees? Do you do a lot of research beforehand?

Ian – Yes. Because it's six months real traveling condensed into two and half weeks, you have to know when to go, when the festivals are. You have to have a rough idea things of who you're going to interview. So the producer will go out there for two weeks and try to pinpoint people. And then a director will go a week later and write a script. And then we'll come out, rip the script up and start again. About 50% of it is spontaneous. It has to be or else it wouldn't work.

Q – How big are your crews?

Ian – Five people. Me, camera and sound, a producer and director. Plus we usually have a fixer, who can sort things out

GUERILLA FILM MAKER SAYS!

Some Interview Techniques

1. Relax your interviewees by telling jokes or talking about non-subject issues.

2. Don't schedule more than two or three interviews a day so that you stay fresh.

3. Keep your subject from saying things in pre-interviews. It's hard to recapture that magic in the second go around.

4. Be honest with your subjects and they will open up to you.

5. Keep eye contact. This keeps your subject engaged, so don't look through your notes while they are talking.

6. Don't speak while your subject is speaking. Active listening is good for day to day conversations, but it will wreak havoc in your edit sessions if your voice is there - unless you're part of the film.

7. For more formal interviews, have your subject repeat the questions as part of their answer.

8. Try not to be too encumbered by people and equipment when interviewing. It's intimidating otherwise.

9. If a subject is lying to you or being difficult, you can confront them on it as long as you know you're right.

10. Don't speak too much. It's not your question that is important – it's their answer. Also it's a human reaction to fill in silences so they might give you more if you keep your mouth shut.

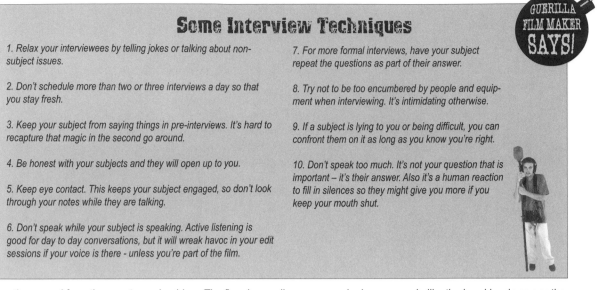

on the ground from the country and a driver. The fixer is usually someone who knows people like the head herdsman or the guy who trains the eagles. And if they don't, they'll go find them.

Q – Do you always use the same crew?

Ian – No. You have to use different crews or you'll go insane. I can't even go around London for three days with my mates with out us driving each other mad. Imagine three weeks away. Oi!

Q – How important is it to have the right team on board when filming?

Ian – Oh, God, yeah. There might be incredible things going on all the time in incredible places with incredible people, but your crew might be a couple of assholes. It doesn't happen that much. Every now and again it has been a nightmare. Like in Tunisa and Libya, this director was an asswipe. I couldn't work with him. Bizarre as after doing this for seven years, you realize how vulnerable you are. I lost all my confidence. It was like the first job I did.

Q – Can you choose whom you work with?

Ian – To a certain degree. I try to work with people that I've worked with before. But it doesn't matter if there are new people. And there has to be new people to freshen it up. They bring new ideas to it. If it were the same director, then after three or four programs, the thing would be identical. You wouldn't even be aware that you were slipping into patterns of where to stay or what to do.

Q – You also shoot some Super 8mm stuff as well, right?

Ian – Yeah. And we have a small back up digital camera to go along with the Digibeta. I love those small cameras because you can really get in there even though the quality is not as good. Sound is a bit of a hassle as well. But soon, you'll be using a matchbox and half the people will be unemployed. And with HD, it's frightening. But that's why I like working with big crews because everyone is concentrating on their job. Then you get the best because you're not doubling up and losing quality. These days we're struggling to even make them because every broadcaster wants them cheaper, but of the same quality.

Q – How may times a year do you go off and shoot a program?

Ian – At the beginning, it was about six or seven months. Not all at the same time or else you would go insane. Now I only do about two months maybe three.

Q – Sometimes on the show you have to eat really weird stuff like sheep's eyes. How do you deal with that?

Ian – In a way, you have to just swallow it! Literally! It's not going to kill you. And whether the camera is on or not, in those situations you have to try anyway. And most of the people are not going to be offended. They know that you have never eaten that kind of rubbish in your life. They're almost chuckling to themselves. But if you're in a small village in Morocco and they're giving you lamb and that's what they eat, then that's more likely to cause offense if you don't like it. You just have to chew, chew, chew.

Q – What is the worst thing that you've had to taste?

Ian – A cockroach. That was in Cambodia. I had to spit that out on camera. But probably if you served that up and you didn't know what it was, it probably wouldn't taste too bad. But because you have that thing coming toward you and it's just a cockroach that you have down in your fridge, it's a different ball game. Before I did the program, I used to be a vegetarian. That was one of the hard things about doing the show - knowing that I would have to eat the meat!

Q – What are the some of the risks involved when doing travel documentaries such as dealing with unstable political situations?

Ian – We haven't had much trouble because we do research on that. But things do crop up. Stupid things. Like in Haiti where we were driving in government vehicles and the crowds were out on the streets at midnight. Any crowd situation can be a bit scary. Other shows we've got caught up in a couple of riots and stuff like that. Globetrekker isn't politically motivated and only skims the surface. We only give you a taste of the country. And I don't want to go to a country that is potentially volatile anyway. It's only a lighthearted travel program. I'm not going to die making television.

Q – Have you had any weird situations with animals?

Ian – That's a bit personal, don't you think?! I did get stung by a two-inch size ant and that hurt like hell. That was in Guiana. They said we wouldn't see any wildlife. That was when I put my hammock on a tree that these ants were going up. And of course at night, I put my hand on it. They had these fingers coming out of their abdomen! I had to put my finger in a cup of water for a couple of hours. Also, we went to Katmandu to film in a monkey temple. The director stepped on a baby monkey. These things are big and could rip you to shreds in a couple of minutes. Ten of them are snorting at you. The director's hiding behind me and they're grabbing my trousers to get to him because they know it's him. A monkey jumped out of a tree and onto the back of his trousers and took a little bite. He's only been filming for two hours and the director's already been bit up the ass by a monkey. He's like, *"It's OK. It didn't cut the skin."* Then he looks down and there's blood everywhere. We took him to the hospital and he got rabies jabs. He was alright, but he was a jinx, that guy. In Madagascar, he fell down a sewer walking backwards while he was doing a shot. He also got mugged in Rio on the beach while snogging some girl.

Q – Do you have any advice about taking equipment into foreign countries?

Ian – Keep your bloody eye on it.

Q – Do you take it on the plane with you or do you put it in the cargo hold?

Ian – God, no, we couldn't cart it all. What we take on the plane is the rushes (dailies), the tapes, the cameras and the sound equipment. I've had stuff nicked in Sweden in a posh five star hotel. It doesn't matter where you are. You have to keep your eye on it. We've had a $20,000 lens nicked in Uzbekistan from the back of the van. We get back and there are a bunch of fourteen-year-old kids waiting for us asking us how much we are going to buy it back for. They didn't know what it was, but we had to give them $200 to get it back.

Q – Have you ever had any delays in getting things in and out of countries?

Ian – Oh, God yeah. In Syria, they wanted to go through all of our tapes to make sure there wasn't anything bad on them. But I think even they got bored of looking at them. I would. Forty tapes at a half hour each of me yakking on. It was more protocol really. But there were times when your kit doesn't turn up. So we're waiting in the airport for 24 hours and going mad because we're losing days. But then the kit turns up and we've lost a day and we're buggered.

Q – Do you do the voice over in the country?

Ian – No. We do it in London. You have to cut the whole thing up to know where anything comes in. I hate voice over. If you listen to my voice over it sounds like a different person is reading it.

Q – Do you write it?

Ian – No. The voice over has to be right because it is facts and figures. It's not a personal journal, the voice over. It's more information lead.

Q – Do you sit down with them and go over it?

Ian – Not really. They're picking up information all along. They know roughly what they want to say in that segment. People ask me if I go into the edit room. Who wants the bloody presenter in the edit room? Worst nightmare for anyone. And that's not my job. I don't know what the director's vision is.

Q – How much footage do you end up with on a three-week shoot?

Ian – Some directors squirt, and squirt and squirt and then try to patch it together in the edit suite. The one we did on Alaska, I think we had 17 half hour tapes, which is the shortest ever. That's only eight and a half hours for a one-hour show. So that's extraordinary. Because when you're interviewing someone, I'll be chatting to someone to get stuff and you're going to use a minute or less in the program. Sometimes we'll come back with 40 hours of tape, which is crazy.

Working With Animals & Children

GUERILLA FILM MAKER SAYS!

Docs involve real life, so even if you're not intending on shooting a nature doc or using kids - they may surprise you or you find that you're having to film them.

Animals

1. Do research on the animals you are going to film. Find out about their habits, mating cycles, hibernation cycles, etc.
2. Prepare to spend a lot of time in the field. Most nature docs take 6-18 months for production.
3. Keep a safe distance between you and the animal. If they are nervous or feel threatened, they will come after you or not give you their natural behavior.
4. Some animals can be attracted by food, but rarely can you get them to do tricks or stunts. Besides, by you doing this, it is not a natural performance.
5. Do not try to help animals in distress. You will just end up causing more of a disaster and potentially open yourself up to disease or attack.
6. Work with trained professionals whenever possible who can help you get those great shots.

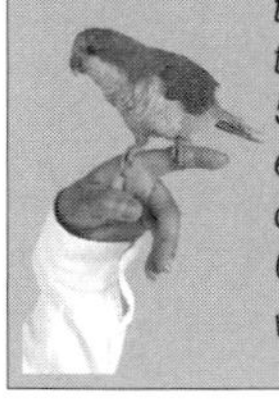

Children

1. Don't patronize children. Talk to them like adults or they will turn off.
2. Children don't have long attention spans so keep your questions simple and short.
3. Children get tired and hungry easily. Be prepared for short sessions and mood swings.
4. Some children are shy so giving them a prop to play with can open them up. Sometimes it helps to let them use the camera for a while.
5. You must get a release from the child's parent or guardian in order to use the interview.
6. With older children, be prepared for them to say the most intimate things right away. Sometimes they may see you as a confessor.

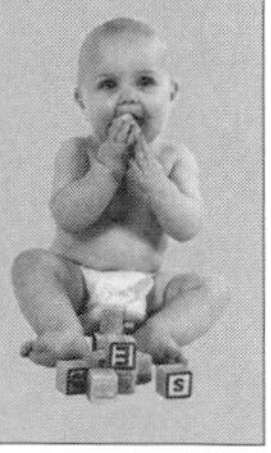

Q – How long is the actual post period?

Ian – When they come back they have three weeks to edit.

Q – Do the producers pick up any indigenous music to put in the program?

Ian – Oh, yeah. They have some great composers who put it all together.

Q – Do you have any advice for a travel documentarian about to do a film?

Ian – The worst crime is a lack of imagination and a lack of flexibility. When you're traveling you cannot be rigid because you can't control situations. You can't be rigid to your script. You might write a beautiful script and no one turns up. You have to be in a state of flexibility or you're going to be shafted and everyone is going to be on each other's nerves. You have to have the balls and the experience to say, *"That's crap. Let's try to do something else."* They're the best directors for me. We went to a festival where there were four Peskies with a top hat and a feather coming out. Coming up to the camera making noises and going backwards and forwards. And I was saying, *"Am I jaded? Have I seen too much? Or is this bullocks?"* No, this is bullocks and they're just taking the piss and I couldn't stop laughing. You can get into that when you're abroad. You have to have patient like you've never had to be. Forget filming, just the logistics of traveling. That's why most of the people on this are people who have done a lot of traveling. But then again, sometimes the spontaneity of someone who's never done it before is exciting.

Q – Is there anything you would tell people to avoid?

Ian – Hippie travelers. Avoid them like the plague! I always travel with a hippie baseball bat wherever I go just to clear them out. Those dirty, crusties that sit in the corner and tell me that they're the only ones really experienced in the country. *"We're all fake and they're all real."* They're so free. That one cracks me up because they're the tightest group you're ever going to meet. They've got such a long list of criteria that you have to fit before they'll talk to you. What pisses me off is that I've actually heard one of them say that they were just as poor as the locals. That's an insult. They're there because they are the new middle class rich colonials. And their money will last a hell of a lot longer. They drive me insane. In reality, 95% of the people on this Earth couldn't even dream about stepping on an airplane. So if you can travel, you are rich. So have the balls to say that you are rich and lucky.

Q – You must meet some amazing characters when you do your shows?

Ian – Oh, yeah. You are humbled every time. We were walking around the back of a town in Mongolia and this guy comes out of a shitty little garage covered in oil. We started chatting and he has four degrees in metallurgy, speaks seven languages and is working for two pence an hour. And here I am walking around in my stupid shorts and I can't even speak English properly. Or the A-bomb victim who survived Nagasaki. It's a once in a lifetime thing to meet these people. Every single job, I thank my lucky stars that I'm on it. I cannot believe that I do this. If you do the trips that I have done you will talk about it and bore people senseless until the day you die. I have done 55 of them. I'm the ultimate travel story bore. I have no friends left. No, not really.

Russ Suniewyk
Colorlab

THE LAB

Q – How can documentary filmmakers make their lab experiences better?

Russ – Go out and shoot a test roll of film with sync sound so you can work through all the potential shooting locations and see how they impact the camera and sound recordist. Otherwise, we may have to unravel a lot of technical issues for you and that can be expensive. You should also shoot lens tests if you can. Lens tests can tell you if the camera package is damaged or needs adjusting. And when you do these tests, do not screen them on a computer screen or on an Avid. Ideally, screen some film work prints of tests and absolutely of early principle photography rolls so you can see any potential focus problems. This is especially true if you're shooting 16mm or Super 16mm, for example. You don't want any surprises when you see your first blow-up print.

Q – When should a filmmaker approach the lab?

Russ – Usually a few weeks before production. It gives us time to know when and how much film we'll be receiving from a producer and in what intervals. Also it allows you to get us the delivery requirements from your distributor if you have one so we can plan accordingly. If you wait until the start of principle photography, the stress can make people forget details. So set down the rules before you start and then we can cut down frantic telephoning back and forth. That's how you lose money and time and get everyone on the set in an uproar and feeling bad about themselves and each other.

Q – Are Super 16mm and 35mm treated the same way when you process it?

Russ – Yes. The most important thing when originating on 35mm is when you crack the mag off the camera between takes to check for hairs and scratches, you mark sync and then put the mag back in sync with the camera. That way we don't have to do reframing. If you present us with camera rolls with reframing issues, the colorist has to stop the telecine process when transferring the video dailies, name new camera rolls within camera rolls on the flex files according to where the new camera starts are – all due to having to reframe. Telecine of film footage is all about data management. It's more important than how the picture looks from the editor's perspective. It needs to have valid time code, with an A frame edit at the head of every tape so that the lists don't get corrupted. If you don't do that, your record ins and outs in editing will be hit or miss because of the 3:2 pulldown. This is something that people who don't shoot film every day forget. Then the dailies come back, the data are screwed up and all of sudden, the first camera roll that was 400 feet becomes six different camera rolls. Then the editor and subsequently the negative cutter get really confused.

Q – What is pushing and pulling?

Russ – If you're underexposed and you want to get back one or two stops, you push the film in processing. We increase the temperature and the time of the processing. Pushing increases the grain somewhat and should be done very gingerly and as last resort. Some people like the look of the increased grain and texture. The blacks change so it's hard to make it match a roll of film from the same scene that was developed normally. Pulling is the opposite of pushing. It's for when you know that you have overexposed the film. In that case, we reduce the time and temperature of the film in the machine.

Q – What can you do to fix a scratched film negative?

Russ – We take advantage of the roll in and out by taking a few feet from the end of a roll and head of each roll and tape it to the film can before processing. It's the footage used to thread up the camera body. There's no picture on it, but it has been through the camera. That way we can see if there's a scratch on it before processing and notify the DP or AC…they can use the camera reports and trace the problem to the offending mag. If we find one on the emulsion side before processing, it's going to be very hard to remove it. It'll have to be done via electronic means in telecine. If it's post scratched by the negative cutter, we can rewash those negative scenes that have that defect on the emulsion and actually swell the emulsion up around the scratch so that the light refracts through the hump of the swelling and isn't stopped by the scratch. If it's on the base side of the film, liquid gate printing does the same thing of refracting the light around the dirt or the scratches and creating and image on an intermediate or print stock that doesn't have the scratch. The rewashing is $.20/foot so it's expensive, but you only rewash what you need. The wet gate print isn't very expensive at all. You want to get dry gate printing or transferring for your dailies and then figure out which ones are scratched and then make plans to deal with them in post. Electronic fixes can be expensive to not expensive, depending on what technology is used. It's not the end of the world. It's just something we have to deal with.

Q – How should film be protected from X-rays?

Russ – Film should be wrapped in lead-lined containers and never put through as baggage but carried on, because the X-rays in baggage security checks are stronger than what your carry on goes through. They may make you open your baggage and show them what's inside. Try to avoid that, but one quick exposure of normal ASA film isn't going to fog the film. Fed Ex is another option because they usually don't X-ray their packages. That may change if we have another terrorist attack, but for right now that's a way to go. Also the higher the ASA, the more susceptible it is to X-rays. The best resource for checking this is the Kodak website. If you're shooting outside the US, it might be a good idea to get the film processed where you're shooting so that you can put your mind at ease.

Q – What are key codes?

Russ – A machine readable bar code expression of the manufactured latent edge numbers. The negative cutter uses those numbers when he/she cuts. There's a dot near the letter prefixes called the zero frame dot. This is also expressed in the bar code data, which is machine read in telecine and goes into the flex file. The frame opposite the dot is known as that frame only (even though the entire letter prefix and number spills over onto underneath the next frame)…the next frame is known as that number +1. When we make an A frame edit in telecine, we start it on that zero frame. All the frames after that number will be labeled with the key code zero frame number plus the amount of frames it is from the zero frame—for example, key code +2 or key code +3, naming the second and third frames and so on. When it gets to the next key code number, it starts over again. In telecine, the machine reads that barcode and puts the numbers into a flex file.

Q – What is a camera report sheet?

Russ – It's a hand-written log of every time the camera starts and is slated. You can go to our website and under our 'Film School" see samples of this and other camera and film reports. The lab that you are doing business with should give you a stack of these forms and they should be in duplicate. An example of what kind of information you put on the camera report would be if a take is MOS or with sound. Other kinds of information are the camera roll, what camera shot it and what mag was used, the production name and the director and DP's name.

Q – What do you do your dailies out to these days?

Russ – Betacam SP, DVCam, Mini-DV, hard drives, and Digital Betacam.

Q – What is the colorist's role in the video daily?

Russ – It's important that the director and the DP talk to the colorist and the facility early on…way before principle photography begins. Hollywood directors watch film dailies not video dailies. The reason why is when you take film and transfer it to video and the colorist sees something out of focus, they know the amount of resolution the film is going to be scanned with and they immediately spot the problem. At that point, they should immediately pick up the phone and call the production office and say that the roll isn't sharp. Then all hell breaks loose as everyone tries to figure out what caused it. The telecine colorist doing the dailies who isn't advocating for the director is going to take the contour button and increase it a little bit so it looks in focus so they don't have to deal with a hailstorm of people pointing fingers at each other. If you do that, then problem film will look soft when subjected to a blow up. You have to make sure they won't cover that up so that you can nip the problem in the bud. And also tell the lab that you know chances are it's not their fault and you will not yell at or sue them if it's an on-set problem. There must be trust and daily candid communication between the photography department and the lab! If the colorist is not taking the initiative to call in daily camera reports to the DP or AC, you need to find another lab.

Q – Is there any reason why anyone in North America would telecine in PAL?

Russ – It cancels the 3:2 pulldown. In NTSC, there aren't the same number of video fields as there are film frames in a second's worth of time at normal speed. And sometimes it's 3 video fields representing one film frame and other times there are 2. That comes from there being 30 video frames to 24 film fames. In PAL, it's the same number every time because you are in 25 frames per second. The video looks more like Betacam or film transferred to video in the UK because the brain is not seeing any 3:2 jitter, symptomatic with 24fps exposed film living in 30 fps NTSC video. There's no jitter because there is a 1:1 transfer relationship. Because of this the data management is a lot easier to control in post.

Q – What are the common mistakes that you see documentary filmmakers make?

Russ – The biggest error is in training. Film is very technical and many film schools do not adequately teach their students how to use a film camera and shoot sync sound. So when the filmmaker gets to use them, we sometimes have to unravel lots of problems. And because of this, filmmakers should hire experienced DPs and sound recordists.

Q – What advice would you give a new documentary filmmaker?

Russ – Be objective…this isn't about you, listen to your subjects! You have to be able to write well. When I see high school kids dripping with talent, and they ask about whether to invest in film school, I urge them to also consider the English department. I know this may seem odd coming from someone who owns a film lab, but I think it is possible to reach a level of high validity with a project even if you don't originate on film. The aesthetic suffers with video origination and plenty of well-versed folks think video origination is very problematic. There's also so much one doesn't learn about the glories of originating on film. But if fiscal realities force you into a place between shooting on tape or not telling your story, then tell the story. You can always get your story back to film…ideally with someone else paying for it.

GUERILLA FILM MAKER SAYS!

Lab Reports

If you are lucky enough to shoot some or all of your doc on film, you will use various lab reports to tell them how you want your stock processed. There is a sound report (how the sound was recorded and where it goes), the camera report (stating what is on each roll), the drop-off report (how much film you have, what kind and do you want any special processing) and the telecine report pictured below (courtesy of Colorlab), which tells the colorist how you want your film processed. You can download samples of all these forms from www.colorlab.com.

COLORLAB LABORATORY AND TELECINE SERVICES

5708 ARUNDEL AVENUE, **ROCKVILLE, MD** 20852 / P#: (301) 770-2128 / F#: (301) 816-0798
27 WEST 20TH STREET SUITE#307, **NEW YORK, NY** 10011 / P#: (212) 633-8172 / F#: (212) 633-8241

TELECINE SPEC SHEET

CLIENT NAME: ____________________

FILM TITLE: ____________________

PHONE: ____________________ **EMAIL:** ____________________

COMPANY/SCHOOL: ____________________

FILM FORMAT: circle one REG 8mm | SUPER 8mm | 9.5mm | REG 16mm | SUPER 16mm | 35mm

VIDEO DAILIES: circle one ONE-LIGHT | BEST-LIGHT | SCENE TO SCENE (Unsupervised)

FRAMING: circle one 4:3 | 4:3 center | Letterbox type - 1.66 - 1.78 - 1.85 - other____ | 16 X 9 Anamorphic | Framelines in Underscan

FILM WAS SHOT @ ____ FPS FOR TRANSFER @ ____ FPS

TIMECODE: circle one NDF (non-drop frame) DF (drop frame)

TIMECODE START @ HR: ________ (TC will start at hour 01 unless otherwise indicated)

MASTER TAPE FORMAT: | Betacam SP | Digital Betacam | Mini DV | DV Cam small or BIG **shell tape** (circle one)

DUBS: | DVD | DigiBeta | MiniDV | _" | S-VHS | VHS | DV Cam small or BIG **shell** | Hard Drive

AUDIO: YES NO

SYNC or TRANSFER (if yes, please circle your audio format) | _" Nagra | TC DAT | 16mm mag |

WILL YOU BE MATCHING BACK TO FILM: YES NO

* If you are planning on film matchback, Colorlab can record Keycode during your film-to-tape transfer session. You have options as to how you would like this information presented on your videotape. Timecode and/or Keycode windows can be "burned in" inside tv safe, outside tv safe, or you may choose to have a clean picture (not burned in) with Timecode/Keycode information on the address track of the videotape and a floppy disk called a **Flex File**. (Keycode reading is available for an additional $50/hr)

AATON LINKER:	**YES**	**NO**	**3 LINE VITC:**	**YES**	**NO**
KEYCODE READING:	**YES**	**NO**	**FLEX FILE:**	**YES**	**NO**
KEYCODE WINDOW:	**YES**	**NO**	**TIMECODE WINDOW:**	**YES**	**NO**

WINDOWS (on MASTER) : circle one | NONE | **OR** (INSIDE or OUTSIDE) **TV SAFE**
WINDOWS (on DUBS) : circle one | NONE | **OR** (INSIDE or OUTSIDE) **TV SAFE**

PLEASE CHECK ALL THAT APPLY:

Camera report/s included with film Sound report/s included with film (for sync dailies only)
Tape stock included with film ____________________
If yes, please indicate the type and quantity of stock
Notes/instructions included with film ***(strongly recom'd for BEST LITE & SC-TO-SC transfers)***

____
____
____
____

THE DIGITAL LAB

Q – What services do you have at Duart that are relevant to a documentary filmmaker?

Larry – As a full service facility, we have a lab where we develop and prep film and four telecine machines to transfer your film to video. If you're shooting video, we can down convert your footage to get you started on your editorial process. We rent edit suites, we have staff editors that you can hire and we also have a list of recommended freelance editors who specialize in documentary. We offer all the post-production services that you will need, including color correction, online editorial, titles, sound editorial and mixing. If you want to record out to film, we can do that, too. So we can go film to tape and tape to film. If you were lucky enough to shoot on film, we can transfer your selects from your offline to HD and then do a digital intermediate conform out to film.

Q – When should a documentary filmmaker approach you?

Larry – As soon as possible. Once they know what they're shooting on, how many frames per second, what aspect ratio they're shooting and what their deliverables are down the road. Just keep things in mind when you start. You're not going to shoot a 2:35 movie if your deliverable is full frame TV. Remember you can't go back and it's a big blow up to get a full frame version from a 2:35 ratio.

Q – What other things should a filmmaker be thinking about if they shoot on a film format?

Larry – Do you want to use the film as an intermediate or do they want to use the film as a final deliverable? Meaning if they shot 16mm or 35mm, they can put sound on it and then they have a finished film. If they shot Super 16mm, that's just an intermediate step because you cannot put sound on Super 16mm. Let's say you shot Super 16mm. That has an aspect ratio of 1:66 to get the whole image of the Super 16mm or you can do a 1:77 aspect to match HD. If you plan to project this film, then you want to frame your shots for 1:85 aspect. So you really want to keep in mind proper framing.

Q – And if you're shooting and editing on DV or HD?

Larry – Let's start with 24 frames versus 30 frames because that's what a lot of people are shooting these days. If they shoot at 24, do they shoot with advanced pull down or do they shoot normal pulldown? The answer to that is what editorial box are you going to be using. For instance, Final Cut cannot take out a normal 3:2 pulldown upon digitizing. It can only take out the advanced pull down. Whereas, the Avid can take out both. What looks better in my opinion is to use normal pull down because even if you are shooting at 24, the tape is recording at 29.97. Normal pulldown looks like any other 24 frame telecine transfer. You don't see as much stutter as you do with advanced pulldown. We also recommend editing at 24 if possible and if you use Final Cut, use Cinema Tools to convert to a 24-frame sequence. Editing at 24fps gives a 1:1 frame relationship if you are going to go out to film.

Q – What is normal pull down and advanced pull down?

Larry – Normal pulldown utilizes the same 2:3 or 3:2 pulldown cadence long used to transfer 24fps film to NTSC video. The first 24p frame is written to two fields of 60i video, the next is written to three, the next to two, and the next to three again. Advanced pulldown uses a 2:3:3:2 pulldown cadence to stuff 24 frames into 60 fields. It creates 1 dummy frame every 5 frames to get from 24p to 60i.

Q – What about framing your shots for the medium that you're going to watch the film?

Larry – Now you can shoot 4x3 and on some cameras you can shoot 16x9. But be careful about choosing a video camera to shoot 16x9. You can do a true anamorphic 16x9 or there are some lower end prosumer cameras that do a squeeze 16x9. The camera stretches the images and softens it dramatically. You want your camera to do the former. If you're going to shoot 4x3 and you know it's going to be a film-out down the road, you want to frame for 1:85 and keep the full frame safe of booms and lights. In post you can reposition your images up and down and make them safe for 1:85. If you do not frame for 1:85 and you have booms and other unwanted things in the shot, it's going to cost you more money down the line to get them out.

Q – Can a 16x9 anamorphic lens give you the picture that you want?

Larry – The only problem with that is that are you keeping in mind what you actually see in the lens? Your video-out might look one way versus how it's going to be recorded. You might have a 16x9 anamorphic lens, but then you're going to have a lot of vignetting on the side. Then you're going to have to blow up your film 12%-14% to get rid of the vignetting from the camera, especially if you zoom out all the way.

Q – When would you suggest someone shoot PAL versus NTSC?

Larry – Three years ago we used to see a lot of people shooting on PAL to get the extra 100 lines of resolution. The only caveat with PAL is your sound because a lot of American sound houses want their sound at 29.97 and their Pro Tools systems are set up for NTSC and not to handle PAL, so you have to do a conversion of your picture to match against to get your sound in sync. If you do a film-out on PAL, most facilities will just keep everything at 25 fps and let the projector slow it down to 24 fps. 99% of the time that's fine, but music and maybe comedy timing can get thrown off.

Q – What are the various kinds of HD?

Larry – There's two kinds. There's SMPTE standard HD, or field based HD, which you get from the Panasonic Varicam 1280x720 or the Sony Cinealta that records 1920x1080. Those are the two high-end ways to shoot HD. For documentaries, you can almost shoot film for the same amount of money as renting the above gear. In HD, you aren't paying for the developing and prep of film, but what you are paying for is downconverts to standard definition. You shoot HDCAM, but in the edit bay or on your computer at home, you're not going to have a $150,000-$200,000 HD deck to load your footage. So you have to downconvert your tape to DV to digitize. You will also be paying for sync and layback as you would in film. You won't be shooting run and gun with a Cinealta camera. Those things are more for interviews and dramatic events. They look great and if your whole film is that way, it will come out beautifully. The other kind is HDV, whether it's Sony, Panasonic, JVC or Cannon. It's an MPEG stream. If you shoot at 30 fps, you can just ingest it right into you Final Cut Pro or Avid Express and away you go. But most filmakers don't want to shoot at 30fps because they think 24fps looks more filmic. Right now neither Avid or Final Cut can digitize 24 frame material from HDV, so you have to use a 3rd party acquisition MPEG to uncompressed codec converter to fix it. You digitize into that 3rd party program and then transcode that clip to something Final Cut or Avid can read at 24fps. Imagine doing that for a whole documentary! You have to digitize it twice. So while it would appear more videoish shot at 30fps, if will save you time and money in the long run.

Q – Is HDV true HD?

Larry – It's lower resolution. There's a hell of a lot more compression. It's not frame based – odd and even fields, progressive versus interlaced. It's an MPEG stream. It's not HD in reference to a true 1920x1080. It's a prosumer version of HD.

The 3:2 Pulldown

GUERILLA FILM MAKER SAYS!

Film runs at 24 frames per second. In North America, NTSC (National Television Standards Committee) video runs at 29.97 fps (commonly thought to be 30fps). If you did a straight transfer from film to video, the motion would appear too fast and the audio would quickly become out of sync. In order to fix this problem, the 3:2 pulldown is used in the telecine process. Here four film frames are distributed over five video frames which over one second gives six additional film frames allowing them to run in sync. The term pulldown refers to the idea of an intermittent shutter mechanism that "pulls down" a frame of film, holds it for a certain amount of time and then advances on to the next fame. Because NTSC video runs at 29.97fps, or 0.1% slower that 30 fps, the telecine house doing the 3:2 pulldown must slow down the picture and the audio on the film side down by 0.1%.

In non-NTSC parts of the world, the 3:2 pulldown is less of a problem. Both PAL (Phase Alternating Line) and SEACAM (Sequential Color with Memory) standards operate at 25fps. In a PAL world (most of Europe), films are shot at 25fps (film and digital) and post at 25fps making it an easy transfer for DVD and broadcast. So if you know your doc is going to end up on TV or DVD only, shooting PAL, even in the US, might be the way to go. Know, however, that if you do go theatrical you will have to slow down your film 4% to get in back to 24fps and that can throw off music and comedy moments. If you know or plan to go theatrically, you want to shoot and post at 24fps.

Q – Does PAL, NTSC or SEACAM mean anything in the HD world?

Larry – There is a 1080/50 which transcodes back to 25 fps, which is PAL. But those three formats are Standard Definition TV formats.

Q – What are the differences between progressive and interlaced scans in HD?

Larry – When we talk about HD, field based HD – an interlaced image has two fields of video. There is motion between the two. So if your hand moves from point A to point B, you'd see physical motion between field 1 and field 2. A progressive frame or 1080 psf, which is partially segmented frames. That means field 1 and field 2 are identical and when those two fields are combined they become a progressive image. A progressive image is cleaner as you don't have the interlacing motion artifacts that you have between field 1 and field 2. However, if you are shooting sports or something with high motion, you want that interlacing because with 60 fields instead of 30, there is more information that can be captured. The motion looks cleaner and smoother.

Q – Is there anything special to think about when dealing with audio in HD?

Larry – Audio likes even pairings. For instance, if you're shooting at 24 frames per second, record your audio at 30. If you are shooting at 23.98, record the audio at 29.97. So if you're shooting with a 1080, 23.98 system, you're going to record your audio at 29.97.

Q – Are there any problems that can occur if you digitize a variety of media formats into your editing system and then go out to film?

Larry – When you do masters for film-out, you usually have film-originated material video originated material and also archival. For the film-out, you have to frame blend the 30fps material. Because it's interlaced and running at 30 frames per second, you have to get it down to 24 frames and make it progressive for a film-out. Going back to that 3:2 pulldown that we mentioned before, to get back to 24fps for film originated material, you just take out the 3:2. For a proper film out from varying frame rate materials you need to process like frames per second material. So what we do is we take all the 30 frame material and process that by itself and make it 24 frames. Then we go all the film material and take out the 3:2 pulldown. Now we have two sequences. Now let's say you have 25 frame PAL, take that out and convert that to 24. Load everything back into a 24-frame timeline so that when you cut between your film and video everything is running at 24fps and you don't get the tearing and the flipped fields.

Q – Is there a way that a filmmaker can avoid this situation?

Larry – Your first decision is what is your majority of your footage. If most of it is 30 interlaced video material, then cut everything at 30 fps. If most of your footage is film or 24p video, then cut everything at 24 frames. To split the difference, what is helpful is cut your sequence, run everything at 30 fps because that is what the tape is going to be running at, then when you are done, make two sequences. Put all your 30fps video originated material on a higher timeline in your editing program and put your 24 fps film stuff on a lower timeline. And then differentiate between your 30i and your 24-frame video material And only do this after your locked picture. One thing, if you're seeing something that goes from 24fps to 30 fps and you think you want to try a dissolve – don't. Keep is as a cut.

Q – How long does a film blow up from HD take and how much does it cost?

Larry – Cost is simply supply and demand. When there used to be three or four houses that used to do this, it was a lot higher than it is now. It's still an expensive process depending on the length of your film. If it's coming from HD the nice thing is that HD's aspect ration is 1:77 and you are blowing up to 1:85. It's not a big jump. You don't have to worry about dropping the heads as if it were 4x3 full frame material. So how it looks on HD is how it will look on film. You have to re-color correct for film because of the contrast and the color spectrum, but that is about it. A 90-minute film normally takes about a week.

Q – What is telecine?

Larry – It's taking your film-originated material and putting on a machine that transfers the film originated material to video for you to work with. When it passes through the color corrector, you have several options. You can do a one light transfer, which means one light of information is passed across the image and it's transferred onto tape. It looks flat. You can also do a best light or also known as scene to scene which allows you to go in and tweak the color and make things sharper. That gives you a cleaner, pristine and prettier picture for your daily transfers. At this time you can sync the audio in the suite, or you can lay it down silent and sync it later. The telecine process is when the 2:3 pull down is inserted to get 24-frame film to 30 frames of video.

Q – Can you fix anything that is out of focus in telecine?

Larry – No. You can fix underexposed and overexposed. There are softening filters, but that is not the job of the telecine process on the first pass. The process is to give a visual representation of how the DP shot the film. So if you put in a lot of enhancements and color and bring up everything that looks underexposed, the DP doesn't correct anything, and so he cannot make it better during production. So the first thing you want to do is put up a chip chart and determine how the image was captured. After editorial if there are things you want to clean up you go into the telecine suite for a second time and do a pass for tape-to-tape color correction. You can add enhancement, different masks to the image to brighten things up or darken them. You can do something called power windows where you want to make the upper corner darker and keep everything else less, or you can change the color of someone's shirt. But you don't want to spend money doing that on your initial transfers.

Q – Is there anything you can do by playing around with frame rates?

Larry – If you did overcrank or undercrank your film, you could always transfer it at a different rate like 18 frames or 16 frames – but you would do that going back to the film and then to tape, not once you already have it on tape. If you shoot slow motion and then transfer it at a faster film rate like 16, it would look faster.

Q – Are titles and opticals part of the HD world or are they a thing of the past?

Larry – In the HD world, your resolution is 1920 by 1080. For a film-out or tape to tape, you are creating 2k files. We still do 2k files for end rolls or intricate title design work, but blowing up HD to 2k versus doing a 2k titles and lower thirds, there's not much difference. But then at the same time, if you're doing a very intricate title design, you want to work at 2k so you don't lose any of the information.

Q – Are there any rules of thumb about what looks good and bad with titles?

Larry – Since HD is so close to 2k resolution, what looks bad on HD looks bad on film. You don't want to use a lot of edgy fonts. If you do use a serif font, you want to make sure it's visible against the background.

Q – What is pan and scan and does that matter in the HD world?

Larry – Yes. Normally for TV deliverables, they're going to want a full frame master. Even the HD that is simulcast over the air, unless it is available in widescreen, is going to be 4x3 pillared HD. That means if you have 16x9 HD, you have to make a 4x3 full frame master. The easiest way to do this is a center extraction. Statistically 70% of the film can be corrected this way. For the other 30% of the film you have to do a pan and scan to get the actors in or the points of interest on the edges of the frame into view. The cost of it is mostly editorial time. For a 90minute film, it takes 6-8 hours to do depending on how far apart the points of interests are.

Q – What should one think about when doing animation or motion control?

Larry – The nice thing about animation is a second is a second is a second. No matter what you originate on 25, 24 or 30 frames, going out to film doesn't matter – a second, is a second is a second. The only caveat on that is you want to make sure that speed of the animation is to your liking. Motion control cameras are going to be recording film and running at 24 fps. Think of it as if you were shooting regular film footage. Or if you are doing an After Effects program, what do I render my animation out to? If you are shooting HD, what you need to render at is 1920 by 1080 at 23.98 or 720p, but you should also render out a lower resolution draft so you can see how it plays.

Q – Are there any ways to get deals from a lab?

Larry – Sure. The more things you do at one facility, the cheaper those things become. It's also good to stay in one facility as much as you can because if there are problems, it's easier to trace them.

Q – What are the common mistakes that documentary filmmakers make?

Larry – I hear a lot of, *"I wish I would have know before I started."* Or *"Next time!"* Well if you don't make your first film as good as it can be, you are not going to get the next one. Try to find out as much as you can before you start your documentary. Unfortunately, documentaries can take several years to complete and the technology always changes. So try to keep up on the industry trends and ask questions.

Q – What advice would you give a new documentary filmmaker?

Larry – Before you rule out film as being too expensive go through the cost analysis of doing a full production in it versus HD. You only acquire the image once, so the better equipment you use to acquire the better your finished process will be. Make sure you spend the money wisely. It's always harder to find the story when you don't know what it is going in. One of the joys of documentary filmmaking is starting out to make a story about X and then Y came around. That's great. But don't let it get to distracting or encompassing for your finding that extra story if the one in front of you is there all along. And don't skimp on the post process or all the hard work that you did to write, shoot and edit the film can go out the window.

High Def Video

Every day seems to bring a new technology or debate. Is HDCam better than Film? Is HDV better than DVCProHD? Is Avid better than FCP? Should I shoot 720p or 1080i and do the film look in post? Of course there is never a definitive answer, and certainly not one that will apply over time, even a short period of time. It's always getting better, faster, cheaper... Right now, HD is rapidly taking over the world and becoming cheaper and cheaper by the minute to use. DV is on its way out, but that's not to say that it's time is up. If it comes to hanging around looking for the right camera and missing your story as it's unfolding – grab that DV camera and shoot! Always remember it's content over technology. Here are some points to bear in mind when shooting HD:

Feed your sound directly into the camera via a sound lead. Set this link up in advance and check it, making sure recording levels can't be accidentally nudged by the camera operator.

Have plenty of blank tapes standing by as you can rip through HD tapes at an alarming rate.

Never over expose or under expose as this limits your ability to grade the image later.

Shoot a 'flat' image, planning to do your 'extreme' look in post-production. You can always add to a look, but it's harder to remove a look.

Use the very best format you can get your hands on, that means start with HDCam, then DVCproHD, then HDV.

More important than the format, is the camera and lenses. Generally, the better formats will be supported by better cameras though.

Why spend $3k or $5k on a prosumer camera when you can rent a top end camera and lenses for the same. I know you can keep the prosumer camera after, BUT the pro cameras will distinguish you from 95% of the competition. You will also attract a higher calibre of crew.

If your project uses a lot of slow motion, shoot with the Panasonic Varicam on DVCproHD, or any new format that supports true slow motion. If you can't, shoot any slow motion shots at 1080i, as the interlacing will give extra information that will look like film when slowed down on a computer.

If you plan to use a lot of green screen or bluescreen, don't use HDV, shoot DVCProHD or HDCam as it has better colour sampling and will make better mattes when compositing.

Plan a post production route where you can be editing within hours of ejecting the tape. Don't put this off until after the shoot. DON'T!

When editing, don't work at full HD resolution, convert tapes to DVcam and work at that resolution, using a cheaper edit station and only a few hundred gigs of Firewire storage. There is no need for terabytes of data storage just yet.

Don't waste precious time and money making HD backup tapes. Just don't hammer your master tapes, and use your DVCam copies for editing. But DO look after your master camera tapes, everything is encapsulated on them.

Do your final online with professionals, and NOT at home, unless you are a professional and know what you are doing.

Research what sales agents require finished films to be delivered on.

Don't get sucked into the Avid or FCP debate. Both are fine tools and the one you should use is the one you get cheapest or free.

If you really can't afford to rent a pro camera, and you have tried and tried, use the cheaper prosumer HD cameras shooting HDV.

Only take advice from people who have actually got their film to the market place. And then use a pinch of salt.

If you decide to back up your audio on DAT, the camera input recording level should should be set to match the DAT output level and then locked so it can't be changed accidentally. Both camera and DAT should use Time Of Day timecode so that they share exactly the same time code. This will mean that later on in post, if you wish, you can go back to your DAT tapes and automatically reconform the audio from the master DAT tapes (which should take a few hours at most).

It's a good idea for the sound recordist to periodically check playback from the camera to ensure there are no technical problems with the sound, and if there are, they have the DAT as the back up.

Paul Crowder

THE EDITOR

Q – How would you describe the relationship between the editor and the director on a documentary?

Paul – It's paramount that you're on the same level as far as communicating. The way I like to work is for people to leave me alone more often. Let me do stuff and then let's watch it and sit and talk about it. While I'm making it, you can come in at any time and sit there. You can say, *"Try this shot or use that song."* I love all that. Give me all that. But also don't question anything I am doing until I say, *"What do you think?"* There's nothing worse than when I'm editing and someone says, *"Why are you doing that?"* It's not a cool question meaning what I'm doing is great and how am I doing it. It's more like, *"That seems wrong."* I prefer to be at my own pace and time. But the director and the editor must know what each other are striving for.

Q – How much is the editor doing the directing of a documentary film?

Paul – That's an interesting question because the film I'm doing now, *Once In A Lifetime* I was hired on as the editor. And halfway through the project they gave me the director's credit. There had been a director involved who shot the stuff, but had since moved on. They felt that I'd created a style to the piece that was non-existent in the first draft that the director had created. Martin Scorsese got a co-directing credit on *Woodstock* even though he was an editor because he created the look and style of that film. So there is a point where the editor is directing the proceedings. The director will say whether he likes it or not and ultimately the director has the final say. It's all down on him and he's the one who has to deliver. You need to do what he wants as that's the chain of command. But again, that's where you have to communicate and say, "This is why I think we should do this." So it's a fine line between editing and directing, but ultimately you're doing what you are being paid to do. Stacy Peralta directed *Dogtown & Z-Boys* and *Riding Giants* and I edited them. He told me how it had to look – gritty and raw – then he gave me the footage and I gave it to him. He came up with songs, I came up with songs, he had ideas, I had ideas; it was a collaboration, but almost like jamming as musicians, we had an amazing relationship working together, we just click, but as far as those films go. It was all his direction.

Q – With digital technology allowing directors to shoot forever, how do you organize all that footage and is there a danger of shooting too much?

Paul – You can never shoot too much. The only problem with shooting too much is watching and logging it all. The thing is when you're making a documentary, a lot of what you have you are not shooting yourself. You may shoot interviews on your subject, but you have to go collect footage as well. And it comes in on all formats. You have to organize yourself in the best way possible. I need to know where everything is. I need to know it's in these four bins and I stick locators on it. Or if I have an assistant, I have them sort it all into bins and label them. So on *Once In A Lifetime*, I'd have a bin labeled "Pele's goals" or "Cosmos footage". I also do these photo strips where I take stills of the footage and put them up all over the walls. I put the time code on them so I know where I can find it. This way I can walk around the room and go, *"Oh, that's that shot I want."* Sort of like visual index cards. When we did, *Dogtown* we had them all down the corridor so we'd just take a little stroll and look around. It's very inspiring that way for us.

Q – When footage comes in on all sorts of formats, what are some tips for not getting it mixed up or lost?

Paul – You should write down where it came from and what you get because once it gets into the Avid, you need to be able to trace it back. Because 9 times out of 10, it won't be a master. It'll be a screener from ITN Archives that has ten different news stories on it. You have to make sure you digitize each clip with relevant information. They'll send you all of this with the clip and you just have to put it in. That way you'll know tape #100 was a bump up tape that was digitized from VHS and it came from ITN Archives, for example.

Q – Are there any problems with getting footage on lots of different formats?

Paul – Yes. When we did *Dogtown*, it was perceived that it was going to go straight to DVD. Maybe TV. So they shot on Super 16mm and they started telecining in 4x3. Then we get four to six weeks into editing and they want to make it into a film, send it to festivals. How are we going to do this? We've shot everything at 24 fps, but we've transferred it all to NTSC. So in that case, it was finish your film and transfer it later so at least then we would have a video format. All the various kinds of video and film formats would then be on one singular NTSC format that we could then transfer to film. You can't do that easily. And when you have lots of motion and interpolation, you get horrendous film transfers and you have to rethink it all. There're two ways of doing a transfer. One way, all the film footage, Super 8mm, Super 16mm and all the interviews, it removes the 3:2 pulldown and that looks beautiful. All the video footage looks horrible. It's all streaky and terrible. So for that, the other process is called 60:24 – 60 fields to 24 frames. It's much cleaner with less interpolation and you get smoother transitions. But, it made it 4% longer. So we created this new 24-frame project, we did all the transfers of each reel, C2 and the 60:24 and got masters of every reel. So two formats. I used the C62 as the master and over cut the 60:24 version, in the places where the video footage was, I want to keep the film stuff from C2 because that looks lovely. So then all the video bits go in the holes from the 60:24 transfer. But I have to trim by a frame or two to make it all fit, as it is 4% longer. There're so many cuts in *Dogtown* and I had to fix each one. But I ended up with a master that looked good.

Q – Did you have the same problem on Riding Giants?

Paul – It was a multiple format film, but we were going to HD. So we did all of our telecine to HD. It looked beautiful. No problem. But, we go to Mavericks, and all the video footage comes in on Hi8 and stuff like that. So we transfer that to HD with a Teranex and it looks fine in the Avid and on Beta. We get to the online and all the video footage we transferred through the Teranex including the Super 8mm that wasn't shot at 24fps, it was at 18fps, had this horrendous interpolation that wasn't visible on those other systems. It was blurred and breaking up. We discovered that The Platinum Alchemist software had the correct HD transfer rate and it handled the interpolation. It made it a lot more stable. So we had to transfer it all right away with about a week before Sundance. The other problem was that we had to get all that footage back that we had sent back to people to cut it and retransfer it. We had phone calls with people like, *"What tape did I send you? This one? No the other one!"* So when you get all these different formats in like Beta SP, Digibeta, Super 16mm, U-matic 3/4 inch even, you have to be aware of the interpolation when you are getting it onto your master format. Also, the older formats – like on *Once In A Lifetime*, we had U-matic 3/4 inch tape where the oxide was stripping off the tape as it was going through the heads. We were losing the tape in the transfer. Fortunately, it was going across the play head and we could see it and we could bump it up to Digibeta. But it was the last time that tape was played.

Q – When you and the director sit down to structure the story, do you think in three acts?

Paul – You have to break it down into what your plot points are going to be. And that isn't always apparent. Dogtown did not turn out the way we pre-thought it. We weren't really sure what the structure was. *Riding Giants* was very consistent to the three acts that Stacy wrote out on cards. But within that three-act structure, we had to build these chapter pods. This is the section where we talk about this, this is the section where we talk about that. Then we start laying the pods together with maybe some music cues. It starts changing and then you realize this one goes into this, which goes into this, which goes into this. That's kind of what happened with *Dogtown*. We start with the pods and then figure out how the story is going to break out. Some of the stories overlapped each other, so we would have to go back on ourselves a bit. We'd get this much of the story told before we can tell this part of the story, even though the first thing happened way after. If we don't lay out this attitude, then this isn't going to play as well. Where do we put the Del Mar section? It would normally go here, but it works better there because we now know these guys better. So we put all the pool stuff first so we could see how mischievous they were. That sets up Del Mar when they go there and become bad asses on skateboards. *Riding Giants* was the same way to an extent. The first act was all Greg Noll. It was a much easier three-act structure because we had three heroes we were going to be talking about.

Q – Do you have problems killing your darlings?

Paul – I call it removing limbs or murdering children. The film gets too long and you have to start cutting things that you love. Or you lose songs. You have a song and you see it and you say, *"This is a must never go."* And then it's gone and you realize that you have probably lost your favorite moment in the film. You just want to kill someone. You have to move on and you can't think about it.

Q – When you edit, do you think character first or story first?

Paul – Story is the most important thing. You have to know what story you want to tell and it better be clear. You have to know why it has to be told, why it is compelling and how to tell that story in a way that it is compelling. You have a film about skateboarders. You have a film about surfers. You have a film about soccer players. You have to make it interesting to people who aren't surfers, skateboarders or soccer players. You have to make it so it is not as Stacy would say, *"surf porn or skateboard porn."* And yet, you have to keep the integrity of the subject matter. Once you know that, then the next thing is the characters. You watch the interviews and you say, *"This guy is fucking hilarious! Make sure we get plenty of him."* Or this guy has got all the information, so we will use him to bridge us. And you try to develop those characters to get within the story. So in this film, there is a guy called Clive Toye who gets sacked by the company he works for halfway through the story. So we try to make it that you can tell he is getting pissed off. He actually was getting pissed off in the interview retelling the story. It was bugging him and you build on that so that by time he gets sacked he is really pissed off. So in documentary, hopefully you are telling a story that has these people that get excited. They don't have to be excited by what they are telling you, but they have to be emotionally involved. They have to be passionate in some way or you have to make it feel like they are. Some people are dreadful talkers but they have great info. In *Riding Giants*, a lot of those guys were laid back talkers and they would get sidetracked and I had to make that slow guy come to life. So it is cutting around "ums" and "ahs" and when to keep them up on camera. When he is focused, he is on camera. The rest of it we can snip it all up to bring back the energy of what he said.

Q – That leads to the next question – you as the editor have a lot of power on how to make someone appear. Are there any dangers there?

Paul – Documentary-wise, you have to be true to the reality of it. You're trying to make a document of fact. You would hope that documentarians aren't trying to warp the truth. I do love Michael Moore's films, but I do find them at time to be a little too opinionated and using editing to give the wrong impression about something that happened. I just didn't like the thing he did with Charlton Heston. He took a Charlton Heston scene out of context and used it to say what he said in Denver about prying the gun out of his dead hands. He said it somewhere else as far as I can tell. At least, if he did say it, they didn't use the Denver footage. That's manipulating of the facts, I find it a little too Fox TV. So with the power that you have, you have to be true to the truth. You need to be true to that person and not have them come off as a complete idiot. Or put words in their to suit your story.

Q – But you can also get a bit of character by playing with things like in Dogtown when you sped up that one verbose interviewee.

Paul – Yes. I developed that at VH-1. You have a bite and people are telling you something, they get sidetracked and then they come back and finish the story. In the old days, I'd keep the beginning and the end and snip out the middle then cover the edit with a picture or something. But in this case, I didn't have any footage to cover that guy. I was in a bind. So I had to be creative in order to get out of it and sped him up. I made a minute last ten frames. It looks wacky and it looked great. I told Stacy, *"What do you think of this?"* He said it was great and we left it in.

Q – Dogtown and Riding Giants have really cool openings. How important is the opening of a documentary film and how important is the ending?

Paul – They are both huge. The ending is the film's climax. You have to have a poignant way to button the film. You need the shot and you need the bite. The last thing that you go out on has to knock your socks off or sum up the film. Or if you don't have that bite, you have to have a thought that comes from dialogue or VO. And with the opening, you are setting the film. Maybe it's because I did a lot of TV to start with and there's always that cold open to start. But with a documentary, you have to clue people in to what they are going to see. In *Dogtown & Z-Boys* outside of the skating world before the movie came along, who really knew who and what they were? So to open, I needed a good piece of these guys who are crazy, outside the box, no rules people that had a moment where they shone really bright and there was a big reaction to it. We have to let people know that happened. Then I needed a song that supports it and Glen Friedman suggested the Hendrix track. I put it on and two seconds in I knew it was the song. One of the things I did there was that I'd roast Stacy a lot when he interviews people and he fucks up, I'll put together a sequence for him of it. And I noticed that I had all these guys giving him grief about the questions. Five or six people saying, *"Man, that is a shit question,"* or *"I don't like that question."* They're very honest and I realized that attitude and that honesty is what this film is about. And we are going to let people know that right up top as the music is playing. So we have that as the guitar is playing and when the drums kick in we go into the montage. It makes people think something happened here and I missed it. What was it? I want to know. And *Riding Giants* was something similar. We wanted to get people scared of these waves. These guys are mad and these waves will kill you. So we had big waves and huge sound and then we go into hard music as people wipe out. It gives you a sense of what you are going to see. That is what an opening should be.

Q – Are there any sins in editing documentary films – things you just should not do?

Paul – You should never put words into people's mouths. You should never lose sight of the story and what you're trying to say. But sins...that's a hard one because I don't really know if there's anything you can't really do. I'm always one for not worrying about the rules. Oh, here's one that always looks pretty bad - cutting from a wide shot to a wide shot. A stadium to a wide of a street to another wide of a street – you should go tight at one point to break it up. And also you should never cut to the same shot again. And don't cut for cutting sake. It's one of the hardest things to do as an editor, but one of the best things about filmmaking is the longer you leave that shot up the more believable it becomes. The longer it's up the longer you can take it in and everything around it becomes real. But if you're trying to create energy, then you want to be cutting a lot. And if you're doing it to stay in time with the music, because there's a good drum beat or whatever, make sure that the next shot is a good one.

Q – What makes you decide to take on a film?

Paul – I've got to enjoy the subject and it has to be something that will benefit from my style. It doesn't mean I can't do serious stuff, but there are certain documentaries that I wouldn't be right for. Like *Born Into Brothels* and movies along those lines are not suited to my style. I like things that have a lot of music in it, have high energy and are funny. I try to make all my films designed to be watched at least twice. In *Dogtown*, there's so much action and I don't worry about the fact that you are missing stuff. Watch it again.

Q – When should a producer approach an editor?

Paul – I guess it depends. I came on *Dogtown* when they were raising money for the film. *Riding Giants*, they had started shooting already. In fact, they had just about everything collected and they brought me in. I'd like to be involved early on. The earlier on you are involved as the editor, the more you can talk to the director about what they could shoot or find.

Q – What in your opinion makes a good edit?

Paul – The easiest ones are on motion. Sometimes a natural wipe by the camera looks good. Maybe someone walks across frame and then you cut as they walk and they cross in the edit and that always looks pleasing. If you're wide and you go tight, that's always a nice, straight ahead edit. I don't hate dissolves, but I don't like them because they are easy fixes. Beginners get in trouble and they hit the dissolve button because it looks good. But too many of them look naff. There's a saying in editing, if you can't solve it, dissolve it. That's why I try to stay away from them. Then again, there are times when a dissolve is the perfect thing to do. If you're doing a montage, matching motion and matching shots is good. So if you have a guy getting hugged after scoring a goal, then the next one is maybe a kid hugging his friend. The shots feel like they belong together. Another thing I like to do is if the camera is focused on something and then it makes a small move to the right, then the next shot you find something where the camera is moving left. You edit on the movement.

Q – What do you like to get from the director in order to make your job easier?

Paul – The tapes need to be organized well. A good thing is to have a series of numbers that belong to a type of footage. So the 100's will be interviews. Photographs will be the 200's. B-roll is on the 300's. Your screener B-roll is on the 400's. Apart from that, being a documentary, it is going to come as it comes. If you can organize it so that all of one guy's photos are on one tape, then brilliant, but it is going to get messy.

Q – Are you involved in the selection of music and what are good ways to edit to it?

Paul – In my past work of *Dogtown* and *Riding Giants*, Stacy and I compiled all the music. And short of a couple of key pieces that Stacy thought would be good or have a specific idea, I pretty much selected the songs for the cut. Then I'd show it to Stacy who might say, *"That one isn't working for me."* Then I'll have to find another one. Or if we can't clear it, then it has to come out. Music is so important – especially to my style. I like to edit on the beats. I like to make sure there is a snare drum here or a guitar twang or keyboard or horn stab there to get the rhythm. And sometimes the action is in time with that rhythm. Stacy's son, Austin, played piano on this piece and it's over a shot of slow motion surfing. A guy is coming down the wave and the surfboard is bouncing along. I saw that if I lined up the first few hits, the bouncing was in time with the piano playing. So I try to find places where action is in time with the rhythm of the song. And if things are a few frames off, you can soften it to the point where it feels like it is hitting on the beats. If a picture is going to zoom in, it starts stops on the beat – not a few frames before or after.

Q – When you work with a composer, do you tell him the kind of rhythms you want?

Paul – Absolutely. I try to work very closely with the composers. I usually get a budget for songs and then I run out of budget and the rest has to be scored. I will put in all known music if I don't have any pre-score and then I will give it to the composer stating that I want something that will match tempo, grow and die at the same time. And I give him the picture to go with it so it's pretty clear how I want the song to be.

Q – Do you supervise the sound mixing, Foley and other post sound sessions?

Paul – Yes. Even in documentary, there's always basic Foley or sound effects. On *Once In A Lifetime*, we did a lot of sound effects. Crowds cheering and foot hits and the like. I'd do the same cheers and hits over and over again and then show the sound guy how I wanted it laid out and he created new ones. It's good to have your editor

GUERILLA FILM MAKER SAYS!

Temp Music

While you are editing, you will want to put some kind of music track down to help set a tone, find a pacing and liven up dead spots of your film before you have any actual score. Music editors sometimes call this "tracking". At this point ANY music is fair game for you do not have to pay royalties. Many film festivals will accept temp music in your submission for entry, with the stipulation that you will have permanent score in place should you get into their event.

There is a double-edged sword, though, when it comes to temp music. On one hand, it can be very helpful to your composer to have famous music tracks as temp music in order to give them a concrete example of what you want from the score. On the other, you may grow too attached to that style of music and not open yourself up to alternative ideas.

there in the mix and the online edit sessions because they can make sure things are going as you want them to.

Q – What are some tips for dealing with bad sound?

Paul – Get a good sound engineer. Get all the plug-ins Pro Tools has. If you have a lot of background noise, get more. Then we can add it when we cut the interview up, you can get around hearing the edit. If a car goes by, get another car going by that is hopefully a little louder and then we can put that on another track to cover the edit. Good filters are essential. If you have cicadas right next to you, there is a hum throughout the whole shot. It's at the same frequency and you can filter it out. Bad recording of voice is almost impossible. Try not to use the camera mic – you have to have close micing on dialogue – you just have to. Get a boom and lav mic and separate them left and right. Don't mix them.

Q – Do you attend test screenings and do you recommend them?

Paul – Definitely, but not studio screenings. I like test screenings with people whose opinions I really trust and respect. I don't like them when they are a bunch of kids who saw it one Saturday night with their popcorn and they didn't get it. I know that is the audience you want, but it's not the point of my film. I like to have two or three screenings with people that I respect. And I will listen to their critique and if you find that people are consistently saying something about your film, then those are issues you should look at. Whether you do something about it or not is up to you.

Q – Do you ever see directors or editors that just don't know when to stop?

Paul – Oh, God, yes. This 70's show that I did for ABC, we must have cut that thing 12 different ways to get it how they wanted it. We ended going back all the way to where we started. That is really the only time I have experienced it. But there are people that do not know when to let go. I think there may be a line in there where if you go over a year of editing, you may fall into that trap. There is a guy cutting a film right now who was 18 months into his edit when we started *Dogtown* and he is still editing. He told me that he is almost done. He has a great subject, but he cannot let go. There is a point as a filmmaker where you have to say, *"That's good. I've done it."* You can always find a better shot and bite. But if those bites are working and that shot is great, let it go. It will lose all of its character and what it was if you over think it.

Q – What are some important things to think about as far as editing equipment is concerned?

Paul – It's important to know your equipment. The big thing now is are you Avid or are you Final Cut Pro and it does matter. Some guys like myself are reluctant to take Final Cut jobs because I know the Avid. I'm not that good at Final Cut Pro. I think it's genius the way it integrates all the other Apple programs. I love the fact that it is so cheap. But it is twenty times harder to organize footage because it doesn't think like an editor. Avid does. It has a lot of ways to organize the footage like color and locators and lots of ways to sort things. You don't have that freedom in Final Cut. Some people will not touch Avid for the exact same reasons that I don't touch Final Cut.

Q – What are the common mistakes that you see documentary filmmakers make?

Paul – Picking the wrong music. Most of the documentaries that I find disappointing usually miss an obvious thing in the structure. They either have placed something wrong or they have repeated themselves several times. It's about finding the places where you can condense it and make three repetitive moments, two moments. And sometimes they manipulate the dialogue for the wrong reasons.

Q – What advice would you give a new documentary filmmaker?

Paul – Always follow what you believe to be right. And at the same time, always be prepared to listen to everyone's point of view. Believe in what you do and understand that 99% of the other people out there that are doing what you want to be doing and are successful, don't know what they are doing as much as you don't know what you are doing. Be as creative as you can and don't copy ideas. Or if you do, enhance the idea and make it your own.

Miriam Cutler

THE MUSIC COMPOSER

Q – How different is composing music for documentaries as opposed to narrative films?

Miriam – When I'm working on a documentary film I feel an incredible responsibility to the characters of the film, in addition to my responsibility to the director. These are real stories and people who are revealing a lot of amazing stuff. The filmmaker might make a choice to have some scenes music-driven, but a composer should always be careful not to detract from the reality of what's going on, and be respectful. As with all filmmaking, one can manipulate an audience with music. Music can change the nature of any scene. As a composer, you must remember you're always giving your point of view, even if you're representing someone else's point of view.

Music also opens people's hearts and makes them receptive to the message of a film. So sometimes, if you're scoring a difficult scene - maybe something bloody or really painful to watch - there're ways of easing that a little for the audience with the music. You can certainly push it, too, but you want the film to be watchable. If it's too harsh, people won't watch it. On the other hand, you don't want to detract from the seriousness of what's going on, either. One big difference with documentaries and narrative is that when there's a lot of emotion happening on screen in a feature you will most likely push the emotion, or put in a song, but with a documentary you will most likely pull the music out. For documentaries, you have to be really sensitive to protect the integrity of the story that you're telling. Documentaries need to be pure, not gimmicky.

Q – When should a filmmaker come to you?

Miriam – In the old days before all the digital stuff, people would come to me with a locked picture. Because of the new technology, a composer can get involved very early on because we can start working with footage while it's still being edited. I think it's better for the film to bring the composer on as early as possible. It's not cost efficient for the composer, but I do think it's beneficial artistically. With *Lost In La Mancha*, I got a rough assembly of 15 minutes, and I wrote one long piece that we ended up using for most of the themes within the film.

Q – How long do you need to do a documentary score?

Miriam – On top of the writing and bringing in musicians, I need a week or two to record and a week to mix. If you give me a long picture, I can write it in 3 weeks, but if you're going to make changes I can't guarantee such a quick turnaround.

Q – Is it difficult for filmmakers to let go of their temp scores?

Miriam – It can be. Directors are so visual and composers are aural. Often, when filmmakers try to communicate in musical terms, it doesn't work very well unless they're actually musicians. So temp scores are a way of communicating nonverbally. My job is to find out from directors what works for them and what doesn't, and to try and understand what they're trying to accomplish with the music. The other way to bridge the communication gap is to discuss emotion and intention: what would you like to have the audience experience while they're watching this scene? Do you want to just drive this point home? Do you want some irony? Do you want a contrast? Is it happy? Sad? Do you want to slow it down? Speed it up?

With every person I work with, we develop a unique relationship. It's almost like dating, because when you first start working together you don't really know each other. Sometimes that can be really fantastic and sometimes that can be a disaster! So the most important thing is to figure out what's going to be your bridge - which is why a temp score can be very useful. Sometimes directors can become very attached to a temp score. But it usually doesn't take too long before they start seeing the value of an original score. That goes with the use of songs, too. I've experienced many filmmakers wanting to use lots of songs, but once they start to grasp what scoring can do - how much more control it gives them - then they start getting more comfortable and by far prefer it.

Q – Do you find with documentaries that the director does have a specific vision of how they want the score to be?

Miriam – A lot of times directors think they don't, but they do. It's the one place they feel out of control in the filmmaking process, and they feel frustrated when they can't easily express their ideas. I keep reminding them that they have a very strong vision for their films and their instincts will kick in about the music as well. Truth is, they know when they hear it if they like it or not. And I would never make someone accept a cue if they don't like it. As a composer I have to be open-minded and open-hearted throughout the creative process. Every score I've done has been very different because everyone I work with brings something completely different to the process. In documentaries, people care so much about their films. They may have risked their lives, spent five years or more working on it, mortgaged their house and so on. So they're going to get a thousand percent from me. They believe in what they're doing and so I believe in them.

Q – How do you look at a score for documentaries?

Miriam – The music needs to be part of the storytelling. It should do everything to support the storytelling. I consider music to be like punctuation - an underline, a parentheses, exclamation point, etc. It can speed up a scene, slow it down or make it feel like time is standing still. It can solve problems in the cut, or sound issues. If you look at all the great classic movies, the scores are really strong compositionally; there's thought and structure. I always think that if someone hears a certain theme - if I've done my job - they won't really recognize why but they'll be prepared for what they're seeing on the screen. There used to be throwaway cues in some of my scores but I don't do that anymore. Every note should have a purpose.

Q – Do you sit down and spot the film with the director?

Miriam – Frame by frame, yes. It used to be that I'd spot the film and then go home with copious notes annotated with timecode. But these days, by the time I'm writing the score, the film has changed ten times, so my notes become more a point of reference. Now I find that I do a lot of catching up on the phone, or get together with the director more often. There are a couple of directors from whom I get minimal notes, but mostly I find that filmmakers are very hands-on.

Q – Do you discuss the themes of each cue?

Miriam – When we start we talk in broad concepts - where we'll have a theme and where we might use that theme, even though we have no idea what it is. Some directors can envision that and others can't. So then I'll try and get at the emotion they're after without talking in musical terms at all. I'll just say, *"What is it that you want the audience to feel here? Why do you think it should be here? What do you want it to do?"* The scoring really starts coming together once I mock up cues with MIDI and samples. That's when they can hear a close approximation of what it will sound like and respond to it. We go back and forth, refining the music, and after they approve all the cues, I get ready to record. I explain the recording process and that they're going to have to trust me to execute our ideas because my job is to make the music the best I can. But I prepare them for the possibility that it might also change and evolve through being performed by musicians. I try to assure them that if it's not what they want, I'll change it.

Q – What percentage should producers budget for the music score for a documentary?

Miriam – I've heard that in Hollywood it's 1%. If you have a big movie budgeted at $60 million, then that's a lot of money but if you have a $200k to $500k picture, then 1% is nothing! So it's hard to do a percentage. There has to be a bottom

Music Cue Sheet

This document lists all the music cues in your film, including the title of each music segment, the duration of each segment, who the composer is, who the publisher is, who the record company is, the main use of the music (whether it's background or featured), and the Performing Rights Organization that the performer is affiliated with. The Performing Rights Organizations such as ASCAP/BMI/SESEC determine from the music cue sheets how much royalty gets paid to its members, and they take responsibility of it's collection domestically and internationally. Your sales agent and distributor will insist on a copy of the music cue sheet in their delivery requirements. They'll pass this on to buyers such as broadcasters who will determine the fees they must pay the relevant collection society. If the producer is paying the appropriate composer's fee upfront, they usually retain the publisher share of the music while the composer retains the writer share. If this is the case, the producer needs to set up a publishing company and they will recoup the publishing royalties. However, if the producer is unable to pay the composer an appropriate fee upfront, a composer will often negotiate to keep the publisher's share of the music. It's recommended as a producer to try and retain at least 50% of the publishing rights but it depends on the cache of the composer. In which case, the music cue sheet could then ensure an unexpected subsidiary income further down the line.

Sample Music Cue Sheet

Series/Film Title: *Urban Skies*
Episode Title/Number: *Grape Soda (#12)*
Estimated Airdate: *1-12-99*
Program Length: *60 minutes*
Program Type: *Comedy series*

Company Name: *Urban Skies Productions*
Address: *7920 Sunset Blvd., L.A., CA 90027*
Phone: *1-800-662-4490*
Contact: *Chris Moll*
Network Station: *Showtime*

Cue #	Cue Title	Use*	Timing	Composer(s) Affiliation / %	Pulisher(s) Affiliation / %
1	Urban Skies Theme	MT	0:16	Rhonda Sims (ASCAP) 100%	Urban Skies Music (ASCAP) 100%
2	Running Home	BI	0:08	Rhonda Sims (ASCAP) 100%	Urban Skies Music (ASCAP) 100%
3	Backwards Love	BI	0:13	Rhonda Sims (ASCAP) 100%	Urban Skies Music (ASCAP) 100%
4	Uptown	BI	0:09	Rhonda Sims (ASCAP) 100%	Urban Skies Music (ASCAP) 100%
5	Skies the Limit	BV	1:03	Terry Oakley (ASCAP) 33 1/3% Larry Joyce (PRS) 33 1/3% Ennio Blake (APRA) 33 1/3%	Terrycotta (ASCAP) 33 1/3% Larry Joyce Music (PRS/ASCAP) 33 1/3% Ennio B. Music (APRA/ASCAP) 33 1/3%
6	Synthroid	BI	0:05	Rhonda Sims (ASCAP) 100%	Urban Skies Music (ASCAP) 100%
7	Coffee In Bed	BI	0:32	Rhonda Sims (ASCAP) 100%	Urban Skies Music (ASCAP) 100%
8	Roll With It	BI	0:15	Rhonda Sims (ASCAP) 100%	Urban Skies Music (ASCAP) 100%
9	Knock Me Down	BI	0:01	Rhonda Sims (ASCAP) 100%	Urban Skies Music (ASCAP) 100%
10	Spinach and Ham	BI	0:16	Rhonda Sims (ASCAP) 100%	Urban Skies Music (ASCAP) 100%
11	Swing to Live	VV	0:34	Jerry Fin (ASCAP) 100%	Fins Alive Publishing (ASCAP) 100%
12	Good Luck	BI	0:11	Rhonda Sims (ASCAP) 100%	Urban Skies Music (ASCAP) 100%
13	Hot Water Beaches	BI	0:36	Rhonda Sims (ASCAP) 100%	Urban Skies Music (ASCAP) 100%
14	Polar Opposites	BI	0:02	Rhonda Sims (ASCAP) 100%	Urban Skies Music (ASCAP) 100%
15	No Way Jose	BI	0:01	Rhonda Sims (ASCAP) 100%	Urban Skies Music (ASCAP) 100%
16	Yes Way Jose	BI	0:03	Rhonda Sims (ASCAP) 100%	Urban Skies Music (ASCAP) 100%
17	Café and Tea	BI	0:08	Rhonda Sims (ASCAP) 100%	Urban Skies Music (ASCAP) 100%
18	Picoline	BI	0:10	Rhonda Sims (ASCAP) 100%	Urban Skies Music (ASCAP) 100%
19	The Pelican	BI	0:15	Rhonda Sims (ASCAP) 100%	Urban Skies Music (ASCAP) 100%
20	Red Hearts	BI	0:13	Rhonda Sims (ASCAP) 100%	Urban Skies Music (ASCAP) 100%
21	Infested	BI	0:15	Rhonda Sims (ASCAP) 100%	Urban Skies Music (ASCAP) 100%
22	Course of Empires	BI	0:08	Rhonda Sims (ASCAP) 100%	Urban Skies Music (ASCAP) 100%
23	Oxford Tins	BI	0:04	Rhonda Sims (ASCAP) 100%	Urban Skies Music (ASCAP) 100%
24	The Ground Is Cold	BI	0:06	Rhonda Sims (ASCAP) 100%	Urban Skies Music (ASCAP) 100%
25	Streamline	BI	0:20	Rhonda Sims (ASCAP) 100%	Urban Skies Music (ASCAP) 100%
26	Green Hearts	BI	0:14	Rhonda Sims (ASCAP) 100%	Urban Skies Music (ASCAP) 100%
27	Absolute	BI	0:05	Rhonda Sims (ASCAP) 100%	Urban Skies Music (ASCAP) 100%
28	Carpet the Walls	VI	0:45	Henry Doe (SOCAN) 75% Rhonda Sims (ASCAP) 25%	Go Doe Music (SOCAN/ASCAP) 75% Simster Music (ASCAP) 25%
29	It's All Too Weird	BI	1:20	Rhonda Sims (ASCAP) 100%	Urban Skies Music (ASCAP) 100%
30	Spagetti Eastern	BI	0:26	Rhonda Sims (ASCAP) 100%	Urban Skies Music (ASCAP) 100%
31	Markets of the World	BI	0:24	Rhonda Sims (ASCAP) 100%	Urban Skies Music (ASCAP) 100%
35	Urban Skies Theme	ET	0:10	Rhonda Sims (ASCAP) 100%	Urban Skies Music (ASCAP) 100%

*Use Codes: **MT** = Main Title **VI** = Visual Instrumental **BV** = Background Vocal
VV = Visual Vocal **ET** = End Title **BI** = Background Instrumental
T = Theme

Note: If music cue sheets aren't done correctly, the country will keep all the monies and split it amongst their own members.

Music cue sheets should be sent to these following organizations for US doc makers:
ASCAP – American Society of Composers, Authors and Publishers. www.ascap.com
BMI – Broadcast Music Incorporated. www.bmi.com
SESAC – Performing Rights Organization for ngwriters and Publishers. www.sesac.com
MRI – Music Reports Inc. www.musicreports.com.
Sample Music Cue Sheet courtesy of ASCAP.

line, and that unfortunately depends on whom you talk to. My personal opinion is you should budget between $15k-$30k as an all-in package for a feature doc. I don't think producers or directors should even try to get a good score for under $15k - not if you want live musicians and an experienced composer. For many years I did the $5k-$10k score, but that's really difficult to do if you want high-quality music. The hardest thing for me as a composer is trying to figure out how to make a living working in indie docs. I might have a really good music scoring budget but by the time I'm done with all my musicians, music prep, recording and mixing, I might not have much money to pay myself for this hard work!

Q – Live musicians can be expensive?

Miriam – Yes. Most people won't do much live recording for low budget projects because it can cost a lot of money. I can do it because I do it in my own studio. I put in way longer hours, I record it myself, I engineer everything and I take it out of my own hide. Package deals are just very hard on the composer. More and more what's happening is that I'll get hired to do a film, then they decide to change the film dramatically and it gets put off 6 months or longer. I've taken the deposit already and now I'm on to other things. Then they want me back, they want rewrites, and more rewrites and the film keeps changing - so it's hard on the composer! But with the quality of the work that I want to do, I'm not willing to compromise. I could make it easier and hire two musicians, but I want to hire ten or more.

Q – Do you ever have an orchestra?

Miriam – Generally traditional orchestras aren't affordable for independent docs. Just the music preparation can cost thousands of dollars. I've achieved the effect of a small orchestra on a $30k budget. With 15 musicians, a lot of overdubs, and long hours of recording and mixing, it's doable, but the charts still cost a lot of money.

Q – Some filmmakers have wall to wall music, is that good or bad?

Miriam –That's usually when they're insecure about their film. Most confident filmmakers don't want wall-to-wall music because they know it will ruin their film. There are types of films that should be wall-to-wall, such as a nature show like *March of the Penguins*. It makes sense because the music is the narrative, like a musical or like listening to *Peter and The Wolf* or *Peer Gynt*. I think it's appropriate sometimes, but it's important to know the difference. I'll let some first-time filmmakers see what it's like and they'll usually see that it's not working.

Q – Are there any rules that you just don't do? Say, you wouldn't have a talking head shot with music over it?

Miriam – There are no rules. Look at Errol Morris's *The Fog of War*. The film has it's own music structure. A film I'm doing now is a really intimate story about family relations of a Holocaust survivor and I was given a rule: no music ever on talking head interviews! Well, we're telling the story, there's archival, then talking head, then archival – and we realize that if we stop the music during the talking head it makes it more distracting. So, yes, tone it down, make it breathe when your interviewee is on camera, and then bring it back in.

If I'm involved early enough, I can influence the structure of the film. If we use the music this way, we can begin to build sections like this, and then the whole process becomes really collaborative and creative. I send music, they cut it in, edit it, move it around, send it back to me. I incorporate their ideas, make changes, send it back. In some cases the director acts as more the overview person and the editor is the one who interacts with me day to day. Every project is different.

Q – In terms of physical elements what do you need from the filmmaker?

Miriam – It's constantly evolving. Digital video or Quicktime are both fantastic but sometimes there are issues getting the versions to work together. My system needs a certain version of Quicktime. MP4 seems to be the new standard nowadays, which I open in Quicktime. Otherwise, digital video is fine as I can convert to Quicktime myself. There're so many different editing systems out there - old Avids, new Avids, various versions of Final Cut Pro, pc stuff – and depending on what filmmakers can afford, or what they have, or what the footage was shot on or cut on, or what drive it was digitized onto, I just never know what I'm going to get. There can be technical glitches, so it's very important to get everything started on the right foot from the get - go. Figure out your compatibilities and your incompatibilities. Also, as a composer I need window-burn timecode and it must be put in a place that doesn't interfere with the picture. I need the audio to be split. If there's any music that's staying, it stays on one side, and the temp music and any other music that's going to be discarded stays on the other side. Be careful when splitting the audio. Sometimes it works, sometimes it doesn't because of a bad cable or a loose connection. Filmmakers should do a dry run with the composer and write down how you got it to work. If it's Final Cut Pro or Avid, there are different ways of doing the output, different compressions, etc. It drives me crazy because every time I get an updated cut it has to be compatible. And as the picture is evolving, I might get new scenes on different formats – filmmakers have to be organized and stick with the same format throughout.

Q – Do you go the final mix?

Miriam – Sometimes I'm invited and sometimes I'm uninvited! Some people have a fear of having the composer at the mix. They think that we can't separate ourselves and see the whole movie. A lot of finessing can still happen at the mix. The filmmaker might decide to change cues, which I can help with. I'll try to protect something if I think it's being made worse, but I'll do whatever I can to make it how the filmmaker wants it to be. Sometimes composers are accused of misbehaving at the mixes but I only speak when I'm spoken to and go out of my way to make it known that I'm there to help. Often it's good to have the composer there to make sure start times are correct, as cues can get moved around by mistake.

Q – What do you deliver on?

Miriam – I can turn in a data and/or audio CD to the final mixer. I also deliver online at my FTP site a lot. The sound guys love it. They just download it and are really happy to have one less detail to attend to. The one downside is that uploading onto the FTP site takes me a long time, especially AIFF files. However, if you have your own server there's no upload time, so you can just stick it on there and they can access it. It's also a great way to get feedback on my work quicker than by Fed Ex or mail. I'm working with people in New York right now and I can make changes and re-upload them within an hour.

Q – Some documentaries are shot on different formats, does that cause any problems?

Miriam – No, unless I get started in the wrong format. It can cause problems if an editor, sound person, and/or composer aren't working in the same format. As long as I get the right information at the start of the project, it's fine. I'm working on a PAL show right now. Digital Performer can handle film 24 fps, PAL 25 fps, NTSC 29.97drop, NTSC 29.97non-drop, 30 fps. Generally it's either PAL or NTSC, and mostly NTSC here in the States. And there's drop and non-drop.

Q – What's drop frame and non-drop frame?

Miriam – This is a very technical explanation, but for a composer's purposes, we just need to know whether it's drop or non-drop. Black and white video ran at a true 30fps (non drop). When the color signal was added, video engineers had to slow the rate down to 29.97 fps for technical reasons. Because of this, non-drop timings did not accurately correspond to real time – i.e. an hour long program in fact will run 59 minutes and 56.4 seconds. The solution to this problem was drop frame – which allows 29.97 frame rate video to correspond accurately with real time by dropping the extra frames. Then it distributes the drop frame effect evenly across each hour. The count drops two frames each minute except for each tenth minute – that is, no frames are dropped at minutes 00, 10, 20, etc.

Q – Do you find a lot of low budget filmmakers ignore sound?

Miriam – I've met some directors who don't realize how important and powerful the score can be and therefore don't care about the score. That's a shame. I try to illuminate them if I can!

Q – If you're doing a film set in a certain country, do you use a lot of indigenous music?

Miriam – Oh, yes. I've done a lot of films like that and I love world music. Even though I studied anthropology in college, I'm not trying to be an ethnomusicologist or be too precise. For example, I can't possibly develop an expertise in music from all the regions of India but I can help my audience identify generally where we are. If you want a truly authentic Indian score you should probably hire an Indian composer. My filmmakers can be very helpful in familiarizing me with music from the regions where they shoot. On a recent project, the filmmakers went all over Afghanistan filming and collected music as they traveled and then presented me with a stack of CDs. I listened to the music, tried to absorb it and identify elements that I thought would enhance the score. You have to be especially careful with vocals. There are all these great samples with Indian or African chanting. I don't know what they're saying, and it could be something inappropriate for the film's story. Also there could be certain instruments that can only be played for religious purposes. For instance, even though I'm Jewish and I know the Kaddish, the prayer for mourners, I had to check and make sure that it was appropriately used in the film I'm working on. I don't want to be wrong. So I checked with the Cantors, the Orthodox people and luckily we were okay.

Q – With documentaries there's a lot of voice over, how does that affect the score?

Miriam – Think of it like a musical where you have people doing exposition.They just are narrating instead of singing.

Q – Do you as the composer have any control over soundtracks?

Miriam – In my contract they have to come to me if they want to do a soundtrack. But not many documentaries have soundtracks. People have asked for my soundtrack to *Lost In La Mancha*, so I've decided to release that and other soundtracks on CD Baby. In the past, you needed a record company to distribute the stuff but now once you get on CD Baby they license the music to all these digital download places. So if you have it listed as a soundtrack, people who collect soundtracks can download it easily. In this whole new world, it's going to be bye-bye to record companies. You'll be able to find all the obscure soundtracks that you want online and download them.

Q – When you compose a score, do you sit down at the piano?

Miriam – I have two Giga studios and with that I can access a tremendous amout of instruments and sounds. There are about 8 pages of 16 instruments each on each PC. That's a lot of possibilities! I don't even have to play piano sounds. The computer has changed my brain; I'm completely different than I used to be. In the old days, yes, I'd sit down at the piano away from the picture. One of the film scoring classes I took many years ago was taught by the beloved composer, Don Ray (*Hawaii 5-0* TV series), who would tell us to look at the picture once, then put it away and go to the piano and write. Now it couldn't be more opposite. I don't go away from the picture for a minute. If I write a composition and draw from it and then start looking at the picture, that's great, but a lot of the time I start writing and the picture tells me what to do. In classic Western music there's a strong tradition of how you write and structure compositions. But I remember in college listening to Laura Nyro, a wonderful singer/songwriter, who created songs that didn't adhere to any structure. Her wonderful pieces just kept evolving, telling her story. In film you're not tied to any compositional structure. The film is defining the structure of the music and the challenge is to make it sound musical. You can go along and do a waltz and then suddenly you're in doubletime. But the key is to make it appropriate to the film and natural sounding.

Q – What common mistakes have you noticed with documentary filmmakers that could be avoided?

Miriam – The most common I've seen is when they start shooting on one format and then switch to another, leaving all this different footage to deal with. Or someone starts shooting in PAL and then comes back to the States and shoots NTSC. Also, when filmmakers do the initial digitizing of their footage wrong, on an old system or don't format the drive properly, it really causes problems. As far as music mistakes, I try and keep them from making mistakes! But oftentimes a filmmaker gets attached to some Bob Dylan song without considering whether there's a chance of getting rights to it. A lot of filmmakers try getting music clearances on their own, but I highly recommend working with someone who knows what they're doing. If you screw it up it's going to come back and haunt you later.

Q – What could a filmmaker do to make your life easier?

Miriam – All the stuff that makes my life hard—the changes, the constant refining—are usually good for the film. So that's ok with me. What isn't good for the film is when filmmakers don't leave enough time to focus on the music and work with their composer. They're too busy to come over and go over the material because they're in post-production and it's all going insane as they prepare for their online and mix. But if they make some time for their composer, they'll be more likely to get what they want. If they're not in the same city, then they should take copious notes with time code numbers so the composer knows precisely what they mean. It's not enough to say, "*You know when Joe picks up the hat…*" Is it the frame where he's first picking it up? When he's got it in the air? Halfway up? Be as specific as you can and take that extra time to provide what your composer really needs: your input.

Q – Any advice for filmmakers?

Miriam – My advice is to just follow your heart. The world is in the mess it is because there're too many people not following their hearts. I'm disappointed that artists aren't leading the way more; most of us spend too much time being bummed out about things rather than inspiring people. To me, documentary filmmakers are like a beacon. They're inspiring us to care. So I say, keep at it! Stay independent!

Mark Rozett

THE SOUND MIXER

Q – What is the job of the re-recording mixer?

Mark – The re-recording mixer is responsible for the finished soundtrack of the film. He takes the edited sounds – dialogue, music and effects – and blends them together to tell the sonic story of the movie. There's no "right or wrong" in the execution of this – only basic principles, conventions and personal taste.

Q – What are the main differences between how a documentary film is mixed and a narrative film is mixed?

Mark – Because of the "guerilla" nature of most documentary filmmaking, the primary difference between mixing is in the condition of the production track – the sound recorded when the picture was being shot. Usually these tracks are much noisier and more inconsistent than those recorded under the relatively controlled circumstances of a narrative film. Therefore, they require more attention to make them intelligible and smooth. In addition, you usually do not have such elaborate sound effects and Foley tracks in documentary mixes.

Q – What materials do you need for the final mix?

Mark – The re-recording mixer is normally provided with a set of sound "tracks" which contain all of the sounds that will appear in the final mix. They've been edited for their proper synchronization to picture, and grouped together according to whether they're dialogue, music or sound effects. The mixer then views these tracks while watching the picture, and adjusts each of the sounds through a mixing console.

Q – Do most documentary filmmakers ignore sounds or use the wrong ones?

Mark – Actually, I've found most filmmakers of today have a very sophisticated sense of sound and its use in film.

Q – Can you do a proper mix with home editing software?

Mark – Yes, in the same way that you can completely mess up a mix with a million-dollar console. It's not so much about the equipment as it is about the mixer. The principles of good mixing far outweigh the technical side, because sonic quality has improved so greatly in the past 20 years. But that having been said, most home editing software is tedious to use considering there are literally thousands of adjustments to be made to produce a finished track. If you're doing these one by one with a mouse and keyboard, it will take quite a long time, and you'll find it difficult to get a "flow" going. That's why consoles and control surfaces are so important.

Q – Is there any kind of paperwork a filmmaker or producer should be aware of in terms of the sound mix?

Mark – Other than the payroll check? Seriously, there was a time when the console was filled with "cue sheets" telling where all of the sounds could be located, according to the sync and also the track layout. That's all been made obsolete because of digital audio workstation playback, where all the tracks are easily viewed on computer monitors.

Q – Are there any differences in terms of the mix between films that were shot on film versus video?

Mark – How the picture originated – film or video – is much less important to the mix than how it will be viewed. If it plays in a theater as a film presentation, the audience will be much further from the loudspeakers than they will in a typical home video presentation. In addition, a movie theater's sound system, especially if it's THX, will offer a wider dynamic range and frequency response than a home system. For these reasons, adjustments are sometimes made in the mix to compensate for these limitations, if the primary venue is to be video.

Q – How many people are present at the mix?

Mark – I've had anywhere from 0 to 20 or more. Sometimes it's just the director, or the picture editor or sound supervisor. At other times it's a full house with all the related parties. There's no rule here, except that the more people who get to offer their opinion, the longer the mix will take. It tends to work best when one person is clearly in charge and has the final say as to the myriad of decisions encountered in a mix.

Q – What is a pre-mix?

Mark – A pre-mix is a step done before the final mix where individual dialogue or sound effects, (sometimes music) are isolated, adjusted and smoothed out before combining them with the other elements of the mix. This allows you to devote attention to problems within those tracks before the conflagration of the final mix takes place – where the complexity and overwhelming nature of the process makes it more difficult to deal with the minutiae. I call the pre-mix "picking fly specks out of pepper." It's a pains-taking process that usually drives everyone but the mixer crazy. Sometimes him, too.

Q – How much should you use surround sound?

Mark – Whatever is appropriate to your film. What's important to keep in mind, however, is that the surround speakers are a sound "field," not point-source monitors like the front speakers. That means the same sound comes out of multiple speakers in the surrounds. That makes it good for ambiences and reverbs and music, but less appropriate for say, a voice – unless you want somewhat of a disembodied effect. My feeling is that if a sound from the surrounds makes you turn around, then it's probably a mistake because it will take you out of the picture. In general, I like to use the surrounds to "fill the room" – but in an unobtrusive way.

Q – Is it common for documentary films to be over-scored and do composers come to the mix?

Mark – The amount of music in a film is a personal choice, and if that's the intention of the filmmaker, then who's to say it's right or wrong. My only feeling is that if you become aware of the music, then something isn't completely right. In fact, if a sound mix is completely successful, you won't be aware of any of it - you'll just love the moods and emotions of the film. Composers do sometimes come to the mix, and I've had it be both a boon and a bane. It's great if they're able to illuminate something that's not obvious in their tracks, but it can also be difficult if they're not able to keep in mind that their music is just one of the elements of a soundtrack. The tendency is to want to hear all the nuances – and that's simply not always possible or even desirable when combined with dialogue and sound effects. It's the overall impression that's important.

Q – What are the common tools that you use?

Mark – Pro Tools is usually involved in most of my work some form or another. More often than not I am mixing on control surfaces that directly manipulate Pro Tools – Pro Control, Control 24, D-Command and ICON. The advantages of these systems over conventional console mixing are huge in that the automation and processing are part of the session and can easily be taken from system to system, edited or manipulated in ways that were not possible until now.

Q – Do you do the M&E mix?

GUERILLA FILM MAKER SAYS!

Sound FX Libaries

These come mostly in CD packs that can vary from 2 to 40 in number. Also, some companies offer various brands that they have purchased over the years. You can also download laser (needle) drops from the web. Either way, your price includes all rights to use the effect.

Creative Sound Design
www.therecordist.com

Gefen Systems
www.gefen.com

Hollywood Edge
www.hollywoodedge.com

JamSync
www.surroundeffects.com

JRT Music
www.jrtmusic.com

Killer Tracks
www.killertracks.com

Manhattan Production Music
www.mpmmusic.com

Omnimusic
www.omnimusic.com

PowerFX
www.powerfx.com

SFX Serafine Collections
www.frankserafine.com

Sound Dogs
www.sounddogs.com

Sound Ideas
www.sound-ideas.com

Valentino
www.tvmusic.com

Mark – I sometimes do, but frequently that is assigned to a separate effects mixer.

Q – Do you normally do Foley on a documentary film? If so, what are some things to think about in terms of Foley?

Mark – Foley is usually involved in some form or another – if only to fill in missing production effects. If a fully filled M&E is required, than a complete Foley pass needs to be done. For documentaries, this isn't usually the case – they tend to be sub-titled more than dubbed.

Q – Is there anything a filmmaker can do to make your job easier?

Mark – Having a clear vision of what he wants in his soundtrack, and being consistent in that vision is most helpful. Barring that, an open mind is also a great asset. Mixes are collaborative efforts – but they benefit most from having a unified vision.

Q – How much time should a documentary producer budget for the final mix? How do you get good rates?

Mark – Attempting to mix a feature-length documentary in anything less than a week will lead to serious compromises. Extra time spent in the mix room leads to further levels of refinement and detail. It can also alleviate a bit of the stress on the mixer who has to make every minute count.The best way to find a good rate is to do a package "all in." That is, have the same company do your sound editorial, Foley, ADR, mix, etc. so that they can discount your rate. It can also eliminate finger pointing if there are any problems.

Q – When should a documentary filmmaker approach you?

Mark – Anytime during the process. Usually I'm contacted when the picture is close to being "locked".

Q – What are the common mistakes you see documentary filmmakers make?

Mark – Not giving enough attention to the hiring the production sound mixer. The very difficult job requires an experienced and creative professional to deal with the impossible situations that will likely be dealt him. And his tracks will almost certainly be the centerpiece of the final mix. If the voices are off-mic and buried in noise, there's virtually NOTHING the re-recording mixer can do to fix it. And nothing brands a film as less-than-professional than poorly recorded voices. Spend the money on the production mixer – it will be well worth it.

Q – What advice would you give a documentary filmmaker?

Mark – Don't forget to have some fun along the way.

GUERILLA FILM MAKER SAYS!

Post-Production Sound

1. Make sure that you previously recorded the best production sound you could – especially when it comes to dialogue. This will reduce the need for subtitling or even ADR and any other post tricks you might have to do.

2. Put your interviewee's voices on separate tracks so your re-recording mixer can set their levels once for each track instead of having to move up and down as each person talks.

3. Put any effects on a separate track from your dialogue and music so you can adjust them separately. Same goes for any Foley if required.

4. A good ambience track (atmosphere/environment) will act like filler in the cracks, smoothing over your edits. Choose your atmospheres with care.

5. Emphasize any sound effects if necessary to add to an existing effect but also to cover any natural sound problems.

6. Your various tracks should compliment each other and not compete, so don't have important sound effects or voice over and a really loud music score at the same time.

7. Too much music can make the audience 'music deaf' and so your score ends up having no impact. Know where to place the music for the most dramatic effect.

8. Taking out your score when you have interviews could be jarring to the film, so think about whether it's best to fade it down but still keep it in.

9. Appreciate the power of silence. Sometimes the best tension is created when nothing is being heard.

10. If you need to edit some music, cut on the beat. In some instances, you can just cross fade your music and it will be fine.

11. Get to know your dubbing mixer before you start working so that you can talk about what kind of sound and effects you want. Also, defer to his or her expert opinion when you are in doubt. They do this day in and day out and know what will and won't work.

12. If aiming for a theatrical release with your doc, your final mix should be done in a studio that handles feature films as opposed to TV programs or news. While these other studios may be cheaper, you will not get the best-shaped sound and end up in the more expensive suite anyway. Most of all you are paying for the person whose fingers are on the faders, not the cool stuff.

13. Make sure to save enough money to pay the recording studio/ dubbing studio so that they will not keep your tapes hostage.

14. If you plan to track lay yourself, don't underestimate how much time it will take. Six to ten weeks is a good guide.

15. Work out how you're going to get your audio to the mix. Avid can export an OMFI file which is often the best way, but do tests as without them, it won't work on the day.

Now at the Final Mix!

This is when all your music, dialogue, sound effects, room tone, ADR and any Foley are mixed into one. It's the most exciting moment of the whole process, as your documentary film seems to leap to life.

1. Sound studios are expensive. Make sure you are prepared, your charts are clear and any creative decisions have been made. Have a list of creative enhancements and problem areas you wish to concentrate on to save time.

2. Mix in stereo. Docs rarely benefit from a surround mix, but if you want it you can opt for analog Dolby, but you pay a license fee. There are other digital formats such as DTS, which some say sound better, but again docs rarely need it.

3. Tape hiss is not a problem anymore because everything is digital. The old Dolby "A" and "SR" noise reduction systems are a thing of the past.

4. It's possible to mix a documentary in 3-5 days (with M&E). Don't let the mixers persuade you into 3 weeks.

5. If camera noise is a problem (film only) most of it can be filtered out, but not all. Either post sync the dialogue or lay in a heavy atmos track over it, e.g. a plane flying over, or a printing press.

6. A Foley artist is a person who adds the rustles, footsteps, etc. You probably won't need too much of this on a doc (if at all), but a day session might give you a much livelier sound track.

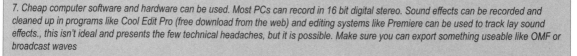

GUERILLA FILM MAKER SAYS!

The Final Mix Cont.

7. Cheap computer software and hardware can be used. Most PCs can record in 16 bit digital stereo. Sound effects can be recorded and cleaned up in programs like Cool Edit Pro (free download from the web) and editing systems like Premiere can be used to track lay sound effects., this isn't ideal and presents the few technical headaches, but it is possible. Make sure you can export something useable like OMF or broadcast waves

8. A Music and Effects mix (M&E) is a mix of the film without any dialogue, to be used for dubbing in foreign territories. All fictional films need this to sell their film. In documentary land, it's looser because creating a filled M&E for a doc is a time consuming nightmare. Most docs are a single camera with people talking and walking, so you'd need to recreate each and every rustle, step, fart and cough. A 90 min doc could take 8 days with a really good mixer/editor. Weigh up with your sales agent if it would suck that bad having subtitles and replacing the voiceover for foreign versions.

9. Work out what kind of stock you need for your master mix and buy some before you go to the studio. They will try to sell you the tapes at an increased price. Alternatively, do a deal including stock (which is pretty common these days). Don't underestimate how these charges can add up.

10. The Dubbing Theater is the best environment you will ever hear your film. What may seem like an over the top sound effect may be too subtle on a TV speaker. Make sure all plot sound effects or dialogue are clear and correctly emphasized.

Tim West
POP Sound

And One More Thing...

Here are some questions from sound mixer Tim West for you, the client, to think about before you start your mix.Thinking them through will save you time and money!

1. Is it to be theatrical mix? 5.1? Stereo? 5.1 with a stereo fold down? 5.1 with a standalone stereo mix?
2. Where is this going to be played? Theatrical /DVD/both?
3. Are you going to record a Voice Over? How much? Does the mixer cut it in or will it be done by an editor? Will it be finalized prior to recording?
4. Are you going to have to record any ADR? Exactly how many lines? Which scenes? How many people?
5. Is the music going to be delivered final or is it to be edited in the mix?
6. Can the picture editor deliver OMF?
7. Will all dialogue be delivered by OMF?
8. Sound design. Which scenes are sound designed montages? How many? Which scenes will the mixer be re-doing? How much of the editors design is to be used? How much of the sound design that is already done does the client like?
9. Does the client want to be present throughout the entire process, or come in for a final playback, or get updates in progress by quicktime etc?
10. Do you want foreign versions? Do they need filled M&E for foreign dubbing?
11. Does the client know what they want or do they want to "experiment" with a variety of ideas in the mix sessions?
12. Would the picture be locked prior to sound editing?
13. Who has final say creatively? Does the director need to get approval from anybody else? Will a committee be producing this or just one person. This would affect our time dramatically.
14. Can the director/committee be flexible? Can a session be postponed if a commercial session comes up? In which case you can get much better deals.
15. When is your delivery deadline?

ANATOMY OF A DOCUMENTARY SECTION 11

FILM FESTIVALS & MARKETS

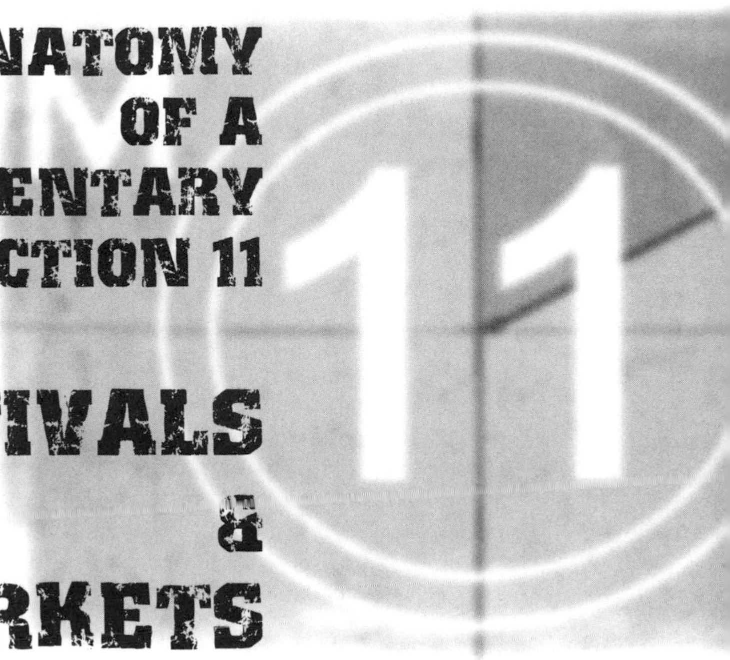

FULL FRAME FILM FESTIVAL

Q – What kind of films do you program?

Nancy – We have two basic components of the festival. One is called New Docs: New Films in Competition and those are films on any subject from around the world made in the last two years. They go through a screening committee and are chosen as official entries into the competitive program. Then because documentaries by nature have information and messages that deal with the state of the world, we have curated programs that bring some of those issues into focus.

Q – What are some examples of the themes?

Nancy – We've looked at class in America. Then we had a sidebar of films that came out of the Hurricane Katrina incident in New Orleans. We have had programs on tolerance, coming of age, science and technology, women's leadership issues and one on hybrids – docs that incorporated fictional elements.

Q – What wouldn't you program?

Nancy – Industrial, ethnographic or promotional films that purport to be documentaries but have other goals. There are many documentaries that are stretching the boundaries. This increases every year and we find it challenging to decide when they cross over the line. Is this film based enough on reality to call it a documentary? So really it's a case-by-case basis on that subject. But we believe there's tremendous diversity in the documentary universe in terms of style and subject matter and we're very inclusive of that diversity.

Q – How does your selection process work?

Nancy – The films are submitted and distributed amongst a selection committee of about thirteen to fifteen people. After a number of months, this committee meets and begins to discuss the films. Then we cull it down to the films that we feel strongly about.

Q – Are the people who select the films staff?

Nancy – We do have a programming department, but the selection committee is made up of expert curators, scholars and filmmakers who've been associated with our festival. They're all volunteers. They're chosen by our staff to participate and frequently change from year to year.

Q – What kind of formats can you project?

Nancy – We can project any format, but we do not project at the festival DVD or VHS. But anything above that is good. We project HD, 35mm, 16mm, Digibeta and Beta SP.

Q – What is the Full Frame Institute?

Nancy – We recognized that there's a need to continue the discussion of the issues of our panels and films after the four-day festival is over and therefore we created traveling opportunitites for the films and related panels. It's a little bit bigger than an outreach program. Because we create new programs around the world. The Institute also has an exchange program funded by the State Department to bring Turkish filmmakers to our festival and send American filmmakers to Turkey.

Q – What are the Full Frame Fellows?

Nancy – That's a program that started in 2003 to offer the rich experiences of the festival to film students around the country. They come to all the panels, we have special screenings just for them and talks with some of the really great legendary filmmakers like Albert Maysles, D.A. Pennebaker and Ken Burns.

Q – What kind of panels do you like to program?

Nancy – We put an emphasis on panels that deal with the content of documentary. We try to be as thoughtful about these panels as possible so it isn't the predictable panels that you often see about technique and how much money one needs. So one year we did a panel on the soul of the story and we talked about the stories that get told in documentaries and how the filmmakers deal with those stories. How hard it is to tell those stories because they're real. They can be really very moving and can enlighten the audience on and how much passion goes into making these films.

Q – Since 9/11, have you seen any trends in the types of documentaries that are being submitted to you?

Nancy – There have been great changes in technology so we've been seeing more films shot on video. That's a good thing and a bad thing. It opens up opportunities for more and more people to tell more and more stories and not have to mortgage their first born to do so. But they might not be as technically efficient. So the ratio of good films to bad films is pretty much the same. I think documentary filmmakers have always tried to be relevant and try to respond to the issues that are critical of our society, so in the last few years we certainly have seem more films about the Middle East, the Muslim world, war in general. We received a lot of films about the 2004 Presidential election here in the US with the divisive political climate and we continue to see those films. We're living in a time where people are incredible critical pro and con of our administration and I think this country is more divided than ever. We have films that reflect those divisions.

Q – How can a filmmaker make the most of a festival or prepare for a festival?

Nancy – They should always go to the festival website and read about, not only the content, i.e. the panels and films in the festival, but also how to navigate the festival. Every festival has their own guidelines and rules about ticket purchases and pass purchases, what one pass includes as opposed to another, how one secures a place in a theater. If they're filmmakers who have their film in a festival, then they need to read the literature that's sent to them from the programming department. Pay very close attention to it because there are requirements in terms of formats, deadlines, publicity materials and information that that department needs. Sometimes filmmakers are so excited about getting into the festival that they feel like once it's in there's nothing more for them to do when actually that is not true. It's just the beginning. They need to attend to all the things that programming department needs in order to have a successful screening. They also have to be mindful that the programming department is dealing with hundreds of films and they're not there to just service that one filmmaker. They need to be considerate of that department, especially as they get closer and closer to the film festival.

Q – What can a filmmaker do to make their screening go well?

Nancy – They have to be very clear about the format that they want to offer the festival. They shouldn't change that format because the programming department often chooses the theater it's going to play the film in based on that. So if they make last minute changes it disrupts everything as it has a domino effect. When they're requested to send in publicity materials and stills and other types of information, they need to do that as quickly as possible. One of the challenges of the festival is putting out the written program that gets handed out at the festival and they have to rely on filmmakers for some of that information. They'll be contacted by people in the travel department and if they can't give them the date that they're arriving or if they start changing those plans at the last minute, that becomes very difficult to deal with.

Q – What kind of publicity materials people should people bring to a festival?

Nancy – Stills, posters and the like all have to be sent before the festival begins. Stills need to be sent as soon as they learn that their film has been accepted into the festival. It's usually a requirement. And they have a very quick turnaround. So if you're off in Afghanistan shooting your next film, you need to make sure there's somebody at home who the festival can reach that can send those materials. If we don't get your stills in right away, then we can't put a picture in the program. And then they'll complain that we didn't have a picture in the program, but that is because they didn't send it to us. There's a letter of agreement that they have to sign as well that has to be done quickly so we can move onto the next step of putting the festival together.

Q – Have you seen any publicity styles that are effective at getting people to a documentary screening?

GUERILLA FILM MAKER SAYS!

Festival Do's And Don'ts

Do research on as many festivals as you can before you start to submit. Find out what kind of films they program, when they program, who attends and what resources they have available to entrants.

Do be mindful of entry fees. Sometimes you will find one that is free, but most likely they will be between $25 and $50. Don't enter a festival that is over this amount. Sundance is $50 so why should anyone else be more expensive?

Do budget for your stay at a festival. This way you'll have money put aside for hotel, food and transportation as most festivals provide none of these things for entrants. You can always get a bunch of friends together and pack one hotel room. Makes for great stories.

Do not pay to be part of the festival program. You should be included since they have chosen you to be in the festival. In fact, some festivals will pay YOU to screen the film. Ask!

Do advertise your film as much as possible yourself. Bring press kits, VHS or DVD copies, flyers, posters (some festivals forbid postering buildings and passing out flyers), hats and anything else you can slap the name of your film on. Be creative as well. If your documentary is about cowboys, dress one of your friends up as a cowboy and have him walk through the festival handing out flyers.

Do bring as many of your subjects along as possible. It will really liven up the Q&A afterwards.

Do get a publicist, but ONLY if you are going to be at one of the larger festivals were there will be a lot of press. It also may be helpful for foreign country festivals as the agents will be more familiar with the press agencies.

Do make sure that your print is in a format that the festival handles and that any special requests, such as HD players, are taken care of two weeks in advance.

Do make sure to get your publicity materials to the festival headquarters as soon as possible so they can create their program.

Do schmooze with the festival operators to find out where the free food, drink and best parties are.

Do not freak out if the projector blows up or the sound drops out of your film. Remain calm and professional. Usually it is a volunteer running the projector with very little training. Don't blame them.

Don't monopolize the film festival depart staff. You aren't the only filmmaker at the festival.

Do not stay too far away from the festival center. The pace of most film festivals, especially the larger ones, is draining. Having to drive half and an hour or more to your hotel at the end of the night just sucks.

Nancy – Bringing the subject of your film, particularly if they are well known, will draw a big audience. If the person isn't well known, but the story is a poignant story about someone or dramatic and that person is there, it makes for a very strong screening experience. People will always remember it and talk about it for a long time. We have an Outreach Committee at the festival. We'll help come up with ideas on developing an audience for them. If they choose to, they're welcome to bring the subject of their film, particularly if the person is well known.

Q – What distributors come to the festival and do you to put them together with the filmmakers?

Nancy – Yes. In fact, what people like about our festival so much is that although it isn't a marketplace, it's a great opportunity for filmmakers and distributors to get to know each other and interact. It's an intimate festival. The theaters are close together. The parties are parties that everyone goes to. It's not ten parties spread out all over town. There may be a few small cocktails here and there, but there's usually one large party where filmmakers and distributors can be together. It's virtually impossible not to meet most filmmakers or distributors at the festival. There are also lounges that make it possible for them to meet each other. We have badges that indicate whether they're a filmmaker or if they're industry. We have an industry handbook that lists everyone from the industry at the festival and how to reach them at the festival.

Q – What are the common mistakes that you see filmmakers make when dealing with film festivals?

Nancy – All filmmakers are entitled to service and care and we like to think of ourselves as a filmmakers' festival. We want them to have a terrific experience at Full Frame. That said, we have so many of them, we have to spread the wealth so it's very hard to give any one filmmaker more attention than anyone else. So they have to appreciate that. The other thing is that on rare occasion, there's a technical problem. It doesn't happen often as we have very good projection and a good track record with making filmmakers happy with the projection. As far as getting into the festival, the story and the craft are everything. It has to be a compelling story and it has to be well told, which means that the craft has to be very good. We know that we're going to be looking at rough cuts, so we know we're not going to see seamless films. We won't accept anything until we see a fine cut, but we are mindful when we're looking at a rough cut as a opposed to a fine cut. If a film isn't well edited and structured, that works against it. Typically, documentaries tend to be too long. Documentary filmmakers need to be really hard on themselves and have other people come in and take a look at them and the film. Sometimes films don't get in, not because they aren't good, but because there is another film about the same subject that is a little bit better or we showed four films about that same topic the year prior. They shouldn't get discouraged and they should definitely submit the film the following year as we have a two-year window.

Q – What advice would you give a new filmmaker?

Nancy – As in any art form, one should look at the very best of that art form. You need to look at the finest documentaries and ask yourself why do those documentaries work when others on the same subject matter don't. You need to perfect your craft, but keep in mind it is the story and the passion behind the story that is going to drive the film. So pick stories that you really, really care about. Know that you are going to be living with that story for years. Don't pick a story because you think it is going to play well in the marketplace. But if you do have your heart set on a theatrical release, then do incorporate into your judgment things that are more marketable. I don't encourage that because what makes documentary different from studio films is the story and if you are not committed and passionate about that story, you are not going to make a good film. And the market is very unpredictable anyway.

IDFA

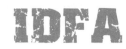

Q – What are you looking for in the documentaries that you program at IDFA (International Documentary Festival Amsterdam)?

David – Creative documentaries of any length completed after September 1st of the previous year are eligible for the next IDFA.

Q – Is there any particular style that you are or aren't looking for?

David – No, as IDFA develops more sections that focus on hybrid works on the border of documentaries/fiction works, the distinction between genres or styles gets less important.

Q – Must all the documentaries have social relevance?

David – No, pure cinematic or experimental works are also shown at IDFA.

Q – What is your screening formats? Do you screen HD?

David – In general, we screen 16mm and 35mm, Beta SP PAL and DigiBeta PAL. All other formats have to be discussed but are possible.

Q – Is there a fee to apply to the festival and what is the process of selecting films?

David – There is no fee required for entry. All films entered are viewed by professionals in the documentary field. The final selection is made by director Ally Derks at the beginning of October. Films entered at the first deadline (May 1st) may have to wait till then to get a final answer. For films entered for the second deadline (August 10th) the beginning of October will also reveal inclusion in the festival or not.

Q – What are the competition programs and what awards are offered?

David – There's the Joris Ivens Competition, which is restricted to films and videos longer than 60 minutes and only European, international and world premieres are accepted. The winner receives the VPRO Joris Ivens Award, 12,500 Euros and a work of art. The jury has the option to grant a Special Jury Award as well. Then there's the Silver Wolf Competition. That's restricted to films and videos between 30 to 60 minutes and again, only European, international and world premieres are accepted. That winner gets the Silver Wolf Prize -10,000 Euros and a work of art. After that, there's the Silver Cup Competition that's restricted to films and videos up to and including 30 minutes and only European, international and world premieres are accepted. The Silver Cub Award is 5,000 Euros. The First Appearance Competition is open to first-time or second-time directors of both film and video documentaries of any length. Again, only European, international and world premieres are allowed to participate. The First Appearance Award is granted to the best debut in First Appearance 2,500 Euros There are two other prizes handed out at the festival, which also include non-competitive films. The festival audience has the possibility to express their appreciation for new documentaries. The highest-rating film receives the Audience Award - 4,500 Euros. An independent jury singles out the best of ten festival films that are nominated

Docs For Sale

Adriek van Nieuwenhuyzen

Q – What is Docs For Sale?

***Adriek** – Docs for Sale is a 10-day market for creative documentaries of any length (except series) which takes place alongside IDFA and the FORUM at a venue in the center of Amsterdam. Over the last years we've had a catalogue with approximately 450 titles. TV Buyers, distributors and festival programmers have access to the 40 booths of Docs for Sale. Those who offer their documentaries for sale have access to the Docs for Sale lobby to meet with the buyers, they don't have access to the booths. Of course it's not obligatory to attend Docs for Sale if you have a film in the catalogue, however Docs for Sale offers a unique opportunity to meet with those who purchase documentaries.*

Q – Can anyone who's looking for a distributor/sales agent, screen their documentaries at this market?

***Adriek** – Yes as long as the production finishes after September 1st. At the time of entry one is requested to classify the documentary in one (or two) of the following categories: history/politics, art/music/culture, human interest/social issues, author's point of view, youth documentaries. The catalogue offers buyers indexes on the basis of these categories.*

Q – How much does it cost to participate in this section and how does one apply? What is the deadline?

***Adriek** – Entering for Docs for Sale is only possible by means of sending the entry form and preview material of the documentary. The prize per title is 185 Euros. For documentaries also selected for IDFA there's a reduced fee of 100 Euros. Deadline for entry is October 1st.*

Q – What screening formats are available?

***Adriek** – Up till now video (PAL and NTSC) and DVD were accepted, but presently we're working on digitalizing the market. For more details check the website - www.idfa.nl.*

Q – Is there a way to inform buyers at the market or beforehand what films are screening when and where?

***Adriek** – The IDFA/FORUM and Docs for Sale guest list is online some weeks before Docs for Sale, the festival and the FORUM start. The Docs for Sale catalogue is available online about ten days before the event starts.*

Q – What is required for the catalogue?

***Adriek** – We need a synopsis of 150-175 words which will be published together with contact details and information like length, formats etc.*

for the Human Rights Film Award. Amnesty International picks the nominated films from the festival films and the prize consists of 5,000 Euros and a limited release in key cities in the Netherlands.

Q – How can a filmmaker make the most of the Festival; for both those attending with films or those visiting the festival?

David – Inclusion with a project in the FORUM is very handy but it's good to visit IDFA with new projects anyway. The attendance of possible funders or co-producers makes for good networking opportunities for filmmakers and other professionals. IDFA and Docs for Sale offer the possibility to watch new films and documentary classics. IDFA features a lot of debates and attending filmmakers will participate in Q&A's after the screenings of their films.

Q – Do you provide publicists for the invited filmmakers?

David – No, all films are available for the press to view either in special screenings or at the press desk and posters of films are distributed during the festival. TV programs do like to screen clips of films screened at IDFA, so it's always good to send clips on BetaSP-PAL.

Q – Do you pay for the airfare and accommodation of invited filmmakers?

David – The festival will provide free hotel accommodation for five nights for the directors whose documentaries have been selected for the Joris Ivens Competition, Silver Wolf Competition, Silver Cub Competition and First Appearance. There's a limited budget for travel costs and additional accommodation.

Q – Have you noticed a trend in the documentaries that you've been screening in the last few years?

David – The main trend we notice is that both the audience and broadcasters are especially interested in topical documentaries. But they also appreciate a true cinematic experience.

Q – What common mistakes have you seen by filmmakers that could be avoided?

David – Don't send too many work-in-progress tapes. Make sure you can deliver the film in time for the festival dates and then decide to apply or not. Sometimes it's better to work on the film a bit more then to rush things and send a preview tape that doesn't give a good impression of the final film. Make sure you send enough information along with the preview tapes. It does make a positive difference if a synopsis, biography and some background information are included in the application.

Q – What advice would you give a documentary filmmaker who's attending the festival?

David – See as many films as possible and meet as many people as possible. Attending IDFA can be exhausting but as most of the decision makers and creative people in the documentary field are present it can be a truly inspiring experience.

Jan Vrijman Fund

Isabel Arrate
Jan Vrijman Fund

Q – What is this fund and why was it set up?

Isabel – *The Fund supports documentary filmmakers living in developing countries. Our aim is to help develop and preserve an independent film climate in countries where because of political or economical reasons the production of documentaries is difficult. We do this by supporting documentary film projects but also by supporting or collaborating with festivals in developing countries.*

Q – How do applicants apply and what are you looking for?

Isabel – *We look for creative documentaries. There are no requirements concerning themes or length. Projects are selected twice a year. The deadlines are always 1 February and 1 June. We've 3 different categories for documentary film applications and a 4th category for festival or workshops proposals. To apply it's necessary to fill out the online entry form, and send the required materials by email, courier or regular mail. All materials have to be in our office on the day of the deadline at the latest. So not postmarked the day of the deadline. On our website www.idfa.nl there is an extended list of the materials to send in.*

Q – What does IDFA consider a developing country?

Isabel – *Each year the Organization of Ecomonic Co-operation and Development publishes the so-called DAC-list, listing the countries that receive Official Developing Assistance. The countries are listed according to the income per capita. As one of our main financiers is the Dutch Ministry of Foreign Affairs we follow the official policy they have for development aid.*

Q – Can a producer from a non-developing country who's teamed up with a producer/filmmaker from a developing country apply?

Isabel – *Only if there's a co-production agreement between two production companies, one in the developing country and the other in the non-developing country. The director has to be a citizen of and live in a developing country. Besides this, the application has to be done by the producer in the developing country and if the project is selected the contract with the fund will be with this producer. A general requirement of the fund to keep in mind in such a case is that a contribution from the fund has to be spent in a developing country.*

Q – Must all applications be in English?

Isabel – *Yes. We only make exceptions for applications from French-speaking Africa.*

Q – What do you require to accompany the producer's application?

Isabel – *An application doesn't necessarily have to be done by a producer. It can be a director that isn't attached to a registered production company. When sending a project it is best to read the regulations on the IDFA website, especially the Jan Vrijman Fund page where we have a section with frequently asked questions that helps to clarify the requirements.*

Q – How much money can one get from the Fund?

Isabel – *It depends on the category. For script development we give a maximum of 4,000 Euros, for post or production a maximum of 15,000 Euros, for distribution and sales a maximum of 7,000 Euros and for festival applications a maximum of 15,000 Euros.*

Fleur Knopperts
Managing Director

IDFA FORUM

Q – What is the FORUM and why was it set up?

Fleur – The FORUM is a three-day market that aims to support independent producers in finding international co-financing and/or co-production deals for their new documentary projects. It was set up in 1993 with this specific aim and also to create a network of documentary professionals throughout Europe, which didn't exist back then. Now, the FORUM's network has expanded as more and more producers, filmmakers and broadcasters from North America, Australia, South Africa and the Middle East find their way to the FORUM.

Q – What is the criteria to get into the FORUM?

Fleur – The FORUM looks for projects that are either creative author-driven documentaries or high-quality television documentaries. We select up to 45 projects from around 200 applications. The formal criteria state that projects need to have at least 25% of the total budget financed, but no more than 75%. Of the projects we select, 90% need to have a broadcaster commitment. Also, only up to 15% of the projects in the selection are non-European. The FORUM is partly funded by the European Union's MEDIA Program, which means we have to focus on the European audiovisual industy. You'll find detailed information on the selection criteria on our website: www.idfa.nl.

Q – How does one submit to the FORUM?

Fleur – The entry form is available online. In addition to that, we need copies of letters of commitment or contracts from broadcasters already attached to the project. Also, we need a synopsis, a treatment, a budget and a company profile and director's CV. If available, we like to receive visual material as well, like a trailer, a showreel or previous work.

Q – What are you looking for in the documentary projects?

Fleur – The projects need to have an international scope, meaning that the project should potentially interest broadcasters from different countries. There isn't a specific genre we're more interested in, but we hardly ever select science or nature/ wildlife projects, unless they have an original twist.

Q – What is the pitch workshop? How much is divided into pitching, networking and meetings?

Fleur – Each pitch team has 7 minutes to pitch their project followed by 8 minutes of Q&A with the panel of commissioning editors. There are up to 30 commissioners in the panel. The pitch sessions are presided over by two moderators. They do the introductions, stimulate the discussions after each pitch and are there to support the pitch teams. Every day, pitching ends around 2pm when we serve lunch for all participants in one location. There, the pitch teams do follow-up meetings and all the other participants can network. Since most of the afternoon is dedicated to networking and meetings, I'd say that the division between that and pitching is almost 50-50. To prepare the producers and filmmakers and to improve the quality of the pitches at the FORUM, we organize a pitch workshop during the weekend prior to the FORUM (the FORUM is Monday through Wednesday). The pitch teams try out their pitch on a panel of experts and get feedback. In addition, the pitch trainer gives general advise on the presentations. Participating in the workshop isn't obligatory.

Q – When pitching is it advisable to have a trailer to show?

Fleur – Opinions vary a lot on whether or not to show visual material. Some people say that we work in a visual medium and therefore it doesn't make sense to only verbally pitch a project. Others argue that a trailer doesn't necessarily give potential financiers the right impression of what the final film will be like. My personal opinion is that it all depends on the project and the material you have available. For example, if you're making a film about one specific person that isn't famous, broadcasters will want to see that person to see if he or she has charisma. On the other hand, if you plan to make a film on the Yanomami Indians in the Brazilian Amazon, it's acceptable that you're not able to show something.

Q – Do you help introduce the attendees to commissioning editors/broadcaster?

Fleur – We have two matchmakers on staff who help with introductions. They also give advice on which broadcaster is best to contact for a specific project.

Q – Do the same commissioning editors and broadcasters attend the FORUM each year?

Fleur – There's a list of the broadcasting companies that were represented at the FORUM last year. Almost all of them are there each year. For many commissioning editors the FORUM is a fixed item in their calendar, but each year we also welcome quite a few new faces.

Q – Are the consultants that you have on hand at the FORUM for individual meetings, all on the distribution side of the business, or from any other field of the documentary filmmaking process?

Fleur – The consultants are distributors and sales agents, but also producers with a wide experience in international co-productions.

Q – How can the FORUM help new documentary filmmakers and producers?

Fleur – The big difference with other markets is that the FORUM has public pitching. If your project is selected to be pitched, you'll have the attention of a large number of commissioning editors and other financiers at once. For a filmmaker or producer that's new to the international market, this is advantageous because you not only pitch your new project, you also present yourself and your company. Especially if you do a great pitch, people will remember you. As a result, it will be easier to get meetings with broadcasters and financiers afterwards. Not only here in Amsterdam but also at other markets where you do follow-up meetings.

Q – Can anyone attend and be an observer to see how the FORUM works?

Fleur – Yes, every producer and filmmaker is welcome to attend the FORUM as an observer. It's restricted however to one person per company. Also, we receive more observer applications each year than we can admit, so we have to do a selection. And, like with the projects, we take more European than non-European observers.

Q – How much does one have to pay to either attend the FORUM or to be an observer?

Fleur – The observer fee is 300 Euros/per person, the project fee is 575 Euros, which admits two people. Both fees include access to the pitching sessions, the lunches and the FORUM receptions. All participants also get the FORUM catalogue, the Program & Participants Guide, the EDN-TV Guide and a free pass for the festival.

Q – How can producers get the most out of their FORUM experience?

Film Festival Necessities

PREPARE..

Get your airfare, accommodations and rental car (if necessary) squared away early. See if festival has some deals worked out for filmmakers.

Save some cash so you can have a good time and relax.

Get business cards printed to pass out at festival.

Create a website to promote your doc online.

Create stickers, flyers, a press kit (b&w, color and digital photos), posters and postcards to pass out at the festival with times and locations of your screenings. The press kit is the most important followed by flyers and postcards.

Take several copies of the film's EPK (electronic press kit) to pass out to distributors. DVD is best.

Make a trailer to include with the press kit.

Pack some fancy clothes for parties.

Don't forget your cell phone. If you are going far away, call your wireless company to see if you can get a good long distance rate.

Have a next project to talk about!

If you can afford it, get a publicist to help you create a media strategy (do this only for the big festivals like Sundance or Hot Docs).

WHEN THERE...

Meet as many people as possible – filmmakers, distributors, journalists, agents, etc. Get business cards, pass out yours!

Create a buzz for your film – pass out your flyers and postcards. Do a cheap (or, not so cheap) publicity stunt. Get your subjects and friends to help you.

If you can afford it, throw a party for your film. Team up with other films to reduce cost.

Talk to everyone you can and find out where the parties are – then crash them!

Use your digital camera to take pictures of you there to put up on your website.

If you are on a budget, hang out at the film festival office. Everyone goes there and they usually have free food.

Hand out your promo items to journalists, distributors etc.

Follow up with everyone you meet.

Talk about your next project and try to get as many people as interested as possible.

Don't sign any contracts while you are there unless you have your attorney present.

Collect ALL press and reviews.

Go support other doc filmmakers by watching their work.

HAVE FUN!

Fleur - Before pitching a project here, it's a good idea to first attend the FORUM as an observer to find out how it works. That allows you to get to know some of the people and to find out who the main broadcasters are and what they are looking for. Secondly, is informing yourself. Do your market research. Before approaching any broadcaster or financier, make sure they're the right person to approach with your particular project. It goes without saying that producers selected to pitch, should be well prepared. But, the same goes for those observing. Even if you're not selected to pitch your project, make sure you have a short pitch ready for informal meetings you have here, even for that very brief chance meeting during the coffee break!

Q – How would you describe the state of the European documentary market, particularly in the last few years where documentaries have been doing well financially at the box office?

Fleur – Some documentaries have done well at the box office, but I wouldn't say many. Also, the ones that do well, were in most cases not predicted to be a success. Take *Darwin's Nightmare* for example. The main financier for documentaries in Europe is still television, and of course national funding mechanisms. In most cases, distributors don't take on documentaries until they are finished.

Q – What are the common mistakes you see documentary filmmakers doing? Either related to the FORUM or documentary filmmaking in general?

Fleur – It's important to have realistic expectations when you attend a market like the FORUM. When you do your market research you'll know better what you'll be able to get out of it. Maybe even more important is to do your follow-up after the FORUM. If a commissioner showed interest in your project, send them additional information, get in touch with them after the FORUM. Don't wait too long. Many producers complain about the time it takes to get an answer from a commissioning editor, but, at the same time, I also get commissioners complaining they never heard back from a project they were seriously interested in.

Q – What advice would you give a documentary filmmaker?

Fleur – For filmmakers attending the FORUM, I believe it's most important to find out what subjects and approaches broadcasters are looking for. Observe the pitches and find out what the stories or approaches are that get broadcasters really excited.

Handling The Press

1. You are never off the record with the press. If you don't want something printed, don't say it!

2. You'll be asked the same questions over and over again. Be prepared with responses that are concise, intelligent, humorous or profound. If you can swing it, try to get the interviewer to show you the questions in advance.

3. If you are being recorded, pause before answering. This will give the editor a clear editing point.

4. Try to answer the question with the question in the answer. For example: "What was working with an elephant like? " is answered, "Working with an elephant was amazing…"

5. Say the name of your film as many times as you can without becoming annoying. Try to avoid referring to the doc as "the documentary" or "the project". If people don't know what it is called they won't go see it.

6. Wear something interesting so that at the very least you will stand out.

7. It is not a bad thing to avoid answering confrontational questions, especially if the reporter has a grudge against you. Politely decline to answer or shift the conversation back to the doc itself. However, it is true that creating controversy about a film based on a feud can, and often does, help the doc at the box office.

8. Always have your publicity stuff on you – press pack, EPK, stills, posters, etc.

9. Telling good, relevant stories is always better than giving boring standard information.

10. Make sure you know how long the interview will last so you can organize yourself to get the maximum amount of information out at the time.

11. Have business cards printed up and give one to the interviewer so that they can always contact you and get your name spelled correctly.

12. The interviewer may want you to say something particular or in a particular way. Try to be flexible here and let them put words in your mouth - as long as they are accurate!

13. Always be complimentary of other filmmakers and their work and others you have worked with. Truly, if you've nothing nice to say, don't say anything at all.

14. Try to avoid talking about the budget of your doc unless it was truly a remarkable feat such as you made it for $7,000 from money generated by having medical experiments done to you.

15. Do as much press as possible to raise awareness of your film. And don't just do entertainment press – go for media that is relevant to your doc's topic or message.

Patricia Finnernan
Festival Director

SILVERDOCS

Q – What is SILVERDOCS and how is it different from other film festivals?

Patricia – SILVERDOCS is a documentary film festival presented by the American Film Institute through an alliance with The Discovery Channel. It's based in Silver Spring, Maryland, which is just outside of Washington, DC at the AFI Silver Theater, a state-of the-art three-cinema complex. It's dedicated to celebrating and expanding the audience for documentary film. It's an international competitive film festival and it takes place in June each year.

Q – How do you program the festival?

Patricia – First we have a huge outreach campaign to the independent film community around the world. In addition, The Director of Programming, Sky Sitney and our Associate Director, Amy King, and I travel to various festivals around the world to uncover new work and foster relationships with filmmakers and other documentary professionals. We create special programs inspired by the documentaries in the line-up. One of our core values is to take the issues explored in the films and create programs that expand beyond the film. This gives an enhanced experience of the film. Bringing in the filmmaker is very important to us as is bringing in the subject of the film, but we also work with the community and bring in journalists and other content experts into the discussion. We show more than 90 films over six days, but the environment is intimate. We have a particular interest in international films. We do special sidebar programs, which change each year. The first year included a sports side-bar. One year we did road movies. Last year we focused on music documentaries and comedy. What was interesting was a lot of the music documentaries dealt with freedom of expression and civil rights. So free speech became a theme of the festival and we created a raucous panel discussion on comedy and the limits of free speech inspired by the film *The Aristocrats*. In 2006, we presented special programs on South Africa, Global Health, and another music program.

Q – What is The International Documentary Conference?

Patricia – Within the six days of the festival, we have three solid days devoted to professional development workshops that bring together program executives, sales agents, public media, public broadcasters along with filmmakers to do discussion about what is going on in the world of film. In our first year, we focused on international development issues and partnered with The World Bank. This year our theme is the future of real. So we're looking at public media from a number of different angles. What we mean by public media is what Al Gore – who will be our keynote speaker - has said is "the marketplace of ideas," and how documentary filmmakers fit into that future. Documentary filmmakers are so important in looking or commenting on ideas or issues in a long form, investigative way that you can't often get on mainstream media. And at the same time looking at how distribution is changing, from Ipods and cell phones to VOD and broadband internet streaming. How does that affect storytelling from the prospect of funding and as well as craft.

Q – How does one apply to get into SILVERDOCS?

Patricia – You apply online at www.silverdocs.com or through www.withoutabox.com and then send in your film. Our deadline is in the first week of March and our late deadline is at the end of March. We do a lot of outreach to other festivals, filmmakers that we have worked with in the past and special communities. So we do request films.

Q – What excites you about a documentary film and makes you want to program it?

Patricia – I'm interested in a strong directorial vision and strong storytelling. It really helps if you have an engaging central character. I love stories that speak to universal principles by telling a personal story. As a festival director, I work with a programming director and we try to address a wide variety of types of films. But films like *Darwin's Nightmare* and *Murderball* really excite me.

Q – How does one get into the Conference?

Patricia – Anyone can come. All of our filmmakers in the festival go to the Conference as our guests. People in the film world can just buy a pass for $400 for the three days and we offer discounts to the many organization we work with such as IFP, IDA and AIVF.

Q – What are your "strands"?

Patricia – We take on specific themes and ideas each year and this year we have chosen global public health. We have titled it Docs Rx and it was a fairly large and unusual endeavor for us in that it really stepped it up a notch in terms of participation and challenging subject. Docs Rx will have between six and eight films and it'll have a special evening program that's open to the general public that will be inspired by one of the films and then there will be a discussion afterwards. In the past, we did a big political night where we had someone from ABC News, the filmmaker and a character in the film speaking. This year it might be a film about HIV/AIDS in China and then you'd have the chief science correspondent from NBC News there, someone from the World Health Organization there, the filmmaker and someone from the film and then have a discussion and open it to the audience. The strand is then brought into the Conference. So we'll have a case study on marketing of social issues documentary – specifically public health films. How a non-profit and an advocacy organization can work with documentaries to advance what they are doing.

Q – What is Sunny Side Of The Doc?

Patricia – It's an international co-production market that takes place in France, founded by Yves Jeanneau, who was head of documentary at a leading French broadcaster. It's a unique thing and a nice marriage for us in the way that Reel Screen, MIP or any of these really big commercial TV markets are not. Sunny Side of The Doc only deals with long-form creative documentary. So it might show a high-end series like *EMC2* that was about Einstein that appeared on PBS. They did a case study on that because it was an international co-production between the BBC and France and WGBH in Boston. So it's kind of high-end documentary storytelling and there are all these programming executives from Europe. At the end of the day, the European commissioning editors are still very important in terms of funding either one offs or high-end series. It's a really interesting place for Americans to go and understand that market.

Q – What is their Rendezvous?

Patricia – The 'Rendezvous' is a specialized pitch market. Sunny Side came to Washington and there were about 200 people total; French and American broadcasters and filmmakers as well as Canadian. Over three days, a network executive would say in five minutes what was happening at *Wide Angle* or the Discovery Channel, for example. Then they would pitch a project for co-production. So the filmmaker would be there with the broadcaster and they would show clips and describe the vision for it. What we did, because we are in many ways in the business of independent filmmaking, was a special outreach and brought in 20 projects from independent American filmmakers whose projects were in the catalog and they had the chance to network with leading commissioning editors in this very intimate environment.

Q – Had they started shooting their projects at that time?

Patricia – Whitney Dow who did *The Two Towns Of Jasper* pitched a new project in development and I don't think he had

Sunny Side Of The Doc

It's always difficult for independent filmmakers to get the attention of broadcasters and commissioning editors. For this reason, Sunny Side Of The Doc (SSD) was started as a market to bring these two sides together. For several days in June, at a site that moves around the globe each year (though its home is in La Rochelle), over 1,500 producers shop their wares to more than 300 buyers. And if someone likes your project, they will invite you to a private lunch or dinner to discuss it further. All genres are allowed as well as all formats. There are screening rooms and a digital video library available as well. There are panel discussions and workshops you can participate in which discuss everything from pitching to new technology. One thing to keep in mind is that the official language of the market is English so all publicity materials must be well translated prior to coming to SSD.
www.sunnysideofthedoc.com

shot a lot of it yet. It really varied where they were in the process. Shannon O'Rourke's film *Maybe Baby* had 180 hours already shot. She had been working on it for a couple of years. Most of the people who pitched were more established filmmakers. We do things for emerging filmmakers at our Conference and at the Festival, but not this, as that is whom the broadcasters want to work with at a development stage.

Q – Is the Rendezvous an ongoing thing or was it a one off?

Patricia – It was a one time special thing for us this year. Last year they did it in Canada at Hot Docs and next year it is going to be in Montreal and then it will be in Boston. So it moves. But we'll go wherever it is and we'll collaborate with them in showing independent filmmakers' work. It's a great environment because the broadcasters are focused and not hiding. You realize that when you talk to any filmmaker, even one with a track record, it's not easy to get your films funded. So to have this opportunity and then to go and try to make a deal at networking lunches and follow ups, it serves an important purpose. Especially in giving American independent filmmakers access to the European market.

Q – Are the filmmakers invited to Sunny Side or do you just pay and anyone can go?

Patricia – The filmmakers submit proposals and then our internal review panel chooses the ones that we want to take to Sunny Side. The broadcasters are just invited by the organizers. They present projects that they have already invested in and are looking for international partners.

Q – What are the common mistakes that you see documentary filmmakers make?

Patricia – Not having top quality camera work, sound recording, editing and paying attention to details. It's particularly frustrating when a filmmaker has found a story that's really incredible or has access to it, but did a mediocre job with the story and technique. One must also be aware of what other films are being made or are out there. You are about to invest probably two years of your life and if we look at our submissions and go, *"Oh, look, there are three different films on the same subject,"* know that only one of them is going to make it into the marketplace. Then I'd also say that the market has gotten very competitive in distribution and the festival roll-out has become really important in so far as where a film is premiered and in how many festivals it plays. First time filmmakers can sometimes not be as savvy as they should be. Make sure you have your premiere at a major festival where there are buyers and press so you can really launch your press. Do your research and know what festivals are out there, who goes and where your work will be best received.

Q – What advice would you give a new documentary filmmaker?

Patricia – Pursuing your passion is the key because documentary filmmaking, and even being in the documentary film business, is challenging. It really helps if you love what you're doing.

GUERILLA FILM MAKER SAYS!

Main International Doc Markets

FEBRUARY

Australian International Documentary Conference, Australia**: Masterclasses, lively panels and an extensive marketplace. You can apply for the pitching forums, submit your documentary to the videotheque and much more. The market component includes the Australian DOCUmart (a day long pitching forum), Pitch and Punts with a development prize up to AUD$20,000, Rendezvous, and the hundreds of one-on-one informal pitches enabled by the AIDC. A broad spectrum of the industry attend the conference from filmmakers, commissioners, industry suppliers, funding agencies, broadcasters, distributors, educational institutions and students.* ***www.aidc.com.au

The European Film Market – Berlin**: Aimed at sales agents, acquisition executives, producers, distributors, exhibitors of films as well as professionals active in the areas of video/dvd and TV sales and acquisitions. Running alongside, and requiring separate accreditation is The Berlinale Co-Production Market - a three day event for producers, film financiers and film distributors, and for operators of film funds, international distributors and TV channels looking for international co-productions.* ***www.berlinale.de

FESPACO - Ouagadougou, Burkina Faso
Home of the African International Film and Television Market (MICA) that facilitates the screening of all African films, enables contacts and exchanges among film and audiovisual professionals and contributes to the expansion and development of African cinema as a means of expression, education and awareness raising. ***www.fespaco.bf***

MARCH

Thessaloniki Doc Market – Greece**: Takes place alongside the film festival and for the five days scheduled is devoted to intensive screenings, participation in the festival activities and facilitation of meetings and negotiations.* ***www.filmfestival.gr/docfestival/uk

APRIL

MIPDOC – Cannes, France**: Held two days before MIPTV, MIPDOC brings together industry leaders in creation, development and financing to debate the hot issues affecting the production and distribution of documentary and factual programming. Trends in programming, co-production agreements and international financing are covered.* ***www.mipdoc.com

MAY

East Silver Doc Market – Prague, Czech Republic**: A specialized market in the Central and Eastern European documentary film field. East Silver is a unique opportunity for documentary film producers and filmmakers from Central and East Europe to promote their films internationally; meet key European broadcasters, distributors and festival selectors. Each year East Silver gathers key European buyers, distributors and festival program directors. This forum allows access to otherwise difficult to find documentary films from Central and Eastern Europe.* ***www.eastsilver.net

The Documentary Forum, Hot Docs – Toronto, Canada**: A unique presentation forum that assists independent documentary producers from around the world and their market partners raise co-financing from the international marketplace. For buyers, the format offers a slate of pre-selected projects in development and production by some of the world's most interesting filmmakers. Over 100 key international broadcasters from Europe, Australia, the USA and Canada regularly attend.* ***www.hotdocs.ca

JUNE

The International Documentary Market, Sunny Side of the Doc – France**: A 4 day duration where participants have access to a wide range of resources with meetings between buyers, commissioning editors, producers, co-producers and high-level international decision-makers at the forums and presentations.* ***www.sunnysideofthedoc.com

SEPTEMBER

The IFP Market – New York, USA**: The IFP Market is a great networking opportunity attracting 1500 filmmakers, screenwriters, distributors, television and home video acquisition executives, domestic and international buyers, agents, managers, development execs, and festival programmers from the U.S. and abroad. Docurama, FilmsTransit International, HBO Documentaries, IFC, PBS, POV, 7th Art Releasing, Sundance Channel, are just a few of the buyers and sales agents who regularly attend to discover award-winning documentaries at the Market.* ***www.ifp.org

OCTOBER

The Asian Film Market – Pusan, South Korea**: A new market that takes place alongside the Pusan International Film Festival. The market hopes to act as a bridge between the Asian film community and the world. It provides various special programs to support international co-productions, information on works-in-progress, and meetings for co-financing, including panels and seminars.* ***www.asianfilmmarket.org

NOVEMBER

Docs For Sale – IDFA, Amsterdam**: An extensive internationally-oriented documentary market offering a limited number of selected documentaries. Visitors to Docs for Sale are predominately purchasers from international TV stations, film festival programmers and distributors looking for new products.* ***http://www.idfa.nl/dfs_content.asp

Sithengi - Capetown, South Africa**: Promotes the development of and trade in African film and television products. Exposes African film and television products to the international arena.* ***www.sithengi.co.za

SUNDANCE

Q – What is your job?

Caroline – I'm a senior programmer of the Sundance Film Festival. I'm one of the people who selects which feature length films are ultimately included in the festival program.

Q – How does the selection process work for documentary films?

Caroline – Every film is carefully handled. It's our job to find the gems, so we take all submissions very seriously. Anyone can submit their film to us. The official feature film deadline is in mid-September. You go online to www.sundance.org, fill out the application form, send in your tape or DVD and we evaluate it. Every film gets watched twice at Sundance. In the first round, we've excellent pre-screeners who watch and write coverage on every film (the way narrative screenplays get covered by production companies). In round two, one of the programmers then screens the film. It's our job to evaluate each film, both on its own merits and in the context of the many, many other films we've reviewed in our time.

Our philosophical approach to programming is that we're compassionate viewers. We know how hard it is to make a film, so we're always looking for a positive angle. If the second viewing by the programmer is a favorable one, that programmer will then share it with his or her colleagues on the programming team. Here's where the positive approach comes in. Let's say it's me that's excited by this film: I'm going to give it to the colleague whom I think will like it best. And they'll pass it on to the next person, and so on. So I'm in effect building support for it, or at least making everyone aware of it, so even if my colleagues disagree with my opinion, the film will be discussed carefully. And then the film goes up on the proverbial Board. The Board is our list of films that at least one person on the team believes should be considered strongly for the Festival. Films on the Board are debated hotly on at least a weekly basis.

Q – When do you start cutting the list down to the final set?

Caroline – We confirm the program at the very end of November, around Thanksgiving.

Q – What gets you excited about a film that makes you want to program it?

Caroline – I think when a film can stand on its own, and by that I mean when I'm watching it I'm nowhere else, I'm completely drawn in and I know I'm in good hands. That's one experience of a great film. There can be a film on a fresh topic we've never seen before, and even if the execution is rough, that's a film that we're still going to consider. Or sometimes the material is more familiar, but the filmmaker has a special point of view or unique access to the subject matter, and that makes the film really important. Or a filmmaker might be formally experimenting, and that can get me excited. At the same time, a film might be slick, by a seasoned team and it's a project that took 10 years that takes a conventional approach to an important figure or historical movement – that's also something to really respect and want to champion.

Q – Is there anything you would never program?

Caroline – No. One of the definitions of the programming profession is to be open to anything and remain elastic it terms of our taste. It's important not to have preconceived notions of what's acceptable or what works in a documentary. Because you never know – people are always blazing new frontiers in all different ways, both formally and in subject-matter.

Q – How important is the first five to ten minutes of a documentary film in terms of getting you excited?

Caroline – A film doesn't need a flashy hook to grab my attention. I'm always going to stick with a film for a significant amount of time to get a sense of where the story is going. Otherwise how can I evaluate it properly? Besides, some feature documentaries really take their time. I'm reminded of *Into Great Silence*, which screened this year in our World Cinema Documentary Competition, and won a special Jury prize. It's mostly a silent film about the monks of Chartreuse who take a vow of silence. It's a spare film that really takes its time, which is exactly the right tone and pace for the subject matter. So as a programmer, it's my job to be open to that aesthetic.

Q – Once a documentary gets into Sundance, what's the process at that point?

Caroline – There's a flurry of activity and they connect with the different Sundance departments such as our press office, our guest services office and print shipping department. The programming team is there to help filmmakers strategize how they can maximize the festival. We have orientations for the filmmakers in Los Angeles and New York. We explain what to expect, how to navigate the Festival, and most importantly urge them to have a good time and not stress out!

Q – Is there anything filmmakers should have ready to go?

Caroline – You can never have too many good still photographs. The photograph speaks volumes about the film and is in some ways the most important tool in marketing their film to the press and future audiences. So during the shoot, I highly recommend that filmmakers hire a still photographer not just for one or two days, but for five, seven or ten days so they can really capture moments that will ultimately become the key images with which to engage viewers.

Q – Who writes up the blurb of the film for your program?

Caroline – The programmers write the program notes. These are designed to give the audience a picture of what to expect– style-wise and story-wise—from the film. At the same time the notes give us programmers a chance to wax poetic about what we admire about a particular movie.

Q – Do you have a preferred projection format?

Caroline – No. We can accommodate 35mm, 16mm and HD CAM. Sundance has been a leader in allowing filmmakers to project their films digitally. Half or more of the films at the Festival are projected on HD.

Q – What are the various programs that Sundance has for documentary films?

Caroline – Sundance has a major commitment to documentary cinema and has since the beginning. The core of the Festival is four competitions - each comprised of 16 films. And unlike any other festival in the world, two of these are documentary competitions. There's The American Documentary Competition and, new in the last two years, the World Documentary Competition. Then there are several other sections that can accommodate non-fiction filmmaking. "Premieres," which tends to be higher profile films, features docs and we even opened the Festival with a documentary – *Riding Giants* – a couple of years ago. Also, there's always room for non-fiction work in our Frontier, Midnight and Spectrum sections as well.

Q – Does Sundance program documentary shorts?

Caroline – Absolutely. Every year we play 75-85 shorts in the Festival and there are always documentaries among them.

Agent Or Manager? Large Or Small?

While getting representation isn't as important for a documentary filmmaker as it is for their narrative cousins, it can still help with brokering deals and finding funds. You may get approached by representation at a festival, don't sign with them in the heat of the excitement. Think about it and talk to them afterwards, they'll still be interested in you for weeks or months. But don't string them along either. Managers usually are easier to get because they come looking for you, while agents pick and choose. A good manager can find you an agent.

AGENTS

Large agencies (ICM, CAA, William Morris) have a lot of power and a lot of clients. That s good because your agent can get your work to any producer anywhere, get you a meeting with almost anyone, get your project to any financier. The downside is that you are one of many and unless you are a marquee client, you won't get all the attention of one who is. Also, you may get placed with a servicing (younger) agent, who has less clout and experience. These places usually won't take chances with first time filmmakers unless they have major heat such as doing well at Sundance.

Smaller agencies (Gersh, Paradigm, Innovative) have less power and fewer clients. You will get more attention from your agent, but they might not be able to get your project to as many places as the larger ones. However, they'll fight just as hard for you and they're more open to first timers.

Boutique agencies are very small and only have a handful of clients. They take chances on first time filmmakers hoping that they'll stay with them if they break big. You'll get plenty of attention, but the larger players in town know that their clients are inexperienced and don't take them as seriously as the larger agencies.

MANAGERS

Managers are another way to go. They come in large, small, and boutique varieties and the good and bad points of those types are the same as the agencies. However, there's one key difference between the two. Managers can be producers, agents cannot by law. As such, managers tend to collaborate with their clients more thereby potentially making a stronger piece of work. They become personally involved in your project and will fight for it harder. Finally, because agents want to package projects with clients from their agency, you might want to consider a manager who is not tied to such thinking.

Both managers and agents take commissions from what you earn. Both take 10%. You only need both if you want to have maximum coverage for your projects and your career. You don't need either if you have a really good, well-connected entertainment lawyer who can get your projects to producers and wants to act in a dual fashion. Most don't, however.

We usually have a shorts program that is dedicated to documentaries. And then there are also documentary shorts that play prior to features. There are so many great ones that come through.

Q – Do you talk to the Sundance Labs when looking for films and do you discuss your program with the Sundance Channel to promote distribution?

Caroline – We do, but we don't have influence over each other's decisions. So if I talk to Shannon Kelley about a documentary project that I really hope he'll consider for The Documentary Fund or Lab, I can share my enthusiasm, but it's not my decision. And likewise, if he wants to recommend a film to the Festival, I'm going to take that very seriously. But he cannot make the final decision. It's a nice check and balance. We share ideas with the Sundance Channel often as well, but certainly don't directly influence their programming.

Q – Do you find that most of the docs in your programs are self-funded or do they have some sort of financial backing?

Caroline – I think there's a real mix. There always seem to be a few funded by HBO or ITVS because those bodies are the key sources of financing for quality documentary projects in the U.S. Also there are more companies getting interested in fully financing or co-financing documentaries (like Participant, Netflix, IFC or ThinkFilm). Even the big talent agencies are beginning to "package" and rep doc projects. And then of course there are always films that come out of nowhere and are completely self-funded, or cobbled together with equity and small foundation grants.

Q – How about on the international side?

Caroline – The Europeans have a lot wider basis of public and broadcast funding for documentary, so I think there is a higher percentage there of films with formal funding behind them.

Q – Do the broadcasters lobby you to get their films in?

Caroline – We're certainly in touch with key people at the broadcasting companies. We're always looking for recommendations from people we trust and respect. That doesn't mean that if someone suggests something to us we're necessarily going to show it. A recommended film doesn't become any more important than a film we've never heard of that comes in without any personal "connection" to Sundance. Each film still has to speak for itself.

Q – Do you ever solicit films from filmmakers?

Caroline – Yes, we're always reaching out to filmmakers, producers and companies to see what they have in the pipeline. We keep careful tracking lists and we check in on films that we know are in the finishing stages. On the international front, because we are dealing with the whole world and there are so many countries--each with their own national cinemas and output of product – we do a lot of outreach work with sales agents, film commissions and production companies.

Q – What are the common mistakes that you see documentary filmmakers make?

Caroline – In my opinion, most documentary films run too long. I see so many documentary films and I've been through the editing process as producer on a documentary feature, so I know how painful it can be to cut. But I think people need to bring more discipline into the editing process.

Q – What advice would you give a new documentary filmmaker?

Caroline – It's really hard, perhaps impossible, to make a living as a documentary filmmaker, so be realistic, but don't take your eyes off the prize. If you've got a story to tell, don't be deterred.

GUERILLA FILM MAKER SAYS!

Useful Websites For Sundance

Sundance Film Fesival main website:
www.sundance.org

Accommodation help: Resort Quest Park City: www.resortquest.com
Tel: 1-435-646-6606
Toll Free number: 1-800-243-2932

Park City Condo Rentals: www.condoparkcity.com
Info@condoparkcity.com
1-888 4 Park City (1-888-472-7524) or 1-435-658-2227
(offers free transport from and to Salt Lake International Airport and your condo, also offer 2 free local Park City taxi rides to the condo unit per day.)

Travel help:
Express Shuttle: 1-800-397-0773 and 1-801-596-1600
(provides round trip shuttle service between Salt Lake International Airport and the Festival in Park City). Vans depart the airport every 30 mins.
Park City Shuttle: 1-800-724-7767 and 1-435-658-2227
www.parkcityshuttle.com

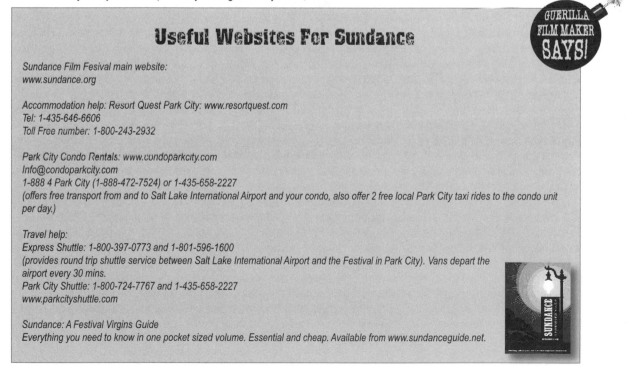

Sundance: A Festival Virgins Guide
Everything you need to know in one pocket sized volume. Essential and cheap. Available from www.sundanceguide.net.

Josh Braun
Submarine Films

THE PRODUCER'S REP

Q – As a producer's rep, what can you do for a producer and their film?

Josh – It really depends on what the project is and what stage it's at. We've become involved in projects when they're little more than a trailer. The things that are hardest for us to jump on board are the ones that are purely at the pitch stage. We'd have to create momentum with the filmmaker. It's tough to create something from nothing although we've certainly done it. It's not impossible, but we rarely have taken on projects like this unless we feel we have the time and energy to devote to get to that point where you're getting financing and the film is being produced.

Q – So you do help find financing?

Josh – Yes. There are projects that come through here where we've signed them and they're usually already shooting or there's a trailer so there's something to get a sense of what the filmmaking is like. We come aboard as executive producers and help raise financing. But the most typical way that we work with filmmakers is that they come in with a more or less completed film and it's about to go to a film festival. We sign to get the exclusive rights to sell the film on behalf of the producer.

Q – What do you look for in a documentary film that makes you want to represent it?

Josh – The truth is that it's not any formula whatsoever. In an ironic way, with the success of films like *Spellbound* and *Mad Hot Ballroom* there are films that have come through here that have tried to echo films that have been successful and that makes me less interested in being involved with a film. The thing that really excites me is a film that comes out of left field and seems to be like nothing else that I've seen. The perfect example is *TV Junkie*. I didn't know much about it. I sat down with our little group of people that assess the films we take on – my brother Dan, Roger Kass, a co-repping partner who also does the legal work and Harry Geller who works in our office. The film was 111 minutes and after 111 minutes our jaws were on the floor. We were speechless. It was such a unique, powerful and amazing film. Those are the ones that you live for. You see a ton of films that are bad and they are really easy – you hope to give the people advice to steer them towards something that can help improve their film, but you can't work on it. Then there's the hardest middle category of films that are good, but you have to make a judgment call, are they good enough? Because we're independent we have the luxury of picking a film that may not be that saleable, but that we absolutely love because it is great filmmaking or it's important. There was a film I signed called *Boys Of Baraka* that we sold to ThinkFilm. When we came on, we knew the distributors were luke warm about its commercial possibilities. I knew it was going to be a challenge, but I really wanted to do it.

Q – Do you find that distributors are more open to documentaries than they used to be?

Josh –The serious attention and consideration is very real and different than it used to be but there's also caution. Distributors are starting to take the first screening of a documentary at Sundance or Toronto as seriously as that of a scripted indie feature – especially if it has a lot of buzz going into it as *Super Size Me* did. So that has definitely changed. My sense is that distributors are as jaded and skeptical as they feel they need to be, but just like I do, they leave themselves open when they find that thing that really excites them.

Q – When is the best time for a filmmaker to come to you?

Josh – On the calendar, the festivals that represent the best sales opportunities and are the most structured are Toronto, Sundance and Cannes but less so for documentaries in Cannes. So for those festivals, filmmakers almost don't have to track me or my competitors down because we're all highly aware of all the films that are chosen for those – and all the other festivals. We signed *Super Size Me* with Cinetic before it got into Sundance. The *MC5* documentary was signed before it got into Toronto. So the best time is when you believe it's really good and it makes the statement that you want it to make even if it's in a rough state. So I tell filmmakers, if you don't feel the film is as good as it can be, don't send it out yet to anyone. At the same time I tell filmmakers to send it to me. I've seen so many films, I've a fine sense of what works and what doesn't. There was a film that ended up premiering at South By Southwest a few years ago called *The League Of Ordinary Gentleman* that I did with Cinetic. We advised them over a series of multiple cuts – screening every single one - to get it to the point that it was ready to submit and likely to get into South By Southwest. When we first saw it, I wouldn't say it was a mess, but all the potential was there - it clearly just wasn't the right cut. Even right now, there is a feature that we signed that was in a messy state that we are directly re-editing ourselves on behalf of the producers with their blessing. I'm a filmmaker and a producer. I was an executive producer on *A History Of Violence, Easy Riders, Raging Bulls, Kill Your Idols* and others and Roger and I recently sold a graphic novel called *Button Man* to Dreamworks that we are producing. I think it can be very helpful for a producer or director who has been working in obscurity and is just emerging into the world to get a little feedback from more seasoned filmmakers and since we work collaboratively we can probably help them in different ways.

Q – How important would you say festivals are for documentaries and do you strategize with the producers on how and what festivals to go to?

Josh – We absolutely do and they are extremely important. We've had the experience of films that didn't get into any festivals because for whatever reasons programmers didn't quite respond. For those films it's really hard to get attention when they aren't given a public platform to get attention for themselves. Then every distributor that looks at it even if it's at a screening that we set up or gets a copy on DVD, they question why it hasn't gotten into any festivals. The festival strategy for any given film can be the key to its success because every film is different and the timing of when it's finished will also dictate what festivals are likely for the film.

Q – Do you do test screenings and focus groups for the films?

Josh – No. We do internal screenings with the three or four people that are here and then we discuss amongst ourselves. But not in a structured way like an actual focus group.

Q – Do you instigate the meetings with distributors?

Josh – Yes. Once we take on a film, all the interface, communication and the interaction with any potential distributor is all through us. We handle all the negotiations, deal making and the legal.

Q – What kind of fee do you take?

Josh – The standard fee is 15%, but sometimes we are flexible depending on when we are seeing the film, how much potential we think it has and if there are competitors going after it.

Q – Are there any problems selling a film if is shot on a digital format?

Josh – It doesn't really make a difference. Sometimes if the content makes it a really good film but the filmmaking is rough, it can be perceived as a little bit of an obstacle. Magnolia Films, who have their HDNet, prefer that films are shot on HD because if they are buying all the rights they can have a window on their channel. But for instance, with *TV Junkie*, the film has been shot on and off for over 10 years, so there's no control over the quality of that image but it's still so deeply

The Next Project

GUERILLA FILM MAKER SAYS!

Now that you've finished your first film and are either enjoying the film festival circuit, a great distribution deal or both, you should remember that people are going to be asking that old question…"so, what's next?" Being prepared here can make a huge difference in your career as people will hopefully be excited by your current film and want to be first in line to work on your next one. We know that marketing your film can be as time consuming as making it, but try to do one of the next few things so that you can strike while the iron is hot!

Try to have another documentary subject story in mind. If you can have some support materials like footage, articles or a treatment etc. ready to go for those meetings youre going to have. But try not to shotgun spray all your ideas. Have one or two that you really want to do.

Try to stay within the genre of your first film. This builds a track record for you and makes financiers more likely to trust you with their cash. Once you have established yourself, then you can start changing genres.

It takes months or years to make a doc or get funding for it, so the more prepared you are, the faster you can get onto your next gig.

Try to be self critical when you look back at your doc. What can you learn from your mistakes.

Understand that you are "hot" for a short period (but longer than in narratvie filmmaking), so whatever you are going to do, get on with it.

haunting and powerful. Ever since the emergence of reality TV, people are used to the handheld look so it generally doesn't matter as much any more as long as the film is good.

Q – Does it help to have marketing tricks to help get the film out there?

Josh – I personally don't think so unless it connects to what is inherent in what makes the film good. If you're trying to create something that is artificial that the film doesn't sustain, I don't think you can get by on pure marketing. It's one thing to have a bad film with some stars in it where you can put their faces on a video box and some people will buy it because it has a recognizable star. But I think it goes to thematic appeal and niche appeal which documentaries often have. If their subject matter has a built in audience, no matter how small, then if the marketing can reach those people, the film can at least be a reasonable success.

Q – What can the documentary filmmaker do to help with the press at festivals?

Josh – It definitely helps if you can get your subjects there. That can get a lot of attention. We had a film called *51 Birch Street* at Toronto last year and the interest in the film was magnified by the subjects being there. The film brings up universal questions about the drama of this one particular family's life and then the people in the movie are there to answer the audience's questions, It can be a very powerful and intimate experience. And then there are the obvious things that may or may not work like posters, postcards and things to build pure awareness that the film is screening. At Sundance, it's almost a waste of time because there is such marketing overload. However you can't just throw your hands in the air and give up, you just have to be a little smarter. We had an unfortunate setback with a film this year called *An Unreasonable Man*. It's an amazing documentary about Ralph Nader. He was going to come and we had a solid week's worth of national press and promotion because he was going to attend and see the film for the first time at the festival. Two days before the first screening, his mother passed away. Fate intervened, but the amount of attention we were going to have when Ralph Nader was going to be there versus when he was not there was noticeable. Luckily the film is great and got great reviews and people were talking about it anyway and we are now close to a deal with a theatrical distributor.

Q – What are the common mistakes that you see documentary filmmaker make?

Josh – It isn't a good idea to show a film to a distributor before it gets to a festival. Distributors will call filmmakers if they hear about a film and and before they know any better, they'll send out copies. There will be a small percentage of films that are good enough that by doing that will end up with someone being interested in the film. But by and large what they're doing is giving one or two distributors an incredible advantage to see the film in a completely relaxed environment where they can get a cup of coffee or take a phone call and perhaps not give the film the attention they'd give it in a room full of other distributors. They may not necessarily get why the film could work with an audience or miss something pivotal that they'd have seen at t a festival. They're mostly very smart people so if they see a film early and pass early they may very well have passed anyway. But then the danger is that the information gets out that a distributor passed and suddenly there's a bad buzz about your film. If you're making a film about musical artists, make sure you get all your clearances before you make the film or cut it and bring it out to a festival. That has been a constant problem. It never seems to go away.

Q – What advice would you give a documentary filmmaker?

Josh – Pick a topic that you're totally passionate about and try to present it in a way that you think is your own voice. Make the best possible film and put your heart and soul into it and hopefully that will be good enough. And if you are happy with it, that should be enough of a reward. If it doesn't happen with your first film, maybe your next one will hit. In the end I think the films that work best are the ones where you seem to be watching it through the eyes of the filmmaker.

Stills & Image

Most posters for documentary films have a single image that captures the essence of your story and target audience. Here are some tips of creating great stills and images for your publicty and creating your own poster.

Stills

1. If you can afford it, hire a professional photographer to shoot your stills. It really will make a difference.

2. Make sure to get shots of the director in action.

3. Always get plenty of stills of your primary subjects doing whatever it is they do.

4. You need to have about 10-12 good photos to give your publicist. Try to shoot ten times that amount to give yourself options.

5. Digital or film doesn't matter so much, though digital tends to be easier for the press to handle - no scanning needed. You can also put digital images on a CD or DVD and on your website.

6. Make sure you get all rights to use your stills from the photographer in perpituity – that includes for publicity, the DVD cover and any future media.

7. Make sure you get the rights in perpituity of the people being photographed, as you don't want them suing you down the road for using their image without their permission.

8. Your stills need to be as high of resolution as possible. Any decent digital camera should be fine, but if you are scanning film positives, make sure your scanner is set to the highest setting.

Image

1. First create the photographic image. This could be a still from your movie or stills that you'll manipulate and edit. Adobe Photoshop will become your best friend. Images created with Photoshop are made of individual pixels or dots. That means that if you make the image bigger, so the dots get bigger too. That's why you have to work at the very highest resolution you can get your computer to do.

2. Secondly, you'll need a vector editing program to handle the graphical elements - your film logo, a Dolby logo, MPAA rating etc. The industry leader here is Adobe Illustrator, but there are cheaper programs that will do the job. These vector based images aren't made of pixels or dots, and if you make them bigger, the edges will look clean and sharp. The only bummer with vector art is that it can't be used for photo realistic images, for that you'll need Photoshop.

3. Thirdly, you need to combine these two – photographic image and logo images – in a layout program such as Quark Express. Again, there are a number of alternative packages that you can use, but Quark is THE industry leader and whatever files you create, need to be accessed and printed by professional printers. Don't get fazed by the PC or Mac debate – both should be able to open files created on either system (although moving from Mac to PC is more problematic). In essence, you could easily create all your elements on a PC – images in Photoshop, logos with your Vector editing program (maybe Illustrator) and text in MS Word – then take them all to a designer with Quark and a Mac, and ask them to lay it out, then save the file and burn a CD for sending off to the printers.

Before you can start any creative work, get all your elements together. Type out your credit block and tag lines in MS Word. You don't want to do this when laying out in Quark, as you will make spelling mistakes that won't get noticed until 200 posters are plastered outside your premiere screening. Get all your pictures together – they should have been scanned already, the key images having been scanned from the photographic negative or transparency, ideally at a professional scanning bureau (although desktop scanners are very good now).

David Magdael
TCDM and Associates

THE PUBLICIST

Q – What is your job?

David – I do media relations and publicity for documentary and independent narrative films. I get press to review films. The good thing about docs is they are more issue oriented, we can go to places off the entertainment page. I work with a lot of first time filmmakers many of whom have never been through the festival circuit or dealt with distributors, so I do a lot of hand holding. They aren't sure what to expect and they don't want to make a mistake or take a misstep. So we do a lot of confidence and trust building. In addition to press, our team works together with the film's producer's rep/sales team. It's important for all of us to strategize and understand what's important in positioning the film. I also look at the marketing aspects for the film so we can build both press publicity and audience awareness for the film. If it's at a festival like Sundance, then it needs to have additional marketing and publicity muscle working together with the sales team creating a whole marketing, sales and publicity strategy. Strategy is the key.

Q – When should a filmmaker approach you?

David – If you're going to be at any large festival where you think you're going to want a presence, you should get in touch with a publicist. Sometimes I'll get calls when people are half way done to get my opinion on the project and see if it's something we'd consider working on once it's finished. Often times, we help them think about different scenarios for getting their film out. Do they need a sales rep or do they need to go the festival route, etc? Or if they get a theatrical release they can come to us for more out of the box publicity instead of the traditional cookie cutter publicity that most releases get.

Q – Do you help create the image of the film?

David – Yes. My philosophy is that the director must be part of developing the publicity strategy as they're the one who had the idea and spent those 2-12 years of their life filming. He/she has a very strong idea of where they see their movie. And that is the first question I ask when they approach me. For example, last year we had a film called *35 Pounds Of Love*. They asked me to see their movie and they didn't have distribution yet, but they thought they needed a publicist. I said, *"Are you in any festivals?"* They told me which ones they were in and I asked if they had gotten anything from them. *"Not a whole lot,"* they said. So I asked them where they saw their film. Is your goal to be on the big screen or are you content to go to film festivals and get picked up by TV? They said they wanted to see it on the big screen. This helps in creating a strategy and managing expectations. In this case, we looked at marketing and publicity that would help drive the film for sales/distribution rather than just for reviews.

I like working closely with a producer's rep because we are working with the same goal in mind – creating awareness, publicity and sales for the film. At the end of the day, the most important thing is that the film gets sold. Then you'll get the reviews later when it gets distribution. If the film gets sold, then the filmmaker becomes hot property. Then you want to position the filmmaker along with the film. With documentaries, you're positioning the filmmaker because they're more often than not the one who came up with the idea, and you are dealing with people who have passion.

Q – How do you choose what films you work on?

David – There has to be a connection between myself or someone on my staff and the film. One that I turned down was *The League Of Ordinary Gentlemen*, which was about bowling and won the audience award at South By Southwest. I bowl, but I didn't know bowling. It was interesting and entertaining, but I couldn't get my arms around it. I felt weird about turning it down, but I've done two films in my life that I didn't really connect with and that wasn't good. For documentaries, you have to make sure that the publicist who is on board really gets and loves the film. You want them to take care of it the way you'd take care of it.

Q – How do you charge for your services? Is it a flat fee?

David – For festivals, it's a flat fee. If we're consulting, it's a flat monthly retainer fee. If it's with a studio, then they have their set rates of what they're going to pay an outsourced publicist. Sometimes, it depends on the amount of work that we're doing. If I get a call from a filmmaker and he only needs help at one festival, then there's a straight up festival fee. However, if it's for one or more festivals or as a consultant then that fee structure would be different.

It's important that filmmakers include publicity in their budget. Publicity and marketing should not be an afterthought. If they are going to go to a place like Sundance, then most people charge about $8,000-$10,000 for their fees. And rightly so. Many of the established publicists at Sundance are working hard beating the streets for the film to help raise the profile of the film or to get a key reviewer to see your film.

Q – How do you discuss strategy with the filmmaker? Is telling them to re-cut it part of this?

David – We'll look at that, but usually by the time they get to us, they've a producer's rep on board or they've done some test screenings. Test screenings are extremely important during the edit process. Especially, if you're going to be sending the film to festivals. You need to know if your film connects with people. You need to show it to people you don't know - people who don't have to be nice to you. That way you can get honest opinions and answers.

Our initial meetings are pretty much comprised of listening to the vision from the director and what he/she sees as a strategy. We talk about positioning and share ideas and angles to make sure that we're all on the same page – so we are pitching the film correctly and positioning the film in a very marketable way. What's great is when a filmmaker can express exactly why he/she made the film. This helps us shape the press materials, the publicity strategy and marketing of the film. We try to follow their vision and make suggestions as well and develop a complete strategy that encompasses everyone's ideas.

Q – For example?

David – Say there's a filmmaker who wants specifically entertainment press like *Entertainment Weekly* and *Filmmaker Magazine*. But they have done a topical film on doughnut eating. Pitching a story on doughnut eating in *EW* or *Filmmaker Mag* could prove to be difficult. What we then do is dissect the film more and think about current events that might work to get a successful pitch there. Maybe someone famous died from doughnut eating. Then we take a look at eating in general and other places that they haven't thought about.

With the film *Rock School*, when it was at the Los Angeles Film Festival, they had John Sloss' Cinetic Media office on board who were taking care of going out to all the buyers. But what we needed to do was create a presence in LA and we suggested bringing out all the kids and having them play right after the premiere screening, as well as at their premiere party. Sloss' office thought the performance right after the screening would be a great added value for the film's presence if the film played well. So we sat down with the *Rock School* people and we all agreed to have the kids come out and play immediately following the premiere screenings Q&A at the courtyard just below the theaters. The kids did three songs and blew the socks off of everyone there in the courtyard. All of sudden everyone was on their phone calling their higher ups talking about the film and how great these kids were. Then, the band played an entire set at their premiere party that same evening and that had everyone abuzz. Basically, the buyers saw first hand how they could market the film and that got them excited and the film played well. Before the festival ended, the film sold to Newmarket Films. It was the only film to sell at the festival that year.

Q – So that was a bit of stunt.

David – Somewhat, but it was one that made sense. I hate calling them stunts or gimmicks, though. Because then people start thinking they should do something on Main Street in Park City. You could, but I need our documentary filmmakers to be smarter about it. I want them to continue the good experience that they have had in the movie theater outside.

For example, we worked on the film *Control Room* when we were at Sundance. Sundance is all about the swag and the free stuff. What swag are you going to put with a film about Al Jazeera TV? We told the filmmakers that their best tool was to bring their film's subjects out to Sundance for the Q&A sessions because Sundance film festival audiences are very high-minded. The Q&A's for the film were outstanding. Here was an opportunity for people from the US to talk with people from Al Jazeera TV, which had been portrayed in our media as the enemy. We had to move these discussions over to a café after each screening because everyone just wanted to talk. It was a true Sundance moment. The filmmakers had the real deal and the audience was able to take that experience with them the rest of their life long after the film was finished. Their subjects became their swag for that film. That same year, we also had *Super Size Me* the same year. Their swag items were Fat Ronald McDonald Dolls, hamburger purses, french fry purchases and other giveaways. For Morgan Spurlock's film those items were great and made sense.

Q – What materials would you need from the filmmaker in order to get the publicity rolling?

David – Photos. I'm finding that filmmakers aren't taking really good, high-resolution photos on set. Not pulls from the movie. We have to have an image that *Variety, LA Times* and *The New York Times* is going to go, *"Whoa we need to have this one."* Filmmaker notes are really important. A synopsis is really important. Bios. A complete credit list. I now have film reviewers who want a complete credit list. They want to know who did the music editing. I have one journalist who always yells at me not to send a press kit to him unless he has a full credit list. Because there might be something in there that triggers something for him and he wants to highlight that.

Q – How many stills would you want to see and should they be digital or film?

David – Lately digital has been the way. It's easy to download. But it has to be high res and 300 DPI. 4x6's are always good. If they can run a 4x6 in the newspaper, how cool is that? And if they shrink it down, it is still going to high quality. How many? Anywhere between six to maybe ten works including either a headshot of the filmmaker or them on set.

Q – Should the press kit be just a Word document?

David – That's what I do. Some people do really fancy things with folders and stuff like that. You can if you have the money. It will help make their film stand out. *Dirty Work*, which we had a few years ago, we put their press kit in a Hazmat envelope. We got additional press on that and it made sense because it was about jobs that people don't want to do like a bull semen collector or an embalmer. Morgan, when he did *Super Size Me*, had a nice press kit that was done in reds and orange – the McDonald's colors. But if you don't have any money, save it. Just put an image of the film on the front. The journalists just want the information. The bios and filmmaker's notes, synopsis. Filmmaker's notes are so important. I always get them to write why they made the movie. Why is the film important? And give me an anecdote. That way if you are not sitting there face to face with a journalist, they can get your thoughts from the notes.

Q – What other publicity materials are indispensable for the press kit?

David – One or two paragraphs descriptions of each of the main players. That way the journalists have additional information that they don't have to go back to the film to see. Sometimes a timeline helps. For *Imelda* we put a timeline of what happened from the time she was born to the time that she came to Manila to the time she was ousted out of the Philippines so the journalists didn't have to research that. *On The Refugee All-Stars*, they did a background piece on what the war was about because how many people here in American know about the war in West Africa? For *Gunner Palace*, I wanted a glossary of military jargon and slang. Also because freestyle rap was one of the big things the soldiers did that was included in the movie, we put one or two of the songs lyrics in the kit. It made it more potent because it talked about their life there.

Q – What is an EPK?

David – It's an electronic press kit. What I like to put on there are at least four one-minute clips of the film and a trailer if you have it. These clips are those that are your best pieces without giving away a surprise ending or anything too important. If you're savvy enough to do interviews ahead of time, include those as well. Often, once a distributor picks up a film, they'll be the ones to put together the EPK. The EPK should be on Beta SP and your publicist should have a DVD or VHS copy. Work with your publicist because they'll know what the TV stations like. Sometimes it's helpful to put sound bites on DVD or CD for radio, which is very important for documentaries.

Q – Are there some publicity items that a filmmaker might think are expensive but aren't and conversely, some they might think are cheap but aren't?

David – I think you should have posters if you go to a festival. You want to create an image that your film is a big film. Posters can be expensive, so if you cannot afford something that's theatrical size, then do something that's 11x17. That way we can mount four of them up there and it looks like the main image. Postcards are good for the publicist and filmmaker to have to pass out and they're cheap. Never leave a lot some place as they get thrown out a lot. Do you need schwag and gift bags? Not if it doesn't make sense for your movie. It will make them talk about your movie a bit, but not a whole lot. We also talk about tee shirts and the like, too. If you can get something for free, great! But I'd rather see the filmmaker put more money into finishing their film and making it look better.

Q – What are some good things to know when dealing with the press?

David – Talk to them first and see what their angles are going to be. And remember you're never off the record. You may say that, but you're never off the record with the press. If you don't want to say something or don't want it to come out, don't say it.

Q – Are there any tips on getting the press on your side?

GUERILLA FILM MAKER SAYS!

The EPK

The Electronic Press Kit is used for publicity, marketing and sales of your project. Here are some things to know to make your EPK look great. Remember the EPK is not a completed production, it's all the elements needed to make a short documentary abour your doc that will be used by TV companies when running aritcles about you or your film.

1. Shoot on HDV, DV or Betacam SP. The EPK doesn't have to look like your film, but it should look like a network news interview.

2. Interview the director, producers and try to get some of your subjects as well. Find a quiet room to do the interviews in.

3. Ask questions of why the subject matter is so important and what attracted them to it.

4. Make sure your interviewees repeat the question in their answer for easier editing. (What is your role in March of The Penguins? My role on March of the Penguins was...)

5. Always get people to state the name of the film.

6. Put on at least four clips from the film that are exciting, but don't give anything away. Leave them wanting more!

7. Beautiful vistas or shocking images look really cool in EPKs.

8. You can include a CD of the score, as long as you have the rights from the composer.

9. Always have some audio clips for radio broadcasts.

10. When editing the EPK, make a Digibeta, Betacam SP or DV master and create DVD or VHS copies with labels for your publicist.

David – It can't hurt to have a personal contact in the press because they are going to be predisposed to the filmmaker. But at the same time they have to be objective because they have to sell the story to their editor without sounding like they have a connection. And they should meet with them maybe beforehand to get to know them. If you don't know anyone in the press, a good movie will always do the trick. Look at *Mad Hot Ballroom*. It wasn't at Sundance. It was at Slamdance. Cinetic had the film and asked me if I wanted to work on it. It blew me away. When I found out it was at Slamdance, I was a little worried because everyone in Park City is focused on Sundance. But this film stood up on its own.

Q – Can you ever have too much publicity at the wrong time?

David – Yes. So you really have to really work with your publicist and producer's rep to manage that. For example, with *Super Size Me*, we knew it was a pop culture film with the McDonald's angle. The description of the film had gotten a lot of play and it sold out right away. So we decided to let it play out and take advantage of it. So what we did is let the audience's carry this movie, not the press. Every time it played we would get calls from the media saying they couldn't get in to the screenings. They were turning away 60-100 people away from the waitlist line and people with hard tickets couldn't get in. We had a screening at 8:00am and I called up Spurlock and said that we knew that people would be lining up at 6:30am in the wait list line. I told him that we should go to McDonald's and go get Happy Meal breakfasts for those first 60 people in the wait list line. So we did that. Spurlock came and delivered it to them himself. We gave dolls to the first five people in line because they got up early. He shook hands with everybody. Nobody got in, but they all got fed. So the story from the waitlist people was word of mouth and consisted of *"We met the director and got breakfast. It was great."* It kept up the film's momentum going peer to peer and it trickled out to the press. It was organic and it worked.

Spurlock is actually a great example of a filmmaker who had his strategy together. He had his producer's rep in place. He brought us on board. He had a whole group of people just to be his warriors at Sundance just to make sure that his posters

Setting Up Press Screenings

1. Give yourself enough lead time. Magazines, television and newspapers usually start thinking about stories 3-4 months before they appear in their publications or on air. Contact them around this time to get things rolling.

2. Create a press release. This is usually a one sheet, 2-3 paragraph statement that tells the press the basic details of your film, when the film will screen along with an RSVP contact number. Contact the publications that you want to show up and ask for the fax number or e-mail to their news desk.

3. Book a theater. Make sure they can screen whatever format you are going to show your film on and make certain there are enough seats for the amount of people you invited.

4. Have press packs made for the screening. This should contain all the basic information that the press need to write a review about your film. This consists of production information, a synopsis, and bios of the key subjects and crew. You can include a statements from other people who may have been crucial for the inspiration for the film.

5. Have a hospitality area set up. The press loves free food and alcohol, and putting them in a good mood before they see your film can't hurt.

6. While not necessary, having the director, producer or subjects around for a Q&A session can be beneficial.

7. Try to get a few "ringers" in the audience (friends, relatives) who will laugh or clap to create a positive atmosphere, which may sway a reviewer's opinion.

8. Many journalists won't make it, so have some DVDs ready to send to them.

9. Find the hook that sets your film apart from the others and then use it to catch the imagination of the press.

10. Follow up your press screening with phone calls to the journalists to thank them for watching and to answer any questions they might have.

11. Remember that your low budget doc is being judged the same as Born Into Brothels – which was also fairly low budget. Expect criticism.

12. There is no bad publicity. Invite as many organizations as possible. Every review helps!

were being replenished. They wore jackets that blazed *Super Size Me*. And he was willing to do anything we asked him to do. It was a dream and it ultimately worked. The film was a hit, got sold and won Best Director that year.

Q – What are some things to think about when things go wrong? What kind of damage control can you do?

David – What I like to do is regroup right away with the principals: the filmmaker, the producer's rep and us. We then figure out what we have to address and what we don't. Case in point, *Super Size Me* was at the Aspen Comedy Festival and that same week McDonald's decides to stop their super sizing. And in their press release they said their "downsizing of super sizing" had nothing to do with that movie. So do we react or not react? I sat down with the distributor's publicist, we pow wowed then called Spurlock and we said, *"They have named you in this. We need to respond."* So we went with The Today Show and the story got picked up with his reaction. We were concerned with the film opening in May, that we would blow our chances too early with a piece in March. However, this was a news story – so it was slightly different. Bottom line, you want to react quickly, but smartly. But in my opinion, there has to be a response because the worst thing you can do in a crisis situation is not react, then speculation just builds and builds and could blow things out of proportion.

Q – What are the common mistakes that you see filmmakers make?

David – Not being honest about what their film really is. They need to be true to themselves to what they really want. It's called having realistic expectations. Also, thinking that they have to make swag and spend money on that for festivals is also a mistake. If you can afford it, great. If not, put that money into post. It's the word of mouth that's going to make someone go see your film, not a tee shirt or hat. Another mistake is not having press materials in on time. Listen to the publicist and the festival office if there is a deadline – meet the deadline. The press kit needs to be done as early as possible with all the elements because it gives us a chance to pitch Variety, which is four or five weeks out from the festival. Be nice to everybody. Be nice to the volunteers and to the people in the press office because they will sell your movie for you. Journalists and real people ask the volunteers all the time what film is good.

Q – What advice would you give a new filmmaker?

David – Make a good film that you are passionate about. That in itself can go a long way. The film can be a little wobbly, but if it has heart, it is going to ring. Don't try to think what the market is going to be. Don't get bogged down in the marketing of your film at this stage. Just make that film that speaks to you! It's yours!

GUERILLA FILM MAKER SAYS!

What's In A Press Kit?

Cover – *Doc title, contact details, press quotes, credits, perhaps a good still image or symbol of the doc and film festival awards.*

Synopsis – *The story of the doc, with a few pics to spice it up.*

Main Subjects & Crew – *Bios of main subjects and crew members with pics and brief quotes about the making of the film. Also a full subject and crew listing.*

Production Notes – *The story of how the doc got made, where, when and why. The press should be able to write a report on your film without having seen it from this material.*

Reviews – *Copies of all your good reviews that you have collected so far. Don't include bad reviews!*

Credits – *Complete subject, crew and technical credits.*

Miscellaneous – *This could be anything else that helps the press understand your film. If there is special lingo or jargon in the doc (say if it is on the military), then a glossary might be a good idea. Or if there is a lot of music, song lyrics could be included.*

Cindy Johanson
PBS Interactive

DESIGNING YOUR WEBSITE

Q – *How important is it for a documentary filmmaker to have a website for their film?*

Cindy – Critically important. As we're looking at how audiences are shifting to use the internet to get information, having an on demand presence related to the content acts as a great way of attracting relevant audiences to the material. The website allows the documentary producer to ensure that they're accessible. When people work with PBS, their internet content is available on this vast archive which currently consists of over 1,800 sites produced by hundreds of producers over the years. That often allows us to appear as the top page of the search engine result, which is critically important as users are looking for particular content.

Q – *What specific things should be on someone's website?*

Cindy – Some standard information such as how to access the content if it's not accessible at a click – such as broadcast dates and times. As we move to an on demand world, there should be a direct click to either receive the content for free or to pay for it. Additionally, producers should include background information about the production, which can range from what the documentary is actually about and/or organizations that deal with related topics. Many producers have included cutting room floor content – such as material that might go on the DVD as extras. At PBS, there are some basic formulaic content that you'll find when you go to a site, but we urge that the story should drive what kind of content the producer feels should appear. There should be bio information specifically about the leads involved and if there's a host or individuals in the film, then include bio information on them as well. You want to have the opportunity to update how the film is going. So if it is in the can, then a website should include updates. People often want to know where the filmmaker or subjects are at this moment in time. An e-newsletter is also a beneficial way to stay connected with the filmmaker for future projects. And then the cutting room floor material I mentioned earlier, which can be video, audio or images. The World Wide Web is about multiple media. And while we will increasingly see video unshackled from its traditional formats and made available on the Internet, we believe just as much value will exist from other forms of media, such as images. One way people come to pbs.org repeatedly is through Google's image search. Having a site developed by an expert that understands how to produce Internet content and apply metadata is important. At PBS, we have a Web resource that describes the process of working with PBS and the kind of content to consider for the Internet. That url is http://www.pbs.org/producers – click on the link to the web manual.

Q – *When should a producer start thinking about creating a website?*

Cindy – In parallel with concept creation and/or production. Some producers are starting to use the internet as a way to share their story ideas in blogs and talk about the actual production process so that audiences are engaged and can give feedback. It becomes a more participatory experience and a way to build an audience that's interested or concerned with a topic. Our ultimate goal isn't repurposing, but pre-purposing.

Q – *Would you recommend that someone build their own website or go to a professional?*

Cindy – My experience has been that professional internet developers are more beneficial than trying to do this for the first time. You want to seek out someone who has a portfolio of sites so that you feel comfortable with their style and approach. And that you, the producer, remain the creative voice and drive the content. Unfortunately, we've had examples of sites where producers just turn over the reins and aren't involved. As a result, not only does the look and feel seem very different from the tone and approach of the documentary, we may find that the facts and source material don't align with the story. You want to make sure that your website isn't the first that a team has produced – don't consider giving your college cousin their "first break" in the internet development business.

Q – How much money should a producer set aside for website development?

Cindy – It depends on the scope of the project. We have internet sites that are produced for anywhere between $10,000-$500,000. Over time, because the content is available on demand at any moment to anyone in the world, we're seeing audiences reached beyond the traditional method such as television broadcast. So while it may seem like a lot of money, four years later, hundreds of thousands of people have come to the website - and your return on investment should pay off. In the last 180 days, we've seen the major networks moving a lot of their digital video to the internet. We're on the cusp of the internet being a primary way that producers make video content available.

Q – Is it possible to make a website for under $2,000?

Cindy – Sure. If you find the right firm who might want an exchange for exposure or some other benefit. Or get someone from a graduate school of internet design. My strong recommendation is to review a portfolio just to be sure you're looking at someone who has produced for the internet before. Check out other sites to see what you like and that will also help you define your possibilities.

Q – What are the common mistakes that you see documentary filmmakers make?

Cindy – Producers sometimes just hand over their content to an outside firm and the producer wouldn't be engaged in the look, feel and content of the website. Remember, it's not just a brochure for the documentary. Your website enables people who have an affinity for you or your content to, not only find out about the documentary, be more engaged. Do identify ways for audiences to connect - to provide input and feedback via an e-mail link so they can ask questions and share their perspectives. Producers also need to think about their website early on in the project and clear rights for the internet.

Q – What advice would you give a new documentary filmmaker?

Cindy – I would urge filmmakers to use other internet sites and understand the power of the World Wide Web. Be experimental, innovate. This is a new frontier and you should go for it during this revolutionary period.

Blogging

GUERILLA FILM MAKER SAYS!

Having a website to support your film is crucial these days. And one way to keep your site fresh and interactive is to add a blog. Blogging allows you to put up a running commentary of what's happening with your film and your life so that your audience feels personally connected to you. You can use it for publicity say to let people know when your film is playing next, to break news or to just share your inner thoughts. But most importantly, your fans can write back to you on you blog and therefore you can give them personal service. You can also blog in groups for an open forum – so if you can get your subject in a room with a computer, people can talk to them via the ether.

Setting up a blog is easy and inexpensive. Just go online, do a search and pick any one of the hundreds that pop up. Try and get one that will let you share photos and connect to other media. But remember – what you write is NOT private! So if you're going to write something inflammatory, be prepared for a backlash in some way.

Domestic & International Documentary Film Festivals

It seems there are as many film festivals in the world as stars in the sky, so choosing which ones to send your doc to can feel daunting. Here are some tips to help you decide as well as a list of the ones that either focus on or have a heavy focus on documentary film. Good luck!!!

1. There are hundreds of film festivals around the world – be selective.

2. Use your World premiere wisely – you only get one.

3. Choose the festivals with competitions; you may walk away with a prize.

4. Try to get the festival to cover some or all of your costs like flights, accommodation and shipping of the prints.

5. Complete and send your application as early as possible.

6. Send a pile of press packs to the festival in advance (including stills and a shot of the director), they will then set up interviews with their press. Take a Beta SP tape with clips (in both NTSC and PAL). Don't leave that tape at the festival or you will never see it again!

7. Remember, if it's a free trip, go for a festival where you actually want a vacation – you could get a week in Asia all expenses paid.

8. Don't get tied up going to festivals. You can just go to what feels like a few and before you know it, a year has gone by, you are no longer a hot new filmmaker and you have blown your window of opportunity.

9. Do research on the festival and the country that you are traveling to. You don't want to end up in the middle of a coup or a typhoid outbreak.

10. If you're going to a festival where the language is different from your own, try to get the festival coordinators to find you a translator.

11. Depending on whether the festivals are now projecting digitally or not, you may well have to have at least one print permanently available for festivals – particularly in some countries who haven't caught up with the technology yet. This print will be shipped around the world from one festival to another and you will probably never get it back. Budget for this print. Keep tabs on that print, you will be amazed how easily it can get lost, especially if you get into making another documentary.

12. Check out the two books listed below!

When it comes to books on festivals there is really only one - Chris Gore's The Ultimate Film Festival Survival Guide currently in its third edition. Most useful is its detailed info on each festival, including info on hotels, maps, even profiles. Gore is a self confessed festival veteran who has first hand experience so you know you aren't reading what the tourist information kiosk would give you. Detailed. Authorative. Humorous.

If you want to understand the inner workings and politics of film festivals from the very large to the very unique, Los Angeles Times film critic Kenneth Turan has put together Sundance to Sarajevo: Film Festivals and the World They Made. For those wanting to get the most out of their festival experience it is a definite must!

JANUARY
Sundance Film Festival
Park City, Utah, USA
www.sundance.org

Slamdance International Film Festival
Park City, Utah, USA
www.slamdance.com

Rotterdam Film Festival
Rotterdam, The Netherlands
www.filmfestivalrotterdam.com

Goteborg Film Festival
Goteborg, Sweden:
www.goteborg.filmfestival.org

The San Francisco Ocean Film Festival
San Francisco, USA
www.oceanfilmfest.org

FEBRUARY
Berlin Film Festival
Berlin, Germany
www.berlinale.de

Dublin International Film Festival
Dublin, Ireland
www.dubliniff.com

Mumbai International Film Festival for Documentary Short and Animation Films
Mumbai, India:
www.miffindia.org/

Bangkok International Film Festival
Bangkok, Thailand
www.bangkokfilm.org/

Ambulante
Throughout Mexico (also March & April)
www.ambulante.com.mx

MARCH
It's All True International Documentary Film Festival
Sao Paulo, Brazil
www.itsalltrue.com.br

Thessaloniki Documentary Festival
Thessaloniki, Greece
www.docfestival.gr

South by Southwest
Austin, Texas, USA
www.sxsw.com

Amnesty International Film Festival
Amsterdam
www.amnesty.nl/filmfestival

Chicago International Documentary Film Festival
Chicago, USA
www.chicagodocfestival.org

London Lesbian and Gay Film Festival
London, UK
www.llgff.org.uk

Guadalajara International Film Festival
Guadalajara, Mexico
www.guadalajaracinemafest.com

APRIL
Full Frame Documentary Film Festival
Durham, North Carolina, USA
www.fullframefest.org

San Francisco International Film Festival
San Francisco, USA
www.sffs.org

Munich Documentary Film Festival
Munich, Germany
www.dokfest-muenchen.de

Hot Docs
Toronto, Canada
www.hotdocs.ca

One World International Human Rights Documentary Film Festival
Prague, Czech Republic
www.jedensvet.cz/

African Film Festival
New York, USA
www.africanfilmny.com

Hong Kong International Film Festival
Hong Kong
www.hkiff.org.hk

Doc Aviv
Tel Aviv, Israel
www.docaviv.co.il

Seattle Arab and Iranian Film Festival
Seattle, USA
www.saiff.com

Wild Talk Africa Film Festival
Durban, South Africa
www.wildtalkafrica.com

All Voices Against Silence
Mexico
www.contraelsilencio.org

MAY
DocFest
New York, USA
www.docfest.org

Seattle International Film Festival
Seattle, USA
www.seattlefilm.com

Tribeca Film Festival
New York, USA
www.tribecafilmfestival.org

Doxa Documentary Film and Video Festival
Vancouver, Canada
www.vcn.bc.ca/doxa

Hollywood Documentary Film Festival
Los Angeles, USA
www.hollywoodawards.com/docs.html

Melbourne International Film Festival
Melbourne, Australia
www.melbournefilmfestival.com.au

London International Film Festival
London, UK
www.lff.org.uk

JUNE
Human Rights Watch International Film Festival
New York, USA
www.hrw.org/iff

Silverdocs AFI/Discovery Channel Documentary Festival
Silver Spring, Maryland, USA
www.silverdocs.com

Florida Film Festival
Florida, USA
www.floridafilmfest.com

Sydney Film Festival
Sydney, Australia
www.sydneyfilmfestival.org

Hollywood Black Film Festival
Los Angeles, USA
www.hbff.org

JULY
Encounters Documentary Film Festival
Cape Town, South Africa
www.encounters.co.za

Karlovy Vary International Film Festival
Karlovy Vary, Czech Republic
www.iffkv.cz

Message to Man International Documentary, Short and Animated Film Festival
St. Petersburg, Russia
www.message-to-man.spb.ru

Jerusalem Film Festival
Jerusalem, Israel
www.jff.org.il

AUGUST
Edinburgh International Film Festival
Edinburgh, Scotland
www.edfilmfest.org.uk

Haifa Film Festival
Haifa, Israel
www.haifaff.co.il

Mexico City International Contemporary Film Festival
Mexico City, Mexico
www.ficco.com.mx

SEPTEMBER
Taiwan International Documentary Festival
Taipei, Taiwan
www.tiff.org.tw

DocNZ: New Zealand Documentary Film Festival
New Zealand
www.docnzfestival.com

Aspen Film Festival
Aspen, Colorado, USA
www.aspenfilm.org

QueerDOC
Sydney, Australia
www.queerscreen.com.au

Raindance Film Festival
London, UK
www.raindancefilmfestival.org

Jackson Hole Wildlife Film Festival
Wyoming, USA
www.jhfestival.org

Vancouver International Film Festival
Vancouver, USA
www.viff.org

Festival do Rio
Rio de Janeiro, Brazil
www.festivaldorio.com.br

Helsinki International Film Festival
Helsinki, Finland
www.hiff.fi

Tri Continental Film Festival
South Africa
www.3continentsfestival.co.za

OCTOBER
Sao Paulo International Film Festival
Sao Paulo, Brazil
www.mostra.org

Yamagata International Documentary Film Festival
Yamagata, Japan
www.yidff.jp

Sheffield International Documentary Film Festival
Sheffield, England
www.sidf.co.uk

Hot Springs Documentary Film Festival
Arkansas, USA
www.hsdfi.org

United Nations Association Film Festival (Travelling Festival in the US)
www.unaff.org

Ukranian Documentary Film Festival
Kyiv, Ukraine
www.molodist.com

AFI/Los Angeles International Film Festival
Los Angeles, USA
www.afifest.com

Pusan International Film Festival
Pusan, South Korea
http:/info.piff.org

Wild Screen Festival, International Wildlife and Environment Film Festival
Bristol, UK
www.wildscreenfestival.org

International Leipzig Festival for Documentary and Animated Film
Leipzig, Germany
www.dokfestival-leipzig.de

Jihlava International Documentary Film Festival
Jihlava, Czech Republic
www.dokument-festival.cz

The Mid East Film Festival
Beirut, Lebanon
www.beirutfilmfoundation.org

Morelia International Film Festival
Morelia, Mexico
www.moreliafilmfest.com

NOVEMBER
IDFA – Amsterdam
The Netherlands
www.idfa.nl

Rencontres International du Documentaire de Montreal
Montreal, Canada
www.ridm.qc.ca

Docudays: Beirut International Documentary Film Festival
Beirut, Lebanon
www.docudays.com

Independent Film Festival of Barcelona
Barcelona, Spain
www.alternativa.cccb.org

International Festival of Documentary and Short Film of Bilbao
Bilbao, Spain
www.zinebi.com

Stockholm International Film Festival
Stockholm, Sweden
www.stockholmfilmfestival.se

Cape Town World Cinema Festival
Cape Town, South Africa
www.sithengi.co.za

DECEMBER
Cairo Film Festival
Egypt
www.cairofilmfest.com

ANATOMY OF A DOCUMENTARY SECTION 12

SALES & DISTRIBUTION

THE SALES AGENT

Q – What is Films Transit?

Jan – We sell licenses and rights of documentary films for people to use them in certain media worldwide. We operate out of Montreal, Canada and have an office in New York (Diana Holtzberg) and Amsterdam (Barbara Truyen). Lots of these media are broadcasters as the market for documentaries is primarily a broadcast market. If you look at the world map, there're about 200 sovereign states and about 40-45 buy the type of documentaries that we're interested in, which are mainly political, social and cultural documentaries. Why only these countries? Because they're the ones with a tradition of some kind of public broadcasting. Broadcasters are 80% of the buys and 20% is other media - theatrical, some festivals, the DVD market and increasingly the silly questions we get for mobile phone rights, although we do recognize that this is a market that is rushing towards us but we wonder if this market means something for auteur documentary as we know it today.

Q – You said you like social, political and cultural documentaries. What makes a good one stand out to you so that you would take it on?

Jan – What we increasingly hear from the theatrical and DVD people that we sell to is that it's important that the viewers in a country can relate to the subject matter. It has to be told laid out in a way that no matter where it comes from, people in all over can relate to it. That's why there's such a small market for experimental films, as these do not really take the viewer into account and only express the filmmaker's individual artistic views.

So what are the subjects that are on top of the priority list? Subjects that people think about. These are things that translate. We just watched a film by a filmmaker from Denver that looks at the commercial American news media. He looked at how they report celebrity trials like Kobe Bryant's. Why is this an important film to distribute? In other parts of the world other than the US commercial media is whittling away the monopoly of the public broadcasters. Once that happens you get a whole different type of news. So those messages are very important. So we like films with relevance. Then they have to be very decently made. There has to be some kind of a filmmaker signature. There are a lot of sales agents out there that will sell whatever they can get their hands on that seems commercial. None of these films are what you would call significant filmmaking. They last 52 minutes, they have a beginning, middle and an end and they are bland. They do well, but it's nothing special, they do not have an impact, nor do they change people's thinking. I like to have films that are just a little special.

We have two specialties as well. We're always interested in documentaries about cinema. We have the best documentary ever made about Lars Von Trier. We took a great doc by Michael Epstein called *The Battle For Citizen Kane* all the way to an Oscar Nomination. And we are always interested in a quirky film about sex. But a film that has something to say. Last year we had a film that we co-produced called *Still Doing It* about sexuality and older women.

Q – What would you not be interested in?

Jan – There's a whole slew of what we call factual entertainment: pretty blandly made films on science, history, food, travel, etc. You know them: image, interviewee, statistic, image, interviewee – a very simple way of filmmaking. There's a lot of docs on exploration. Every single fucking millimeter of the world has been explored and every animal has been filmed. Every time you put on channels like these you see sharks or tigers. I'm not interested in that. I'm not interested in sports unless it's a social issue about sports. There've been some stories about soccer in different parts of the world, which are quite significant. The market has a hard time with shorts, which is stupid and sad. It's not that people don't like shorts; there's just no economics in them. We'll occasionally take on a short because we like it. Whenever we meet a buyer, we show it and they usually buy it, but for very little money. Classical music, dance, opera I'm not interested in because there are well functioning infrastructures for people to co-produce with each other and where buyers for these genres meet each other. There are companies like Rhombus who are experts in the field and make beautiful films. And people in the classic arts have their own well organized market track.

Q – Does it matter these days what format a documentary is shot on?

Jan – It has to be digital. It has to be 16x9. And increasingly, people like to see HD as the shooting master.

Q – Can you still shoot DVCAM and is it acceptable?

Jan – Yes. But you will want to upgrade your master to a better format in post. The broadcast requirements at HBO and BBC who set the trends, are very, very high. Let me give you an example. There was a film in Amsterdam and at Sundance where it won an award called *De nadie*. It's a Mexican film about the horrible things that happen to poor desolate people as they struggle through Mexico on their way to the US. From a content point of view, it's a shocker. The stories are so awful and horrible. But it's a pretty badly made film that when I saw it at IDFA, I had to switch it off after a half hour. It would never pass any technical test. But from a content point of view, it is very powerful. At Sundance, the 150 people watching did not care because they got so sucked into the story and they gave it an audience award.

Q – What are some other reasons that documentary films don't sell?

Jan – It could have already been done a few times and the market says we have had enough. At this moment, we see a very clear flood in the market of films on Middle Eastern issues. Anyone who today wants to make a film on Iraq is making a big mistake, unless you have an angle that is unique. Not only about Iraq, but about the whole Israeli/Palestinian issue. Everyone wants to make documentaries because the world seems to scream at them in all these seminars, *"Join us because it is a great world."* But how different is a tenth film about homeless people? How different is a tenth film about Israelis and Palestinians who live happily with each other on the same street while the rest of the world around them is up in flames? Anyone who is looking for their next subject matter has to think twice. Not just twice because someone else may have done it already, but how can I do it differently. Whenever I do courses or workshops, I always say the moment before you start making a film, you have to do a lot of research and find out if your subject matter is appropriate for a documentary. Maybe it is better to a 20-minute item.

What documentary filmmakers often do not realize is that broadcast in general deals with all the issues that they want to deal with in many other broadcast formats: magazine shows, talk shows, local documentaries and broadcast likes to deal with issues in their own language and in their own culture. It's increasingly important that the films they buy, do stand out, are different, and contribute something NEW to existing material. Broadcasters increasingly ask themselves the question: why would my audience want or need to see this. Filmmakers should ask themselves this question continuously.

Q – Should filmmakers always try to make feature length documentaries?

Jan – A feature documentary has a lot of advantages and a lot of disadvantages. Maybe it's a subject that's better for an hour format. Now you get into the real crucial issues that filmmakers have to think about. If you make a feature documentary, you have to have a story that starts somewhere and goes somewhere. It has to have a beginning of a story that develops all the way to the end. If you don't have that and instead do something observational where you just follow someone, that's not a structure. The other thing I wanted to say is if you desperately want to do a feature doc, we're increasingly finding that broadcasters don't want them. It's not an issue for DVD. It's not an issue for festivals. But it is for broadcasters. There are less and less slots in prime time for long format documentaries. And with the exception of places like The Sundance Channel, ARTE, the BBC, documentaries aren't a priority. Even the Germans, the Belgians and the Fins, they do pay attention to documentaries, but it isn't a priority. That translates into practical issues. If you go to the market with a feature length doc, you'll almost never get it into prime time. It will have to air after 11pm or midnight. If you make an hour version of your film and everyone likes you film, you can get a 9pm or 10pm screening. That's a choice filmmakers have to make while in production. Increasingly, we're cutting down films that were once feature length films. Filmmakers always say they don't want to cut it down because it is too hard or it costs too much and why don't we see if we can sell it as a feature. It's not a good idea anymore. But we think they have no choice and might as well start thinking about this DURING their production process.

Q – How important are film festivals to selling documentaries and which are the important ones for documentaries?

Jan – Festivals are very important. There's a big distinction between how it works in the US and the rest of the world. In the US, Diana has figured out that if you literally plug your film into the twelve key festivals such as Tribeca, Seattle, Denver, Full Frame, Hamptons and SXSW, you'll get a cumulative effect. It means that the film comes floating to the surface and the chances of you making a deal in the US are pretty high. There's a lot of DVD interest for documentaries in the US. Overall there are about 3,000 film festivals. But there are only four that we call launch pads: Berlin, Sundance, Toronto and Amsterdam – those are the launch pads for feature docs. Once you have done that, I'd say there about 35-40 key festivals in the world. Sydney and Melbourne, Yamagata in Japan, the Helsinki Film Festival, the Stockholm Film Festival, The Munich Film Festival, Rio, Hong Kong, Encounters in South Africa etc are part of these 35-40 key festivals. If you don't have a deal yet in these countries, you can try to get one there. If you do have a deal, then the distributor can use the film festival as a national launch pad. This is what our strategy is all about. US, launch pads and key festivals. We do the US. We do the launch pads. We create a strategy for the key festivals, but hand that over to the filmmakers we work with. The producers have to do the work there, but we tell them exactly what to do. Beyond that, there are a zillion other festivals and we don't want to know about them unless it's a nice vacation trip. We also need to have some fun sometimes. The market is not big enough to soak up all the documentaries that are made. So people have to make selections and they select the films that they like or have heard of. So we want all of our films to pop up in all those key festivals in order to create a reputation for them.

Q – What are the important film markets to attend?

Jan – All of the bigger festivals have some kind of facility that allows people to do a bit of business. That's very good. But there are a couple of broadcast markets, which are MIP-COM and MIP-TV. In the broadcast world, these are musts. They are also very hard to deal with because they're huge. Ten years ago, people would walk by and make an appointment and everyone was cool about everything. Now seven weeks before the festival, people start e-mailing their appointments. The only way it works is to go there with an agenda. If you go there just to take a look, you'll get lost. You'll leave town screaming. If you have an agenda with appointments, it makes a lot of sense because people have time for you, they are in the mood and they're concentrating. Then there are the film markets – Berlin, Cannes, Sundance and Toronto. My assessment is that the people that go to these markets are primarily fiction film buyers. People say that now there's a lot more interest in theatrical documentaries – it's still very fragile. What I heard at Sundance, Berlin and other European markets was that there were no real documentary theatrical hits in 2005. We didn't have a Michael Moore. So they're real cautious in 2006. These distributors only buy 15-20 films a year and only one or two are documentaries, if any. We need to keep this in scope. The broadcast markets are very clear. The film markets are very trend sensitive. One big difference that we see between now and ten years ago, is that ten years ago if you went to a market screening for a high profile documentary, none of the theatrical and DVD people would show up. Now they do show up. It doesn't mean that they will buy, but they're going to see the films.

Q – Does it make a difference in the deal if you sell a film at a market or after?

Jan – I'm not so sure. I think it's important to grab the opportunity at the festival if there's interest. The trick after the festival is to solidify the interest and get them to sign on the dotted line. Filmmakers have to realize that in the broadcast world where most documentaries go, the decision to buy is a decision based on content. Everywhere outside of that, theatrical, internet, DVD a decision is made by recent experience or the question: can we make money on it. All decisions are based on calculations, in DVD: how much unites can we turn? They figure out how much it will take in the first month and then at three months and six months. The idea that people love an independent film and are going to buy it because of that – forget it. There's no charity in that world, no pity for the independent filmmaker.

Q – Which window of sale usually generates the most revenue?

Jan – It's either the surprise at the beginning where someone offers you $300,000 for an all media deal in the States, a big worldwide deal, or it is long-term broadcast revenue. There's a saying for all media deals with major companies that every deal you make within four years you will be spending $25k on an audit. Because it's easy to get screwed. Well, maybe that's too harsh. When you look at distribution reports, about how many DVDs sold, etc. but there are very little mechanisms to control those reports. There are only a few countries in the world that have a state operated control system for box office and home entertainment. France is one. It's very, very easy for someone who is very, very far away from you to monkey with the figures. There are a lot of respectable people out there but most of them are just in the business to make money. The more established theatrical distributors, I don't think there is any problem. If you get an offer from a DVD distributor and you look on their website and there are only horror films there, I'd think twice on taking the deal.

Q – You mentioned new media like cell phones, do you think those will become viable revenue sources?

Jan – Who is going to watch a 120-minute film on a mobile phone? I don't know, but we have to put it into our contracts. We also have to put in internet protection clauses because anything that goes on the internet infringes on everything else. If I sell the rights to Holland exclusively and the film is on the open internet, then people in any other country can pick it up from there without paying for it. It's a big issue that is hurtling toward us. The film *The Corporation* can be downloaded from a couple of sites and the filmmaker is in arguments with those sites because he thinks they are doing something illegal. The problem is these people don't think that way.

Q – They don't think it's piracy?

Jan – Nope. They say, *"The internet is a new world. Shut the fuck up."* Not in those words, of course, but if you look at other things like if you sell DVD rights to France and then all of a sudden you find out that a thousand DVDs have been bought in Germany from France and are being sold in German stores, that's also an infringement on rights. If you look at the EEC Free Trade Arrangement, any object that is bought in the EEC can be sold anywhere else in the EEC. And that's a big issue. That's a big contradiction with what we're doing. The problem is that these new rights issues are so complicated and difficult to deal with that the filmmakers won't be able to deal with it. The only ones who can deal with it are the majors and they don't give a shit where the DVDs are sold. On a positive note, filmmakers can look at that dark mountain of piracy on the internet and think that people who steal only have one motivation – to make money. And the films that we're dealing are not the films one can make major money with. So it's an issue, but I think that the numbers that we are dealing with are negligible. You can be very scared and freak out, but the amount of money lost to piracy on independent documentary films is very small.

Q – When do you like to be approached by a filmmaker?

Jan – There are three stages. The idea stage, just before the fine cut and of course a completed film. We really like before the fine cut because it's really important how you start your film in the broadcast world and a lot of documentary filmmakers don't have a clue about that. So they start their film with something very slow and a buyer has already turned it off. If you ever see the film *American Hardcore*, the first seven minutes of that film are dynamite. So smart, well done and to the point. You want to see the rest.

Q – Do you ever fund a documentary film?

Sales Agent Tips

GUERILLA FILM MAKER SAYS!

1. Consider the viability of your film as a salesman – would I want this film and if not, why?

2. Content is more important than style and form in documentary filmmaking. As long as you have an interesting story, good information that satisfies the core audience of your film and some interesting characters, you will find an audience for it somewhere - and your sales agent should know that.

3. Sales agents are tough to deal with – they are professional hardcore negotiators. If they sign your film, they will more than likely want it for 15 years, 25% of sales, plus expenses and refuse a cash advance. The upshot is that you will probably never get paid. Try to get a cash advance, reduce the number of years and percentage. The first one is unlikely to happen, the last two are very negotiable.

4. Keep some territories and windows for yourself. If your sales agent messes you about, this will mean you can approach distributors in a different country and make a direct sale. You will get a lesser fee because you are not a sales agent, but it's better to get 100% of $10K than 100% of nothing.

5. Alongside your doc, you will have to supply a huge amount of delivery items (see the Delivery List on the next page). These are important and often overlooked. Without these items, no sales agent will touch the film or they will fulfill the delivery list and charge you for doing so. Take care of it yourself. Study this list and make sure you know what each thing is, how much it costs and where you will get it.

6. Try not to state how much the budget of your film is unless it is part of the story like My Date With Drew who shot their doc for $1,100 that the director won on a game show!

7. Attending one of the big doc film markets like Hot Docs or Sunny Side Of The Doc will broaden your outlook of sales agents and of how docs are marketed and sold. GO TO THE NEXT ONE!

8. At film markets, look at which ones sell documentaries of your genre and target those.

9. Get a performance clause in your contract. If they don't do a certain amount of sales in a certain amount of time, you can void the deal.

10. Cap their expenses so that they have to get written permission to spend more than you agreed initially. Otherwise they could be free to charge you whatever they want.

11. Be tough from day one. Insist on reports as agreed, prompt payment and accurate information. Make them understand that you will not tolerate complacency. If you make yourself a nuisance, which is well within your rights, they might actually give you what you want.

12. You do not have to go with a sales agent from your own country. Go with the one who shows the most enthusiasm or offers you the best deal.

Jan – We have, but we don't have a lot of money. We may help out a filmmaker with bridge financing if he's getting a subsidy in two months from somewhere. Or in the last stages before a film gets released, we can help there.

Q – If you find something that you want to take on, what kind of deal can the filmmaker expect?

Jan – We have a standard contract that many say is the best in the business. It's a 30% commission and very few deductible costs. The next step is to get the contract signed and then determine where the film starts. If it's for broadcast, then it will start at the next broadcast market. It could start at a major film festival. In February, I'm already lobbying to get films into Toronto in September.

Q – What are the common mistakes that you see documentary filmmakers make?

Jan – Submitting unfinished films to a major film festival. Bad mistake. You better call them and ask for an extension of the deadline. The other one is not thinking of other formats while you are in production. Filmmakers need to have flexibility to create sometimes even two or more versions of their film, maybe one for domestic use and one for export.

Q – What advice would you give a new documentary filmmaker?

Jan – The most important thing is not to work completely alone and to be open to advice and be active in seeking advice. One thing we have found out is that filmmakers have very little access to strategic information like how to submit to film festivals. So learn from each other, phone your colleagues, talk to them at festivals. Other filmmaker's experiences are very important.

GUERILLA FILM MAKER SAYS!

Sales Agent Deliverables

Not all of these items will be needed, (some won't be an option if you shoot digital) but most will. The cost of making this extensive list could be more than your entire film. Speak to your sales agent and negotiate an exact list (which will usually be determined by the distributor) with a budget for making it, BEFORE you sign any sales agreement. This is a LOT OF STUFF!

Release Print
35mm com/opt print (combined optical print). This is used by the sales agent to screen the film at markets in a cinema environment. A 90 minute film will be 5 reels long.

35mm Interpositive and 35 Internegative
Made from the original negative. You have already made this in order to produce your final print, and it will be held at the lab. (90 mins in 5 reels.)

35mm Optical Sound Negative
Made from master sound mix. You have already made this in order to produce your final print, and it will be held at the lab. (90 min is 5 reels).

Sound Master
Master sound mix, probably supplied on either DA88, time coded DAT, hard drive or MO disk. Some agents may request a 35mm sound master, which you should avoid. The sound mix will also be on the DigiBeta on tracks 1 and 2.

Music & Effect Mix (M&E)
Master M&E sound mix used for foreign territories to re-voice the film. Supplied on either DA-88 or time coded DAT. Some agents may request 35mm sound master which you should avoid. This sound mix will also be on the DigiBeta on tracks 3 and 4.

Textless Title Background
35mm Interneg/Interpos/print of sequences without the elements. Used by territories to re-title in their native language. Video versions of the textless background will also be needed.

35mm Trailer
Including aceess to interneg, interpos, optical sound, magnetic sound master and M&E mix. It is common now to produce the trailer on DigiBeta and digitally copy the video onto film. The quality isn't as good, but it may be adequate and certainly cheaper and easier to produce.

Video Tape
Full screen (not widescreen) perfect quality Digital Betacam of the film, including stereo sound (on tracks 1&2) and M&E (on tracks 3&4). You may want to make widescreen versions and 16-9 versions, too, but these will probably be subsequent to the full screen version. You may need to supply a BetaSP so that the sales agent can make VHS/DVD copies. Should also include the trailer, in full screen (not widescreen) perfect quality, including stereo sound (on tracks 1&2) and M&E (on tracks 3&4). You will also need a trailer with texteless backgrounds, too.

Video Tape Textless Backgrounds
Full screen (not widescreen) perfect quality Digital Betacam of textless background sequences, including stereo sound (on tracks 1&2) and M&E (on tracks 3&4).

Universal Master
24P HD master tape (usually HD-D5) transfer of your film, fully graded and cleaned. Hi res and true 16:9 image, means it can be used to make ALL the different tapes required for international sales. Also includes all audio tracks (Dolby Digital 6 discrete tracks) and a stereo track for broadcast TV. This would replace ALL other video tapes required on this list. All textless backgrounds can be included at the end of the tape. THE HD MASTER IS POSSIBLY THE MOST IMPORTANT ELEMENT TO GET RIGHT FIRST!

Stills set
100 full color transparencies will be requested but you can get away with 20 as long as they are good. May be possible to supply these on CD-R/DVD-R now, but they must be very high quality scans professionally done or from a high quality digital camera.

Screenplay transcript
Final cut including all music cues. This can be double column format or traditional screenplay format. An accurate and detailed transcription of all the dialogue, visuals and action. You will need to sit down with your lap top and do it from scratch.

Press Kit and reviews
Copies of the press kit, on paper and disk, and copies of all press and reviews. Don't give them the bad reviews.

EPK – Electronic Press Kit
BetaSP of interviews with subjects and principle crew. Shots of crew at work, plus clips of film and trailer. You will also need a split M&E version so that interviewees voices can be dipped down allowing a translation to be spoke over the top.

Music Cue Sheet
An accurate list of all the music cues, rights, etc. Used by collection agencies to distribute music royalties.

Distribution Restrictions
Statement of any restrictions or obligations such as the order in which the crew is to be credited.

US Copyright Notice
Available from The Registrar of Copyright, Library of Congress, Washington, DC, 20559, USA.

Miscellaneous Paperwork

Chain of Title
Information and copy contracts with all parties Involved with production and distribution of the film. This is needed to prove that you have the right to sell the film to another party. Usually the director, producer, musician and release forms form all other parties involved.

Certificate of Origin and Certificate of Authorship
Available from lawyer. You go in, pay a small fee, swear that the information is correct, they witness it and you have your certificate.

Credit List
A complete subject and crew list, plus any other credits.

Errors and Omissions Insurance Policy (E&O)
Indemnifies distributors and sales agents internationally. Available from a specialized insurance agent (approx. cost $10,000).

Lab Access Letter
A letter giving access to materials held at the lab to the sales agent. Remember, if you haven't paid your lab bill yet, they may not give you this letter.

THE DISTRIBUTOR

Q - Are you finding there is more of a surge in docs than in recent years?

Eamonn – No question. The last couple years have seen a whole change in the marketplace for documentaries. Formerly it was the "d" word. People would try to avoid the use of the word documentary at all costs and now it's badge to wear proudly. I really think that one of the factors is that there've been so many really good, atypical docs. They're not your Dad's documentary – the boring staid, talking head, social issue, PBS, you feel good because you went and endured it kind of documentaries. There have been all these innovative, challenging, unique films that have come out that play like fiction. But I think one of the factors entering into it is reality TV – one decent by-product of what I think is a horrific trend is that people's appetite for seeing real people in dramatic situations has been opened up and people realize that there's dramatic potential in your neighbor next door.

Q – Do you try to have a balance between narrative and documentaries?

Eamonn – No not really. If we're too overloaded then we aren't going to pick up the same thing over and over again. Unlike Hollywood feature films where they try to follow the formula, independent films are exactly the opposite. If they've already seen something similar, people don't want to go.

Q – What makes a documentary work theatrically?

Eamonn – For one it has to have a very strong narrative thread. There are a lot of documentaries that are very nice little snapshots of life and interesting people, but on a theatrical level it's not compelling. You need that drive to keep you engaged. I also think there's on some level some sort of extremity – and I don't mean shocking or outrageous. It's something that's integral to the subject matter. *Capturing The Friedmans* is a great example. You look at this film and you think how did people act that way? There were so many twists and turns to the story that it was hard to assimilate the whole thing. People wigged out – they didn't know what to think at the end of it. The other thing is some sort of promotable aspect. *Control Room* wasn't extreme by any means in the filmmaking, but the sort of effect that it had on viewers was. People were conditioned in the US to think that Al Jazeera were these rabid, American hating, will do anything to help the people plant bombs to get at America, journalists. But no, they're reasonable journalists. We rushed that film out to release. We were taking dates and making posters before we even had contracts signed. We opened the film and we didn't have a trailer. And we set house records for two weeks straight.

Q – Word of mouth worked really well on Control Room.

Eamonn – Yes. I think people appreciated that it wasn't, especially in the environment of that year, this hyper-polarized advocacy on both sides. This was something that reasonable people could go and watch and make their minds up in a calm intellectual setting. It's the age of the cheap sound bite. *"He flip-flopped." "He's a girlie man."* That really sums up the issue. So often, any sort of level of depth is glossed over. It's hyperbole, which has really undermined any rational discourse now.

Q – How do you find the docs?

Eamonn – Mostly at film festivals. We also get invited to screenings, which we always go to. Things come over the transom.

Q – What would you say are the main film festivals?

Eamonn – The big three are Sundance, Toronto and Cannes. I love Toronto in general, not particularly for documentaries, but a feeling that it's a good blend of being curated and a wide array of films with a worldwide scope. Cannes can be more of a grab bag because so much of what takes place is in the market, which if you have $1000 you can have your film screened. There are no barriers to entry.

Q – Does one festival focus more on documentary films?

Eamonn – Sundance always has a very strong emphasis on documentaries. *Capturing the Friedmans* and *Control Room* were at Sundance. I saw *Ramones* first at Slamdance interestingly enough. They didn't even apply to Sundance. The filmmakers were naïve – and they would be the first to admit it. Music rights - what are those? They fashioned for me an unbelievable film, which has a great narrative thrust. I thought it really transcended its subject matter.

Q – What kind of deal can a filmmaker expect and is it similar to narrative?

Eamonn – Pretty much. Our typical advance is around $25K for North American rights. Often times, docs need to sell off the public TV or to HBO rights or something to get started. So that's a piece of the pie that is gone. We're concentrating on getting all rights, which means we may be paying more money for things to enable the filmmaker to come out whole. Frankly, we're going to pay as little as possible and take as little risk as possible. Generally, we have a small distribution fee and that is split with filmmakers. Deals are what you can get. As soon as you put a template down, the next deal you make is completely different and it really depends on the competitive marketplace. What leverage power each side has. We aren't trying to screw anybody, but if we don't have to take a risk monetarily we're not going to.

Q – So expenses would come off the top?

Eamonn – Yes, we'd get our money back before anything else is taken off. As for caps, we agree to them within reason. I generally don't have a problem with them on my own practical level because I don't like to spend a lot of money if I don't have to. If I have to spend a lot of money I think I have a pretty good case of telling the filmmaker why and why it is good for him. And a lot of times most of the deals we do, it behooves us to get into a net position because we end up making more money which helps the filmmaker. We're a lot of times in the same boat in maximizing the revenue.

Q – What are the theaters like for booking documentaries?

Eamonn – The barriers have broken down greatly in the past few years. *Super Size Me* did over $10 million. I predicted early on that *Fahrenheit 9/11* would go over $100 million and everyone looked at me like I had two heads. People have no issues at all. If you're doing business, then you are doing business. We just opened the Patty Hearst documentary, *Guerilla*, which did well and it's a fantastic film. Landmark has always played documentaries, but even their appetite has increased as well. It's all what the market will bear. Regal Theaters, the most conservative, monolithic theater chain was fighting to get as many prints of *Fahrenheit 9/11* as they could. It's not red states or blue states - it's green states.

Q – How do you see digital theaters playing into the future of documentary films?

Eamonn – Landmark Theaters, one of our sister companies, has a big initiative to get digital into as many theaters as possible in the next couple of years. That's an interesting angle coming up because a great cost is blowing up the films, not to mention the individual prints. Right now there's not enough digital theaters to effectively maximize the film theatrically. There will be in a couple of years and I think that's going to be more and more part of the equation. I also think it's going to bring more flexibility to programming. If it's a really good film, and a certain amount of people want to see it, but I can't play it for a whole week, I will play it Monday through Thursday. Or I can switch it out – Thursday night at the theater is doc night were you can bring on special programming and you don't have to go through the expense of making prints to service a whole bunch of theaters for a limited run.

Q – Is the DVD/Home Video market more accepting of documentaries?

Eamonn – Yes, but mainly because of their performance theatrically. Video and the ancillaries lag behind in general. Theatrical is much more the cutting edge medium of people going out to see these things and the video catches up a little bit later. Theatrical performs relatively better than video does – relative to feature films.

Q – What are your biggest delivery standards?

Eamonn – Clearances are a big thing. You want everything locked up because you don't want a subject not liking how they're being portrayed and coming after you.

Q – Does it make a difference what the documentary is shot on?

Eamonn – Yes, to us if it's shot on HD we're much, much more interested in it. In general, just the look of the film makes a difference in its playability. A well-shot film is better than a grainy not well-shot film. But *Super Size Me* was shot with Mini DV that played all over the country.

Q – If you saw a movie shot on video, would you be involved blowing it up?

Eamonn – That depends on the deal you construct. For *Control Room* we put up no advance, but paid for the blow up. Blowups can vary from $30,000 to $100,000. It really depends on what needs to be done and what sort of source material they have and how mature the filmmakers are in actually getting all their materials together.

Q – Is music clearance a big problem?

Eamonn – It's a big problem for all filmmakers. People have their wish list for what they want. *Stairway To Heaven* would be great right here or I want to do all Beatles. That's just a filmmaking problem so you have to be realistic. Also, get a quote for a song, don't execute it, but get a negotiated price so that if Focus Features wants to come in and wants to buy your film, they won't jack up the price. When you get a festival license you can negotiate a real license and try to do as good as you can which may be better than what a company can do because people figure they have deep pockets. Conversely, another company may be able to do better because they have an in with the music company.

Q – Do you see a lot of works in progress and make a decision on that?

Eamonn – If there's some high art film that's going to cost a bunch of money, we won't do that on a production level. Acquisitions are different because you can see and you can judge the finished work.

Q – Would you rather come in earlier if it were with an established filmmaker?

Eamonn – That's more left up to the production companies. Like *Enron* was definitely underway before we got involved. He may have even filmed quite a bit of it before. That is when we took it over.

Q – Are international sales for docs a lot better in terms of DVDs?

Eamonn – Good question. Documentaries in foreign territories are usually the domain of the cable network and broadcasters. All the ones that have a smidgen of profiling the US would routinely get played throughout Europe on TV and that's the milieu where everyone is comfortable watching documentaries. There are theatrically released documentaries. *Capturing the Friedmans* was released in England and it did pretty well. It's hard to say, people are used to watching them on TV and a lot of it wouldn't play on American TV because they're too edgy or bohemian.

Q – And in Europe you really make your money on the ancillaries.

Eamonn – That's especially true in the UK. You think theatrical is bad here? Over there, there are even fewer theater owners. There are two people to call and if they aren't interested then you're screwed. And they dictate the terms of the percentage splits. The United States is getting close to that but it's not quite there yet.

Q – What are the common mistakes you see with documentary films?

Eamonn – Not being ruthless on themselves. Falling in love with certain scenes that don't advance the flow. Make sure you have compelling subject matter. It's a documentary and you're relying on actual things happening to make it compelling, which I always find to be an amazing leap of faith.You're filming a boring patch. On the political side, one of the big issues is people trying to prove a point instead of letting the audience judge. Rigging things so it's one side or the other. Michael Moore is different. He's up front. I hate this President, this is a gross thing and this is why. But when you see films that purport to be objective, yet you see the editorial hand so heavily tilting one way or the other, it's intellectually insulting.

Q – What advice would you give a new filmmaker embarking on a documentary?

Eamonn – Make sure that your film is going to be a priority for the company that you sell it to. It's very easy for a company with a ton of films on their slate not to push yours more than the others. Sometimes it's a lot better to go with a smaller company than one of the majors. If the majors have a big Oscar winning film that they are going to push at the end of the year and you're going out at the same time, they'll love your film and wish you the best, but their energies are going to be more concerned with something that is going to give them a big upside.

Dealing With Debt

GUERILLA FILM MAKER SAYS!

Now that you've maxed out those credit cards to make your film or to survive while making your film, you've got to pay it back. It can be daunting especially if you have rent, car loans, school loans, health insurance and every other bill under the sun. Here's some tips on how to make some cash so you can still work on your own projects.

Work on other documentaries/TV shows/commericals/promos/ music videos/features *- just make sure it's paid work!*

High End Corporate Video *- making training and internal films for companies. Dull and you have to work with people who have little, if any, creativity. Pays really well, though.*

Teaching/Public Speaking *- giving short courses (even getting staffed) and lectures open up to you once you have made a film. And you can sell your film there, too.*

Wedding Videos *– these days everyone wants their wedding filmed. Capitalize on this (especially with relatives) and make some money shooting and editing nuptials. Works for bar mitzvahs, births and just about any other celebration.*

Creative Work - designing websites, journalism etc.

Temping *- takes up a lot of time, pays not that great, but you have flexibility to choose the gigs you want. Plus you meet a lot of people going to different companies.*

Get a job *- takes up a lot of time when you could be working on your projects. You could try to get one in the field of your next doc - instant research and access! Of course, the old standbys of waitering and bartending still exist.*

Medical research *– Robert Rodriquez did it to make El Mariachi. Donate your body to research clinics and you can earn some cash for testing drugs and the like. You can get some good free medical care if you have something nagging like asthma.*

Property *- real estate will always be a money maker - you just have to have the money to buy a house or two. If you live out of a city center, this isn't too bad.*

Ellen Capon
Docurama

DVD DISTRIBUTION

Q – What is Docurama and how did it come about?

Ellen – Docurama is a DVD label based in NYC with a catalog of over 150 classic and award-winning documentary films. We're the only label dedicated exclusively to documentaries in the home entertainment marketplace.

Q – What do you attribute to the explosion of documentaries in the last few years?

Ellen – I think festivals, particularly Sundance, have given documentaries a much higher profile in recent years. And people have taken more chances by taking them out theatrically. There's also been a greater hunger for content other than the standard Hollywood fare. You can look back at what happened with independent film in the late 80's and early 90's - when people sought out films like *Sex, Lies & Videotape* – and you see that things were going in a different direction from what the studios were doing. The documentary boom is similar in some ways – people are looking for something different.

Q – What kind of documentary does Docurama look for?

Ellen – We're a business, so we need to look for something that we think will generate a profit. We typically search for films that have some sort of pedigree. They may have won an award, or have been nominated for an Oscar, or be a classic film from many years ago. Beyond that, we look for films that have a clear core audience. Our customers are either the general documentary enthusiast – the kind of person who likes documentaries regardless of the topic - or the more common subject enthusiast who has an affinity for something specific like Bob Dylan, motorcycle racing or gay themes.

Q – Do you only do the DVD market?

Ellen – We primarily do DVD. We do have a partnership with a company called Shadow Distribution, whom we work with to offer theatrical distribution to filmmakers. We've acquired all rights in the past and sold them off, but our core business is DVD. We also have distribution partnerships with Sundance Channel, IFC and POV.

Q – How important is the DVD market to documentary films?

Ellen – It's critical, first and foremost as a means of distribution. Not all films will get a theatrical distribution deal. And not all films last that long in theaters when they do get one. So rather than television being the only other distribution alternative, DVD offers a continuous open window for audiences to access these films. Companies like Netflix are really important in terms of allowing films to be seen by wider and wider audiences. Second, DVD is important to the documentary filmmaker because it allows them to include more content in addition to the film itself. Most filmmakers record hours upon hours of material that doesn't make it to the final cut. There's a lot that they have to leave on the cutting room floor – a lot more that you as a viewer wished you knew about the subject. So DVD is a way to include deleted scenes and additional material or updates about the people profiled in the film. Lastly, the DVD format can bring some of that great festival energy back into play. The majority of these documentaries are seen at the festival level where you get to have a Q&A with the filmmaker afterwards. You don't get that in a commercial theatrical run. And beyond that, films that don't get a theatrical run sometimes get shelved never to be seen again. That's always been a mystery to us. DVD provides a way for audiences that aren't going to the festivals to see these films. The Q&As that we put on the DVD provide the audience with that sense of interaction.

Q – What kind of deal can a filmmaker expect from Docurama?

Ellen – We structure deals in a variety of ways. We have royalty deals, distribution deals, 50/50 deals – it really depends on the film, the filmmaker, and the sales potential for the film. How much risk the filmmaker wants to assume plays a big part. The price point and how many units we think we can sell all factor into determining the type of deal. Our deals last typically between 5-7 years. We do give advances, but they vary in amount based on those variables I just mentioned.

Q – What do you mean by risk?

Ellen – For example, in a 50/50 deal all of the costs that go into producing the DVD need to be recouped before anyone gets paid. Whereas in a royalty deal, the filmmaker get a percentage, say 25%, from the first dollar of revenue. So there's less upside since it's a 25% royalty versus a 50/50 profit share. But in the royalty situation we are assuming all the risk in terms of the outlay of money to produce the DVD. It's difficult to say which one to choose because it really depends on the film, how many units you think you are going to sell, etc.

Q – Do you do international as well as domestic?

Ellen – No. We primarily focus on the US and Canada. We have acquired worldwide rights in the past, and then we have relationships with foreign distributors that we'll sell rights to. But we're not in the business of manufacturing DVDs for other regions – you know, PAL versus NTSC and all of that.

Q – Do you interact with the filmmker on the artwork and deliverables?

Ellen – No one knows their film better than the filmmaker. That said, we have over 20 years experience in the home entertainment market and often we may have a better idea about what artwork will work best on the store shelf. So we try to harness the knowledge that the filmmaker has amassed to get the right extras content and the right look and feel for the film and then we bring in our expertise to get the final product. Ostensibly, the filmmaker has been out on the road with the film at festivals or the film has had a theatrical release. They know what kind of message works and who likes the film. When we're looking at putting extras on the DVD, or doing the commentaries or an interview, the filmmakers know what information or content those audiences are most interested in. With artwork, sometimes a film comes to us with key art that really works and is now recognizable in the marketplace. *Wild Parrots Of Telegraph Hill*, one of our latest success stories, was out there and did almost $3 million at the box office and had this really recognizable key art. So we replicated that on the DVD. Conversely, if the artwork doesn't work, we may completely change it. But we always do what we do with the input and collaboration of the filmmaker.

Q – What elements do you want from the filmmaker when you put the DVD together?

Ellen – The film, of course. Then we have a discussion about bonus materials. Our approach with bonus features is that they not be some slick, produced content as is often the case with studio films. We want content that is going to fill out the film and complement it. Often times it has been several years since the film was shot, so there has been progress or development with the characters. So we look for new material that has been shot, interviews, recorded Q&As, deleted scenes, etc. We need as much key art and photography as they have. We also ask for a really detailed list of who has responded to this film. Often times filmmakers have a mailing list that they have amassed. That's extremely important in order to get access to the right groups of people that would care about the film when the DVD becomes available.

Q – Do they give you an HD master?

Ellen – We're not quite at the HD stage yet. We're looking to the future and know that HD is coming pretty soon, but there's

GUERILLA FILM MAKER SAYS!

DIY DVD

If you want a great DVD for your film, then that means YOU will need to oversee the production. Leave it to the distributor or anyone else and you will no doubt get an uninspired collection of extras. We would all like our docs to be seen on the big screen, but the way technology is going, it's likely that this DVD is going to be where many see your movie. So make it special!

You can produce all the extras on miniDV or HDV – 'The Making Of...", Director's Commentary, Deleted Scenes, etc. So get interviewing yourself and make it interesting and snappy. Get as many of your main subjects and crew in as possible. This is also a great chance to put in a "what's happening to them now" sequence. Create some great menus in Photoshop etc. If you feel so inclined, you could master the whole thing yourself, though in practice, we would recommend letting a dedicated company with a track record do this. If you give them detailed notes (ideally a flowchart), all menus and backgrounds on disk, and all the video elements on tape (clearly labeled with in and out timecodes), then you should be abot to cut a GREAT deal. Maybe as little as $500.

They will burn you a DVD-R for you to test (it's a dual layer DVD9 disk then they will use two DVD-Rs or recompress to fit on a DVD-5 for testing only), and when you are happy with the job, they will export it all to a DLT tape which will go to the factory that will press your disks.

still a bit to be worked out before we get there.

Q – Is there anything about closed captioning or other languages they need to know?

Ellen – We don't close caption everything. Sometimes it's critical, though. We have a film coming out called *Touch The Sound*, which is about a percussionist who happens to be deaf. There are a number of core audiences for this film. There's a huge educational audience, a music audience and a large deaf audience. But with the deaf angle, to put a film out like that and not close caption it would be the wrong move. But it's a case-by-case decision. In the case of subtitling in other languages, it doesn't make a lot of sense for us most of the time. Why do Japanese subtitles for a film when we only have American rights for example?

Q – Do you do the authoring?

Ellen – We outsource that to several authoring houses in New York City and elsewhere. We may start doing some of that in-house, however. One of the things about authoring a DVD is that it is chaptered. We typically segment a film into 8-12 chapters of roughly equal length. No one knows the film quite like the filmmaker does, so we usually ask the filmmakers to provide us with ideas for how their film might be best split up.

Q – What kind of marketing and publicity do you do for your releases?

Ellen – We have a dedicated publicist who's out there working hard servicing all the regular home video outlets and publications. He also looks to the core markets for each film and tries to get into publications that don't necessarily review home video, but would be appropriate for the specific film. So with *Wild Parrots, Bird Fancy,* the magazine isn't a big DVD reviewer, but it focuses on one of our core markets for the film. And press is clearly the best way to get the word out on a film. We do advertising through the trades so that independent retail and rental stores can find out about the film and order it. We don't do a ton of advertising at the consumer level. For what it costs it doesn't make a lot of sense for us. Then again, sometimes it does if it's really targeted. For *Wild Parrots Of Telegraph Hill*, there is a huge regional market in and around San Francisco. So a 30 second commercial on Animal Planet in the San Francisco region is something we might do. But we are not taking out full-page ads in *Entertainment Weekly*.

Q – Can a filmmaker approach you directly?

Ellen – We have an acquisitions staff that's out there attending film festivals, meeting filmmakers, and sourcing content all the time. But we don't mind getting direct submissions, we just might take awhile to get back to you! We keep track of submissions, try to watch them in a timely manner, and we make sure to get back to everyone. Because the content we look for has some kind of profile, usually we'll have heard of the film before we receive it – but that isn't always the case.

Q – What are the common mistakes that you see documentary filmmakers make?

Ellen – Some filmmakers cannot give a concise synopsis of their film. You have a limited amount of time to get a clear sense of your film across to someone. So have a pithy, direct, cohesive statement of not only what your film is about, but what about your film is going to make someone want to watch it. One of the most important things we can get from the filmmaker is good art and good imagery. I can't tell you how many times filmmakers have not provided us with any photos at all. It's really hard for us to design a DVD package without imagery, and you really need to have clear, professional materials when presenting your film for submission.

Q – What advice would you give a new documentary filmmaker?

Ellen – If you want to get your film out there and make a name for yourself as a documentary filmmaker, I think you really have to think hard about the topics and subjects that you are selecting for your film. If you have this crazy grandmother and you've always wanted to make a documentary about her because it would be a shame not to have captured her on film before she goes, that's fine. But you can't go ahead with that project thinking it's going to be the next Sundance hit. If you're going for a career in documentary, you have to pick subjects that are compelling and aren't so niche that even if they make it into a festival they aren't going to go anywhere beyond that. You have to think about not only whom the audience is but if the final product is something they're going to want to watch.

Test Screenings

Even if a festival deadline is fast approaching, you should have a test screening of your film. Showing your doc to an impartial audience is a good way to tell if the mechanics of your story are working. While the opinions of the people watching your film are just that, opinions, for the most part, if a problem keeps being raised, you should attend to it.

1. Pure human emotion is always the best indicator of how things are going, so watch and listen to your audience. See if they're shifting in their seats, are they fidgeting or looking visually bored? Has anyone fallen asleep? Are they laughing in the right spots? Looking at their watch?

2. Have your editor copy the whole film with all the sound, sound effects, temp music onto VHS, DV or DVD. Where titles or scenes are missing, put up a card explaining what should be there.

3. You may have several test screenings. A small one with people whose opinions you respect would be a good starter to fix immediate problems. These can be people in the industry who can see technical problems that a general audience may not get. Once you make these changes, then have a larger test screening. Invite friends of friends who aren't in the industry and those who would be your target audience for your doc. Avoid family as viewers as they may not tell you the truth.

4. Remember a test screening is all about finding the problems. Don't expect anyone to praise your film, and if they do, ask them what they hated about it. Invite them to be as harsh as possible.

5. If you can't afford a video projection venue, then find someone with a huge TV and buy everyone pizza. Try to create as much of a theatrical experience as possible, so take the phone off the hook and switch off the mobile.

6. Draw up a questionnaire and ask them to fill it in. Do this before you get into a general discussion in order to reduce "group think". Have a big box of pens at the ready.

7. Have a freeform discussion at the end of the screening, and ask questions about the things you suspect may be a problem.

8. Your distributor or studio may require a test screening of their own so they know how to market your film and how much to budget. This will be with a complete unknown group in your target audience, and from all walks of life, to hopefully represent the audience who will eventually be viewing your movie.

9. This can be a harsh environment for directors and producers. Don't let subjects attend unless they are on your advisory board and can help spot problems.

EDUCATIONAL DISTRIBUTION

Q – Your organization focuses on documentaries as a teaching medium, who does your library reach?

Cynthia – DER's mission is to cultivate community engagement with the peoples and cultures of the world. Our programs reach millions of individuals each year through broadcast, film festivals and classrooms throughout the world. We sell directly to educational institutions worldwide including an extensive sub-distribution network throughout Asia. We address the need for tolerance and understanding of people who are different than ourselves. This need is universal and more evident in today's global political, social and cultural climate than ever before. Underlying the diversity of the films is the conviction that documentary and ethnographic films can broaden and alter preconceptions of marginalized and underrepresented peoples and cultures within the United States' population and abroad. We also maintain an archive of historical significance and public interest.

Q – Do you handle the US K-12 grade school market?

Cynthia – While K-12 has historically not been our focus market, we've made workshop presentations to help educators develop ways to utilize our collection in schools. As an example, the head teacher at the Moccasin Community Day School requested video donations to be used by their disadvantaged student body. We donated programs from our collection that feature young people dealing with socio-economic and cultural problems in a wide range of environments throughout the world. In exchange, we asked that the students write essays in response to the films. Submissions were judged and the winning students were allowed to pick a title of their choice from the DER film collection. We used the Moccasin Community Day School Project as a model for the development of a multicultural media workshop for schools and communities struggling with poverty and ethnic diversity. We've made strides in reaching teachers at the K-12 level through workshops and presentations on integrating global issues in curriculum. We have made curriculum and study guide material available as free downloadable PDF files off our web site. We're also starting to offer free programs via Google Video.

Q – Do you deal with museum distribution?

Cynthia – We work with museums in two ways; first many museums rent or buy films from us for their film programs and screenings. They also license footage from our archive that is often integrated in their exhibitions.

Q – What kind of documentaries are you looking for with regards to your distribution library?

Cynthia – While we come from a strong cinema verité tradition, we've broadened our interests to include many other stylistic approaches to documentary story telling such as experimental and animation. What we look for are programs where the esthetic fits the story, where content is king, and where the filmmakers demonstrate a deep commitment to and engagement with their subjects.

Q – What documentaries aren't you looking for?

Cynthia – Formulaic approaches, wall-to-wall narration, unnecessarily long docs and history.

Q – What are the best selling lengths for documentaries in your library?

Cynthia – Length does not factor in on popularity or sales. We have best selling shorts as well as full-length features.

Q – Do you have to become a member of DER to participate in the rental of your films?

Cynthia – No, we aren't a membership organization. We have a tiered pricing structure - institutional with public performance rights, K-12 teachers and Community Colleges, and consumer/home video.

Q – What kind of deal does the filmmaker receive from DER if their film is included in your library?

Cynthia – We offer royalty based on gross sales from all sources. We do not buy out rights. We have a standard contract that's negotiable. If there's competition for a film that we really want to acquire we'll offer a cash advance on the royalties.

Q – Do you license any of your films to broadcasters? If so, what kind of deal does a filmmaker receive?

Cynthia – Yes. 50% of gross is our standard. Again, negotiable depending on the circumstances.

Q – Have you noticed more of an interest and awareness in cross cultural documentaries in America since 9/11?

Cynthia – Absolutely! Interest in our programs has exploded and increased even more dramatically in the past two years. We respond to current events and our archive is historically important. For example, following 9/11 we focused attention on our films from Afghanistan from 1970 to the 1980's to offer in depth information on the geography, people and culture beyond the sound bites of network TV.

Q – How important is it for the documentary filmmaker to look at the community outreach of their film?

Cynthia – This is becoming essential for most funders. It should be a built in component of every filmmakers business, funding, and distribution plan.

Q – Can you help find funding or finishing funds for a documentary filmmaker? How successful is the response to the films seeking donations on your website?

Cynthia – Through our role as a fiscal sponsor we currently support the work of 27 independent filmmakers whose subjects range from an examination of Native Alaskan sovereignty within historical, cultural, spiritual and political contexts to *The Mathare Project* where the filmmaker has been living in and documenting life in an orphanage in Kenya over a period of years. As a result of our support, all these projects have raised some funds moving them closer to completion - others have been fully realized. We have a rolling deadline. To initiate an application we require a treatment (ideally two pages), bios of the production team and a budget. A trailer is not required, but previous film work may be requested.

Q – How important is the internet in today's distribution of documentaries?

Cynthia – Essential! Without the internet, we would have been out of business several years ago.

Q – How does a filmmaker approach you if they have a film that they'd like to be included in your library?

Cynthia – E-mail is a good start. They should first visit our website to see if they feel their film would be at home with us.

Q – What common mistakes do you see with documentary filmmakers that could be avoided?

Cynthia – We often get DVDs or other previews for acquisition with no indication of how long the piece is. Also, often there isn't sufficient contact information on the material sent to us.

Q – What advice would you offer a documentary filmmaker?

Cynthia – Know whom you are talking to! I hate it when a filmmaker wastes our time by sending us programs that are clearly not anything that would interest us. Do some research before you make that initial contact. Go to a distributor's or funder's web site before you make your first phone call or send an email query to them. People appreciate the fact that you took the time to do this. It also saves everyone time in the end.

GUERILLA FILM MAKER SAYS!

Distribution Agreement Pointers...

1. An advance. Rarely given, usually only if the film needs completion money, in which case the distributor/agent might take a higher commission.

2. Number of Years for the rights to be licensed to the Distributor/ Sales Agent: From 5-35, standard is 5-10 years. NOT in perpetuity. Try to have the initial term be relatively short (say 2 years) with automatic rollovers should the distributor deliver a certain amount of revenue in that time and/or a specified slate of theatrical releases occur, which in the US should include New York and Los Angeles screenings. If those performance requirements are not met, all rights would automatically return to the filmmaker.

3. Extent of Rights being requested by Distributor/Sales Agent: i.e worldwide, worldwide excluding domestic to be negotiated between the parties.

4. Fees/rate of commission: Usually between 20-25%. Sometimes 30% depending on the extent of input by Distributor/Sales Agent and this should be limited so that the Distributor takes only one commission per country.

5. Ownership: Make sure you, the producer, will still own the copyright to the film – not applicable if you are selling the doc to the Distributor. If you are licensing the rights to certain territories you will remain the copyright owner.

6. CAP on expenses: Make sure there is a maximum limit (a ceiling) on expenses and that you are notified in writing of any large expenses i.e. over a specified amount, that you are able to refute if necessary.

7. Direct Expenses: Make sure that overheads of the Distributor and the staff expenses are not included in Distribution expenses and will not be added as a further expense.

8. Sub Distributor Fees: Make sure that these fees are paid by the Distributor/Sales Agent out of its fees and not in addition to the Distribution expenses.

9. Consider your position on Net Receipts: i.e. monies after Distributor has deducted their commission and fees subject to any sales agreements you enter into with a Distributor. Make sure this is clearly delineated in the contract with no loopholes. Remember that taxes should be taken out of gross receipts not net receipts.

10. Errors and Omissions Policy: See if this is to be included in the delivery requirements as this could be an added unexpected expense. Distributors are often willing to absorb this cost and recoup from gross profits. It is important that you as the filmmaker are added as an additional named insured on the policy.

11. Cross Collaterization: Where the Distributor will offset expenses and losses on their other films against yours. You don't want this.

12. P&A (Prints and Advertising) commitment from the Distributor: Negotiate total expenses that will be used on P&A in the contract i.e. a fixed sum. Include a Floor and a ceiling.

13. Domestic Theatrical Release: Negotiate what print run is expected, and in what locations. Specify what locations so that you don't find a clause in your contract such as 'your film will be released in three of the top one hundred markets'.

14. Distribution Editing Rights: Limit for only censorship requirements although if you are dealing with a major Distributor this will not be acceptable.

15. Producer's input in the marketing campaign.

16. Trailer commitment: will this be another hidden additional cost? Make sure theaters have this in plenty of time.

17. Release Window: Get Distributor to commit to release the film within a time frame after delivery of film to Distributor.

18. Audit Rights: The Producer has the rights to inspect the books with a ten-day notice re: the distribution of the film. The Filmmaker should receive statements (either quarterly or monthly) from the distributor with any payment due to the filmmaker.

19. LIMITATION ON ACTION: You want to make sure that you have enough time to act on any accounting irregularity that you may discover. Fight to have at least a three- year period from receipt of a questionable financial statement, or discovery of any accounting irregularity, whichever is later, in which to file a demand for arbitration.

GUERILLA FILM MAKER SAYS!

...Distribution Agreement Pointers cont.

20. If the Sales Agent intends to group your film with other titles to produce an attractive package for buyers, ensure that your film is not unfairly supporting other films or that you are receiving a disproportionate or unfair percentage.

21. Make sure that the rights revert back to the Producer in case of any type of insolvency or if the Agent is in material breach of the agreement.

22. Check the Delivery requirements very carefully.

23. Indemnity: Make sure you receive reimbursement for losses incurred by you as a result of distributor's breach of the terms of the agreement, violation of third party rights, and for any changes or additions made to the film.

24. Lab Access Letter: Distributor should not be permitted to remove masters from the lab nor take possession of the original negative and any other original materials. They may have a lab access for supervised use of the negative and other materials for duplication or promotional purposes.

25. Termination Clause: If the distributor defaults on any of its contractual obligations, the filmmaker should have the right to terminate the contract, and regain rights to license the film in unsold territories as well as obtain money damages for the default. Filmmaker should give distributor 14 days prior written notice of default before exercising the right to termination.

26. Arbitration Clause: This ensures that any contractual disputes may be solved through binding arbitration with the prevailing party entitled to reimbursement of legal fees and cost by the losing party. For the best results, the parties should submit such action to binding arbitration with the AFMA (American Film Market Association) arbitration division. The Distributor will fight for Arbitration to take place near them locally. If they're not local to you, either fight for arbitration to occur locally to you or in a place of equidistance to the two of you.

27. Filmmaker Warranties: Filmmakers warranties in regard to infringement of third party rights should be to the best of the Filmmaker's knowledge and belief, not absolute.

28. LATE PAYMENTS/LIEN: All monies due and payable to the filmmaker should be held in trust by the distributor for the filmmaker, and the filmmaker should be deemed to have a lien on filmmaker's share of revenue. The distributor should pay the filmmaker interest on any amounts past due.

29. SCHEDULE OF MINIMUMS: For each foreign territory for which a distributors or foreign sales agent who licenses foreign sales rights, there should be a schedule of minimum acceptable license fees per territory. The distributor is not permitted to license the film in each territory for less than the minimum without the filmmaker's approval.

30. FILMMAKER DEFAULT: The distributor should give filmmaker 14 days written notice of any alleged default by filmmaker, and an additional 10 days to cure such a default, before taking any action to enforce it's rights.

John Vanco
IFC Center, NYC

INDIE THEATER

Q – Are there any criteria for the kind of documentaries you show at the IFC Center?

John – Because I'm in New York, I have the luxury of being able to program what I think is the best, without having to make any concessions for commercial concerns. If we program films that get support from the press, they might only appeal to a niche audience, but in New York those audiences run pretty deep. Also there's a passion driven aesthetic is how Noah Cowan and I picked films for Cowboy Films, our distribution company. So I'm not really limited by anything other than my own aesthetic.

Q – Do you usually screen the films before you show them?

John – Yes. And that's true with most art house cinemas in New York. You have to think long and hard about what audience a film is going to have. The films we do don't have a lot of P&A dollars behind them so there's a lot of pressure on the film to provide it's own marketing engine to attract audiences without the marketing tools that more mainstream releases get. We spend a lot of time trying to figure out what kind of reviews it will get. What kind of word of mouth is it going to generate. How are we going to get people to come out to it? So looking at the film is the first step in all of this.

Q – Do you help advertise the film or is that mostly on the filmmaker?

John – It's mostly on the filmmaker, but in New York many theaters do ads in the weeklies and the *New York Times*, which are small and basically list the days programs. But if someone wants to do some display advertising on top of that, that decision and expense is on the filmmaker or distributor.

Q – Have you seen any special advertising that filmmakers have done that were unique?

John – There're a lot of grass roots promotions that come into play for documentaries all the time. That goes especially for social issue documentaries that have a core constituency that really cares about those problems. People do special screenings for those groups and then go to places where those people are and hand out post cards and so forth. Then of course there's the internet and there've been a lot of success stories with how people can get out, fairly inexpensively, information on their movie.

Q – Whom do you usually deal with in getting films into your theater?

John – Usually the distributor. We'll take on a film from a foreign sales agent when there's no US distribution. In which case we'll do the publicity and marketing of the film ourselves. There are situations when we deal directly with the filmmaker when they have retained the rights and aren't working with a sales agent or a distributor.

Q – What is the standard deal that you do with a distributor?

John – For a new film, we usually do a locked run of one or two weeks. There's always the possibility of holding over beyond that if a film does really well. In terms of revenue, we do the standard New York theater deal which is a 90%/10% split. It's a little more complicated that the deals around the country, but basically the theater will retain a house allowance for a film playing for a week. The house allowance is like rent. After that house allowance, which is sometimes called the house nut, the payout is 90% to the filmmaker and 10% to the theater. If you don't make the house allowance, then there is a floor of 25% that goes to the filmmaker. And if we did publicity or press screenings, we'd deduct that from the amount that goes to the filmmaker. Also the filmmaker bears part of our directory listing cost.

Q – What is common in the rest of the US?

John – The amount to the filmmaker is based on a flat percentage. It's usually around 35% and there may or may not be expenses taken out of that. For the bigger theaters and the chains it is still based on a percentage, but you might get a sliding deal. So the first week you get 60%, then the second week you get 50%, then 40% and 30% and it goes down as you get further into the run. But unless you are at a firmed terms theater, which there aren't a whole lot of, it's basically a negotiation with each theater.

Q – What is the gap of time between agreeing to run a film and screening it?

John – Usually it's about a 3-5 month window and that's a little longer than it is for most theaters. Sometimes you open a film on Friday and it does worse that expected. On Monday you're already looking for a new film for that next Friday. It doesn't happen much with us because we're tightly booked.

Q – What is four walling and would you recommend it?

John – It's paying a fairly high fee to own all the playtime in a particular auditorium for a week. So you can give a theater $5,000 and you can play your film for a whole schedule and any ticket sales in that week go 100% to you the filmmaker. If you gross more than $5,000, then you did OK. If you gross less, then you lose money. Filmmakers do four walls most often when they can't convince theaters to play a film in a conventional way. It's usually a last resort situation. And if that's your only option, then it might be because your film doesn't belong in a theater based on the marketing tools that you have at that point. The other side of four walling is if you have something heavily branded like Spike & Mike's tour of shorts, and you know you have a big, predictable audience coming, then you can make a lot of money four walling.

Q – In the calendar year, are there any dates or times that aren't recommended for opening a documentary film?

John – It used to be a little more complicated. For a long time people wouldn't open small, niche films in the summer because that's when the big Hollywood movies took over. And early December was a bad time because it's just before the Oscar movies come out and everyone is Christmas shopping. Now it's changed where every weekend is a bad weekend to open a little movie because it' so crowded. Even early December now that they've moved that Oscars up, everything is not clogged up at the end of December. It's all spread out from Thanksgiving on. A small movie opening in the teeth of the Oscar releases is going to have a hard time. But generally, a good week to open your movie is when there are no other movies opening that are going after your audience. And you can't predict that because everything shifts. You can strategize a bit, but you don't want to be defensively shifting your film all over the place.

Q – When do you start putting trailers for films in theaters and how long are they?

John – A good trailer is between 90 seconds and two minutes. And we'll play a trailer as early as eight weeks prior to the opening. But we'll only play three or four trailers at a time. We give preference to the movies that are playing sooner. So we might get a trailer in and it will have to wait in line until there is room available.

Q – How have documentary films been doing at the box office?

John – Michael Moore's movies have made a big difference in terms of convincing everyone that docs can do big box office. The market place is cyclical. In the 1970's and 1980's there were big docs that did very well. *Woodstock* and *The Last Waltz*, which were music themed and then *Noah's Ark* that did well across the country. Now it seems that the political docs are finding audiences, but it's not really a new thing for docs to find success. We do well with docs. They tend to be more review and word of mouth driven than opening weekend box office numbers driven. We played *Darwin's Nightmare* here last August and it had a good opening weekend and it held really well and stuck around for a long time. Then we brought it back when it got nominated for an Oscar and it held on again. It opened to an $8,000 weekend and throughout it's run it grossed about $66,000 at our theater.

Q – What kind of film and sound formats can you screen?

John – 35mm and HD Digital. We can run that off of HDCAM. We can do PAL or NTSC. We can do Digibeta or Beta SP. And we also run some programs off a server or hard drive. For sound we use Dolby Digital.

Q – Is the hard disk projection becoming more popular?

John – The studios and the big exhibition chains are fighting over who is going to pay for converting the tens of thousands of screens in America to digital. And until the dust clears a few years from now when we know what the standards are, not much is going to change. For us, we are able to show more and better programs and have flexibility by being able to show all these formats. It's fairly common for most art houses to have some form of digital projection.

Q – Is there anything a documentary filmmaker can do to benefit their screening?

John – Use marketing tools like posters, trailers, postcards, flyers, word of mouth screenings and online campaigns. For people who have made a good documentary, I usually tell them to get a distributor or hire a consultant to advise you through the process. You usually only have one shot to do something for your film, so don't hamper your chances. Just make sure the people that you ask help from are experienced.

Q – What are the common mistakes that you see documentary filmmakers make?

John – A common problem is to not take good on set still photography. It's the most basic of deliverables and it becomes very difficult, especially when your distributor is trying to do things cheaply, to do any marketing materials without good art. So get someone who knows what they're doing and have them take good photos. It makes a big difference.

Q – What advice would give a new documentary filmmaker?

John – Watch a lot of great documentaries. Spend a lot of time seeing how people have achieved telling really great stories and new ways of telling them. And be in it for the love of filmmaking and because you are in it to tell the story you want to tell. Don't be in it because you want to make a lot of money or have a stable career with it. Your gratification should come from the work itself.

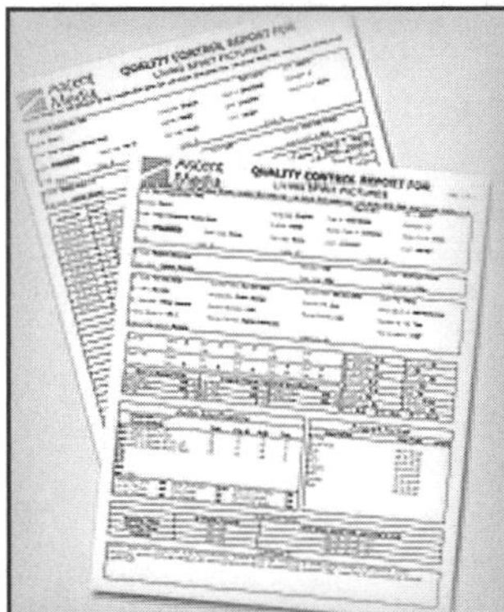

GUERILLA FILM MAKER SAYS!

The QC Report

Quality Control is used by sales agents, distributors and broadcasters, to ensure your film reaches the rigid technical standards required for international sales. The QC report (quality control) is usually two or even three sheets long. The first page is a very detailed list of what is on the tape, it's format and technical information in excrutiating detail. It also lists problems in a summary... and it's these problems that you need to deal with. They will be detailed on the second sheet. Problems are listed, with timecodes, and they are rated in severity. 5 is considered Imperceptible, 1 is considered Very Annoying. Most frustrating is the fact that much of the QC process is subjective. With one company it could pass, yet with another it could fail. Only excellence all round will guarantee a pass. Not all companies use the same paperwork, although it's likely to be very similar to this example here.

Q/C Failure Reasons

Video blanking (rare)
Problem *- this is where a border has been put on the master, either at the top and bottom or on the sides. If it extends too far into the picture area it will fail.*
Solution *- don't put any video bars on your master.*

Crushed blacks (common)
Problem *- the video levels drop below 0.3v and picture information. is lost.*
Solution *- the video signal can be boosted, but this should never have happened if you had kept an eye on the waveform monitor.*

Crushed whites (common)
Problem *- the video signal has peaked over 1v and so picture information in the whites is lost.*
Solution *- the video signal can be clamped down, but this should never have happened if you'd kept an eye on the waveform monitor.*

High error rates (rare)
Problem *- the DigiBeta machine used to master the tape produced too many digital errors for it to play back on other machines, although it would play back the tape itself.*
Solution *- either clone onto a new tape from the original machine or re-master!*

Picture drop-out (medium)
Problem *- distortion & errors, caused by dust or tape problems.*
Solution *- most commonly this will mean transferring to a new tape and cleaning up the errors, either in a paint program or by going back to the source material for the problem shots.*

Audio dropout / spikes etc. (common)
Problem *- there can be errors on the sound which means it may spike or pop, or disappear all together.*
Solution *- go to the original mix and check it. If it's OK then re-lay onto master. If not, you may need to re-mix the audio for that part.*

Audio peaking (medium)
Problem *- the audio peaks and potentially distorts on transmission or duplication.*
Solution *- re-lay the sound pulling the levels down at that point, or pass the sound through a compressor / limitor box.*

Weave (rare)
Problem *- the image weaves from side to side. Only a problem on film, usually S16mm, and most noticeable on titles or static shots. Rare to be a real problem.*
Solution *- not much can be done, short of major digital stabilization. Get your check-book out!*

Joins kick in gate (rare)
Problem *- the physical edit on film jumps on screen. Caused by a cheap neg cut and most common on S16mm.*
Solution *- do your neg cut with a good company in the first place!*

Audio too low (medium)
Problem *- the audio is too low. As well as a technical problem, this may also be because you have a very dynamic mix, or it may be a creative choice.*
Solution *- remix , or pass the mix through a compressor limitor to make the quieter bits louder.*

Too dark (subjective)
Problem *- the picture is deemed consistently too dark. Even if you have made a 'dark' film, this can be a problem.*
Solution *- re-grade the picture brighter.*

Too grainy (common for S16mm without DVNR)
Problem *- the picture contains too much grain, usually a problem from Super 16mm only.*
Solution *- re-telecine, passing the image through a DVNR box, which will dynamically process the image and reduce the effects of grain (as well as dust and sparkle).*

Dust and sparkle (common)
Problem *- Image contains dust & sparkle. Only a problem for film.*
Solution *- passing the telecine through DVNR may help, but most likely you will need a de-spotting session where a technician manually 'paints out' the blemishes.*

Hairs in gate (medium)
Problem *- a hair was trapped in the camera gate when shooting. Only a problem with film.*
Solution *- either replace the shot OR manually paint it out. Any foreign object can cause a similar problem (such as a boom in shot etc.)*

Audio hiss (common)
Problem *- the audio is poorly mixed and has a lot of hiss.*
Solution *- possible to filter some, but you may need to re-mix properly.*

Bo Smith
Museum of Fine Arts, Boston

MUSEUM DISTRIBUTION

Q – Why does the Museum of Fine Arts, Boston program so many documentaries?

Bo – I've always shown a lot of documentaries ever since I started programming in the 1970's. There's perhaps a larger audience for a non-fiction film than a fiction film within alternative venue presentation, such as museums as there are more people committed to certain issues and subject matter than there are generally committed to supporting independent narrative features.

Q – Are you looking for anything specific in either genre or theme when you program?

Bo – I look for great films, number one. And then after I find great films, I have to find a way to effectively program them so that there's a responsive audience that's drawn to see them. I have to reach organizations that support the culture or a subject matter of the film. Many of the screenings that we do, I'm already familiar with these places so I don't have to reinvent the wheel many times. Other times, I do and I have to find a way to reach them.

Q – Boston seems to have a plethora of groups interested in documentary film?

Bo – Boston is a great town to program in. We have a population that generally wants to learn. And Boston has many educational institutions that we can work with in order to add a scholarly slant to our presentations.

Q – How do you find the films that you program?

Bo – We go through distributors. Sometimes people come to us. And sometimes we go to film festivals and find things we like.

Q – Can the filmmaker come to you directly?

Bo – Sure. And many do.

Q – What kind of deal would they get from you if they came in direct?

Bo – I think that if people come to us directly the deal is more likely to be more advantageous for them than if it were through their distributor. It's a deal that is usually fair for all sides because there is more room for flexibility.

Q – Is there anything unique about showing a film in a museum setting?

Bo – Yes. We have people predisposed to art and to appreciating and wanting to learn more about artistic experiences in general. That's our advantage. People come here with that in mind. So if there are films that relate to art and artists, and there are a growing number of them over the last 25 years, that's a big terrain for us to focus on.

Q – What kind of formats can you screen?

Bo – We prefer 35mm - we have Surround Dolby - and NTSC Beta SP. We don't have Digibeta and we don't have PAL Beta SP. We haven't done Hi Def, yet. Really, we can project anything on video as long as we can rent a deck or make a transfer. And we'll organize that for the filmmaker.

Q – You seem to have a lot of film festivals that come through the museum.

Bo – There's a big difference between a festival that we organize and one in which an independent festival organization uses us as a location. So the French Film Festival, the Gay and Lesbian and the Iranian Festivals, we do all the legwork on. While the Jewish, the Independent Film Festival and the Roxbury Festival have independent organizations that do the legwork. For the most part, we stick with an annual pattern because the media and the public are expecting it and it pays off to have something that people are anticipating without you starting from scratch to promote it.

Q – How did you come involved with the African Film Festival?

Bo – It came out of a New York organization, the African Film Festival, that for a good number of years has made their festival available to other sites. So that's a case of a touring package that gives us the core of a festival and then we supplement that core with other films. This year it's about half and half.

Q – Are you involved in curating exhibitions in other areas of the museum that may contain documentary film or video presentations?

Bo – I have been involved a little bit in things that enhance an exhibition, but for the most part I am not too involved. I might direct people to different films that would be useful.

Q – What are the common mistakes that you see documentary filmmakers make in getting their work shown?

Bo – This weekend I looked at some films and saw that there's a growing body of work of these personal essays that have been fairly successful in getting modest support from foundations. It's work that I really like, but it's work however, that as a programmer where I have to get people in seats and pay for admission, it's tricky. I don't know if it's obvious what the subject is and while a lot of people would enjoy the work, I don't know if you can attract people if they don't know it's about an issue that they care about. It's a big bugaboo with documentaries in general that there are very few people who have on their list that they have to see a documentary today. The only people that you attract to documentaries are the people who care passionately about that subject. I guess there's hope now that there have been enough successes in the marketplace that people will understand that documentaries can be fun and rewarding. And I think younger people might have a slightly different attitude than older people about that.

Q – What advice would you give a new documentary filmmaker?

Bo – Have some sense of who the audience is going to be for your film. Or if you're making a film for screenings to people who are on the very margins, understand that it is a really tiny crowd that comes to them because they are academically committed.

GOOGLE VIDEO

Q – How can Google Video help a documentary filmmaker?

Jen – Google Video provides an innovative way for filmmakers to distribute their work and discover new audiences around the world - without forgoing their rights. We have an open model where filmmakers control how their work is offered to viewers, from setting the price and free preview to geo-targeting and copy protection. Through the power and simplicity of search, documentary filmmakers can easily reach new viewers, even if their work appeals to an extremely small niche.

Q – What kind of content is Google looking for?

Jen – Google Video is all about giving users access to video content that was not previously accessible. To fulfill that goal, we're open to content from all types of professional and amateur content producers.

Q – What content does Google never want?

Jen – Google Video's policy disallows the use of material that may promote hatred or advocate against any group such as religion, sexual orientation or race as well as any content that infringe copyright.

Q – How does one approach Google with a film?

Jen – Any producer - large or small - can upload their content onto Google Video via https://upload.video.google.com/

Q – Does Google solicit films from filmmakers? If so how do you find them?

Jen – The content acquisition team actively works on getting filmmakers to upload videos onto Google Video. We don't discuss our specific acquisition strategy or methods.

Q – What kind of license fee does Google give a filmmaker? How long does the deal last for? What rights is Google buying?

Jen – Google does not charge a license fee to filmmakers. We host, serve, and index their videos for free. If they decide to sell their film on Google Video, they will get a 70% revenue share. The content owner retains all rights to his content.

Q – How long does the film stay up on Google Video?

Jen – As long as the filmmaker wants. If they use the self-upload service, they can delete their film whenever they want. They retain complete control on how and when they want to distribute their film.

Q – What format does the film have to be delivered to Google on? Does Google help with compression and the technical aspects?

Jen – Our preferred formats are AVI, ASF, QuickTime, Windows Media and MPEG formats. Specific video codecs we accept include H.264, H.263, MPEG 1/2/4 and motion JPEG. One thing to keep in mind is that the higher the quality of the video you can provide to Google Video, the better your video will look on our site. I have have content originating from camera phones, webcams, etc., please upload your file as is from those sources. For content originating from a DV camera or other high quality source, we recommend encoding at full-frame size and a high bit rate (you won't go wrong with interlaced MPEG2 at >5Mbps and 720x480 or 720x576 resolution).

Q – How long of a film can you accept?

Jen – In the spirit of openness, producers are welcome to upload a film or other content of any length.

Q – What other cross-promotional things can a documentary filmmaker do with Google?

Jen – Depending on the quality and uniqueness of the content and its value to our users, Google will often consider doing various promotions with the filmmaker.

Q – What are the common mistakes you see documentary filmmakers make?

Jen – That they don't do all their homework on all the ways they can promote, distribute and monetize their film above and beyond the traditional vehicles.

Q – What advice would you give a new documentary filmmaker?

Jen – A new documentary filmmaker should learn all the new ways to promote, distribute and monetize their film(s) and that the internet has evened out the playing field for all large and small filmmakers. There are tremendous opportunities out there if they choose to be creative - ultimately, they may no longer have to sacrifice art for profit.

GUERILLA FILM MAKER SAYS!

When Disaster Strikes

1. Don't avoid legal issues or leave taking legal advice to the last minute. Get on them as soon as they arise.

2. If you think your distributor is being dishonest, at a minimum, write them a letter stating what you think is wrong. Be nice at first and then get progressively more adversarial if they resist. Copy the letter (cc:) to your attorney so that the distribution company knows you are involving them.

3. A contract agreement cannot force someone into action, but a good one has remedies so if someone is dishonest, you could get monies or your film back.

4. Try to have your contracts made in your company's name instead of your own so that any bankruptcy or lawsuit issues do not affect you personally.

5. Have a clear paper trail of who owns the copyright on a project so you can defend yourself.

6. Have a bankruptcy contingency clause in your agreements stating that if your distributor goes under, the film copyright reverts back to you.

7. Arbitration favors the wealthy. If you don't have any money, avoid going to arbitration if you can and sue them instead.

8. Sometimes the only recourse is to ride out the deal and get your film back. If it is a valuable title, you will still be able to sell it. If it is too old and no one wants it, try a gimmick like making a director's cut or adding new commentary features to attract sales agents.

9. If you are owed money by a company that goes under, stay on the person's bankruptcy proceedings. People will try to get away with things if they are not checked.

10. Actors and crew cannot take their names off films if they have a contractual obligation to do so.

11. As a last resort, you can get an injunction to stop a film from being released. They are VERY expensive and should only be done if you know you are right and the end result will be hundreds of thousand or even millions of pounds.

12. Bankruptcy does offer you an out to your problems, but you will have a bad credit rating for a long time, which may effect your ability to get a mortgage or an auto loan.

OUTFOXED: DIY DISTRIBUTION

Q – Many documentaries take the traditional path of distribution - theatrical, TV, and DVD. Do you think this is dying model?

Robert – How much trouble do I want to get into with all my friends who do this for a living? I think that clearly we're in the most revolutionary time of distribution that any of us been through. You can't read the papers fast enough to keep up with the changes. A year and a half ago if you'd talked about CBS selling TV shows on Ipods you'd have been arrested. To the degree that documentaries have limited audiences, and there are exceptions, I think the technology in general is going to be more helpful. That's why advertisers are having heart attacks, but they'll eventually get there in terms of targeting whom to reach. So I think theaters will always be an element of it in varying degrees. But whether it's on the same day or with *Outfoxed* where we went into theaters after the DVD was out or *Wal-Mart* where it was simultaneous - I think it behooves everybody to be wide open to doing it differently. Nobody is smart enough to know exactly what that's going to be, but I think the people who stick out their tongues and have a hissy fit and say they are only going to do it the way it has been done are in deep trouble.

Q – Did you originally want to go down the traditional path with your documentaries?

Robert – The first one I did which was *Uncovered*, I started June of 2003 and my partners were political folk, they weren't filmmakers. I ran out of money and I went to some people for help in July and they wanted it for the beginning of August. They didn't know film and I said it was impossible. But it was actually great because it shifted my thinking. What I realized was that I was making a film that people wanted to impact a current debate. Not 5, 10 or 15 years later. So I geared myself and whatever motley crew I had at the time and we got it out in October/November. So with that timetable after having made 55 movies with the traditional system, it never occurred to me that you could move that quickly. They're right. The country was debating the war and what went on. I had two partners. One was the Center for American Progress, which does think tank and access to opinion makers and the other was Move On. So I took my new partners and my old notion of an opening day and put it all together. We're going to have one screening in DC with opinion makers and that same day we are going to use Move On, Buzz Flash and Alternet and The Nation to open online. So we had a new model of an opening day. And to my shock and amazement, not shock and awe, it worked.

Q – And because of the success of that you decided to continue that model?

Robert – It was two things.I didn't have to ask anyone's permission. It was the most liberating thing in the world. I didn't have to go begging these people to show it in a theater, a film festival or television. Now the thing that has come clear to me after *Outfoxed* and *Wal-Mart* is that if you're interested in impacting social change, it's a non-argument that this is the way to go. Who's going to pay $7-$10 to see a documentary on subject that you disagree with or don't care about? But if it's playing at your school, your relative invites you over, it's at your church - all right, I'll go see it. So we're reaching people that you'd never reach if we went traditional. I've made this transition and I'm passionately committed to it.

Q – What does that grass roots distribution entail as far as strategy?

Robert – Unbelievable amounts of work. I hired a grass roots organizer before I shot anything on *Wal-Mart*. Everybody hates Wal-Mart - a thousand groups hate them. So she started calling them and building partners. Then we committed to a date. We committed to having a series of issues that we'd touch upon in the movie, labor, environment, etc. - so they'd know their issue would at least be part of it. And we worked out a system where they'd get money for every DVD they sell.

Q – What are these house parties that you encourage?

Robert – We set up a website and people can sign up to be a host. Some of these groups would then host at a church and we'd have over 8,000 house parties in our opening week. We would've had 700,000-800,000 people watching the film in the first week. If you want to go to a house party, you go to the website, put in your zip code and you can find one near you.

Q – Is it all projection or does it stream over the web?

Robert – It's all projection because we still need to sell some DVDs. Plus the technology isn't completely there to download a movie off the web and play it. But one day I hope to get some funding and do tha with some of the political stuff.

Q – Do you notice a rush of sales after a house party?

Robert – What we've tracked is if people would do it again, and would they take political action – these are the key issues for us. Certainly, when there's publicity and a lot of attention, we sell DVDs, but if your model is just to maximize every dollar, then you shouldn't do the house parties. It's 800,000 people and only 8,000 have paid for the DVD. Now if we had money we could ship DVDs to all the screenings and then people could then buy them. We don't have those resources. But people are committing to take political action after seeing the film.

Q – What are some good tips for free or cheap publicity?

Robert – Well, the website doesn't cost much as you know. Having a webstie is more important than the film itself. The trick is if you have a targeted audience, say nuns who ride on motorcycles, then you go searching for those groups and you start connecting and linking to them. If you've done a documentary about a terrific young woman with red hair who comes of age, it is tougher. But if your audience can be specified, then it's possible with little money and a lot of time on the web, to get to them. Chat rooms are good, too.

Q – Should you give your project over to someone else to promote?

Robert – I think the days of giving it over to someone else are almost gone, even in the traditional world. If someone picks up your documentary to be in theaters you are going to be on tour. You don't have to sell every copy yourself, but you are working on it. Even with big studio movies, you have to do three months of press. I'm sure collectives will grow up; documentary filmmakers will get together to do it. You just have to seize the idea that the old is either changing or over.

Q – Any other tips on self-distribution?

Robert – Here's my theory: if I'm going to put in 18 hours a day, I'd rather put it into distributing my movie myself than trying to convince somebody to distribute my movie. Either way you're going to put in the time. One is calling people who don't call you back and the other is building a website and connecting with groups, going out speaking, creating a trailer and the like. That's my preference. We all have the fantasy that we're going to make the film and then some big daddy or mommy is going to come in and take good care of it. And we're going to go on and make our next film. There are probably two or three people in the world for whom that happens, but for the rest of us who are mortal - give it up.

Q – How are the new medias going to affect distribution?

Robert – It's already started. Kodak has the contest to make two-minute short films and you can make a movie and put it on Google. I think there are a huge new distribution channels. The question is can you make a two-minute documentary

Going Under

GUERILLA FILM MAKER SAYS!

1. Make a deal – if your creditor thinks they won't get paid. Offer them half or even less and they may take it, but you will have to pay there and then.

2. Offer to pay it off at a small amount of money per month. If it is vaguely reasonable, they will accept.

3. No one wants to force you to go bust, it costs a lot, takes a long time and often, no one wins.

4. If you do want to go into insolvency, let them push you into it. They'll then have to pay the liquidator or receiver rather than you.

5. If you go into liquidation, you will have to supply all your books and records which will be scrutinised. Make sure you didn't do anything illegal or undeclared.

6. If serious negligence or fraud is discovered, you will be barred from being a company director again.

7. Hopefully you will have made your film under a company as if you didn't, you can be made bankrupt and everything you own can be taken, bar the tools of your trade.

8. Keep talking to your creditors and it may not even get that far.

9. Seek legal advice immediately – let's hope the company forcing you into liquidation isn't your lawyers.

10. Going bankrupt gives you a bad credit score. Bankruptcy details remain on people's ratings for up to six years, so it will take a few years of good credit practice to return a rating to health.

on a cell phone? I'd love to, but I don't know what it is yet. What do you do for a podcast? What's the difference between watching something on your cell phone versus a computer monitor? Generationally, it might not matter. My son who is 13 doesn't differentiate where he sees something. Totally platform agnostic as they say.

Q – Would you recommend a new documentary filmmaker find a grass roots company to help distribute the film?

Robert – I don't know that there's a grass roots company. There are kind of advisors you can find. But I think with no money, which generally means you have some time, you can find and connect to the people in the world who would have an interest in your film. And theoretically, when you did the documentary you were immersed in that world. I love the political stuff that I'm doing so I build these alliances. I know everyone in the Wal-Mart universe now. So it's not a stretch to work with them and get the film screened. Any other subject could do the same, too.

Q – And you are better off if you can cut out the middleman.

Robert – Psychologically, I certainly am. I would rather be frustrated at my own efforts than be angry at trying to get some middleman to do something. And in general I think that's the way the world is moving. If you sell a hundred copies of your DVDs on your website and you are charging $12 or $15 and you are able to keep $8 or $9 of that, it's good. But you want to keep the cost down as well because people will take a chance buying a DVD if you keep it under $10.

Q – How did Outfoxed get its theatrical release following its DVD release?

Robert - The irony is that I had made this transition on the documentaries even though I came through the traditional world and I wasn't even thinking about a theatrical release. And then a distributor said that they'd like to take it out. I said, *"You know it's out on DVD?"* And he said, *"Yeah."* But I think there are both audiences.

Q – Did you do a different cut of Wal-Mart for the international market?

Robert – Yes. The movie was too long. But I had some DVD extras and there was stuff from the UK and I think one was from Canada. We thought we could put this into the international version, which is a more traditional way of thinking so that the international people see that it is an international story. But I just got back from touring around Berlin, London, Edinburgh and Dublin and the consist comment was, *"Thank you. You showed us something about the United States that we didn't know or understand."* So in retrospect even though we did it that way, I don't think it is necessary. I think the thing that the sales people and the distributors will learn is that if you make an interesting film the audience will come.

Q – Do you think it would have made a difference had you released the international version here in America?

Robert – I don't think so. There wasn't that much of a difference. Had I done a huge recut, maybe. I am embarrassed by how much footage I shot on this movie. I could have a 20-hour version.

Q – One of the great things about DVDs is that it allows you to put all the extras bits on it.

Robert – Yes. It's great. And as I am working on my next films, and as I did with *Wal-Mart*, I would say set this piece aside for the DVD extra. To me, it is built into the creative process and exciting.

Q – Did you create the DVDs and the packaging yourself?

Robert – No, we shipped that out because the numbers got too big. We actually bought a little duplicating machine, but then we sold 20,000 the first day. And we commissioned someone to do the artwork.

Q – Any mistakes that you notice with documentary filmmakers that you think can be avoided?

Robert – I can't speak for them, but I can for my own work. I've made almost every possible mistake that you can. I committed to a release date before I knew how long it would take. I committed to a date before I had all my interviews lined up. Not doing transcripts. It ended up costing me more and taking more time because I had to keep editors on longer because I didn't do a really refined paper cut. On this one now where I have much less money, I'm trying to do it. I'm very visual by nature and a lot of it is feel for me, but I have to do it or else it is a killer. And on sort of an abstract level, with *Outfoxed* and *Wal-Mart* - you give those films to ten different filmmakers and you get ten radically different movies and going into them I didn't know what the story was going to be. I should have given more time before I involved more bodies. Of course the research told me what the story was so I might take that back. I don't know if I could have done it any differently.

Q – How much time would you recommend devoting to self-distribution after the film is done?

Robert – A couple of months full time doing nothing else. And do every piece of press no matter how big or little.

Q – Any advice you would give a new documentary filmmaker?

Robert – Find a way to make it. Get the price as low as possible. Get your own camera. Steal an editing system. And just go make it because the energy that you are going to spend convincing someone else to give you the money sucks the blood and energy away and it turns you into a salesman and not a better filmmaker. So given how cheap the technology is today, just find a way to make it. Even if it's only 10 or 15 minutes long.

GUERILLA FILM MAKER SAYS!

Grass Roots Distribution

1. The most important thing to have is a website. You can provide information on your film, link to relevant websites and most importantly, sell your film from it.
2. Docs usually have built in audiences based on the subject matter. Connect with or link to the websites of those organizations and people during production and keep them informed on your progress.
3. Create a massive e-mail and name list of everyone you meet, e-mails you or buys your film. These are your "customers" for this and other films.
4. Non-theatrical distribution is huge for docs and you can do it yourself. So colleges, conferences, churches, youth groups, synagogues, mosques, national organizatons, etc. are all fair game.
5. House parties can be good way to get large groups of people together to see your film and buy your DVD. People can organize them off your website or with an organization.
6. Save money for lots of DVD stock and postage.
7. It takes a lot of time and effort to self-distribute. Budget 3-4 months of doing nothing else after post.
8. Get into as many film festivals as possible. You can make connections, get reviews and raise awareness easily at them.
9. Hire an advisor who does grass roots marketing to help you.
10. For foreign territories, it's still best to get a sales agent. But work a deal with them so that if they don't sell a territory after 12 months, you can sell there yourself. If they end up selling it, then you can stop.

ALTERNATIVE DISTRIBUTION

Q – Is the traditional route of distribution dying?

Peter – Traditional independent distribution is broken. It may be working for the people who benefit from having the filmmaker's movies, but it's not working for the filmmakers. In the old model you relied on middlemen to get your movie to audiences. In the new model, you take a hybrid approach where you choose certain companies to work with in certain areas. In other areas, you take more control of the distribution of your movie. You sell directly to TV, not to some other company so there's no money coming off the top and they aren't cross-collateralizing the money with other revenues. They aren't putting your film in a package. You can then make choices about who is really excited about your film and can help raise its profile. The second way the new model is different is that we're redefining distribution, which is no longer territory-by-territory – now it's global. So in the old model, if you made a film in the US and wanted to show it in France, six grumpy French distributors watched your movie and if none of them were persuaded to pick up the movie, nobody in France got to see it. Now we have a situation where a filmmaker can make a documentary, have a website and anyone with internet access and a credit card can get the movie on DVD or via a download. So if there's a core audience in France for your film, you can reach it.

Q – Do you even need a foreign sales agent then?

Peter – You can work with a foreign sales agent and have her sell your film to whatever territories she can. Whatever territories aren't sold at the end of 12 months, you get the right to sell into off your website. If your foreign sales agent ever sells another territory, you stop selling into that territory from your website. Another thing that's different from the old model is that filmmakers can now have a direct relationship with their audience. In the old system, when Alfred Hitchcock made a new film, his fans went to see it in theaters, but he didn't know the names and addresses of any of the people who watched it. Today, if someone buys a film off your website, you have the name and e-mail address of that person. You want to convert that person from a consumer of the product into a patron of the filmmaker. A filmmaker can send out an e-mail to his core audiences once every three months, letting them know what he is up to. Now you have a two-way relationship. I can't quantify the value of the feedback you can get from those people. It's not going to cost any more money to buy a film from a filmmaker's website, and the impact on the filmmaker is so much greater than if it was purchased at Blockbuster.

Q – So now marketing becomes the biggest hurdle as you need to get people to your website.

Peter – It's critical. The fifth change in distribution is that instead of targeting a general audience, core audiences are targeted. From the time you get the idea for the film, you should be thinking about who the core audiences are, where they are, what organizations they belong to, what periodicals they read and where they hang out online. As you do your research, you start collecting e-mail addresses and creating a mailing list. You launch a website that lets people know the film is coming. You give people an incentive to sign up to your mailing list. Then you begin outreach to websites relevant to your project and exchange links. You encourage people to write, discuss, argue and talk about the movie. The film doesn't have to be brilliant for them to like it. It just has to give them the content that they want or need. Once the core audience embraces your movie, your possibilities are fantastic. The other thing we have to do is get people to think of the internet as global instead of national. If you do that, your opportunities are greater.

Q – What are some of the pitfalls of the look of a website?

Peter – Sometimes filmmakers create websites that are uninspired. Websites need to be dynamic, not static. You have to give people the idea that this is a changing, growing, living place and if they bookmark it, it'll be different when the come back later. The websites need to be personal – the filmmaker's persona needs to be there. One thing I hate is when you click the "contact" link and you get info@XXX.com. People are missing the boat here. Forget info@. Have two e-mail addresses if you want a private one. My third suggestion is that you have a bigger idea for your website than just a promotional tool for your movie. Your film can be at the center, but other films and books can be there, too. Your website should complement not undercut rival websites. If people come to your website and see useful information, chances are they will come back. To make websites dynamic, you can have: changing video material, a blog, an active link series, etc.

Q – Are doc filmmakers more prone to this as they're more concerned about getting their messages across?

Peter – I think every filmmaker would like the possibility to be in a movie theater and I think they've the right to be in at least one. And more and more filmmakers are starting in one theater to test the concept. If nobody comes, well you tried and may decide not to put any more energy into that. If a bigger audience than expected shows up, you can arrange a service deal to get it out. You can always four wall your film in a small market, which may not be that expensive. Alternately, if you can find a theater to book your film and they can do some press for you and utilize their mailing list, what's the downside?

Q – Getting into theaters makes it easier to attract press.

Peter – Yes. Getting into theaters is about raising awareness to help with video sales. Every filmmaker should try to get theatrical release but should not trade their distribution rights for that possibility. For example, I just got an overall deal offer for a film I'm involved in. Instead I said that we'd consider selling them video rights. They offered to do a theatrical release and pay for it, but I said no. That may seem counter-intuitive, but if we do theatrical ourselves, we can control the money spent and don't have all those expenses going against video revenue. When you understand the new distribution models well enough to be able to turn down offers, then I think your possibilities are going to be much greater. The old model was very reactive and that's a recipe for disaster. So how about having a proactive model where you work backwards from the audience and you think about how to split the rights up and how you're going to make direct sales off the website? You can decide who is going to be a good video or TV partner. Then you think about theatrical and see what makes sense. Then when you get offers after festivals you can say – well, you're offering us a $100,000 advance for all rights, but we know that if we sell 5,000 copies off of our website at $20, we can make the same amount of money and retain all the rights. Then you're at a point where they can say, *"How about $500,000?"* If they say *"$100,000 is as high as we can go."* Then you can tell them it was nice meeting them and maybe you'll be able to work with them on another project. I was talking to an indie distributor recently and said I wanted to send him a movie, but I didn't want to make an overall deal – only a service deal. He was confused until I told him I knew the value of the film video rights and that it didn't make sense to put them through an overall deal. He said OK without a fight. So know the value of your film. Don't take a bad deal if you can do better.

Q – What's wrong with the traditional model specifically?

Peter – They can put your film in theaters and give up on supporting it as soon as it premieres on the first Friday night. The second problem is that you don't have any control over the marketing. Third, they get to choose the video company – most likely a subsidiary of their own company, which may not be the best choice for your movie. Choosing your video distributor is crucial because that's where the most potential money can be made. Fourth, reporting is not always up to snuff. Money comes in, but it never gets to you. There are honest distributors with accurate reporting, but cross-collateralization can easily result in little or no money being paid to the filmmaker. This contrasts with a model where the viewer buys a video right from your website and the money comes directly to your bank account. Say you sell your movie for $24.95, which is common. Shipping and handling is about $4.95 and the replication of the DVD is $.95, so you can make a significant profit. This contrasts with a retail DVD distribution deal in which you get a 20% royalty. 20% of the wholesale price of $12.50, so $2.50 that may come to you some day. And if you sell it on your website, you get the name and e-mail address of every buyer.

Q – Should a filmmaker consider four walling?

Peter – A better approach would be to book your film in theaters. If an exhibitor sees value in your film, he'll give you a deal. That's the no-cost approach. Rather than approaching theaters directly, you can work with a booker. You should be able to find a booker who can open your film in five cities for $10,000. Plus you'll have to spend money on prints and advertising. You could easily get up to $100,000 for everything. Most people don't have $100,000 burning a hole in their pockets. In that case, you can go to private investors and ask them to fund your theatrical release in return for putting them in first position on video sales from your website. If you're sure you could sell 5,000 copies of the DVD from your website, you could pay their $100,000 investment back. That doesn't include possible revenues from TV sales. Hopefully you'll also receive some revenues from theatrical distribution so that the cost of being in theaters is less than the $100,000 you spend. In the final analysis, I don't think theatrical is essential. But it's definitely worth trying in at least one city.

Q – Given what you said about a global market, how do you get your film sold internationally?

Peter – Work with a foreign sales agent. For documentaries, it makes more sense to hook up with someone who just sells TV rights. I wouldn't recommend that filmmakers attempt to do their own foreign sales.

Q – What about house parties?

Peter – They're becoming more and more popular. Organizations like house parties because it allows them to work at the grass roots level and it doesn't cost the organization much. And it may get their members to take action. Movies lend themselves to different kinds of house parties. Some work better on campuses, others in church basements.

Q – Are TV companies receptive to the filmmaker selling directly to them?

10 Points To Look For In An Agreement

GUERILLA FILM MAKER SAYS!

Set out below are some very broad considerations which you should give to any agreement. Of course, each circumstance will require more specific attention. If your liabilities under the agreement could involve you in substantial expense, seek legal advice.

1. Ask yourself first what interests you need to protect and are they sufficiently protected.

2. Do you have any existing contractual obligations to other people and if you enter into this agreement are you going to be in breach of those existing contractual obligations?

3. What are your liabilities in this agreement and if things go wrong, what are you liable for? Look out for clauses which make you personally liable even though you may be contracting through a company i.e. are you being asked to give a personal guarantee for a loan which is being made to your company?

4. What is the agreement asking you to do and is it reasonable and within your power to deliver or achieve?

5. If you are required under the agreement to do something, ask to change any reference to your using your 'best endeavors' to 'reasonable endeavors'.

6. If you are providing your own original work or any intellectual property owned by you under the terms of the agreement, what happens if the project does not go ahead? Do you have the chance to regain or repurchase your property?

7. If you are due to receive any royalties or profit share under the agreement, make sure that the other party has an obligation to collect in any revenue derived from the film or project, that they must show you their books and you have the right to audit those books. Check also your share of Net Profits (as defined in the agreement) is as agreed i.e. are you receiving a share of the Producer's net profits or a share of all net profits?

8. What are the possible sources of income to you from the film or project and are all those sources being exploited and if so, are you getting a fair share of that income?

9. What sort of controls do you have over the conduct of the other party? Are the promises they are making under the agreement sufficient to cover your interests? What happens if they are in default of their promises?

10. Remember that if the agreement is being provided by the other side, the terms will be very much in their favor. This does not mean that they are necessarily trying to stitch you up, this is just business.

Peter – I don't recommend doing it yourself—better to work through a producer's rep or sales agent. It's not impossible to do it yourself but it's harder. Filmmakers can call up acquisitions people, send them the movie, and make a deal. Neither is a guaranteed route. One thing, I'm constantly surprised at how many filmmakers sign deals with producers reps or agents and don't first talk to people who are doing or have done business with them. Filmmakers will talk to you. If they've had a horrible experience, they'll try to keep you from having the same experience.

Q – Are film festivals still important to the distribution process?

Peter – They are in some ways more important than they've ever have been. Festivals are a way to get reviews and to build some awareness. I think it's important for filmmakers to see their film with audiences that aren't their friends and family before submitting to festivals. They should also understand which festivals have press and distributors at them and which have neither. Filmmakers need to pay attention to the order in which they apply to festivals. They shouldn't let the Sundance deadline determine when their film is finished. And if they think festivals are going to look at their film twice, they're sadly mistaken. The film festival world isn't a level playing field. That's not to say it's crooked, but it's political. If someone can put in a good word about your film to a programmer, it helps it get seen at the highest levels. One thing many filmmakers don't know is that you can get screening fees from many festivals. Let's say you can divide the world into A, B, C and D festivals. C and D festivals will pay screening fees and some of the Bs will, too. They'll only do it if you ask and often when first asked, they'll act like they don't understand your request. Then they'll go check with someone and get back to you. If they don't pay screening fees, that's one thing, but if some get fees, you should also if you ask.

Q – What do you think about new media distribution?

Peter – Portable media distribution will be important. The idea is that you pay for to a feed from a filmmaker that downloads to your computer or portable media player. For shorts, animation, trailers and other promo things, this will be very helpful.

Q – Are there any technical issues people should know about when doing internet distribution?

Peter – Regional codes on DVDs can prevent things that play in the US from playing in the UK or Japan. I recommend that filmmakers encode their DVDs for region 0 so they will play in every region. As far as TV standards like NTSC and PAL, my sense is that many DVD players overseas can convert NTSC DVDs to PAL. Or you can distribute your film with PAL on one side and NTSC on the other. I think language is a bigger problem and that's a matter of seeing where your demand is. If French people want to see your English language film, then you have to think about subtitling or dubbing.

Q – What common mistakes do you see documentary filmmakers make?

Peter – Music rights. This fantasy that having that Bruce Springsteen song over the end credits of the film is going to make a big difference is ridiculous. I recommend that filmmakers use original music from an up-and-coming composer. That way you control your music. Licensing archival footage can be a serious issue for documentary filmmakers. Pat Aufderheide at The American University has done good work with Fair Use that filmmakers should be aware of. Filmmakers should think clearly about their core audiences and build relationships with key organizations and websites these audiences frequent.

Q – What advice would you give a new documentary filmmaker?

Peter – The possibilities have never been better to get movies out widely and effectively. While filmmakers need to understand that it's still harder to get a film into the world than it is to make one, they now have the opportunity to go around the gatekeepers and reach viewers directly. If filmmakers can convert them from consumers to patrons, they'll be able to build core personal audiences that could provide vital support throughout their careers.

Katy Chevigny

MEDIARIGHTS.ORG

Q – What is MediaRights.org?

Katy – We started out as documentary filmmakers making movies and quickly learned that there's so much good documentary filmmaking out there, but there's limited ways to distribute it. And even those who had good distribution for their documentaries, often that distribution didn't help it get to the widest possible audience. Often it was short lived. You might have a broadcast and then an educational distributor, but tens of thousands of people who might want to see it, might not if they missed the broadcast or didn't know of the educational use catalogue it was in - they might not know it exists. We used to feel that there were a lot of documentaries just sitting on shelves and if they could just connect to the people who could use them, they could have a much longer life. We aggregated all the distributors of documentary film that we could find and we created an online database of all these films, which has now grown to over 6,000 social issue films. Right now it's the only way you can find a lot of them and you can search by topic, title and filmmaker. We also have articles and resources to help people use documentary film in their community work to advance the efforts of their non-profits and to show that if documentaries are shown in the context where there is active audience and a facilitator who can help guide a conversation that documentaries can lead to social action.

Q – Why only socially oriented documentaries? Why not all documentaries?

Katy – There's a great book called *Directing The Documentary* and the author of that book says that the documentary form is designed to shed light on a social problem. That's his definition and sort of historically that's the case. We didn't want to be responsible in the website for documentaries that didn't have any social issues focus whatsoever. For example, some are strictly for fun like an animal documentary. Our mission was to link documentary films with people who are trying to use them to talk about contemporary society. We have nothing against those documentaries, we were just trying to find a problem the scale of which we could take on. For that reason we also mainly do domestic films. We do have a lot of international films in our international film category, but we couldn't set out to include all documentaries in the world because we just don't have the capacity.

Q – Many films don't get a theatrical or broadcast release. What are some alternative ways filmmakers can distribute their films – even at the grass roots level?

Katy – One of the main reasons we set up MediaRights.org is that there are not enough broadcast outlets and distribution outlets, traditional ones, for the amount of good documentaries being made. There are a certain number of slots at *POV* every year. There are a handful of slots at HBO and PBS. So a grassroots means of distribution is the way many filmmakers can get their films out there if they don't hit the jackpot in those kinds of broadcasts. Filmmakers can self-list their films with us even if their work is still in progress. We set that up initially so that filmmakers who want to connect with other filmmakers and non-profits, or documentary viewers who might be interested in their film, can start to have exposure for their work. As a MediaRights member, they can get the newsletter and learn about other outreach strategies. Sandi Dubowski's film, *Trembling Before G-d*, is a great example of a grassroots program that started before the film was finished. We try to convey to our filmmakers to not wait until their film is done to start thinking about finding an audience for it. That should be done right at the beginning of your filmmaking process. Like contacting groups who are working on similar issues you're interested in. You'll end up doing better research on your topic knowing what else is out there from people who have been working on these issues forever and can make your film better. One of the weaknesses of many documentarians is thinking we have discovered something new. But really it's just new to us. There are people who have studied this stuff for thirty years and we need to avail ourselves of their resources. Otherwise, we're not doing the film justice and we are not giving credit to the people who have done work in that area. The other thing we encourage filmmakers to do through MediaRights.org is to reach out to non-profits and community groups in our database who are interested in using media. And we also encourage them to use Guidestar.org to locate other organizations that are working on issues that they are interested in so that you can partner with them. Also, you may get some grassroots organizations that know about you in advance and are sort of championing your film. They can help your film have a life after the broadcast. They can help you set up screenings afterwards and talk to their constituencies about how your film can be used.

Q – Outside of groups that have an active interest in your film, what are other places that you can show it?

Katy – Every film is different and you have to create your own plan and talk to as many people to help you design that plan. So for example, what Sandi Dubowski did was different from what anyone else had ever done. He created something that was special in terms of how he got his film out there. You couldn't really apply that to any other film. Certainly some of the enthusiasm that he had you would want to apply. We have the Outreach Journal that we have on the website just about every month. It gives a filmmaker's perspective on how they distributed their film. They're very varied, but it often inspires people to design their own. A couple of years ago a filmmaker showed her film in beauty salons as a way to reach women to say what she wanted to talk about. She arranged to screen it in all over the place and nobody had ever done that before. From the strictly marketing standpoint of how to get famous or rich, making your film isn't so much our focus as it is trying to figure out how to make your film have a greater impact with the people who really want to know about it. We believe that self-distribution can be really effective and even if you have a distributor, you have to take initiative on your own to make sure that it is reaching all the people that you want it to reach. There are a lot of independent groups that do a lot of community screenings of indie films that young people go to e.g. Rooftop Films in New York. Often the hardest thing to do when you're a filmmaker, after you've filmed your subject and it's been just you sitting with it in your bedroom, is to build a base for your film from scratch than if you had been networking with people and thinking collaboratively about how this film might be in the world. Say you were doing a film on cancer and you're in California. But there's an organization in Arizona that focuses on cancer. You can call them and say, *"Hey, I want to do a screening. Do you know a place that wouldn't charge me a fee to show it and you can bring an audience?"* And they might say, *"Yes. I know this and in fact, I know the local film festival programmer."*

Q – Do you have any tips for when you talk to non-media organizations about getting them interested in working with you or showing your film? Is it different from how one talks to broadcasters and distributors?

Katy – When you talk to broadcasters and distributors you're in pitch mode. You're making an argument as to why your film is good enough to be included in their catalogue. When you're talking to other groups, I'd say that you need to make an argument that your film is important and has something special to say and is well crafted. You have to do that because you want to distinguish yourself as someone who has done careful work on the subject as opposed to something that someone just threw together. When you're setting up screenings with non-media people, it's best to do more listening then you might with a broadcaster or a distributor because you're talking about more than just your film, you're addressing how your film might fit into a larger dialogue. Sometimes you want to partner with groups that work on this issue and then you want to call them and say, and again I recommend this happen at the very early stages of the game, *"I am so and so. I am developing a film about X, which I understand your group deals with a lot. I would like to talk to you a little about some of the things that I am including in my film and maybe some other things that are really pressing to you and your community to make sure that I am making a film that is timely and effective."* You want to make sure that you are not making something that is oblivious to some central concerns going on in your field of interest. Another thing you could do is set up an advisory council of people who are experts in the field or, alternatively, they don't have to be experts, they can be mentors. That also helps because if you are coming from a position where people don't know you or your work, it helps to let people know that you are taking this seriously and you have allied yourself with people that they know. So with our film *Deadline*, we had this great advisory board and we said we are making this great film about the death penalty and we want to focus on the story of so and so, what do you think? And we got incredible advice. It really helped shape the film. They said you should look at this angle and we thought we wouldn't because of X, Y and Z reasons and they would say that the work that they're doing would be pushing things that way so it would be important in a couple of years. We wouldn't have known that so we shaped the film that way and they were right.

Q – What is the Independent Producers Outreach Toolkit?

Katy – That is one of our products, which is a service to do all the things that we've been talking about. It offers a bunch of how-to steps to create an outreach program. You start at the beginning of the film. You assemble an advisory council. You try to ally yourself with people who are already working on the issue to see how your film could be of use to them. We also have case studies in the tool kit of many successful outreach programs. And we have them in a variety of sizes of budgets and types of films. We also have interactive budgets so you can plan an outreach campaign. If you only have a certain amount of money, you can plug in those numbers and it will suggest how you might want to use those dollars in terms of doing this outreach.

Q – Do you handle documentary shorts as well?

Katy – Yes. Shorts are also part of the MediaRights.org database. So if you have one you can list it. We started the Media That Matters Film Festival five years ago as a proof of concept of our idea that media when used effectively and placed in context can really have an impact. People were not sure what we meant. They would say, *"What do you mean media has an impact? People go to a movie, they feel something and then they go away and it is over."* It doesn't have to be that way. So with the Media That Matters Film Festival we curated a set of 16 films that a jury selects and they are all 8 minutes and under. The reason that we chose that length is because we wanted them to be streamable on the web and able for most people to watch them. So when you watch the film on the web, there are a set of "take action" links listed below. The point of which is to harness the feeling you have after watching this strong, interesting short where you have learned something new about an issue. You can harness that emotion because the things that I am thinking and feeling now may make me want to get more involved – say to volunteer at that organization or just learn more about the topic. This way the film is a doorway to the issue and to motivate people to make a difference.

Credit Report Companies

Experian Consumer Assistance
PO Box 2002
Allen, TX 75013
(888) 397-3742
www.experian.com

Equifax Credit Services
PO Box 740256
Atlanta, GA 30374
(800) 685-1111
www.equifax.com

Trans Union
2 Baldwin Place
PO Box 1000
Chester, PA 19022
(800) 888-4213
www.transunion.com

Q – Is there anything else unique about shorts?

Katy –You can use them in lots of different ways. We produce a DVD of all the festival films every year because we have a lot of demand from educators and community groups and youth media groups to show the festival. And one of the things we have found particularly with educators and community groups is that the short format is a great way to start a conversation. You don't have to have people in a room for 90 minutes and then have a discussion. But if you want to show three shorts about environmental sustainability that run a total of 25 minutes and then you can have an hour discussion and it becomes more about the issue. In addition, a variety of different groups can show the films in modular ways. You could show one because a young person made it. You could show another because it is an example of how to use animation.

Q – How are you funded? Do you take a cut of the films?

Katy – No. We are a non-profit and we don't take a percentage. That is part of how we encourage the distributors to be involved. They, especially the educational distributors, have a small profit margin as it is. At the time we started MediaRights.org it was a radical idea and people were kind of suspicious. We really had to explain that we were trying to expand the reach of their listings. We are also supported by foundations and government funding and in addition we do some consulting work and we sell the DVDs. And we sell the toolkit. We get corporate sponsorship for the festival.

Q – Do you do fiscal sponsorship as well?

Katy – Yes. We can be a 501 (c) 3 sponsor for filmmakers as well.

Q – What is Youth Media?

Katy – We discovered that young people are interested in the web and social issue filmmaking and independent media. And partly because we had this shorts program through the festival, we found that we were getting a lot of interest from young people. An enormous percentage of our submissions for the festival are from young people. We didn't set out to be that way, but every year our jury would pick a lot of youth-made films for the festival. It wasn't a quota. They would just emerge and rise to the top. So we show a lot of their work on a website called www.ymdi.org. There are a lot of programs for training youth in media in the US, but not in the distribution aspect of getting their stuff to a wide audience. That was the gap that we filled in.

Q – What is Big Mouth Films?

Katy – That was the kernel that started all of this. It's our documentary film producing arm. We have produced six documentary films. Our most successful was our most recent one, *Deadline*, which was about the death penalty and went to Sundance and was broadcast on NBC. We also produce social issue shorts for non-profit organizations. These are pieces that will help those organizations advance their reach in the community. We usually do our own ideas. We generally don't work with the producers who come through MediaRights and we are not a funding source. We don't have the resources to do that for so many feature docs.

Q – What common mistakes do you see documentary filmmakers make?

Katy – One thing is that I don't think documentary filmmakers realize how important it is to work and play with others throughout the process. That doesn't only mean being collaborative through the production process. You are not building a house that you are going to live in. You are making a piece of material that is designed for a mass audience. It is designed for other people to get something out of. You need to engage with other people even if you don't agree with them. You need to be aware of the public. Both the constituency of the people who would interested in your film and those who wouldn't be. We get approached by a lot of filmmakers who have been working in isolation. Maybe they are a couple who have been working on it for five years and they have only shown it to a small circle of people. That is generally not the best way to make a film or get it out to an audience. That may come out of the auteur aspect of filmmaking where people don't want their film tainted by another's way of thinking. And it might be just insecurity. But you need to strike a balance and let the world in a little bit while you're making a film. Because the world will get involved when it's done, hopefully, anyway.

Q – What advice would you give a filmmaker?

Katy – For a first project, take on something that is complete-able. I am all about taking on ambitious topics and doing things that haven't been done before, but I think there are so many people that start films and then don't finish them because they're trying to hit the jackpot or they're trying get into Sundance. I am going to be one of those one-tenth of one-percent of people who are going to make this film in their garage and then it's going to go on to wide theatrical release. The likelihood of that is very small, so for your first film I think you should find a topic you know you can sink your teeth into or you know you have contacts to. It is approachable. And do it in a way so that you are not going to have to raise millions of dollars to finish it. It's not going to require a whole lot of magical things to happen to finish it. Maybe you make a short and submit it to film festivals and try to build up your work that way.

US Documentary Film Box Office Grosses (2001-2005)

Title	Distributor (USA)	Country of Origin	US Box Office Gross
The Aristocrats (2005)	ThinkFilm	USA	$6,377,277
Enron: The Smartest Guys In The Room (2005)	HDNet Films	USA	$4,064,421
Grizzly Man (2205)	Lions Gate Films	USA	$3,174,085
Mad Hot Ballroom (2005)	Nickelodeon Movies	USA	$8,044,906
March of the Penguins (2005)	Warner Independent	France	$77,413,017
Murderball (2005)	MTV Films	USA	$1,523,883
Rize (2005)	Lions Gate Films	USA	$3,278,611
Why We Fight (2005)	Sony Pictures Classics	USA	$1,436,279
Born Into Brothels (2004)	ThinkFilm	USA	$3,410,863
Control Room (2004)	Magnolia Pictures	USA	$2,586,511
Darwin's Nightmare (2004)	International Film Circuit	France	$195,048
Fahrenheit 9/11 (2004)	Lions Gate Films	USA	$119,194,771
Metallica: Some Kind of Monster (2004)	IFC Films	USA	$1,222,708
Riding Giants (2004)	Sony Pictures Classics	USA	$2,276,368
Spellbound (2004)	ThinkFilm	USA	$5,728,431
Super Size Me (2004)	Samuel Goldwyn	USA	$11,529,368
What The Bleep Do We Know (2004)	Roadside Attractions	USA	$10,941,801
Aileen: Life and Death of a Serial Killer (2003)	DEJ	UK/USA	$85,992
Capturing the Friedmans (2003)	Magnolia Pictures	USA	$3,117,985
Coral Reef Adventure (IMAX - 2003)	MacGillivray Freeman Films	USA	$24,600,000
The Corporation (2003)	Zeitgeist Films	Canada	$1,879,301
The Fog Of War (2003)	Sony Pictures Classics	USA	$4,193,943
Lost Boys of Sudan (2003)	Shadow Distribution	USA	$120,651
My Architect (2003)	New Yorker Films	USA	$2,748,981
Touching The Void (2003)	IFC Films	UK	$4,581,222
Tupac:Resurrection (2003)	Paramount Pictures	USA	$7,707,563
Amandla! A Revolution In Four Part Harmony (2002)	Artisan Entertainment	South Africa	$398,981
Bowling For Columbine (2002)	United Artists	USA	$21,244,913
Comedian (2002)	Miramax	USA	$2,744,253
The Kid Stays In The Picture (2002)	MCA/Universal Pictures	USA	$1,434,436
Lost In La Mancha (2002)	IFC Films	UK/USA	$734,514
Dogtown and Z-Boys (2001)	Sony Pictures Classics	USA	$1,293,295
Trembling Before G-d (2001)	New Yorker Films	USA/France/Israel	$619,612
Winged Migration (2001)	Columbia/TriStar	France	$10,762,178
The Endurance: Shackleton's Legendary Antarctic Expedition (2000)	Cowboy	Sweden/UK/ Germany/USA	$2,452,566

ANATOMY OF A DOCUMENTARY SECTION 13

THE LONG VIEW

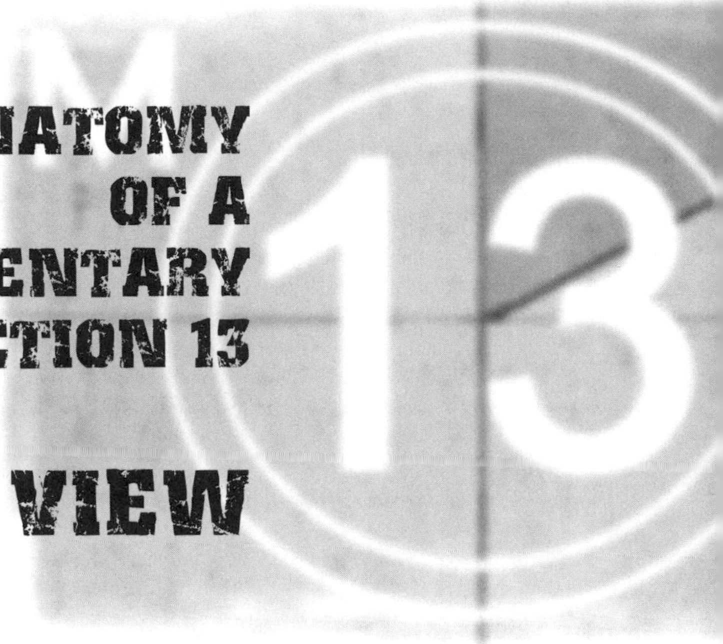

Nick Broomfield

THE DETECTIVE

Q – What does documentary film mean to you and what excites you about it?

Nick – It covers an enormous genre of very different films. Some of which have very little to do with one another. You can lump films like *The Weeping Camel* in with documentaries even though it has nothing to do with documentary at all. So I guess the term is really inadequate and confusing in and of itself. Subsequent terms like cinema verité or observational filmmaking are slightly more accurate because they define a particular style or approach. I suppose the thing that excites me about them is their rawness and spontaneity and the uncertainness of the interaction between the filmmaker and the subject. Those amazing moments that are completely unique to that form of filmmaking – that only otherwise happen in real life encounters where you're in conversation with someone and/or something quite remarkable and unexpected happens. Fiction tries to imitate that, but very rarely comes up with anything as complex or as amazing. I think documentary encourages filmmakers to be very flexible in their approach. To not go into subjects with a thesis all carefully worked out. They have to be open and on a voyage of discovery themselves and take the audience with them.

Q – Your style has something of that, as your films tend to be about you making the film as well as whatever your subject matter is.

Nick – That's implicit in any film as the filmmaker goes on a journey. It's just off camera to a greater or lesser extent. Making documentaries is a very intimate relationship between the subject and the filmmaking and the extent that the relationship is successful is completely reflected in the film. I feel it's easier to acknowledge that relationship and use it as a very positive structuring device. Sometimes, not always. I think there are certain films that don't require that kind of structure. Films from institutions or films of processes or films of events that have a built in beginning, middle and end don't require another structuring device like the filmmaker telling the story. But if you're doing a film that seemingly has a lot of arbitrary connections and those connections only seem to connect in the filmmaker's mind and require those connections to be made explicit, then it's very useful to have the presence.

Q – Do you tell your interviewees that you're going to walk in with the cameras rolling?

Nick – I say that I'm making a home movie and I'm filming everything. If I come in with a film camera rolling, don't be surprised.

Q – With your style, you're able to get things from subjects that they probably wouldn't say in a conventional interview. What tips would you give new documentary filmmakers on interviewing subjects?

Nick – The main thing is not to box the interviewee into a corner and to not make the situation so formal that it's inhibiting. Or in any way to make the interviewee feel inadequate. They can't feel as if they or their house are messy. They have to be made to feel absolutely OK with exactly whom they are, which is exactly what you want for your film. So the main thing is to make people relaxed with you and to enjoy to a certain extent, your presence. I'd say have a very tiny crew. I think the ideal size is two – one on camera and one on sound - and just to get on with it. Don't say too much about what you're doing and why you're doing it. You're obviously there to make a film.

Q – Do you think going in with the camera rolling gets a gut reaction from the subject?

Nick – The initial meeting with people is often the moment at which your first impressions form and those are the strongest. You resort to an almost animal instinct in your judgment of people. It's almost before your intellect has started working. You go on what they're wearing, how they look at you or if they're fat or thin – all these animal things that have nothing to do with their political position. They all influence your reaction to them and indeed, the audience's reaction to them. And as you're taking the audience on a journey that you're involved in, those initial meetings are essential to the audience because they're meeting them for the first time, too. They want to see the houses that they live in and the kind of curtains that they have in their windows.

Q – You don't seem to ask rapid questions. You give them a chance to breathe.

Nick – Maybe that's because I think of them as conversations or interactions. And hopefully you've done enough work where you can be fluid and flexible in the order in which you ask your questions or steer the conversation. Realistically, unless you're structuring the film around one interview, you're only going to cover a couple of main topics. It's very rare, in my films for example, that an interview will last more than three to four minutes. So in that time, you only can cover a couple of things. I prefer to go back and re-interview them on different questions rather than stand them up and ask the same thing, which creates a static feel as you keep going back to the same interview throughout the film. I think maybe your first interview is wide where you're covering lots of different topics and you're getting to know them and you are asking a lot of background stuff, but subsequent interviews become more and more specific and more and more centered around one or two topics.

Q – How important is it for documentary filmmakers to listen to their subjects?

Nick – That's the reason you're making the film.

Q – Sometimes when someone interviews a subject, they end up filling in the blanks for them.

Nick – I know what you mean, but I have never done it.

Q – When you're recording your phone conversations with your subjects – do you have to tell them that you're doing it?

Nick – I think you're probably supposed to.

Q – Have interviewees ever said that they refuse to let you use what you shot of them?

Nick – I've never had that problem, but I 've occasionally decided to not use footage in order to protect someone.

Q – Would you suggest that people pay their subjects for interviews, as that sort of proposes a contract that they have agreed to do it?

Nick – If you're taking up a great deal of someone's time and you're invading their house and eating their food, it'd be a customary form of the society we live in that you'd offer them something. But if they're super rich, then you might be insulting them. Most people kind of like to receive something. Not always. But some people feel it's appropriate. It shouldn't be something that would change their objectivity or that they would in deed start telling you things that they wouldn't have or they start to perform and make you happy. You don't want to pay people money and that changes the basis of your relationship.

Q – Do you need to have clearances for selling the film?

Nick – Yes, you do need to have clearances. And sometimes you need to have clearances so that the people in the film acknowledge that they've in fact given you their permission and that there won't be any argument later. I suppose if you don't have hidden cameras and a big camera is pointing at them, they know you're making a film and they carry on. There's an implicit agreement for them to be filmed. And obviously, if it's someone who's serving in a public capacity like a policeman, schoolteacher or politician, somebody who in a way has sacrificed their private persona because they are fulfilling a public function and as such are accountable. With other people who are very private and you're in their home or whatever, it's appropriate to get a release form them. And also I suppose in terms of Errors and Omissions later, it's generally useful to have releases. Although, I think that everyone would agree that a release is not watertight. If anyone wants to sue you, they'll sue you anyway. It's interesting – every TV station has very different releases. HBO I remember were very scornful of the BBC release. The BBC has a different release from Channel 4. No one really agrees as to what a correct release should be. And if you pull out a complicated release that is pages and pages long and people feel they have to read it all and they don't understand the language, it doesn't make your job easy.

Q – You seem to like lightening in a bottle characters, like Courtney Love. Do you think character first before story in order to get a more personal approach?

Nick – I don't think you start with a character and then find a story. I mean that film was to be a study of Kurt Cobain and it turned into a story of Courtney Love because she was such a monster and she was trying to stop the film. So it was the only story I could tell. I think you have to tell a story about what's happening rather than the story you may have originally set out to make. Terreblanche – I did know about him before, but the film was going to be about him and the AWB. He is obviously a very colorful character, but I was more interested in his driver and the driver's wife than I was in Terreblanche.

Q – You seem to push the interviewees a bit to the point where it seems that your life may be in danger. Do you find that you get more out of them this way?

Nick – I think you're generally on a quest for truth of answers. And I think any filmmaker is in the capacity of an odd father confessor figure. The subjects very much see you that way because you're asking them about their lives and this is their moment of truth. Their moment to define themselves. It gives you the ability to ask questions that you wouldn't do in normal conversations probably. Or certainly in a more blunt fashion. I think it is an acknowledgement of what's going on. Films always make things larger than life, partly because they're seen by so many people and are on a big screen. The mere fact that you study something that has been removed from life and is being shown back produces something that takes on another significance. Asking questions that are more pointed than normal just acknowledges that.

Q – If you are not getting what you want out of a subject, do you ever jig things up a bit?

Nick – I remember once with Victoria Sellers who was giving me nothing and lying to me, I turned off the camera and said, *"I'm tired of this shit you're giving me. We aren't going to continue unless you start answering some of the questions and telling me the truth."* That had the desired affect. She was very drugged out at the time. So occasionally I think you have to do that.

Q – Is there anything you do while you're filming in terms of trying to get more out of your subjects?

Nick – Not really. I think you try to find out what connections they make between things. And you try and copy those connections in the way you interview. If that makes sense.

Q – In your documentary on Terreblanche, the driver comes out with an "out there" theory and it seems in your response that you're playing dumb. Is that what you're doing to get a further response out of him?

Nick – No, with some of his weird theories, I really don't understand him. I suppose it gives him an opportunity to really express what he's going on about. They are certainly nothing I know about because they're weird theories about the Jews or the Bible. But those things you need explained. Those are genuine questions of not understanding what he's talking about.

Q – Ethics in documentary filmmaking is a hot debate. How would you advise filmmakers to handle this?

Nick – I think they need to answer their own consciences and do what they are comfortable with. I think a good test is that when you sit through your own film, do you feel comfortable about certain things that you have done which might not be fair or might not be representative of the situation? Or might not have been a reasonable way to behave? That's a very subjective thing. People have a very different ethic about things. I think one wants to get away from there being a McCarthy ethics board documentary. And there have been moments of that and there have always been bad times for the form. There can be a slight religious quality to documentary sometimes which can be a little too Puritan.

Q – Are there any ethical boundaries that you wouldn't cross?

Nick – What? Like sleeping with my subjects? (laughter) I'm sure there are plenty. I think all the time you're assessing what you think is appropriate in the same way you do on a day-to-day way of living. You try to do good things that you can justify to yourself. I think it's very important to be aware of the reason you're making the film and what you feel the bigger picture is. That'll justify certain things that you wouldn't be doing otherwise. It's a big responsibility in a way.

Q – You've shot most of your movies on film. What do you think of the quality of digital video?

Nick – The main thing really is the story that you tell – much more than the means by which you tell it. I love film, but on the last couple of films I've used HD and I have to say that I like the look of HD. It's very flexible and I like that kind of information. I think it makes film look like from a different era. I'm sure in five years time, we may have moved to a different form, but no one will be using film. I think this is a transitory debate. It's a bit like should we be shooting on black and white or color. And indeed, I like black and white – shot my first film in black and white – but you wouldn't think about black and white anymore. I miss very much cutting on film against in a digital way because that's how I learned to edit and I'm quite frustrated editing the other way. I think it's important that one has the best resources at one's fingertips. HD certainly is.

Q – Do you think there's a certain discipline missing today because people aren't learning how to shoot film?

Nick – I suppose they will learn that discipline in the cutting room because sooner or later you have to work out what your story is and how to structure it. And maybe that's more painful when you have shot so much material and have to cut it down. I'm sure you shoot less the next time.

Q – Are there any mistakes that you see documentary filmmakers make that can be avoided?

Nick – With myself, there are a couple of films that if I had carried on filming for a couple more weeks, I could've had a really remarkable film. And by not carrying on, I shortchanged the film. That is one really big mistake that one shouldn't repeat. I suppose the other one is in second-guessing oneself. I remember when I was making a film about Lily Tomlin, I never thought she was funny. But everyone else thinks she is funny, so she must be funny. And the film wasn't funny. I should've really listened to my own feelings.

Q – Any advice for new documentary filmmakers?

Nick – If there is a subject that you really want to make, on your first film you just have to go out and make it without having proper financing. Then use that as your passport to make films that are funded in the future. It's sort of a vote of confidence in yourself that you'll do that and it might take many months and it is a big gamble. But it's better than sitting around waiting for money that probably will never come.

LISTEN UP!

Q – What does the term "documentary" mean to you?

Michael – That's a very important question these days with the rise of reality TV. One of the hazards these days is that, reality is perceived by some people as documentary. If reality goes down the toilet as it surely will, as all things are cyclical, will documentaries go down the toilet with them? So it's nearly impossible to define what a documentary is. But I suppose I'd call it the observation of real life in a non-interventional way. It's important to see the difference with reality, which is at its heart, contrived. Some of it is very successful and illuminating, but it's contrived to put people into situations and see what they do. A documentary has them in a natural setting.

Q – What advice would you give a documentary filmmaker about choosing their subject matter?

Michael – The great thing about documentaries is that it's totally democratized. At very little cost you can go out and shoot, cut and finish a documentary. Before, it was a whole huge investment deal. That's the good news and the bad news. There are a lot of terrible films made because they don't think it through. *"Let's make a film about my grandmother,"* and off they go and do it. I think the important thing is not the choice of subject - it's your approach to it. Before you approach your documentary, you should figure out a very elementary structure to see what and where you want to go with the idea. The excitement of a documentary is that it's a real thing happening in front of you – you aren't working with a script in a way one does in fiction. But my advice would be to plot out a story so that it does have some purpose to it. Just don't go out there and shoot a ton of stuff on a subject and then hope you or someone else can come in and make sense of it. While it's much easier to make a documentary, it's much harder to get them seen. So if you want that to happen, you have to be doubly thoughtful about what it is.

Q – What advice would you give to new documentary filmmakers on the topic of interviewing subjects?

Michael – I've found that the best way to interview people is not to be very well prepared. You know what the subject is and you know what is going on, but to run through a list of questions is usually deadly. The only way to interview someone is to have a conversation with them and listen to what they say. This is best if you want something emotional and intimate. If you want the facts and you need it done crisply and cleanly, then of course, go in as crisp as you can. For all interviews, don't say very much. There's nothing worse than an interviewer who has diarrhea of the mouth. Keep the questions short and don't be afraid of silence. Sometimes silence is your best weapon. People will want to fill a silence and when they do, maybe they will come up with something for you. And don't go through the interview with them beforehand, as you only get it fresh and interesting once. If you blow that by driving in a car or having a cup of coffee with them while planning it out, you're dead. You'll wish that you'd been filming that time in the car or at coffee because you will never be able to capture that moment again.

Q – Is it difficult to be objective with subjects that you've been following for a long time?

Michael – You can't be objective. The word objective is bizarre. It means going in and being cold and formal with an interview in a documentary. That's not the way to do it at all. You have to build trust with the person. They have to know they're safe with you. You have to be emotionally involved. You need to be subjective. That's not to say you do whatever they want to do or agree with whatever they say. My point again is that you have to know what you are after. You have to know what your end result is even if it is a circuitous route to getting to it. If objective means distant and cold – forget it. If objective means being even-handed and fair minded, that's another thing and sometimes even that is irrelevant. If you are making a very passionate film about what you think is an injustice then you don't want to be even handed. But you have to be honest at least with the people you deal with. Then the way you approach them depends on what you are doing. If you want anything emotional or revealing then you have to be very much at one with your subject so you will give them the confidence to be open with you.

Q – Are there any differences when you interview children?

Michael – I find the best thing with children is not to patronize them. Treat them like adults. Once you start putting on funny voices or talking down to them, kids resent that.

Q – What advice would you give to new filmmakers on ethics?

Michael – It's a private matter. I don't think you can legislate for it. You have to be honorable. You have to tell people what you're going to do and do it. Don't cross any line to them. Don't lie to them. Don't deceive them. You might think I'm going to have to do something because it's very important that I get some statement out here and I may have to misrepresent it. Maybe you do, but it's a question of your personal ethics. I love arguing with people that documentary is a pure form whereas narrative films are contrived. But every edit you make is a judgment. Making a documentary film is full of judgment calls and therefore full of ethical calls as well. And I don't think doing something like paying people compromises things necessarily. I paid people on the *Up* films because it's a business and someone is trying to make money out of it and therefore why shouldn't they. If people are only doing it for money or they're being paid a lot to say something then there may be a strong ethical breach. Then you're buying information. But if you're paying people for their time or the exposure they have to deal with, there's a difference between those two things.

Q – To what extent should a filmmaker be thinking about their audience?

Michael – Always. We are in the business of entertainment. And too many documentaries show no thought of some end result. You have to make it for people. You are trying to communicate something. You don't patronize the audience. You don't confuse the audience. Pay attention to their needs. Know who your audience is so you can talk the right language to them. You're never making it for yourself.

Q – What are the common mistakes that you see new documentary filmmakers make?

Michael – The structure issue. The thought that all you have to do is shoot a lot of material and somehow the story will emerge. It's true with experienced documentarians as well. And it's become more endemic with the relative cheapness of stock and digital. Have some sense of the structure and the end product in your mind.

QUEEN OF THE DOC

Q – What does the term documentary filmmaking mean to you?

Barbara – For me it's about taking the time to go beneath the surface and find the heart of the story. I think documentary film makers struggle to create unforgettable and entertaining films that introduce people to characters they might never know. Or show a different side of people that maybe we thought we already knew. I think that documentary films and filmmakers sometimes take you halfway around the world or just to the other side of the tracks. Any way you sort of go with it, it's a journey that can change you forever. I think what makes this journey possible is the collaboration you have with other directors, with camera people, with editors, with sound people and the subjects of your film.

Q – Do you think it's important for a documentary filmmaker to go to film school?

Barbara – I didn't go to film school. I learned by doing. I got to work with the Maysles brothers. I got to do sound, editing and got to see how things came together. I just wanted to be out in the field. I wanted to feel it, taste it and be part of it in whatever way I could. I was voracious in learning so that no one could ever say to me you can't do this. I needed to be able to say, *"Yes, you can."*

Q – What advice would you give a new filmmaker in choosing subject matter?

Barbara – The subject matter you choose is something you're hungry for. It should have a diverse perspective and a story that makes the film come alive and turns the viewer on. Maybe it even fills a void. Something that makes you, as a filmmaker, want to go out into mainstream media, to use every device you possibly can, to make a film that means and says something to you. It makes you laugh or cry. Or the people that you follow are so fascinating that they just jump off the screen.

Q – How can you get subjects to trust you especially when you are treading on sensitive ground?

Barbara – You have to be real. You have to be true to who you are and put yourself out there as a person, as a filmmaker – be part of whatever you are doing. There are no agendas to go by. I think you just have to be as truthful as you can with your subjects.

Q – How do you diffuse tense situations with subjects or crewmembers?

Barbara – I'm extremely patient and if somebody flares up, I don't take it personally. What I struggle to do is to go underneath who that person is and try to figure out what could've possibly made them flare up. Then I try to go at it around a different corner or from a different perspective. And suddenly everything else will stop and it's about figuring out why they're in that place, whether it's a cameraperson or sound person. I always let them talk and I never come at anyone from a place of anger. I just listen and try to take them in a different direction.

Q – Are there any ethical boundaries that you feel shouldn't be crossed when making a documentary?

Barbara – Not that I want to skirt the issue, but you never know until you're in one. It's difficult to tell you. In eastern

Kentucky, when we were doing *Harlan County*, the issue was trying to stay alive. And trying to stay on that picket line. We're always trying to film in a way that would ensure nothing would happen to anybody on that picket line and to these people that I'd come to know and care about so much. I think it just depends on when you walk into it, what you do and who you are. It's almost like making a documentary film, you can't script how you are going to react, what you're going to say or do.

Q – When you were on that picket line was the camera acting more like a shield or a red flag to a bull?

Barbara – It could've been either one. To me it was a shield and maybe to the strikebreakers it was a red flag. I felt protected because I had my Nagra with a mic and Kevin Keating and Hart Perry had their cameras. While you're recording, you feel safe because you can see and are attuned to everything that's going on. But then the people on the other side were pissed off that we were there and preventing them from doing what they wanted to do.

Q – How do you deal with dangerous situations like when you were shot at with machine guns?

Barbara – You just have to be in the moment. You don't think about a schedule of things or get out a list of things to do. You just think about survival. If I do this, what will happen in the spur of the moment? It's like a car accident – everything slows down and you sort of go with it and watch it happen.

Q – Do you have any advice on pitching projects to funders?

Barbara –You need to know what story you want to tell and really do research on the different places that you are pitching. What are the kinds of things that they show? You should tell them something that's within the line of what they're doing, but it's also something they've never heard before. So somehow you're inspiring them to maybe break their own rules or question what they're supposed to be doing. You have to size up whom you are telling it to. Stories are things that we all share together and if you tell them something that you really feel committed to and so vibrant and passionate about, you are going to get them to feel that way. Sheila Nevins, who is the head of programming at HBO, says, *"It may not be what someone says, because in documentaries it takes all different shapes and it goes in all different ways. But if there's passion behind the filmmaker, and if it comes from their heart, I'll probably do it."*

Q – When a filmmaker sits down to start their project, what are some of the main things they should be talking about? Is it important to think about where it will end up?

Barbara – When I start a project and I have no funding, no distributor, and the only one interested in it is me, I don't think about where it's going to end up. I think about who the people are, what the story is, how we can film it, what the style is, the humor in it, the sadness in it. I think more in those terms.

Q – What do you see as the future of documentary film?

Barbara – This is a new era for documentary films and as non-fiction filmmakers we are reaching larger audiences. Documentaries are making more money than ever before. There are entire networks with portions dedicated, for the first time, to non-fiction programming. And there is this new generation that is stepping up to the plate and bringing with it hard-hitting, entertaining and political films to audiences. I just think this is one of the most exciting times I've ever seen for this genre of film.

Q – What should a filmmaker think about as they sit down to edit their film?

Barbara – When I go into an editing room, and particularly if I have been on location, I keep my mouth shut while the editor is watching. That way he or she can feel what is happening. When you're in the field, you have been part of what the editor is watching, and if you start talking about it, you are bringing a lot more to what they're seeing on the screen. After they've seen everything, and I always like to sit where I can see their faces and watch where they smile or get bored, I like to see what the editor takes in. Once they have seen it, then they can stop me dead in my tracks when we talk about structure and what we have in a scene. They can tell me if I don't have something. It makes for a totally even playing field. Editors in documentary films are incredible storytellers and are the people who really help shape these films. They're so important. It has to be someone that you like and respect and someone who is there because they care about the subject matter and the story.

Q – What do you think of the demise of film and the rise of HD?

Barbara – I love film, but it's very costly. The most important thing is to tell a story and to get out there and make the kind of films that you want to make. For me, the content is what is most urgent. Regardless of the medium you're working with, you need to have a DP like Joan Churchill, Tom Hurwitz, Don Lenzer, or Gary Griffin – someone who can really be a storyteller with the camera.

Q – What common mistakes do you see documentary filmmakers make?

Barbara – I don't know if there are common mistakes because you're not in their editing room. You're not in the field with them. You don't know what they have to work with. You absolutely do the best with what you have. I think as a filmmaker, you can't talk too much. You have to have a place that's comfortable for whoever you are filming so that person blooms and is open. You can't push your agenda on anybody else. That allows them to take it to other places, the characters. And they will totally surprise and shock you. It's better than anything you have in your head. So keep quiet and let your characters take the lead.

Q – What advice would you give a new documentary filmmaker?

Barbara – As a new filmmaker, they are taking on an incredible responsibility when they walk into the world of someone else. Making a documentary brings you closer together and shows our collective human spirit. You need to have a personal responsibility to the people you are filming. It's so important. We have to respect them and their story.

What To Do If You're Arrested Or Questioned By The Police...

GUERILLA FILM MAKER SAYS!

During the '70s, a bunch of filmmakers working on the documentary, Weather Underground, were harassed by the government. Not only were they wiretapped and put under surveillance, but they were issued with subpoenas, which were then withdrawn. Issuing and then withdrawing subpoenas was a very powerful technique of harassment. Withdrawn subpoenas can be reissued at any time and the filmmakers are subject to immediate arrest. Fearing confiscation of their material the filmmakers were not able to work securely on their film. As we know, wiretapping is now strongly planted back in the government of today, even though it's illegal and violates the Fourth Amendment and other Constitutional protections guaranteed to every American. So could the situation of Weather Underground happen again? If you criticize the government as a documentary filmmaker, are you headed for the wiretapping list? Are pseudo documentaries such as Peter Watkin's controversial Punishment Park going to actually exist? Since 9/11 more and more documentary filmmakers are coming across the new government laws such as the Patriot Act or the Material Witness Detention Policy i.e. Cyrus Kar, who was filming a historical documentary in Iraq was detained by U.S. personnel for 50 days. Rakesh Sharma, a well known Indian filmmaker was detained and harassed by the NYPD while filming on the streets of New York. The ACLU (American Civil Liberties Union) says his is the first suit to challenge the constitutionality of New York's film-permit practices, which in the post-9/11 atmosphere expose low-budget and independent filmmakers to risk of arrest simply for documenting public places. Here are some tips of what to do when facing a similar situation...

1. Never admit guilt, in fact, do not say anything while being arrested. Remember you have the constitutional right to remain silent. It is NOT a crime to refuse to answer questions. Although the only question you should answer is your name as you can be arrested in some states for refusing to provide it.

2. You have the right to speak with your lawyer, whether or not the police inform you of that right. As soon as you request to speak with a lawyer, the police should stop asking you questions. Even if you don't have a lawyer, you must still request a lawyer and the court will appoint one for you. The police should offer you one phone call, where you should call your lawyer, or your most responsible relative/friend/producer who will either come to bail you out or hire an attorney.

What To Do If You're Arrested Or Questioned By The Police... Continued

3. Anything you say to law enforcement can be used against you and others. Remember your Miranda Rights: "anything you say can and will be used against you in a court of law." Lying to a government official is a crime but remaining silent until you consult with your lawyer is not.

4. You have the right to have your lawyer present during your interview, and you can stop the interview at any point to talk to your attorney.

5. Unless you are charged, they cannot take your photo or prints.

6. Make sure you find out all the charges against you and discuss with your lawyer whether they are criminal or civil charges, and further, if they are felonies or misdemeanors.

7. If the police stop you on the street, ask if you are free to go. If the answer is yes, just walk away. If the police say you are not under arrest, but are NOT free to go, then you are being detained. The police can pat down the outside of your clothing if they have reason to suspect you might be armed or dangerous. If they search any more than this, say clearly, "I do not consent to a search." They may keep searching anyway.

8. If stopped filming on the street by the police, the police are not allowed to confiscate your tapes and camera. If they ask to see your footage you do not need to show it to them. If you refuse to hand over your tapes and your camera to the police, you should not be arrested. As soon as you pass over your camera to them, you have given the police permission.

9. In certain states, such as California, documentary filmmakers are viewed as newsgatherers. And a professional journalist cannot be forced to give up unpublished material, except in the limited context of a criminal proceeding where the defendant subpoenas the material. A grand jury subpoena is a written order for you to go to court and testify about information you may have. However, even then, the criminal defendant must prove to the court that without the subpoenaed material, a fair trial is impossible for him before the court will order the material produced.

10. If the police stop you in your car, keep your hands where the police can see them. You do not have to consent to a search. But if the police have probable cause to believe that you have been involved in a crime or that you have evidence of a crime in your car, your car can be searched without your consent. Clearly state that you do not consent. Officers may separate passengers and drivers from each other to question them and compare their answers, but no one has to answer any questions.

11. Police or other law enforcement agents cannot search your home unless you give them permission, or unless they have a search warrant. A search warrant is a court order that allows the police to conduct a specified search. Do not interfere with the search as you will not stop it and you might get arrested. But you should say clearly that you have not given your consent and that the search is against your wishes. Your roommate or guest can legally consent to a search of your house if the police believe that person has the authority to give consent. Police and law enforcement need a warrant to search an office, but your employer can consent to a search of your workplace without your permission.

12. A search warrant does not mean that you have to answer questions.

13. If agents do not have a search warrant, you do not have to let the police search your home and you do not have to answer their questions. The police cannot get a warrant based on your refusal.

14. If they search your home without a warrant, do not get in the way and if someone is there with you, ask them to witness that you are not giving permission for the search. Call your lawyer as soon as possible. Get the names and badge numbers of the searching officers.

15. If the police or FBI threaten to get a subpoena, you should call a lawyer right away. Anything you say can usually be used against you.

16. If you're treated badly by the police or FBI, write down the officer's badge number, name or other identifying information. You have a right to ask the officer for this information. Try to find witnesses and their names and phone numbers. If you are injured, seek medical attention and take pictures of the injuries as soon as you can. Call a lawyer or contact your local ACLU office.

17. Remember, if you have been taken downtown, unless you've killed somebody, absconded with the entire production budget or funded your film through drug dealing, you should be out of jail within 24-48 hours.

18. DO NOT PISS off the police. ALWAYS be courteous and polite!

For more information, check out the ACLU website: http://www.aclu.com/.

St. Clair Bourne

SEEK TRUTH

Q – What led you to documentary filmmaking?

St. Clair - Basically, it was dissatisfaction with what I saw on TV about the Civil Rights Movement. Many of the times they got it wrong about what they said about black people. When I was coming up, the media was just about to open up for black people. At the time I thought the height of being a documentary filmmaker was being a producer on a national network like CBS. They had the money, the exposure and the audience. And at the time, they actually did, but they essentially didn't have the truth. Through a series of circumstances American public TV created a series called *Black Journal* and it allowed me a chance to make the films I wanted to make and have an audience; clearly not the audience CBS had, but then people started to look at public TV as a place to get new information, black and white, and then brown and yellow, etc. So though I gripe about it now, public TV was a way for me to start projects.

Q – Was this at the height of the Civil Rights Movement?

St. Clair – It was 1968 and the Civil Rights Movement had basically run its course and the Black Power movement was coming in. Black people as a group began to want power to figure out what they wanted to do whether white liberals agreed with them or not. I was able to make films that captured that spirit. And because the power structure didn't really know what we were doing, we could get away with it. That experience still empowers me to this day - the feeling of being able to make a film and have people act on the information you gave to them.

Q – What was Black Journal?

St. Clair – It was the first black controlled national public TV documentary series. What happened happens a lot in America - white liberals started the idea of black show. And they said it was to be by, for and of black people. But in fact, of the 32 people on staff, only 11 were African-American. Most of the producers were white. They were very sincere and had good intentions, but they began to interpret our experience. So we went on strike and literally embarrassed them as liberals. We had press conferences saying they advertised such and such, but this is the reality and they won't give up the power. They backed off, changed the structure and we began to do the work and make the films of the contemporary black social experience in these short documentaries. There were two people who were hosts and then we the producers went out and produced 5 minute to 25 minute film pieces. Sometimes we would have in studio discussions.

Q – It seems like it was breaking new ground.

St. Clair – It very much was breaking new ground. The only reason they kept us doing it was that we had a great audience. It was African-American based, but then white people began to discover it because they could find out things about their black citizens that no one else was saying. So they tuned in and wrote in saying, *"we didn't know this."*

Q – How different is documentary filmmaking now from then?

St. Clair – Back then, because we were doing reports for TV, you couldn't get that fancy with it. We usually had one of the two hosts as the narrators and the interviews were mostly on camera interviews. There were some voice-overs, but they thought that was too avant garde. And in fact, if you apply for co-financing from the PBS series *American Experience* today they will send you the same sheet that they adhered to back then. You must set up what you are going to say with an expert. Show what they're talking about and then have another expert explain what they've just seen. If you're a documentarian in this country, and you are making a film for American public TV, you have to realize the rest of the world doesn't respect that format. So if you're making a film like that for PBS, you really need to think about alternative versions in terms of being able to sell it. Also if you want to sell it to France for example, who have really good budgets, they're not interested in seeing talking heads speaking English. That means they have to add either a voice over or subtitles, so visually it's easier for them if you already have the visuals and have a voice over because they can just put in subtitles. That's a technique that you have to be aware of when you talk co-productions.

Q – Do you use verité style?

St. Clair – Yes. That was en vogue when I started and I like that. And because we were new, most of the documentaries would have a college professor or some expert being interviewed, but we at *Black Journal* would get articulate people from the community to talk. We called it *The Interior Voice* – the voice from inside the community. That's another technique for filmmakers. I'm not saying one is better than the other, but if you choose to do a film about somebody in the community, let the funders know because that's now an added production value. A big difference now is that most funders would like to see the film that you're going to make on paper. In the old days, you could go in and say, *"I have this idea. I'm not sure how it's going to work out. Here are some the elements."* They would say, *"Here's some development money. Go out and let us see what it looks like."* What they really want now is a producer to come in with that on paper and a 5-7 minute trailer. The technology is relatively cheap so you can do it. But it's certainly a difference.

Q – Is that because of this recent explosion of documentary filmmaking?

St. Clair – It's part of it. The other thing is budgets are decreasing Three or four years ago, Discovery would pay $350,000-$400,000 for an hour doc and now it's down to $200,000. So if they commit to development, they're going to make the film. And they want to see if your subject that you have decided to tell the story through is TV friendly. I produced a film for HBO on Gordon Parks who was a world famous photographer, they had me go out and film him to see if the camera likes him.

Q – So it has not gotten any easier for you despite having made 40 plus films.

St. Clair – I have to jump through the same hoops because it has changed from the quality of the idea to demographics. When I go to meetings now, I have to make the subject matter appeal to the 18-26 year old demographic. That means that any historical subject prior to the 1980's, I have to have a way to make that appealing to a young audience.

Q – Does that mean now that these docs will have a one-sided point of view?

St. Clair – That's really the skill of independent producing - making the case that the point of view that you want to put in your film, if it's not in line with what they think, has an audience. Again, we're back to demographics. What I'd encourage filmmakers to do now is not get caught up in the philosophical argument of what is objectivity and should the broadcaster show all sides or not. Figure out where they're coming from and try to adjust your pitch in line with that. They don't want to hear about the larger picture. They turn off.

Q – Have you noticed archival houses charging a lot for clips and not giving in perpetuity lengths anymore?

St. Clair – Yes. What I'm encouraging filmmakers to do is to make contemporary subject matter that alludes to the past. It reduces the need for archival footage and also the stuff that you create becomes archival footage for the next generation. Then you can sell it and you don't have to be as exploitative as these current houses are. But with the clips now, you can purchase different scales. You can buy it for just domestic TV or just for film festival exposure or both. Or film festival, domestic TV and foreign TV. Or one for domestic theatrical. If you can afford it when you do your budget, you should put in a figure for what they call "buy out." That's for rights to all windows. That way, if somebody wants to buy it for, say, Arte, you've got it cleared for everything. And now that there's Fair Use, there's a way for people to not have to necessarily go to archival houses.

Q – Is it still possible to make films about Civil Rights in the way that you want to?

St. Clair – Advocacy was a valid artistic approach in the Civil Rights days. Now advocacy, especially if it's against something the government is doing, is not big. They don't really like that today because of two things, the power of the government in terms of controlling media and also the compression of the existing media corporations and their closeness with people in the government. The way you can get around that is doing what Robert Greenwald is doing. That's to identify your audience and feed them the information directly. The thing about ethnic material is that it's always under attack. Culturally, this country is run with a Eurocentric sensibility. Oddly enough, myself as a media activist of African American descent, I never find a shortage of material. Frankly, I'd rather there wasn't because it would reflect a better society but the reality is that it's on going and it'll probably be on going. And it's just not ethnicities. Gays, for example, have to think about how their message fits into an increasingly conservative environment.

Q – Given today's environment of illegal wiretapping, it feels like nothing's really changed from the 1950's.

St. Clair – The hard lesson that I've had to learn and prevents me from burning out is America is a perpetual work-in-progress. There are always new immigrants coming into the country and that upsets the people who are already here. So there's always turmoil. For a documentary filmmaker, that's really good because there's always material. Secondly, there's a class struggle here that no one talks about. The people who own the means of production and the people who work in that structure of production are always in that battle. One of the reasons we always fight the same battles, is because we always approach it as: once it's won, it's done. But that's not true because nobody really looks at it from a class analysis. I curated a special program at the Full Frame Film Festival on class in America. I looked at over 100 films and I'm very disappointed because even in the progressive wing of documentary filmmaking community, the idea of class is shown via ethnic films. They think a poor black person being helped by a white person is a class issue. There are class elements in it, but what I'm hoping for is for more people to incorporate class in their films. That goes for me, too. I'm basically a race man, but I've had to realize that my films are incomplete unless I put in class. There will still be this battle, but at least you will know why and not get as frustrated.

Q – Do you see a lot of censorship today?

St. Clair – Yes, I do. Two ways. One, it's masked as marketing. They don't say, *"We don't want this material in there."* What they say is, *"Well, there's no audience,"* or *"People won't understand this,"* or *"Our demographics indicate that we don't know who this person is."* For example, there's a guy named Dick Gregory who was a comedian and social activist and I pitched that to several people. They won't say, *"Well, we don't know if we want this black guy critiquing and accusing the government of diminishing the rights of citizens."* What they'll say is, *"Nobody knows who he really is."* The other type of censorship is self-censorship and this is happening more and more. Filmmakers will say they want to make a film about how the government is cheating the citizens of voters. *"Wow, that is going to be hard. Maybe I'll just show one case where one machine didn't work. So I won't indict the system, I will treat it as an individual situation."* That's self-censorship.

Q – There are though those filmmakers like Michael Moore who don't fall into that trap.

St. Clair – Yes. Spike Lee did the same thing when he came up. He became a showman. He marketed his image as a provocative person. In Spike's case, it was a militant, kick ass filmmaker who speaks the truth on behalf of the black masses, which is what he was. In Michael Moore's case, it was this fat guy from Michigan who was a working class hero who struggled to tell the truth against this huge structure in America that was trying to screw the white middle class. And he made them laugh every once and awhile. He's very clever.

Q – Can the documentary community support many filmmakers like that?

St. Clair – No. That's the thing. Part of the way of marketing your film is that you become subject to the understanding of marketing. That's if you have an image, you can only push that image so far because people burn out on it. So either you have to put it out there little by little so that it doesn't or you have to let it go out there, burn out and come up with something new. I don't think the community can support a gimmick or a technique for a long time. The only thing they will support is good information. And even that has to be jazzed up a bit. A good example is *Emmett Till.* It's not a great film, but the information that comes out there is fantastic and in fact, it reopened the case.

Q – So how would you define the term "documentary"?

St. Clair – I'd have said innovative, journalistically based films, but I can't say that anymore because people are using re-creations and animation. It's always changing. In fact, when I first started making films, the camera work that exists in films and music videos today was considered bad camera work. Point of view, shaky camera, lots of angles – you wouldn't be hired if you brought in stuff like that and now the audience accepts and likes it. I think a good documentary should be of service to the audience. They should feel they have more information that makes them think their lives can be better. And there's a commitment of truth to the information that you bring to your audience. After that, anything else is up for grabs.

Q – With news in the US being so concerned about ratings, sound bites and entertainment, are documentaries one of the last places where someone can find truth?

St. Clair – Yes and that's why the documentary has gotten popular in the last half decade. People are getting information from them that they would not get from their regular news broadcast. That's why they're willing to pay for it. People may want sensational docs soon. *Super Size Me* is an example of this. He took that technique and now has a TV series. And it's not bad. As long as they have a commitment to truth and information to make you live better, then it's good.

Q – Can you be objective in documentary filmmaking?

St. Clair – That's a myth. And I think people use that ploy to cool out the truth. *"What you say may be true, but you're not being objective."* Maybe, maybe not, but that's not what I am trying to do. Everybody has a point of view – how you shoot it and whom you choose to shoot – all of that is personal and subjective so objectivity is out the window.

Q – And with so many points of view, it is difficult to know what is right and wrong.

St. Clair – *Control Room* explores that. And there's a new film called *Desire*. It's about a white woman who follows four teenage girls of different ethnicities in New Orleans pre-Katrina. She puts herself in it and she teaches the four young women to make their own films, which she puts in this documentary. And then she allows herself to be interviewed by them. She's trying to avoid being the boss because she comes from a privileged background. If you come at it that way, it's OK. She says this is good information and at the same times lets me know what their prejudices are.

Q – Do you think since 9/11 there's been a difference in documentaries as far as where they're coming from?

St. Clair – More important is how the government has handled it. After 9/11 there was a burst of patriotic films about us being attacked and that was basically white people. People of color said, *"I'm not surprised."* This country has fucked over a lot of people. A lot of Columbians and San Salvadorians remember 15 years ago. What filmmakers have seen is the government try to mould a media concept – to promote fear. So in their films they have tried to counter that. It makes people go deeper than the projected view of American life. Once you do that once, you do that in all your stuff. White America has been coddled. There haven't been that many bad things that have happened to white America other than 9/11 whereas overseas it happens all the time. Filmmakers have to address the fear or puzzlement that they have about American life, and if possible give an antidote to that.

Q – Again, it feels like we have gone back to the 1950's.

St. Clair – It's because people are scared. You would have thought that Oklahoma City would've done it but somehow because it was white people who did it, but they looked at them as crazy white people who don't know how lucky they are. But when people of color do it....look out. People of color are considered by most white people to be inferior or not as smart. And yet they blew up this iconic building. If they had gotten the White House like they were trying, it really would've freaked people out. That's why the Patriot Act gets signed even though it's not right, we don't want to get attacked again.

Q – In the UK, people can really question the Prime Minister, in the US the President is treated with so much respect he doesn't seem to have any checks.

St. Clair – It's not respect, it's fear. That's where the documentary people jump in fearlessly. Their job is to question them no matter who's there. And that's why Reagan started to cut the funding of institutions to documentary filmmakers. They cut the NEA and the NEH by saying these are the *"hate America people."* I was there for this. The press secretary would call the presidents of networks and say, *"The White House was displeased with this report."*

Q – What would be the response of the filmmaker to the President?

St. Clair – *"We can't make this film. I really don't want the White House on my ass because they may instruct the IRS to do an investigation and cause us to explain to our stockholders why the IRS is looking at us."* I'm amazed at the amount of documentaries get made given the pressure to stop that line of inquiry. Usually it's the young people who do it. I can feel myself getting tired. I choose my battles now. Documentarians have to band together now. You have to have a real posse and everyone has to acknowledge their role.

Q – How has black documentary making changed over time?

St. Clair – Back then, there was a feeling of overt political commitment and the battle was to get the resources to fill that. Right now, there isn't a political commitment. At best, it is an attempt to rewrite history so that our role is in it. *Emmett Till* and *Gordon Parks* are exactly that – to go back into the past and show another version. One thing that has been achieved is that a black point of view is integral to talking about America. Diversity is a given.

Q – Do people of different races and socio-economic classes experience film in different ways and how does that affect documentary filmmaking?

St. Clair – Yes. On the race thing, if you grew up as African-American working class, you see how differently the system works for someone who is African-American and middle class. Even though they're still African American, it's at odds with the Euro-centric culture of the country. That comes into play when you pitch to a network or commissioning editor because you have to legitimize the black view. You don't have to do that if it's white. For example, if we talk about slavery then we have to say many years later the working class sees the cars and jewelry as things they were deprived of and now it's seen as achievement. You have to be very clear about what elements you want to put in depending on whom you want to talk to.

Q – How do you feel about minority programming?

St. Clair – At the time, we were so shoved to the side we were thrilled when someone said, *"There must be money set aside for minority programming."* It was an acknowledgment of our existence. Same with Black History month, *"During February we must make sure that information about blacks are on TV."* Good! Now we say, wait a minute. Why just once a year? We're just as American as anyone else. Our sensibilities aren't in the minority. There're more white kids listening to hip-hop now than ever. Some of it is just ignorance because if you confront people on it they say, *"Oh, yeah. You're right."* With Paul Robeson, I lost a battle because I wanted it to air during his birthday in April, but they said no – Black History month. It will change. Black basketball style of playing used to be called black basketball, now it's just basketball style.

Q – Do you miss film?

St. Clair – Yes because of the look. But I've had to shake that off. There are advantages to video. You can shoot more and you don't have to stop every ten minutes to reload. There are technical things you can do like film-look and colorizing. I haven't had the chance to shoot HD yet.

Q – What are the biggest challenges in documentary filmmaking?

St. Clair – Financing. After that, it's the artistic control of it. And then it's outreach. Getting it to as many people as possible as well as getting it to the people who will benefit the most from the material.

Q – Do you think the traditional path of distribution is dying?

St. Clair – I think more and more it's going to go directly to the audience. In 7-10 years, you'll be able to download the films. Just put in your credit card and it will come through. I don't think the traditional way is going to disappear, but I think it just won't be the only way.

Q – What tips would you give documentary filmmakers on having long careers?

St. Clair – You should really have a group that you talk to and work with. I'd concentrate on engaging with material that you're personally fascinated and attracted to. It's really hard to make a film and sometimes the only thing that keeps you going is your personal interest in the material. Have a good accountant who keeps track of all your bills and can tell you when you're over budget. And whatever you do, publicize. People laugh at me because I send something out every week or two. I'm not NBC and I don't have a publicist. So I have a list of people who work for the papers, who are freelance journalists and the word of mouth people. Don't wait until you finish the film. Each time you accomplish a step, announce it.

Q – Is having people around you why you started your organization?

St. Clair – Yes. The Black Documentary Collective in New York and The Black Association of Documentary Filmmakers in Los Angeles. When I started working, I had a whole group of colleagues that I could talk to. But as time went on, some of them fell away – they quit, started teaching or died. When I started doing *Gordon Parks*, I realized in the production meetings that I am the only one from my generation. And I wouldn't be able to talk to anyone about anything and when the production was over, I'd be alone. So I put word out for African American documentary filmmakers to get together so we wouldn't be alone. I would rent a space once a month and people would come. After three months I formed an organization in New York, The Collective and one in LA, West. They're separate and have their own personalities.

Q – What are the common mistakes that you see documentary filmmakers make?

St. Clair – Accepting as gospel the way things have been done before. In the long run, you may have to retreat to that position, but don't come into HBO or Discovery that way because they may buy some of your new ideas and let you try them. They say they are open to new stuff, so take them up on it. That's one thing I see with the black groups. They're so happy to be working after a lifetime of discrimination that they won't shake it up. And a lot of the time, if it's black material, the networks want to be told what to do.

Q – What advice would you give to a new documentary filmmaker?

St. Clair – It may sound corny, but you have to really chart out what you want to do because once you do that, you can go anywhere. You're the center of what you want to do. It takes a lot of heart to do that but it is what keeps you going. Go into Discovery and say I just got out of film school and I've got some new shit. What do you think? So self-affirmation, not big headedness, is important because that informs how you approach the money and other people to work with you.

ACTUAL REALITY

Q – What does documentary filmmaking mean to you?

R.J. – It's a form of storytelling that uses real life and real people to tell true stories. What I learned from D.A. Pennebaker and Chris Hegedus when I did *The War Room* is that cinema verité is a form of documentary filmmaking that aspires to all the things that great scripted movies aspire to. As a documentary filmmaker, I go into a situation and observe and film it as clearly as I can. In the post-production process, I work as hard as I can to tell a truthful a story about what I witnessed. Documentary filmmaking isn't objective. I spent time as a journalist and it's not satisfying or possible to me to be objective. But that doesn't mean my obligation to tell the truth is any less than the obligation the journalist has. I combine the story of what I witnessed with the experience I had while witnessing it. So if you look at a film like *A Perfect Candidate*, if you had witnessed the Chuck Robb-Ollie North Senate campaign for an entire year and had filmed it, what you might have seen would've been the exact same thing that I saw, but the film you made would be completely different. And the difference would be the difference between you and me.

Q – Two of your shows 30 Days and Black. White. seem to invoke social change or at least for people to think about the world around them. Is that important for documentary films?

R.J. – All narrative art gets people to think about the world around them. I'd tell you that I don't consider myself to be an agit-prop filmmaker. I'm exploring things and asking questions. That question might be - what's it like to run a presidential campaign? How come Oliver North is able to raise $17 million and run for Senate in Virginia when seven years earlier he was about to go to jail for lying to Congress? Or what's it like for a white male from the Bible belt who believes homosexuality is a sin to spend a month with a gay roommate with whom he might develop a strong friendship? I know there're others who use documentary to pursue social change. For me, it's really about telling stories of real people by asking questions and exploring the answers from many different angles.

Q – How is working on a feature length documentary film different from working on a season of TV?

R.J. – Film and television have many things in common and many things that are different. One of the things that I learned from Penne is it's important to know what you're doing right from the beginning. In a theatrical environment, your audience has chosen to come see the film. The first thing you do is give them an opportunity to settle into the movie and leave the world behind. TV, which has its own advantages in terms of storytelling and reaching audiences, is very different. Your audience may have made a choice to come to you, but they're constantly conscious of all sorts of other choices that they have. And unless you are working in a premium cable environment or a non-ad supported environment, every 12 minutes or so there's a reason for them to go away. So you're thinking about all sorts of different things in terms of structure — you have to build in what we call act-ins and act-outs. When you're editing a film that's for theatrical release, it's a very different thing because you aren't working with those built-in breaks and you aren't working with those kinds of constraints. I'm not saying that one is better than the other, only that you're thinking about different things. Among the advantages that television has is the fact that you're far more likely to have all the money you need to make your project, or at least you have a big head start. Whereas if you're making an independent theatrical film, the chances are that you're doing it on maxed-out credit cards or borrowed money from friends and family.

Q – What is it that film and TV have in common?

R.J. – The process of making a television series or a theatrical film is mostly exactly the same. The tools you use - character, narrative, interwoven stories, earning the trust of your subject, combining the experience you witness with the one you have – those are all the same, whether you're working in film or television. In both, you always have to be aware that first and foremost the story belongs to the subject and not to you. Lots of things follow from that. If they don't want to be filmed at any given moment, I don't want to be filming them. Why? The story belongs to the subject and not to me. When I'm editing I'm always focused on telling the story as truthfully as possible. Why? Because the story belongs to the subject and not to me. In the field I work very hard to impact the environment that I am in as minimally as possible. Why? Because the story belongs to the subject and not to me. One of the greatest misconceptions about cinema verité filmmaking is that the filmmakers become 'flies on the wall.' Documentary filmmakers are human sized, present and in the room. They don't disappear or fade into the woodwork. What a good filmmaker does is create an environment wherein the subject becomes as comfortable as they would be with a good friend whom they trusted. So the most important thing to do when working on these projects, TV or movies, is to earn the trust of your subject. There are many ways to do that and you have to do it every day. The most important way to earn trust is to be who you say you are. You have to tell the truth.

Q – On American High you gave the kids cameras. Did you train them and is that a good way to earn trust?

R.J. – In getting access to the high school, one of the administrators said, *"What's in it for the kids?"* I said, *"Well, they get to be in the film and they get to work with these filmmakers."* He said, *"OK, but this is a school. What are they going to learn outside of experience?"* That was a damn good question. So I thought, what if they were able to learn something concrete, for instance how to use a camera? Then I realized the way to do it was to teach them to use the cameras so that in those moments where the filmmaker isn't present, we can still capture the experience the subject is having. In fact, the subjects will be able to capture it themselves. The filmmaker's not going to be there at 1am when 17-year-old Kaytee Dodle is thinking about a guy she loves. But if Kaytee has a camera and has been taught the principles of composition, angles and lenses and how they can help communicate, then Kaytee can contribute to the story in a way I never could. I found that the texture of the experience and the contribution of this internal monologue added great depth to the stories.

Q – What tips would you give new filmmakers on pitching TV executives?

R.J. – Don't pitch TV executives, go out and make a movie. If you're really hell bent on selling a TV idea, and if you have a good idea that you really must make, then I'd consider partnering up with someone with a little more experience. It was extremely valuable to me to work with DA Pennebaker and Chris Hegedus when I was first starting out on *The War Room*. Other than that, I'd say, try to sell ideas that you are truly passionate about and you feel that you need to make. It's always going to be very hard, so if you don't really care about it, it's just not worth it.

Q – Is it difficult to give up final cut when working for a broadcaster or studio?

R.J. – Not really. I can't think of a single instance where a network or studio has cut behind me or asked me to change something that I really didn't want to. So really the question is, how difficult is it to take notes from network and studio executives. And the answer is that it's not difficult at all, and in the best cases it can be extremely helpful. You're always going to be getting input during production and post. In a TV environment, hopefully you're working with smart executives whose insight and advice is going to help you. It's always hard to get notes from anyone be it your best friend, your mother or a TV executive. You think you've done it the best you can and done it the right way and someone tells you a scene isn't working – that's hard for anybody to hear. So one of the things you have to learn is how to listen. When I'm getting notes, I always write everything down. I type as I take notes. I want to make sure that I'm hearing it as clearly as possible. Because sometimes my first reaction is they don't know what they're talking about. But then I give myself a little time to reflect. And on reflection I've got to admit that they're probably right. Even if they don't have the right solution to a problem, they've likely identified an issue that needs to be addressed. To me, anyone who is looking at your work before it's done is a potentially helpful resource. It's an opportunity to make your work better. I always say if you look at an unborn child at seven months and you expect it to be cooing, you're going to be disappointed. It's still growing. The same is true of art, and that's why it's hard to show it to people before it's completed. But if you have some friends whom you can trust, you need to show it to them. And you don't even have to ask them about it afterwards, because if you're really honest you can tell what's working and what isn't just by standing in the back of the room and observing. You can tell what's funny and what's boring. You can't avoid the truth when you show it to people.

Q – Any tips on going from managing a small three-person crew to several crews and editors on a TV show?

R.J. – You don't have to know how to do everything, but you do have to know how to get people who know how to do everything. That's what producing is. You get the right team together to solve the problem at hand. On my first film, *The War Room*, he first thing I did was call Wendy Ettinger and ask her to produce it with me. She was my friend and I had tremendous respect for her opinion. She also had great access to the resources to get the film made. The next thing we did was go over to DA Pennebaker and Chris Hegedus and asked them to direct the film. That was just good producing.

Q – Do you usually compensate the subjects for your films and TV shows financially?

R.J. – It depends on the circumstances. When you're making a straight up documentary like *American High* or *Thin*, then no there's no compensation for the subjects. But projects like *Black. White.* where we asked the six family members who participated in it to leave their jobs and homes over a six week period, we gave them a stipend. It wasn't a lot of money – probably not as much as they would have earned in their jobs. But we didn't want them to be unfairly burdened by the fact that they were participating in the show.

Q – What ethics should filmmakers be thinking about when dealing with sensitive material?

R.J. – The story belongs to the subject and not to you. You have to be who you say you are and earn the trust of your subject every day. Acting according to these principles is about ethics. We don't film people who don't want to be filmed. We don't lie about who they are and their stories. We don't steal from them. If we don't get a release from them, we don't use the material.

Q – Have you ever had to deal with censorship or ended up censoring yourself because of TV standards?

R.J. – In a commercial TV environment, the language you can use is restricted, but that's the only limitation I've faced. Of course, I'm always making choices about what I keep in the cut and what I don't use, but those decisions have to do with telling good, truthful stories, or with other considerations that matter to me. I remember the first week we were filming *American High* we filmed with a kid for a couple of days and he went home and told his mother about the things he had said while we were filming. Not that it was anything too bad, but he had told some stories. His mom got uncomfortable and he came to us the next day and told us that he didn't want to be part of the project anymore. We said, OK. And he said, *"My Mom's uncomfortable that the tape even exists."* We said, *"Here's the tape, it belongs to you. It's your story, not ours."* It was an easy decision to make because of the fundamental principles that we work by. If you've identified these principles, it becomes easy to make decisions in difficult times.

Q – How do you see new media affecting documentary films in the future?

R.J. –The thing that I'm most excited about these days is the unintentional documentary. I think it's a whole new genre in doc storytelling. Among the films in this genre are *TV Junkie*, *Capturing The Friedmans*, and *Tupac: Resurrection.* They're three very different movies, but they all have significant amounts of footage that was shot by someone who had no awareness that he was making a documentary. In the case of *Capturing the Friedmans* the bulk of the footage is home movies. In *Tupac*, the entire narration is taken from interviews Tupac did over the course of his lifetime. In the case of *TV Junkie*, the filmmaker is an obsessive videographer, but he's not actually shooting the film that we're watching; he's just filming everything in his life. I'm really excited about all the films that we're going to see that were filmed by accident. We all have cameras. I have a camera in my PDA right now. I can shoot a movie of any moment in my life and download it to my computer. Now the technology exists for people to collect tons of biographical material so the documentary opportunities that are going to exist as a result are going to be extraordinary. In terms of the internet as a means of distribution, I suspect you're going to end up with exactly as many great films as we have now. Great filmmaking is pretty hard and takes enormous commitment and development of skill and talent and good fortune. I do hope though that it will make the medium open to more people and more socio-economic barriers will go away.

Q – What advice would give a new documentary filmmaker?

R.J. – My advice is always to make films. Take advantage of the fact that you live in a time where the technology is extremely affordable. Part of being a documentary filmmaker is being resourceful—so go out and get the equipment and tell the stories that you need to tell. It's going to be hard and painful sometimes, but if that's what you want go out and get it. Don't take no for an answer. I always say that no is the pathway to yes— at least the person saying no is engaging you in conversation! It's an exciting way to live your life and experience the world—embrace it with passion.

GUERILLA FILM MAKER SAYS!

Originality

All of the people in The Long View section have had long careers and one of the reasons for that is that they have always been original in the people and subjects that they've chosen. No one really looked into modern American high schools in the way R.J. Cutler did and St. Clair Bourne was on the cutting edge of bringing the black American experience to public airwaves for the first time. The lesson here is when thinking about your next project either go someplace that no one has ever scene or take the familiar and turn it on its head. DO NOT GO FOR THE CLICHÉ! That is the fastest route to having funders turn down your ideas.

And while technique isn't as important as content in documentary filmmaking, you can still distinguish yourself with unique storytelling like Nick Broomfield's ballsy interview style, Michael Moore's comedy or Stacy Peralta's free for all use of pictures and graphics. Being original is the greatest currency you have when you don't have a track record.

ANATOMY OF A DOCUMENTARY SECTION 14

CASE STUDIES

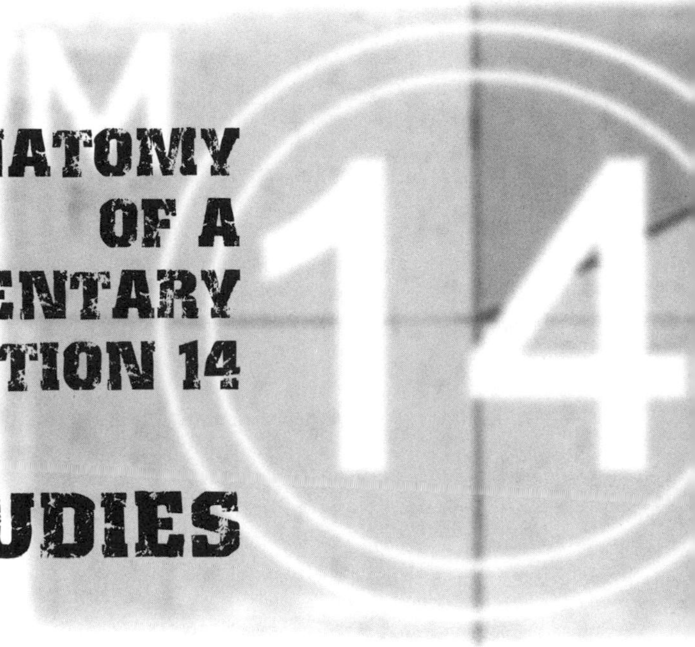

MAD HOT BALLROOM

Q – What is your background?

Marilyn – I was on the other side of production for the first part of my career doing public relations, working with camera reporters and TV crews. I became very interested in capturing stories because I was working with a lot of news-type people. I took some courses at NYU in film and video production and then became an assistant at various production companies that did commercials and corporate videos. There, I learned the mechanics of filmmaking. And eventually I started producing other people's films, commercials, shorts, industrials, everything.

Q – What led you to the subject matter in Mad Hot Ballroom?

Marilyn – I have a very old friend, Amy Sewell who's my producing partner. Amy writes a column in a local Tribeca newspaper. They asked her to do a story on this little elementary school that was doing a ballroom dance course. She followed them from beginning to end and fell in love with the whole progression of the story. Amy had no background in production, so she had me over for a glass of wine and said, *"You have to do this film with me. I want to follow this little school and document this."* I said, *"Let's follow a few schools."* New York City is a place where you have so many diverse cultures – you don't have to travel far to find people from all over the world. So we decided to see how this same experience would unfold with different groups of kids. We picked these three because they offered so much. The kids in Tribeca come from families that are generally more affluent and educated and they were more verbal. I remember when we first went there to introduce ourselves, I asked the 10 year olds, *"Does anybody know what a documentary is?"* And one of the little kids who is in the film says, *"Do you have a distribution deal yet."* In Brooklyn we found this lovely school, with this lovely principal and these lovely kids. And we fell in love with this class. Then we picked the Washington Heights school kids because we wanted a real departure. These kids are mostly immigrants - some of them don't speak English. There is a 97% poverty level in the school and the neighborhood has real challenges. And, win or lose, the teacher, Ms. Reynoso was going to be a great character. She was so driven and passionate.

Q – How many schools in all did you see?

Marilyn – Twenty. And a lot of it was dictated by the schedule. If two schools had dance class on the same day at the same time, then it was dictated by economics. I'd rather shoot one school in the morning and another in the afternoon on the same day so I could maximize the crew.

Q – What did you shoot on and did you personally shoot any footage?

Marilyn – No. I had a DP. Amy had said, *"Oh, let's shoot and edit this ourselves"* but I said, *"If we want anything that anyone can bear to look at I think we need to get a real cameraperson."* This was very challenging to shoot because the subject matter was kids. I had some experience with 24p video, which has a very distinct filmic look and I thought it would work well for this project. It also works well with low or no light. And another thing dictated by shooting these kids was that the Department of Education wasn't going to allow us to bring lights and cables into the schools. Kids could trip over the wires, etc. I'd say 80% of the film is in available light only. Also we wanted to be very intimate – get as close as possible to these kids and not with a big camera that was going to intimidate them . So we shot on the Panasonic DVX100A.

Q – How many people were in your crew?

Marilyn – Four of us. Myself and Amy and we did everything from pick up sandwiches in the morning for the crew, drive the production van, everything. Also, our DP and sound person. And it mostly was four women and I don't know if that means anything except that we developed such a close bond and relationship with these kids that they sort of forgot about us. I guess they're used to women teachers.

Q – Before you started shooting, did you go in and talk to the kids?

Marilyn – We went in once to each school and that's where we had that talk with the kid who wanted to know if we had a distribution deal. We told them that we were going to do a film, but I don't know if any of them really grasped what that meant. But they were amazingly adaptable to our presence. I've thought about this a lot - kids grow up with video cameras. Their parents are videotaping them from the time they're small. It's not really that big of a deal.

I found that there were some techniques that developed in the course of shooting that really helped them be natural. As opposed to talking to an adult where you can do a one-on-one talking head interview, kids did better when they were occupied with something and with each other. That's why a lot of the film is conversations between kids. Having them tell each other whatever it was I wanted them to say really worked. Sometimes I'd say, *"Tell me about the girls in your class?"* and before very long it would turn into this full on back and forth conversation. In the case of the boys who are playing foozball, it was really helpful to have them occupied this way. They would just go at it and be themselves.

Q – Was that something that happened over time?

Marilyn – Yes. But they were much more open at the beginning than I thought they'd be. I finally started saying to them, *"if you look at the camera and you start making faces at the camera, you're not going to be in the movie."* And they'd look away. And after awhile they were so unconscious of it, I was pleasantly amazed.

Q – Especially if there were four of you around.

Marilyn – Usually when we were shooting in the dance classes, I'd send camera and sound only. Especially during dance, there was a lot of movement and Claudia Raschke-Robinson our DP was phenomenal. She really moved around them and it was very difficult in the dance classes to be around her because she was constantly flipping around and I had to get out of in the shot.

Q – Since you weren't shooting yourself, what kind of instructions did you give your DP?

Marilyn – The entire film is pretty much at the eye level of the kids. The camera never looks down at them. So we'd talk about composition and color and we developed a running style that worked for us. Sometimes I'd say to her, find this type of scenario or focus on that because as the classes and the story were progressing - different things were unfolding with the kids. Little conflicts and problems would arise. Like the kid Jonathan at Washington Heights who was acting up and was finally thrown off the team. We started to focus on him because there was something bothering him. In this type of shooting, you're in a room and there's so much happening that you have to be disciplined enough to choose a moment and stay with it and let it play out even though you can hear and see four other things that are interesting to you.

Q – Did you shoot with multiple cameras?

Marilyn – For the bulk of the story it was one camera. When we got into the quarterfinals and semi-finals we shot with two. The kids would be sitting on a bench waiting to get up and dance. One camera would stay with them and one would follow a couple out onto the floor and that person would finish the dance with the couple and then the next camera would go out. It was really important to get all the reaction, cheering and emotions that were playing out. For the final competition, which was the big one, we shot with four cameras. And it was the same kind of technique, one person would stay with our kids, follow them out, come back while the other ones were backstage cheering. One camera was focused on the audience just at the bottom of the stage getting parent's reactions and a wide shot of the audience in general. One camera was on a little riser getting the wide of the stage and CU's as well. In that way, I was able to get everything I needed. This film had a very hard start and stop date because it starts on the first day of classes and it ends on the last day of competition and there is no chance to go back and get anything we missed.

Because of that, I made two decisions. One was to a lot of coverage camera-wise and covering a lot of classes. The other key decision was to start my editor early on in the production. We shot from February to June – I started the editor in March on Avid Express because I wanted her to be there to speak with me every day when I brought her material. We'd go over footage and she was building little scenes and she could say to me, *"I see something here, see if you can follow that"* – so we really collaborated in a big way building the story together as we shot it.

Q – A lot of documentary filmmakers can't do that.

Marilyn – It was amazing. I was very lucky to do that. Honestly, we had so many characters and so many things going on that it was a tremendous advantage to be organizing like that. I wanted from the beginning not to use a narrator. I wanted the story to be told completely through the voices of the characters. So, it was important to find threads that would connect one scene to the next. It was a great way to work.

Q – What was your process for sitting down with the editor during production?

Marilyn – Typically we'd shoot two days a week, sometimes three. I believe we shot on Tribeca in the morning on Mondays and in the afternoon in Brooklyn. On Tuesdays we'd shoot in Washington Heights. So on Wednesdays, I'd bring my dailies and I'd sit with Sabine Krayenbuhl, my editor and we'd talk. We'd look at every frame of the footage and we had all these little bins – the Wilson bin, this foxtrot bin, whatever. We were building scenes and also building tiny stories. So I had my off days to do that, and I was constantly e-mailing Sabine late at night because this film consumed me.

Q – Did you know during shooting how the story was going to end up?

Marilyn – Well it was certainly a lot longer after our initial rough assembly. Out of our 150 hours of footage, we had lots of little story arcs that had to fall away. We did have the basic story structure that had to be followed – from class instruction to the quarterfinals to the semifinals to the finals. And we had all this amazing material with the kids talking candidly about their lives. So, it was a matter of finding a way to make this all flow together. We found ways to condense time like having certain pieces of interviews with the kids serve as voice overs while they were dancing or doing something else.

Q – Did you transcribe any of it?

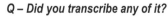

Marilyn – Tons. We transcribed lots of it ourselves, Amy and I. In the end, we used the transcriptions, but we didn't rely on them quite as much as I thought we would. Sabine and I were so used to combing through the footage and pulling out a sentence here, a sentence there. There were certain things that we knew we were going to use, it was just a question of where. Like this line from a little girl Emma who says, *"according to scientific research, women are the more advanced civilization."* When we shot that, I knew it was a keeper, and I had a ton of them, but how much can you put in?

Q – How long was the whole process of making the film?

Marilyn – Amy's article in the paper came out in July and she approached me in August. We started discussing and scouting schools in September. We had to go through a very bureaucratic process with the Board of Education – it was intense. Initially they told us, *"No problem,"* so we hired the DP and bought equipment, insurance, acquired permits, all that stuff. In early January we checked in with them again and this time it was, *"Wait a minute, you're shooting during school hours? No way!"* Can you imagine? We were freaking out. We had to find anyone that we knew that knew anybody that knew anyone else on the School Board and in the midst of this I had done this little commercial job and I came in to pick up my check and the executive producer that I worked for asked, *"How's your film going?"* I said, *"The Board of Education is going to shut us down."* He said, *"My brother has been with the Teacher's Union for thirty years, he knows everybody down there. Here is his number."* So, in this way we were able to salvage our film and get started.

Q – Why didn't they want you to shoot during school hours?

Marilyn – I think New York Public Schools are a little sensitive about cameras going in and recording while school is in session. Maybe it's liability issues or increased security after 9/11. Who knows?

Q – Did you have to prepare a proposal for them?

Marilyn – Amy was really the person who composed a lot of the proposals and letters to administrators. We took the angle that our film was going to highlight this program, which is saying very good things about arts in the public schools. We figured that if they felt it would be a positive statement, they would give in and let us shoot.

Q – So what changed their minds?

Marilyn – A bombardment. We had people writing letters and making phone calls on our behalf. We were always minimizing our presence. We're a tiny crew with this little tiny camera. We promised not to bring in excessive lighting our cables. We forged a relationship with American Ballroom Theater who is the organization that sends the dance teachers to the schools and they advocated on our behalf. We finally wore them down which was good because we were having nervous breakdowns. It was like, *"oh my God, we're shooting in a week and we still don't have the OK".* It was a really bad 10 days. But we got in and that was great.

CASE STUDIES

Q - Did you get any funding for this?

Marilyn – Amy was the grant writer and she applied for a ton of them. A lot of energy was spent and we didn't get one. Nothing. Some private investors stepped up to the plate and told us to go ahead and make our movie. We were so lucky!

Q – Did anyone come on board during post?

Marilyn – Very early on in the edit process we cut a trailer to raise funds. Ten minutes. I was never going to use the end of the story in my trailer because I never wanted to give away who wins, but pretty much early on we had enough material to do a fund raising piece for post-production. Our investors believed in our project, and they said they would help us to the end. It was a very rare situation.

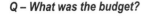

Q – What was the budget?

Marilyn – At this point it will come in at about $500,000. We're still working out some things. There's a lot of music to license. Big hurdle.

Q – I've never seen New York City look so colorful. When did you shoot it?

Marilyn – We shot from February to June. There were a couple of things that I was very intent on doing with this film. One was to show the passage of time using imagery and also I wanted to always remind the audience that was a story about New York. We created what I called the portraits of the city. I always wanted to frame the interior scenes when we moved throughout the city within the context of the neighborhood to remind people of the landscape these kids live in. The mangos in Washington Heights and the street life there is very much a part of the character of that part of town.

Q – We noticed that at the beginning of the film you didn't set the locale of New York City, but went right into the ballroom dancing.

Marilyn – That's true. I guess I wanted a more intimate intro to the characters. Yes, there's this iconic imagery of New York, the skyline, the Empire State Building. I wanted to stay away from those things. I guess I wanted a more personal and particular visual frame of reference than what other people may think of New York City. I wanted more of the guy who was frying stuff on the corner or the fire escapes. I wanted to put the audience into the kids' daily experience. There are all these little characters – the kids - but there are also three big characters. One is Washington Heights, one is Tribeca and one is Brooklyn. If they were visually very distinct, then I could jump from one to the other without introducing it them in any way.

Q – Was there anything else similar to that, that you wanted to include?

Marilyn – Besides the reference of where they are and the angle at which we shot and the color and the music - originally we intended to intersperse the ballroom dancing music with hip hop or the music that the kids were listening to. This was a story of contrast and we wanted to contrast what they listen to with what they're being introduced to against their will. They don't sign up for this class. If your school says we are going to do ballroom dancing and you are in the fifth grade, you are in ballroom dancing. And you're going to put your arms around a girl and dance to Frank Sinatra. So it was always fun to watch them freak out. But I wanted to show the flip side of that which was when they were home and they were listening to whatever it was they were listening to. Certainly not ballroom dancing. But I could never find a place for it.

Q – You knew that there was going to be a lot of music issues, when did you start checking into licensing?

Marilyn – Very early on because this isn't a film where you have certain ideas about what kind of music you can use and you can throw a song over a scene and if it becomes too expensive you can take it out and put another in. We were shooting where music was playing and the voice and the music were married to the picture. We started checking out very early on what some of the music was going to cost because we knew we had to use it.

Q – Did you know what the music was going to be beforehand?

Marilyn – Yes, the instructors have a list of meringue songs, tango songs, etc. and some of them that we checked out were out of our reach. So we asked them for this one semester to please not use that one song. We can't afford it. Can you please substitute it with something else. And they did. We do have some classics in there - Frank Sinatra, Peggy Lee, Bobby Darin, Della Reese. And what can I tell you? Both Amy and our Music Supervisor did a lot of begging and pleading, and continue to do it. They say it's a low budget documentary about New York City kids and most people have been kind. And some have mde us crazy.

Q – How much is it to license a Frank Sinatra song?

Marilyn – We're still in final talks with a lot of these people. We got festival licenses for everything, but it doesn't really help you in the real world because you can't show the film outside of a festival. Also these publishers, the more sophisticated publishers, know that you might get picked up by a major company and if you do, they're going to jack up the price. They say, *"When you have a distributor, call us"*. And the distributor wants you to come in with your music squared away. I'd advise anyone who needs to license music to invest in a really good music supervisor.

Q – How long was the editing stage?

Marilyn – Well there was a lot of playing with time in the film. Because I had this desire to tell the story without using a narrator, it was very time consuming to search out that perfect line of dialogue that would get us to that next scene and connect all three of these scenarios that were playing out at the same time. We had a lot of material and a lot of repetitive material – we decided to introduce each dance by skipping around to show the same lesson being taught at the three different schools and contrast how they were all doing it. So our process was to build this fat story and then trim it back. Also, we built a series of montages of the kids talking about certain subjects – boys and girls, being eleven, their futures, etc. that we used as sort of chapter breaks. The entire editorial process took about six months.

Q – When did you finish your first cut?

Marilyn – Mid-October. We initially had a five-hour cut which was a big step. I mean we could watch the five hours, but no one else in this world could do that! Then we got to a two and half hour cut. And that's when we started to screen it for people. That was around Halloween. We'd tell people it was long, but I wanted to see what was understandable, and what was unclear. Also, I didn't have any titles in my first cuts because I wanted to see how much people could grasp before I felt the need to start identifying things. The very first version was very minimalist. Jumping around from school to school didn't seem to be a big problem. I asked if people could understand that we were doing that. And they did. But people were telling me they were lost in time. How much time is passing? So we started to say this is week five, seven, nine. Then it was, *"It would be fun to see the kids' names. Who are they?"* So we started to identify them by name. The introductory titles at the beginning I knew would always be there. But the feedback in those first initial screenings really helped us to clarify the story and lay it out in a way that wasn't confusing

Q – How many test screenings did you have?

Marilyn – About five.

Q – You made a conscious decision to not show the defending champion Queens school until fairly late in the film. Was there a reason for this?

Marilyn – Well, we had our three selected schools and the story was about them. Our expectation had been that the Brooklyn kids weren't going to get very far and they didn't disappoint. They were awesome, but we knew competition wise, they wouldn't get to the end. We were pretty sure that the Tribeca school could make it to the semi-finals, but when they both got knocked out in the first round, we were like, *"Oh no!"* Two of our three teams are gone. We only have this one last team to take us to the end of the story. And we were like, *"OK, this is going to go where it's going to go."* Amy had wanted to go see last year's defending champions from the beginning, and now that we only had our one team, the defending champs took on a much bigger meaning. They were the counterpoint to the team we were following. And the contrast between their neighborhood and Washington Heights was huge.

Q – When did you finish the film?

Marilyn – January 10. A week before we went to Slamdance.

CASE STUDIES

Q – When did you submit it to Slamdance?

Marilyn – Late in the game. We targeted Sundance first, but they turned us down with a form rejection e-mail. I was very disappointing. But you move on. When you look at the roster of documentaries that are in Sundance. I think that our film didn't really fit with their idea of a story that's topical or political. We have issues in our film. These are urban kids living complicated lives. When you hear the girls in Washington Heights talking about how they don't want boyfriends that deal drugs. And their fears of drunk men looking at them on the street. There are definite issues there.

Q – Slamdance was different?

Marilyn – It happened in one day. We Fed Ex-ed them the film because we had missed their deadline. A day later they called and said, *"Thank you so much for sending us this. We want to make it the opening film."* They were so gracious. And I think in the end it really served us to be the opening film of the smaller festival rather than getting lost in a bigger festival that clearly didn't get us.

Q – What format did you finish on?

Marilyn – We showed Digibeta at Slamdance, but we're also on D5 HD and from that I'm going to go to film.

Q – Did you have any problems with going from 24P to HD?

Marilyn – No. It's important to plan your shoot based on how you're going to edit and what you want your final output to be. I always had high hopes for this film, so just in case, I wanted to be prepared for a theatrical release going to 35mm. So very early in the process I took some footage to Duart in New York and they did a 60 second test. It looked beautiful and they told me don't use advanced mode. Don't shoot anamorphically. Block off the frame in the viewfinder. Shoot in 4x3, but block it off. For us, that was the best way.

Q – Was it difficult to get Duart to do the tests for you?

Marilyn – A year ago, there wasn't that much reference footage that had been shot on this Panasonic camera yet Duart was more than happy to test with my footage and to make a digital test reel because they had no other digital test reels to show other filmmakers. So they were pleased. They made many calls to Panasonic because they saw that there was a problem with the advanced mode and Panasonic didn't know what to say. It was just one of these early kinks. No one knew because it was so new.

Q – So in regular mode you didn't have any problems going to HD?

Marilyn – No, everything looked beautiful. Everything worked really great. I think that Avid Express was the best thing to edit on. I was told that if you're going to finish in the digital world, then Final Cut Pro works better than if you are going to go to film for some reason.

Q – How did the sale of the film develop and who bought it?

Marilyn – It was incredible. A real night to remember. We had our third and final screening at Slamdance, and lots of distributors showed up. There was a bit of a bidding war, which lasted all night long. We closed the deal at 5:30 am. Paramount Classics bought the film.

Q – Have the kids seen the film?

Marilyn – Very few of the kids have seen the film – the only ones who did are the ones who came with us to Park City. At some point we're going to get them all together and show it to them.

Q – In looking back at the whole process, is there anything you would have done differently?

Marilyn – Honestly, the whole experience was so pure. Even our stumbles were great because they were totally ours.

Q – What advice would you give a new documentary filmmaker?

Marilyn – Be as buttoned up as possible in regard to releases, and clearing footage and music. You don't want to have a big problem down the line. Cover yourself from a legal point of view as much as possible. And most importantly, try to surround yourself with as good a team as you can. You don't have to have everything figured out – the documentary process is one of discovery as you go along. Collaboration is the key.

Sheena Joyce Don Argott

ROCK SCHOOL

Q – How did you get started in documentary filmmaking?

Don – I did a two year program at The Art Institute in Philadelphia. I met my former business partner there and as soon as we graduated we opened up a company in Philadelphia. We set out to do creative projects, but reality sets in and you have to make a living so we did a lot of commercial videos and freelance camera stuff and that's when I landed DP jobs with ESPN and Fox Sports. I knew people there so it was fairly easy for me to get gigs.

Q – Did you do any documentaries at that time?

Don – Yes. We started a documentary about a local artist in Philadelphia and that's when I really got the bug. I've always loved documentaries, especially *American Movie*. I cite that as the first time that I realized documentaries could be more than the PBS didactic kind. The subject matter was so enjoyable I thought it would be really cool to do a documentary that doesn't rely on big productions. Something where I could be a lot more hands on. So for me it was a nice transition to be able to pick up a camera and just go and get amazing stuff as opposed to sitting down and working out a schedule and breaking everything out. You get bogged down by the process when all you really want to do is shoot and do it.

Sheena – I went to Bryn Mawr College as an English major. I thought I wanted to be a lawyer until I started working in internships in corporate law. I thought I'd hang myself if I had to do that for the rest of my life, so I started doing internships in television in Philadelphia. I finally came to terms that I'm a whore to pop culture. I love films, TV and documentary and I wanted to get my foot in the door no matter what the price. So after graduating, I went to work for Philadelphia's Film Commission and learned a lot. I was there for four and half years and learned about producing because the Film Commission acts as a producer for films coming in. You make things happen from closing streets to hiring cops to getting good reservations at a nice restaurant. But I wanted to get out eventually and Don and I had been friends for about three and a half years before we started dating. His business partner wanted to move the business to LA and Don and I had a conversation where we realized we didn't want to go. So Don would keep the business going himself and I'd help at nights and on weekends. Then he called me at work and said, *"Don't kill me,"* which is always a great way to start a conversation, and then, *"We're going to do a documentary."* He said that he always wanted to do a film about the program School Of Rock so we were going to go to a show. If we liked what we saw, then we'd do it together, so we went to see the kids play songs by Frank Zappa. Two songs in, we were there! Don started shooting two days later.

Q – Had you seen the shows before or spoken to them?

Don – Never. Talk about guerilla filmmaking! There was no research, no planning.

Sheena – We had a camera and a mic and that's it. We'd write the questions out for Paul Green and the kids at night and then Don would take them in and shoot the next day. He'd come home with the footage and we'd talk about it. We did this for two or three months and I decided that I'd quit my job and we'd try and do this together.

Q – Had people approached Paul about doing a documentary before?

Sheena – Yes, but I think he saw a kindred spirit in Don. Don's a musician. They have a similar sense of humor, but Don doesn't have the abuse. Paul said that he hadn't found the right people to do this kind of project with. He wanted someone who wasn't just going to come in and get footage. He wanted someone who was committed and was going to try and do something with it. Don said, *"I've never started a project that I haven't finished and I will do as much as I can to get this out to as many people as possible."*

Q – Did Paul want to see any of your reels?

Don – I gave him copies the two 70's porno records that I made. I guess seeing stuff that I had produced and put out there was enough for him. Demian Fenton who edited *Rock School*, actually approached Paul saying that he'd like to do a documentary on him and the school. Paul said, *"You're a day late and dollar short. There's someone else doing it, but he's a cool guy and you should talk to him."* He called me up and we hit it off on the phone. I never asked to see a frame of anything he had edited previously.

Q – Did you get any cash from anywhere?

Sheena – No, unless you count maxing out our credit cards and borrowing money from parents.

Don – The difference, I think, between us and other filmmakers who don't have the support of a production company is that we were doing work in the business that could support this project. We had editing suites, camera equipment and freelancers that we could call in favors for.

Q – What camera did you shoot Rock School with?

Don – The DVX-100 and we edited on Final Cut Pro. We shot at true 24p, which presented a whole bunch of nightmares. Film school is great and it prepares you for certain things, but when you get into the business you realize there are so many things you're never going to learn in a school environment such as we couldn't import the 24p footage into Final Cut 3. We had to wait for Final Cut 4 to come out. When you're lucky enough to sell a film, you get that delivery schedule and you're like, *"What the fuck is this?* We need an M&E track. But we don't have an M&E track. We have two tracks of audio. But you need an M&E track because for foreign sales you need to dub it. And also there needs to be a sound effect track. We don't have a sound effect track. We shot with the microphone on the camera so there was no way to separate the music and the voice.

CASE STUDIES

Sheena – We were also Newmarket's first doc, so it was a learning experience for them as far as delivery schedules are concerned. We're not beholden to the same big studio machine standards. You cannot hold *Rock School* to the same standards as *Passion Of The Christ* or *Oceans Eleven* and no matter how cool Newmarket is, the people that do their DVD distribution have their own standards. They don't want to hear it. They say this is the way it has to be.

Q – Did Newmarket come up with any cash for what had to be done on the delivery schedule?

Don – No. They purchased the film and then we used our minimum guarantee to deliver the film. We sold the film to Newmarket for $725,000, which is good money. But you factor in $200,000 just for music licensing and another $200,000 to deliver the film and you factor in two and half years of blood, sweat and tears plus what you owe the business and it comes out to something like $16/hr. But that's cool.

Sheena – We're going to be OK. At the very least, we're going to get out of debt personally and business wise and that's an absolute dream. To not have to worry about how much over the minimum payment on my credit card to pay this month is magic.

Q – What were the problems with going from 24p to HD?

Don – The biggest problem for filmmakers if they want to move forward with this camera is that they shouldn't use the masked letterbox function. I say that because when you sell the film and they want a 4x3 version, you have to go back and blow it up and resize everything. I had the presence of mind not to do that.

Sheena – But who thinks of this? Or a 3:2 pulldown? And how that would fuck up your life for so many months? That's why you need *The Documentary Film Makers Handbook.* It took us 5-6 months to do the deliverables.

Q – How expensive was the transfer?

Sheena – It's safe to say one 35mm print was going to be $40,000. That was the beauty of having a post supervisor who was recommended to us by Newmarket. She was able to get us package deals for indie film fests and lucky for us we had been picked up already so we weren't this little film anymore and we were going to be in Sundance. Then you get a little bit of special treatment.

Don – Actually, the long convoluted process was this – we shot with the DVX-100 and edited with Final Cut Pro 3 in 29.97. Color corrected the film at another facility and transferred it to Digibeta. We projected that at the LA Film Fest and Newmarket bought the film and gave us their delivery schedule. Not thinking there would be any problem we sent the Digibeta to Technicolor to do a test. They said it was all fucked up because you have the 3:2 in here when you upconvert to HD. So what we had to do was go back to our 120 hours of master DV tape and redigitize at true 23.98, which then had to be re-color corrected. The problem was that in the Pogal system that our colorist used, it fired on the A frame all the time so we were off. So they had to do this whole whacked out duct tape fucking thing just to get everything to fire at the right time. There are a lot of cuts in the film and you've to punch in and out every scene to color correct. So they had to run it through an Avid to fix it. In hindsight, we should've taken the 23.98 master and output that to HD and then it would've been in an HD world and could be color corrected in HD. So we ended with a Digibeta master, which was true 29.97 with the 3:2 taken out, which then could be upconverted to HD D5 with no problems. Then it could be upconverted to film.

Q – How much did you sell the TV rights for?

Sheena – We sold the TV rights for $375,000 to A&E Films and then we got $187,500 before all the fees and percentages. Cinetic got wind of us when we were in the IFP-NY Market in September of 2003 with an 18 minute teaser. They wanted to see our stuff and took us on and thank God they did. So they sold the film at IFP-LA five days after the first screening. We were the only film to sell.

Q – Why didn't you approach companies fund the film at the beginning?

Don – It's just not how the business works. And ultimately for a first time film you don't want to have to be under the umbrella of a big company because they'll just own it and take it away from you. Ownership is everything in this business. When you prove yourself then people will come to you and then you can negotiate terms.

Sheena – After IFP-NY we got a lot of offers from TV networks. And when you'e poor, it's tough to resist.

Don – But we stuck to our guns. We had the idea to go theatrical first and we knew enough that if we got TV deals and sold the TV rights away it might hurt us in the theatrical world. And at VH-1, you sit in these big comfy offices and you speak with people who think they know more than you do about stuff. They all say the same thing, *"we think this is good, but you should make it a made for TV thing. Forty-four minutes.* " And we were like, *"no we think* *this is a feature film and you don't know what you're thinking about."* So a key thing for first time filmmakers is to keep ownership of your project – even if you get outside investors.

Q – Would you say that your first film is the only time you can make your film the way you want to make it?

Don – The beauty of doing your first project is that you really get to enjoy the whole thing because everything you did to get it to its finished state was all you – meaning the three of us, myself, Sheena and our editor, Demian. If other people give you money, they want to have input. But if you're smart and have good people around you, then you can maintain creative control. And Newmarket didn't ask to have a cut. They didn't change one thing in the film. It was miraculous. We have been extremely fortunate in that sense.

Q – Did having smaller cameras help when shooting the kids?

Don – Yes. They aren't so threatening. I didn't even have a boom operator. If you have a big camera with this thing over your head, there's no way that you can be real. So I would just mic Paul with a wireless and then have the camera mic for the ancillary stuff. I would be in the corner, not like I was hiding in the bushes, but the kids do tend to forget that you are there because you're there all the time. That's when you get the real moments.

Sheena – One of the mothers told me that someone asked her if it was weird for her kids. And she told them that we had become a part of her family. They could tell that we were not out to make this exposé on the Paul Green School Of Rock. That we had a genuine interest. We had dinner at their house shortly after we started filming and after that it was like Don was the crazy uncle with his video camera - the family member at every birthday party or family gathering who has the camera attached to them. That may have been true for a lot of the kids.

Q – How many kids did you follow and how did you decide to choose them?

Sheena – We followed 8 that were recommended by Paul, although we count the twins as one. It was obvious who was going to emerge as the most powerful characters. There was another girl who was very interesting. She was very shy and Paul was trying to help come out of her shell. But ultimately her story wasn't there and she didn't open up enough to us to make something of it.

CASE STUDIES

Don – There were a lot of cool, unexpected things that happened with the kids that I knew would end up in the final film; like discovering that Maddie had formed a band at her Quaker school called The Friendly Gangstas. And the minute we shot the Guitar Gods show and these little kids were playing *Black Magic Woman*, I knew that was the opening of the film.

Sheena – And the moment of Asa saying *"party on"* to the poignant moment from the kid in the wife beater tee with the lollipop in his mouth saying something with such satisfaction asi if to say, *"Yeah, I fucking nailed that."*

Q – You have a lot of famous music in the film, were you worried about the clearances?

Sheena – We struggled with that. But not as much when we actually sold the film because the buyers expected to see the music that was in the film in the final version that we handed to them.

Don – There were two real big problems that we encountered. One was originally C.J. plays Van Halen's *Eruption* at the Guitar God's show. And then it goes into *You Really Got Me*, which is how it goes on the Van Halen album. That was in the film the whole time - even when we showed it at the LA Film Festival. But we struggled with the rights to that. Van Halen and David Lee Roth were suing each other and they hate each other and all this stuff. So it took a really long time to get it to the right people. David Lee Roth said if we could get Eddie to agree, he'll agree. Van

Halen saw it and he fucking said, *"no."* That was the scariest moment.

Sheena – A kick to the stomach. To get all the way to Eddie Van Halen and for him to say no.

Don – So we thought the deal was going to fall apart because that was a key moment in the film for that character. I mean C.J. did *Sultans Of Swing*, which does not have the same weight as *Eruption*. And *You Really Got Me* was good, but having lived with *Eruption* for so long…

Sheena – If you didn't know that the songs existed and you showed C.J. playing *You Really Got Me* with a pretty kick ass guitar solo in it, you're not going to miss *Eruption*. Also, *You Really Got Me* is much more known to the general public.

Q – What rights did you need to get for You Really Got Me? It's by Ray Davies from the Kinks, but C.J. is playing the Van Halen version...

Don – Van Halen never copyrighted their version. So we only needed the publishing from Ray Davies.

Q – Was Newmarket funny about having to change the cut?

Sheena – They were awesome. I don't have one bad thing to say about Newmarket. They've been so supportive and encouraging. And Newmarket isn't afraid to take chances. They're extremely innovative. Another major studio made us an offer, but said that we had to drop all the cursing and put more pop songs in it. Well guess what? That isn't the film.

Q – Did it take a long time to sort out the clearances and how expensive were they?

Don – It took a long time. The only song that was really expensive was *Black Magic Woman*, which was $36,000. But all the rest of the songs we got for about $4,000 a piece. The second major problem was with the Frank Zappa estate.

Sheena – Here's what we didn't know. Gail Zappa, who is the head of the Zappa family trust and controls all things Zappa, told us that some of Frank's songs are un-licenseable. They can't be played by anyone but Frank. Yet some of those songs were in the backgrounds being played by the kids.

Don – So that forced us to weed moments out of the movie. At the end of the film, Paul says, *"The greatest moment of my life, except for my baby…"* and then it goes to that hand thing...well, originally it cut from that moment to the kids being asked to come back onstage and join everyone else who was part of the festival. Paul makes this beautiful speech where he says, *"When bands play this song, Black Napkins, they never play the ending right. So this is what we are going to do. I am going to count to three and we are going to play the ending right."* So it comes back full circle that he's perpetually teaching. So he counts to three and they play the ending right and they go on to the ending. But we couldn't get the rights to *Black Napkins*. And not only is it playing in the background, he makes reference to it. That was such a hard cut to make.

Q – Was Gail Zappa mad about it?

Don – Yes. We should've known according to her. She's very protective of Frank. That's her bread and butter. That's her thing. And that's OK.

Sheena – We would make the argument with her about how this film would have a positive impact on her late husband's memory. We are introducing Frank Zappa's music to an entirely new generation of kids. And she said to us, *"Frank Zappa doesn't need your help. Frank Zappa is already a legend."*

Q – Was there anything else that came up that you didn't expect?

Don – One thing that we did really well, which Sheena played a big part of, was the releases. She was manically on top of that. You can get killed at the end of the day when you do finally sell the film which you have shot for a year, to go back and not only get releases, but now because people know that the film has been sold, they're asking for more money. So when you're small potatoes, it's very important to get them to sign a release to get their permissions.

Q – How did you organize your footage and did you do any transcribing?

Don – No transcription. We didn't have the money for it. It was all by memory. There's no better way to start than just start, so we started putting scenes together that have a beginning, middle and an end. When we had enough of those things, we wrote them down on index cards and mixed and matched them. So we'd say we need a moment that shows Paul as a good teacher, but he's a goof-off. The biggest breakthrough for Demian and me anyway, was that in the first cut we had all this rehearsal footage. And we thought we should spend a lot of time there in order to set up the Black Sabbath show. But it bogged down every time you ended up there. But there were these great powerful, intense or funny moments that we needed to weed out. So we decided to do that three-minute montage of all the best moments in the rehearsal space. This is how Paul Green teaches – we're going to show it to you now. It took us forever to figure that out, but when we did it was a revelation.

Sheena – Our first cut was 2 hours and 45 minutes where we slapped everything in a line. We developed this system where only two of us would be in the edit suite at any time. So there would always be one fresh set of eyes on what had been edited the night or day before. It was usually Don and me during the day and Don and Demian at night. That allowed us to maintain some sort of perspective. Don and Demian would be up until 1am getting hopped up on Skittles and cutting scenes together, getting all excited about it. They'd show it to me in the morning and usually I'd say, *"What the fuck were you thinking?"* And then we'd fight really hard for an hour and then I'd get pissed and walk away. Then Demian would look at Don and say, *"Shit, she's right."*

Q – Looking back is there anything you would have done differently?

Sheena – I'd have done more research in hiring certain post positions. I would've been less afraid to ask more questions or make our opinions known to the higher-ups who bought the film.

Q – What piece of advice would you give a new documentary filmmaker?

Sheena – This is your film. Trust your gut. Make your voice heard. Even after you sell the film, never be afraid to speak out on decisions that are being made—you know your film better than anyone.

Don – From a technical standpoint, really think things through the entire process. Too often, filmmakers rush into productions and don't think through all the problems that may arise when shooting and have a "fix it in post" mentality. Ask questions, use your resources, do research. Other than that just go for it.

WHY WE FIGHT

Q – What is your background and why did you go into documentaries?

Eugene – I went to Princeton University where I started directing plays. I was very moved by political drama so it ended up being my focus as a student. I'd always been very driven politically. Plays were exciting from my standpoint in having the role of the director, which meant managing the creative endeavors of large team of which we were all equals. There's a great Latin expression, which is sort of like "leader among equals". The notion of having a team that could work together and that one person could be the organizational center and then everyone else had very particular skills and crafts that could be harnessed together into a whole. That's a very exciting idea for me. And in fact it's a political idea because it has a lot to do with the way social movements function. Often, they have central figures that carry the message forward but there's an army of talented people who come together to actuate something.

At the end of college, I made a short film, which got into Sundance and won a student Academy Award. Now Hollywood will start calling, I thought. So I sat by the phone and I got some iced tea and I waited and waited. I moved to Hollywood, thinking maybe they didn't want to make the long distance call. I got a hotel and my iced tea and waited! A studio executive that I had gone to school with, said *"I think it's awesome that you made the trip. But to be blunt with you, you coming out here with that film under your arm or without it, is the same."* That was a huge blow, but he was correct. That town was not ready to embrace independence and find a jewel in the rough. You needed to be like Tarantino and have the next great thing.

Q – So what did you do?

Eugene – I started doing a lot of music videos and commercials. But my politics took their toll. I'm not a commercial watcher nor am I music video watcher per se. What I have found out in life, if you haven't found something that you're willing do die for, then you're probably not going to do a good job at it. So I was in search of the thing I was willing to die for. I started to become eclectic, which really means desperate and taking all jobs that would come my way! I started working in politics because my political interests were brewing. I worked a lot with Jesse Jackson and by chance ended up going to Guantanemo Naval Base where we found out after the fact that the US government had detained a large group of Haitian refugees and quarantined them under an unestablished medical claim that they had HIV. Jesse Jackson went to try and mediate as the Haitian refugees had gone on a hunger strike. I can tell you that Guantanemo was no place to be then, let alone what it has become now. I was allowed into the camp with a camera crew. and when we got back to the US, I found out that we were the first camera crew allowed on the base. So all my footage on Guatanemo Naval base got picked up by the networks. All of a sudden I was in this very sexy position that I never imagined would come from my political interests.

I'd found the scenic route to finding a medium in which I could communicate to people about things that were important to me. And so since then I've made a number of documentaries, which tend to be big P political, whether they're social political, race political, gender political or in the case of the most recent film very much about war and capitalism. I also have done some dramatic films that tend to be small p political.

Q – What are the main differences between narrative and documentary in getting your politicial point across?

Eugene - I think you have to be a superlative dramatic writer to create material that can navigate the very narrow channel through which the distributors and broadcasters of the world will allow you to pass carrying political baggage. In the documentary world, it's expected that you're carrying political baggage of an enormous nature. So what happens when you're a dramatic filmmaker is, as the captain of the ship you start to try and get through that narrow passage, and you start to notice as you go that it's narrowing and narrowing. You're losing prospects of people who once said they were interested. And you start discovering that there's a big difference between the cargo that they're going to permit and the cargo that you're going to jettison. And obviously the compromise issue starts to come in when you start jettisoning cargo that's near and dear your heart. Then there's really no point in taking the trip to begin with – you erode the reason that drove you. I spoke to Steven Soderbergh recently and had an amazing, eye opening talk with him on how he navigates his political subject matter through the dramatic channels. He said quite simply, *"I hide behind a genre."* I'd heard this before – that if you play by the rules of a genre, you can tuck into all sort of small unnoticed corners of your work some of the important themes to you. The question at the end of the day is are you satisfied with that? Is that sufficiently political for Steven Soderberg? My sense is that any artist that's as smart as he is unlikely to be satisfied. For directors, the work is similar.

Q – You clearly deal with political and historical point of view, but you also touch upon personal stories in Why We Fight. Do you think that is your narrative side coming in?

Eugene – In an interview where I was bullshitting I'd say yes! But in reality I don't think the world works that way. I'm a desperate person trying to find a way. And I'm no dummy, if you want to make a political film – you're going to talk politics at the viewer for an hour and a half. And if you're asking them to do that on a Friday night when they've put the kids to bed, worked all day, want a date and just as the guy is trying to get his arm around the girl you start talking high tech politics, the guy is going to go to sleep. So you need something that's going to give them a window into why they are watching. On the other hand, human beings are what interests us – the rest of it doesn't matter. If you forget the human then there is no point dealing with the political side. It becomes theory – a class you take in college that wears on you because it really becomes abstract. So part of putting them in has a strategic side effect which is, human interest is good. At the same time, it's hard for me to make that stuff without really dealing directly with human beings because it becomes too remote. What I like is being the person who brings together a lot of different voices and gives them as much room as possible to self express while also being aware of the needs of the whole. It doesn't matter to me what the substance is.

Q – Do you feel you can change the world with a documentary film? Can you change people like your cop in Why We Fight who is very black and white?

Eugene – I have a friend in New York who's a brilliant restauranteur and he gave me an incredible piece of advice. I'd been talking about what the effectiveness of movies can be from a political standpoint and he said, *"There's a right way and a wrong way to do that. You think you're part of some movement and whether you are or not, I'm not going to debate with you. But in that movement, you're the guy with the flashlight. And so long as you remember that you're the guy with the flashlight you can use it to shine the light into dark corners and illuminate for people information they may otherwise not have. The moment that you get big ideas, that you're going to change the world with your one little film, you're going to start using your flashlight like a bat. You start swinging that flashlight around, the light goes all over the place and it doesn't stay in any one place long enough for anybody to read what is happening or learn anything. So just shine the light and you'll be fine."* That's the limit of my aspiration. It drove the way I made this film and it will drive the way I make films until I figure out some other way to overturn the system. I think you have to be part of a mosaic and let other people take your project and run with it. So if I could inspire a discussion, which is what this film is trying to do, then those people have a discussion piece and who can argue with discussing?

Q – Do you think that's a better approach from Michael Moore's opinionated

Eugene – We were given a lot of pressure to put the film out before the election by the broadcasters involved and I resisted that pressure. Mainly because I thought the subject we were studying - American war making and America's obsession with war is a condition that doesn't relate to any one president or anyone election cycle. And therefore to try and link it to a presidential election would confuse the issue. It would act as though when John Kerry or George Bush got into office that something would've changed or gone away and that's obviously not the case. Of the forces that compel America to go to war, who's sitting in the Oval Office or sitting in Downing Street in Britain for that matter, is but one detail. We all started to realize when we were getting pressure to get it out that it was extremely important to move forward with whoever was in the White House. If John Kerry had won, it would have been a letter to the new President. In this case, it's really about where we find ourselves today. Everybody is always asking me about Michael Moore and thank God for Michael Moore. Michael Moore over the years has consistently pushed the envelope on the viability of documentaries as a form for people to watch in an ever-narrowing landscape of media awareness. So whether one agrees or disagrees with how he does it, whether one likes how he looks, or talks or how funny he is or how he dresses, or whatever – it's sort of irrelevant to me. I don't always agree with lots of things that I think are important or valuable. So thank God for him.

Q – Do you find it easier to get funding for documentaries when you put your political views across than doing a dramatic feature?

Eugene – If I didn't have the BBC and I didn't have funding in Europe I wouldn't be able to make movies.

Q – What made you choose the subject matter of Why We Fight?

Eugene – The reality is you choose the subject that you think you can get done next. And that's a tragic thing to say. There are other things that I was dying to do, but this was the one in an increasingly complicated world of national security and international relations that was a natural to pitch to the world community. It's also something that I really cared about and there's only a handful of things that I care about. We were able to appeal to the BBC, RTE, a large number of European broadcasters and to the European Union itself at a time when there was a zeitgeist for it. I think in many ways it was luck of timing. I feel like an ambulance chaser sometimes – the worse the world gets the more popular my films seem to become.

Q – Do you think America is opening up more with funding for documentaries?

Eugene – We'll see. I think right now they're all looking to see if Michael Moore was a once in a lifetime experience. So the fear of course is that they're going to say, *"Where are all the jokes? Where's all that sexy music and all those embarrassing moments?"* And that's not the lifeblood of a documentary. It's the lifeblood of Michael Moore's work and more power to him. The question is have they made that marketplace open to one particular style of ambush comedy journalism or are they really saying reality sells. I think they already knew that reality sells when they invented reality TV and highjacked and bastardized the form. So I'm not sure that they're up for a brand new lesson of "real things sell." So I fear a little bit that there really isn't a commitment to reality, but there's a commitment to dollars, which we all expect. So the question is going to be based on the performance on these next round of films after *Fahrenheit*. When rap music came out everybody listened to it for a while and they said this will last a week or two. And it was only through the extraordinary perseverance of quality out of the black community making rap, that rap is still around. I'd hope that would happen for documentaries.

Q – Is that the same with political documentaries or do you think that has opened up because of 9/11?

Eugene – I do think there's a ping-pong phenomenon that goes on which is as something like the Bush administration takes hold, we move in a more and more radical policy direction. Many people talk about how history operates as a pendulum – it goes this way and that way. A French philosopher said, *"It really doesn't operate as a pendulum, it operates in simultaneity so what happens is as the forces of the right grow for example, the forces of the left protest in the streets and as the forces of the right shrink, the people have no reason to protest in the streets and they go back to watching color television."* That phenomenon is a much more tragic outlook on the pendulum than thinking we'll get this back again. But at the same time it's very empowering for me because it's a very clear way for me to remind people of how we act politically.

The weekend after Bush won, myself, my wife, my kids and a lot of other people found ourselves marching in a war protest. Had John Kerry won, I wouldn't have been marching in that war protest.

Q – When you did this film, did you find that you were putting your political viewpoint on the documentary?

Eugene – When you make a documentary, your perspective is growing all the time. You're reading a lot, you're learning a lot, you're working with a team of people who's views differ and are informing you. The thing takes a form that it could never take without every single one of those factors coming into the mix. So that stew of impressions and thoughts start to lead toward a finished product. And that's the magic of it – it's an absolute time capsule of a period of time of people in life. Then you look at it and say how strong of a view is that and is that a view that I want to hoist on a viewer.

In some films I can imagine wanting to hoist opinions on a viewer like we have to cure this epidemic now! But a film about a need to think more deeply about American war making is something where I'm trying to encourage thinking rather than share my view. The priority has to be on getting other people to be inspired to have their views. And the stronger I make my view, the more oxygen I take out of the room for them to express views. It's a tactic of trying to create a ventilated room and sometimes I have to pull myself back. For example, I don't narrate the film and I'm not in the film. That's a choice for me to take a step back from it to allow a range of voices in the film to become an example of the spectrum of American and world voices that I'd like to see discussing this issue. The piece itself becomes an example of what I want to inspire.

Q – There's a lot of archival footage. Did you do the research?

Eugene – No, Melinda Shopson and two other people did the bulk of the research and there's an enormous amount of research that goes on. I have the easy job. I wake up at 3am and write and e-mail. Hey, go get me so and so's tax returns or go get me that article that was written in 1999. Then they have to go deal with the librarians.

Q – Are they things that you remember specifically?

Eugene – Yes and it's astounding how well archived the world has been. We are losing that as a society because the American society is cracking down on its own archiving. It's harder and harder to get current events out of archive and that's a crisis in the American media much like other crisis in the media. But in the old days, it's unbelievable how well documented this culture is. There isn't a thing a camera wasn't running on in history in the last 100 years of this country. And it's really the researchers who make and break the film because the magic of their quest to find, not just an example of what I've asked for, but multiple examples from multiple angles just brings those moments in history to life such as, Eisenhower's address. Not only do we show Dwight Eisenhower's farewell address in the film, which a lot of people have not seen, but we have it from multiple angles and outtakes. We have an entire rehearsal of it. We have text that he wrote where his handwriting is on the speech. These are incredible endeavors for people to hunt down and find, but they become invaluable in the film. Even if the shot they end up with is only six seconds in the film, you'd be amazed at how often and audience member comes up to afterward and say, *"That shot was unbelievable. How did you get that?"* And that is half the battle. The rest is connecting the dots.

AFTER INNOCENCE

Q – What is your background?

Jessica – I grew up in a documentary making family as both of my parents made films. I traveled a lot and met lots of interesting people because they took me on all their shoots. I didn't know necessarily that I wanted to make films, but the environment that I grew up in stimulated me. Once I decided that I liked making films and that I was kind of good at it, documentaries were the most amazing way to meet people that you normally wouldn't meet and learn things that you normally wouldn't know.

Q – When you went to film school did you want to make documentary films?

Jessica – I was different. The film students there at USC could quote every Scorsese film and the like and I didn't know any of them because that wasn't what I was exposed to. I did mostly narrative shorts in film school, one of which was called *Los Angels,* which did the festival run and won several awards.

Q – What did you do when you left film school?

Jessica – I worked on independent low budget features from sound editing to director's assistant for Cheryl Dunye who did *Stranger Inside.* Just trying to learn all the different aspects of how a set worked. Starting out I worked for free for two weeks and then I got paying jobs. If you're eager and people like you, you go from there. And then I got a gig on *Crime And Punishment*, which was an NBC documentary series. I was a series associate producer and camera operator, shooting courtroom scenes with robotic courtroom cameras. I learned a lot about the criminal justice system – how trials worked, etc. So that's when I saw how the judicial system worked and how adversarial it is. I was following prosecutors, which is the other side of what my film is about. There are good prosecutors, but I definitely saw that a lot of people are fighting on the side of winning and getting the longest sentence possible. I was really disturbed by that. So when this subject of innocence and wrongful conviction came to me, it seemed perfect. It informed my whole experience making *After Innocence*.

Q – So how did the idea of After Innocence come to you?

Jessica – My producing partner, Marc Simon is an attorney and he was a former student of the Innocence Project. He works with Barry Sheck's group that uses DNA evidence to prove innocence. Through mutual friends, he was looking for a filmmaker and I was nominated for an Oscar for my short documentary *Sing* that I produced. He e-mailed me and I couldn't believe that a film hadn't been made about the subject because it's so compelling. Since I've made this film there've been 30 people who have been exonerated by DNA evidence over the last two years. When I met these exonerated people, I was amazed at how they weren't bitter or angry in the way that I expected and that no one is doing anything for them. I decided I wanted to make this film for them and others.

Q – Had the Innocence Project been wanting to make a film, but weren't sure how?

Jessica – I think that timing had a lot to do with it. DNA technology has been in effect for ten years and most media attention has been towards the first five minutes of fame like, *"Oh, my God, you're out! What was twenty-two years in prison like? What's your first taste of ice cream like?"* Very sensationalist news stories. Then these people were left with nothing else and some are very bitter about the media as well. There's a huge story about what happens after.

Q – Did the Innocence Project come on as executive producers for After Innocence?

Jessica – No, they gave us their blessings but It was Marc and I who made the film independently. Because he was from the project, the Innocence Project supported us, the exonerees trusted us, which was huge for access. So with money saved from my NBC days and a Pacific Pioneer Grant for emerging filmmakers, we started. Then the Illinois Humanities Council came in because Governor Ryan from Illinois commuted all death sentences for life. Then we had a fundraiser and people who wanted the story to be out there got us through 80% of production. I'd jump on a plane when things were happening and just dedicated myself full time to the project. Towards the end of production, Showtime funded the whole thing based on a proposal and an 8-minute short I made.

Q – How much money did you have coming in before you started shooting?

Jessica – Nothing. I'd jump on a plane to Chicago from the money I saved up from my job. In documentary, if something is happening you have to shoot it or else you'll miss it. You can't wait for the money to come. And because of my relationships with amazing cinematographers on *Crime And Punishment*, we have some of the top DPs shooting on the film who believed in the project and some would defer their pay until we were funded.

Q – How long after finishing the proposal did you start shooting?

Jessica – It was about 6 months. At the opening of the film there's a conference, which was the first thing we shot. It was with 30 DNA exonerees - the largest gathering ever. So that was a large casting session. We met Scott Hornoff, a white cop and realized that if it can happen to him, it can happen to anyone. We met Dennis Mayer who was from Massachusetts. He was the most recent person out so I wanted him in the film. We wanted to get different people in different stages of being out. Vincent Moto, the black musician from Philadelphia. He'd been out for seven years and he has been struggling more than anyone because he still has a criminal record. He can't get welfare. We wanted to show different geography, the various reasons they were convicted and the lengths of time they have been in. And of course, they've to be dynamic people. Nick Yarris, the death row exoneree; we met him in the film when you meet him. He happened to call Vincent Moto on the phone and had just been released for a few days from death row and solitary confinement. We met him and he was amazing. It was a perfect documentary moment. Something random happens and they become a big part of the story.

Q – Were any of the exonerees funny about you wanting to tell their stories?

Jessica – This community has no voice. So to have their stories told is really important to them. Beyond that, what they've gone through – the pain of being in prison for 20 years – there has to be some reason for that. And part of that reason is making sure that it won't happen to anyone else.

Q – What tips would you give on casting for a documentary?

Jessica –Your subjects have to be articulate. We met some amazing people who had horrible experiences in their life, who would've been perfect for the film, but they were completely inarticulate.

Q – How easy was it getting access to the Florida prison?

Jessica – We lucked out because Florida is incredibly lax. Other states aren't as lenient with the cameras. Florida loves cameras. It took a lot of negotiating – especially the last shot of the film when Wilton Dedge is being released. That's very unusual to get access to a prison as someone is walking out. It's part of the guerilla filmmaker mentality where you have to be really nice to everybody, but you have to know what you want and do what you need to do to get it. We'd always write a letter explaining what we wanted and threw around the term "Oscar nominated" a lot. "Educational documentary" is another one. Key words that are truthful and help you get what you want.

Q – How long did it take to get permission to show Wilton's case?

Jessica – It didn't take that long. He's one of the most important characters in the film. He's the only one who's in prison. It took us two years to find him. He was very distrustful at first because he's a very private man. But he understood that his story could eventually help a lot of other people. Courtrooms are public, so as long as you get permission from the judge you can shoot there. We got a judge that was very media friendly. We were running around the courtroom and he'd wait until the cameras were ready before he'd start his courtroom.

Q – How did you get Wilton to trust you?

Jessica – We only met him three times. There was that one interview in prison and there was a guard right next to him. That's why when you meet him it's a two shot of him and the guard so the audience knows that he was always there. Wilton couldn't really speak as freely as everyone else and the stress that's on his face is the stress of being innocent and in prison for 22 years and also having someone breathing down his neck who was apparently not a nice guy. Then we met him at his hearing and at his release. We met his family and his attorney who were very supportive of us. Everyone had to be on board with the project and feel OK about it.

Q – Was it easy to get the people out of prison to open up?

Jessica – No, they definitely had to trust us. Scott Hornoff the police officer had cheated on his wife, which is why he became the prime suspect in the murder. Asking people about affairs and why he has trouble relating to his wife now – the emotional walls – that's really heavy stuff.

Q – Any tips on getting people to gain your trust or getting them to open up?

Jessica –The number one rule is that you're a guest in these people's lives and you have to respect that. If they start to feel uncomfortable, you back off. Don't let yourself or your ego get involved in the story. Stay low and wear dark colors. They seem like little things, but they make a big difference. Don't make eye contact with people when you're shooting because that's distracting. For instance, when I do an interview, I never have my producing partner sitting behind me because that might be distracting for the subject.

Q – Did you ever have to back off from a subject when interviewing someone?

Jessica – With Nick Yarris, our death row guy, we had to be low key until he was comfortable with us. He directed the interview in terms of where he wanted it to go. I wasn't going for the sensational stories, *"Were you raped in prison? Tell me the most brutal story of what happened to you."* That isn't what it was about for me. The film's focus was about life after exoneration. I also had Dennis Mayer say things like, *"I didn't know what to expect in prison. I expected to die. I expected to be raped. I expected to never get out of prison."* I think that's more powerful and the audience is going to be thinking what would it be like if you were innocent, rather than describing a gang rape.

Q – How did the prosecutor in Wilton's case act when interviewed?

Jessica – I wanted to get as many points of view from people who were directly affected by this experience of wrongful conviction. Be it the woman who was raped and wrongfully identified someone, to the prosecutor who apologized and was a good guy, to the prosecutor who said, *"We don't owe an apology to anyone. Nothing is wrong with that."* I didn't have to get that juicy tidbit out of him. That's how he felt. They wanted to get their point of view across as well. For the prosecutor in Wilton Dedge's case who is very adversarial – he prosecuted him 20 years ago as well as this time around – he didn't want to admit that he was wrong. He was happy to tell us his point of view. He was right and that was why he was being so adamant about it. He waited around on a hot Florida night when we were all being bitten by bugs and happily answered all of our questions. And I was happy to show it.

Q – How large was the crew you usually took with you to each interview?

Jessica – It would be my producing partner who would help out and get releases and be a right hand person. A cameraperson and a sound person. Sometimes I'd do sound.

Q – What did you shoot on?

Jessica – We shot on the DSR-500 Sony camera. It's a big DV camera. It has fantastic lenses and for my camera people who are very experienced, it's a much better way to shoot rather than a handheld camera like the Sony PD-150. When it is on your shoulder, it's steadier. Even though it's big, you can be intimate and it looks significantly better. We recorded sound right into the camera. We'd have a boom and a lavaliere. In the courtroom scenes, we had a couple extra mics there. We didn't do DAT recording, but we did have professional sound people because bad sound can ruin your film.

Q – Since you weren't shooting, what kind of instructions were you giving your DPs?

Jessica – Before we'd shoot, I'd explain to them what the story was in this scene. And I'd explain the values that I wanted. So I'd say, *"Right now we're shooting Scott Hornoff with his kids and he hasn't been able to be with them for 6 years. So we're focusing on his relationship with them. I love looking at people's faces, so get close ups."* That's the great thing about cinema is that you get to look into people's faces that you don't normally get to look into. We had four main DPs and some additional ones, and that was because of economics and availibility. You want someone who responds to what the film is about and is plugged in emotionally. They know to move in at the right time because they know what the scene or the character is about. I'd also whisper in their ear and ask them to get something – sort of like being their second set of eyes.

Q – In post, did you notice any different styles between your cinematographers?

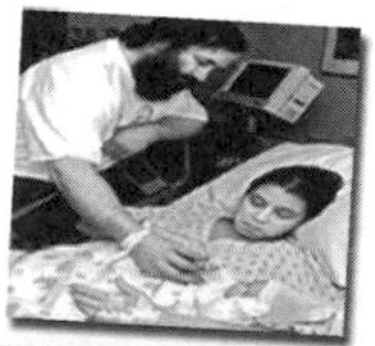

Jessica – Definitely. Penelope Spheeris was my mentor and she told be the most important thing to know about filmmaking is *"know your craft."* It's so true. If you know on a technical level how to shoot and do sound and you understand the editing process, it's a huge part of making a good film and being in control. In the editing room, I knew everyone's style. Some people stay a little wider. Some a little closer. Some are amazing at lighting. Some do better with set interviews. It didn't really present any problems because each character was shot by one DP so it was consistent. And having a slightly different style for each person helped distinguish them from each other.

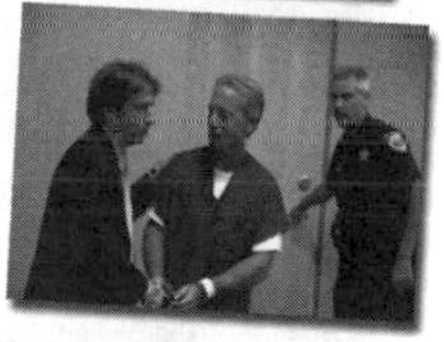

Q – Did you have any instances of long planned events falling apart or something happening spontaneously and you had to scramble to get there?

Jessica – That's the documentary way. You know what you want, but you don't know what will happen. You can't freak out when things don't go your way. We thought that Wilton would be released at that hearing and he wasn't. So we had no idea when he'd be released or if he'd be released. And if he wasn't that'd be part of the story. And Nick Yarris, we had no idea that we'd meet him. He had another film crew following him and we had to kick them out because it was our shoot. You have to have the confidence to know that it will work out and be flexible.

Q – Did you know how the story was going to be structured before or during editing?

Jessica – I have to give props to my editor Brian Johnson who edited *Buena Vista Social Club*. He's the most dedicated, creative person. Basically, from the beginning when I had the proposal, we knew that we'd use a diverse number of people, but the backbone of the story would be someone getting out of prison at the end. And then every other story would resonate off one another so that you wouldn't repeat ideas. In the filming and editing process, I discovered how amazing these people were and that they weren't bitter. They were positive and they wanted to change things. So the whole first two thirds is positive and the last third is about activism, change and preventing this from happening to others.

Q – Did you do any cutting during filming?

Jessica – I cut an eight-minute piece to get grants, but I didn't really start cutting it until the end of shooting.

Q – Did you have any problems in post?

Jessica – The biggest obstacle for me was that I had over 140 hours of footage and only four and a half months to edit. I think 5-6 months is more proper. Brian and I worked 7 days a week 18 hours a day. It was grueling, but enjoyable. Showtime wanted us to make the Sundance deadline and it was good because it forced me to figure out quickly what was the most important part of a scene or character.

Q – When did Showtime come on board?

Jessica – They came on in July or August and by September we had to submit to Sundance. We submitted a rough cut and no one other than the editor and four people had seen the film. And since no one had seen it, it made the premiere at Sundance more epic.

Q – What was the final budget on After Innocence?

Jessica – It's confidential but under $1 million.

Q – What did you master to at that point?

Jessica – Digibeta. We screened at Sundance on HD and then we eventually did blow up to film.

Q – Did you do anything in post to play around with the picture?

Jessica – The most important thing in post is to have a good color correction. Our film out looked as if we'd shot on film. It cost about $250/hr. and we did it for three days.

Q – What were your thoughts on music?

Jessica – I worked with a very experienced composer, Charles Bernstein. If you're on a tight budget or tight deadline, it is good to work with someone who's experienced so you can get fast turnaround on things. I told him that I wanted music that had a positive moving forward theme since that's what the film is about. I had a composer before Charles whom I fired because he kept making it sound like prison clanking sounds. *After Innocence* was about the moments after release, about being in fresh air, having a first kiss and appreciating life's moments. We did the music in about three weeks.

Q – Did you have any songs that you had to clear?

Jessica – We licensed a song from Vincent Moto in the film because music got him through prison so we put that over the final credits. And then, *Happy Birthday*. If you Google it, it will say, *"Use it and we'll sue you."* The scene is a really important one where Dennis Mayer has his first birthday at home and his family sings it to him. It's only two lines of the song and we had to clear it. So I wrote them a letter and explained the scene and why it was important. They gave us a low budget step up rate where we pay a fee now and if the film makes over $5 million we pay them more. We paid about $5,000 for *Happy Birthday*, but I felt strongly about it.

Q – Were you looking for theatrical distribution at Sundance?

Jessica – Yes. We got a sales agent, Andrew Hurwitz, but we didn't sign until Sundance and because we were at Showtime, people probably didn't know that our film rights were available. Showtime very rarely goes theatrical with any of their films, and almost never with a documentary. But I felt strongly about it and put it into the contract that we could do it. We didn't have to give up anything for it. They were supportive of it.

Q – Were you able to relax at Sundance?

Jessica – I enjoyed it, and we brought the exonerees and their significants from the film so we had a large entourage. We all had fun and they all wore *After Innocence* hats and shirts. I told them that when we go to Sundance, you all are just as big a star as Gwyneth Paltrow or Steve Buscemi and you should own it. And they did. People would mob our exonerees as they walked down Main Street. One exoneree went up to Steve Buscemi and said, *"Twenty-three years death row. What's up?"* And then they'd take a picture together with any celebrity they could find and send it back to their friends and family. Look what I'm doing now that I'm out.

Q – Any advice on dealing with the pressure of Sundance?

Jessica – I was lucky because Showtime took care of parties and publicists. Definitely have postcards and buttons to pass out and if you have a documentary definitely have the real people there. It makes a big impact for the audience, is fun for your subjects and is great for press. See as many films as you can.

Q – How are the sales of the film going?

Jessica – Good. We've had strong openings in LA and New York where it played for a month. At the end of our theatrical run it will have played in about 100 cities.

Q – What's happened to the guys since?

Jessica – The film is being used as a political tool, which is more than I ever could have imagined. It's being shown to try and get compensation legislation for the wrongly convicted especially in Florida. Florida has a law to destroy evidence in cases they consider old. Wilton Dedge who was the guy who gets out in the film was awarded $2 million. He now works as a gardener and his girlfriend calls him The Millionaire Mower. He loves being outdoors. Everyone is having babies. Nick Yarris met a British woman, got married and moved to the UK and is expecting a baby. My parents were the wedding videographers. Dennis Maher just had a second baby. Herman Atkins from LA just got married and was featured in the wedding section of *The New York Times*.

Q – What advice would you give a new documentary filmmaker?

Jessica – Find a subject that you are passionate about because it can take many years to make a film and you want to be able to stick to it. And have all your legal aspects, releases, contracts with crew – everything – all taken care of And know your craft. The more you know how to edit, shoot or do sound the more accessible filmmaking will be and it won't be a mystery and you'll be a better filmmaker.

ROMANTICO

Q – Did you always want to do documentaries?

Mark – Early on I knew that I wanted to do film, but I wasn't sure that I was going to make a career of it. I'm not sure when I had my epiphany about documentaries. I think I saw a couple of them and realized that documentary wasn't what I thought it was. I saw *Let's Get Lost*, which is about Chet Baker. It was a beautiful black and white portrait of this guy, very cinematic and visual storytelling. The structure was a bit loose, there were no expert narrators and it was all told by the subject himself and his various wives and girlfriends. It isn't necessarily my favorite film, but there was something about it that was a revelation for me. And then I went backwards and started to see old verité documentaries from the 60's. I saw *Salesman* – all the Maysles films. *Primary,* about Kennedy. Then it was on to Canada to the NFB stuff like *Lonely Boy,* I loved that movie. It's about Paul Anka, this pop icon on the 1960's with all the screaming girls. But they were all these films that were very simple in appearance but very complex because they're edited just with observational material and occasional addressing of the camera. That's the kind of film I wanted to make.

Q – Did you study film in college?

Mark – No I majored in Biology and English. I immediately started angling toward filmmaking right after graduation. Growing up my father used to shoot a ton of Super 8mm and we'd edit our home movies with tape and then add soundtracks and I'd narrate. So after graduation I started volunteering at this production company that made environmental propaganda films. Nothing spectacularly artful, but the films were about the impact of development on indigenous people and rainforest deforestation. I wasn't being paid so I left. I took some film classes and went to Stanford. I specifically applied for the documentary film program because I didn't feel like I was signing on for life. Some people look at documentary as a stepping-stone to making narrative films. I don't. But I didn't quite know how much I loved the work until I started to see some of the more artful documentaries.

Q – How long was the program?

Mark – Two years and it was production intensive. It's a great program. You have two professors and you're constantly making your own movies. And there's no competitive aspect to it in terms of who gets to direct the films.

Q – What would you shoot on?

Mark – The first few exercises were in 16mm. I'm feeling a little old here, but there was some 3/4" editing for one exercise Media Suite Pro, which was the low end of Avid was available to them just at the end, but I was editing on a Steinbeck and a Motorola. Adding a frame of mag back onto the sound squawk box, you'd have to go the right speed in order to hear it. You'd think it was the 50's. It was the best thing because it encouraged my film snobbery in a good way.

Q – Do you think it made you more efficient in your shooting style?

Mark – I suppose if you start off just in the video world it can certainly affect your sense of process and how you go about filmmaking. I know that with the current film that I'm making, I shot super conservatively. *Romantico* started off as a short film, but I'm sure I've internalized the ethic that I had in grad school of shooting film in an economical way. You preconceive to some degree the sort of things that you'd want to get on film. You don't go out there and vacuum. Those films can and should be made where you catch every little moment as it happens. But I'm interested in capturing little moments and not every moment 24 hours a day. Then you can turn the camera off and spend time with the film subjects and consider what to work towards next.

Q – What is Romantico about?

Mark – It's about a mariachi musician, Carmelo in San Francisco who was a migrant worker. He worked as a musician (and also a car washer and baker) for tips in burrito joints and hipster hang-outs in the Mission District. Carmelo goes home to Mexico after three years of life in San Francisco. There, he tries to figure out a way to pick up the pieces of his family life. The question of the film is can he live with his family and take care them at the same time.

Q – Why did you choose this subject?

Mark – I think for me, I never get truly excited about a subject when it's just an idea. I have to meet people. I'm willing to fail – that is, if I meet people and don't find the right subject, I won't start the film because it's too huge of a commitment. But as for the idea, I was thinking about these guys in my neighborhood who walk from taqueria to taqueria and I thought, *"I'll introduce myself to a few of them, no commitment and see how it works."* I started interviewing these bands and I became compelled by this idea that there's a bachelor culture among these musicians and maybe among a lot of the migrant workers. All of these guys have families in Mexico and live together as surrogate families. The accordion player, guitarist and the guy who plays the requinto all live together in these makeshift garages apartments. Or like Carmelo in cardboard box bedrooms in apartment hallways. They're each other's friends and family and they all have kids at home they haven't seen forever. They sing love songs and they don't have loved ones near them. So I was interested in it as subject matter and I thought maybe I'll find the right guy. And I didn't find him until I met Carmelo. I approached Carmelo and his partner Arturo on the street. I think I pulled over my car and started running after Mariachis, which is what I was doing in those days. So I started talking to Carmelo and the guy was very present and earnest from the get go. The way he looked at me was like I'm interested, what are you going to talk to me about? Whereas the other guys where like - why are you talking to me?

Q – Are they all illegal?

Mark – I think all of them are undocumented. Carmelo came over the border from Juarez to El Paso, TX. Arturo came over with a fake green card. I did an audio interview with Carmelo to sort of cement the idea that I was going to make a 10-minute film about him. And at the end of the interview I asked him if he had anything to add – anything I hadn't asked him. He said, *"Mark, I have been waiting a long time to tell the story of my life."* He has this odd mix of humility and this sense of epic scope of his life – I thought maybe this was the guy. Except I was concerned about how was I going to tell his life story in ten minutes. But I started the film because I liked him and I wanted to start this process. I had one shooting week reserved at the camera rental place. Regular 16mm. With a sound person and an assistant following them around the Mission as they played. A lot of walking shots, a lot of music and audio interviews so I wasn't rolling film on a guy who was as long winded as Carmelo.

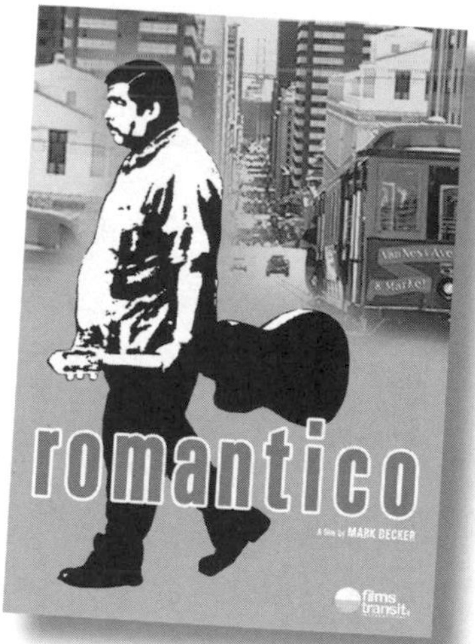

Q – Who was loading the mags?

Mark – I was. I'd have three or four 400-foot mags so I wouldn't be constantly changing them. I was thinking of it as a little festival film, which is why I was shooting standard 16mm at the beginning. Now I'd have shot it Super 16mm from the get go because of how perfectly it corresponds to the HD aspect ratio. Five days into the shoot, three years after he arrived in San Francisco, he decided that he had to go back to Mexico. There was no sign of that at the beginning of my shooting week. I showed up at his apartment with my crew and he was drunk. But the good thing is he's an affectionate drunk – he grabbed my face and he said, *"Mark, I'm so happy that I met you. But I have to go home. I'm sorry. I have to leave the film."* His mother had diabetes and was dying. He had to go and see his family. So I found myself at the airport shooting his departure and that's when the film took off.

Q – Did you go with him?

Mark – I went down later. I couldn't afford it then. I had some luck because I received a grant around then from The Pacific Pioneer Fund. They give money to "emerging" Bay Area filmmakers. I applied and I got $10,000 based on a little trailer I cut from the first shooting week.

Q – Don't you need a small track record with the Pacific Pioneer Fund?

Mark – Yes. I'd done some shorts and cut other people's films. The Jerome Foundation in New York also gives grants to emerging filmmakers, but in New York. And I had moved to Manhattan during production. So I received grants early on from these two organizations. I've friends that have applied that weren't quite emerging enough according to these foundations and others that were too emerged. I think you have to convince the Foundation that this film is a significant step forward in your career and that you don't have too much of a track record. I only had one film out there in festivals. I think during the board meeting I spoke to the idea that this was a big step for me – to make a film that had political subtext – and that it was much more complex than my first film.

Q – Did you have to put together a proposal?

Mark – Yes, and I've been cutting and pasting ever since. I can't believe that first proposal got me anything because by the time you do the 700th proposal you realize how much better it has gotten and the first one looks so terrible.

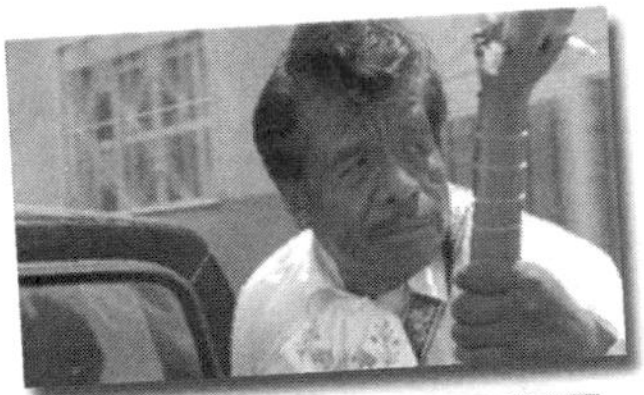

Q – What do they look for specifically?

Mark – I'm not sure. I think it's one of those funds that's a lot about the filmmaker. So they're looking for someone who is actually going to do their project and is passionate about it. What's really nice about The Pacific Pioneer Fund is that you get to meet with them. There are other foundations that are cold and they reject you based on what they don't know and never even ask you. I received plenty of rejections during this process, but when I got that positive feedback it did wonders – giving me a sense of confidence that I could move forward. Whatever they said, it was beyond the money. I felt like OK the film can work. And I had enough money for the beginning of the next shoot and by the time I got back from the second shoot, I think I got another little grant and that was how the whole film was made. Little piecemeal grants. Kind of like an IV drip.

Q – How many in total?

Mark – Seven or eight. Pacific Pioneer Fund. Flieschecker Foundation, Lucious and Eva Eastman Foundation, Jerome Foundation, Sundance Institute gave me the first grant, then California Council for the Humanities, then Sundance came in with additional funding for a work in progress. Then I got a surprise grant. The biggest gift of them all and one that I didn't apply for. At the time, the Skirball Foundation started associating themselves with the California Council for the Humanities and I got a phone call from the Skirball Foundation saying that they wanted to see a proposal. That's the first unsolicited grant I ever received. I worked like crazy for the $5,000 grants. I wrote them a couple weeks later to find out about the process and how long it would be and they said, *"Oh, we're really sorry that it has taken so long, but we're going to give you $50,000."* It's taken two weeks and you are giving me $50,000? And I didn't even apply? It enabled me to not take freelance work and edit my own and finish it. I still only had two thirds of the budget.

Q – How long were you in Mexico the first trip?

Mark – A week and a half. I didn't know what to expect. I was too conservative. I shot too little footage. I got a bunch of scenes that are in the movie, but I found myself wanting to go back to Mexico to have more footage to work with. If I shot 50% more, it wouldn't have impacted the budget that much because I'd already rented the equipment and paid for the travel. When I flew to Mexico, it would be timed with something important – like he had been saving up for his daughter's fifteenth birthday – her quinceañera – and he lost all that money paying for his mother's funeral. So I made sure to show up during her fifteenth birthday to see the fallout of that whole thing. He couldn't give her the big party.

Q – Did you ever wish you were shooting video so you could let the camera run longer?

Mark – No. I guess I'm a bit of a film snob. But I edited *The Lost Boys Of Sudan*, which was shot on Digibeta and was cinematic. It's all about what that film subject is. I started the film thinking it was going to be more of a verité thing and it turns out that wasn't where the great moments were. Carmelo isn't particularly demonstrative around other people. But he's a really good storyteller. So I began to give life to his past, present and his future in a way that demanded a certain amount of stylization. So it became a little bit more about getting Carmelo when he's at his most engaging which is when you're watching him talk. A lot of what is going on with him comes through in his self-conception. He has this vision of his life in grand terms even though he has had a very humble upbringing.

Q – So that is where the dreamlike sense that film can give, works well?

Mark – Absolutely. And there are a couple scenes in the film that are surreal – and the film grain I feel helps that. And I feel like film connotes the past.

Q – Do you think the Latin culture lends itself to this more than say an American culture?

Mark – Certainly in terms of what I was seeing when I went down to Mexico. Everything looked so beautiful and colorful - even a cluttered house. His wife and daughters had collected a million little dolls and they were all along the walls. They didn't even have a roof over part of the house and there was like a yellow sheet that hung from the ceiling and the sun filtered through the sheet and the whole room was yellow. The detail you get with film and the limited depth of field really felt right for this project.

Q – So how long were you down there for and how much footage did you shoot?

Mark – I shot a total of 7-8 weeks total. But I only shot 12 hours of footage. I spent a lot of time trying to become part of their world, which would make them as unselfconscious as possible.

Q – How did you do that?

Mark – With Carmelo it was easy. He's a great documentary subject in some ways because he'd fall into character as soon as I put the camera on my shoulder. If he was going to a gig or something or getting on a bus, he wouldn't wave good-bye. Actually, if it ever came to a point where I wanted to engage him it was a little difficult. Other people were more self-conscious. His wife was. The kids were quiet to begin with. Like in any film, the best moments to capture are when things are happening because nobody's thinking about you. But those intimate scenes at the dinner table when there are just a few of them there, that's when it becomes self conscious and I can only use a few of those moments. I think it was just them getting used to me. You want to spend a certain amount of time with them because you're a guest. So I had to show them that I was there to be with them and not to be parasitic.

Q – How were you storing your exposed negatives in steamy, hot Mexico?

Mark – I was hoping against all hope that nothing would go wrong. The hotel wasn't that warm, we kept the door and curtains closed. Mexico is a pain with shipping back and forth to the US. We lost some stuff in the mail. I wish I could've sent it back early in the shoot to make sure there where no light leaks. I never paid dearly for it, but next time I'd like to do things with less risk.

Q – Were there any issues going down there to shoot with carnets?

Mark – There were some problems especially going down there on the last shoot dealing with getting permission to not having the film exposed to X-rays. But with carnets, no, I'd go to the Mexican consulate beforehand and get permission that this was an educational documentary, not for profit. I never had to pay anything. There're some film services where people will drive your film from where you shot to your home, but it's enormously expensively.

Q – When you were shooting, were you editing in your head?

Mark – Yes. The film started to take shape after my second shoot in Mexico when I got a critical mass of footage to work with. But while I was shooting I was thinking about what I needed, no doubt. I wanted some sort of scene to play out in front of the camera where Carmelo would figure out he was going to come back to the US. And I happened to get this scene where he was talking to an advisor in his hometown about how you go about getting a visa. The advisor tells him all he needs for a visa is just to show proof that he's economically well off enough that if he goes to the States he has a job to return to, that you show your national and international credit cards and proof of ownership of your house and vehicle. It's one of those scenes where through the main character you see his dilemma: he can never go over to the States legally. I worked really hard to get those scenes so I wouldn't have to construct that stuff.

Q – How long did the edit take?

Mark – Well I was constantly editing in the beginning for the proposals. Always feeling like why am I editing for proposals and catering to their needs when I want to be editing the movie. That was always a little bit of a frustration.

Q – What did Sundance do for you?

Mark – The first grant I got which was development monies was theirs. It was a Godsend. And they started to engage me in their Labs. That was great because I was editing my own movie and that's an impossible task. All my battles were completely internal so I just tortured myself. This gave me a chance to get some feedback.

Q – What is the experience like at the Labs?

Mark – I was involved in three distinct labs. There was a brief one in 2004 where I sent a rough cut of my film to three or four sales agents, distributors and filmmakers and we all met at Sundance. That helped with some initial contacts with people, getting some feedback on my film and forcing me to make progress in order for me to have this meeting with those people. The second lab I did was the editing lab, which was the best lab in terms of the ramifications it had on my film. It forced me to make significant progress within one week by showing the film and editing it and showing it again with people in the room. It accelerated the process plus I met a bunch of people there. Independent filmmaking can be such a solitary endeavor – especially in post. Then there was the Composer's Lab. Again, you show your film and end up getting feedback on it. Then you learn to work with film composers. I ended up using the person with whom they paired me up in the lab.

Q – What were the amenities there?

Mark – They pay for you to get there, room and board. You stay in a cabin with a couple of the advisors or the other filmmakers. You have your own room and it's this insular world on the side of a mountain in Utah. It's only about your film for one week. You have no other life distractions. You eat every day with the advisors and the other filmmakers and you drink with them at night. You work in these little modified trailers that have all this editing equipment in them. It's like a film school experience that you aren't allowed to have as an adult. It's definitely a privilege.

Q – How did Jan Rofekamp get involved as your sales agent and how have the sales of Romantico been?

Mark – It's still a work-in-progress. I met Jan first when I got money from Sundance in January 2004 and they invited me to show a rough cut of my film to some people and Jan was one of them. Then, when I was doing the Composers lab at Sundance in the summer of 2004, the beginning of the lab overlapped with the Producer's Conference. Diane Weyerman who at the time was running the labs hooked the lab participants up with some of the participants. And one of them, again, was Jan. That isn't the usual route. Usually someone sends him a film saying they got into a festival like Sundance or Berlin and want to know if he'd represent it.

Q – So where is the film now?

Mark – The film will be on the Sundance Channel in 2007. And Jan is selling it internationally. The first broadcast will actually be in Finland of all places. And it looks like I'll start a theatrical run in the fall of this year (2006). The tough news with my film is that I made a foreign language documentary – not the most commercial property around. The good news is that it got nominated for a couple of International Spirit Awards and that's helped as my film has been renewed in a way. So I now have offers from some small to mid-sized distributors to get a theatrical run in the US.

Q – Did Jan want you to cut down the film to an hour length for broadcast?

Mark – I'm sure we had that conversation and it completely makes sense. Jan understands that I don't have the budget for my film to cut another version. I've had nothing but positive experiences on this film, but it hasn't proven terribly profitable. But it's my first film and it has gone beyond my original hopes.

Q – Now that the film has garnered critical acclaim, are you finding it easier to get in doors that were once closed?

Mark – I feel that I have the ear of a bunch more people now. That probably happens for everybody. With my film, no matter how difficult it is on the distribution end, people have liked it. So regardless of how they feel about being in business with my film, they think that I did a good job and I get work offers. And the editing and shooting work that I get has gotten much more interesting.

Q – Looking back on your journey with Romantico, is there anything you wish you would've done differently?

Mark – I'd have had a little more fun at Sundance. It's such an overwhelming experience. And given it was the first festival and there were sales opportunities, it was a little stressful. Maybe I could've taken a step back, but that's easier said than done. Otherwise, I had a couple of opportunities to get some private funding from individuals. For some reason it made me uncomfortable. And given that I'm still in debt with then film right now, it seems like a foolish decision. I have a two-year old daughter. It changes how I feel about debt.

Q – What tips would you give new filmmakers?

Mark – I believe in taking a risk. Put yourself out there. For me, *Romantico* took on a life of it's own. I didn't preconceive it to be how it ended up, but I stayed open to what was unfolding before me. The most inspiring aspect of making documentaries for me is the improvisation – responding to what's in front of the lens, and on your monitors. If I hadn't kept an open mind to Carmelo and what he was offering me, *Romantico* would have never come to life.

David Redmon

MARDI GRAS: MADE IN CHINA

Q – What is your background and how did how end up in documentary film?

David – I grew up in Mansfield, Texas and had no formal introduction to politics or anything because my parents were really young when they had me. They worked for the city of Mansfield and that's what I did after high school. I worked like 40 odd jobs from grocery stores to telemarketing. My parents were working class, so I was really aware of these inequalities and differences at a really young age. I just didn't have the language to express it. After high school, I was working construction and got picked on because of my size. I immediately drove to a junior college and I said that I wanted to go to school. They asked me if I had taken the SAT exam. I said no and wanted to take it right there and then. They started laughing. So I went to night school at junior college and then got a soccer scholarship to Texas Wesleyan. I transferred to Texas Christian University where I studied sociology. I got the bug and I went to Texas Woman's University where I got a Masters and I ended up getting my Ph.D. at the State University of New York at Albany. I loved it. I was introduced to all these things like globalization. That's how I got involved in filmmaking. I started going to all these demonstrations on globalization out of curiosity. And I went to an indiemedia center where people were filming and I saw a film called *Zapatista*. I met the director and producer and we started talking about making films.

Q – Is that where the idea for your film came from?

David – Yes. I thought I could tell a story about globalization by connecting it to Mardi Gras. I started doing research on Mardi Gras beads and the history connected to them. The Soviet Union invaded Czechoslovakia and put the glass bead factories out of business. Entrepreneurs were forced to go to China and Hong Kong. So that's where I knew I had to go.

Q – Why did you settle on that Chinese factory?

David – That was the only factory that I could get into. I called ten bead companies in New Orleans and two people let me interview them. The one guy in the film, Dom Carlone told me to come out and see him. I drove from Texas to New Orleans at least five times because he said he was ready for an interview. I didn't have a camera at this time. I was just going to write some articles. Now the first three times, he wouldn't let me interview him or turn on the camera when I got one. But he saw I was persistent and he finally said, *"OK, what do I have to do?"* I told him and I turned on the camera and we started talking. Then Dom put out a challenge to me. *"If you can find out who makes my beads, then I may call him in China and say that he should let you interview him."* So I did two months of research on the internet going to the Hong Kong Chamber of Commerce and typed in key words like "plastics" and "celebration." I narrowed it down to five people. It was midnight in Texas, I called Hong Kong and luckily got Roger, the factory owner on the phone. He spoke English and I said, *"Hi. My name is David and Dom Carlone asked me to call you. He said that if I find you, I could make a film about your company."* He said, *"Dom Carlone? Dom is a great guy. He made me rich. Any friend of Dom's is a friend of mine. When do you want to come out here?"* I looked on the calendar and said in four weeks. He said that he would meet me at the airline gate. I said, *"But wait. I want to make a film about your company." "No problem."* The next day I bought a Canon GL-1. I flew out to Hong Kong, stayed with him for a while and interviewed him. Then we flew to mainland China.

Q – How many times did you actually sit down with Dom?

David – I showed up at least three times when we'd sit down and talk. But he wouldn't let me turn on the camera. Then he'd send his son in who would tell me these outrageous stories. And I still couldn't turn on the recorder or the camera. Other times I'd show up and he wouldn't be there. I didn't know what he was doing. Maybe because I looked so young he thought it was a joke. I interviewed him three times. Two times before I went to China and one time after. He wanted to know why I wanted to come back and I told him that I had been to the factory and I had a lot of questions. So I did an hour interview with him on camera. The New Orleans bead industry is very competitive. So like anyone, he was looking for exposure just to get the edge. And it's true when he says in the film, *"If I didn't do it someone else would."* It's capitalism. If he leaves his company, then someone has to fill his position. That's an important part of the film.

Q – He seemed a little scary. Almost dangerous.

David – He brought me to a room once and I started getting nervous. He told me to pick up a can. I didn't know why, but he kept telling me to pick up the can. All these people then started to stand around. So I did and it shocks me. I started going, *"What are you doing?"* They all started laughing and patting me on the back. *"We got you. Just remember this."* So he said, *"Let's go do this interview."* Two years later after I had made the film, I get this Death Bead from him. He sends me this e-mail with viruses and an image of The Death Bead. And the e-mail said, *"Let's be friends."* Then I scrolled to the bottom and there was a JPEG of a skull and bones and crosses. It freaked me out, but I never heard from him again.

Q – Why do you think he sent The Death Bead?

David – I had presented the film as a work-in-progress at the University of Chicago and they put it up on their website. It said, *"Sociologist David Redmon investigates sweat shop abuse and connects it to New Orleans entrepreneurs."* Then I got the e-mail.

Q – But nothing else happened?

David – Well, I don't know if I was being paranoid, but a Mass Media Conference was being held in New Orleans one year and they invited me to speak. This was six months after The Death Bead. They were advertising in the newspaper and on local TV. Everyone had a badge except for these two people in the front row. They were staring at me the whole time. Are they with Dom? So I was like, fuck it. What are they gonna do? Kill me in front of everyone? No. I'm going to show the footage and then leave. So I show the footage and people were outraged. The two people in the front row were looking directly at me and they were shaking their heads. The reason that I thought they were working for him was because as the next person started speaking all eyes shifted except for theirs. And I'm freaking out – they're going to hurt me. I tapped the moderator on the shoulder and asked him to call security because I was feeling really uncomfortable. He was looking at me like I was insane. Security comes in and escorts me out while the other guy is giving his talk. I just ran as far as I could go. I never heard from him again.

Q – Sometimes China can be funny about letting filmmakers into the country because they don't want any bad press about conditions there. How easy was it for you?

David – I didn't go as a filmmaker. I went as a tourist. I took 100 Mini DV tapes with me and they did ask me through a translator why I had so many tapes. I didn't know I had to have a license. They all looked at me, congregated and talked and I had no idea what they were saying. They came back and told me to go ahead.

Q – A license for what?

David – To practice journalism. I went to the factory in rural Fuzhou alongside some mountains. It was a beautiful area. I stayed for about three and a half weeks. Finally on a Sunday the workers were allowed to leave and I followed them around as they shopped.

But what I didn't realize was that I was being followed. I stood out like a sore thumb naively filming the workers buying things. A government official told Roger that I had to leave or else they were going to arrest me. He sat me down and said that I had to leave first thing in the morning because I didn't have a license to practice journalism. When I went out, they looked at my tapes and they didn't really say anything. They just asked me what they were. I told them that I was a tourist and I was filming people riding bicycles and playing in the park.

Q – How much had you shot in the factory?

David – At that point, about 55 hours.

Q – It's hard to believe that Roger the factory owner picked you up at the airport.

David – It was confusing because in China, Dom's son-in-law called while I was at the factory and Roger looked at me. He said, *"David, that was Dom's son-in-law. He doesn't know that you are here. You told me that they knew you were here."* I said, *"They did. They said if I found out who you were, I could come out here and make a film." "But they don't know that you are here."* He never said anything else and just carried on.

Q – When Roger first met you was he excited because he thought you were going to show his factory in a good light?

David – Absolutely. But you have to understand, when I went to China I just wanted to make a film about globalization. I didn't know how the factory was going to be. If it was great, I could knock down all these stereotypes.

Q – So you were discovering things for yourself as you were doing the filming.

David – Yes. I didn't know what the workers were saying. We were communicating through a dictionary and via playing with the camera. It was a toy we were using to get to know each other while I was living in the factory. One day Roger took me out to eat at an extravagant restaurant and I left my name and the address with someone at the front desk and said, "*Hey. My name's David. I'm a US Citizen and I am making a film and I need someone to translate for me. English. Fujinese and Mandarin. Please have them come to this factory and I will pay them $10 US an hour."* About four days later someone showed up at the factory.

Q – When you got the translator on board did Roger give you free range?

David - That's when it stopped. *"Why is she here?" "Well, Roger, the workers have to say wonderful things about you, too."* So he said it was fine, walked away and came back with a supervisor. And he followed me everywhere I went and listened to the kind of questions that I asked.

Q – Roger states that punishment is good in order to make the factory work properly. Then the girls tell you exactly how it is. Could they say that with the supervisor there?

David – They didn't say anything then. What happened was the factory became very busy because it was the peak season of production. The guy who was watching me had to leave and he realized that the questions that I was asking were so harmless. So when he left, I knew it was my chance to ask rigorous questions. The first one I asked was the first one in the film to Liolia. She said, *"Roger told us not to say anything bad about the factory or we're going to get punished."* So I asked her why she was telling me. She said, *"I get punished so much, it doesn't matter. I'm stuck here. I'm going to tell you."*

Q – How long did it take for the workers to trust you?

David – Some were instant. They kept calling me over to play. What I found out through the translator was the only time they were allowed to talk in the factory was when I was there. It was this time out moment that suspended the norm and the rules. So they were talking to me while they were working and they said how good it felt to talk. The translator was trying to get me to leave. *"You don't want to talk to these people. They're migrants. They don't have any important stories to tell."* She was middle class and couldn't get it through her head. She didn't translate everything clearly and she didn't speak English very well. So what happened was when I got back to the United States, I hired someone to translate the footage for me and that's when I found out that what the translator was telling me wasn't exactly what they were saying. I couldn't believe it so I got hired a few more translators to come in and make sure the translations were accurate.

Q – Do you think that had something to do with Roger?

David – Maybe. They had a few isolated conversations. But I think it was also because she felt kind of ashamed. Here is this guy coming in to film and she wanted me to show China in a good light.

Q – How different was what they were really saying?

David – Very. I'd ask how many hours a day they worked. And she'd say they only worked 8. And then I found out they were saying, *"No, we work 15 and if we can't finish our quota, we have to work overtime."*

Q – What were the men doing in the factory?

David – The men were supervisors. In the cafeteria, there were two lines – a boy's line and a girl's line. The girl's line was so long, they had to wait for a long time, then sit down and rush to eat. The guys could go in front of the girls and get the food when they wanted to. It was a way to taunt the women. You can see the women's frustration.

Q – What other psychological abuse was going on?

David – Roger would be yelling and shaking someone. He'd look at me and I'd pick up the camera and the worker would be crying and saying no because it would be doubly shaming her. Roger would say to me, *"See how stupid they are? See how dumb they are? David, I'm so sorry that these workers are not doing their job correctly. What do you think of this?" "Well, Roger, they're kind of young and it's hard work. I think you're being a little too hard on them." "You think so? Really?"* I didn't want to say that he was fucked up and what he was doing was illegal or else he'd have kicked me out of there. I had to compromise.

Q – Did you start editing when you went home after the first visit?

David – No. I didn't have a computer. I had to do the translations through the TV – just watching everything. When I had the translator, that's when I got glimpses of what was really going on.

Q – When Roger let you back in the second time, had he spoken to the workers or did he have a problem with you?

David – Yeah, he had a problem. He was upset because I turned up out of nowhere. He was in Hong Kong and the security people at the gate let me in. He came back and asked me what I was doing there. I told him that the story wasn't finished because I had to leave last time. We had stayed in contact over e-mail. I told him I was coming back, but I didn't say when.

Q – Did you do that deliberately?

David – Yeah, I think he'd have said no. Anyway, I went at that time because it was Chinese New Year so I could go home

with one of the workers and get their parent's perspective.

Q – Why was there so little footage with the parents?

David – Because they only get to stay home for 2-3 weeks for Chinese New Year. So the way the film is edited is to show the redundancy of work. That's what they do in the factory. In comparison, when they go home it's just for that momentary time and that's why it got that much time in the film.

Q – How far away were these villages?

David – Some were as far north as Beijing. Some were only 3 hours away. I wanted to go home with one worker and Roger told me, *"No. They're backwards. They're going to beat you up and steal things. And if you do go with her, I'm going to fire her."* So he pulled us all in and told her what was going on and she started crying. I told Roger that I really needed to go home with a worker and I don't want them to get fired and I don't want you to punish them. I told him that I really needed the parents' perspective on their daughter coming here to work. He said, *"Fine, but I'm going to choose who you go home with." "Don't you think she should have a choice on whether she wants me to go home with her?" "No. I am going to choose."*

Q – How long did you stay in the village?

David – Three days. Then I left China.

Q – Did you explain to the workers what you were doing there in the factory?

David – Yes. I sat the workers down in the dorms and through the translators explained what was going on. The one thing that happened was that the woman that I went home with said that she was quitting after the New Year and didn't want the film shown for two years for safety. So it has been four years now.

Q – How much footage did you shoot and how did you organize it?

David – I shot about 200 hours. I had two journals and a case where I kept all my tapes. I catalogued every shot and used the camera as my deck. I used colors to highlight certain entries to associate that with a particular shot. If it's hands working, it was purple. If it was a long distance shot it might be red.

Q – Did you know the story before you left China? Or did it come to you while looking at the footage?

David – I was trying to connect what I knew at the time about the factory and Carnivale. There was also this supposed global anti-capitalist movement developing. I wanted to show the anti-capitalism carnival and then compare it to the Carnivale of Capitalism and then have the workers in the middle. Show Mardi Gras the carnival of consumptions. Then show the factory workers and then go to this other carnival that's happening against capitalism. Beads are worn at the anti-capitalism carnival as well. So I wasn't saying this was the way to go, I just wanted to show how the beads are used. I showed the film to Judith Helfand who made *Blue Vinyl* and she said that it looked like I had too much of an agenda. I told her that this is where I followed the beads and she told me to take it out. Then my friends saw it and though they like the images, they said I had two stories.

Q – What were the images that you took out?

David – I went to the World Trade Organization meetings in Cancun where I snuck in and interviewed delegates about China. They said China is fabulous right now. It's going under this process of development. And then I just contrasted that with saying that China is modern now, but not everyone is benefiting because migrants aren't benefiting.

Q – So it was more political than a personal story about girls working in a factory.

David – In my opinion, I was trying to put the personal with the political. When Colin Moore and Nick Chatfield-Taylor, two New York film students who helped me, came in with fresh eyes, I didn't know what they saw. Maybe they saw it as an overt political presentation. When I first showed them the 95-minute cut of film, they said it had an agenda. I went to China. I saw the factory workers and this is their life. Text giving information backing up the images. They said that no one wants to see this. You can't just go in a straight line. You have to bounce around and go on tangents and then somehow connect everything at the end.

Q – Did Nick or Colin edit any of the film?

David – There are two scenes that they edited: the three women dancing around with the beads and the opening sequence. They were very open to sitting down and telling me what to do.

Q – Would you advise other documentarians to have fresh eyes look at their work?

David – Yes. You get too close to the footage and you aren't objective anymore. We went to a friend's house in Boston and showed the film to people to listen to what they had to say. I wrote down all their interpretations and took what they said to heart. I also sent it to at least 15 different academics and sociologists to see what their comments were. They'd all tell me what things worked or what was irrelevant. The most common feedback was that the film felt long. Not that it was too long – that it felt too long. But that was my intent to somehow show that these workers worked this long and therefore you as an audience, although we can never fully empathize, can get some tangible sense of the wrongness of it. It was a sharp stun But it made me more open. And I made the changes.

Q – Did you finance the film yourself and what was the final budget?

David – Yes. Ashley Sabin and I. She came into the film a year or so later. When I met her, I had applied for a grant and had been rejected by IFP. I got rejected by some other grants. Then I called ITVS and they told me to send something in, but I never finished it. If you include everything, the budget was $30,000.

Q – When did Ashley come on board?

David – Well, she's my girlfriend so as soon as that happened she became involved in the making of the film. She did a little bit of everything! She took an editing class and it helped because it was hands on. She went to New Orleans and was the one holding the camera during the cultural exchange sequence. And that is how she learned how to film. She shot the people's faces as they were looking at the footage.

Q – Do you think your documentary will be screened in China?

David – I submitted it to the Hong Kong International Film Festival as a rough cut. I don't know if they're going to take it.

Q – Do you get the sense that Americans have any concept or are starting to get a concept that the world is so varied after watching a film like yours?

David – My interpretation is that it's fabulous that we in the United States have many documentaries like *Super Size Me, Fahrenheit 911*, etc. but problems arise once one sees themselves as becoming an activist simply by screening a film. Even though they've provided a platform and this space to get out information that journalists are ignoring and rendering invisible, then it becomes all to easy to just to show up and say, *"Thank you for this information. I feel more enlightened. I feel entertained. I'm going to go back home and that's it."* People have 2 to 3 jobs or they work part time. They have their own responsibilities. But what I'd hope is that somehow I could make a trilogy between this one, one in Mexico and one in the US to understand why they're working 2 to 3 jobs and don't have any health insurance. It's directly related to this global economy. It doesn't just happen out of thin air. It's political bureaucrats who are elected who manufacture something like this.

Q – What do you find challenging as a documentarian when you are out shooting? Or what do you find exciting?

David – There's something excessive about doing it and that's exciting. It overrides who I am and what I am in my body. I'm there and it's knowing that somehow I'm able to navigate through all these layers that existed to keep us out – whether we have done it by breaking the law, following the law – somehow we're there. Then you have to come to terms with agreement. What is too much? What is not enough? And then there is the idea of walking on the edge of surprise. We never know what we're going to encounter. That is what I like. I love destroying the inequities that exist through conversation. Like what I did in the factory, I was already destroying or circumventing the obstacles that were designed to keep them out.

Q – What were your music decisions in Mardi Gras?

David – We didn't have any money. Ashley's friend Matt did the score so I told him we had all these sounds from the factory that are really interesting. I asked him to compose something out of them. And he loved the idea. The other person who gave us music is called Bingo Music. They're from New Orleans. I sent them the film and they loved it and they let me use their music anyway we wanted to. I eventually purchased the music rights from another company. I chose public domain music, which saved me thousands of dollars.

Q – What kind of instructions did you give your composer?

David – I said that I saw this movie called *Dancer In The Dark* and the main character worked in a factory. And when the workers are repeating things over and over again, they look like they're dancing. So I asked the composer to create music that corresponded to the repetition of the factory and he did that through sound and machine.

Q – Now that the film is finished, is there anything you would want to change?

David – Yes. There's always something. I paid $700 to transfer the film and I realized that I misspelled the word "Canada". Shit! Then at the last minute, Nick calls and says that I should really put the wedding in. So I put it in and paid another $700. You asked me where I got financing. I was in Illinois and I met a couple in an elevator. At that point, I was selling the film for $1 or $5 out of my suitcase. We'd go to meetings or conferences and I'd set up a monitor or a computer and show it. People would want to buy it, ask how much and I'd say whatever they wanted to donate. So I met this couple named Deborah and Dale Smith and they gave me $20. Thank you! Now I can get on a bus and go somewhere.

Q – Was this a rough cut?

David – Yes. It had the military in it. It had this long footage with interviews with soldiers in New Orleans and how they like to beat up Iraqis. So they bought the film and called me three days later and said, *"Wow. We really love your film. We want you to have any creative control over your film. We want to give you $5,000."* It took me about a week and a half to say yes. Then just sent me a personal check with my name on it.

Q – Did you feel that you had a responsibility to finish because someone put in money?

David – A bit. But I used that money to buy another hard drive because I could no longer render the film. So I bought a hard drive and submitted the film to a lot of film festivals. And I retained some of that money to help pay for the hotel in Sundance. If I hadn't gotten that money, I don't think I would've submitted it to a lot of festivals, especially Sundance because it was too expensive.

Q – How did you feel when you got in?

David – I was pretty excited. Is this real? I think they were wondering why I was so quiet on the phone. I was stunned. Fifteen festivals had rejected the film - why does Sundance want it?

Q – Did others call after you got into Sundance?

David – The next day. Then Slamdance called and I almost went with Slamdance. But Andrew Hurwitz from the Film Sales Company called and we went with him because he said, *"I won't make us any promises. The film may sell or it may not. My purpose is to get this film out to an international audience because I have the license to sell it internationally. I sold Born Into Brothels and I am still selling My Architect."* He had a good reputation and he used to be the head of acquisitions at Miramax. I got the sense that he wanted to do this the way we wanted to do this.

Q – What is the deal that you get with him?

David – He wanted 15%. I called Sundance and they said that was quite normal for an international sales agent. He said that he wanted $6,000 of the first sales and again, Sundance said that was normal. And they said he was one of their most recommended agents. As much as I hear people bash Sundance, they called me every day, even when I was there to ask me if I needed anything like extra tickets or an extra badge? They were really helpful.

Q – Has anyone bought it?

David – Yes. The Sundance Channel bought it as well as several international channels. It's been screened in over 200 festivals, 200 colleges and we are booking it personally into theaters ourselves. This method of self-distribution has resulted in consequences that have surpassed our original goals.

Rosadel Verela Jehane Noujaim

CONTROL ROOM

Q – What is your background and how did you get into documentary filmmaking?

Jehane - I went to school to be a doctor but after almost failing out of Chemistry I switched from pre-med to a visual arts and philosophy degree. After school, I received a grant from the Gardiner Foundation to make a short film in Cairo and a year later I moved back to the US to New York where I worked as a director's assistant - I was terrible! I remember the director saying to me, *"There are gardeners and there are flowers. I think you're a flower…so go out there and bloom."* It was the sweetest way anyone had ever fired me! So I took a job with MTV on a show called *Unfiltered* where we sent cameras to kids around the US who had issues they wanted to film and share with the viewer. I helped them tell their story and I learned how to edit quickly and work on a deadline. The job was great fun, and that's where I met Rosadel.

Rosadel – My first few jobs were internships at ABC in New Orleans and in New York. There, I got a job at MTV and I stayed there for four years as a freelancer. I met Jehane as I interviewed her to work for *Unfiltered.* She seemed very passionate about working on the show, so we hired her! We had similar compassions and sensibilities and we very soon became friends. I then applied to the DGA Assistant Director program and miraculously got in. They serve as your agent for two years and place you on different TV shows and features in NYC or on location. I worked in the assistant director's department where I did everything from getting coffee to working on the online edit. After doing that for two years, I decided to go independent. That's when Jehane and I decided to partner up.

Q – You worked with D.A. Pennebaker and Chris Hegedus on Startup.com. How did that come about?

Jehane – My roommate, Kaleil started an internet company, Govworks, with his best friend, Tom and they were hiring friends to work with them. Funding checks were flying in for thousands of dollars when there was no product to invest in yet. Two friends with very different personalities, hiring all their friends and raising millions of dollars - I felt there was a story there and started to film. I met Chris and Penne (Pennebaker) because they'd been interested in making a film about the dot com world and had been looking for subjects. The marketing director for Govworks, David, was a friend of Penne and Chris' and asked whether they'd want to come in and meet the company and me. David thought they'd also know how to raise the budget for the film. At that point I'd put everything on credit cards. We hit it off immediately and I was excited to be working with such great filmmakers and wonderful people. It was great to have their guidance.

Q – What was your role on the film?

Jehane - I did a lot of shooting because a lot of the story happened in my apartment and throughout the night in bedrooms, bathrooms and gyms. Penne and Chris suggested I stick to Tom and Khalil like glue as they were the story. When they separated, Chris would follow one and I'd follow the other. I was comfortable with the shooting part of it, but I relied on them during the editing phase when we had to deal with over 380 hours of footage. Penne and Chris had some great advice about when to stop filming, *"You stop when you get bored."* So when the internet speak got heavily technical, that's when I'd shut off the camera. Chris took the lead in the editing room and I'd help her identify chunks of possible scenes and we put together a basic storyline. When we had a three hour cut, Erez Laufer then came in and helped to make the fine cut.

Q – Did you learn anything special from Penne and Chris?

Jehane – I learned a great deal - not all of it tangible. When I first met Penne he showed me one of his favorite films. It was a 20-minute film of this musician named Victoria. He told me that many of the films on his shelf, people had never seen, and yet they were some of his favorites. There was something about this legend of documentary filmmaking being unaffected by commercial success that was inspiring. Fear of commercial failure can hold you back at times, and Penne's attitude taught me a lot about the importance of following what is fascinating to you rather than the rest of the world. Chris' every day filmmaking advice and friendship taught too many lessons to list here. She was a filmmaker who juggled taking care of a large family, teaching film at Yale, keeping up with a demanding film career, making films with her partner in life and work - Penne, and then walking the dog – she's a living example of someone that just made it all work.

Q – Did you get the idea for Control Room before the war?

Jehane – Yes. Al Jazeera as a channel always fascinated me because it started in 1996 and was championed by the US government as a wonderful movement toward democratic thinking. No state government could censor it because it was available on satellite. Many Arab governments despised it because they were exposing corruption and discussing issues that had never been brought up in the news like women's issues and religion. In villages, you'd see people living seven to a room and pooling money to get a satellite dish so they could watch Al Jazeera. Then when 9/11 happened, and they showed Bin Laden tapes, it became labelled the mouthpiece of Osama Bin Laden by the US. I felt that if these journalists were now pissing off most governments across the world, they must be doing something right…or at least have some interesting characters working there! As the war was starting, I knew that my family in the Middle East were getting a very different story that I was in the US. People in the Middle East were questioning how we could achieve peace through war and saying that this war was the last thing we need after all these sanctions. Then I'd watch US coverage - about how this was going to be a clean war, with surgically precise bombing and soldiers going to be greeted with flowers as they walk through the streets of Baghdad. I knew that the people in the end who were going to suffer were the civilians of Iraq and the United States. I knew that if I were ever going to make a movie about Al Jazeera – now was the time.

Q – How did you manage to get access to Al Jazeera?

Rosadel – We'd sent faxes to them, but we didn't get any response. So in true documentary fashion, Jehane went over to Doha and sat in the guard's office for a long time just trying to get access, and little by little she did.

Jehane – I think that sometimes you just have to show up and knock on the door. I get there and all the journalists are staying at the Ritz and the Sheraton waiting for the war to happen. I went to this cheap motel where it was mostly Indian and Pakistani workers. I couldn't get an Al Jazeera pass to get in the gate, so I called Abdullah Shleifer, the head of the media department at the American University in Cairo. He got me a meeting with the editor-in-chief who asked me how long I needed. I told him that the filming of the last film I made lasted for a year and a half. He was shocked - the longest they had let people in, was for a couple days. *"We are getting ready for a war,"* he said, *"It's not a good time to have a camera around."* In addition, the BBC was making a film and had exclusive access to the newsroom. So how was I going to make a film about a news station when I didn't have access to the newsroom? I asked the editor-in-chief to allow me access for just a couple of days and I told him that I didn't have any lights and that I only used a small camera. Hani Salama, who filmed with me joined a few days later and we started filming in the cafeteria because that was the only place I could get access to, but it turned out that that was also where all the interesting conversations were happening. That's where I met Hassan and Samir. Samir and I had a long talk and he said that he knew the kind of film that I wanted to make, but I was going to be talking to savvy journalists and there'd be no way that they'd give me access like that (especially knowing the power of editing).Hassan and I hit it off right away and he pledged to get us access. After a few days, I think the journalists saw that we weren't

funded by anyone but were independent, and they saw that we cared about this story. As we hung around all day and night, they started to let us in. Hassan and Samir began to help us get into important places, open up to us, and because they liked and supported us - other people started letting us know what was going on.

Q – So that was the tipping point?

Jehane – Yes. You need a champion on the inside that's going to get access. They talked to the management and somehow we kept getting passes day after day to stay there. But we had to get a new pass every day. We could've been in the middle of a big story and if the secretary was in a bad mood that day she could not have given us a pass.

Q – Did you both go to the Middle East to shoot?

Rosadel – No. I stayed here in the US and sent out equipment to them and looked for funding. I couldn't really be much help to Jehane there since I don't speak Arabic nor am I very technical. Hani was much more suited for the job.

Q – How long did you actually shoot in Qatar?

Jehane – Six weeks. At CentCom, we couldn't get in because we needed proper journalist credentials and our letters from MTV didn't work. I took a job with Pacifica Radio so I could make some money and have a journalist pass but that didn't work either. Once again, Abdallah Schleifer came to the rescue. He got in through a pass from the American University at Cairo and interviewed Lieutenant Josh Rushing and told him about our attempts to get in and make a movie about the media. Josh Rushing said all we had to do was show up with our passports and we could get a day pass. We couldn't ask questions or have a firm location in the briefing room, but we could come in and spend as much time as we wanted to there. So we did that every day.

Q – When the war began, did the journalists remain objective or did nationalism arise?

Jehane – For the most part tensions were high.The Al Jazeera journalists knew and cared deeply about what they were covering - many had family and friends in Iraq. So there was some nationalistic and emotional reporting there. On the American side, most of the expert journalists on Iraq went to Iraq and weren't hanging out at Central Command. Most of their understanding of what the Arab world was thinking came from conversations with the Al Jazeera journalists. Most of the journalists at CentCom were bored with the coverage because they weren't getting information from the military press officers. If you talk to Josh Rushing now he'd say that no one pushed very hard. He thought there was this nudge, nudge, wink, wink, barely getting the job done attitude going on, where the journalists would tell the officers what they'd be asking them - perhaps to get in good graces, so that they could get some information. To understand the position of the journalists, many said if they'd asked any tough questions, they wouldn't get their questions answered and they wouldn't be called on the next day. They'd get into trouble with their bosses for not getting answers. There was national pride that surfaced on all sides. Foreign (non-US) journalists often commented on the very nationalistic reporting on the US side. But in terms of us filming the journalists and their personal feelings, most had all signed contracts with their companies saying they would not give their personal opinions. People were nervous about their jobs - especially because Peter Arnett was fired after talking to Iraqi TV. I spoke to a photographer who said he was taking the same pictures as the Arab photographers - but his pictures were not being picked up. And he said he couldn't say that on camera because if he did he would be fired and never get hired in the industry again. So someone like Tom Mintier, who had been through the Vietnam War and was the bureau chief for Bangkok, seemed to live outside that careful treading that many of the younger journalists felt the need to do. Tom was frustrated with the fact that he couldn't report on what he wanted to report on. He said there was a lot more freedom in covering Vietnam.

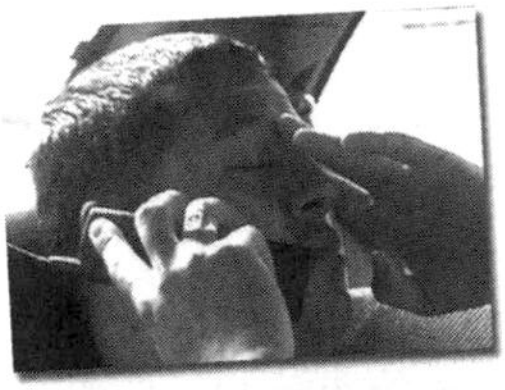

Q – Either there or in Qatar, did anyone stand up and say, "No. That's censorship and we will not tolerate that."

Jehane – The print press is able to do a lot more investigating than the TV press which relies on quick sound bites, appealing to advertisers, and making sure ratings stay high. One might think that you'd get high ratings from showing something controversial, but there seemed to be a different attitude during war. They believed that the country gets very sensitive and patriotic. They seemed to feel that showing the casualties of war- on both sides - was 'in bad taste'. I always thought this was a little weird - was it in bad taste to drop the bomb and kill people? Or in bad taste to show the results of that bombing on television to show what war was really about? Even Jessica Lynch had to come out herself and say that her story had been exaggerated and manipulated. It was a shock to me that the Jessica Lynch story in our film had people (some lefty filmmakers too) questioning my "patriotism" when I showed a 20 minute cut of the film right after the war. Tom from CNN questioned his order from above to show the video of Jessica Lynch's rescue. He felt that it was a diversion of attention. Some saw this as a scene which questioned Jessica Lynch's bravery, rather than one about Tom's claim that the military was hiding information by diversion. That same day, the three main journalist headquarters in Baghdad had been bombed so it was a legitimate question for Tom to ask. At the end of the scene, Tom called his bosses at CNN and asked why he was covering her story when troops were marching into Baghdad. His boss said it was what all the other networks were covering and what the American public wanted to hear about. They felt that people would change the channel and ratings would go down if they didn't report on it. But did people say this is censorship? No, they wanted their jobs, they wanted their questions answered, and the best way to get this, they felt, was to play nice. There were definitely grumbles but journalists didn't see the lack of information as censorship but as legitimate manipulation of information that any military would partake in during war. Tom often said that he couldn't rely only on what he heard at CentCom to tell a story—that that would be naïve.

Q – Did you have any issues being a woman or an Egyptian-American person in this environment?

Jehane – I sometimes think with filming it can be easier as a woman. Maybe we aren't taken as seriously and so we're able to slip in a little more. I think it comes down to, whether you're a man or woman, having the willingness to sit down, listen to people and make the effort to understand where people are coming from. One Al Jazeera journalist said that their experience with foreign journalists was that they'd come in and take shots of the veiled women behind the control booth. But there are also women in jeans in high-powered positions, so why wasn't that being shown? So when they saw that we were trying to tell the story in all its complexity, it helped with building trust. I think it helped that I was Egyptian American because I wasn't from either side, really. I was from both sides. I think it helped that Hani was there because he's Bosnian-Egyptian and had been through the Bosnian War. I never felt being a woman held me back in any way.

Q – What cameras did you use?

Jehane – This is a "do not do this in your own movie" comment! I went there with a VX-2000. It was NTSC and the lighting in the room would flicker on our tapes. I couldn't leave the country to get my equipment once the war started. Then I found out there was one PD-150 PAL camera in all of Qatar so I bought it. We shot most of it with the PAL camera, but the cutaways were on the VX-2000. When we got to the final film, we tried to replace all of the NTSC shots because they're not of the same quality. And we had to transfer all the NTSC tapes to PAL.

Q – Was that a nightmare?

Jehane – Yes! We transferred them very basically and then when we got to the final film, we transferred them at a higher quality. The reason we had to transfer them was because we were using a Final Cut Pro machine where you had to choose PAL or NTSC. I think now you can go between both in the latest FCP. I had two radio mics and an overhead mic. Hani and I were constantly piecing equipment together. I was tempted to temporarily borrow from certain news organizations. When you're sitting at CentCom late into the night and you have Fox News with their fantastic equipment lying around, you're thinking, all I want to do is borrow that microphone for a couple of hours to get some good sound. But we didn't. We were lucky because Hani is a musician and knows sound well. We had to figure out how to make our boom wireless. So we went down to the local electronics guys in downtown Doha who helped us build one. They fixed connections so that we got some fantastic working sound equipment. It would've cost thousands of dollars to get this contraption made from any standard equipment store and we built it out of odds and ends! We looked a little strange and even used a broomstick for a boom pole on one disastrous day - but it worked out.

Q – Were you able to get releases and clearances from people?

Jehane – You're supposed to get a release before you start filming someone. But when you first meet people, it's not the first thing you want to do because it seems so legalistic. So we didn't get releases until the end. There are some people who don't care how they come across - they say this is me, this is how I felt and if I have any integrity I'll stand by what I said. I tried to follow characters that were like that. I had a gut feeling that Samir, Hassan and Josh wouldn't go back on what they said. And I felt the same way about Tom from CNN and David Schuster from NBC - they all had great integrity, even though allowing themselves to be filmed and opening their lives placed them in precarious positions. I'll always be grateful for the trust they put in us.

Q – Did anyone say they wanted to see a cut of the film before they gave their approval?

Jehane – No. I tried at one point with Al Jazeera and the US embassy to give them some say over some specific footage because I wanted to film some meetings between Al Jazeera and the American Embassy. When they said no, I offered to let them look at the footage afterwards and have a cut over it. I think it's worth it to give that up if you're trying to get something very difficult and they aren't going to give it to you any other way. And if they have great demands on the cut, then you don't use it. But Al Jazeera took an attitude of journalistic integrity - They said, *"We'd never allow anyone to cut our footage and we would never ask anybody to allow us to cut their footage. But you also cannot have access to the meeting because the US embassy will not allow it."*

Q – Did you ever feel that you were in danger while you were there?

Jehane – Not until I recently heard about the memo between Bush and Blair that Bush wanted to bomb the headquarters of Al Jazeera - and that's exactly where I was.

Q – How did you fund the film?

Rosadel – Initially, the BBC was interested and they were pretty much on board. But they soon realized they were already doing a story about Al Jazeera internally. One department didn't talk to another basically. And the BBC and Al Jazeera have a relationship as many people from the BBC left to go work for Al Jazeera. So we had to put the flights on credit cards and tried to use equipment that we had from before. At the beginning, we really didn't need much money and Jehane would stay at friends' houses. Once we had a ten-minute trailer, I shopped it around to different people and networks here in the States but so many people said they couldn't program it for the year 2004 because we wouldn't be talking about the Iraq War in 2004. It would be over! Many of the networks said they already had a Middle Eastern story so they didn't want another one. They thought it was too much of a current event. So we got some loans and did it independently.

Q – What kind of loans?

Rosadel – From family and friends. Our only option was to try and do it as cheaply as possible. We found amazing interns who we couldn't have made the film without, BJ Perlmutt and Julia Bacha, among others, and gave them credit as compensation. That got us through the first stages of editing. Also we cut the first half of the film in Egypt because it's much cheaper than New York City. So we were creative and did it as quickly as we could. Since it was a timely piece, we were a bit afraid that we wouldn't get it out in time. Fortunately, the film turned out to be a timeless study on media during war.

Q – How much did you spend on production?

Rosadel – We don't know the exact number of the total budget yet because we still have bills coming in, but so far it has come in under $1 million.

Q – Were there any problems getting equipment in a foreign country?

Rosadel – We had to buy a lot of stuff here in the States and send it over. Sending it to the Middle East is extremely risky and expensive. You don't know if they're going to get it or not, and you're taxed when it comes in and out of the country.

Q – How long did it take to edit?

Jehane – 8 months. We also decided to edit the film in Egypt because we felt it would be easier to get the Arabic music I wanted to use. And we knew that we had a lot of Iraqi Arabic to translate, which would be tremendously expensive to do in the US. My parents had a house at the Red Sea so we took it over and ate, slept and edited there. Rosadel bought a bunch of drives in the States and sent them with B.J. and Julia. B.J. was a film student at Columbia and Julia was a Middle East history and politics major. Julia's orginal plan was to go to Iran, but she couldn't get a visa and thought this was a good stop on the way. Mona El Diaef, my old boss at MTV, loved the project and came out as well to live and work with us. So after a month of prep work at the American University in Cairo we each took our laptops with Final Cut Pro and we all moved to the house. Hani, who had filmed with me got into a car accident on the way to joining us in the Sinai—so after a stop in the hospital, joined us with a broken leg and set himself up on the couch, leg in a cast, editing system on his lap. B.J. taught everyone the basics of Final Cut. I gave everyone a character to work with, and we began logging, loading and cutting the best footage of our characters.

Q – How long did that take?

Jehane – May to August. By August, each of us had 10-20 scenes with each of our characters. Then B.J. had to go back to school and began e-mailing us his sequences from New York. Mona had to leave the Sinai editing madness in September and go back to New York. She left us with a number of sequences of conversations between Hassan and Josh. Julia stayed at the Red Sea and cancelled her trip to Iran. She had become immersed in the editing process and with learning Arabic. When her Visa finally came through for Iran in September, I begged her to stay and finish the film. It didn't take too much. Hani was with us working on music and editing - his leg still in a cast. At this point electricity in the desert was sporadic, and we were having terrible technical problems with sequences coming from 5 different computers and now being e-mailed back and forth overseas. We moved back to Cairo to try to find technical help. We attached all 8 drives to one computer and the whole editing system just crashed. This, in addition to the power surges, no sleep and watching a twirling ball on a Mac, left us with our head in our hands half of the time. Because we could only use one computer, we worked in shifts around the clock. Julia, Hani and I took turns working from 8am - 4pm, 4pm - 12am, and 12am - 8am. It was a labor of love. We hired two editors who helped us cut together Arabic scenes and one who helped improve our technical problems. By October, we had a three-hour rough cut with no music. So we decided to go back to the US to try to find serious help.

Q – Did you have any problems leaving the country with your footage?

Jehane – Getting footage out of Egypt is always an issue. You need to pass through censorship and have a number of permissions granted. Finally, we were allowed through. But we packed all the drives in carry-ons and hand carried them to New York City. Our Executive Producer, Andrew Hurwitz called Sundance and got us an extension. An intern at Sundance wrote back and said, *"We look forward to seeing the film, just give us a call when you get to the States and have something to submit."* Hani, as a young male Egyptian Bosnian, couldn't get a visa to the US, which was sad as he had to watch the film go without him. Julia as a female Brazilian was easier and we got her one. So Julia and I finally arrived in the US in November, needing someone to take over the editing for a bit so we could sleep.

CASE STUDIES

Q – Who did you find to help you edit?

Rosadel – Lilah Bankier, Charlie Marquardt, Alan Oxman and Andrew Rossi came on board and put together all of the previously edited pieces and it was that hour and a half that became our submission to Sundance.

Jehane – We had some confirmation that we had something interesting because people who would visit Julia's apartment where we were editing, would be glued to the footage. So a week after we got to the US, we called Sundance to let them know we were sending the package. They said that there was no way they could accept it at this point—we were way too late. I told them about the extension and they said that extensions were only given for two weeks and we could submit again in 2005. I couldn't believe it and forwarded them the e-mail we received. It turned out the intern was not supposed to have said what they did. So basically this intern at Sundance saved us and the film! All the films in competition had been decided upon, but they told us to send it in anyway. I got a call the next day from Diane Weyerman who said that she had just gotten back from Amsterdam and watched our film at 2am. She was excited by it and asked if we thought we could have a finished cut by January. If so, we'd be in the American Spectrum.

Q – What month was this?

Jehane – Mid-November. I was flipping out! No one had slept for weeks! I called Andrew Hurwitz and told him we were all at the end of our ropes and we needed editing help and music. So he called his friend Alan Oxman who came in to watch the film with another editor Lilah Bankier. They saw the potential and said they'd do it, but that technically we had created a complete disaster! Well, they saved the film's life. They took the film to their offices at The Edit Center - an incredible place to learn how to edit - and worked straight through the holidays. Lilah was amazing on the machine and fantastic with music and picture. And Alan had brilliant advice to give on the edits. They set up two identical systems so we could work at the same time. Charlie worked on one machine and Lilah the other while Alan became the Edit Supervisor. B.J rejoined the group and worked as a Producer. Mona rejoined the group to start choosing the music. Rosadel was finally there to add structure. And for the next month and a half we worked day and night.

Q – With so many editors, did you have problems coalescing it into one editing style?

Rosadel – Definitely. And that's where Jehane really stepped in as director. She knew what she wanted in the film. She knew what style and tone the film should be. And the editors were very sensitive to the fact that they had to work in a different way. I'm not sure I'd recommend having so many different editors for a film like this.

Q – Did you transcribe any of the footage?

Rosadel – Not everything, but most of it. We used interns and editors to do the transcription. We'd highlight different bites that we wanted to use and put them on the back of note cards with the scene it was to go into. We'd cut some transcript logs and then have another copy of them that wasn't cut so we could read though it continuously. It was important to have both sets.

Q – Did you cut anything during editing that you wished you'd kept in? Or did you have to cut anything for legal reasons?

Rosadel – Out of the 300 hours there were millions of bites that I know Jehane was very sad to see go. I, as the producer, had to be like, *"Whatever. Let's move on."* At the end of the day you have to do what's best for the film. We thought that maybe we might do a three hour version in order to use those bites somehow, but we never did. Why ruin a good thing? There was nothing that we cut for legal reasons - maybe sensitivity reasons. You want to make the characters as honest as possible and not embarrass them. At the end of the day, Jehane wants the characters to be happy with the film. Samir really didn't love one quote we had where he says, *"If I got a job at Fox, I would take it."* It's the one quote that everyone talks about. Jehane thought about not putting it in, but in the end he wasn't saying anything bad.

Q – How did you deal with music?

Rosadel – Music we got from friends and family or any kind of public library. Anything cheap, free and easy. So we sent e-mails to musician friends of ours and said that if they wanted to submit their music to be used in a film, without charge, feel free. So we got a bunch of CDs in and our fantastic music supervisor, Mona Eldeif along with Jehane chose the songs. We did try to have a couple people compose the whole score, but the problem was that the film was never really finished enough for that to work. The CDs were great and as we were used to making a ton of different songs feel united from our days at MTV, it ended up working quite well. We wanted to balance Middle Eastern music with American music and we didn't want to be heavy handed by having the lyrics state exactly what was going on.

Q – Did you ever meet Michael Moore and talk about your two different styles handling similar material?

Jehane – We had dinner together after the Critic's Awards with our characters - Josh Rushing and Hassan. But I don't think we ever talked about the comparison of our films. I think Michael Moore has given a real gift to documentary filmmakers, especially for the international release, because you seldom saw documentaries in theaters prior to *Fahrenheit 9/11*. I tend to enter situations where I know very little about the subject matter - I didn't know much about the media in the Iraq War. I didn't know anything about business or the dot com world. It's a journey of discovery for me. I want to find characters that are immersed in the story and that can lead me through it. I'd be worried taking a viewer on a journey by myself as the leading character unless I was an expert on it. You have to be willing to play the tour guide through the story. And Michael Moore does an incredible job of this, and of attracting a wide audience and asking probing and difficult questions. He tells a story through his journey of investigation. And I think this works well for many American audiences who like to have the hero take you through a series of questions and interviews and adventures. Michael Moore is that everyman's hero. And he has a wonderful sense of humor, timing and ability to lead audiences on a journey.

Q – Did you do test screenings when editing?

Rosadel – Yes. They were very helpful and we took their notes and amended things. We handed in a film to Sundance that we were happy with, but not completely to our satisfaction. That didn't happen until the film came out in theaters.

Q – Did you have all your clearances in place before Sundance?

Rosadel – Not exactly! We had a lot of them, but it wasn't until we sold the film that we pulled it all together. Remember we didn't even know what the film really consisted of until the last minute when we went to Sundance. We had the main characters' releases and the songs all cleared. Every time something went in, I consciously made a note of whether it could stay. You want to avoid having to rework things as much as possible.

Q – What format did you screen at Sundance?

Rosadel – HD. It was easy to do, but a bit expensive for us – around $700. They delivered the tape to my apartment at 4am and my flight to Salt Lake City was at 7am. It was a close call! We arrived Friday afternoon and our first screening was Saturday morning.

Q – How was Sundance?

Jehane – It was intense and the screening was amazing. Hassan came out for the first screening. We were so scared that people wouldn't be open to it because the images of the war were so different than anything they had seen previously . All three screenings were sold out with long wait lines outside. We had a Q&A that lasted long after the screening and went out into the hallway. We had liberals, conservatives, military people, filmmakers - even a couple viewers from the government – the movie provoked such intense discussion between everyone.

Rosadel – It was unbelievably busy, crazy and exhausting. But how can you complain? Your film is playing at Sundance! Everybody is going to see it including all the distributors. And at the end of the day, what we wanted was people around the world to see the film. We didn't want fame and glory. We got great feedback, which was wonderful as we hadn't shown it to many people. We learned a lot in terms of the sales and what our options were. We didn't sell it at Sundance, but a few weeks later. That was good actually because we could come back to New York and think about all our options – see what company we wanted to go with. Also we got to talk to a lot of other filmmakers who went through the same thing and we got to meet a lot of creative, interesting people.

Q – Who bought the film?

Jehane – Magnolia. They actually came up to us at Sundance right after the first screening. I was very impressed by their courage and excitement to take it on. They offered to pay for the finishing of the film, and then do a split after their costs were reimbursed.

Q – Is Magnolia handling foreign?

Rosadel – No. International is being handled by TV-2 Denmark and they've sold the film to numerous territories and are still working on selling it to more. They're very supportive and behind the film. The film has done OK internationally but could still do better.

Q – How did it fare in the Middle East?

Rosadel – Great reactions - very different reactions. Many were very curious about Josh Rushing when they wouldn't have even spoken to an American in a uniform before the film. There was also intense debate about Al Jazeera because they know so much about it.

Q – What about America's reaction to the film?

Rosadel – I was blown away by how many people came up to me, telling me they had seen the film. Not friends and family but strangers. I had a baby recently and the people at the doctor's office were talking to me about it. That was random. I love that people are talking about the film and the issues in it. All the awards we have gotten and all the things that we have been able to do because of it, has been overwhelming.

Q – Are you finding it easier to get your projects made since Control Room?

Jeahne – It's easier, but it's not an open door.

Q – Did Chris Hegedus and D.A. Pennebaker see Control Room?

Jehane – They were the first people that saw it after we felt we had finished it. I told them they had to be honest. They watched it in silence. And then Pennebaker says, *"I wouldn't change a fucking thing. It's perfect"* Chris said that the film had pulled her in all the way through – she liked the characters, but found the content of the footage from Iraq difficult to watch sometimes. I said, *"But there are parts that are kind of clumsy. I don't feel for example that the story arc is as clear as Startup.com."* Pennebaker said something like, *"So what if parts are clumsy – If Jesus broke his leg and had to limp around, he'd still be Jesus! It makes me think of how I would feel if Chicago was bombed."* My interpretation was that it may not be the perfect story arc - little in real life is - but it got at the crucial issues and it made you sit in another place. Their opinion was so important to me and I was very happy as I left their office. It made me feel ready to put it out there.

Q – Looking back on the Control Room jounrney, is there anything that you wished you had done differently?

Jehane – It would've made the experience better if we had someone who knew what they were doing technically. We doubled or tripled our editing time because of it. Having a very experienced editor to begin with would have been helpful. And the rush to finish it, left us with a couple of unforeseen clearance issues, which we dealt with during festival time. Maybe if we hadn't been going so fast to get the film done, we could've avoided them.

Rosadel – We did it a little too guerilla and it was quite difficult doing it that way. But at the time we didn't have the money or the resources to do it any other way. I think I'd have got a little more advice beforehand from people who had made documentaries in the same way.

Q – What advice would you give a new documentary filmmaker?

Rosadel – Talk to people in the industry who have done this over and over again. Then go ahead and trust your instincts and do it. Make a plan of what you want to accomplish, talk to these people about how you can accomplish it and then go out and do it.

Jehane – It was incredibly helpful to make my first film with filmmakers that I deeply admire. That's not always easy to do, but you don't have to be co-directing with them. You can be a production or editing assistant on a film they are working on. You build a confidence in yourself when you work with people you admire and they show confidence in your gut feelings. That was the biggest gift Penne and Chris could give me. They would tell me to trust my gut and get on flights for interviews for Startup.com even if I didn't know if I had access - if I felt it was important. Chris would always say, *"You never know what is going to happen so if you feel it, go for it!"*

Ross Kauffman

BORN INTO BROTHELS

Q – What is your background and how did you team up with Zana Briski to do Born Into Brothels?

Ross – I was a film editor for about eight years doing mostly verité docs. Towards the end of the 1990's there wasn't much that excited me in either TV or documentaries, so it was hard to find great projects with good budgets where you could do decent work. I was ready to quit the documentary industry all together. Zana had been going off to the red light district in Calcutta for a couple of years to teach photography to the children. She knew that I wanted to direct and asked me to "document" the classes. I said, "no." as I knew how difficult a road it was and I'd seen so many filmmakers try it and not come out for the better. I turned her down many times and finally she shot some footage in Calcutta and sent it back to me. I saw it and felt a strong connection to the kids, loved the material and had to do it! So I ended up directing, producing, shooting and co-editing it. Zana was co-director, co-producer and co-cinemtatographer, and Nancy Baker was the co-editor.

Q – Did you go to film school?

Ross – No. In college I was lost, but I graduated with a marketing degree. I was working as a waiter one summer and picked up a book about film in a second hand store called *The Elements Of Film* by Lee F. Bobker. I read the whole book in one night and loved it. So the next day I picked up some more books, started watching movies and moved to New York. I got a PA job and discovered that a good way to learn filmmaking was in the editing room.

Q – Did you plan the story of Born Into Brothels or did you find it in the editing room?

Ross – We had no plan whatsoever. That's the way Zana and I like to work. We want to react to what's going on around us. She's a still photographer and that's how she shoots, and I come from an editing background, and that's how I edit. I never want a story in mind when I enter the editing room. I just want to see the footage, let it wash over me and take it from there.

Q – What cameras did you shoot on?

Ross – We had two Sony PD-100's and I had a wide-angle adapter and Zana didn't. In terms of sound equipment I had a Beachtek adapter with a radio mic on one channel and a Sennheiser shotgun ME-66 on the top of my camera. Zana had an ME-64 and that was it. We didn't have any other crew. And many times it was me alone shooting trying to figure out the best way to get good sound. Sound is so important. If you have bad sound you're pretty much done for.

Q – Did you use the radio mic a lot?

Ross – Yes. I usually put it on whomever the main character of the scene was at the time, whether it was Zana or one of the kids. And I used the ME-66, which covered me most of the time. I have to say when you have a documentary with a lot of subtitles - it helps when your sound is lacking in quality. In addition, I was thinking about the subtitles on the bottom of the screen while shooting, so I was framing for that.

Q – Were you grabbing lots of cutaways and B-roll given your editorial background?

Ross – Sometimes the editorial background helps and sometimes it hurts. Occasionally I found myself thinking too much while shooting, thinking about the shots that I might be missing, and at that very same moment, I'd miss the shot that was happening right in front of me. So I'd have remind myself to concentrate and feel what's going on in the moment. Don't think so much. And a lot of the time I didn't have a translator with me so the shooting was a lot more fluid and natural. I just had to feel what was going on.

Q – Had Zana built up a relationship with these families when she went out prior?

Ross – Yes. She started in 1997 working with the women – photographing them and living in the brothel a week or more at a time. She naturally built up a relationship with the children to the point where they asked her to teach them how to use her camera. She never intended for any of this to happen. She was reacting to a need.

Q – Was it difficult for you to come into that situation and have to build up your own trust with them?

Ross – The kids and I had an instant rapport. I remember the very first day I arrived in Calcutta. I got off the plane and pretty much went with Zana straight to a photo class in the red light district. The kids were great and we had an immediate connection.

Q – Since they were used to cameras were they fine with having the video camera in their faces?

Ross – They never really cared about it. They had fun with it and I with them. I'm never the kind of person to say make believe the camera isn't there - because the truth is, that the camera is always present. I'd show them footage, let them use the camera so they'd be comfortable with it. It was also fun to see them have a great time with the camera!

Q – Did you have any technical problems with the camera or the sound?

Ross – The PD-100 has only one channel audio input, and the only problem I had was with the Beachtek, which is an adapter that goes onto the bottom of a camera so you can split the audio into two channels. One of the cables in the Beachtek broke and I had to solder it back together.

Q – Could you take the PD-100 on the plane with you?

Ross – We got visas to go into India, but it wasn't as journalists. We were totally under the radar for the whole project. But taking the camera through the airport and making sure your tapes aren't x-rayed. It's a pain in the ass. I've heard that it doesn't matter if you X-ray your tapes, but I just don't trust those machine. It's just a matter of being vigilant and tenacious and telling the security people "no". Our first trip was before 9/11 and our second trip was after 9/11. After 9/11 it was of course much more difficult.

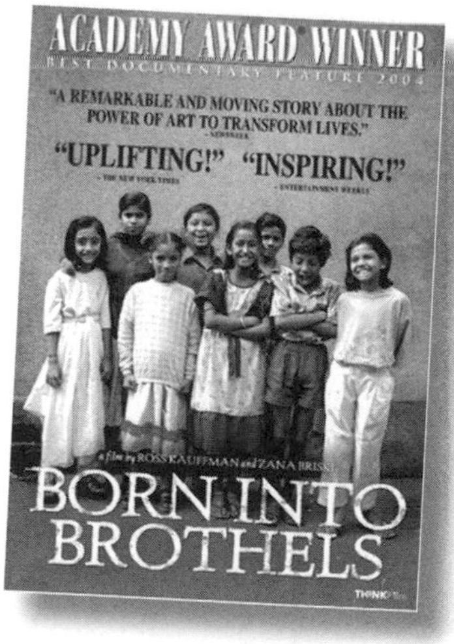

Q – How many times did you go out to India?

Ross – There were 2 trips for about 3 months each over a 2-year period. We also shot in New York whenever the situation arose. We shot in Amsterdam as well. In total we shot about 170 hours of footage. We then spent about 7 months raising money, and spent almost a year editing.

Q – Did you start editing in between trips?

Ross – No. I believe the editing process is one where it's extremely difficult to stop and go and stop and go. That said, while in India, I had a laptop and I logged a lot of footage. I knew I'd have to make a trailer of some sort to get funding. But I went through the footage very quickly just to get a basic idea of what I would use in the trailer.

Q – How did the kids' mothers react to the cameras?

Ross – They were fine. Every so often a mother wouldn't want us to shoot. They totally trusted Zana and myself. Zana was teaching their children, giving their children something interesting to do, and the mother's appreciated and respected her for it. Most of the time I'd defer to her about what we could and couldn't shoot. In the film, there's a fight scene where people are yelling and screaming. We were sitting in Shanti and Manik's room and just outside the room, we heard some screaming. Their mother was screaming at Manik. This kind of screaming happens all the time, but Manik was shoved across the doorway. I looked at Zana and said, *"Should we shoot?"* I wasn't sure what she'd say, but it happened all the time so it wasn't a problem. So we started shooting and at a certain point they closed the door. They were a little bit ashamed. It wasn't so much that they were saying we couldn't shoot. They just wanted to close the door. So I walked out the door into the courtyard where the fight was happening, and Zana handed me the camera through the window and I shot the whole scene. It's an important example of why these kids shouldn't be in this environment. I think the most important thing is that you have to keep asking yourself the question of should I or shouldn't I shoot. *"Is this pertinent, is it necessary"*. If the answer is yes, then it's important to keep shooting.

Q – Was it awkward to be a male in the red light district?

Ross – To this day, Zana and I will dispute this, but I have a feeling that when I arrived in the red light district, Zana went from being this crazy woman who was alone... to a woman with a "man" with her. In a lot of cultures, if a woman doesn't have a man with her it's a little strange. And everyone there knew that we were dating at that time, so in a weird way the people in Calcutta felt a little more comfortable with her. The day I got there was the first day Zana was invited into the main brothel – we both were. So I think it helped, especially with the Mafia that is present in the red light district. They're a little more comfortable with a man, which is ridiculous because Zana is a strong as any man in her character and ability.

Q – Did you have any funding in place when you went out there?

Ross – No. Most of the funding came from Visa and Mastercard. Zana's the queen of rotating card balances so that you get 0% APR. We bought our own equipment and paid for the flights ourselves. When I got back I bought a laptop and Final Cut Pro. I edited some footage, showed it to some people, and we went back to Calcutta again in 2001. We returned to NYC and I edited a longer trailer, applied for grants and we finally received our first from the Jerome Foundation. We were ecstatic. And then we received a New York State Council For The Arts grant. But the grant that helped us out the most was the Sundance Institute. That money enabled us to hire an editor and actually make the film that we wanted to make.

Q – Was the grant application process easy?

Ross – They're not difficult, they're just extremely time consuming. And that's the hard part - trying to make a film and raise money. And neither Zana nor I are producers. I have to say the best part of doing grant applications with this "new technology" was that I could cut and craft each trailer for each grant. It really helped tremendously. So for the NYSCA grant, it was a more arts oriented grant so that's what I concentrated on. Same with the other grants. And that's not to say that the film isn't represented fairly in those different trailers, it's just that different parts of the film are highlighted.

Q – Are grant foundations looking for similar things?

Ross – I'm not an expert on grants. I don't know what they're looking for. We applied to ITVS three times and they rejected us. I think they were about to accept us the 4th time when HBO said they wanted to buy the film and we went with them. Grants are difficult, but like anything, you have to earn your money.

Q – What was the final budget of the film?

Ross – It was between $350,000-$450,000 depending on a multitude of things.

Q – How did you start the editing process and were you both in the editing suite?

Ross – We started a year earlier by getting every word of footage translated. I knew we had to do that because these kids come up with all these amazing little things all the time. At one point in the film, Puja is walking up the stairs and she's trailing behind Gour carrying his bag and she says, *"I'm always carrying this guy's bag!."* There was just something so human about it. I would've missed that had I not had everything translated. Zana, myself and Nancy Baker, the co-editor, sat down and watched all 170 hours of footage for five weeks. For me, I want to see every frame of footage and know what's in there. Taking notes, getting impressions of the footage and talking about it. What was great was that we all reacted to the same basic material. Then we left Nancy alone for a while. My assistant editor Eric Welsh did an amazing job getting everything translated and organized. Nancy put together some selects, and then did an assembly.

Q – Was it cut linearly?

Ross – It wasn't linear at all. It was more like here's the footage and the scenes, let's create them and see what happens. We had our index cards with scene names up on the wall and Nancy and I'd shift them around – we'd worked together quite a bit playing with structure for months. That was the only way we could figure out what the story was.

Q – Had you always wanted to bring in an external person to edit the film?

Ross – Yes, absolutely. I love the process of editing, but it drives me absolutely nuts. And I knew bringing in the right editor is so important. Editors bring so much to films, documentaries especially. They bring ideas and structure. Nancy worked on the film for 7 months and then she took another job with Barbara Kopple. Nancy thought I should edit the rest of the film and I thought she was crazy. We were running out of money and couldn't really afford to hire another editor. Zana and I were co-directors, and we were handcuffing Nancy, making it difficult for her because we were really starting to argue about what we liked and didn't like. So I finally ended up editing for the last 5 months of the film. It was a struggle editing my own footage, but Nancy knew it was something I had to do and she was right. A film will either take that turn in the last few months or it won't. The film did; and it worked out great.

Q – How did you and Zana work as co-directors?

Ross – It's funny, Zana and I worked pretty well together in the editing room. We have a similar aesthetic. We knew it was going to be a hopeful film. We both thought that the music should play a large part in the film and it should be more like narrative film music. We had similar ideas. What we brought to it merged well and we both complimented each other. That goes back to the shooting as well. She's a photographer and I come from editing. She's looking at beautiful shots so she'll shoot a moth against a light for ten minutes. Whereas, I'm also shooting for story and those two styles merged together well. That's not to say that we didn't want to kill each other every now and again!

Q – How long was the whole editing process?

Ross – Eleven and half months. We finished the day before the Sundance Film Festival. So no test screenings. I arranged the editing schedule so that we'd just make the Sundance deadline. Not to say that Sundance is the end all be all for documentary films, but I knew it would be a great platform to premiere the film. And because we received the Sundance grant, we were invited to the Composer's Lab.

And all of this by no means guarantees you a spot in the festival. We were just crossing our fingers. Sundance is so much more than just a festival, and our film benefited tremendously from the labs and Sundance's continued commitment to our film.

Q – Did you go to the Composer's Lab while you were still editing?

Ross – Yes. Nancy kept editing and Zana and I took three scenes to the Lab and just worked with the composers there. It wasn't so much about the end product as it was about experimentation and discovery.

Q – Did you do anything additional in post?

Ross – We had a really great sound mixer named Tom Paul. It's all about casting. You're casting the right editor. You're casting the right sound editor. Tom was a wonderful mixer and very sensitive and caring in terms of the story. We also spent a fair bit of money as we had a sound editor working for about a month. I'm a real perfectionist in regards to getting the sound that I want. You can only do so much in the field. The same goes for the film blow up. The quality has to be the best that it can be. And many times, if you're being funded by a distributor they're going to tell you that you don't need this and you don't need that. They always seem to be looking at the bottom line and they often try to skimp as much as possible. But in the end it shows. People feel it.

Q – Who composed the music?

Ross – A composer named John McDowell. He was trained in classical and eastern music and he had never really done a film before. He seemed like the right person. I was a little hesitant to hire him, but we went for it. Most documentary films spend $10,000-$15,000 on a score, but in the end, we spent over $20,000.

Q – Did the grant monies you received pay off your credit card debt?

Ross – We paid off some of the credit cards, but the grants in general covered about 30% of the total budget. That's not including the film blow up or any of the other theatrical related expenses. We had to raise outside money for that. We had an angel come to us in the form of a woman named Geralyn White Dreyfous. We had heard about Geralyn and we invited her down to the editing room. She knew that we were in dire straights and she said she'd help us raise the money that would enable us make the film we needed to make. I don't think we could have done it without her. She's incredible and so committed to doing good work. She helped us get in touch with other filmmakers, to talk with them and learn from their mistakes. She was my date for the Academy Awards and we had a great time. But to answer your question...with the sale to HBO and international sales we finally made our money back and made a profit.

Q – When did HBO come on board?

Ross – I'd been in touch with HBO for a year and half showing them trailers and cuts. During the summer of 2003, Sundance held a producer's conference alongside the Composer's Lab. Lisa Heller from HBO was there and she wanted to see my 2 hour and 45 minute rough cut. And I wouldn't show it to her. Everyone thought I was crazy. *"HBO wants to see your cut! Show it to them!!"* But I wasn't going to show it to anyone before it was ready. So we edited for another month and got it down to an hour and half and then I showed it to Lisa. HBO loved it and they wanted to license it. So we had a decision to make – do we have HBO license it and then possibly get into the Sundance Film Festival with HBO in our corner or do we say no to HBO and roll the dice, hope to get into the festival and have a great screening and hope there is some bidding war? In the end, we felt that this was our first film and I have always enjoyed working with HBO, so let's go with HBO and keep a theatrical window in case we have distributors that are interested. Many sales agents didn't want to rep us because they thought that our "ship had sailed" including our sales agent, and that by letting HBO buy it before Sundance we'd never get a theatrical release. After we won the audience award at Sundance, we had a couple theatrical distributors interested – Miramax being one of them, but they all fell through. I gave a tape to ThinkFilm in March and told them that the theatrical rights were still available if they were interested. And finally, after we won the Audience Award at the Full Frame Film Festival In April, ThinkFilm called the next day and said they wanted to distribute it theatrically.

Q – Was everybody happy with the cut you had or did you have to make changes?

Ross – We didn't make any changes we didn't want to do. HBO gave us two very brief notes; one from Sheila Nevins and one from Lisa Heller. They were things we agreed with totally. ThinkFilm came on so late there's nothing they could say.

Q – Did the HBO deal help you with the ThinkFilm blow up?

Ross – Most people think that the distributor bears the cost of the blow-up. In the end, Zana and I ended up paying for the blow-up because ThinkFilm wouldn't pay for it. So yes, the money made from HBO did help out with the blow-up.

Q – When did you have your theatrical run?

Ross – Our theatrical run started on December 8th, 2004. We had a very basic strategy that we worked out on paper. This was 2004, an election year, and we knew that we either had to get the film released months before the elections or just after because the elections saturate the media. So we chose to release it after the elections and before the end of the year. We premiered on December 8th at the Film Forum in NYC starting with a two week run. Most people thought we'd get an Oscar nomination and we hoped it would stay in theaters until the nominations came through in late January. The film did well enough at the box office, so the Film Forum held on to it. When *Born Into Brothels* received an Oscar nomination, the film was released into more theaters and when we won the Academy Award ThinkFilm put it out a lot wider. I think at one point it was on 125 screens. We haven't seen much money from ThinkFilm but hopefully that will change with the DVD sales. Though I've been told that we won't see much. ThinkFilm's advertising budget was minimal at best. I spoke to one of the top people at ThinkFilm in Toronto about it and at one point he said, *"I don't believe in advertising, it's all about word of mouth with a film like this."* That makes total sense for a film that's solely word of mouth. But once it's out there and people know about it and are talking about it, you have to let people know that it is still playing in theaters. So they dropped the ball by not putting enough advertising money behind it. I asked Marc Urman at ThinkFilm, *"If you had more money, would you advertise it more?"* And he said of course he would. So I ended up raising another $62,000 privately for additional advertising and it helped tremendously. Among other things, we put a quarter page ad in the New York Times. Everyone saw that ad. But in the end it wasn't enough. But they were great in terms of collaborating on the poster and the trailer. But when it comes to anything regarding money, they're horrible. That was really depressing.

Q – And how was your experience with HBO?

Ross – They were great. They're smart and they care about the right things. ThinkFilm didn't take advantage of the fact that this was a non-profit venture and that we were trying to do good and help people. In the end ThinkFilm's lack of consideration in regards to the humanitarian angle helped HBO because once the theatrical release was over, HBO used it to their advantage in order to drum up publicity for their broadcast. ThinkFilm got so caught up with the fact that this was a film, and they treated it like a regular film.

Q – Who controlled the DVDs?

Ross – ThinkFilm. They wanted to cut every single corner when it came to the DVD and I fought them tooth and nail to put out a DVD that we could be proud of. For a filmmaker, the DVD is the final product where most people are going to see their film. It is extremely important to the filmmakers. For example, at one point the same person from ThinkFilm in Toronto told me, *"It doesn't matter how many deleted scenes we have on the DVD as long as we can say on the back cover that we* *have 'deleted scenes'."* Of course, that was a very depressing conversation for me.

Q – What happened when you were nominated for an Oscar and then won it?

Ross – I feel very fortunate and the truth is we didn't make this film to make money. But if other people are making money from your film, you'd like to think you'd make some. We have made enough so that we can live a bit. So I shouldn't be complaining too much. The Oscar will definitely help me get films made in the future. Plus it makes my mom very happy!

Q – It would be nice to think that some of the film's revenue would go towards helping the kids.

Ross – Right. And from the beginning we wanted to make sure that whatever we were doing, these kids would be the beneficiaries of it in some way, shape or form. We traveled for a year and half selling their photos at festivals and raising awareness of the kids' situation. In a weird way, everyone seemed to win – just because we were doing something good. We're funding the kids' education, and we're raising money to start a school in Calcutta. So in the end, the kids have an opportunity for education, we have Oscars, and ThinkFilm has an Oscar. Everyone did well.

Q – Did you get bumps in your contract?

Ross - In the whole deal making/contract phase, I went to other filmmakers for advice and one of them said that I should put bumps - a small percentage of the gross income from the film - in the contract. I told this to my sales rep and he kept telling me that *"that is not normally done"*. And I kept telling him, *"I don't care if it is normally done! Because what is 'normally done' is that the filmmaker gets screwed!!"* Let's push the envelope a little bit. That's a hard battle to fight. In the end, we finally got bumps, and it is the sole reason Zana and I made any money from the theatrical release and it will help us to continue working with the kids and to make more films. People wonder why it is so hard to make good movies. I feel like if the financial model were fairer towards the filmmakers, it would allow them to make more films of quality. But when you come away from an experience like this and can't afford to live, your desire to make a good film lessens.

Q – Can you say roughly how much you made from the film?

Ross – It grossed $3.5 million at the box office. I'm not sure how much it has done in DVD sales. So in the end, Zana and I split a little over $200,000 from domestic and Canadian theatrical. International sales are still coming in.

Q – Has winning the Oscar raised awareness of the kids?

Ross – In a way it helped and in a way it hurt. I've just returned from Calcutta where I was looking at land where we are going to build a school. But more publicity makes life more difficult in certain places in India. A lot of times it's better to be under the radar. But the kids are doing well. Most are going to school and are in good homes.

Q – Have you begun another documentary?

Ross – I've been so inundated with this film and I'm the kind of person who needs to decompress. I can't jump from one thing to another. I have a couple of films that I'm executive producing, helping younger filmmakers get their films made. There was a guy who worked on my DVD – Jeremiah Zagar, he is 23 years old and he is so talented. He's making a film about his dad who is a mosaic artist in Philadelphia. I saw his footage and I loved it. It's so rewarding that with my recent success, I can help him get it made, and get it made well. When the right project comes along for me, I'm sure I'll jump into it with as much tenacity as *Born Into Brothels*.

Q – How about Zana?

Ross – This is a woman who has dedicated 8 years of her life to this and she's pretty burnt out, I think. And she hasn't taken a photograph in years. She's going to start again and she's going to Borneo to continue her photography. I'm picking up the reigns with Kids With Cameras.

Q – What advice would you give a new filmmaker?

Ross – The most important thing is to be tenacious, persistent and just keep with it. Seek out the counsel of others. Talk to as many filmmakers as possible and get their feedback. But most importantly, just keep making your film.

GENGHIS BLUES

Q – What is your background?

Adrian – I began making films with my brother Roko in elementary school back in Chicago. In junior high we had a bicycle business, in high school a house painting business and so by the time I got to college I was ready to go out and shoot a movie and make billions. However, after talking to the school counsellor, I realized the probability of that happening wasn't likely. So instead, I studied political science and international relations. I'd also take business and film classes on the side – audit them or just sit in on them. After school, my brother and I worked a bunch of odd jobs and traveled around the world. My license plate on my car says, The Journey. That's what it's all about. Traveling and telling stories.

Q – How did Genghis Blues come about?

Adrian – When we were in high school, we saw a documentary called *The Last Journey of a Genius*. It was a BBC Production shown on *NOVA* on PBS. It was about Ralph Layton and Richard Fineman who were famous American physicists and their attempt to get to a place called Tuva. We had never heard of Tuva. So after college we called Ralph Layton who was the head of Friends of Tuva. Rich Fineman had died and no one else knew what Tuva was about. We told Ralph that we were documentary filmmakers and we had been making films for 15 years. Luckily there were no videophones and he couldn't see that we were 22 and 24! So he started telling us about Jurgs, and Yaks and shamans and throat singing and these Penatuva rings vibes in the Siam Mountains somewhere north of Mongolia. Then he told us about a guy named Paul Pina, a blind African American blues musician who lives in San Francisco who played with T-Bone Walker and BB King and Johnnie Lee Hooker. He wrote the song *Jet Airliner* that the Steve Miller Band made famous. Paul had heard throat singing on short wave radio eight years ago and taught himself how to do it; met some Tuvan throat singers and was going to go to Tuva next summer – would we be interested in filming that? We were like, hell yeah! We had fallen asleep to too many documentaries about extraordinary places, fascinating people and incredible adventures but told in the most dry and boring ass way. People thought we were lying when we were pitching this. One, Tuva doesn't exist because it's not on the map. Two, no one can sing with four or five voices. Three, there ain't no blind blues dude who heard something that can't be done on short wave radio who met some people from a place that doesn't exist and now is going to a world festival that happens every three years. Who the hell are you? So we went and maxed out our credit cards!

Q – And, followed him?

Adrian – To try and boost our cache with Ralph, he liked us, but he hadn't met us yet and we seemed to be getting along, but at any time he could have decided that we weren't the guys for this. My brother and I were in Europe and we decided that one of us had to get to Tuva and try to prove to Ralph that we could go to Tuva, shoot something and come back. My brother went to Tuva the winter of 1994–1995, and came back with footage and that kind of sealed it. The BBC was very keen on this project because they had done the original *Last Journey of A Genius*. We were sort of going neck and neck with the BBC. And, here we were two guys with no education in film. Six months before the adventure was going to happen in the summer of 1995, Ralph called us up and said the BBC were unsure about it, so why don't you do it? We went in the summer of 1995 with Paul.

Q – Did you have any money to do it?

Adrian – We didn't have jack shit. Credit cards. Visa and American Express. Maybe we got a 10% discount on something.

Q – How many cameras did you have?

Adrian – We had two 16mm cameras, a Russian one with a nice array of lenses and then an old wind up Bolex and 3,000 feet of film. But *Genghis Blues*, which has now 30 35mm prints in Dolby SR sound and has played in 50 countries around the world, was actually all shot on a little High 8 camera that I had in college. A Sony TR-101, a nice High-8 single chip camera that I'd shoot my soccer matches on. Literally days before we left, a video house in New York that we had been schmoozing for a few months sent us overnight one of first Sony VX-3s, the three chip Hi-8 cameras. The idea was to shoot film of all the beauty shots and then video of all the interviews. So even though we took the film cameras, we had no time to even think about loading film so we shot everything on video. I think it was a year later that we gave away the film stock that we carried to Russia and to Tuva and back! So, it was actually good that we didn't shoot any film because it would still be sitting in my mom's refrigerator and that would be it.

Congrul Lundar who is sort of the co-star of the film, and the most famous throat singer there is, flew back with us to the States. Every year he does a little tour of the West Coast/East coast gigs doing throat singing. He was already coming and Ralph Layton timed it so that he came back with us. So once more we contacted all of the people whom we'd contacted over eighteen months to try and find money for the film and told them that we'd returned with the most famous Tuvian throat singer and would they like to have tickets to his performances? Some of them actually showed up and were impressed but they still didn't give us any money. So, we had 180 or 200 hours of footage and no money.

Q – How long were you in Tuva?

Adrian – Five weeks. And, granted, of the 180 hours 40 or 50 was purely archival stuff. We shot every performer at the competition. Documented full sheep slaughters and how they prepared the innards of the sheep for someone. So we edited some of it and had to cut most of it out because it was starting to gross people out. So we had the stuff and we had no money, we had no clout and most people didn't believe us. So we drew up a nice budget - $180,000 or something like that. We realized that the editing would be $80,000 or something. And, then realized we could look at that two ways. One, either we need $80,000 US dollars or we need an editing system. We put the word out to everyone we knew and we found out that Ralph Layton wife's sister worked at an architectural firm that redid an in-house post facility in San Francisco. He said give this guy a call. 3 hours later, this guy was showing us the whole facility. We told him that we needed to transfer the Hi-8 tapes to some sort of more stable format, Beta ideally but we had no money. He said *"I'm going through Beta tapes like people go through water and once we master, we throw the Beta tapes away and I'm always looking for somewhere to give them to."* So that got us into a two-year odyssey of nights and weekends at this post house editing. By 5:30pm, everyone would go home, no one got in before 6:00am and no one was there all weekend.

Q – So you spent two years putting it together and working to survive...

Adrian – The key thing for anybody who wants to follow their passion, filmmaker or otherwise, is that in a communist society, freedom is found by leaving it. That's what my parents did in coming to this country. In a capitalist society, freedom comes when you're able to design your life when more money comes in than goes out. Also, if you're able to have more money coming in than going out, you aren't beholden to anybody. When we did *Genghis Blues* we lived above a shithole auto body shop in an office that had no shower or kitchen. We made a shower that was hose on top of the toilet. It was kind of ingenious, actually. That's how we lived for two years, but we were within bicycling distance of where we were editing. This guy Buff LaBeauf, who ran the post facility, saw that we weren't slackers, we were

presentable and that we were somewhat clever and could learn things. So, as we started to learn skills in this editing suite, he started giving us jobs.That guy not only believed in us, not only gave us editing facilities, not only consulted and stayed many late night helping us out with technical issues, but also gave us jobs in order to survive for two years.

Q – Do you have to be obsessed to do filmmaking? Did you have a life other than the film?

Adrian – Not really. But, we really didn't care. Yeah, we live in San Francisco. It's a fabulous town and there's a billion cool things going on. We could go to a bar and sit around and stay there until closing or, we can go hang out with Paul and Congral and look at Tuva and craft our passion. Some people might call it obsessed, but it was logical for us. We had fun.

Q – So what happened when you finished the film?

Adrian – We finished it at the end of summer of 1998. Three years. We had no investors or studio asking to meet a distribution deadline. No one was expecting anything. The way we figured it, we had 60 years to make this film. So, three years later it was done to our satisfaction. We then applied to a bunch of festivals and we also sent it off to a couple of people who over the course of making the film we got to know and trust in the film industry. Man, I remember we got a call back from a couple of them and they said, *"Who's seen this film?"* We told them that we'd sent it to a few festivals and Hawaii and the Hamptons wanted it. As we were just nasty, pasty, out of shape dudes, a few days in Hawaii would be great. They told us to not send it out to anyone else because we should apply only for Sundance. We weren't sure as at that time there was no video stuff in Sundance. We'd shot on High-8, not even Digibeta. But, we trusted these people and it sucked cause I had to call up Hawaii and the other festivals and turn them down. So instead, we applied to Sundance and I remember in 1999 you could only apply 16mm or 35mm, so we checked off 35mm. What the hell. The big dream.

Q – What did you hear from Sundance?

Adrian – We were driving from California to Oregon for Thanksgiving when we got a message on our pager. We stopped at a gas station as the sun was setting. The message said, *"This is Sundance, please call us."* And, we thought, *"Man, we forgot to send something in. We screwed something up and they're giving us a chance."* We're thinking, ok, one of us drives down to San Francisco and the other goes to Thanksgiving. So, we call them up and they tell us that they love the film and want to see the 35mm print as soon as they can. We had previously called the few labs that could do this transfer at the time and they told us that we needed $50,000 just to begin with for the transfer and then $7,000 for the color correction, sound etc. That was more money than the two of us had earned in our entire lives collectively! So as soon as we got the call from Sundance, we celebrated for 3 minutes and then we were like, *"we are totally screwed. Now, we have to come up with $60,000 in a few weeks or else we can blow Sundance."* So I got back on the phones and we started to scrape some money together. A week had gone by and I think I only collected $350 and I thought that this seriously wasn't going to work. But then by calling around we got into this A list of money film tree. One person I called gave me a name and number to call of someone who might be interested. So I had someone on my behalf call this person and recommend me. I then got a call from them saying, *"I hear you're a great filmmaker, how much do you need?"* I told them that I needed $60k. *"I don't have that much money, but I can introduce you to some people. You know it's a lot easier to get $10,000 than it is to get $1,000."* And, I thought, man, I am talking to the right crowd! So, I pieced together $50,000, and we talked to the lab and schmoozed them down to $47,000.

Q – Did you have a lot of investors?

Adrian – We had five people who gave us ten grand each. It was a gift.

Q – They didn't want a return?

Adrian – No. But what we did do was get a non-profit status 501 (c) 3 through the Film Arts Foundation, so people can donate and get a tax write off. So we cobbled it together. This one lady have us $10,000 and it almost became like an action. Got ten, need twenty. The lab needed $16,000 to begin so when we got our second ten thousand my brother went down to start the process, and they are like, *"Do you have the rest of the money in a cashier's check?"* Yeah, of course we've got it! So now we thought we were really fucked. Now we were $16K in the hole. The colorist guy had told us it was going to be more like $7,000. They gave us a lucky break, gave us a discount and moved us to the overnight shift. It so happened that the overnight colorist was the guy who did *Hoop Dreams*! This guy went and busted his ass for us and never got paid. My brother went there and slept there with him on the floor and brought him food. They were really great people. Then the whole other issue we had was that we had committed to 35mm when Sundance had accepted us, so we were told that we had a choice of what type of transfer to do – either Kenoscope, which is basically a film camera pointed at a very high level TV. And that costs $22-$25K. Or a 4MC transfer, which was a lot of high tech crap and more expensive. As this was three years of our life that we were talking about, and we'd got into Sundance, we went for the more expensive one.

Q – So how did Sundance go?

Adrian – When we got into Sundance we were short by $60,000 and we only had 30 days to raise it. We had no handlers, no agents, no studio, no manager, no PR people. Nobody. Where were we going to stay? I was trying to find $60,000, my brother was doing research on labs... I'm fond of saying independent filmmaking is the biggest misnomer in the English language because there is no more independent form of story telling created than independent filmmaking. We depend on all kinds of people. We have a lot of debts to pay. Everyone who came on board knew that we were never going to repay them, but hey, let's go to Sundance!

Q – Doesn't the festival put you up?

Adrian – No. Sundance is booked a decade in advance by the big studios and there aren't a lot places to go find stuff. And, we knew we couldn't be in Salt Lake City and drive back and forth. I'd call the places and what was available was small, expensive and far outside of Park City. Also, how were we going to get there? How could we treat a few people like Buff LeBeauf and Ralph Layton, and how could we market the film? So I started looking at Winnebagoes and motor homes. Everyone could pile into the motor home in San Francisco, we'd drive into Park City and then park along the side of the street and put big posters up and give out schwag. I called Park City who told me that we couldn't park overnight, we'd have to park outside of town in these RV places. The RV places then told me that the shower facilities freeze up and you have to walk a ways in the snow. I couldn't do that to these old people and adults that were coming. However, with all my phone calls, I got to know some people in the Park City City Hall offices and fire department and finally a guy in the police department told me about a friend of his who owns a piece of property in the center of Park City. He was going to build a house there but we could use it. Great! We could bring in a jerg, a Mongolian conical tent, and live in it.

Then I spoke to a friend of mine, Marcel, who tells me not to pick up the phone again until he calls me back in half an hour. So I'm sitting there waiting and he calls and says there's a lady who's going to call you, she's a good friend of mine so talk to her. He hangs up and the next day she calls and says that she lives and deals in property in Park City, what did I need and how much did I have to spend? I tell her that we need a place for about six people and that we have about $2,200 (which is what I calculated the Winnebago gas and rental would cost). She tells me that she has a place. It has 8 or 9 bedrooms, four game rooms, a Jacuzzi that fits 10, and three other rooms downstairs. I tell her that we can all fit into one of those rooms and be really quiet. And, she says, no, no, for the whole thing! And, I said, you're very kind, but we only have $2,200 for the ten days, not a day. She thought I was nice and gave us a deal. We had 40-60 people camping out at that place!

Q – That many people?

Adrian – At least. Paul Pina's birthday was in late January so we threw him a birthday bash. And, I remember taking a photograph of all the boots that were in the entrance hall - which was bigger than my bedroom. It was just covered in boots. In the morning, everyone is crashing out and my Mom is cooking up gourmet.

Q – Did you do your own publicity?

Adrian – Yeah. We thought about making guitar picks with *Genghis Blues* stuff. But, we were like forget that, we've got to bring Congrul from Tuva. It was going to be about $5,000. Where are we going to find $5,000? We had almost maxed out the Discover card for our plane flights. I called a friend who had done Russian American studies stuff at UCLA and asked him if he had any ideas. He gave me the name of the president of the East-West Foundation of the Rockefeller Foundation. So I called him up and told him that I wanted the most famous Tuvian throat singer to come to America for the film festival. He told me he didn't do movie stuff but did cultural exchanges. Cool, I told him we'd bring Paul and we'll do cultural exchange stuff. He said, *"Ok, I'll give you a $5,000 check out of a slush fund that we have!"* So Congrul came. I called Sundance to see if they could set anything up for publicity and they said that all they could do was a 20 minute gig. I was not about to put Congrul on an eight-day journey for a 20-minute gig. So I get back on the phone, *"Does anybody know anyone who knows a place in Park city where we can do a gig?"* We ended up getting a chapel in Main Street, Park City, Utah and we played there for three nights.

Q – When was your first screening?

Adrian – 8am Sunday morning of the first weekend. Not the best time. And our other times weren't that great either. So we postered the town and handed out flyers for three days.

Q – Sundance doesn't usually let you put up posters, right?

Adrian – True. But we were smart about it. We always asked permission. We'd try to get stores involved by passing on the excitement so they felt like they had a role in it. If our posters got tacked over, we'd replace them elsewhere. You poster over someone's poster, you're asking for trouble. And just talking to people really helped.

Q – How did that first screening go?

Adrian – We had the concert the night before and people kept coming in. It was packed. The most memorable thing for my mother was that Harry Belafonte showed up and gave her a CD. We had a huge standing ovation. It still gives me chills. Then it snowed like crazy. I figured no one was going to show up at the screening but thought, *"Wouldn't it be cool if I ever made a film that people would wait in line in the snow on a Sunday morning to see?"* And there they were! 500 people standing in line! And that was the first time we had seen the transferred print. In the opening part of the film, Paul wins the competition and the audience in the film starts clapping. I turned to my brother and said, *"That Dolby Surround is sweet. The clapping sounds like we're there!"* He said, *"No. Look."* And the audience in the theater was clapping!

Q – How did the Q & A go?

Adrian – Amazing. We got on stage and brought on Congrul in full Tuvian regalia. No one could believe it. It was like he walked off the screen. Another standing ovation! Then he started singing acapella through the audience. Every screening after that was packed. Fortunately, we won the Audience Award so we got an extra screening on the last Sunday. We packed it out and we called Paul, who was sick and couldn't attend, and he did Q&A over my cell phone speakerphone. The crowd went nuts. One of the great things about *Genghis Blues* was that in the beginning people thought we faked it. Tuva doesn't exist and there's no such thing as throat singing. Wow, that's powerful storytelling. When these people cannot tell what is real and what's not. We used that to our advantage in marketing. Nowhere on any of our literature will you ever see documentary stated unless it is in a catalogue. There's the old saying – there's no such thing as bad publicity in the entertainment industry, it's all on how you spin it.

Q – What did you shoot your sound on?

Adrian – We had a sound guy named Lemon DeGeorge. He had done a lot of Paul's recording. We had a DAT machine and a couple of microphones. But when we landed in Tuva, things moved too quick and we like to make films as they happen. No narration. Often, Lemon was too slow. He's a tech guy and wanted it perfect. So when we went to edit, all the sound came from the camera mic. It sounded OK because we got really close to the subjects.

Q – What about the score and music?

Adrian –The music was off CDs that Paul and Congrul had recorded and we got the rights to.

Q – What about distribution?

Adrian – At Sundance, we met a lot of people. Then again at Rotterdam. And at Berlin we sat down with people. We went with Roxy for domestic and Jane Balfour for foreign. We knew that we would have to go with smaller distributors who would allow us to stay in the film's marketing decisions. Roxy was very passionate about it and they were in San Francisco so we could just walk into their offices and ask them things. It played in over 100 cities in the US. We had a great lawyer who really looked over our contracts and got us good deals and educated us on how the distribution deals worked.

Q – How did you become Oscar eligible?

Adrian – All you have to do is show the film in a theater and sell tickets to the public for one week in either LA or Manhattan. So we four walled it and then sent in the paperwork to the Academy. Then we got a call that said we were on the short list. We were in Mongolia in February at a festival – 12 hours ahead of Beverly Hills. My cell phone rings and on the other end is our lawyer screaming that we got nominated. I don't know how anyone knew where we were, but we had reams of faxes telling us *'Congratulations!"* We lost to *One Day In September*, but damn, it was our first film.

Q – Did you get offers to do other things after the nomination?

Adrian – Yes. Some narrative feature things were talked about. We got pigeonholed though. All we got was weird music themed music. For documentaries, too.

Q – What is your next doc?

Adrian – It's called *Beyond The Call,* about a guy named Ed Artis, a Vietnam vet with three purple hearts and his two buddies, Jim Laws and Walt Raderman. They were delinquents as kids. Ed was busted for robbery and was going to prison until his uncle worked a deal where he would go into the military. He became a paramedic and would go out and treat the local population. The war ended and Ed never stopped. He goes all around the world doing this. He met Jim and Walt who were doing other philanthropic work like that and they created Knightsbridge – an organization that gives medical help to underdeveloped areas. We followed them when they were in Afghanistan just as 9/11 hit. We had to fake our way into the country as press. The US was bombing all over the Northern part of Afghanistan. All of that is another story!

Q – What advice would you give a new documentary filmmaker?

Adrian – You've got to love it or you aren't going to make it. And surround yourself with some key people. Worry about the things you have control over and keep your eye on things you don't understand.

Leonard Helmrich Hettie Helmrich

SHAPE OF THE MOON

Q – What are your backgrounds?

Leonard – I finished film academy in Holland as a director and editor in 1986 and then in 1990, I made my first feature length drama for cinema. The reviews were good, but the audiences wanted things like *Spiderman*. I grew in up the 1970's so I wanted to have messages in my films and therefore I focused more on documentaries. It also allowed me to be able to do my own camera work.

Hetty – Leonard is my brother. Our parents always took us to the movies to see things like *Ben Hur* and Cecil DeMille's *Moses*. We'd always analyze them. Then in 1982, I met an important filmmaker from Holland, Pim de la Parra and asked him to give Leonard an internship and he did. When Pim finally got financing for his film, Leonard finished school so he could be paid for the job. I saw the problems of getting a film made. So I decided to take a management course to learn the business of film. When I was done, I produced Leonard's first feature film. Then I produced his documentary *Moving Objects*, which won the Golden Gate award in San Francisco. And now I have directors coming to me to produce their films.

Q – What type of documentaries do you do?

Leonard – More of the cinema verité type. I've developed a certain style that I call "Single Shot Cinema." It's a style that brings you closer to the subject and one for which you don't need a big budget. It looks like how I made movies before I went to film school. Then, it was 8mm and I was doing the shooting myself. I went to film school and they told me I needed all these people and I had to deal with actors. People had to be put in little boxes of the job they did and I didn't like that.

Q – Does Single Shot mean that you're doing everything yourself or does it refer to the actual shooting style?

Leonard – It means that I'm doing longer takes that I condense with editing. With Single Shot I don't think about the shots beforehand. I try to put my own personal emotion into the movement of the camera. Because what you normally see in direct cinema or verité is that the camera is only trying to register a moment. I say the moment isn't the most important part. The important part is how you register the moment. You're part of the moment, so you have to put how you feel into the camera shot. Try to anticipate what will happen with the next moment and be there with the camera. That will allow you to edit properly. And because you're moving it makes it easier to edit. Cutting movement to movement is much more fluid. I never use lighting – always available light. I always say the lighting is always perfect; you just have to find the right angle. So you're always adjusting as people move around while the event is taking place. But you do have to move in a smooth way so that it works in the editing.

Hetty – And it must be very close. Not a wide angle.

Leonard – Yes. Stay close because when you use a wide-angle lens close up you get distorted faces. That's not true to life. You need to have the face normal and have things in the background giving perspective. Everything in it is real. There's no narration because the story has to explain itself. The footage has to say everything.

Hetty – And no one ever looks at the camera. So it's like you're there. We don't interact with the subjects. They only interact with each other. It's kind of like a moving fly.

Leonard – Yes. In direct cinema they don't want to interfere either, but you always get these profile shots. I hate that. I want to see their face and their eyes. I like to go in front of their face in a way where they don't even notice. I like to go into the aura of the person. And if they can't feel me, then I'm not close enough.

Q – Do you have to get your subjects used to this or does it come naturally?

Leonard – It comes naturally. Most people after a few minutes of shooting are used to it. In fact, in the film there's a fire and all the people came up to me the next day and said that I missed it. They were surprised to learn that I was there.

Q – Other than the camera, do you use anything else?

Leonard – Many things. I build a lot of devices to help get shots you normally couldn't get. For example, there's a man walking across a bridge and I built a tall crane like device that allows me to get a shot many feet over my head. We spend a lot of money on grip equipment. It doesn't mean that I'm going to rent grip, but rather that I'm going to invent grip. I built that crane device out of bamboo because there was no way I'd be able to rent something like that in the middle of Indonesia.

Q – Other than things like that, did you shoot purely handheld?

Leonard – Yes. And when it's not handheld such as with the bamboo crane, I make it look handheld. I built some sort of control that I can use with my hands. It's never a machine. It's usually just a steering wheel, string and a hi hat on the top that swivels and it feels like hands on the camera. You get the feeling that I'm there 40 meters above the ground. You get vertigo. Especially when you watch it on a big screen.

Q – Have you used this technique before?

Leonard – Yes. This is the second film of a series of three we're making. The first one was called *The Eye Of The Day*. It's about Suharto who was the President of Indonesia for 32 years and was brought down by the students. I wanted to make a story about students and my lone crewmember who was taking part in this. What was happening in his life represented what was happening in the whole society and his family.

Hetty – Leonard was in the middle of some demonstrations with the military on one side and the students on the other.

Leonard – Yes. I had to shoot without a crane because of what was going on around me.

Q – What did you shoot Shape of the Moon on?

Hetty – Mini-DV 900 and the Sony PD-150. We transferred it to 35mm for theaters and Sundance.

Q – Are you both of Indonesian descent?

Hetty – I was born there, but it was a Dutch colony. Our father was Dutch and our mother was Javanese. We had to leave the country in 1957. We went to Holland and Leonard was born two years later. Leonard was really resistant to shooting anything in Indonesia. He asked me, *"Give me one good reason why I should go there." I told him, "Your roots are from there. I was born there."* And when our mother died, I told him he could learn more about her. And then two weeks later, someone called me from a production office of the Dutch Film Academy and asked me to go to Indonesia for the production because I could speak the language. I couldn't go because I have two children. But they said they also need a cameraman. So Leonard went and he saw the country. And he didn't even speak the language.

Leonard – I spoke a few words. Enough so that the crew thought I did.

Hetty – When he came back, he changed his mind. So we did some research. It was very difficult to get financing in Indonesia because it was a documentary and because we were Dutch. It's the same kind of thing as between France and Algeria. When I approached film commissioners from the Dutch broadcasting companies, they said, *"Why Indonesia?"*

Q – That's strange because you generally think of Holland as being so open.

Hetty – Yes. So we financed it ourselves with very small funds. And then Leonard was captured.

Leonard – I was doing research by following these students in 1995 with just a little Hi-8 camera two years before Suharto went down. But in the students, something was boiling already. So I was shooting a demonstration against Suharto and the police caught me and put me in prison for four days. It was like *Midnight Express*. It was terrible.

Q – Even with a small camera like that, they were suspicious?

Leonard – Yes. They thought I was with the demonstrators and they wanted to know who the leader was. They couldn't do too much to me because I was a foreigner. I had an assistant who was given to me by the students to carry my bag. He was caught and he was tortured. He did get out, but they used electricity on him.

Hetty – They wanted to use it on you, too. And they wanted to shoot you.

Leonard – When they took me from Yogyakarta to Jakarta in the middle of the night, which is about 500 kilometers by car, I was sitting between two militaries. I told them, *"Shit, I have to take a leak."* They stopped and pointed me toward a tree. I was handcuffed and I knew that one of these guys had a gun. I knew that if I got out, they'd shoot me in the back and say that I was running away. So I stayed in the car.

Hetty –The other good thing is Leonard is known as a filmmaker in Jakarta so the Dutch Embassy knows him. At that time, it was right before Indonesia Independence Day and the Queen of Holland was coming there for first time ever. Leonard was at the police station just as somebody at the Embassy saw him and he was able to warn them of what was happening to him.

Leonard – I wrote a letter in the toilet and I folded it. I was standing behind the guy from the Embassy and he didn't see me, but I put the paper in his pocket. I tapped him on the shoulder and he was glad to see me as we had arranged for me to shoot the Queen at an art school. Then my friend saw these two guys in the military uniforms. I said in Dutch so they wouldn't understand me, *"I don't think I can make the shoot. Read the paper in your pocket."*

Q – Then what happened?

Leonard – He immediately phoned up the Embassy and told them I was there. The military was angry because they wanted to take me somewhere else. But because the Queen was coming, all the Dutch foreign ministers were there already as was the Director of Foreign Affairs. So it was easier to get me out of the country that way.

Hetty – He was there for four days and he had to pay a lot of money to get out. He also got stamped on his passport "persona non grata" so he cannot go back to Indonesia. And this was in 1996. We had to wait three years and then I called my elder brother and said that we had interests in the films there, can we do something about it. He went to the Embassy and finally he got them to remove the stamps.

Leonard – I had a letter from the Indonesian government after Suharto went down, so it was easier to go back.

Q – So you got lucky with timing.

Hetty – That's always how it is with our films. We finished *Shape Of The Moon* in July and it was Oscar eligible. It opened IDFA in November and it won the prize there so our Dutch distributor decided to open it on January 6th. He had plans to open it in Acheh over Christmas, but we couldn't go because we won that prize and that is when the tsunami hit. Another thing, in the movie, one of the first shots is of this wave. And I saw the audience go WOW! How did you do that?

Leonard – I wanted to express what is Indonesia. You see an Islamic society and a sea of people in a mosque praying and there is one guy who is crying. At the moment, the priests are saying, *"Save our country,"* the guy looks back and you see this white wave that matches the white they wear to mosque. At IDFA, this was before the tsunami; they wondered what it was a symbol of. I didn't know. But here at Sundance after the tsunami, people are saying it's too obvious. I tell them it has to do something with the moon controlling the waves and the sea. But with history, it has a new meaning for people.

Q – How did you handle the music to Shape of The Moon?

Leonard – We don't have much. Mostly what was on the street. There are many times where the people speaking at mosques have Arabic music behind them. I also like to have real sounds because that gives you a feeling of where you are. So crickets and a dog barking in the background. The one thing with music is that you have to deal with a composer and the rights and all of these things.

Hetty – In *Eye Of The Day*, in the beginning, it's very beautiful. You see a beggar who's singing on the street with an instrument that he made himself as he goes from car to car. It's beautiful and we translated the song.

CASE STUDIES

Q – Do you play around with the images much in post?

Leonard – Not in the sense that in editing I alter things. And we don't really alter the colors. We do play around with the transitions a bit.

Q – Can you give us an example?

Leonard – There's a scene in *Shape Of The Moon* where a woman decides to go to the countryside and she goes by train. The train goes through a tunnel and then you see a little light far away and it's getting closer and closer. But it's spinning around a little bit. And it looks a bit like the moon. You get closer and closer and you hear the train sounds echoing. Then you come out and you find out you're in a bucket that has come out of a well.

Q – When you shot Eye Of The Day, did you know you wanted to do a trilogy?

Hetty – No. We had a step outline of the film and after editing we had so many things that didn't belong to the story that I said we should just make some other films, a sequel and maybe a trilogy out of it.

Q – Did you do test screenings of the film? Also what did you edit it on?

Hetty – Final Cut Pro. It's very easy. It costs almost nothing. But yes, we always have viewings after a few weeks of finishing a cut.

Leonard – You can ask people how it's working. We show it to people who like film or to our colleagues and get their opinions. It doesn't mean that I will do what they say because I might know the personality of the person and if he's the opposite of what I like, then I do the opposite of what he says. So we show it to 5-6 people.

Hetty – We have a friend in Amsterdam who has a small theater and he allows us to screen whatever we want. It only has 20 seats and it's very relaxed.

Q – Were all of your films personally financed?

Hetty – For *Eye Of The Day* I got a small amount of money from the media in Brussels. It was research money and we did the whole film with that. When we finished it, we showed it to the Dutch Film Fund and they loved it. They said we needed to do more and wanted us to have an editor finish it in a month and blow it up to 35mm. So they gave us some money and I put in a little and we did that.

Q – How much was the budget for Eye Of The Day?

Hetty – About $20,000. Then the blow up was expensive. It was about $40,000. It's so slow. They do one minute a day. It took them seven weeks to transfer the film back then. Now they have a new system and they can do it in seven days.

Q – You had to bring on a new editor after editing the film yourselves. What was that like?

Leonard – We hired one person before this, but he wasn't experienced enough. With the film fund money, we were able to hire the woman who edited my first film which one the prize in San Francisco.

Q – After finishing Eye Of The Day, what in the remaining footage was the storyline for Shape Of The Moon?

Leonard – We had all these darlings that we had to kill from the first film, so we strung them together and it didn't work. Plus, I was still shooting *Shape Of The Moon* and I realized that what was happening in the family at that point was much more interesting than what I had shot before. So we decided to focus more on what was going on at that time and made a step outline for the plot. I then figured out what I was missing.

Hetty – I was at the Australian Film Conference and then made a stop over in Indonesia for two weeks. He showed me what he had at the time and then said that the old woman was planning on going to the countryside. This would be great because he has this Christian woman dealing with life in a Muslim community. Her son falls in love with a Muslim girl and he has to convert because he cannot marry a Muslim girl or it's like prostitution.

Leonard – We also follow a line of drama. We start the story and then in 25 minutes we have a twist in order to keep the audience focused. Then in another 25 minutes ther's another twist. We did this in *Eye Of The Day*, when we show people trying to catch a snake before they start harvesting rice. I was able to get really close to the snakes and it gave a good shock effect. I needed something like that for *Shape Of The Moon* and so I did the guy walking on the bridge with the crane.

Q – How did you organize those 200 hours of footage and did you transcribe any of it?

Leonard – I transcribe everything. A year's worth of footage. Every day as we were watching it, I'd write down what I see and also the time code and the scenes. And I'll make notes on it if it's really interesting. It takes time to do, but it saves you a lot of time in editing. I don't use a special program to organize it – I just do it in Microsoft Word. Then you can just search for "snake" or whatever and find the shot I want.

Q – Were you cutting while you were filming?

Leonard – No. Well, we did have that one editor at the beginning of *Shape Of The Moon*.

Q – How long did it take to edit Shape Of The Moon?

Hetty – I think it was about one month for the first cut, but we weren't satisfied. We found out that the marriage was going to happen and the son converted and had to be circumcised. He had to get it. Afterward, he came back with another editor and it took them four or five months and it turned out great.

Q – When was it complete?

Hetty – In June and we had to screen it in order to make it Oscar eligible. Then we sent it off to the South By Southwest Film Festival and Venice wanted it as well. Then IDFA said it'd be their opening film, so I dropped the others. Then Sundance wanted it, but they realized it was important for us to screen it in our country first.

Q – Any idea of the title for number three?

Leonard – Something to do with stars. That way we have the sun, the moon and the stars. It will be about the rich people in Indonesia. They control the entire economy and I want to show how that affects the people of the country.

Q – Is it tough to get funding for documentaries in Holland?

Hetty – If you're just starting out, yes it's tough. But if you team with a company like mine, Scarabee Films, that has a track record, it isn't as tough. I can then become an advocate and convince broadcasters to get money. The main money comes from places like The Rotterdam Film Fund, The Dutch Fund. Sometimes it's a gift and other times you have to give them money if the film makes money.

Q – Are there a lot of broadcasters In Holland that support documentaries?

Hetty – Yes. In Holland we're fortunate. We have more than 25 public broadcast companies A.O. VPRO and NPS and even a Buddhist Broadcast company.

Q – What advice would you give a new documentary filmmaker?

Hetty – If they want to make a film they have to realize that it's difficult, of course, and they should find the right person to help them. I don't think Leonard could make so many films if he did them all by himself. Also, choose documentaries that come from your heart. A filmmaker that really wants to tell a story in the way they want to tell it is something that producers and financiers like.

Leonard – I'd try to find someone to help you do the business side of it. It's best to separate the artistic from the business. When you're shooting, trust your own intuition. Be yourself at the moment you are shooting.

THE EDUCATION OF SHELBY KNOX

Q – What made you want to do documentaries?

Marion – When I left college, I knew I wanted to work in film, but I had no idea what the animal was. I majored in English and I came from a family that didn't have a television. We were readers. I didn't recognize actors. All my friends thought it was a hoot that I wanted to go into movies because I was so ignorant. I'm not proud of it. It doesn't prove that I'm an intellectual. It just proves that I had no idea. My parents who were an engineer and an academic said, *"That's nice,"* and scratched their heads when I said I wanted to go into film. They said they knew someone who could help and they would send me off to meet someone who was utterly inappropriate. I'd arrive at the office and I would look at them and they'd look at me and they would say, *"What do you want to do?"* I'd say, *"I want to work in film."* They said, *"Well, what can you do?"* And I'd look at them like a deer in the headlights.The one skill that kept me in good stead was the ability to articulate an idea. To write, to communicate. I also had a very passionate interest in politics and current affairs. So the fit from that into documentaries was ideal. I wound up at cinema studies at NYU and I got a to make a film in another department and I got it solely on writing abilities. I understood the issue and I had a real story. I went out and took stills of this small town that was hit very hard by the closing of the steel mills. And with a grant I was really on my way.

Rose – I came in a different way. I was majoring in art history, was going for a masters, fell in love with film and realized that I didn't want to be an academic or a critic, which is where I was heading. I wanted to make films. I got a job as an intern for a documentary filmmaker. He let me do a lot such as edit and shoot. I was very lucky. Then I got an opportunity to work on a feature and I got caught up working on features. I went out to Hollywood as an assistant editor. I'm a New York, Jewish, intellectual and I really didn't take to Hollywood. I didn't want to drive. I wanted to walk. And everyone thought I was a hooker. So I said I wanted to go back to New York where I can sit in cafes, read books and walk. I could have gotten into the LA union, but I decided not to do it. Was I a fool? I don't know. It's the road not taken. But I love New York and at the time I thought I was Woody Allen. So I came back and I worked on features that were cutting in New York, but I also loved documentary and wanted to make my own film. The more I worked as an editor on other people's films, the more I knew the temperaments and I knew I had to do my own thing. When I met Marion, it was a marriage made in heaven.

Q – What are the advantages to working with a partner?

Rose – It's great because there are so many important decisions to make. Creative, practical, business wise – so having someone that you are compatible with is like making a good marriage. We'll often differ in opinions, which is great. *"This is scene is great." "What do you mean, that scene is stupid."* We'll argue and arrive at a compromise or one of us will come up with another solution. When we really care about something, we'll trade off – she'll get this decision and I'll get the next one.

Marion – This is really strange in listening to this because it shouldn't work in a creative process because you can't compromise when you're putting together a film. It either works or it doesn't.

Rose – But creatively you have to have the same likes.

Q – Why did you choose the topic of sex education?

Rose – We have an interest in it. In 1998, we did a film on RU-486 – the contraceptive. In 2000, we did *Live Free Or Die* where we followed an OB/GYN who does abortions and is fighting a Catholic hospital merger and he is fighting to stay in a school where the right to lifers are trying to kick them off from being a volunteer teaching sex ed at the school the kids go to. It's a very fundable topic.

Q – When you think of an idea, do you think what would make a good documentary or what can get funded?

Rose – We think about what can get funded and there's a wide range of ideas there. Plus we know that sex-ed community. Once you make relationships with funders, those are the people that you go to because you know what their interests are. You fold that into your thinking about what's your next project.

Q – Why did you choose the topic for Shelby Knox?

Rose – *Live Free or Die* centered on an abortion doctor in New Hampshire fighting a Catholic hospital merger. The doctor was also fighting to continue teaching sex education at the local high school. Through that, we learned the amount of federal funding going to abstinence-only sex education programs and decided it would be a good subject for a documentary. We also both had kids who were asking questions about sex, and we wanted to explore the process of sex education on America.

Marion – *The Education of Shelby Knox* is a "social issue" documentary that uses a human-interest story to explore abstract political and cultural issues. In this case it's sex education, gay rights and the role of religion in setting school policy. We chose the topic for *Shelby Knox* for two very simple reasons. One is "the house's a' fire" idealism. We think the issues the film deals with weren't that well known at the time, and really important. The other reason is the topic is fundable.

Q – How did you find Shelby? How important is casting?

Rose – We started looking for a town with a fight around sex education, but after a year hadn't really found one that had a strong story. In 2001, we got a phone call from the adult advisor of the Lubbock Youth Commission detailing the efforts of twenty-five teens to get better sex education into their conservative high school. Shelby was one of a core group of teens really working on the issue. When most of that group left to work outside the confines of city sanctions, she stayed and decided to run for mayor of the youth commission. It wasn't until very late in the process that we decided to use Shelby and her family as a vehicle to tell the story. Casting is very important because the characters have to really have something to say and be interesting enough to engage a wide audience, especially if they're to carry the film.

Marion – Casting a documentary like *The Education of Shelby Knox* is crucial. The central character has to embody issues, has to want very much to participate, and has to be willing to form a lifelong relationship. In the case of *Shelby Knox*, we got the money to make a film about abstinence till marriage sex education from foundations before we found the story. We then embarked on a yearlong search that involved networking in over 20 states in close to 30 communities.

Q – What did you shoot on? How many hours of footage did you shoot?

Marion – We shot almost 200 hours on Beta SP and mini DV. As we hone in on a story, our shooting ratio gets more and more efficient. I'd think that's the case for most filmmakers. At first the ratio is high, reflecting false starts, shooting things that don't pan out, following characters who may be terrific, but don't integrate well. Gradually, the ratio gets better and better. If you're lucky enough to be editing while shooting, the ratio is eventually very efficient.

Q – Did you edit while shooting or after everything was done?

Rose – We started editing after shooting for about a year, but moved slowly. When the bulk of shooting was finished, we launched into a serious edit that lasted about a year.

Marion – Editing and shooting are always governed by the masters of time and money. In the best of all possible worlds, we can edit, let things sit, show them around, ruminate, shoot some more...a process both luxurious and desultory. In the worst of all possible worlds, we have to shoot, edit and push the film out the door at breakneck speed. In the case of *Shelby*, we were sometimes on the first schedule (rarely), sometimes on the second. On the first, slow pace, whenever we ran out of money worked on other jobs, or waited for events to happen. On the second, fast pace, when we were making screening and finishing deadlines.

Q – Did you have any problems in production or post - technical or personal?

Rose – The hardest part about this film was getting all the releases, especially from teens that were fearful that their parents would somehow see them. It also posed a problem when teens were too young to sign releases for themselves, but were scared to ask their parents to sign for them. Because the subject of the film was so sensitive, we had to do a lot of explaining to parents at each step of the way.

Marion – Music was an "I wish I'd known" situation. With our earlier films we simply took the fine cut to a composer, who wrote original music. End of story. But in the case of *Shelby Knox* we cut many scenes to popular music. There was no problem using this music for the PBS broadcast, as PBS has several blanket agreements that essentially let producers use music at no charge. But we had to clear music for all the other uses – festival, international, cable, and so forth and we started addressing it at the point we usually do, when the fine cut was finished. Big mistake! Leave enough time and money to deal with music. *"Yeah, sure you can use it,"* even if it's in writing, does not pass muster. Every piece of music has different entities attached to it who must release the music. From composer to performer to the record label to my uncle playing the fiddle, cover every base. Some of those releases can be accomplished with enough persistence and money, but not all. In which case, scrape together the money and hire a music supervisor to find replacement music that's reasonably affordable. In the end, we went with music with a Texas twang – kind of like Shelby's.

Q – Did you face any problems as New York Jewish women going to Texas?

Rose – There's a lot of mistrust of "Yankees" in Texas, so we had to contend with the stereotypes of typical New Yorkers. As women, it was almost easier to fly under the radar because no one had any real expectations that two females would somehow manage to finish a film. As for being Jewish, a lot of people in Lubbock felt it was their Christian duty to convert us to Christianity. There was a misunderstanding about Jews and Judaism. For instance, Shelby cried because she thought we were going to hell for being Jewish!

Marion – I think audiences expect, and would like, a telling anecdote expressing cultural dissonance, the experience of being an outsider. In fact, I feel very clearly that the biggest hurdle for a filmmaker is never that of being from "out there," it's always about being the un-invited guest. And once you wrangle your way into the party, you're a guest with a camera, asking questions with the intention of making people's answers very public. Knowing this on the way into a situation leads me to be as sensitive as I can. My sensitivity is compounded by the fact that I grew up in Poughkeepsie, and hated having New Yorkers think we were "hicks." In Lubbock, I think people made more assumptions based on how we behaved than on who we were. As to Shelby crying because she thought I was going to hell...I was raised Quaker, I'm culturally Jewish, and when she told me the story, it took awhile for me to believe she wasn't kidding.

Q – How did the sale of the film go?

Rose – PBS has the rights to the film for four years. Our international distributor, Jan Rofekamp, has sold the film internationally, thus far to England, Holland, Spain, Canada, Israel, Finland, Taiwan and Virgin Airways.

Marion – Because ITVS provided finishing funds, with a commitment from PBS/POV to air the film, broadcast rights were taken. Luckily we still had all the other rights, which are being exploited in a range of ways. Over a year after our premiere, we still have not, for example, finalized our home video debut, but Shelby is coming to you via Netflix any day now.

Q – You seem to get a lot of grants for your films. What are the various kinds you've received?

Rose – Our first grant was from The Ford Foundation for $50,000. At the time it seemed huge, but in looking back now it is a drop in the bucket. One thing, we learned from that was to know the mandate of the funder. That was for a film on men in terms of being involved or not involved with raising kids either jointly or as a working family. We had this proposal about how men need to help women all throughout. We sent it around and it wasn't getting funded. I heard about this foundation that was into children and we sent it in. We went in and took out the word "women" and replaced it with the word "children," and we got funding. That in a nutshell tells you that you have to target what peoples' mandates are. You can't go, *"I have this great idea and I am a great filmmaker and this is an important subject."* You really have to bend with the wind. How do I fit? Some people may think that's too much of a compromise, but that's how the world works.

Marion – I got a very small grant to do a film on a toxic waste treatment plant in Ohio. We started shooting that and fundraising for that one and editing out of some borrowed offices. We did that through the summer and then came across a story about the French abortion pill RU-486. One of the things we learned on the film called *Toxics* and the RU-486 one is that they were both issues that foundations were putting money into. *The Toxics* wasn't funded as much because it didn't address a big enough issue. What I didn't know then was how to take a small issue when I'm talking to a foundation person and show them how it fits their big issues. Environmental racism was still a new topic. Questions about what you do with your garbage, shipping it to other places really had nothing to do with the film we were making.

The article we found on RU-486 was clearly something that people in the foundation community were quite concerned about. They all realized it was symbolic of a large issue and that film about it could affect policy. There were certain policies in place that were curtailing its production and had to do with health and life on a large scale. With that in mind, we wrote a proposal framing this big picture and got our first grant from the Ford Foundation. We were in that office that Rose describes and we got a call that we got $99,000. I couldn't believe it. I had to ask the program director to repeat it. I thought she was saying $9.99! Then we had the Fatherhood project and the one on RU-486. The Fatherhood project funding was a bit of a fluke because it addressed working family issues and that's a soft issue.

Q – Any other tips on dealing with foundations?

Marion – One thing to remember is that people who work there are experts on an issue. No matter how much you think you know, they know more. You must assume that you're writing to an expert. You have to show that you know the basics, but you also have to show that you understand things on a more sophisticated level. And you can do all of that and still not get funded. One thing to do is start shooting a little piece and try to get people to see it. Start going to conferences and networking with people in that field.

Rose – With funding, sometimes you get a little bit from here and there. You have to throw ten balls in the air and maybe one happens. We were very lucky through the 90's as it was a very prosperous time thanks to Bill Clinton. So we could get money for one project and some more for another, but not ever enough to commit to one fully. We still had to juggle.

Q – Many new filmmakers have no track record of making films. Does that matter to foundations?

Marion – Track records don't matter so much. If all you have is a camera and you pass yourself off as media, you'd be surprised how many experts will lend their name to your project and be on your advisory board. Those experts also know an awful lot of people including funders. So what you want to do is know enough about your subject so you can approach them. Usually, those big people are thrilled that anybody is going to give media coverage to their issue. On the filmmaking, you can attach an executive producer who does have a track record so you put what you don't have into a package.

Q – How closely do you have to stick to your proposal that you put forth to a foundation or funder?

Marion – You do have to deliver, especially if you want to go back to them again. They do have great expectations, but those expectations are that the film gets out there to their constituents. They have other grantees that they fund and you have to plug into them. For instance, for *Shelby Knox*, there's an organization called Seakist and another called Advocates For Youths. Seakist, which deals with issues of sexuality and issues with young people. The National Campaign Against Teen Pregnancy, as well. The Red Cross even.

Rose – So what we have to do is have them put us in their newsletter, have them link the film to other organizations. Get it into high schools. This is the important work that you have to do because foundations think, *"If I am funding media, it isn't the direct link to people, how can I prove that the money I am giving will be used properly?"* It's their responsibility to make the film prominent in that way. So if you can do that, then you can go back and show then, *"I did that. Now give me money to do this one."* But through the creative thing, this is gold. You don't have an executive producer over you. You have complete editorial control. We come with an abstract idea like sex education and we can make any film we want to make, but then we have the hard part, which is to find somebody like Shelby. But that's the task as a filmmaker.

Marion – If I had my druthers, I'd stay with foundations instead of more commercial places because when you ask what you have to deliver, we do describe a film. We set a controversy in a small town over sex ed and I gave a couple of towns as examples where things happened in the past. Then I tell them what our main character will be like. This way you aren't just describing issues, you're going to put a human face on the issues. When I say that we have complete freedom, we generally are in complete sync with what the foundation's goals and objectives are. So we aren't going to make a film that's wildly out of sync with what the foundation is trying to do. And for that reason a very conservative foundation wouldn't fund something about a controversy over abstinence and comprehensive sex education to two filmmakers like us. Somebody might do one from the opposite point of view and go to these conservative foundations and their presentation is going to be completely different. The thing about getting foundation money is that it's very slow. It's a crap shoot. Funders don't come up to you and say they'd like a film made. You have to go to them and that's what makes it hard.

Q – How long does the process take?

Marion – Years.

Rose – Well, sometimes, if you're doing something they are very interested in it can go faster. Our last film came together quickly with the funding. There are big funders that launch you and then other funders come in with the $20,000-$30,000. We have been lucky to have healthy budgets – sometimes half a million dollars.

Marion – But that's over years.

Rose – But that's our responsibility if it takes that long to do it. It's part of the crapshoot. There are stages to the cross here. Like at HBO, they don't give you the money all at once. They parcel it all out to you. But you know you're going to get it. And with tough, independent films like this – and the nature of our lives because we have kids we didn't want to go and live in Texas.

Marion – The other thing is that we do this full time. You can make a film on much, much less. Rose and I are completely self-sustaining. We have to pay for our health insurance and our overhead. You can make a film for much less money if you have another job, if you have a spouse or live with your parents or have a trust fund.

Q – Do you work with any specific fiscal sponsor so you can get money from foundations?

Rose – We're a fiscal sponsor. We set up our own non-profit, Cine Qua Non.

Marion – But finding a fiscal sponsor is a piece of cake. We did it because we didn't want to give a way the fee percentage to anyone else and when you're talking about hundreds of thousand of dollar budgets, that can be $5,000-$7,000. It's usually 5%. But it's a lot of work running one of these non-profits, so the people that charge that have to do this extraordinarily thorough and expensive audit to be a non-profit.

Q – Looking back, is there anything you would have done differently on The Education of Shelby Knox?

Rose – Hindsight is 20-20. I try to avoid this kind of thinking.

Q – What are you working on now?

Marion – We're in the development phase of a number of stories. It's too early to tell which one(s) will take off and become films. So I don't like to jinx things by singling out any one until it is hatched.

Q – Do you have any advice for new documentary filmmakers?

Rose – Love your story or topic or character. You'll have to spend a number of years committed to it, so make sure it's right for you. It's also a good idea if it's an important subject; people finally want something that speaks to the times. It's also easier to fund if it has topical significance. And finally, don't be afraid to take a point of view; it's an illusion to think that you can know how to shape a story if you don't commit to your point of view. And that is certainly not the same thing as doing propaganda.

Marion – If you're going to be an independent documentary filmmaker, and don't have outside means of support, do think seriously about it as a lifelong career. It's like choosing to be in the fine arts, a painter, or a writer, with the illusion, because there's so much media out there, that it pays more. If you still decide to do it, then find people you like to work with and do your own project. That's the only way you'll get close to all the steps of researching, writing, shooting, and editing. Work at something else while you do it, work weekends, just find a way to do your own project, scary as it feels. This will train you and give you a calling card. It will tell you if it's what you really want to do and if you are good enough at it. In addition, the same skills that make for success in anything apply here. Know how to write, how to communicate, how to come through.

THE UNTOLD STORY OF EMMETT LOUIS TILL

Q – What is the story of Emmett Till and how did that affect you as a boy growing up?

Keith – Emmett Till is like the Anne Frank of the black community. He was a 14-year-old black Chicago youth who in 1955 went to the Mississippi Delta to visit with his southern relatives. Within a week's time, Emmett was abducted from his great uncle's home, tortured and murdered for one of the oldest taboos of the South, addressing a white woman in public. Two men, Roy Bryant and J.W. Milam were soon arrested but later acquitted in the court of law, by an all white, all male jury. Four months after this crime, Roy Bryant and J.W. Milam confessed to the murder of Emmett Till to a reporter who published their story in *Look* magazine for $4k. This sparked outrage across the country, which later mobilized the American Civil Rights Movement. Because of Till's death, Rosa Parks refused to get up from her seat on that bus in Alabama. Because of Till's death, it lead 26 year old Dr. Martin Luther King Jr. to take on the Montgomery Bus Boycott. I learned about the case of Emmett Till at the age of ten when I was in my parent's study in our home in Baton Rouge, Louisiana. I came across a *Jet* magazine photograph of Emmett Till from 1955. And like many of us who saw that photograph for the first time, it shocked me tremendously. You had on one page the angelic face of a fourteen year old kid, the mirror image of myself, and then on the other side, you had the brutalized photograph of Emmett. When I got to high school and I was interracially dating, my parents would often tell me, *"don't let what happened to Emmett Till, happen to you."*

Then I had my own wake up call with racism. Two weeks before my high school graduation I was beaten by an undercover police officer for dancing with a white friend of mine. That's what spurred me into wanting to do something towards fighting injustice in this country. I began to study criminal justice at Southern University of Baton Rouge in hopes of becoming a civil rights attorney. But during my junior year, two of my childhood friends moved to New York City and started their own production company and that's when I was introduced to the entertainment industry. I began to produce and write music videos for them and eventually directed music videos. Then I had my opportunity to work on a feature and the first thing I thought about writing was the Emmett Till story. But because of the overwhelming evidence that eyewitnesses were now coming out with, it grew into a documentary. We thought that producing a documentary was the best way to get the new information across out so that it could be used as a stepping-stone to getting the case reopened.

Q – When did you decide to make the feature into a documentary?

Keith – Mrs. Mobley, Emmett Till's mother had a bit to do with it. She saw that since I was a first time filmmaker and didn't have the finance in place to make a feature, it would take a long time to produce. Also Mrs. Mobley and I realized that a narrative film wouldn't get all the facts out. We wanted to practice realism and felt that producing a documentary and giving a platform for the eyewitnesses would be a great way for accomplishing that goal. Documentary filmmaking is the new wave of activism. Why should we rely on speaking about social issues that plague our communities when we can show it?

Q – Do you think it's easier to make socially oriented documentaries?

Keith – The atmosphere is open in mainstream media. But there's nothing better than being an independent filmmaker. I had a lot of opportunity to go to studios but I wanted to have control of the film so I could use it as I saw fit. I was trying to start a movement. So I raised money for it by showing a work-in-progress to people for about a year. People like to feel involved in the process of making a film that's trying to be part of a solution. It was a grass roots movement, which was needed to help push this documentary along. But unfortunately even through that process I wasn't able to raise enough capital. My parents actually gave me the finances that I was supposed to go to law school with to produce the film. I tried to go through the grant process, but I was in Mississippi, I needed money right then and there, and I had exhausted my account, so I just went back to the basics. The same basics that many filmmakers go to - especially black filmmakers. They get credit cards and fill them up to the limit.

Q – Why do you think you had problems with grants?

Keith – It was timing. Grants always have grant periods and I just couldn't deal with the fact that I had to put together the proposal, had to wait and not know if you're going to get a grant. Coca-Cola promised me $75k.The second week before I was supposed to get it; they told me that they had made a mistake. They were over-budget for their last grant period. That turned me completely off grants. And that's when my parents came to me and told me that they had money that they had set aside for school and we ended up spending $567,000 to produce the film.

Q – How did you get in touch with Emmett Till's mother?

Keith – Technology is a wonderful thing. I went online and did research. I didn't know Mrs. Mobley of course, but I knew that she was still alive. I just typed in Emmett's name and found out that she had a foundation where she was still fighting to get justice for her son. I wasn't going to go through with it unless I had her blessing. I had to have her involved with the process. The first time I called her I was afraid to talk to her - I hung up on her actually. I didn't know what she'd say to a young kid calling her up and talking about her son who was brutalized in the manner that he was. The following day I called again, introduced myself and apologized for what happened the night before. She insisted that I relax and talk to her. And I went through everything about how I found out about the case, what happened to me and why I'm interested in telling the story. She was so captivated with speaking to someone so young who wanted to deal with a case that happened before his time. Someone who not only wanted to produce a film to raise awareness about her son, but who hoped on getting the case reopened with her. We became very close and I was able to work with her for 8 years until her passing in 2003.

Q – When you started doing your research were you able to get your hands on any original records?

Keith – All the 1955 court records were destroyed so we didn't have that to go to for research. Two copies were made but they were both missing. They were destroyed so no one could go back and try and reopen the case. Adam Clayton Powell and Charles Dixon of Detroit tried in 1956 and they weren't able to do it. The only thing that existed at the time was a Master's Thesis written by Steven Whitaker and it wasn't enough information. I had to go back to all the microfilm on the case. Emmett Till's case started the media revolution in this country. It's the only case that's completely documented by archival film, archival photographs as well as archival microfilm - thousands and thousands of articles. I was able to piece together the story and I found out names of different eyewitnesses from the time. I searched those names to see if they were still alive and found out that they were. But my missing link to the whole case was the relatives of Emmett Till. They were still alive. I interviewed Rev. Wheeler Parker, who went to Mississippi with Emmett Till from Chicago. There was also another gentleman named Simeon Wright who was a cousin who stopped talking for many years about the case because of his family being blamed for the kidnapping and murder of Emmett Till. His father was Mose Wright. They were the family that Emmett Till was visiting in Mississippi. Simeon didn't want to talk about it and it took three years to convince him to talk to me. The reason it took nine years to make the film was because witnesses didn't want to speak to me. I had to put the filmmakers hat aside and become friends with these people so they could trust me enough to be able to tell me their story.

CASE STUDIES

Q – How did you manage to get Simeon to open up to you?

Keith - I think Simeon's wife had a lot to do with it. I called him and he didn't want to talk to me. He didn't want to talk to anyone from the press because of what the press had written about he case. And I just kept calling, I kept calling and I kept begging. His wife told him one night, *"Why don't you talk to that boy? He's trying to tell the story the right way and he can't tell it the right way without you."* And he came back to me and granted me the interview. Because Emmett was her child, a lot of Mrs. Mobley's eyewitnesses hadn't come forward because they felt that she should be the only one talking about the case. It was just a no-no subject. They never discussed it, even if they were around each other. When Simeon spoke to me, the other eyewitnesses came forth. They just needed someone to talk to and when they trusted me, they came out and they're spilling their guts. You can see all the raw emotions. It was wonderful, man. It's something, being able to tell the world the story that you learned at the age of ten the right way by the eyewitnesses who were there.

Q – Did your research help you as well?

Keith – Yes. I had to know my subjects before I interviewed anyone or else I had no chance of getting them to talk to me. But more than that, I had to know the places as well. So I went into the Delta and Chicago. One of the first things I wanted to do before shooting was go into the same place that Emmett Till was in back in 1955. I told myself that I wasn't going to be biased. I need to find out both sides. I need to understand why this could take place. So I began to read up on the history of Mississippi and specifically this area.

Q – How did you get to Al Sharpton?

Keith – Al Sharpton was a friend of mine before the project. He was a good friend of Mrs. Mobley so he told me whenever I got ready to produce the film, that he'd get involved with it and help me as much as he could. Although, I didn't use his name to get me in doors because at the time he turned off a lot of people. But when I produced the film, I was ready to interview everybody - white side, black side, regardless what you thought about a person.

Q – How did you approach the white side?

Keith – Unfortunately, I wasn't able to really get the other side. I confronted Juanita Milam the wife of J.W. Milam and she told me that her ex-husband and Emmett Till were dead and that the story needs to be dead. I tried to get the camera on the white woman that Emmett Till whistled at. And every time I got close to her she'd move or change her name. Then Ed Bradley at *60 Minutes* did a piece on me and was able to bring her back into the spotlight. Now we could visually see her.

Q – I'm surprised she didn't want to talk about it. In the footage from the time, Juanita seemed so upset when J.W. was acquitted.

Keith – The story was a thorn. It ruined their lives. Roy Bryant, J.W. Milam and their families became outcast. They weren't able to hold jobs. The chain of stores that their family had all over the delta in Mississippi catered to black field hands. So when the case happened, the black people protested. They practically were run out of Mississippi. When that confession came out, it blew everybody's mind – especially the whites.

Q – Did Mrs. Mobley ever get to speak to them?

Keith – Mrs. Mobley was on a phone conversation with Roy Bryant and a reporter. Roy Bryant didn't know she was on the phone and Mrs. Mobley kept quiet. The reporter asked Roy Bryant if he had it all over again, would he still have murdered Emmett Till. He said, *"Yes."* These people never had any remorse for what they did to Emmett. Mrs. Mobley always wanted closure and she never got it even though she fought for 47 years to her last breath. But you're totally forgetting about the other victims - the cousins who were there. Mose Wright was the first black man to testify in a court of law in Mississippi and live. He had to deal with the pain as well as his kids and other family members who were there. They're victims, too and that's why closure needs to happen.

Q – At what point did you start shooting and what were you shooting on?

Keith – I started shooting in 1999 on a Sony DVX-1000. I brought in two other cameramen one shooting on Beta SP and the other on a Canon XL-1. Thank God technology made it easy for us to pick up a camera.

Q – What did you edit on?

Keith – The first version that the FBI saw was 90 minutes and that was done on Final Cut Pro. The ultimate film was cut on Avid Express. Final Cut Pro was more difficult than Avid Express to use. Final Cut Pro has so many other things to do than the Avid Express. You don't have to be a great editor on FCP, it's just that Avid Express has a lot of things done for you.

Q – How many hours of footage did you have over the nine years?

Keith – I had 120 hours. But I didn't edit the film. I had to step away from it. I was never a big fan of editing and I surely didn't like looking at the footage I'd already shot because I thought everything was good! So I brought in an established editor who's a good friend and mentor of mine, David Dessel. I had a good treatment where I wrote what my objective would be and he looked at the footage with that in mind.

Q – You had the story pretty early on – is that what it ended up being or did it change?

Keith – It changed because of the passing of Mrs. Mobley. It's more of a memorial piece that I made for her now. She's basically narrating. I've never been a fan of narration for documentaries. I used to sit in school and watch narrated documentaries all the time and it was just boring. Plus, you'd think the words he's saying is the Bible! I decided to go another route and just let the eyewitnesses tell their own story. Because then there would never be any debate on what transpired in 1955 because I had the people who lived it telling their own story. So Mrs. Mobley ultimately through her interview brought you from one scene to the next, intertwining with the other interviews. It was more passionate and human doing it that way. You have to play on people's emotions in order to make a movement happen. And that was my objective, to wake up another movement within this generation because I thought it'll be a catalyst for change today. Even all the way up to making the decision of using the photographs of Till's coffin in the film. I wanted people to have that same shock that I had. And the picture has woken up the past generation, this generation and the generation under us because nobody can imagine that something like that could ever happen to a 14-year-old kid. That's why Mrs. Mobley made that ultimate decision to have an open casket because she knew it was going to start something.

Q – Since you were trying to start a movement, was it hard to stay unbiased as you started out to be?

Keith – I was kind of leaning one sided in a way. But I didn't want to make it biased whatsoever. I wanted a story that everyone could relate to. David was able to bring that to in the film. He's a Jewish guy. He was an eye outside of my race, and that helped produce a film that everyone can relate to it.

Q – Did you think you would actually be able to reopen the case?

Keith – Not while I was alive. Here you had a woman who fought for 47 years to get her son's case reopened and nothing happened. And here I come in with my little 9-year period producing the film; I never thought it'd have a profound effect. This film wasn't just about me learning the truth about Emmett Till's murder, it was about me finding my place, identity and mission in life as an African American male in this country. Emmett's mom was nurturing me into an activist without me even knowing it. She gave me my purpose in life.

Q – What did you think of the PBS documentary on Emmett Till?

Keith – I didn't want to go the historical way that PBS did. One thing I can honestly tell anyone who's producing films or documentaries, produce your film completely first before you start talking about it in the public. Keep it a secret. Don't open your mouth until you've entered the editing phase and you completely know what you're doing. Because of PBS, I had to come up with a new way of telling the story and reopening the case proved to be that.

Q – How did you use it?

Keith – City councils over the country passing resolutions in support of my effort. And it wasn't just New York City Council that you see in the film. The Chicago City Council was the first to pass a resolution that supported my efforts. Then Congressman Bobby Rush got together with other members of the Congress and passed a resolution supporting my film and efforts. Then you have Senator Schumer's involvement in lobbying the federal government to reopen the case. He was able to help navigate any problems with the justice department because of budgetary reasons in a way that I couldn't have. The Senate sent resolutions direct to Ashcroft's office. My mother is a member of Delta Sigma Beta sorority; one of the oldest black sororities in this country and the national house wrote a resolution supporting my efforts with their 50,000 members. Mrs. Mobley told me that there're two tactics to use to become successful. She said, *"First, get the media behind you and then get the people behind you because the evidence won't stand by itself. Those are the same tactics that I used back in 1955." The New York Times* wrote a huge editorial piece on me in 2002 which began to spark interest around the world about what I was doing and that began the momentum.

Q – There's a lot of archival footage in your film. What were your experiences with it?

Keith – The greatest thing about the archival footage was there was a lot of it. Every major network covered the case in 1955 as well as different universities. UCLA for instance shot a lot of footage. You also had a lot of international stations and networks that covered it. Most of my footage came from CBS so you're talking about $2,800 a minute for usage. But that said, another image that I used was Fox Movitone. There was footage there, but I had to get everything transferred from 16mm to videotape in order for me just to look at it. That cost me $7/$8k to just do the transfer not even knowing that I was going to use it! But it was rare footage that no one had ever seen before. I got very cool with Peter Bergman who was the director of Fox Movietone and he just began to find footage that was in unmarked boxes. CBS then helped me out. When I did *60 Minutes*, they asked me if there was something they could help me with. I begged them to release that footage to me and they released it in perpetuity. That was something like over a $160k worth of footage. But there are a lot of things that documentary filmmakers need to be aware of when using archival footage. There's a Fair Use clause in the constitution under freedom of speech and that would apply when anyone wanted to use archival stuff, as long as you do it to benefit the community and not in a way that's going to be derogatory. The people who made *Eyes On The Prize* just went through this. They're able to get around it with the Fair Use clause. That goes for photographs as well.

Q – What were your thoughts on music for the film?

Keith – I initially had staple music that was already done by a composer, but it was very expensive. I brought in a composer, Jim Papoulis, who could build music around the film. He gave it a lot of emotion. He brought in his friend, Odetta who's the voice and singer of Civil Rights, and they put a spectacular soundtrack behind the film. The greatest thing about Jim is he writes on the spot. We're sitting in his studio and the movie's on the big screen and he's playing to the big screen. Whatever came to mind, whatever he felt, he wrote it there and then.

Q – How long did editing take?

Keith – First, David did it on the love of me. He didn't charge me anything. But because of that, it took about a year because he had other projects. I wasn't rushing to push the film to come out. The only time I did was when I started to make moves within the justice department and I needed it as a tool to galvanize the public. If I'd released it sooner than I did, it wouldn't have had the same effect.

Q – Did you have any problems with the audio?

Keith – Only on one interview. Simeon Wright's lav gave out. There was only one track playing, usually there's two. So the most important thing I now know is to have a sound engineer with me to check that the sound's OK. My problem was that I couldn't have anyone else there with me, because none of the eyewitnesses trusted anybody. The other problem I had was that I wasn't in a controlled environment. In Simeon's interview, he had an air conditioner on and it really messed up the sound. You need to check out all the sound in the room before shooting.

Q – Who approached you to buy the film at the film festivals?

Keith – HBO and Court TV wanted to do deals with me. HBO told me to hold out and messed up my deal with Court TV and then HBO decided they didn't want the film. I was out on my ass! But Mark Urman at ThinkFilm was watching me for a long time since the Hamptons Film Festival. He saw how people were galvanizing behind me and the film and saw that there was a movement going on. He picked the film up after it was released at the Film Forum.

Q – What deal did you get?

Keith – A 50/50 deal after expenses.

Q – Did you do a theatrical run?

Keith – Yes. The problem was that we didn't have any marketing dollars. We were very successful getting people to come out, but it was a task because of the socially oriented subject matter. That was something I had to battle with. Here you have Michael Moore's *Fahrenheit 9/11* and everybody went to see that, but it does nothing to your community. Bush is still in office. I'm a big fan of Michael Moore, but it did nothing. And then you had my little film that's changing the laws as we speak and nobody went out to support it. Every filmmaker should make sure that you have marketing dollars.

Q – Your DVD commentary gives a lot more information than what was in the film?

Keith – That's because of the investigation. You have to understand that my goal was to get the case reopened. There's a lot of footage that I would've loved to put in - like eyewitnesses I discovered after the case was reopened. But I didn't want to harm the investigation in any way. A number of critics came out and said, *"Well, we heard that you got the case reopened this way, but it's not in the film!"* Most of it is actually seen in the film. You have to understand the case to really know that it speaks about other people being involved. My whole job was not being a filmmaker first. I was seeking justice for Emmett Till, so I left a lot of material out of there. The commentary was rushed. I wish I had taken more time. I was traveling and I had a one-day break so they put me in the studio. I went through it two times and I was so tired. I wanted to be more prepared, but the engineers said I should speak from the heart.

Q – Looking back, is there anything that you would have done differently?

Keith – I was so into the creative aspects of the film that I forgot about money. But the great thing about documentaries is that you don't necessarily need a lot of money up front. I wish I'd have developed a team to help me, but no one wanted to because there was no money in it for them. Then again, with this case, I might not have been trusted if I wasn't by myself.

Q – What advice would you give a new documentary filmmaker?

Keith – To produce a film of this nature, you have to be very, very patient. It's not going to happen overnight. You have to realize that there's a process and you cannot rush it – especially if you're tackling a social problem or issues that deal with everyday communities. Documentary is a new wave of social activism. No longer do you have to speak above the atrocities that exist in the community. You can tell these stories visually and that hits the people more. That's a lot of power. And I believe the only revolutions in society today will happen through the arts because we only believe what we can see and touch. It will not just happen through leadership speaking about it.

WAVES OF REVOLUTION TO WAR AND PEACE

Q – How did you come to start making documentary films?

Anand – More or less by accident. I was on a scholarship at Brandeis University in America from 1970 to 1972; it was in the middle of the Vietnam War. The Anti-War movement was at its peak and I became immersed in it. On my way to a demonstration in Washington DC, I borrowed a 16mm Arri BL and a hand cranked Bolex camera from our Theater Arts Dept. and filmed for a few days. This never became a finished film but later I made my first film just before the Bangladesh War. Bangladesh hadn't been formed yet and there were East Pakistani refugees streaming into India. Conditions were terrible and there were lots of human rights violations. To generate money for the refugees, we asked people at our university not to eat for a day. I filmed students and professors asking whether they were eating and what they thought about the fast. People gave excuses for why they had to eat and this became the film *Business as Usual*. I joined an anti-corruption student movement in North India. I borrowed a Super 8mm camera to film police atrocities on non-violent student protestors. So, all my filmmaking came out of immediate concerns of the moment.

Q – What was that film used for?

Anand – We just wanted to keep a record of police violence and document the peace rally. Later on we decided to make more out of it and I projected the Super 8 film footage onto a little screen and shot that with a 16mm camera to blow it up. The frames between Super 8 and 16mm didn't quite line up and caused a flicker so the footage was far from professional but quite dramatic. Then a friend with a hand crank 16mm camera joined me and we went back to shoot more footage. I ended up making a half hour film about the movement called *Waves of Revolution*. The film soon went underground because there was a state of Emergency in India and all the people I'd been filming were in jail. Democratic rights were curtailed. I had to go into exile after a few months or face the prospect of jail. So I couldn't show the film publicly, barring a few underground screenings. I cut the film into pieces and smuggled it outside the country through various travelers. I then got admission to do my post-graduate studies at McGill University, Canada, where I finally pieced the film all back together. I toured the film through North America, UK and other places where there were Indians fighting against the Emergency.

Q – Were you shooting any sound?

Anand – Yes. In both *Waves* and the Brandeis film I had sound equipment that I borrowed. But *Waves* was shot on outdated black and white stock that other filmmakers gave me and the soundtrack was largely recorded on a cassette recorder. It wasn't real sync sound. So a few frames would match and if you had anything longer than a few minutes it would go out of sync. There was only one sequence in Delhi that was shot with a proper sync camera that I was able to borrow briefly.

Q – What did you do when the Emergency ended?

Anand – I returned to India and made a film about political prisoners called *Prisoners of Conscience*. That was technically a little bit better but still black and white.

Q – Where were you getting the money to process the stock?

Anand – I didn't have money. These films were made with almost non-existent budgets and the good will of all the people around me. I borrowed footage from other filmmakers. Labs gave me outdated stock that they were going to throw away.

Q – Did you edit the film?

Anand – Yes. I managed to get free editing time at places at night when everyone had finished work.

Q – What was the next project you worked on?

Anand – I came back to Montreal in 1979 to finish my degree in Mass Communication. At that time I made a film with a Canadian filmmaker about Indian immigrant farm workers in the Vancouver area called *A Time to Rise*. The first time I went to America in the 70's, I'd worked as a volunteer with Caesar Chavez's' United Farmworkers' Union. This time when I went to Canada I found Indian immigrant farmers trying to form a union. So we invited Caesar Chavez to come to Vancouver to meet the Indian farmworkers. Our film when completed was well received specially by the labor movement. As we had Indian and white workers jointly battling the farm owners lobby, our film became an example of how to fight racism in the workplace. In the end, the film was distributed by the National Film Board of Canada.

Q – What was your approach stylistically in that film?

Anand – Jim Monro, my Canadian co-director, interviewed the white farmers while I did the interviews of the workers so we got great access this way. Apart from this there was a lot of cinema verité of the struggle as it unfolded. In all my films there are a lot of times when the camera mainly observes what's going on and a lot of times when the camera intervenes in what's going on depending on the circumstances.

Q – Are you ever in front of the camera?

Anand – Almost never as I'm usually the cameraperson. My voice is often in the story, asking questions, arguing, but rarely my visual. Some documentary theorists have made a fetish out of self-reflexivity but I believe this shouldn't be a matter of theory. It's something that if it happens, it happens and it need not be edited out.

Q – After A Time To Rise you went back to in India.

Anand – Yes, I went back to India in 1982 and made a film, *Bombay, Our City* about the slums of Bombay where people's homes were being destroyed. It was made over three years and it made a bit of a stir because the elite weren't used to hearing street people talking on camera. They regarded them as eyesores. The film allowed the homeless to articulate what they were going through and the homeless came across as far more human, dynamic and intelligent than many of the so called "respectable" members of society who were revealed in their self satisfied heartlessness.

Q – Did you have any funding support?

Anand – I've never had proper funding for any of my films, preferring to be independent rather than enter into co-production contracts. If you see these films there are no listings in the credits for funders, either government or private. In the beginning I raised help through people who supported the cause, grass roots movements or individuals who gave small amounts of money. Later as the films got known I became able to survive on sales. I like this better because I don't feel tied to anyone and have a lot of freedom.

CASE STUDIES

Q – Are most documentaries in India funded by grants or state funds?

Anand – No. Documentaries are rarely funded by the State. Of course the government does make documentaries through the Films Division or Doordarshan, our national TV, but these are mostly propaganda films. There are some trusts now that are putting small amounts of money into documentary films, but it's rare. One thing that happened is that in 1982 *Prisoners Of Conscience* and *Time To Rise* were shown on Channel 4 in England. These films also won a £5,000 award at the Tyneside Film Festival so I was able to recycle all this into making another film.

Q – You must have accumulated at lot of footage over three years. Do you edit as you are shooting?

Anand – I never work with a script as such. Although I do research while I'm making the film, I don't pre-judge the film before it's made. Often there's not even a guarantee that what I'm shooting will become a film. I often film things that are interesting and eventually may be useful - sometimes I'm right and sometimes I'm wrong.

Q – How did you gain the trust of the homeless in Bombay?

Anand – It happened slowly. In the beginning, they didn't know who we were or why we were there. There's a sequence where an old woman whose home has just been bulldozed attacks me and asks: *"Why are you filming us? Are you just going to become rich and famous? Nothing is going to change for us, so don't take pictures of the poor."* But over a period of time, a trust developed. And in fact, that person that attacked me loved the film when it was completed. These kinds of films where we depict injustice and hardship are voyeuristic and you always have to ask yourself what gives you the right to film? And you should only go ahead when you know that what you're doing is going to be of some use to the people that you're filming.

Q – Do you have any tips on interviewing people?

Anand – There's no trick or formula. People are intelligent. They gauge where you're coming from. If I identify with the cause of the people I'm filming the distinction between the people being filmed and the people doing the filming is reduced. They're happy to be filmed and inform us when things are happening so that we'll be there with the camera. Of course there are others whom I film sometimes with whom I'm not in sympathy or in agreement and here there's a different relationship, sometimes antagonistic, at all times more cautious.

Q – How do you deal with more hostile interviewees?

Anand – First of all you have to get access, so you have to figure strategies to do that and these differ according to the situation. I don't use hidden cameras and things like that, but I might pretend to be a TV crew. Right now in India there is so much TV that people are used to the presence of cameras.

Q – Did Bombay Our City get a theatrical release?

Anand – No. Only *War and Peace* got a theatrical release. In Bombay we got two multiplexes to release it for a week each and it was pretty successful. We got a lot of publicity because it was the first time that a documentary of this kind was being released. We even had full houses on the last day. We could've run longer, but the contract was only for a week. Documentaries almost never get theatrical releases in India. It happened with *Fahrenheit 9/11*, which didn't do as brilliantly as it did in America. Perhaps because American accents are difficult for Indians to follow and documentaries are more demanding than fiction. At least it showed that documentaries could play in the cinema.

Q – Your next films In Memories of Friends and In The Name Of God seemed to have religious overtones.

Anand – Anti-religious is more like it, or at any rate, anti-fundamentalist. They were about religious violence and the rise of fundamentalism in India. Broadly from the 1980's and still through today, we're going through a bad period in terms of religious fundamentalism. The reasons for this are global as well as local. Since the war in Afghanistan when the CIA imported Bin Laden from Saudi Arabia and went in and taught Moslem villagers in Pakistan that their Islamic duty was to wage jihad against Communism, the whole region has been completely turned upside down. They put religion on the agenda. And when Islamic fundamentalism began to grow across the border, Hindu fundamentalism began to grow in relation and reaction. Of course Hindu fundamentalists existed prior to this as well. They were the ones who killed Mahatma Gandhi, but they had to go into hiding after that for many years and were able to revive slowly during the Cold War.

Q – So you were documenting a lot of the violence?

Anand – My films were trying to reassert a kind of democratic, egalitarian outlook rather than a religious outlook. They were trying to counter the rise of fundamentalism by reminding workers of their identity as workers. I interviewed both sides, many sides in fact. We didn't have just one religion that had become fundamentalist. In *In Memory Of Friends* you see the rise of Sikh fundamentalism. *In The Name Of God* is about the rise of Hindu fundamentalism. And *Father, Son And Holy War* is about both Hindu and Moslem fundamentalism. *War and Peace* describes the point at which fundamentalism and militarism in the sub-content reaches the dangerous and macabre phase of nuclear nationalism.

Q – How has censorship come into play with your films and how do you handle that?

Anand – I've had censorship battles from the beginning. My first film went underground and emerged many years later. And virtually all my films – in fact if you go on my website, www.patwardhan.com you can read about some of the litigation in brief. I've had censor board or legal troubles. When BJP, the Hindu right wing government came to power about 10 years ago, the attack on civil liberties and my kind of filmmaking increased. *War and Peace* faced this because the BJP populated Censor Board asked for 21 cuts and we went to court. Finally, I won the court case and I didn't have to cut anything. In fact, I've won all my battles against the censors over the years and not a single frame has ever been cut. I also won five different court cases against our National TV because they kept refusing to show my films. The mandate of our government run public channel is to show the best films in the country. As several of my films won national awards I was able to argue in court that the government cannot refuse to telecast a film that its own jury has awarded as the best film of the year.

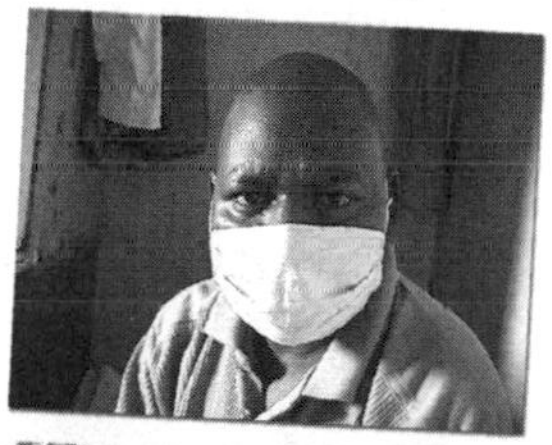

Q – And National TV probably doesn't want to show the dirty underbelly of the country?

Anand – Criticism is unwelcome everywhere. My films are critical of the state and expose what the fundamentalists have done. They show the kind of manipulations that take place and point out how religious fundamentalism is just another form of politics – it has nothing to do with religion. Different governments that have come to power in India have always tried to brush this under the carpet.

Q – There's a sort of subtle censorship here in the US...

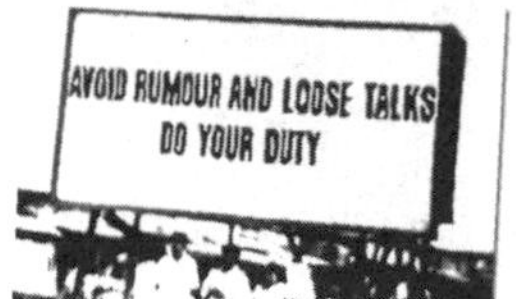

Anand – I don't think it's that subtle. For instance my films almost never get shown on TV in America including on PBS. This is partly due to political censorship but mainly due to ethnocentricity – the rest of the world is just not important. The irony of democracy in America is that people think there's freedom and that's the beauty of the system. But

CASE STUDIES

only a few carefully regurgitated ideas circulate amongst the majority. The fact that Bush won twice doesn't show a high level of comprehension. Even after all the lies of the WMD's he got re-elected! It could only have been achieved through a controlled media. In fact there's global censorship. Most images from Iraq aren't being circulated anywhere in the world, certainly not in America. I'm not saying that the system in America is all bad. You do get the occasional film that is critical. Michael Moore's films are shown and a few others like *Control Room* get out there, but they are still not able to reach out and change the reality.

Q – How did War and Peace come about?

Anand – I was disgusted with the fact that India did nuclear tests in 1998 when the whole world had almost stopped testing. India had been one of the original countries that had been fighting for a test ban treaty. So for India to turn around and do a test of its own and declare that we were a nuclear weapons state was a tragedy. It was out of the depression of that moment that I began to film. So I followed both the people who were thrilled with the tests and those who were upset and started a peace movement in India and Pakistan. I also belong to an organization that is trying to make peace – The Pakistan-India Forum for Peace and Democracy and we have been trying to arrange people to people visits for the last ten years. So I went to Pakistan a few times with my camera. I also filmed in Hiroshima and Nagasaki because some of the survivors of the atom bomb came to India and Pakistan to tell us about their experiences and invited me to come back with them. After I filmed in Japan, I wanted to film in America as well because I wanted to find out what prompted the first use of the bomb. I went to the Smithsonian and learned that a whole exhibit about the 1945 bombings had been censored in America. This was an official exhibition in the National Air and Space Museum. They had planned a 50th Anniversary of the Atom bomb exhibit and they got a lot of historians to work on it. All of the research was scrapped because what it was revealing was that America didn't need to use the atom bombs at all. The bombs were used for Cold War purposes – to tell the Soviet Union how strong America was. So in a way 350,000 people were sacrificed for this. Many of the American military generals at the time including Eisenhower were opposed to dropping the bomb. The real impetus came from scientists who wanted to test it out and the defense establishment.

Q – So the film was your journey through this depression?

Anand – Yes, in a sense. It starts out where I talk about my uncles who had been part of the non-violent movement against the British led by Gandhi. So the film was about the ideals of someone like Gandhi and how we have degenerated into wanting weapons of mass destruction. It's also about Big Brother and how Indian and Pakistani elites always try to emulate the United States. And about the United States, which sets a terrible example to the world with its ideology of Might is Right. The US has the biggest-by-far number of nuclear weapons on this planet and they have not reduced their stockpile even after the Cold War. So when the US tells other countries not to build weapons, no one takes it seriously.

Q – Did the average Indian or Pakistani care about what was going on?

Anand – I found that the ordinary people in India and Pakistan wanted peace. But they would become jingoistic at any point in time if they were manipulated. It's mainly the elites in the countries and the middle class that gets up in arms and starts jingoistic jargon about nationalism. The working class - they want to survive, pay the rent and put food on the table. They know if you spend all your money on weapons you won't have anything left over for other necessities.

Q – What do you look for in a subject when you make a film?

Anand – I don't get into a film unless I'm highly motivated and something bothers me a lot. That can take a long period of time. And as I said I often film just to have things on record and not for a film per se. If I get a critical mass of that over time, then I might sit down and think about making a film.

Q – Any traits that you look for in your main characters?

Anand – In most of my films, there are many, many characters. They're often films about events and large happenings, so they aren't biographical. Some people become characters over a period of time, but that's not pre-decided.

Q – What do you do with music?

Anand – I use a lot of music, but it's always integral to the film, rather than music from the outside. I never use a score or mood enhancing music. I've used music from the people in the film. If I'm following a peace march and people are singing, that's the music I'd use.

Q – Do you find inserting music fake?

Anand – For me sound is documentary evidence almost as much as the picture is. Just as we decide not to write dialogue and reenact stuff as we aren't doing fiction, so it is with sound. Occasionally some moments that we couldn't capture live need illustration, but then I indicate clearly that it's a re-enaction. This gives the film a kind of credibility. So similarly with the soundtrack I think it adds credibility when you don't put in lots of special effects and external music.

Q – Do you have to pay for music clearances in India?

Anand – Yes, if you use pre-recorded music you have to get clearances.

Q – Do you have any philosophies on your editing style?

Anand – In a very general sense I do take care not to depress my audience. The situations I film are often depressing so I have to be careful that my film doesn't rob energy and get people so down that they feel there is nothing they can do about it. I try to find moments of resistance, the silver lining in every dark cloud.

Q – Do your films look for the hope?

Anand – If I couldn't find hope, I wouldn't film because I'd be too depressed. That happened to me a few years ago after the pogroms in Gujarat. I looked hard for the silver lining but found none. Luckily others went in and documented the horror of the anti-Muslim violence that took place there with full state complicity, so that there's a valuable record, however hard it may be to watch. It isn't that such horrors are not documented in the films I make, but as I said, these moments are interspersed with moments of resistance, so that the over all impact is not debilitating.

Q – What are the common mistakes that filmmakers make?

Anand – People think you have to move a lot. Because you're excited you tend to do a lot of moving with the camera, panning and zooming or whatever. But the kind of stuff you get with a long take with a wide angle is often more interesting because what's interesting is what's in front of the camera and not the camera's own movement. In any case I don't like gimmicky camerawork or editing that draws attention to itself. I prefer a more direct approach to documentary filmmaking.

Q – What advice would you give a new filmmaker?

Anand – Don't get into it unless you are absolutely passionate about the issue you are filming. Documentary filmmaking is not a career option unless motivation is high as it is not easy to make ends meet. The best films I've seen weren't necessarily made by professional filmmakers but were films where people really got involved.

MARCH OF THE PENGUINS

Q – You trained as a biologist, so how did you become a documentary filmmaker?

Luc – I'm a filmmaker by pure chance because in 1991 after my Masters in biology from Lyon University, France, I had the opportunity to go to Antarctica as a biologist. Two months before leaving, a Swiss film director called and asked if I'd film some penguins for him. My experience in Antarctica was a revelation. It was a chance to mix science and a more sensitive point of view. When I came back, I continued my biology studies, but I didn't want to be a scientist anymore. I wanted to become a filmmaker. For me it's interesting to mix everything in your own job – the taste for adventure, the taste for biology and also the pleasure of making a good film.

Q – Your film doesn't feel like a normal nature documentary. It's much more personal. Was that intentional?

Luc – Yes. I don't like to make the same thing as everyone else. And I'm still a researcher inside, so I wanted to try something new. It was very intentional in this documentary to put strong human feeling into the film.

Q – How easy was it to get the funding for the film?

Luc – It was a nightmare! My producers did an absolutely wonderful job because they covered me. When we decided to make the film, they said, *"We will deal with this part of the process."* So I was just on the creative side. The production company was close to bankruptcy just before the Cannes Film Festival in 2004. They gambled on it though. They said that they didn't want to sell everything. They wanted to keep the rights on the film and that I was going to keep final cut.

Q – Did you start filming and then raise money or the other way around?

Luc – I met my producers for the first time in August 2002. They fell in love with the idea. I told them I have a window to go to Antarctica next year because of my special relationship with the French Antarctica Institute. We decided to go that year and not to wait, so we had to build the film with the means we could find quickly. The first means was the TV rights in France. But it wasn't enough for the whole film. The goal for us was to be on the boat in January of 2003 and to get the best quality for the money we had. It was always a balance. Now, when you go to Antarctica, you can't easily pop back and also you have to take everything with you. That's why we chose Super 16mm. It wasn't the best, but it was good enough to do a theater release. The cameras were smaller, so we could have a crew of two guys for one year.

Q – Did Super 16mm make it easier to film in the cold?

Luc – It was easier to handle and it was cheaper. The weight was an issue because everything was carried by humans. Each kilo more in the bag or on the sled was something bad for the film.

Q – Did you write the script before you went to Antarctica?

Luc – A rough treatment and we did a shot list. For me the story was quite obvious. I wanted to film it first and then narrate it. When I wrote this script, I had ten years of experience filming and making documentaries in Antarctica. I was very well prepared for the logistical stuff, because everything was ready in my mind. I wrote this script in less than one day. I also knew that this film might be a hit because the landscape was so amazing and the story itself was so strong.

Q – How did you protect the film stock from the cold?

Luc – The unexposed film was kept at 4° Celsius in a fridge. The exposed film was kept frozen in a freezer at -18° Celsius. We did that to slow down the chemical process of the film because it had to stay unprocessed for one year. We didn't have any problems with the exposure or any of the technical aspects but the film was dirty. The air there is very dry so you have a lot of static electricity in the camera. So all the dust sticks to the film. It was a nightmare in post-production to clean it.

Q – How much equipment did you take down with you?

Luc – We took two of everything. Two bodies. Two long lenses. Two tripods, etc. We had two zooms and two prime lenses. We didn't have a lot of equipment. We took some lights, a small crane and a small dolly.

Q – What other problems did you have with the equipment being in that environment?

Luc – We weren't really filming in extreme temperatures. In the mainland of Antarctica, you can have extreme temperatures up to -90° Celsius – that's like being in space. But we shot on the coastline. The ocean has a warming effect so it was never colder than -37° Celsius. The average temperature was around -20° Celsius. So you can still work with normal gear, but you have to bring oils for the camera body. The biggest enemy is the wind – up to 180 km/hr. Forget sound and picture, it was difficult just to stand. Sometimes it was extremely frustrating because the scene was there, but impossible to film because it was too windy.

Q – How big was your crew?

Luc – Two cameramen during 13 months of shooting. I was there for one month at the beginning of shooting, to install them, to explain things like where to shoot. And then I was there for the three last months with an underwater cameraman. The two main guys were in charge of all the technical aspects of the equipment. They fixed everything and kept it dry for the whole time. Jérôme Maison was in charge of underwater shooting with a pole cam. He was in charge of the sound recording and still photography. For me the choice of these two guys was important. Jérôme was my assistant for three years, so I knew him and he knew me. He's a biologist and a very tough guy. He's very adaptive. And Laurent Chalet has the other aspects I was looking for – he was a feature film shooter. The goal was to find a summary of all needed knowledge in two people.

Q – Where were they based and did they do the long march?

Luc – They were based at the French scientific station Dumont d'Urville. It was built in the 1950's on the coast of the French part of Antarctica. The station is only 800 meters away from the Emperor's penguins' colony. It's a 20-minute walk when weather conditions are fine outside and three hours when they're not. It's very close. Without this station, there wouldn't be a film.

Q – Was it easy to get permission to use the station?

Luc – Relatively easy because I had been there before, and knew the responsible persons. When the French Polar Institute said we could go, I asked my crew if they wanted to go and for me, they had to say yes immediately. It had to be their first feeling because you must have a huge determination to go there. It's very painful to live in Antarctica. Sometimes the wind goes at 100 km/hour for one week. So sometimes it's hard just to wake up and go outside. And the task was to go outside and work every day. So you must like that and be married with the challenge.

Q – How many people live at the station?

Luc – About 30 during the winter. During the summer it can be up to 100. And in the summertime there's one boat per month. There are no boats during the winter.

Q – Are the penguins used to humans because the station is so close?

Luc – Yes, they've been familiar with humans since the 1950's so it was easy for us to approach them.

Q – Did you have to get any special insurance for the equipment to go to Antarctica?

Luc – It was difficult to find insurance because it was so risky. But for this kind of film you have to push all the limits because the normal process of filming just doesn't work.

Q – Did you take anything else to make your stay easier?

Luc – The station is very comfortable nowadays. After 50 years existence, you now have thousands of DVDs and videotapes and you have a very good cook! It's not a normal situation, but it's very comfortable considering you're in Antarctica. It's a small village with two main buildings. It's a summary of all human kind. You have a guy who can fix cars, a computer guy, a biologist, a physician, a cook, a plumber, etc. Having these people around also keeps you sane.

Q – How did you shoot the underwater sequences?

Luc – There were two techniques. One was a pole cam. It's a small DVD recorder on a perch that was put in the water inside a crack in the ice. The second was the cameraman who went into the water with the camera housing.

Q –The water must have been extremely cold.

Luc – Yes, but they like it like that! I think it's a privilege to dive in such an amazing place. It's not normal. The sounds of the seals, the whales and the water are amazing. The light glimmering inside the iceberg is amazing. So while diving is painful, it's fascinating as it's another world.

Q – Did you have any problems when shooting the penguins?

Luc – Sometimes they were so curious it was difficult to shoot them. Or we'd have to wait a week to get one shot. But that's normal for wildlife filmmakers. But really 99% of the time we didn't have a problem.

Q – Did your crew have any problems with storms?

Luc – Yes, Jérôme and Laurent were lost in a very serious storm and were very close to dying. A team from the station rescued them. Only because they had a GPS transmitter on them could be found. Even if you're familiar with this place, it's very dangerous because a storm can rise very quickly. The snow whips in the air with the wind and you're in a thick dust.

Q – Did you focus on shooting one particular couple of penguins?

Luc – No, we did that in the editing process. You cannot distinguish them. It's impossible.

You cannot have empathy for a crown – they cannot explain anything. So one of the difficulties of the editing process and the narration was to follow something quite clear within this mess.

Q – When you are with wildlife long enough, do you get to know little subtleties about their body language?

Luc – For sure. It's more a feeling. You know something is going to happen. You're with them all year so you have a strong recognition about their humor and temper. Sometimes you feel they're nervous and you don't know why, but they are. This morning they're friendly. We called it security distance – how close you can get to them safely. Every day it changes. You learn how close you can get because you can detect their small behaviors. There was a time when a cameraman would stand up and start shooting and I would pull him down because it was violating the security distance. All of this is the first stage of your job when you work with wildlife be it lions or penguins.

Q – How close could you get?

Luc – Two meters. Sometimes it was ten meters. You don't choose. They choose. You're in their world. You feel it and then you put yourself there. You go there to film natural behavior. If they're stressed or afraid because of you, then you have nothing.

Q – What other tips could you give to new filmmakers who want to shoot animals?

Luc – It's important to have a lot of knowledge about natural history. And you should get a lot of naturalistic field experience. You need to be able to read what's happening around you.

Q – Is there any way to manipulate your shots in order to get what you want? Say by giving them food?

Luc – You can't do that with the penguins because you have no food to give to them. Sometimes it might work with lions or bears to attract them, but penguins are so out of the normal experience. And really, penguins are so generous with their behavior that you don't have to interfere. What's interesting is that you don't have one actor doing the same thing ten times. You have thousands of actors playing the same scene for a long time. So all you have to do is be there. Once you have the footage, then you can manipulate in the editing room.

Q – Did you ever want to intervene to save the eggs that would get frozen?

Luc – Anything you do for them you're going to make a mess. The first rule is to be neutral and invisible in the landscape. For example, if you were to put a lost egg on the leg of the father, you'd have to go inside the colony. You'll then make them all nervous, they'll move away from you and then you'll have hundreds of lost eggs. You must tame your own emotions. It's very human to try to do something, but Antarctica has been going very well without human interference. You must keep yourself at the right place even when you see birds dying.

Q – How much footage did you end up shooting and how long did you edit for?

Luc – 140 hours of Super 16mm. And 30 hours of underwater footage. It was a nightmare for the editor. We cut from the beginning of March to September, so about 6 months.

Q – What was your process in editing?

Luc – For me the first stage was to organize all the footage. Second was to try to express the scene and to find a balance between what you want and what you have. Sometimes you have to make a curved line to go and keep what you have because sometimes you get an amazing shot that was not expected. So after this expression of the footage, we cut and cut and cut again in order to find a rhythm and the story.

Q – How did you end up cleaning the film that was dirty?

Luc – We did it after we locked the cut because it was so expensive. We did a computer restoration for the parts that were too dirty. The wet gate alone didn't work because sometimes we had artifacts in the film itself.

Q – Did you do any color correction?

Luc – Yes, because the light was so different on many of the shots. One sequence was shot in January and the next in June or July. So sometimes the light would be green and in other shots it would be pink. The color grade was absolutely necessary and a big job. We didn't do any special effects in the lab.

Q – The American version of the film is very different from your original version. What are the differences?

Luc – There are three differences. There are three minutes less in the American version. Some shots that weren't needed – mainly the most violent predator shots of the film. The second difference is the narration type. The French narration is made with three voices – one male, one female and one chick. They use first person narrative, *"I" – "I feel that", "I do that"* – they're the "spokesmen" and tell the story on behalf of the other birds of the colony. The voices were done by well known French actors. Whereas, in the American version, there's a more classical documentary voice-over narration, remarkably well told by Morgan Freeman! Warner Independent brought him in. The words between the French and the American version are to a major extent the same. But the point of view is different. The last difference is the music. The music in the American version follows a more classical film music inspiration. It's well done. The French version's music is a more experimental, electronic music. Maybe it was too experimental for an American audience? I really don't know. When Emilie Simon, the French music composer chose to do the music, she used English voices for the songs. In France, we had no problem with that, as they didn't detract from the French narration in the film. In the American version, I can imagine that Warner Independent didn't want to have a new meaning parallel to the narration using the songs.

Q – What instructions did you give your composer about what you wanted the score to sound like?

Luc – I didn't have the opportunity to work with the American composer. But for the French musician, she had to give me the color of the fairytale. She had to give me the beat of the landscape. The screen is two-dimensional and Antarctica is impressive because of that third dimension. So the music had to give me that third dimension. The same went for the sound design. Emilie Simon is a young composer and she could give us the soft touch of the tale. It was interesting to mix the tough experience of Antarctica with her soft touch. From the beginning, it was not my goal to make something tough, but to make a fairytale.

Q – Which version do you prefer?

Luc – The French version. I admire Morgan Freeman's voice and it's amazing to think that I could work with such a talented person and Alex Wurman did a very good job on the music. But when you make a film, it's yours and you like that one best.

Q – When did National Geographic become involved?

Luc – They were involved in the distribution on the North American territory, same as Warner Independent Pictures. The first producer is the French company Bonne Pioche in co-operation with the private producer APC; Buena Vista Intl. France was our distributor in France, and the French company WildBunch was in charge of the international sales.

Q – How are most documentary films funded in France?

Luc – We have the CNC, the French governmental center for cinematography. Then there are the TV stations.

Q – Are more documentaries being made in France these days?

Luc – Yes. Most documentaries are made for TV and there a few that make it into the theaters. There's a new age of documentaries though coming into the theaters. It started with *Microcosmos* – which opened the door. And also there was Jacques Cousteau and his films. It's interesting to see and to try understand why many nature feature documentaries are coming out of France. It's part of our documentary history I think.

Q – Are more films being made because of the digital revolution?

Luc – Yes. It's easier to escape from the normal production line with the small digital cameras. It wasn't so simple years ago, so this opens the field of what you can say. And it doesn't matter if the picture isn't the best. If the story is interesting, you will sit through it. So it's a big change, what you say is more important than how it looks.

Q – Can you get closer to the wildlife with the smaller digital cameras?

Luc – No, because the animals aren't afraid of the cameras, but of the humans behind them. For my next film, I'll use both techniques. HD for the weight, for its convenience to handle and its capacity in low light conditions; but also 35mm for the slow motion shots, but mainly to show the esthetical quality of the landscape and the wide shots. It's too early for me to abandon film. Also I couldn't use HD in Antarctica because the electronics would have frozen and video isn't good in the extreme lighting conditions there.

Q – Did you intentionally want to talk about the greenhouse effect on Antarctica?

Luc – It was intentional not to put a direct political message in the film. Everyone on the planet nowadays knows about global warming so to tell it directly again, was not the objective of my film. Maybe for me it's more important to give something to love before I give the lesson. Ten or twenty years ago it wouldn't have been the same situation. Back then, the goal was to put into people's consciousness the basic ecological problems of the planet.

Q – What traits are good for a wildlife documentary filmmaker?

Luc – Emotion. If you don't feel something when you're out in the wild, there's no film. That's the basis for everything.

CASE STUDIES

Q – What are some of the problems that can be avoided when shooting wildlife?

Luc – The obvious problem with wildlife production is time. We need a lot of time to make our films – you can't direct animals as you can do with actors. For wildlife films, you need approximately one year for the shooting, sometimes more, you are not done with six weeks as usual for feature films. And it's not traditional to have time nowadays. You need to wait and see what nature is willing to give you, you need patience. To maximize your chances of catching good shots, you have to be prepared as much as possible and need to know exactly what you are looking for.

Q – What advice would you give a new filmmaker who wants to embark on a wildlife documentary?

Luc – To have luck, to have luck, to have luck. One third of your own work comes from your own emotion, that's the basis. One third comes from your own energy – making such a film demands your total devotion. And one third comes from pure luck. There are thousands of good films made and why some are more successful than others, no one can say. If you look at the history of a film like *March Of The Penguins*, it's amazing to see how in all stages of the making you need luck. You need luck to be in the right place, at the right time, together, with the right people.

Sandi Dubowski

TREMBLING BEFORE G-D

Q – What is Trembling Before G-d about and where did you get the funding?

Sandi – It's about homosexuals in Orthodox Jewish society. The initial grants came from The Jerome Foundation, The New York State Council On The Arts and the Paul Robeson Fund for Independent Media. Those kept the production going and allowed me to cut a little trailer. I was working a full time job at Planned Parenthood and it took awhile for me to sort of leap into the unknown and do the film full time. Then I went to the IFP Market and I met a sales agent who put in some funding in order to be the sales agent and we were off and running.

Q – You didn't shoot your film yourself, what made you decide to let others do the camera work?

Sandi – I wasn't a trained cinematographer. I felt it made sense for me to step back and focus on the directing, building the relationships with people and developing the characters and the narrative.

Q – Did you use the same crew wherever you went?

Sandi – No. I was shooting around the globe. I had a few Israeli cinematographers in Jerusalem and Tel Aviv. I had a key London cinematographer. I had key people in New York, LA, Miami and San Francisco.

Q – Did you have any problems shooting in any of the foreign countries?

Sandi – No.

Q – What was your process of gaining trust with your subjects especially given the sensitive subject matter?

Sandi – I think the thing about shooting documentaries, especially with people who are very vulnerable is they want to be reassured you'll be there for them when the camera is turned off. Not every gay Orthodox person has had trauma – some people are happily integrated. But these people have had very tough lives with a lot of pain. So to go to that place where you have to reopen those scars is hard. You have to be there to comfort. I spent thousands and thousands of hours with people when the camera wasn't on at all. It was just us connecting or me spending time in the community. I was a referral person. I was a matchmaker even. I was a shoulder for people to cry on. I was a peer counselor. I was a friend. I helped kick start a support group in Los Angeles. Many documentary filmmakers don't do that.

Q – Is it hard to maintain objectivity when you get so tied to them?

Sandi – That's why you have an editor. You're the one who carries around all those experiences and the editor watches it via the footage. It's not what you have captured of them - it's only what they see on screen. That's really helpful to have that relationship. Susan Korda who edited the film did an extraordinary job. It was almost like she had gone through it herself. The editing room became like a Yeshiva and we became study partners. She didn't know the words, the language, the ritual, the theology, the philosophy or the taste of the culture. So I had to relay all of that. And we had disagreements about the characters and who they were. In the edit room, you're like a psychologist. You're analyzing people's motives and intents. And how they try not to lie to themselves. People have these self-images, but sometimes footage speaks differently.

Q – Did the choice to use the subtitles for Hebrew and Yiddish words grow out of Susie not understanding the language?

Sandi – For any non-Jew or liberal Jew who didn't understand Orthodox and Hasidic Judaism, I think it was essential to have a film that could translate. It's not like they're speaking in Hebrew or Yiddish. They're speaking in Hebrew and Yiddish phrases. It's a very unique form of translation - having a sentence in English and then an italicized word that represented the word that needed to be translated.

Q – How many hours of footage did you have?

Sandi – 450 and we had to reduce it to a 90-minute film.

Q – How long was the production process?

Sandi – We shot for five years and we edited, including fundraising trailers, for fourteen months. So towards the end, we were shooting and editing at the same time. I went to Miami to do a fundraiser and then decided to do an interview there. They turned out to be so amazing that I went back and shot for four more days. And they made it to be one of the six main characters.

Q – What was the thought process behind the silhouettes?

Sandi – So much of this world is hidden so I had to figure out how to make invisibility illuminating. So we threw up this 14 foot screen on an NYU sound stage and I invited the community to form their image behind the screen. It was just beautiful. We had this virtual shtetl and all the community came. We're talking lesbians who had to sneak away from their husbands who brought their kids to the set. And their husbands had no idea they were lesbians, let alone in a movie. We had people who were Orthodox, people who left Orthodoxy, people who were married or singles. We had straight Orthodox people come. The silhouette tableaus were to represent holiness, which is hard in language to represent. And the tableaus were these mythic shadow worlds. They have a different texture and language from the rest of the film and I love them. I think they bring an altered space to the movie and act as like connective narrative tissue. We had no voice over so they helped bind the film together.

Q – They also seemed to elevate your film and make it larger in scope.

Sandi – They made it more cinematic and helped distinguish it from a normal verité driven documentary. I'm really interested in hybridization and pushing documentary language, so that was an exciting experiment. We tried all sorts of ways to do silhouettes. We used curtains, throwing their shadows on walls, using different textures. Putting them in front of a curtain and behind a curtain. Lace and patterns. Lots of different ways. Susie and I co-directed those sequences and we shot on DVCam.

Q – How did you organize all that footage?

Sandi – Everything was transcribed. We had a whole team of interns transcribing for us and I paid some people. We did an elimination of a lot of characters and it took time. But we really worked from transcript books and index cards.

Q – How long did you edit for? And did you make just a final cut or did

you make many different cuts?

Sandi – I created a half hour work-in-progress midway through the process that we used for fundraising. Actually, we created a 10-minute trailer and then came back and edited some more. All in all, we edited for 14 months and I think it was critical to work with an editor. I was really into feedback screenings and that drove Susie crazy. I put together three feedback screenings. One was for Orthodox and Hasidic gay and lesbian people. Another one for Orthodox and Hasidic straight people. And a third for non-Orthodox and non-Hasidic people who were mostly secular Jews and general audience people from the film industry. So we got three radical takes on the movie.

Q – What were the takes?

Sandi – *"This film makes Orthodox Judaism look so beautiful."* Then, *"This film defames Orthodox Judaism." "The characters in this movie have incredible courage and we have fallen in love with them." "These people can't get their lives together. Why are you representing the community with them?"* So it was navigating all the identities that had a stake in the movie and then dealing with the universal audience. So when I was editing, I had two eyes. I had the universal audience eye and then the Orthodox police. I edited it from within and then I edited it very wide.

Q – You worked with a composer. What were your instructions for the score?

Sandi – We started off with a temp score of Jewish music. It wasn't what I really wanted so it wasn't hard to separate from it when we took it out. I heard John Zorn's CD and I was blown away. I didn't want klezmer composition. Every Jewish movie has klezmer. I wanted something that had a minor key. Something that had a sense of doubleness - that something is deviating from the norm. We had a meeting with John and he really dug the film. He could've scored to time and that would have been very expensive. So to keep costs down we decided that he'd create a body of music that the editor would just edit from. So we gave him the amount of time we'd need for each piece and its emotional resonance. Susie played a huge role in this, as she's great with music. Then we decided on instrumentation. We chose an organ, clarinet and percussion. The organ makes it sound Goth and churchlike – that automatically puts the film in another realm. And he just created this awesome score that he released on his own label. We had to go back once to redo some stuff. But it really elevated the film to another level. Music also came from the characters. We called Mark, one character in the film, the melody of the movie. He's always singing. And on the DVD I have *Mark The Musical* and it's Mark singing through the Hasidic world.

Q – Did you do anything special in post?

Sandi – It took a long time to do all the subtitling and we did special sound work because it was all over the place. We got a big sound mix given to us in kind. I worked with an amazing title designer Andrew Capelli who did a five minute credit roll at the end, which might be the longest one in history. What he designed was so graphically striking and elegant. It's sad that on video and DVD it doesn't come through as well as it does on 35mm. The titles also reflected the silhouettes.

Q – What was the cost of the film in the end?

Sandi – Around $750,000.

Q – When you finished the film, what happened with regard to festivals?

Sandi – We submitted it to the festivals and we waited. And then *Trembling* got into Sundance and then we got into Berlin. When we were strategizing for Sundance, we thought we should creatively shape our experience at the festival to reflect the film's core meaning. So we did the first ever Shabbat at Sundance. In Utah! We koshered a restaurant in Park City and had a beautiful meal with Rabbi Steve Greenberg who was the first openly gay rabbi who is in the film. We had over 60 people come – producers, Sundance programmers, Tilda Swinton, critics and local Utah Jews. It was great. A mix of gay, straight, film, not film, stars, not stars, Christians and Mormons. We met this guy in Park City who was a chef and had a condo and he not only gave it to us to house our team but cooked a Shabbat dinner for 60 himself. We also convened a Mormon-Jewish gay dialogue on homosexuality. We had people who were ex-communicated from the Mormon church drive from all over the state to come. This family came – a husband, wife and two babies and no one knew why they were there until he raised his hand and said that he had a boyfriend before he got married. *"The church told me to get married and be devout and it will go away. Well, five years later we're still married and have two kids and it still hasn't gone away and we don't know what to do."* We didn't know what to do either. These people were facing a crisis in their lives publicly and with dignity. That's when I first realized that the film was not just for Jews – it can touch any outsider.

Q – How did the screenings go?

Sandi – The same. The people who went to the dialogues went to the screenings and the testimonies just poured out. A guy came up to me and said, *"I'm Muslim, I'm from Pakistan and I'm straight and this film is about my life."* We got a lot of press about these events. It distinguished us from other films and gave us a higher profile.

Q – What did you do after Sundance?

Sandi – We got into the Berlin Film Festival and we did a Shabbat in East Berlin where we had 60 people come together from Holocaust survivors to German gay Christians to film industry people. Then we won two awards – one was the Teddy Award for Best Documentary.

Q – Did you have a sales agent at this point?

Sandi – We had a team already. We had a publicist, mPRm, in LA who were great. Then we had Michael Roban and Linda Hanson who acted as producer reps/sales agents. They were responsible for domestic. We signed with New Yorker Films in April. I didn't just want a distributor; I wanted a partner because I wanted to be an active participant in the distribution. I had the best experience with a distributor that one can have.

Q – What was so great about it?

Sandi – We did the New York premiere at the closing night of the Human Rights Film Festival and we had to turn people away. The energy in the room was so intense. People were laughing, people were crying. After the film, all these people in the movie, including some who were in silhouette, got on stage and we did a Q&A. It was electric. The next day Jose from New Yorker said, *"Sandi, we need to have a meeting in the office tomorrow!"* I was nervous. He said, *"It's clear from last night that you have created a family and this film must move like a family."* We were going to do a traditional release where we open in New York, then a week later in LA, then a week later in San Francisco. But he said he wanted to open New York in October and not go to another city until January and let it build in New York at Film Forum. It was such a smart move. We turned Film Forum into a town hall and scheduled three weeks of events both in the theater and surrounding places. And we did this ongoing engagement for weeks, which meant we packed the cinemas because every event was co-sponsored by different organizations and they would mobilize their membership. We did an African American/Orthodox Jewish dialogue on homosexuality. We did events where I put together a coalition of eight Orthodox synagogues that sponsored two dialogues. We did events with senior groups and filmmakers at AIVF. We did Catholic/Jewish dialogues. And I'd have kept going but we had to open Amsterdam and Israel.

Q – Who paid for all of this?

Sandi – From various sources – the distributor, individual donors, volunteer in-kind work. The movies were in the cinema and then we walked somewhere in a five block radius to the follow up. Some of them we did in the cinema as well, but you don't have time because you are trying to pack five shows a day. We broke box office records at Film Forum and that allowed us to book other places like the Laemmle Sunset 5 in Los Angeles. And we replicated the New York model there and in like 80 cities. And I hired outreach coordinators in every city to get people mobilized.

Q – Did the film find its way into medium sized towns or rural parts of North America?

Sandi – Eight million people have seen the film. It's played tons of small towns. And in documentary you have a huge life in non-theatrical. That's defined as screening outside the cinema space, so conferences, colleges, churches, synagogues, community centers, etc. That's huge in terms of revenue and community. It created community wherever it went that had lasting impact beyond the screening. There was a palpable sense of excitement in a city when we came to town. I can't tell you how much the film got propelled by all those people. I took all those people's e-mails and built a database of close to 18,000 people. I send an e-mail out saying we are going to tour Eastern Europe and we need support – boom! I get responses.

Q – That's also a base for future films.

Sandi – Definitely. You build relationships. It's hard. You go to a city, you show the movie, it's so emotional. People share very intimate life stories from the audience and you have this very intense relationship with people for five days in Austin, Texas. Then you're gone.

Q – Did you find it to be lonely?

Sandi – Yes, sometimes Rabbi Steve would come. Or Michelle or David. Filmmakers should really consider if this's really the model for them because they might not have the personality to want to be public and continually engage with audiences. Or they may want to move on to their next film quickly. Also, it's expensive and fortunately we got grants. The Walter and Elise Haas gave us a huge grant to do Bay Area programming with the movie. So we're able to have this incredible Shabbat for 120 people. There's a lot of advance planning that needs to be done for things like that.

Q – How much did you make in your theatrical run?

Sandi – I think we broke $1 million.

Q – Who did your foreign sales?

Sandi – Philippa Kowarsky at Cinephil. I met her while making the movie. She was responsible for foreign TV and she has done a good job selling it everywhere. We did some theatrical in the UK through Martin Myers at Miracle Films. He is so gung ho. He'd jump into the car and he, Steve and I would drive to Brighton or Manchester for shows. We did theatrical in Germany and Israel – that was tough because it was during suicide bombings. We did South Africa, the Czech Republic and Canada. And then of course lots of non-theatrical worldwide. I went to the World Parliament on Religion in Barcelona with 7,000 religious leaders and teachers. It blew their minds. We were the only program to deal with homosexuality. One thing we did was train 11 facilitators in Jerusalem and they went out and did closed door screenings for 2,000 principals, administrators and teachers in the entire Israeli school system – both secular and religious. So that is an even deeper level of engagement with a movie, but we wanted to prepare teachers in Israel for when the film goes on TV. Because when it does we might have tens of thousands of people coming out. We also held the first ever Orthodox Mental Health Conference on Homosexuality.

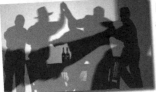

Q – How do DVDs help this model of distribution?

Sandi – I have done over 800 live events with the film. I documented a number of the dialogues and events. So we created a three-hour DVD about the making of the film and its movement around the world – *Trembling on the Road*. Much of it is documenting the change in people's lives. We have the protests in Baltimore with Orthodox Jews and Evangelical Christians together. We have footage with a hostile response in Mexico City. We have some of the eight Orthodox synagogues at Film Forum. I created nine new films. I was able to include 40 minutes of interviews with Orthodox rabbis. We have more with Rabbi Steve Greenberg, the first openly gay Orthodox rabbi. In the film, he has three clips. On the DVD he really has an extensive interview. I did *Behind The Silhouettes*, which was about the making of the silhouettes. I include my short Tomboychik. New Yorker Films underwrote all of this, which is pretty incredible. And we have a beautiful deluxe two disc set. Now I just have to say go to Amazon.com to get my movie instead of taking someone's card and e-mail them that the next screening is in St. Louis.

Q – Looking back on this whole journey of the film, is there anything that you wish you had done differently?

Sandi – I think I might have leapt on the tech bandwagon earlier and started a blog.

Q – Have you had to deal with censorship?

Sandi – In South Africa, we got a theatrical release in Cape Town and Johannesburg. The Chief Rabbinical Court of South Africa tried to stop us. They canceled the screening in the Chief Rabbi's community center and the prevented us from advertising at any Jewish community center or going into any schools. It completely backfired. We ended up getting nationwide press – radio and TV. We did dialogues with Imams and people who had fought Apartheid. Whenever you censor something it often backfires in your face.

Q – What are you working on now?

Sandi – I'm producing a documentary about Islam and homosexuality.

For more information on screening Trembling Before G-d for your group, go to www.tremblingbeforeg-d.com! Spread the word!

Pirjo Honkasalo

THE THREE ROOMS OF MELANCHOLIA

Q – What is your background and why did you go into documentaries?

Pirjo – I'm from Finland and I went straight to film school when I was 17. I was much more involved with feature films when I was younger and I did everything. Driving the car, making the coffee, taking care of the drunken directors. Lying to their girlfriends and wives! For 10 years I worked for feature directors and then I directed the most expensive film made in Finland. It was a two and half hour historical feature on the Civil War of Finland in 1917 and an anarchist who was involved in it. So I didn't start little! For another ten years I went on like that making features. Then I started to ask myself, *"Why don't I live the way I think."* At the time, we didn't have proper feature film producers, we had to produce our features ourselves and I felt that my life was just that of a small businessman. Always talking about the one million you don't have and that very soon it will be seen on the screen. So I stopped the company, declared that I'd never make films anymore, packed my backpack and went to Mexico and India. For three years I didn't do anything. I was writing articles and photographing and paying for my traveling that way. Then a friend of mine asked me to go with her to a convent in Russia. She had a sewing machine that she wanted to donate to the nuns. So I went with her. It was a Russian Orthodox convent and we stayed there for almost two months helping the nuns take horseshit out to the fields or whatever they were doing. And at the same time, reading about the religion and getting to know them. It was still the Soviet Union and so the convent was illegal because Russia didn't like religion.

Q – Was getting into Russia a problem?

Pirjo – It wasn't difficult for Fins to get visas to the Soviet Union. But they had destroyed or closed most of the monasteries and convents. But our convent was on the border of Estonia, which was part of the Soviet Union, but as it was a few kilometers on the Estonian side so they didn't touch it. I went back to Helsinki and I met a Swedish producer who asked me what my plans were. I heard myself say I'm planning to make a film in Russian convent. I hadn't even thought about it! Then she said, *"How much money do you need?"* I told her and she said go ahead and do it and that's when I started shooting documentaries.

Q – Your films have a lot of mood in them. Has cinematography always been important to you?

Pirjo – Yes. When I went to film school, we didn't have departments. Everyone was together and I was never afraid of the technical stuff so I ended up graduating as a camerawoman. I was the only one who didn't want to be a director. So it was a good way to learn the skills of camera.

Q – Do you find that your dramatic films share a similarity in cinematography to your documentaries?

Pirjo – Yes and I don't shoot my dramatic films! In feature films the machinery is so heavy and it's so frightening and inhuman that if the director is talking all the time about the lenses, voltages and cables then the actor becomes a victim of the technique. There must be someone who safeguards the actor from the technique so the actor doesn't have to see or feel these things going around. But then of course, I choose cameramen who think in the same way that I do and I prepare them well so I get the same image I want. I think it's a bad idea to shoot your own feature.

Q – How big of a crew do you use on your documentaries?

Pirjo – Usually because I'm the director and the camerawoman, I have a camera assistant so that there's someone loading the magazines. I also have a soundman who's a sound designer as well. Then I'll work with a local production manager or producer unless I produce it myself.

Q – How did you build up trust and intimacy with the kids in the Academy?

Pirjo – You instinctively know if you have a connection with a person. It's chemistry. Something non-verbally travels from your soul to the other soul and you feel it. So in this film, I didn't talk to the principal and find out who had the most tragic story. My only thought was that if I have a non-verbal contact to a child then I picked on those children and then it's as if there's no camera. They forget it immediately. It doesn't really have anything to do with filmmaking.

Q – How long were you with the children in the Academy?

Pirjo – Not long. I made several trips and because children grow up so fast you can't be with them for too long. With Popov, I was there when he first got into the school and he was sitting on a bench and I was just looking at him and so amazed that he doesn't blink his eyes. He was following everything so carefully. I fell in love with the way he looks. How he observes. It wasn't necessary to ask him what he thinks. There's a lot going on in his head and it doesn't get better if I ask what exactly he's thinking now. I realized that he's an observer and there're no expressions on his face, but you see from his eyes that he's extremely intelligent. Then he checks me. It's kind of love at first sight.

Q – Even though it's a very cold and lonely subject matter, you're capturing humanity with the children.

Pirjo – I'm fascinated and curious about the silent moment. That's what art is about – about what we cannot talk about. It's a unique medium to communicate on that level. We don't have many other languages to communicate at that level.

Q – Why did you choose choral music as your soundtrack?

Pirjo – It's actually modern choral music and not classical. I had the thought that the music is the seer. I gave it the nickname Arch Angel Gabriel. Gabriel told the Holy Mother that Jesus is coming, Gabriel dictated Koran to Mohammad. So that was the working title. I wanted it to be in the background and leading its own life and sometimes when it gets too bad it takes a step closer. So it becomes a character itself.

Q – Why did you decide the structure of three rooms and title them the way you did?

Pirjo – For some reason it was clear to me that this was a picture – like an author painting in three parts. On the left you have Russians, on the right the Chechnians and in the middle you have evil. And that was determined in the early stages of editing. And then I started to see them more as rooms. Three rooms which have to be in the film as linear principles because film is a linear medium. Hopefully, the audience would know that these things are going on at the same time and can interact with each other at any point. Unlike Michael Moore, I didn't want to edit things for the audience. I just give them the three separate parts and I don't help them because I don't want to interfere with what they see. People see things in different ways. On the surface, the three rooms have nothing to do with each other, but it's up to the audience from which room to which room do they walk through each door.

Q – How were you able to gain access to the Academy? And were there any dangerous situations in Chechnya?

Pirjo – No, there were no dangerous situations. Access was really easy. We just walked in! Part of it I can't talk about because I'd risk the lives of some of the people. But of course we fooled the Russian Army because the script we showed them is not what the final film turned out to be. But we had permission from the head of the Russian Navy and if you manage to fool the Russian military you shouldn't be ashamed of that!

Q – It didn't seem as though there was anything that reflected them in a negative way?

Pirjo – To be connected to the Chechens is negative, even in a film – the hate of Chechens in Russia is such that just to show a Chechen as a human being is a problem. They openly call them animals. You can kill animals, but you cannot kill human beings. Putin, before his advisors told him to shut up, when he started in his speeches, he said that he was going to shit on them and he's going to kill them if he finds them - things like that. So just to be in the same film is an insult.

Q – How did you meet the orphanage worker, Hadizat?

Pirjo – I read an article about a Lithuanian priest who takes care of some Chechen children. So I thought it would be much easier to go to Lithuania and maybe something opens up for me there. I traveled there and there was no priest, but there were children. And they were Hadizat's children. She had managed to get some of the older children to stay in Lithuania and go to school because if they're in Chechnya they can't go to school. Then they told me about this woman Villan, who when she was 14 was in the ruins after her mother died. She didn't say that she was raped by the soldiers, but it was likely. Hadizat had come to her and said, *"Would you like me to be your mother?"* Hadizat's from an orphanage in Grozny – a Russian orphanage where she was not allowed to use her own language. So she hates orphanages. If she promises to be a mother then it's like a home. It's not an institute.

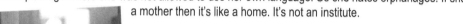

Then I organized permission to go there which wasn't so difficult because this was before 9/11. The President of the neighboring state where the refugee camps were gave us a car and border cards and pointed us to a hotel where it was guarded by soldiers. We were there for a few weeks doing research and unfortunately we didn't shoot because we didn't realize that everything would get so difficult. But after 9/11 as Putin joined the war on terror, the European community and the American society decided that whatever happens in Chechnya is an internal affair of Russia and nobody should interfere. Luckily, I got permission to go again, but to my surprise the hotel which had been full of human rights workers like Amnesty International, Red Cross workers and journalists, were now all gone. It was empty. I think it was an accident that they let us in. After two weeks they threw us out. They came to us and said you have 24 hours to leave. Everyone knows what that means. Americans could never have guessed that Russians joining the war on terror gave Russian the right to practice acts against human rights. And they immediately used it.

Q – How much footage did you shoot?

Pirjo – It was Super 16mm. The first part is Fuji 500 Daylight, which I tested and at that time was the best film. Normally you don't change film in the middle of production, but because there were three separate parts and there was no inter-cutting, I could change. Kodak came out with this wonderful product Vision 2 500 - which was so much better. This film's shooting ration was a little less than 1:4.

Q – Did you have any idea how the story was going to unfold while you were shooting?

Pirjo – I had the trifict already. But because it's a documentary you never know what will happen. You write the script just to get the money and then you throw it away. Then you're writing the script the whole time you're making the film. I try to do my homework so when I'm behind the camera I sense, I don't analyze that this shot belongs to this film or it doesn't. It might be that there's a murder going on my left side, but I keep it as my private memory.

Q – Do you have any advice for new filmmakers?

Pirjo – I think the difference with young filmmakers and me is that that they can go on and piece pictures endlessly. I come from a generation that when I have the camera on my shoulder I can hear the film catching the magazine. I know that every frame is too much. I don't believe in shooting endless amounts of material. It's a fake philosophy that documentaries are made at the editing table. Frequently you see that young filmmakers haven't considered what the beginning and the end of the film will be and when the cameraman has been shooting, there hasn't been an effort to raise the intensity of the situation – so that in a single moment they can show more. When you shoot as little as I do, you focus on that.

Q – Do you feel video is the main catalyst of this?

Pirjo – I think that it's a positive revolution that we have digital cameras. It's easier to show your talent than before. Also very different kinds of talents can enter the film field. Even dreamers. Before it was impossible because to show anything you had to be an economist to organize the finances. But you have to realize that you're not Dostoevsky overnight. It's still the same skill that you need even though this new medium is available. For example, I was on the jury of the Amsterdam Film Festival. Watching five feature length documentaries a day, you'd think that you'd come out with an artistic catharsis, but you come out with an epileptic fit because the camerawork was so bad. I was reading a Norman Mailor article the other day. He was writing about how having commercials every ten minutes on American TV affects children's concentration. He says that children could read two or three hours in a row before, but because now in story telling they're interrupted, they're kind of forced to lose their ability to concentrate, which affects their ability to learn and to make art.

Q – Do you notice a difference between American and European films with that factor?

Pirjo – In Finland, we have four main TV stations of which two are public stations where there are no commercials. So a filmmaker can think dramaturgically along long shots that'll hold the attention of the audience. But as a young American filmmaker if you know that you're never able to show it in one piece, without yourself realizing, you start to censor yourself. There's a difference in thinking in the European cinema where film is considered to be a work of art - like a symphony or a book. I have actually been very surprised because I normally don't watch a lot of TV, but while I was at Sundance I kept it on out of interest and I found out that Norman Mailer is right. I'm always interrupted and there are no real programs anymore. It's bits and pieces. Having this consumer economy is the sense of America and having commercials is endangering the talent. It's a Catch-22. And it really affects documentaries because the place they show them most is on TV. I also think pitching ruins the art. It encourages intellectual dishonesty. Young people are so eager to make films and they learn what things can be pitched and what can't. And they only make the ones they can pitch.

Q – Does Finland have a dedicated industry to documentary films?

Pirjo – Yes, Finland is very strong for documentary – one of the strongest. There's less financial support than in Sweden, but we have an extremely good situation in that we've had extremely intelligent and good people on the TV side. And they don't interfere. They have opinions and that's fine. It's not the money, it's that we have the right people at the right moment at the right place. And we have exceptionally strong female filmmakers.

Scott Dalton

LA SIERRA

Q – What is your background?

Scott – I have a degree in journalism from the Universtiy of Texas. After college I was hired by the Associated Press as a staff photographer. I was stationed in Panama for three years, a year in Guatemala and three years in Colombia. I quit to do *La Sierra*.

Q – Why Latin America?

Scott – After graduating college, I went to El Paso, Texas and I didn't have anything else to do. I stayed with some friends, was doing photos on the weekend and I bumped into an editor at AP, showed him my photos and he offered me the Panama job on the spot. He didn't even ask me if I spoke Spanish!

Q – How did you meet your co-director, Margarita Martinez?

Scott – Margarita worked and still works for the AP in Bogotá, Colombia. She was one of the reporters and I was a photographer so we worked and traveled around a lot. I knew I wanted to do a documentary, but I didn't know on what. And I knew I wanted to team up with someone because I didn't know what I was doing. She had a contact in the neighborhood and got me a job doing photos there for a Canadian newspaper. When I was there, I realized this was it. This is the documentary. It took me a while to talk Margarita into it, but that's how we started.

Q – How were you able to get their permission to shoot and shoot safely in La Sierra?

Scott – It was a little tricky because the town is in the middle of a guerilla war run by teenagers. We had to go through national paramilitary leaders and the head of that group was a good contact of Margarita's. She asked him if we could go into that neighborhood and film and he gave it to us. No conditions, too. Go shoot and if the guys want to let you do stuff, then OK. We filmed over the course of the year. The first couple of trips it was people checking us out, seeing what we were up to and getting to know us. Little by little they started to open up as we built trust.

Q – How long would you stay with the people in the neighborhood?

Scott – It would depend on what was going on. A trip might be three days or it might be a little under two weeks. Margarita still had a full time job, so her time was limited so sometimes I'd go up there and hang out. I'd go house hopping and walk through the streets on the hill and just spend a lot of time with the people.

Q – Even with the paramilitary leader's approval did you feel safe?

Scott – We knew that with these guys, we were safe. They were told to let us be there and how much they wanted to let us film was up to them. But when you're in another neighborhood, which is under control by different groups, then there was a little bit of concern. But I'd been in Colombia for six years now, traveled all over, been to all the crazy places and knew the people, so I knew how to handle things. But it's true; I'd only been in that neighborhood to do one story on them. But it's still the same thing you see all over Colombia – young guys with guns and the conflict. The rural areas are a little different, but not really.

Q – Other than being there a lot, was there anything else that you did to build their trust?

Scott – It was just kind of getting to know them. A funny thing happened there, too. I was doing a story there for *The Los Angeles Times* in another part of Colombia and was kidnapped. It was big news there and even made the international news. I was kidnapped by the rebels, who were their enemies, so I think they thought that I was with them. I was held for a little under two weeks.

Q – Did you ever feel like you had a price on your head?

Scott – Colombia is one of the most dangerous countries in the world. Over 100 journalists have been killed there in the last 10 years. Usually they're local reporters and not international ones. So I never felt like I had a price on my head. With the kidnapping, we were just in the wrong place at the wrong time. And we eventually got out. And even after that, I took a few weeks off to be with my family and then went right back.

Q – Does one get used to being in dangerous areas?

Scott – You get used to being in those situations. But when people are shooting and there are bullets flying by, personally, that's not something you get used to. It's scary. You know that the guys who are with you aren't going to shoot you, but they're being shot at so anything can happen.

Q – How far into the year of filming was it when your lead character, Edison, was killed?

Scott – It was about halfway in. That was a traumatic experience for us and we took a little bit of time off, then went back and finished up. Working for AP, we've covered all these horrific events – massacres and funerals. And you're always affected by it. You feel for the people, but you don't know the people. That was one of the frustrations. You always felt like you weren't digging that deep to get to know the people.

Q – How did you finance La Sierra?

Scott – We didn't have any contributions at all. I took my pathetic life savings at the time, which were very minimal, and bought the camera, the microphones, the tripod and the laptop and just winged it.

Q – What did you shoot with?

Scott – My friends recommended the Sony PD-150 and so I ordered it, read the manual and went out shooting. I was glad that it was small enough that I could run with it.

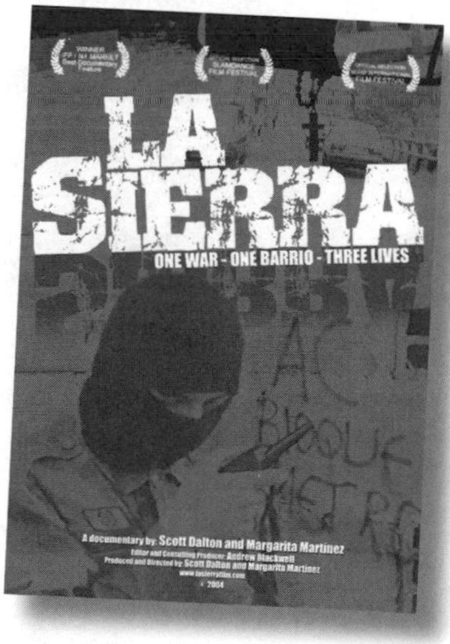

Q – How did you handle the microphones when running around?

Scott – It was all very minimal. For the interviews, we had a lavaliere mic and the rest was the camera mic. We didn't have a sound person or anything. A lot of times I was there by myself with the camera and strapped the tripod to my back. Most of the times I didn't have time to use the tripod.

Q – Did people get used to the camera because it was so small?

Scott – Yeah, they got used to it really quick. And it did seem less intrusive, especially without a large crew.

Q – Were you editing as you were shooting?

Scott – No. We shot about 120 tapes and weren't really sure about how to put it together. Luckily, this American editor moved down to Colombia to be with his girlfriend and was looking for something to do and we were looking for someone to edit. We didn't know him before and then he spent the next six months in my apartment. I'd spend the morning looking through the sound bites and figuring out what to put together, then he'd come in the afternoon and we'd work for eight hours a day putting it together scene by scene.

Q – How did you organize your footage?

Scott – Chronologically. After we'd go do a shoot, we'd come back and look at the tapes and make a rough log and label the tapes so we knew what was there. After that, I figured out what the story was, how all the scenes were going to work out and what we needed to get. We got all the interviews transcribed, so we could read them over and I'd just highlight the quotes that I wanted. Then we'd go look through the logs for B-roll or interview footage to support them and put them together in Final Cut Pro.

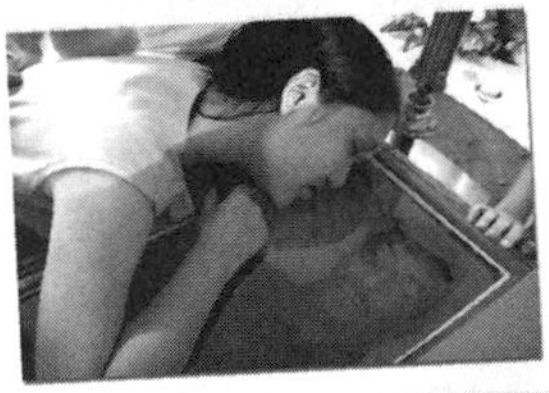

Q – Did you go back and shoot anything during the editing period?

Scott – A little bit. I went back and got some exteriors and general shots. Also the last scenes with the wrap-ups, that happened while we just started editing.

Q – How long was the whole process of making the film?

Scott – We had one year of shooting, but we were going back and forth and there were times when we wouldn't go for a month. We had about three months of editing where we worked eight-hour days, five days a week to get a rough cut done. Then we spent a couple of months fine-tuning it. At that point, we had a 110-minute version, which we sent out and got into the IFP Market in New York and won Best Documentary there. Everyone was telling us that we needed to make it shorter, so we went back in and cut 15 minutes out and got it down to 95 minutes. Then we wanted to cut it down even further, so I did telephone editing sessions with my editor in Connecticut. We got it down to 86 minutes. Then we started working with Films Transit and besides that version, they wanted a version between 50-60 minutes for European TV who have one-hour time slots.

Q – When did Film Transit come on board?

Scott – We met them at the IFP Market and they were interested but not committed. So at the same time, we sent it out to different people. When we were at Slamdance we had some offers from other people, but we really wanted to be with Films Transit. So they said, *"Let's have a cup of coffee,"* and they wanted the film.

Q – How much did everything cost from beginning to end?

Scott – It's hard to say. If you consider buying the equipment, the time involved and turning down jobs to finish it. The rough figure we're playing around with is $50,000.

Q – What format did you end up on?

Scott – Most places we're showing it on Digibeta. We aren't doing a 35mm transfer. We can't afford it. One thing that they wanted especially for English broadcasters is a letterbox version. We didn't shoot it letterbox, so we're going to have to go in and do that. Then we needed the two different lengths. They wanted all the legal clearances. We didn't realize that when there's music playing in the background that you have to pay for those rights. And of course, the clearances for the people in the film. It has turned into a little bit of a problem. We had to go back and get clearances from all the people when we had almost finished editing. We went up to the neighborhood and got everyone to sign releases or their surviving family members to do so. Or the mothers of the young boys.

Q – Was that difficult to do?

Scott – We were a little concerned about it because you have these guys doing drugs and shooting things up. But everyone signed right away, they didn't think twice about it.

Q – What kind of problems did you have with the music licenses?

Scott – Since we didn't have any money, we replaced the music. A lot of the environmental music that's there is kind of expensive. They want $3,000 a song. We were going to have a $25,000 bill that we don't have. So we got in touch with a Colombian music rights company and they helped us find songs to replace them. So we ended up paying $1,500. It's unfortunate that we can't keep it and certain scenes we're going to have to cut because of this issue. For example, there's a scene of a guy singing at the funeral, but we have to cut it because you cannot put other music over that.

Q – Did you get an advance from Films Transit?

Scott – No.

Q – What kind of deal did you get with them?

Scott – It's divided up. They've a US side and then a rest of the world side. You can decide to do both or one. We decided that it would be easier to do both. The deal is 70%/30%, which is standard. With the US deal, we could've gotten 80%/20%, but that would have meant that we have to do all the deliverables for the next year. And it kind of gets to the point where we have to move on and work on other things. And they're a company that you can trust. We are really happy to be with them.

Q – Did the IFP Market put you in contact with distributors?

Scott – Yes. They do screenings, set up meetings and it's closed to the public so it doesn't count as a premiere. It's a place to go to get feedback and to make contacts. We sent ours in as a completed documentary and that way they don't really set up any meetings for you. They have a couple of sessions of what they called speed dating, where you meet with HBO and A&E and PBS. They bring in the important people from there and you sit down at a table and they say, *"Go. What is your story?"* And you try to get them interested. They've another section for works-in-progress that works a little differently. It seems almost better to make contacts that way because people are getting on board to help get it done. People from places like BBC will read about your project and they will request meetings. *Mad Hot Ballroom* was at the IFP-Market with us as a work in progress and they had like twelve meetings with people. It also allows you to find out who is who and schmooze, which I'm not too good at.

Q – Did you get anything for winning the best documentary prize at IFP?

Scott – $10,000, which has helped a lot. And they took us to Berlin and did a market screening there called Best of the Fest. It's to help us meet buyers.

Q – Did Films Transit give you any notes about what they thought you could cut out to meet their length?

Scott – No. They were really good about letting us do it on our own. We talked to some other people and got some opinions because we got to the point where we could hardly look at it anymore. Taking time off and coming back with fresh eyes really helps. The 86-minute version is the best its been. Had we been a little more experienced we might have had a little better luck with getting into other festivals with a tighter version.

Q – Did you do any test screenings?

Scott – We had test screenings in the sense that we had our journalist friends in Colombia watch it. But it's difficult with your friends because a lot of the times they just want to say, *"Great job! Let's get a beer."* They don't want to be too critical. But we did get some good criticism along the way. Maybe we were resisting some of the cuts because we were so close to it that everything that is in there seems really important. With some time and coming back, you realize that not all of it is essential.

Q – How were you able to separate yourself from the emotions of the subject?

Scott – I think it's the opposite. If you separate yourself, it's going to be noticeable. I hope our film comes across as being intimate and caring about these people and not an academic observational piece. There was never a point where I was like I'm here just as a journalist or as a filmmaker. You try not to get involved in their lives or change them at all, but sometimes, they'd ask you to give them your opinion. And especially working with this subject matter you aren't working with angels. They're an illegally armed group and they have done some bad things in their lives. But you realize that people aren't black and white and that's hopefully something that comes across in the film.

Q – Most of them were kids who were playing war for real.

Scott – That was a big motivation to do the story. They have grown up in this culture for forty years. They don't know a world without war. Yet, they live in a large city and can get down there where there are free universities. But they aren't exposed to those things. They know there are neighborhoods and conflicts and the way to become somebody is to become involved in this. And nobody is going in to change things or offer alternatives to this lifestyle. It's a cycle of violence.

Q – So everybody leaves them alone? Nobody goes up there?

Scott – There's nothing to go up there to do. If you're there, you live there. You don't go to La Sierra to go have dinner. It's a very poor neighborhood – almost nothing exists in that way. La Sierra is at the top of a mountain, above it is nothing but peaks. You can see the distribution of wealth there by going down to the city. In La Sierra, there's a bus stop and a little tiny restaurant, which you wouldn't really call a restaurant. There's a little pharmacy and a place to get a beer. Then as you go down to the city, you start to see places to eat. And the crazy thing is that in a taxi, it'd take you 10 minutes to get downtown.

Q – And all the violence is contained to this area?

Scott – When we first started filming it was in little pockets all over Medellin, which is a pretty big city of maybe two million people. When we started filming, the rebels controlled part of the city, another by a paramilitary group and then a part by the Bloque Metro. There was fighting between the various paramilitary groups against the rebels until they took control. Now La Sierra is more peaceful than it has been before because the one paramilitary group consolidated power and had a peace treaty with the government.

Q – When you did the interviews did anyone ask for money?

Scott – No. No one asked for money or anything. There were people who didn't want to be interviewed. Some really wanted to be interviewed. I was surprised at how candid they were from the very beginning. Some times they'd be like a politician and gloss it over a little bit. I think that when most people go to do a story on the Colombian conflict they just do talking heads with the paramilitary leader or the government officials and that isn't what we wanted to do. We wanted to interview the kids and know what their lives are like. And nobody had ever shown that interest in them and they appreciated that.

Q – Did you have any technical problems?

Scott – When I first started shooting, I had the problem that I was going in as a still photographer. So I had that mentality of move around and get that shot and then that shot. So it took me some time to realize that I have to go slower and let some seconds pass by to get shots. And looking at the footage helped that, too. We had some sound problems at the beginning because I didn't understand the settings on the camera. There was a setting on the PD-150 that says one audio track or two audio tracks. So when I had the lavaliere microphone, I assumed that I should do two to have one on each channel. But what it does is give even sound on both channels. So some of the first interviews were bad and the sound bites aren't as good as they could be.

Q – And post problems?

Scott – We had problems with trying to make VHS copies from Final Cut Pro where we had sync problems. At that time we were dealing with a 110-minute track and as the project was playing it would get out of sync. Maybe it was because the computer was processing information. So there was a lot of tweaking involved and I didn't really understand it all.

Q – Any ideas on what your next project is going to be?

Scott – Yes. I'm doing one on the US-Mexico border. So I bounce back and forth to Colombia in order to get photography gigs to support these docs I'm doing. I wanted to shoot them on one of these new HD cameras, but I don't have money for one and even if I did, I started shooting with the PD-150 and I'm afraid that it'll look weird going between the two formats.

Q – What advice would you give to new filmmakers out there?

Scott – To be patient and persistent. And choose a story that you care about and think is important. There are a lot of different styles to documentary filmmaking. Some people can go in for a month and finish something up. It depends on what you want to do. But the stuff I want to do you need to spend a lot of time to see the highs and the lows as everybody's life has an arc to it. And keep shooting.

Kerry David Brian Herzlinger

MY DATE WITH DREW

Q – How did the idea for My Date With Drew come about?

Brian – I've had a crush on Drew Barrymore ever since I was 6 and saw her in *E.T.* After college, I came out to LA to make movies. Instead, I worked on several TV shows like *Ally McBeal* and the pilot to *Grey's Anatomy*, but soon found myself unemployed. I went on a game show called *Taboo*, ended up winning the game show and the prize was $1,100. And the winning answer that got me the prize was the name "Drew Barrymore". At that point I sat down with my friend Brett Winn one Friday night and we decided to take that money and make a film about my dream – to try and meet Drew Barrymore. My other friend Jon Gunn brought Kerry David in and we started that Monday.

Kerry – After working for Tom Cruise and Nicole Kidman for three years, I had started my own production company and executive produced a few films like *Agent Cody Banks 1 & 2* and a Lifetime movie called *Perfect Romance*. Then my business partner Jon Gunn who went to school with Brian and Brett, told me about their desire to document a movie where Brian would try to meet Drew Barrymore. I related 100% because I had the desire to meet Tom Cruise. And the moment I met Tom will be engrained in my mind forever and I thought it would be fun to help Brian out.

Q – How long after the game show did you start?

Brian – Maybe a month.

Q – This documentary has a lot of the structure and style of a narrative film.

Kerry – What you're talking about gave us a lot of trouble with sales and distribution. It's a documentary. It wasn't manipulated. And it was sculpted in post like most docs. But Sundance didn't know what category to put us in. None of us had made a documentary before, so we started shooting and using six degrees of separation to make this happen. I knew Tom and Nicole so that must be able to help. Brian knew Lucy Liu through *Ally McBeal*. So we thought these things would help us and they didn't. It was all documented. It's a romantic comedy wrapped up in the body of a $1,100 documentary.

Q – I would have thought that would have been a great marketing tool.

Kerry – We thought so, too. It's a love letter to Drew. I don't think it would have worked if it wasn't Drew and it wasn't Brian. She's an A list actress, but people don't think of her that way. She seems so accessible. And Brian had this crush on her since he was six and he was willing to be so vulnerable and honest on screen. That's what a documentary needs: honesty and accessibility.

Brian – We got the camera free from Circuit City. We didn't have any lights or a tripod. No microphones. We didn't know what was going to happen day to day on the journey. We had a couple of tent poles. We knew we were going to have a test date because if I were to succeed in this I didn't want to look like an idiot. And the only other thing we knew was in those 30 days, the *Charlie's Angels: Full Throttle* premiere was going to happen and I had to get in to ask her out. We didn't know what was going to fill in those moments. So we had to go through all the footage afterwards to find the story.

Q – What was the camera that you bought at Circuit City?

Brian – It was a Panasonic three chip Mini-DV camera. It was $1,400 charged to Brett's credit card. And then we returned it 30 days later for a refund when we were done. They don't have that policy anymore. Now they have a restocking fee.

Q – Did anything happen with them when the movie got out there?

Kerry – Well, very early on we got a release from them. We told them we were making a documentary and that our budget was $1,100. When they heard that, it didn't sound threatening. So I approached them with a release that I typed up that was for "worldwide, throughout the Universe" and "in perpetuity" to cover whatever needs would come through distribution. And we used that release for everyone in the film. It took a while to get it signed as it went up the ranks and through the departments.

Q – Did they ever come back to you on it?

Kerry – We came back to them. After we won all the film festivals, Jon and I had a brainwave of trying to get Circuit City to come in and sponsor us so we could release it ourselves. So we contacted them and they said, *"Could you remind us what we signed?"* They decided they didn't want to do anything and we moved on. We had a lot of stories like that along the way. Brian called Jon Bon Jovi at home when we were trying to get clearance for one of their songs. Jon actually gave us the right to use it, but Universal Music squashed it by charging us about 30 times our actual budget. It was around then that Universal Music said that we'd never have a Universal song in this film. Jon called Eric Carmen's (who did the song *All By Myself*) mother at home after he got her number from a friend. She directed him to Fred Carmen - Eric's brother and lawyer- who sat down with his brother and their wives to watch the film. They loved it and the next day he called the head of Universal Music personally and said they wanted *All by Myself* to be in our movie. There was no other song that would've fitted more perfectly for when Brian returns the camera than that song. What we'd like to share with any other indie filmmakers reading this book is that no one wanted to help us or wanted us to make this movie. It's your job to turn no one into someone, and someone into many!

Q – When you were shooting these things or using songs in the film did you think they'd be problems later?

Kerry – We knew we'd never pay for them ourselves. We needed a distributor to pick all that up. So we just cherry picked all our favorite songs and put them in.

Brian – The movie that played in movie theaters or that you see on DVD is the movie that we made. We had final cut. All the songs that we have in there we're ecstatic about. If we didn't get one originally, we found another that was better.

Q – Did you have any problems with the camera?

Brian – Number one. Don't shoot a movie on auto focus. And taking that into consideration, when you're shooting digital video, it's 30 frames per second and eventually you're going to blow it up to film, which is 24 frames per second. So, you have to blend the fields to compensate for that. We didn't shoot 24p because it didn't exist yet. And when you blend the fields, it blurs a little bit. So if you have a shot that's even slightly out of focus, it makes it hugely out of focus when you blow it up onto a big screen. But that's part of the charm of the movie. The story we're telling lends itself to being told this way. The camera is part of the plot. The sound mix was fun because we didn't have a microphone. Everything was married. We had some great friends at Sonic Pool who helped us out with that.

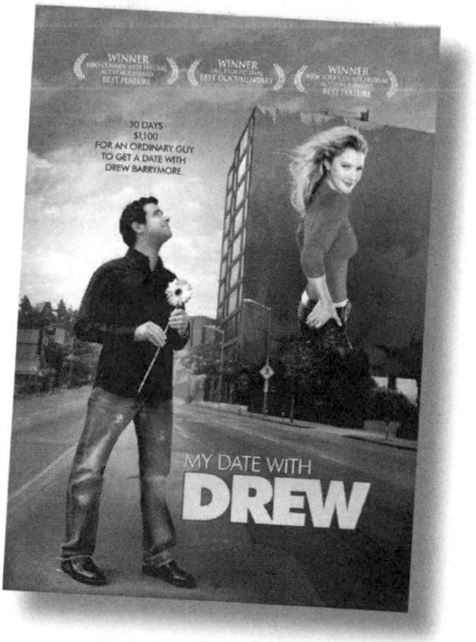

Kerry – At one point, we had spent a lot of money and there was a hiccup in the distribution contract. And we were thinking if this doesn't go through we are going to owe $300,000 and we're going to have to leave town!

Brian – Yes. Our $1,100 movie ended up costing $300,000. But the movie that was in the festivals and competitions was made for $1,100. We sold it domestically for $650,000. And we parlayed everyone's fees into marketing.

Q – During production were there any happy accidents that happened?

Brian – The whole film is a happy accident. When Andy Dick shows up, that just happened.

Kerry – Not being able to take the camera into the *Charlie's Angels* premiere was a happy accident because I think there's so much drama that comes out of just staring at the display on Jon's phone during one of the most pivotal moments of the film! I wasn't there that night. Jon called me and said Brian was freaking out and didn't want to do this or that. I told him that if he gets kicked out that it'd be awesome footage - equally as valuable as him not getting in. Also, when Drew showed up to shoot, we had a situation with Jon that involved an impromptu visit to the bathroom. When he came out of the bathroom, and she walked into the restaurant, the camera battery light started flashing. It was like something out of a horror story after all we'd been through to get to that moment – but Jon turned the camera off and then on again and it behaved perfectly! I was mic-ing Drew at the time, so I didn't realize any of this – I was just focusing on the fact that I knew Drew hated being mic-ed and that I hoped I could do it quickly and painlessly so as not to upset her!

Brian – It wasn't the battery. It was the clean head warning light. And when that is on the camera won't record.

Q – What was the situation then?

Kerry – Jon had to uncontrollably poop.

Brian – One disaster almost happened. While shooting the phone call from Nancy Juvonen, Drew's producing partner, the "tape end" warning starts flashing. So at one point when you see it cut, it's because Jon stopped the tape, rewound it and recorded over what we shot earlier in the day. He didn't even know what he lost. It was one of those big risks that actually paid off.

Q – How long did Drew stay for?

Kerry – She agreed to 45 minutes and stayed for an hour and a half. She was incredibly gracious. She was great with Brian. We had two cameras that day because that was something we couldn't afford to have undocumented.

Brian – For that, a buddy of mine drove up from New Jersey to New York with lavaliere mics because we didn't want to risk not getting audio on that. And it was a good thing that we did because next door a buzz saw was going off. You can hear it when you watch the movie. Also, my ex-girlfriend who kept calling...we weren't planning on that.

Q – That was an interesting part of the film because as you were breaking out of the rut, your ex was now getting jealous and angry. It was very much something out of a narrative film.

Brian – We just had to make sure we were telling a story. The first string out that we had was over 5 hours long and we thought all of it was pertinent. Like when I was trying to get in touch with Lucy Liu to get in touch with Drew, that went on for days and it came to a crushing dead end. We had nothing else going on. I thought that was going to be it. So there were plenty of things that when even stretching it, they all connected.

Q – How long was the whole shooting process?

Brian – We started on May 30th, 2003 and shot for 30 days.

Kerry – But it wasn't until day 87 that we finally got to Drew. Then we edited it for just over two and half months on Brett's laptop computer with Final Cut Pro 3.

Q – How did you organize your footage and did you transcribe anything?

Brian – We digitized all the footage and then we'd label the sections that we thought could be used later. The majority of our money was spent on storage and videotapes. We had seven hard drives. There were a stack of them and the computer would crash every five minutes because it was too much information.

Kerry – We did have to transcribe the final movie, but that was a distributor deliverable, not for organizing the editing.

Brian – The distributors require it for closed captioning and subtitles. But in terms of taking that 85 hours and organizing and structuring it so you can find it later, I mean we were cutting while we were shooting. We actually cut about an hour of the movie before I found out that I got the date.

Kerry – At one point we realized that even if we didn't get Drew, we had a story. It was about a quest. We'd have sculpted the piece into pursuing a life long dream – and how just doing that had changed Brian. We did have an alternative ending, though. We were going to have Brian in a hot tub and we would slowly pan back and Brian would say, *"I finally got my date with Drew."* And then he would be in there with Drew Carey. And then Drew would raise his beer to camera and say, *"Ain't love a bitch?"*

Q – Do you think that would have played as well as getting the real Drew?

Kerry – When we get to Day 30, people think that we didn't get the date but they always burst into applause, regardless! This happened in all the screenings that we had and they all had this reaction because they were so with Brian at that point. So we would've had them I think, but it would have been less satisfying from our perspective.

Q – Did you do any test screenings?

Kerry – Yes. We started off with our own and then once we had a distributor involved, they held theirs too. The difference of opinion in marketing from our perspective, against the distributors, was that we always marketed our movie for what it was; a small indie documentary that had won every festival we entered in to. The distributor wanted to market the movie as a big Drew Barrymore movie and we felt that duped the audience since she's only in it for five minutes. They wanted to put her on the video and the one sheets.

Q – Between Day 30 and Day 87, did your new job at E! pose any problems for shooting or finishing the film?

Brian – Two things about that situation. One, the show I got hired onto was called *Love Chain*, which chronicles celebrities and their past love relationships. The episode I got hired to work on was the one on Drew Barrymore!

Q – That's just freaky weird.

Brian – I know. We couldn't get the footage, though, because we weren't allowed to take the cameras up into E! It was me in my little cubicle with all these black and white photos of all her old boyfriends around. It was one of the lows. I had no idea what was going to happen. If it was going to be a no, then I wanted to hear that. But when that call came, and we were up and running again, I quit the job at E! I had been working as an assistant for 8 years, so to go back and be a PA was not happening. A few weeks later I was being interviewed at E! and they had me sign their wall of celebrities.

Q – What was the website you created?

Brian – We created it to get access to Drew and get her people to see the trailer. But what we didn't know was when we put that trailer up, how many people around the world would respond to the idea of it and write in our guestbook, *"Go for it, Brian! If you can get a date with Drew, can you get me a date with Charlize Theron?"* Within two weeks we had 250,000 hits and within those e-mails were film companies like Fox Searchlight and Artisan asking us when the movie was coming out.

Q – What was the tipping point of getting things going again?

Kerry – 98.7FM, a radio station here in Los Angeles, talked about it at peak time.

Brian – But we also told a lot of our friends to get it out there. We sent out mass e-mails and six degrees of separation started all over again. Then CAA and William Morris sent us e-mails stating that they heard about the movie and they would like to meet with us. So we went into CAA and they loved the movie and thought we should sell it to TV. We didn't agree with that, but we let them do the distribution screening. They got all the major movie studios there and told us, *"Don't be surprised if people walk out of the movie and only three or four of them say that they are interested."* No one left and we got a standing ovation! So over the next few days, Kerry, Brett, Jon and I took two DVDs all over town to show it to various distributors. We didn't want to leave it because we thought it might get pirated. And one by one, every studio loved it, but didn't know what to do with it marketing-wise so they passed. So CAA wanted us to go with the lucrative TV deals and said that we didn't spend that much on the film and we could have made a lot of money.

Kerry – Before the HBO Comedy Arts Festival, CAA took out a two-page spread in the trade magazines congratulating all their clients who had attended; except us. We actually won the Audience Award for Best Feature and they didn't mention that at all! CAA called with an offer from NBC on the table that was for a lot of money, but we had just won the festival and were excited to see how that might help us. They'd never truly been in support of *Drew* being released theatrically, and had said so many times. So we agreed to part ways with them on the theatrical representation and decided at that point to try and find a theatrical distributor ourselves. If we failed, we agreed to come back to CAA and let them take us out for the TV deal they felt it was best suited for.

Q – So what happened after that?

Kerry – Andy Reimer at DEJ had seen it while we were on our journey. He was saying that this was a project that he wanted to take on because it still had the allure of Drew Barrymore. They also had an output deal with Blockbuster in their back pocket so they knew it would rent forever and they'd make their money back that way.

Q – Did Drew Barrymore's Flower Films help you at all?

Kerry – No. They were totally disassociated from us. Nancy Juvonen agreed we had done so much on our own that it would belittle everything that we had done if they helped us.

Q – When did they see it?

Brian – After it was cut. We had some major concerns about showing it to Flower Films because my Mom calls Drew a slut in the first ten minutes. And I'm sneaking into the *Charlie's Angels* premiere so it's kind of a how to guide on doing that. But during the premiere sequence Nancy was on the edge of her seat yelling, *"Get in! You can do it!"* And then when Nancy called me in the film, Gwenn Stroman, one of her producing partners, was crying. They took us all out that night for a great sushi dinner.

Kerry – They started telling us stories from the other side of what we were going through. They were hearing about this project chasing them saying, *"Who are these people?"* It was great to get their perspective. But apparently, it was after Brian did the interview with John August, that John called Nancy and said that he had met us and said, *"They're filmmakers. They aren't stalkers. Don't be nervous."*

Q – You did all the narration, Brian. Did you write it and how did you record it?

Brian – We wrote it all together on the laptop. We put the scenes together in the order that we thought would tell the story the best. And wherever we needed spots to segue, that's where we put voice over. The voice over would come out of the threads of the story that we were talking about. As far as recording it, I spoke right into the camera mic sitting on Jon's couch. That's it. Originally, we were going to have me on camera doing the voice over, but we decided after a couple of screenings not to do that. So we just took the audio part.

Q – There were some fun graphics like the money countdown and the six degrees of separation maps. How did those come about?

Brian – We wanted to keep a running tab throughout the movie of the money to show how we were losing it. As for the six degrees, we wanted to show that everything was real. We didn't assume we could do it, so we showed the path. A designer who worked with Brett did the graphics. He also did the opening graphics of the pictures. They were all favors. That was a $10,000 job that we didn't pay for. They got to use it for their reel and we lucked out.

Q – What did you finish the movie on and what was DEJ's deliverable schedule like?

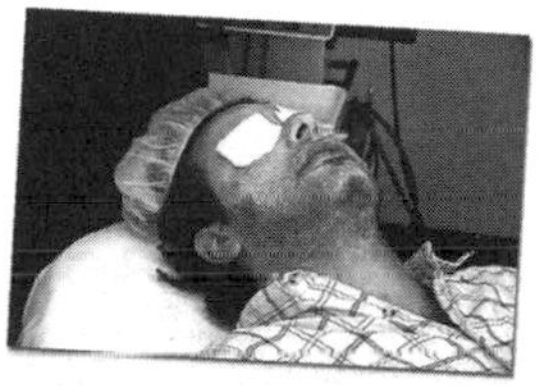

Brian – We finished up on Digibeta and then E-Film did the intermediate. The biggest problem was the field blending. A lot of the darker scenes like in people's homes, unless there was a graphic on there, we'd have to take the field blending off. And fortunately, the camera wasn't moving so you couldn't tell. Without the field blending, about 40% of the movie is out of focus. The deliverables were standard.

Q – Did you play around with any of the color in post?

Brian – Everything was color corrected. You can never expect everything to go right the first time. One time the machine wasn't calibrated properly. We went shot by shot and color corrected it, but the machine was off by one frame. So the last frame of shot A would bleed into the first frame of shot B. So we had to go through it over and over again. And the sound mix we had to do over again. That's a good example of when you take standard techniques and apply them to a movie that's shot on 35mm or HD. With ours, you couldn't do that. We did the opposite of convention and it worked great. For example, getting rid of room hiss, you're not supposed to bring it down to a certain db because it screws around with the timbre. So we're doing that and driving our sound mixer nuts, but it sounds better that way.

Q – How long was your sound mix?

Brian – 6-8 weeks. We did a pre-mix in Final Cut, but we had to start from scratch. We went through it once and that took a while. Then we'd play it at a screening and realize that something was not right.

Kerry – We were asking them to do things that they didn't know how to do. We had no money and we were pulling in favors from the mixers. We were going in between their projects so it was off and on. It probably would've been a lot quicker had it been condensed into consecutive days.

Q – Any problems in the sound mix that could have been avoided in production?

Brian – Using proper microphones and sound equipment! That's why half the movie is subtitled.

Q – How did you handle all the celebrity interviews?

Brian – Everyone was really great! Of course, I was a huge fan of Corey Feldman because of *The Goonies*. So for me it was just asking questions that I would've always asked Corey Feldman and how he knew Drew. Eric Roberts knew Drew from a party and that was enough for an interview. John August worked with Drew.

Kerry – What gets glossed over was that on the day of the date, Brian had to be interesting. Behind him there was a hedge and there was me, Drew's assistant, our friends Pam and Lisa and the wait staff. He has Jon and Brett filming him and he's meeting for the first time the woman that he has loved since he was six. They both handled it so well. I would've passed out had I met Tom Cruise under those terms. It would've been Drew Carey in the tub.

Brian – You see me pacing back and forth. What you don't see is the hour before that where I'm pacing inside while Jon and Brett were setting up the shot. While I was in there, the one thing I kept thinking was the worst thing that could happen would be uncomfortable silences. I created three failsafe topics of discussion to go to just in case. Then Drew shows up and I forgot all three. To this day, I don't know what they are.

Q – One thing that did feel sort of set up was in the grocery store when you happened to see Drew's engagement announcement in Star.

Brian – No, it was real. That happened on Day 29. I was sitting there shopping and sick of being filmed. All I wanted to do was get food and then to see that there… But I see what you mean because of my Mom's catch phrase in the film about *Star* magazine. But it was real. Actually, since this film came out, my mother loves Drew now. And she'd love to apologize to Drew for calling her a slut.

Q – Were there any other things that you wish you'd have done differently?

Kerry – I wish we had gone about the music clearance differently. Our mistake there was that we had no budget so we hired somebody to work for free because they wanted the experience. There are just some key areas in film where you have to hire professionals.

Q – You guys did all your own marketing and publicity?

Kerry – All of it, up until we signed our deal with DEJ.

Brian – We did more publicity than our actual publicist did!

Kerry – Yes. With the exception of AOL and Yahoo, most people contacted us directly through the website. That was because we had done all this guerilla marketing and cold calling. That's what you do as independent filmmakers. And when we were no longer in control of that aspect of the process after we sold the film, we felt that the marketing performance stopped. We would have done things so differently, but it was their baby then. But for documentaries, you can do it yourself. With the internet and word of mouth, it is not about big dollars anymore.

Q – Why did you go with DEJ?

Kerry – They gave us enough money to finish the film. So there was no real choice.

Q – Did anything else go wrong with distribution?

Kerry – One thing we did wrong was that we got a foreign distributor and a domestic distributor on board at the same time. That was a mistake. We should've gotten the domestic first and sorted out the foreign later because the foreign distributor wanted some of the same territories as the domestic distributor and had expected to have them in the deal and we had to go around a couple of times to keep everyone happy. Given that the foreign could've waited, next time I'd sort the domestic out and know exactly what was left to offer the foreign.

Q – Did you get an advance from the foreign distributor?

Kerry – Yes. We paid off our outstanding bills with it!

Q – Have you seen any other monies come back as of yet?

Kerry – A little. It made $225,000 or so at the box office. But the filmmaker is rarely the entity that reaps the rewards in these deals – we're just thrilled so many people around the world are now getting a chance to see it and be inspired by it.

Q – What was the deal that you got from the distributor?

Kerry – It wasn't quite the standard 70%/30%. Foreign wanted some English speaking territories but we had sold them already to domestic. Domestic wanted Canada and Australia which is also what foreign wanted. That was problematic and it made us drop our foreign. Our domestic deal was fairly complicated. Part of our deal was that we parlayed all our fees into the marketing of the movie so we didn't actually make any money up front. Had we done better business at the box office then that money would've been returned to us in full.

Q – Has the film opened other doors for you?

Brian – Yes. We're represented now. I'm a now correspondent for *The Tonight Show* now. And we have a TV show that spun off of the movie. A reality show.

Kerry – We give people $10,000 and they have 30 days to make their dream come true.

Q – What advice would you offer a new documentary filmmaker?

Kerry – There has never been a better time to be a filmmaker. It's always about the story and our movie showcases that by how we shot it. So as a young filmmaker pick up a digital camera and go out and shoot it. It's accessible and affordable. Just make sure you have a good story. Story is king.

Brian – And don't take no for an answer. High schools and colleges have equipment now that's leagues better than what we made the movie on so the only thing stopping you from making the movie is yourself. And you have to be more passionate about the story than anyone else because they're not going to care. You have to make them care.

Sean McAllister

THE LIBERACE OF BAGHDAD

Q – What is your background?

Sean – I left school at 16 and worked in a factory in the UK. An interest in film provided me a way out of that lifestyle. I left the factory and went on the dole (welfare) for about 9 years and during that time I went to a community center and found video cameras. I was never really interested in cinema or film or documentaries or television, but there was something about the range of mad characters that I met in the factory. The jobs I'd do were very boring, but the best part was the people that I worked with. And that's what I like to show in documentaries – the ordinariness of people's lives portrayed in an extraordinary way.

Q – What was the program at the community center like?

Sean – The films were very obvious and issue based about local concerns. Housing problems and the like. They weren't character based. I did that for about three years. Then I applied to Bournemouth Film School where I discovered the assholes of the industry all rolled up into one public school boy concoction of nonsense. I started working each summer in a Bird's Eye pea factory and I wanted this to be my first documentary film. I pitched it to the guys at Bournemouth and they wanted to take a film crew with HMIs and all of this nonsense. I had just discovered Video 8mm and doing it yourself and they're like, *"No, filmmaking is about collaboration."* So I fucked it off, really. They take on so many students who want to make films through this factory process and only two or three people ever get to direct. So I went through it and then I applied to the National Film School along with all of Bournemouth's top boys who had gone through the factory with their polished 16mm films. I was the only one that got in – with my little Video 8. The guy who would become my guru said that they felt sorry for me.

Q – Did you have a better experience at The National Film School?

Sean – The guy who was running the course had a cinema verité approach to filmmaking, which is what I like. The documentary program was the only thing that was completely separate from anything else in the school. You produce, shoot and edit your own films. It was great. There were four students and two tutors. I was there for four years. Colin Young, the main guy, was saying things that were the opposite of Bournemouth. He said, *"This isn't the place to play it safe. Take risks. Fail. Fuck up. Because you ain't going to be able to do it when you leave here."* It's changed a bit now. It's more like Bournemouth. And now you have to pay for it. Back then they were paying me £100/week to be there.

Q – Once you left film school did you find it easy to get a job?

Sean – No. I went straight back on the dole and I was depressed. But that's when I went to Iraq in May 1995 for a voluntary thing, which started my love affair with Iraq. I went on my birthday, which is the same as Saddam Hussein's. So I heard *Happy Birthday* piped in everywhere I went. All fucking day long.

Q – Why Iraq?

Sean – Oh, I was up for anything just like I am now. Anything could've happened there after the 1991 war. Ironically, it's a more dangerous place now than it was back then. I went with a political action group who wanted to raise awareness about the UN sanctions. So we did all of this hard hitting filming babies dying of diarrhea in hospitals. Very strong stuff. There was a blackout of news coming out of Iraq then which helped demonize the Iraqi people so we didn't have a problem bombing the fuck out of them in 1991. I was there for a month filming this stuff and when I came back to the UK, the BBC said it wasn't a story. ITV said it wasn't a story. I was shell shocked. In retrospect, the group I was with might have been too left wing and the story wasn't balanced. But what I learned quite quickly was that to raise awareness of genocide or dying babies, you don't necessarily have to shoot dying babies. We had become desensitized to it. I went back to make a film for Channel 4 on the Gulf War Syndrome and again what was happening when we turned the cameras off with the Iraqi guards or minders was so much more revealing than the little interviews that we were filming. So when the war came in 1998, I was able to get a visa through a connection with the Iraqi authorities and that was my calling card for the TV show *The Modern Times* to commission me to go and do *The Minders*.

Q – What are minders?

Sean – When you shoot in Iraq, Saddam's Ministry of Information gives you a minder – someone who watches you to make sure you don't do anything the State would object to. It's difficult to get any truth in that way. And the way I like to make films is in a one to one relationship. If I had that one to one with my minder, he could become my character. He could invite me to his house and I wouldn't need any other minders. So I managed to make a film with the minders.

Q – Did the BBC want something on the minders in general?

Sean – They didn't care. The idea of the minder was sexy enough. It was a postcard of the modern times. And I was still able to explore the effects of the sanctions on Iraqis as everyone did suffer – even the minders. So I have one very effeminate, sort of camp minder and another one who is a temporary minder who hasn't worked in five years and is struggling to get by. He loved British football and Kevin Keegan so I instantly had all these connections. So the film becomes about my relationship with him and he gets fired because of his association with me. He took us to a football match and kindly to his home. There's this 15 minute scene in his home where there's this real strong moment of truth where he shows me around his empty house as he had to sell all his furniture during the sanctions. As much as we all try to understand what it's like, you could never live it. He took me to his bedroom and he shows me a wall with blue tack on it and he says, *"Here was Kevin Keegan."* He said that in 1991 when they had no heating he had to burn it.

Q – What did you shoot The Minders on?

Sean – The VX-1000. It was great. It's small. It doesn't intimidate anyone. And because it's video, you don't have to only shoot ten minutes at a time. I learned from DV documentary that you have to think on your feet. It's a liberating way to work because it allows me to take part of the experience and that's what it's all about. And if you're honest and in it for the right reasons, then there's no question that your subjects will trust you.

Q – Do you feel that you need to have some objectivity, to be slightly removed from them, or is that not necessary?

Sean – Yes. I go mad at times. I shoot in three blocks now when I shoot for eight or nine months. I shoot for three months and then come away for a couple of weeks for fresh air and then go back in. *The Liberace Of Baghdad*, part of it is a straight narrative about my subject, the pianist Samir. Is he going to go to America or isn't he? Is the hotel that we're staying in going to get mortared? Are we going to die? And then who is Samir and what is our relationship? That gives it warmth and humanity. That's important and it all comes from being there and living. DV allows for that to happen. You don't have that if you have a crew. I've filmed Samir going to sleep. You can get that with DV.

Q – So your stories were more following your relationship with these people?

Sean – Yes. There are two things going on. A narrative that you can see and a journey of me into someone's world.

Q – Do your subjects get used to the camera because you're there all the time?

Sean – Yes. It became a friendship, a relationship, a genuine journey with experiences, the only difference is that I have something here on my shoulder or in my hands.

Q – What happened after Minders?

Sean – I got bought out by Channel 4 at a lucrative £60,000 retainer. They sent me to Jerusalem because they wanted me to look into this story about Christians who were going to kill themselves at the Millennium. I went there and met a Palestinian guy who was a tour guide. When you went on the tour, he always started talking about his politics. How settlers are moving into the Arabic part of Jerusalem, so that became my story.

Q – What did you shoot The Liberace of Baghdad on?

Sean – My dream camera. The Sony PD-100. I even moved away from radio mics and shot all sync with a good on board microphone. What initially took me back to Iraq was to do some research on the trial of Saddam. I took out a second mortgage on my house to survive and got into a lot of debt.

Q – Do you cut as you go along?

Sean – No. I tried to do that, but I work with one editor that I worked with on my very first film and we have developed this system. He's my second set of eyes and in many ways is the co-director. I trust him. I'd go away on holiday and give him a list of the footage that I thought was great and then he would digitize it and make a long assembly of scenes. And then as we were closing in on the cut, we would go back to those scenes that we got in and shift through it to find fantastic, little touches that we missed. And that is the objective eyes. You have to have trust there.

Q – So there was no other money?

Sean – The total budget fully waged was £120k and we took out the wages to bring it down to the level that we could get started at £50K. TV2 in Denmark gave me £4,000 for development to go to Iraq and then £16,000 advance for them to be the world sales agents on the film.

Q – How did you find Samir?

Sean – I checked into the hotel were he worked. I'd go out each day looking for a story and each night sit and listen to him play. We got talking and I soon realized he was my story. He had half his family in Iraq and other half in the US and was waiting for a visa to join. Actually after meeting his daughter in Iraq, who loved Saddam and didn't want to go to America, I knew I had the conflict I wanted.

Q – How important is finding the right subject?

Sean – Very important. Without the right person, I don't have a documentary. When researching, I'm living in a place, getting a feel for what people think, what's going on etc. Slowly I start to get a feel for what it is I want to say. So then it's about finding a person interesting enough to keep me and the audience engaged for 70 minutes. I'm looking for a number of angles, sub stories. For example,

I knew Samir wanted to go to America, but deep down felt confused about what America was doing in Iraq. His daughter who loved Saddam, showed the conflict he and all Iraqis feel about what is happening in Iraq. Their dilemma is many Iraqi's dilemma. Deep down hating Saddam, appreciating liberation, but hating occupation. Also you need someone brave enough to let you film at random without being guarded and someone you feel something for genuinely. I'm now in Japan looking for that person on my next film. It's nearing 2 months and nothing so far. It's hard.

Q – How many hours of footage did you shoot?

Sean – I shot about 70 hours over 8 months.

Q – How long was the post process and did you do any special tricks there?

Sean – No special tricks. I edited with my regular editor Ollie Huddleston in 10 weeks. I only edited when I was done shooting as I never knew the end point to determine what the story is. So many of the scenes have a number of unfolding storylines, all which mean nothing until there is some conclusion somewhere.

Q – How many trips did you make to Baghdad for this project?

Sean – 3 trips to Iraq, around 12 week trips. First by road, then by air on a dodgy little aircraft making corkscrew take offs and landings to avoid surface to air missiles. Great fun!

Q – Did you have any problems in production either from a technical standpoint or from the Iraqi government?

Sean – No never, but I never bothered them so they had no reason to take my tapes I guess.

Q – How did you handle the music in the film?

Sean – I made clean recordings of Samir's music on DAT, and had him sit down playing pieces at his piano with coverage shots as I knew I'd need them. What's used was the really good sync scenes. Ollie and I would go through the rushes together and decide what to digitize into the Avid. We trace my journey, decide on the best moments and create an unfolding story as we digitize, then I leave Ollie for a week or so to cut scenes down, and make a long 3 hour cut which we both watch and then get stuck into it.

Q – Has the film sold anywhere besides the presales you got?

Sean – This film has won more awards then any other film I've ever made but it has been the worst sales ever! We won best documentary award at the British Film Awards 2005, and were nominated for the Directors Guild of America Most Outstanding Documentary.The Sundance Channel will buy it for rubbish money $37,500. The sales in Europe have been bad as well. Arte in France have always bought my films but not this one. They say they didn't like Samir.

Q – What advice would you give a new documentary filmmaker?

Sean – If you can find an easier way of living - do it. To make real insightful documentaries you have to give your life, family, bank balance, sanity, day to day existence as an ordinary human being. The rewards are there if your ego is big enough to drive you to this, if not, don't worry, it wasn't really worth it after all.

Daniel Gordon

A STATE OF MIND

Q – What made you choose North Korea as your subject for your documentaries?

Daniel – My interest in Korea has purely come through football! I'm a football fanatic. I grew up with this knowledge of a North Korean Football team from 1966 that had somehow bonded with the people from Middlesbrough. I'm from the north of England as well. They had beaten the Italians that year in the World Cup and when the Italians got back to Italy they were pelted with rotten tomatoes. But what actually happened to the North Koreans after that point was unknown because they never played at that high level again. I started working at Sky Sports doing documentaries on a much lesser scale. I produced and directed a 15 part series on Premier League clubs, and I was asked what I wanted to do next and I said, *"Definitely to go and find the North Korean football team."* And everybody said, *"There's absolutely no way that you can get to North Korea."* I actually studied History and Politics for my degree, but I didn't really know about the politics of North Korea other than the basics. I had no idea of Kim Il Sung or anything like that so I came purely from a football fan angle. The more I looked into it and the more people said it can't be done, the more I thought we're going to do it! It took four years to get the permission.

Q – Most foreign journalists can't get access to North Korea, where did you go to get permission to film there?

Daniel – I went to Nicholas Bonner, my associate producer who's based in Beijing and is an Englishman. He runs this company called Koryo Tours, which has been running cultural exchanges and tourism to North Korea since 1993. He wasn't sure about me initially. Was I a journalist pretending to go and do this doc as a lot of people do? As soon as we met, he kind of realized I was sincere, and that this was going to be a great film and the North Koreans would go for it. They trusted that I wasn't going to go in pretending to do a football story and come saying North Korea is a terrible place. I play football so when we went out with the North Korean players I'd get hold of a ball, juggle, do the various tricks and actually play and they realized that I was genuine. So if they did have their guard up in any way, it soon dropped. The more I went, the more I thought this is like no other country on Earth. *The Game Of Their Lives* is huge in North Korea. It's been on TV ten times. There's only one channel out there so we get 100% ratings every time! So because of our success, we realized that we could get access to the Mass Games. They opened themselves up for us and really wanted to be involved with us.

Q – Why did it take four years?

Daniel – I had to go back and forth with faxes. They'd say, *"Send us your work, so we know that you're genuine."* So I did. The worst thing was after about three years when they said yes, the independent production company I was working for backed out. So I left them, formed my own company, raised £90k from private investment and went out to North Korea. No broadcasters would back it, no regional film people, no national film people. I had to go and do everything. I met John Battsek in London, who had just produced the Oscar winning doc *One Day In September.* He loved the idea and gave me the best possible advice – just get out there and get the footage. So Nick, the crew and myself went in October 2001 because we were saying we can get in, get out and we can get amazing footage. What we got exceeded our hopes. We did a press conference with the footage and suddenly the phones started ringing. John Battsek came on board fully as our Executive Producer – he has been brilliant in that role for us for all our films since. The BBC gave us completion money and from then on all the films we've done have been with the BBC.

Q – So once they saw that you really did have access they backed you?

Daniel – Yes, and we had amazing archival footage as well. The North Koreans had shot a lot when they were in England. In 1966, they took a four-man crew and spent £3,000 on equipment and £500 on film. They sent their rushes down to the Kodak laboratory to be processed overnight so they could make their film. And I knew that would still exist because one thing that socialists do is keep their archives in really good order. When we first saw it, it was unbelievable. Not only did they show it to us, they printed us a brand new positive from the original negative! They told us they'd pay for the transfer because they wanted us to make the best possible film. That would never happen anywhere in England! Nick and I took 13 cans of film on the train from Pyongyang to Beijing, which is 25 hours. When we arrived in Beijing, we couldn't even carry the thing. But basically they trusted us. It's considered national treasure and it had to go through a hell of a lot of form filling to allow us to actually take it out of North Korea. Again we have a very special relationship. The woman who we deal with, who's like our guide, we've worked with her for the past six years and become friends. She's been to my house in England when we brought the football players back there. It's become very personal.

Q – Who does she work for?

Daniel – The Korea Film Export/Import Company who have been our partners from the very beginning. They're a state film company who have the responsibility for dealing with foreign film companies. If we need more access than they would ordinarily like to give, they understand that and basically fight our battles for us with the necessary governmental people before we arrive.

Q – Do they work as a co-production company or do they get a fee?

Daniel – It's co-production in that they helped to produce it, but not a co-production as in any money. They just get a credit. In *State Of Mind*, we were filming in Kim Il Sung Square. We got there and we didn't have any permission to go and it was on one of the major nights. When we arrived, the official wouldn't let us film because we didn't have the official permit. But they then told them that we were the guys who made *The Game of Their Lives* and suddenly it was like the Red Sea parting. They were like, *"These people must come and film"*. Our guys asked about the permit and the visa, and they said, *"Forget the permit, they don't need a permit, they made Game Of Their Lives."* Suddenly we got the best spot, the state cameraman was moved away and they allowed us to go into the center of the crowd. We realized that we were very lucky and had very special access.

Q – Was there a big difference from filming your first film to the second?

Daniel – The main thing is you start to ignore the blatantly obvious. The first time you go there, all you see is the monuments to the Great Leader. You see all the propaganda murals. You see the fact there's barely any neon lighting and everything looks very similar and grey. Then the second time you go you actually don't notice it anymore. And you don't spend your entire time gawping out of the window.

Q – Did you have any problems filming as a Westerner?

Daniel – No. They've never been funny. The great thing is you don't get a whole crowd of kids interfering, so that's really good. But also we've never been interfered with at a government level.

Q – Did they ever want to see any of your footage?

Daniel – They want to see it more from a creative point of view. There are certain rules with filming that we respect. For instance, if you film the statue of the Great Leader, they don't want you to pan up from the feet up to the head because in

Asia that's a lack of respect. If there are portraits of the Leader in the background, don't film them cut in half. We respect that as we would if we were making a film in the Vatican and they wanted it filmed a certain way. They know we're mindful of that and they know if that doesn't get adhered to then it won't go in the edit because it would offend them. With *Game of Their Lives* we actually had a big problem when they saw the film on how we turned the Korean War. We got the same complaints from the South Korean Embassy in England too. So they both have a problem with the Korean War as officially the other one started it! For all the films we do on Korea, I'm not bothered who started it. I'm bothered about saying what a brutal war it was and how it affected our protagonists. The team goes from a country that's been completely flattened and thirteen years later, they're at the World Cup. And for *A State Of Mind*, it's three generations. One who was ten years old during the war, one who grew up just after the war, and the youngest is at the same age the granddad was during the war, but has never experienced war.

Q – How big is your crew when you film? Do you hire any locals?

Daniel – No. We had a crew of five - two cameramen and a soundman for the *Game of Their Lives* and myself and Nick. For the first part of *State of Mind*, it was just Nick and myself because we were really recce filming. Then it was just Nick Bonner, Nick Bennett my cinematographer and me on sound. For the latest one, it's four of us, camera, sound, myself and Nick. I like to keep small because it's lighter, obviously less expensive and you can move easier in whatever given situation. But I don't like being shorthanded, which is what we were for *State of Mind*, which actually caused a lot of problems.

Q – Hadn't the BBC come on then?

Daniel – For *State of Mind* they were on board from the beginning and they've been brilliant ever since *Game of Their Lives*, especially our Commissioning Editor Richard Klein, but the finance was a little under half the budget. So we had to get ARTE from France and WNET from America to both come in with the next 55-60%.

Q – So when you first went there you didn't have everything and you had to keep it low?

Daniel – Absolutely. And when we got out there we realized that we budgeted for two, maybe three trips and it ended up being four. We were extremely pushed for everything. Half way through filming, the SARS outbreak happened and we had to get out of North Korea as they were closing down the borders. We had no idea when we'd be able to go back. Even when we did go back and we got as far as Beijing, North Korea was still closed. So we had to kick our heels in Beijing with nothing to do for a week and all we could see was time just ticking by. The country was completely sealed for three months - the only country in the world that did so.

Q – Do you or any of your crew speak Korean or did you have an interpreter?

Daniel – We have an interpreter with us at all times. And that's actually quite useful. Nick and I are both very pigeon at speaking Korean. Every time I've gone I've wanted to learn the basics but I've never had any spare time to learn. But now I can read Korean and Nick can too, although we can't tell you what it means!

Q – This Korean Film Export/Import Company, did they help you find your subjects for your second film?

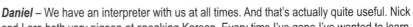

Daniel – We went back in May 2002 to screen *Game Of Their Lives* to the North Korean football players which was the most nervous I've ever been or since in a screening. It was weird as we only had the English version and had no time to translate it. So they basically watched the film in English with bits in Korean. The next day we went out and had lunch with the Film Export/ Import Company and they told us they wanted to do a feature about Mass Games and a couple of gymnasts who really want to perform, but they're not that good and they have to train and you see the tears and all the problems they have, and it all comes right in the end. It was exactly what we wanted to do, but as a documentary. But we made it very clear from the start that we were after real life. We told them that we were going to come back in September and asked them to find us the best gymnast for the Ball Discipline. They came back saying that they'd take care of it. So we started semi-filming with them in February. We were planning on doing a bit of filming in every season, so we were planning to stay for a year on and off, not for a full year. We suspected that that girl had been chosen because it was a model family and then we met the family and realized it wasn't really the model family. It wasn't the Walton's or anything like that. And while we're filming with the girl, she kind of mentioned that she had this friend who's a bit younger than her who she coaches. She's part of a family, has sisters and we thought it might work. We've got this relationship between a girl who has no family, no sisters, a very adult family and she's got this mate in a block of flats next to them who she goes round to for a bit of loving.

Q – When filming in the girls' homes, how did you make sure that you captured the normality of their lives?

Daniel – The first day we got there was a nightmare. There was a crew of three. Then, my dad had come out just because he likes to go out there for a bit of a laugh. The film company had our two usual guides. A couple of people from the company who were quite high rank came in to see the filming. The woman from the apartment who was in charge of the block came. The woman from the elevator wanted to see the film. Mates were coming round and I was like this is a two room flat! We had 20 odd people there and from that point on we said from now on, it's just Nick the cinematographer and me. So we carried on filming and we had absolutely no idea what they're saying as we didn't even have our interpreter there. They got it pretty straight off that we were just going to film them. For all we knew they could have been saying, *"God, these white boys are idiots."*

Q – You didn't have your translator with you?

Daniel – No. We had absolutely no idea what we were recording. The family kept wondering why we wanted to film them making dinner or telling their daughter off as it was so normal to them. And we just told them to carry on.

Q – The North Koreans show an open hostility to the US. Did you encounter any of that as a Brit?

Daniel – The British are more welcome than the Americans because we have diplomatic relations and there's a relationship that goes back to 1966 with football and when we took the players back in 2002 where we've become minor celebrities. It's very bizarre to have a random North Korean shout out *"Dan,"* in the street. They don't do autographs, but it's very funny. The only time we're reminded of our nationality is if we're in the war museum or at the border. I think people recognize that if you're in the country and you have the minders there, then you're doing something good. Americans are allowed in on occasion. The North Koreans claim that they make this distinction between the American people and American imperialism.

Q – It seems that they live daily with air raid drills?

Daniel – Yes, that was in 2003. It was a very tense time. The US military build up was happening in Iraq. The nuclear inspectors were there and everyone knew America was going to have a war. And Rumsfield said as a direct threat to North Korea, *"We can fight a war on two fronts."* And Bush's State of the Union speech where he named North Korea as part of The Axis of Evil was widely reported there. They were pretty certain the US was going attack and in April when we were there the Saddam statue was toppled in Iraq. We thought North Korea was next and had Iraq gone differently, that may have been the case. They didn't want war, but they were ready to defend their homeland.

Q – Did any of your subjects want to know what life was like outside of Korea?

Daniel – To a degree. They're interested in family life. They're interested in the footballers. We took them a video of what our lives and families were like. I think they contextualize everything in terms of being in North Korea and that is the best place to be.

Q – Did they ever express anything negative about their country?

Daniel – I never heard a North Korean be negative about the country. Even when the radio is manditorialy pumped into their kitchen's all the time – it's just a part of life. News and propaganda movies are on all the time. I stop noticing it after awhile.

Q – Do they show anything from outside of Korea on TV?

Daniel – They show sporting events. The main thing they show is natural disasters. The east coast is prone to flooding. They showed the World Cup in South Korea. I saw some Italian football matches on North Korean TV. All the feature films that are made in North Korea must adhere to the cinematic arts that are demanded by Kim Jong Il. He's written a book called *On The Art Of Cinema* and that's the main text for how films should be made. They need to breed revolutionary consciousness. You can have anything else, action, romance, but it has to have that and a love for the leader. The people seem to genuinely enjoy them when they watch them. The waitresses in this one restaurant that we know are glued to the screen when they come on. I've seen the film five times with them and they still cry at the same spots!

Q – Did you have to do any self-censorship?

Daniel – There's always a sense of self-censorship in any documentary. I got close to the girls and there are times when I don't want them to feel too uncomfortable. It's not as big a deal as you think. The only time I really thought about self-censorship in *A State Of Mind* was when the girl was quite scathing about her granny and how she pushes her. I knew it was true, but whenever we go there that woman was great to us. If I put it in the film, I have to face the granny. Then sure enough a month later we interviewed the granny and she said she had to drive the girl and be brutal on her. That was such a relief! They both went into the film. However, in our latest film we are using some South Korean archival footage and the people who gave it to us don't want us to portray South Korea as a villain. At times, the western broadcasters have wanted us to take a stronger tone with North Korea. So there you see the propaganda from both sides. I told them that the commentary will say what they believe and the audience can make their own mind up.

Q – Has filmmaking in North Korea gotten easier since your first trip there?

Daniel – It never gets easier. We started with a very neutral, feel good story. Then we went into daily life, which no one had ever done before – even North Koreans. Then we went for a political hot potato in talking about defections and life in America, North and South Korea. And yet the cooperation still comes from the North Koreans.

Q – Is this the first time people have talked about defection?

Daniel – Absolutely. There was always this rumor that Americans were living in North Korea, but the information was impossible to get. The North Koreans first said it wasn't true, and then they said it was true, but it would be impossible to film them. I took that as, *"Yes, it is possible."* But it took two years to do it. These people lived in America, went to South Korea and then defected to the North in the 1960s. It's an amazing story.

Q – Are there movie theaters in North Korea?

Daniel – Loads. We took *Bend It Like Beckham* to North Korea and screened it in a theater that holds 2,000 seats. It was the most bizarre thing you could imagine. 20,000 people saw it. I actually gave a speech that opened that film festival and a man came up to me and said that he never thought he would live long enough to see an Englishman give the opening speech at the film festival. I was the first one. When you stop to think about it, that's kind of significant. In Pyongyang, there's the International Cinema House, which is the main one and there are half a dozen others in town. Then in the suburbs and every town and village, there's a cinema. They are part of the propaganda machine.

Q – Are there any documentary organizations there to help filmmakers?

Daniel – There's the Documentary Film Studio where we source a lot of our archive. We have a great fixer from there who finds anything and everything. He found the men who arrested the Americans in the 1960s in North Korea for us. He went through an amazing process to do it.

Q – Could you and Nick ever walk around freely?

Daniel – We have done. But it gets a little tiring after awhile. We wanted to walk to an evening meal one time and it took over an hour to walk there. So you don't do it out of practicality. And there's no street lighting. We came back in pitch black. I wished I had a torch (flashlight), but if I had one, everyone would know I was a foreigner. It's an absolutely safe place. I have never felt threatened in North Korea. We've actually lost camera equipment and had it delivered to our door the next day! Not sure that would happen in the UK.

Q – Are things like supermarkets and shops very different?

Daniel – Until recently, it hasn't really existed in a way we would recognize markets and supermarkets. Even now we buy all of our provisions in China and bring them over. We've all had varying degrees of difficulty with the food. Some of it is purely that we're stressed and homesick and the time difference is difficult if you want to talk to anyone back home. It's expensive to call home, too. But now we have it down and know how much chocolate and baked beans to bring over from China. We take our HP sauce to remind us of home. I have a jar of Hendersons Relish, which is particular to Sheffield where I'm from. That's in our hotel restaurant! We would bring jars of peanut butter down to breakfast and people would laugh at us.

Q – Do they have normal leisure activities that we're all used to?

Daniel – Sure. People want to walk in the park and swing on the swings. They want to take boat rides. It's the same as the rest of the world. But it's more like how England was 50 years ago where Sunday, the day of rest is the day of rest. It's very difficult to get anyone to work on that day.

Q – Do you think the outside world has painted a really bad image of North Korea from what it actually is?

Daniel – From a people level, yes. The people have been demonized alongside everything else that is going on in the country. But equally they think everyone in America is bad because of George Bush and that's just as wrong.

Q – What advice would you give a new documentary filmmaker who wants to shoot in a political hotbed country?

Daniel – Have no preconceptions and be very open. But you have to be aware of the country and don't be surprised if you're surprised. Be very open and honest with people. They trust us completely now and we have a lot of fun when we're out there. In fact, when most people go there, they think you have to be serious. The North Koreans are very funny people. They love practical jokes. They're very close to us Brits that way. And of course the biggest advice in documentaries is don't take no for an answer. Everything is possible.

CAMEROON TO FRANCE

Q – What is your background and what led you to documentary filmmaking?

Jean-Marie – I grew up in Cameroon and I came to France to continue my studies in audio-visual communication where I got a Master's degree. I wanted to make films to talk about life in my country. Because there was heavy censorship on words I thought films would be the right medium. So the films that I wanted to make were about everyday life – about people's lives.

Q – You mention censorship, did you have problems making your films?

Jean-Marie – No. I never really had problems. The censorship was really on the written word – the newspapers and some radio journalists. At the time, there was no TV in the country. There weren't so many images. I wanted to write and to talk about life around me, but images seemed more appropriate.

Q – Would any of your subject matter normally be censored in the newspapers?

Jean-Marie – Yes. I lived in a country were people were saying everything was beautiful and wonderful, when basic issues were not addressed. Like running water. More than 70% of the people didn't have it and the issues were not being dealt with. On the radio, they would be saying that you live in a beautiful country and our President is the best President. We thank him for making a new stadium or whatever. But no one was questioning why there weren't enough good schools? Why the hospitals were in such a state? Why doesn't everyone in the country have clean water? They were not the kind of issues that the government would want to address.

Q – When you made your films that did address these issues, did you have problems showing them in Cameroon?

Jean-Marie – Not really. People at that time weren't used to watching documentaries. When I showed my first documentary, which was called *Bikusti Water Blues* - a 90-minute documentary that I showed in the cinema, people said I was showing them things that they already knew and that they wanted action films! Some people would say that it's good to talk about these things and others would say that I shouldn't show trash taking over the city because that is not good. We need to see beautiful things. The cinema is a place where people go to dream. So it wasn't censorship so much as it was the public. When I showed the film in the cinema there were 30 minutes of previews of things like *Rambo* and American films where people were shooting and cars exploding and all these Hollywood things. And then you would have a documentary on everyday life - people were frustrated.

Q – How difficult was it to get the theaters to screen your documentary?

Jean-Marie – It wasn't difficult because there weren't that many African films being made. I'd just go to the theater with the print and bring them my posters and ask them to show it. Then we would split the money. They were just glad to do it. But I could only show it a few times.

Q – Was it difficult to raise awareness of the film?

Jean-Marie – No. I hired a guy with a loudspeaker, put some posters on a car and drove around the city announcing that there was going to be a screening of an African film tonight. Then I went to the radio station and asked them for advertising.

Q – How did the screenings go?

Jean-Marie – The first screening was quite successful, but people were upset because they saw a film about everyday life. I couldn't understand it at the time and I was very frustrated. I wanted to make documentaries different from what I had seen when I was a kid. I tried to make them lively. Having music, having a storyline – a beginning, middle and end. I tried to make my documentaries look like fiction films. People followed it, but in Europe people would say the structure was very odd. It's a story of someone telling a story of another one telling a story. Sometimes that was a little too complicated. I was mixing documentary and fiction and some of the things were reenacted.

Q – It's interesting that France who has been at the forefront of new styles of filmmaking didn't jump on it.

Jean-Marie – The place of the African in France is very complicated because most of the films challenged the official vision and discourse on Africa. The French were supposedly helping African cinema so they were promoting a vision of Africa that was almost like Africa from the villages - the Africa where you would go and spend this nice holiday. Exotic Africa! By making films that gave the reality and the everyday problems of people in African cities, I wasn't popular. And at the same time, the tendency toward documentary wasn't this way. Cinema verité was in the 60's and 70's. And when I did *Africa, I Will Fleece You*, for me it was a really difficult moment because I was addressing the French colonial history. So instead of looking at the film that I did, people started saying that my film was a pamphlet, a collage – it had nothing to do with cinema. They didn't consider me a filmmaker. I was just someone who was putting things together. The appreciation of the film also conflicted with the discourse of Africa and what was acceptable for an African filmmaker to say regarding the French Holy Mother Land. How could he say all these horrible things about France? I had a lot of difficulty at that time showing and promoting my work. Actually, *Africa, I Will Fleece You* was just released in the cinemas in 2003. It was shown on TV when Arte was still a cable channel. When I showed it in the cinema, people discovered the film and were really surprised at the modernity of the approach ten years or so after the fact.

Q – How do you think living in France has impacted the kind of stories that you tell?

Jean-Marie – Actually, I'm grateful for living in France. I live in a place where I have a chance to affirm my position as a black man. It has always allowed me to keep Cameroon and Africa in my creative space. If I were living in Cameroon, I probably wouldn't have made the films I've made because I'd always have the pressure of the police on my back. But at the same time, living in France didn't allow me to work as easily as I should have because making everything, for me, is a nightmare.

Q – Is it easier for you to make films these days?

Jean-Marie – I do have a network of cinemas that keep inviting me back - maybe 50-60 French cinemas. But still, I need to make a film that will give me some financial stability as making documentaries independently makes it very hard to make ends meet.

Q – Do you find that people in France are more open to looking at the situation in Africa properly?

Jean-Marie – No, I don't think so. Even with all the education that people receive, I don't think the openness is there. It's almost like people are trying to put their head in the sand. Two days ago there was an article in the newspaper because one of the big public stations were going to appoint a black journalist to present the evening news. Everyone is saying that this is a sign that society is changing. This isn't true. Nothing is changing. They're just trying to be like the BBC. They suddenly realized there have been black journalists on BBC for a long time.

Q – You have written that occupied people are forced to learn other people's identities. Do you think documentaries are a modern way for people to retain their identity?

Jean-Marie – Cinema has always been used as a way for people to portray themselves. To help people identify themselves and give them a sense of dignity. That was one of the aims of African cinema from the beginning – to counteract the brainwashing of the colonial culture. I believe documentaries are important for people to express themselves and to question society around them. They have to make a statement and assert a position of where they are. And have a broad look and opinion at everything happening around them. By doing that, people are obviously reclaiming their own identity through the diversity of looks and reflections people have on situations and things. When you give a unique view on things, it's a very dominant and oppressive vision because that is what's being forced on people. During the colonization period we had the feeling that the image we had even of ourselves was a false image. Now when people can speak out and talk about things and express themselves, it's a way to regain your own identity.

Q – How big of a crew do you use?

Jean-Marie – It depends. I had a larger crew on my first documentary because it was shot on Super 16mm film. Gradually, I went to video. For *The Colonial Misunderstanding*, when I was shooting in Germany, I had a two-person crew: a cinematographer and me doing sound. When I go to Africa, it's a two-person crew and most of the time it would be a one person crew. I'd hire an assistant and I'd do camera and sound at the same time.

Q – Do you take your equipment to Cameroon or do you hire it there?

Jean-Marie – I take my camera with me because I had so many problems when I started. I had to rely on people locally and it was always a nightmare. It's also a nightmare to go through customs, but that's less than getting there and not knowing if you're going to have a camera and if you do, what state it's in. You always have to do tests and then send the film to a European lab before starting to film. So it's best to take equipment there.

Q – What do you shoot with now?

Jean-Marie – I shoot in DV-CAM and with the next project I might shoot HDV or HD.

Q – Is there an arrangement between France and Cameroon to show films in unaltered cuts?

Jean-Marie – Yes. It was that a Cameroonian film would be considered a French film. It's protection for Cameroonian filmmakers in facing censorship.

Q – Are there are lot of documentaries on TV in Cameroon?

Jean-Marie – Most of the documentaries on TV there are reportage. They will film traditional dancing or how to make a drum. There are very few true documentaries that have a point of view. People are not really trained in making documentaries because it's a school of freedom. It allows people to express their point of view and when you have television that's state television or you have a private television that's trying to copy the national television – documentaries don't have a place. But with satellite, people will watch a documentary on Cameroon. I am always surprised at that.

Q – Is it easier for a young filmmaker to start a career in documentary films now than when you started?

Jean-Marie – When I was kid, to be a filmmaker was difficult. Today so may people can take cameras and go out and make films. But the big problem is that there's no training to explain to people what is a real documentary and what is reportage.

Many kids would say that they want to make a documentary about the wood industry or how to make palm oil. Gradually, I hope, people will learn and make documentaries.

Q – Have you filmed in any of the neighboring African countries?

Jean-Marie – I went to South Africa, Namibia and Togo. The documentary filmmaking there is still in the beginning stages. A lot of the festivals are more and more trying to promote documentaries. It's amazing. When I look before me, there were maybe two documentary filmmakers on the whole continent of Africa. Now I am almost considered the older generation of documentary filmmakers. There are many young people coming behind and they're really very talented.

Q – How do you fund your films?

Jean-Marie – Big question. I try to fund them through European TV, foundations and institutions. The budgets vary. My last film had a budget of 250,000 Euros. The one before had no budget because I did it on my own. And the one before that had budget of about 190,000 Euros. And the one before that had no budget. It was just me and the camera and I edited it, but really it was about 80,000 Euros when all was said and done.

Q – Are there any funding organizations in Cameroon that help with funding films?

Jean-Marie – Yes. The Ministry has started giving some money to filmmakers. They may give 10,000-15,000 Euros. There are no tax relief schemes or anything like that yet. There are co-productions as well. I did one with Germany for *The Colonial Misunderstanding*. It's great because I can find a lot more funding this way before starting.

Q – Do you have to pay a lot for your archival footage?

Jean-Marie – Yes, large amounts. It's a shame to pay so much for our own images.

Q – Is insurance difficult to get when shooting in Cameroon?

Jean-Marie – No, but most of the insurance companies in the country are part of foriegn companies.

Q – Have you ever been in any danger when shooting your documentaries?

Jean-Marie – Not really, actually. When I'm filming in Cameroon, for instance, people don't know what I'm filming. I look like everybody else. But my most frightening experience was when I was in the US, New York, once with a friend. He took me to a place where you weren't supposed to be with cameras. It was a drug place and we had to get out of there as quickly as possible. He was a white director. But I have forgiven him now.

Q – What are the common mistakes that you see documentary filmmakers make?

Jean-Marie – I don't see a common mistakes, I see common passion and I like some films better than others.

Q – What advice would you give to a new documentary filmmaker?

Jean-Marie – Be yourself and good luck.

DOGTOWN & Z-BOYS TO RIDING GIANTS

Q – What's your background and how did you get into documentary films?

Stacy – In my 20's, I had a very successful skateboarding company and we did a lot of very creative advertising work - we worked outside of the box. We wanted to figure out a way that we could reach kids that were buying our products around the world in a way that magazines couldn't provide. We thought up this idea of doing a skateboarding video – this was before the VCR revolution. The video became *The Bones Brigade*. We hired a Hollywood crew to make this video, but they didn't treat me or the kids with the respect that I thought they should. So after the first day of shooting, we parted ways. I was living in Hollywood at the time and I rented a 3/4" U-Matic camera and a recorder and I had a Sony 5850 3/4" editing system put on my dining room table and I started shooting. I had no idea what I was doing. But the one thing that I knew was that I understood how I wanted skateboarding to be photographed and presented.

Q – Was there anything out there at the time like it?

Stacy – Nothing. From what people tell me, this was the first "action sports" video to hit the market. Prior to this there were surfing movies and ski movies that were shot on 16mm and projected in auditoriums. People in Hollywood, producers and things like that, noticed that their kids were watching my videos over and over. I started getting calls from Hollywood to be a 2nd unit director – to direct action sequences for motion pictures. From there, I started to get opportunities to do comedy and documentary style stuff for TV because I had a style that people liked. One thing lead to another and I had to make a decision of either staying in the skateboarding business or becoming a filmmaker. And I decided in '91 to be a filmmaker.

Q – Was it fascinating to see how Hollywood movies worked?

Stacy – Yes because I could see how much more money and deliberation time they had to spend on lighting and set up and rehearsal, where I was basically used to stealing every location. If I couldn't go in and figure it out right there on my feet, I couldn't get the shot because we'd be either kicked out or threatened with arrest. But what was weird is that I really didn't want to do those films anyway. I wasn't inspired to do them. I just wanted to do my own thing.

Q – Where did you get the music from for the Bones Brigade videos?

Stacy – It was all self produced. A friend of mine who was one of the founders of a band called The Surf Punks, Dennis Dragon, came from a music family. He was not only a musician, but he was a music engineer and a producer. He worked on his own outside of the music industry and had his own giant truck filled with music equipment. I'd cut my videos to music that I'd buy at Tower Records and I'd go to Dennis and say, *"Can you make something that sounds kind of like this?"* And he'd build soundtracks for me. We'd make 20-25 original songs per video that were either inspired by something I heard or came from an idea that I had. Occasionally kids would give me music that I'd put in the videos as well, but not often.

Q – What did you shoot the videos on?

Stacy – We started with 3/4" video, which was a very cumbersome thing because it's a big camera with like this big hosepipe to the recorder. The tapes were gigantic. They were bigger than today's cameras! It made it difficult to jump over fences and run from police! The big trick with that equipment was how we could get moving camera shots. And they didn't make wide-angle lenses for those cameras. They made wide-angle adaptors that screwed onto the end of the lens, so it wasn't a perfect picture. But what I figured out was that if I put the recorder in a backpack and wear the backpack and I could hold the camera and shoot down NYC and San Francisco streets carving through people. The shots we were able to get with these big cameras were so amazing that - that's why I started getting work in Hollywood. You couldn't get these shots with a dolly. Even with Steadicam, they couldn't get the speed that I was getting on a skateboard. The producers who got me on to these projects would say to their camera departments, *"Just let the kid do what he does."* The camera department would look at me on my skateboard and they'd say there's no way we are going let this kid carry this Panaflex camera. But they did and I'd be going backwards and forwards and darting through people. And they'd look at the footage and they were like, *"We could never have gotten that shot."*

Q – But you weren't happy doing just that?

Stacy – No. I wanted to tell stories. So I started getting offers in television. The first couple of TV jobs I got, I actually liked. But as I started doing more opportunities in TV, I realized that it was an awful business. It's the most uncreative business, everything is by the numbers. I'd direct a show that I was very proud of, but if no one saw it, if it didn't get ratings, I couldn't use that show to get another job. But if I did a show that I was embarrassed by, and it did good numbers, it would propel me forward. I didn't want to work that way. So I sat down and had a day of reckoning with myself. What are you going to do? You're in TV and you don't like doing this. I didn't want to be a rock video director because I don't like rock videos but that was the normal way to become a feature director then. And I didn't like TV commercials. What am I going to do to get what I want? I thought what has always served me in the past had been my ideas. So I decided to teach myself how to write screenplays. I'd direct a TV show for three months, take that money and take two months off and write a screenplay. As soon as I was done writing, I'd do another TV job for three months. I did this for about three years until I had about five screenplays. And that's when the Dogtown experience presented itself to me.

Q – How did that come about?

Stacy – There was a 7-page article in Spin in 1999 about us guys in the Dogtown experience. It was called *Dogtown: In Search Of Skateboarding's Founding Fathers*. It was quite a good article. It was very rock and roll and subversive in the nature of the way the story was told. When the article hit the newsstands, Hollywood producers called me and a lot of the other Dogtown guys that appeared in the article to buy our life rights to make a fictional movie. A number of the Dogtown guys sold their life rights, but I wouldn't sell mine. I told the Hollywood producers; *"If you let me write this or at least let me be involved in the writing of it, I'll do it."* They said no. But they kept coming back to me saying that they needed me in the story because I balanced the story. They kept saying: *"You're the straight guy and you help balance Jay Adams and Tony Alva."* I told them that I still wasn't going to sign on unless I had something to do with the writing of it. And they said, *"We can't give that to you."* That's when I sunk into this great depression. I took a hike one day behind my house in the mountains and said, *"I'm just hitting zeroes here."* I couldn't sell my screenplays, I hated TV, and now the story that I always wanted to tell is being taken from me. What's next? Are they going to steal my identity? So I said, screw it. Let the Hollywood studio make the fiction film, I'll make a documentary on our experience. In the end, I finished the doc before the feature film and in fact, got to write the script for producers Art and John Linson – who were great!

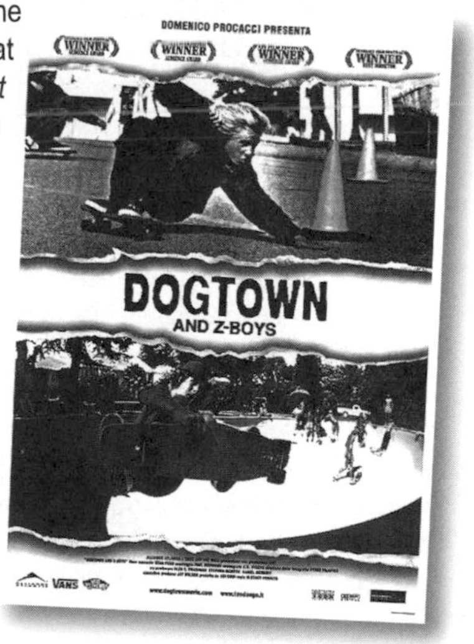

Q – When you started Dogtown did you have an outline?

Stacy – No. When I started making *Dogtown*, I thought my career was over. I was going through a divorce. Losing the house of my dreams. I really thought I was going to end up in a restaurant as a waiter. But I knew I wanted to make it, had to make it and I was excited to make it. I had in my head all the chapters and all the questions that I wanted to ask everyone because I knew that with documentary films they're written four different times. The first time you write is when you conceive your questions. Ultimately, if you don't conceive good enough questions, then you won't illicit good enough narrative. As you're doing the interview you come up with follow up questions that help build the narrative. Once you've your narrative, then you go through it and piece it together based on your transcripts. That's the second form of writing. Then you write your voiceover bridges that connect one area of thought to another. You get into editorial and you start rewriting there. So my instincts worked well for me on that because I asked the right questions, but I never knew how the doc was going to lay out.

Q – What do you mean by that?

Stacy – We cut the movie in chapters not in any particular order. We cut the Bicknell Hill segment, the POP segment, the Zephyr shop and the Del Mar segments as stand alones. One day I put them on 4x6 cards and thought about what would be the best way to lay out this film. Parts of it worked and parts of it didn't work at all. It was at that point, that I started moving things around and Paul Crowder, the editor and I found the narrative sequence of the film.

Q – Did you start off by going chronological?

Stacy – Yes, exactly. Originally, we had the pool segment in the later part of the film and it didn't work at all. But what I was afraid of was that if I put the pool segment earlier in the film there would be too much skateboarding action, back to back. When we were making this film, everyone kept telling us, *"Who gives a damn about a bunch of '70's skateboarders? You have to have current skateboarders in there today. You have to have Tony Hawk."* You can get that modern stuff at any skateboarding shop! I was afraid to put too much action in a concentrated area, yet it's what the film demanded. One thing you learn when you make films is that the film at a certain point will dictate what it wants. I did learn very early on that the best ideas come out of happy mistakes. And you have to be very careful as a creative person not to get too pissed off if things don't work out the way you had originally planned. Don't get too dogmatic. And that's when you have to watch your instincts because those will be the defining moments of finding the brilliance.

Q – Do you find that when you come to a block that you can get through it easily or do you have to walk away?

Stacy – It's different every time. For instance, in *Riding Giants*, which was a three-act film, we thought the third act, which we edited second, was going to be a slam-dunk. We thought this thing was going to cut like butter. We cut it together and it was a dog! I wasn't expecting that at all. But I had enough confidence at that point not to panic. Paul and I had a good second act that we were both happy with. So we decided to put down the third act and go to the first act, which we thought might be a bit weak. Paul said, *"I'm just going to slam this thing together based on the editorial story that you have put together."* So he cut it together really quick and we looked at it a week later and were like, *"Oh, my God! This is fabulous!"* It ended up being really good which we weren't expecting. That gave us a little breathing room. All the while, I ruminated on the third act – asking myself; *"what is wrong with it?"* About six weeks later I realized that we had to redo all the music and we needed to restructure the drama of the act in a new way. But unlike *Dogtown*, on *Riding Giants*, I did lay the film out at the beginning of production - from start to finish on 4x6 cards exactly how I wanted it to be and in the end it came out to be about 90% of what I originally intended.

Q – Did you follow the same editing style of your skate videos?

Stacy – There are some similarities. Paul and I had worked on a couple of TV shows together and had the same disappointing experiences. The executives say, *"Look we're bringing you in here because we want you to think outside the box."* And every time you take it out of the box, they go whoa, wait a minute – this is too much. So when *Dogtown* happened, we both had a synergy about where we were going to let it all go. For example, if there was a long-winded passage of someone speaking and we wanted the first part of a bite and the last part of the bite. Paul just sped it up instead of doing a dissolve. I looked at it, laughed my ass off and said, *"That's staying, that's fantastic."* From that point on he realized that there was a freedom where anything goes. And the people that we were making the film for didn't get in our way. In fact, we took them to lunch one day and wanted to show them a segment of the film and Jay Wilson, the president of Vans said, *"We don't want to see anything. Just make sure you finish the film on time."* Jay was the executive producer and guardian angel of the film.

Q – Vans put up all the cash?

Stacy – All the cash. We originally went to Rhino Films. Rhino said they were interested but they wanted someone to co-finance it. So Agi Orsi, the producer said she knew someone at Vans and went to Jay Wilson. Immediately, he said yes as they were interested in producing films. We went back to Rhino and they said, *"I'll tell you what. Have Vans finance the whole film and when the film is done, we'll pay our half."* Vans was like, *"Are you serious? There's no way we're going to do that."* So the film died. Six weeks later Agi says that Vans called and they're going to finance the whole thing alone. They put up $400,000 and it cost Vans less to make that film than it does one of their TV commercials. They can't lose.

Q – How did you get all that great music?

Stacy – Vans interrupted us during editing and said that they needed us to cut a 7-minute trailer so they could show what was coming down the pike. We estimated it would've taken 4 weeks out of our already tight editing schedule. But Vans needed it and we were really pissed off. So Paul started working on that and 3-4 weeks later we had this trailer that was the best piece of filmmaking that any of us had been involved with. It was so good that we thought, *"Damn, the film will never live up to this."* So we gave the trailer to our music supervisors, Debra MacCollach and Marc Reiter and they got it to Jimmy Page and the Hendrix Foundation. These people saw it and said, *"This is hot. Yes, you can use our music for paperboy wages."* So the trailer ended up opening many avenues for us. It helped us create momentum for the film early on.

Q – Normally, your whole budget could have been just for music on other films.

Stacy – We got the deals of the century. And because we got Led Zepplin and Hendrix early on, others like Rod Stewart and others like him were, *"Well, if they're doing it we'll do it..."* But what else that trailer did was inform us as to what the film wanted to look like. It instructed our style. It became our road map.

Q – Was the film as kinetic before you did the trailer?

Stacy – It was kinetic. I was an editor for ten years and it's the way I cut and it's the way Paul cuts. One of the things that we did in *Dogtown* that people commented on was the treatment of photographs. We used a traditional matte camera to shoot all of our still photos. But we did it differently. Typically you lay the photograph down on the matte and then they program the moves of the camera with a computer. I told the operators that I didn't want any programming. I just wanted them to operate the controls as I scream orders at them. And we didn't stop the tape. Normally they stop the tape when they're done shooting each and every photograph and then they start it again when the next photograph is laid down. I'd just throw photographs down saying, *"Do this! Do that!"* And it would be going all over the place and they'd be saying, *"But I'm getting the edge in the shot."* But I didn't care. I just kept them going. It was this freestyle way of doing it and Paul embraced that in the cutting. He got the fingers coming in and the photos underneath one another. We just wanted to show the deconstruction of the whole documentary process. It was fun. We were finally let out of the box.

Q – In Riding Giants you took the photographs to another level with the 3D movements. How did that come about?

Stacy – In *The Kid Stays In The Picture* they took the flat image and gave it a 3D look. Paul was at a wedding and saw a friend who said that he knew the 3D style and thought he could go even further. Our thought was to take the big waves and do that 3D idea to them. We gave him, Rick Greenwald, a couple of images and he came back a few weeks later and just knocked our socks off. It was a very time consuming and expensive process, so we were very selective in where we used it. There was another section at the head of the film where we had to tell two minutes of surfing history. It was kind of a dry but we had to do it in order to set up a prologue. I had Paul cut some traditional photos together and they looked flat. This was the head of the film. This was a very valuable piece of real estate here. It has to be better than this. So I took the photographs to a company called Blind Propaganda who are the same title graphics people we used for *Dogtown*. I asked them to animate an old, one-dimensional historical photograph of Hawaii. They took that concept and made it almost look like animation. Bingo! They designed this two-minute piece based on the historic photos that became this 3D trip though time that allowed us to rise up a notch. Then there are other areas of the film where we did drawings because we couldn't get under the ocean to show guys wiping out under 40 foot waves - we drew what we thought the experience might be.

Q – Did you use the same graphics company throughout?

Stacy – Yes. We couldn't give them a lot of money, but we let them work out of the box. That's one of the ways that you can get deals. You're promising creative expression in exchange for a low paycheck. With Vans on *Dogtown*, we weren't able to pay anyone much money, but we were able to give them free shoes. It's really weird what a person will do for free stuff!

Q – How did you get to Sean Penn to do the narration?

Stacy – An associate of ours said that he knew a guy who knew Sean Penn's assistant. We all laughed at the absurdity of us actually getting Sean. But then we thought what have we got to lose? So we sent the trailer to Sean's assistant who took a look at it said, *"Sean is going to love this."* So a couple days later we got another call and Sean's assistant said, *"Sean has seen it and he loves it. But he doesn't know that the film is going to stand up to this and he might want to meet with you and see what you have."* So we're working down to the wire on a Saturday and Agi answers the phone and I see her eyes light up. She looks at me and mouths *"Sean Penn!"* She hands me the phone and he asks where we are. He said he'd be there in 20 minutes. He shows up and we're nervous as hell and he wants to see what we've got. But he said, *"I only have 10 minutes so show me the best stuff."* We show him ten minutes worth and he wants to see a little more. We show him more and then he wants to see even more. About an hour later he was really hooked and he said, *"I have to go or I'm going to start crying."* He gets up and he goes. And we were like is he in or out? A few days later his assistant calls and said that he loves it and he wants to do it. So we went to San Francisco and we recorded him while he was doing the mix for *The Pledge*. He'd be upstairs mixing and then come down and read about ten minutes of the film, go back up, come back down, go back up… At the end of the day, he said that he didn't want any money for the film. He just wanted a couple of signature model skateboards from Tony Hawk for his son. It turns out *Dogtown* was a mirror of his own childhood. He grew up 20 minutes north of us here in Santa Moncia. He went to high school with some of the guys on the Zephyr team.

Q – Did you write the voice over?

Stacy – Yes. Writing narration for a film is very tricky and difficult. You can't be too dry and you can't write in too much of a style. It has to fit in between. Usually I'll write a piece of dialogue and write it again, again and again. It'll take me two to three pages to write two lines. Refashioning it over and over until it comes out with a punch. And when we were going to record it, I assumed that Sean was going to say, *"I could do this line a different way."* But he didn't change anything nor did he ask to change anything. He just read it like it was, which really surprised me.

Q – The moment when Sean clears his throat during the narration would've been cut out of most movies, but it felt so right.

Stacy – That stuff just fell into place. The mistakes seemed to enhance the film. And he was cool with it. But I have to tell you something - we never thought *Dogtown* was going to be successful. We thought it might get a second tier run on cable TV. It was one of the first films of its style to break out. Prior to that, documentary films were about poor Palestinian people or kids starving in Africa. Not to put any of those films down, but that is typically what a documentary film was so we had no intention of getting into Sundance. But this camerawoman said, *"You have to submit this film to Sundance. It's going to get in, so you're going to have get your team in order."* I went back to the office and suggested this and everybody said, *"What do we have to lose?"* So we submitted it and we got in much to our surprise!

Q – Did you gather all the stills and photographs used in the film?

Stacy – All of it. One of the things of being involved in that world is that I hadn't destroyed too many brain cells to forget things over time. I remembered all the photographers and cinematographers from back then and I knew who to go to. One thing you never want to do in a doc is to have too many talking heads. You have to have support visuals because they give you the authenticity and they strengthen your narrative style. My theory as a director was to get a lot of coverage so Paul would never run out of material. At one point during production, I hired a detective to find some of the people that I needed to find and he was really, really helpful.

Q – What made you decide to hire a detective?

Stacy – I'd drive to work every day and there was a detective's office on Venice Boulevard. So I decided, heck, go in and see what he says. He found some of the Z-Boys for me. And he found them immediately. He was charging me $300 a shot to find someone and he was doing it really easily. I knew there had to be some sort of public databank that he was accessing. So after a few times, I went to him and told him, *"Look man, I don't have a lot of money. I know this is really easy for you. Give me a deal."* So he fessed up and gave me a much better deal.

Q – Were you editing as you were going along or just at the end?

Stacy – Both. For both films, we made them in nine months time, which is really fast for a doc. Because I know so much about post-production, I'd get segments put together for Paul – the narrative story line and the photographs and the music. And while he was working on one act, I'd be working out on the next act, be it shooting, obtaining the materials or whatever was needed. We worked in tandem like that on both films.

Q – What formats did you use for both films?

Stacy – All of them but primarily Super 16mm. There was actually something in *Dogtown* where we ran into a nightmare when we did the film-out of the Meridian Avid to HD and then transferred it to film. The matte camera material was shot on the Beta format, then we had Super 16mm for the interviews, then Super 8mm and many other sources – but all of these different sources were having problems calibrating properly. So there were blur trails in the final transfer to film process. Paul figured out a way to fix it. He had to go back and redo certain parts of the film that were in video at a different frame rate in the Avid that looked bad. We had a similar problem with *Riding Giants* where we had to go through an interpolator for some of the source footage.

Q – With Dogtown, did you know you were going to finish on film?

Stacy – No. We never thought we were going to succeed with *Dogtown*. Sundance was a total surprise because I thought they only took really serious films. We were excited to have got in, but then someone sobered us up saying, *"You have to fill those seats up there in Park City. You're going to get six screenings of your film and if no one shows up, no one is going to buy it."* In other words, your film is finished. So we went up there all ready with posters and the first day we found out all our screenings were sold out already. It turned out to be a dream experience.

Q – And Sony bought it at Sundance?

Stacy – Yep.There were other companies that were interested, but Sony presented the best deal. It wasn't necessarily the best financial deal. But they guaranteed opening it in a certain amount of cities on a certain amount of screens.

Q – Documentary films usually don't make a lot of money in world-wide sales. Was yours financially successful?

Stacy – I'm assuming it was very successful for Sony Classics because they had a lot of people bidding against them for *Riding Giants*. I only made $30,000 for three years of work on *Dogtown*. It took a year to do the treatment, the budget and the planning. It took another nine months to make the film and another year to release it. I had to go on the road talking to journalists to help sell it and get bodies into theaters. I did 600-700 interviews selling that film. There are so many hats you have to wear as a documentary filmmaker. You have to be a salesman to get the film financed. You have to be a filmmaker to make the film. And then you have to wear the marketing hat. And you really have to know your stuff because if you don't the film companies aren't necessarily going to want to get in business with you again. It's so tricky selling these films. They need all the help they can get, which is really incumbent upon the filmmaker to get down and dirty and be very resourceful.

Q – Which is why there is usually such a big gap between doc filmmakers films - how long was the gap until you did Riding Giants?

Stacy – After Sundance 2001 and we assumed Sony Classics was going to release it the following June. But they said they wanted to wait a year so they could put it into every film major film festival - that way everyone, everywhere on the planet would know about the film. It premiered in the spring of 2002 and opened wider by that June. It was also in June of that year that I got the idea for *Riding Giants* – we quickly put together the financing for it by the end of the year, and started production in early 2003 and premiered in January 2004 at Sundance.

Q – How did you sell Sony Classics on Riding Giants?

Stacy – We didn't have to. They wanted it from the get go. In fact, we found out afterwards from Tom Bernard, the head of Sony Classics, was that he clandestinely flew to France to see an early copy of the film because he wanted it.

Q – How did the French financing come about?

Stacy – Laird Hamilton who was one of the featured surfers in the film had been in the process of trying to get a docu-drama about tow-surfing made and he had this relationship with this Frenchman who made a lot of money in French game shows. Canal Plus was buying the Frenchman's company and they wanted him to stay on board. So he said that if they wanted him to stay they had to finance his documentary films. He and Laird tried to get the docu-drama financed but they couldn't because they couldn't figure out the story. So I knew that I needed Laird Hamilton to be in *Riding Giants* and Laird said *"you should talk to this Frenchman."* So I pitched him, Franck Marty, the story and he said that it was what he wanted to do. So he financed the film. It took his company a long time to get the financing in place. In February, Agi and I realized that if we wanted to make Sundance, we'd have to start production now. So she and I financed the film for six weeks and the quickly realized that it was a big mistake. Eventually the financing came through and we went into official production. I think by putting up our money first, we ended up jump-starting the process. And we were able to make the festival date.

Q – Did you get any backend deal on Dogtown?

Stacy – I'm supposed to have some tiny little bit of someone else's tiny little bit, but I know the reality of the business – I'm never going to see a penny. I didn't do it for the money. If I do earn anything, it'll be a complete surprise bonus. For *Riding Giants,* I was actually paid a decent wage to make that film. And I got a similar backend deal as the other one. Unless you are someone like Spielberg, you're not going to get serious backend money. The one thing that I learned in this business and in life in general is if you're doing what you like doing, then that's the bonus. Try to get a good salary out of it. The backend goes to the people that can hide the numbers.

Q – In Dogtown, you interviewed a lot of your friends and with Jay Adams, it was a very touchy situation. Was it easy or difficult to talk to them?

Stacy – Difficult. First of all, I hadn't seen Jay in maybe 15 years and I was shocked at seeing the condition he was in. I was figuring out in the interview how far I could go with him. He was very open to going places that I didn't expect. My son was with me who was 9 at the time. He's a very perceptive kid and I'd told him a lot about Jay. He was frozen when he first saw him. And it was a very eerie situation on an obscure side of Oahu where we met him. The way that we'd gotten to him was we had contacted a guy who told us to call a number at 5pm. Then we called at 5pm and another guy answered and told us to call at 6pm. Then we were told to meet somewhere at a specific time. We'd show up some place and there would be a couple of guys there who'd tell us to go to this house at this time. It was like finding Osama Bin Laden. We get to this house and it's dark and there's lots of pot smoke. It was like a dungeon. I ask, *"Where's Jay?" "Oh, he's in another room. He'll be out in a minute."* Everyone is cool but it was weird. And finally he kind of stumbles out of this room and he's like, *"Hey, Stacy."* It was like no time had gone by. It was very strange.

Q – Do you have any philosophies on conducting interviews?

Stacy – When I interview people, I never want to look down at my notes. I always want to remain in eye contact with them, laugh at everything they say and show genuine interest. I try my best to keep them engaged because I want them to give me everything they got. But if you look down at your questions when they're talking, you lose them. Your people on camera are the most important things in your film. They're who you tell your stories through. If they bore you during the interview then chances are they'll bore the audience. If they're inspired chances are they'll inspire the audience.

Q – So casting your documentaries is something one must get right?

Stacy – Yes. If your main character is not entertaining, you'd better orbit him with people who are entertaining to make up for his lack of exuberance. And I believe as documentarians we have to make our films as good as fiction. And that mandate has to come out in every aspect of the film – the music, the visuals, the style, the story, the characters etc. I got the idea to make *Riding Giants* because I had to interview Greg Noll for another film. Greg is featured in the first act of *Riding Giants* and I found him to be this fantastic interview subject. At the time, I asked him if anyone had ever made a film on big wave surfing. He said no but they better do it soon because all of us old guys who started this thing decades ago are about ready to do the big kick out. Which means they're about ready to die. Agi and I had been planning on doing another movie on another surfer called Mickey Dora and we had everything set up but he unfortunately died shortly thereafter. Got cancer and in three months was gone. After that interview with Greg I got into the production van with Agi and said that I knew what our next film was going to be. She said, *"Great! And after Greg, let's go get Laird Hamilton."*

Q – Did you know Laird?

Stacy – I had met Laird once before, but we didn't know each other. The beauty of a guy like Laird is that he can bring people in to surfing who aren't part of that tribe. Too many documentaries fail because when you're making a film about a "closed society" like skateboarding or surfing, you can't allow your interviewees to speak in code. You want the people whom you're making the film about to feel like you've treated their subject honestly, but you also cannot go so far their way that it leaves everyone else out. You have to design the film in such a way where it's realistic to the hardcore but open and welcoming to the general public. If you lose one of them or both them you lose the drive of the film.

Q – What advice would you give a documentary filmmaker?

Stacy – You don't have to have confidence to be a filmmaker. To me what you need is an idea and the ability to wake up every morning and deal with that idea and the many facets of bringing it to life. Also, I feel that ideas travel in the subconscious atmosphere the same way viruses travel in the physical atmosphere. Ideas land on us as impressions or subtle hints and you have to be really careful about sharing them too early because inevitably those whom you share your ideas with won't understand what landed on your shoulder because you barely do. You have to sit with that idea in that state of absolute insecurity and unknowing and just deal with it, day by day, until that idea begins to take shape. And it can take a long time. That to me is one of the most difficult aspects of the creative process. I can feel the idea, but I can't make sense of it. I can sense it but I can't see it. You can't expect others to see it because if you try to get their acceptance and validation it, the opposite will happen. They'll say, *"I don't see it. That's a bad idea."* You stay within yourself and embrace the unknowing.

THE MAN WHO STOLE MY MOTHER'S FACE

Q – How did you start out in documentary filmmaking?

Cathy – It was very much in my blood as my father was a filmmaker. I myself, started in community and Youth Theater in Sydney where I found the love for story and directing. I had a passion for storytelling and I loved how documentaries enabled you to tell stories and keep it real. It was very accessible. Hi 8 cameras came out soon after that and they enabled new filmmakers like myself to get my own camera and go out and start shooting. Once I knew how to edit I was on my way.

Q – Was it helpful to you starting out as an editor?

Cathy – The more you know about editing the more informed you are of the process. As an editor I learned how a scene comes together, what components you need. Editing is the kitchen where the film is made. You may have gone to pick some great tomatoes and lettuces, with the footage being of prime quality and just ripe. But it becomes a meal as a result of how you put it together in the edit room, how you lay it out, what spices you add, what bits you cut off and throw in the bin. To me editing is where the real art form takes place. And it's helped my shooting skills.

Q – How did your film Losing Layla come about?

Cathy – *Losing Layla* began as a project by a friend of mine who was documenting her desire to have a baby and a partner who was unwilling to be a father. She documented it video diary style. She asked me to film the birth of the baby. It was the one scene that she simply couldn't film herself and 8 hours after the baby was born, the baby died. It turned into one of the most extraordinary experiences for me because my friend asked me to keep filming. So we filmed for the next 4 days - the grief of the parents and the family after losing this baby. She kept the baby with her for 4 days. It's actually a parent's right to have access to the body of their child after it's died. Same as you can with anyone who dies in your family. She wouldn't let it go. She kept bringing it back out of the freezer. Finally, she buried her baby. It became an incredible documentary about loss and grief. That was one of the many paths that *Layla* blazed, helping women who had their babies ripped from them and never saw them after they died. That grief can go on for 20-40 years if they don't do the grieving at the time.

Q – When you first thought about filming My Mothers Face, were you intending on it being a catharsis?

Cathy – The story of what happened to my mother was obviously with me very profoundly since 1988 when she was attacked and raped in her own house. I attempted to put it in film form a number of times over the subsequent years but broadcasters rejected it saying I wasn't experienced enough to tell that story. With *Losing Layla*, I saw how the film could both be a healing process for me and my mother, but also that it could be a way of engaging with audiences worldwide on a very important topic that isn't discussed. And by going into this personal story about me and my mother's urgent need for justice seemed like a good way into the story. It always pained and frustrated me that I hadn't got any justice at the time. So I went back to South Africa just to simply see if could get the case reopened and to see to whether the guy was still alive and if there was any chance of getting justice in this new South Africa. Under Apartheid, the country was in chaos and there was no interest in prosecuting a young white teenager for raping an elderly woman in the suburbs of Johannesburg when the country was falling apart. But when I went back in 2002, the country had changed and sexual assault was a priority. One in two women are raped in their lifetime meaning there's a rape happening every 26 seconds in South Africa.

Q – Why do you think that Johannesburg, more than any other city in the world, has such a high rate of rape?

Cathy – It has a history of violence that's beyond comprehension and that violence goes into every aspect of society. So there's a culture of violent response and rape of course is a violent act. There are also historical issues relating to loss of power and loss of self-esteem in the black community and in the white male community. So it's complex but you know what's surprising is that yes, we're all shocked that we hear those figures in South Africa but when I looked at Australia, the figures are one in four women can expect to be sexually assaulted once in their lifetime. That shocked me to the core. I have a 13-year-old daughter and between her and her three friends, statistics say that one of them will get raped. In the US the figures are shockingly high and in the UK the statistics are astronomically high. It's the fastest growing and the most hidden crime in the world because most women don't report. And they don't report because either it happens within family and friends, or they realize that they're not going to get any justice through the system. So it's not just South Africa, it's really a global problem. But South Africa is so up front about it and the government had taken it on as a priority issue.

Q – So in 2002 you went back to South Africa and you started your investigation?

Cathy – Yes, I returned in 2002 armed with determination, the budget, an assistant and stayed for 3 months.

Q – Did you have any problems being in the country?

Cathy – One of the very first things I did when I went back in 2002, was to hire a personal bodyguard, Moshadane, who became my friend and part of the film. It was because of having him by my side, I was able to go to places and meet the people and not get robbed or mugged. It was a reality that anyone walking around with a camera or even a handbag was at risk in some of the areas that I went. But Moshadane had a gun and he was with me all the time. I couldn't have done it without him. He was also fantastic with connections and getting me to meet great people.

Q – What was your plan when you went back?

Cathy – My plan was that I'd find the guy and when I told him who I was he'd break down and cry, confess and tell me that he was really, really sorry! I realized afterwards that was a very naïve hope. One of the things about South Africa is that if you're found guilty of rape, it's a life sentence. It's a very, very serious crime. So when I found him and confronted him, he went into a denial sequence, which is really quite fascinating. He was frightened and very, very confused. But he certainly didn't confess and then he shut me off completely, refused to see me, put a lawyer between us, and started threatening all sorts of things. My hope of having that restored justice wasn't met, but for my mother, the most important thing was that she wanted him to know that she still knew it was him and she wanted him to know the damage that he had done. The fact that she was heard and acknowledged by her neighbors and her son became more important than getting this guy locked up.

Q – Am I right in saying you used a hidden camera?

Cathy – Yes. That was one of the more bizarre parts of the filming; realizing that I had to do the hidden camera thing. That's not my style. I always engage with my subjects, get releases and make sure they see the footage, so this was very different. First of all I cleared it ethically and legally with a lawyer to make sure it was all above board. If he had confessed, that footage could've been used in the trial against him. So it was important for me to gather as much evidence as I could. In fact the police did use the footage. They gave it to a psychologist to assess whether he was lying or not and all the indicators were that he was lying.

The police completely believed my mother and were convinced he was guilty but they didn't have any hard evidence.

Q – How did you feel yourself when you confronted him with the camera rolling?

Cathy – It was probably the most frightening thing I've ever done. I didn't know whether this guy would turn violent and attack me because he's being confronted with something that puts his life at risk. As it turned out, the camera is in a tiny little buttonhole and a strap I was holding and I was supposed to be pointing it at him. But at the first part of the conversation I kept pointing it into a window that was behind us so he was reflected in the window. It was actually really good because you see me confronting him. It was an accident that turned into our advantage in the editing. I did eventually go inside the office with him, I got the camera right and got the footage. But we had to blank him out for legal reasons, because technically, according to our law, he's innocent until proved guilty.

Q – Did you ever think because you were so close to the subject matter that you were acting in a way you might not have if you were one step removed?

Cathy – There's no doubt that I was performing two roles. I was both the subject of the film and the director. And most of the time I handled the duality okay. But clearly the fact that I was making the film influenced what happened because people who I dealt with clearly responded differently because there was a camera following me around. Therefore maybe I got things moving faster and more attention than other daughters would in a similar situation. But also the fact that I was making a film motivated me to keep going when perhaps otherwise I might have given up.

Q – How did your mother react with you filming her?

Cathy – My mother said, *"I'm happy for you to do it, I'm very pleased, amazed and honored that you're interested enough to do it but I actually don't want to be in the film."* The first interview that we did, she was in silhouette, in the dark. Over the three years we made the film, she saw bits of it. Then things started to emerge and my brother apologized to her about his reaction to what had happened. She had been locked away like a hermit since it had happened but then she started to get up and go out the front door, engaging with the world and meeting people. The more she went out, the more she was in the film, so by the end she wanted to be in the film. She even agreed to one of the most harrowing scenes in the film where she's sitting in her bedroom looking her absolute worst and she said that the scene has to be in the film because people have to understand how low she went. So she was glad to be in it. She wants me to make a sequel! My mom's 76 now, she's so fit and healthy, she walks every day and has lost 25kilos (55lbs.). She teaches, plays tennis and has experienced love again. It's been a miracle what this film has done for her. There's no doubt in her mind that it came about through the acknowledgement she got from the film.

Q – What size crew were you shooting with?

Cathy – It was just me, a production manager from Australia, a sound recordist from Jo'burg for the whole three months. Moshadane, our security guard who was with us all the time. Then we hired another cinematographer for the scenes that I was in. So essentially a crew of four, sometimes five.

Q – What did you shoot on?

Cathy – I shot with the PD-150. So many documentary filmmakers have used this camera - such as Morgan Spurlock on *Super Size Me*. It's very small, very light, very unobtrusive and looks like a personal handycam. And for a lot of the situations I was in, it was absolutely ideal because it wasn't a big intimidating thing. When I filmed the police officer who clearly is caught out lying about the case - if I'd gone in with a big Betacam camera, that scene wouldn't have happened.

Q – You did some recreation in your film. What do you think about using recreation in documentaries?

Cathy – When the crux of the story is something that happened twelve years ago, I think it's really important for audiences to get a strong feeling of what happened that night. And I felt that I needed to start the film with that story and just having my mother tell it isn't particularly engaging. So recreations are obviously a very important aspect. I did it in the street where the attack happened so there was an authenticity about the place, even though the street had changed quite dramatically in the last twelve years. I storyboarded that scene and shot it like a little drama.

Q – Are there any ethical boundaries here that could be violated?

Cathy – As documentary filmmakers we need to expand our storytelling capacity so we can meet those demands without losing the integrity and heart of our story. I'd never go to extremes because broadcasters say audiences want it. There are enough people out there who do that. We do need to look at the engagement and entertainment aspects of documentaries because audiences are really getting into documentaries if they're well told and structured. I'm keen on recreations as long as you maintain the integrity of the story and it doesn't start to become more about style.

Q – Any tips on recreating footage?

Cathy – Scripting and storyboarding as you would a drama is very necessary. Have lots of time to plan. Lots of documentaries are made on low budgets and are rushed so give yourself that breathing space to do it well because bad recreations are awful! The other thing is to find a style that suits the style of the rest of the film, so they don't stand out and look like some kind of bizarre attachment that doesn't quite fit.

Q – Any tips on archival footage?

Cathy – I love archival footage. I've just made a film about the comedian Spike Milligan, which involves a huge amount of archival footage. But that archive cost so much money because we had to pay a variety of people who owned the rights. It was really a nightmare. But we used primarily film of Spike's own home movies and that to me was the best of the archive and the most accessible because the family collaborated on the film. In my own case, yes, my dad was a filmmaker and I was very lucky to find the old home movie of him and my mother on their honeymoon. That turned into a device for us to talk about her marriage and how monumentally unsuccessful it had been. It's great to see my mother as a young woman. To see her face and her attitude when she was younger because the whole attitude of her face after the attack becomes really important.

Q – Did you have any funding when you first started the movie?

Cathy – I had the whole film budgeted and funded when I went to South Africa the second time to shoot. We have a wonderful situation here in Australia where we have to raise half of the budget and the Australian Film Finance Corporation will put in the other half. So I was able to find half the budget from the presale to the ABC channel, the license fee, and our distributor Jan Rofekamp from Films Transit. He actually took *Losing Layla* and when I pitched this film to him he believed in my capacity as a storyteller and actually put money into the film. We got a Distribution Guarantee. It's very unusual these days but it does happen when people believe in something and want to see it happen. It was a very hard film to pitch to broadcasters before it was made because they weren't sure what they were going to see or what was going to happen. It's about sexual assault, so it's a big turn off in many ways. We got money from Films Transit, ABC, some state agency money that made about half of the total budget, which was $380k Australian, and then we got the rest from the FFC.

Q – Did you find your story while filming or in the editing room?

Cathy – The story emerged as it was happening. I wrote diaries and scripts all the way along the line. I mocked up a script of what I needed to look for and what I was hoping for, but obviously a lot of that changed. I wrote a diary every single day of what I was doing and what I had done. And a lot of those thoughts became the first person narration. In this role of playing both director and subject of the film, I would say - where am I in the story? What do I need for the story to work in the edit room? And knowing editing, I knew how I had to look for that footage. For instance, the scene with my brother - I filmed him and he storms out yelling at me, *"This is all rubbish, bullshit!"* I knew that I needed to stay with him; personally because as his sister I needed him to understand what was going on with our mother. None of that footage would have been useable if he hadn't got it - if there hadn't been some redemption and turning point within him. And finally I asked him to sit in front of the camera again and to talk to me. I knew as an editor that I needed that payoff and then when he apologizes on camera, it's incredibly moving. It wasn't made in the edit room, it was made in the shoot. But I had a brilliant editor in James Bradley who's an award-winning editor in Australia. He was fantastic because he really understood the men's part of the film. So often sexual assault stories are made by women, about women and generally appeal to female audiences. And James really got the male angle of this right.

Q – What is that difference?

Cathy – It's for men to understand the impact of their response when their mother, girlfriend, daughter, or lover is raped. When they go in and say, *"Why did you do this, why did you go there?"* That "why" question becomes a blame statement and causes so much damage. They need to understand that and a lot of men didn't get that. The other thing is when the black actor in the film, Bongani, talks about his girlfriend being raped and the impact it had on him. He's such a powerful male figure in the film so when he talks so emotionally and strongly about how wrong sexual assault is, I think it really helps a lot of men understand that this is men's business, this isn't a woman's issue.

Q – Any tips for writing narration?

Cathy – Narration in a film like this is very important to get right. I had two narrators, which is tricky. I had my mother narrating the first part of the film and then I stepped in as the narrator when I came into the story. That was unusual, but it did work. The second thing was that I felt the narration needed to have a liveliness and even a bit of humor to it because it's such a tough story. So I really tried to keep my narration away from too much heaviness and keep myself out of the story as much as possible and just focus on what people need to know. I got a narration consultant, an experienced documentary filmmaker called Mike Rubbo and I also had a consultant in Canada, Barry Stevens, who also had made a fabulous film with himself as the subject of the film and he kept his narration very light and very engaging.

Q – What were your plans for music?

Cathy – I started off wanting an entirely South African score but my mother is a classical pianist and after the attack she stopped playing. The piano just sat in the corner and became neglected. At the end, she starts playing again and plays Chopin. Chopin was a very big part of my childhood so I really wanted his music in there. The third element was this suspenseful thriller aspect to the film, so I wanted this kind of understated thriller tone raising the question of *'what's going to happen next?'*, which is hard to get from Chopin and the African music, so I ended up with three styles. I was told you can't have three different styles of music in one film but I think I pulled it off by playing the styles purposely where they're needed in the film and they work!

Q – How did you organize your footage?

Cathy – I'm a Virgo and I just kind of organize it as I go along! When I shoot, I label every tape, keep a log so by the time I got home I had 100 hour long DV tapes all marked, what they were and logged in order. We transcribed some footage outside of the edit suite. Then basically the editor started watching the lot and imported what he thought was going to be the raw material. We probably ended up with more like 10 hours of material that became the basis of the film. In the end we did a 74-minute version and a 55-minute version. The 74-minute version being our festival version that the Sundance Channel bought and the 55-minute version was the ABC and broadcast version.

Q – How long was the edit process?

Cathy – Fourteen weeks and then two weeks of online. I live on a rural property of twenty-five acres, half an hour from Byron Bay in Northern NSW. We have our own edit studio with an edit suite, which is a German system called Silver. It's an Avid lookalike. It's a very clever system that also allows us to produce DVDs. When we go to our online, which is the grading, sound mixing and the final graphics, we go to a fully furnished Sydney production house. We finish on Digi Beta.

Q – Did you do the festival circuit?

Cathy – Yes, Jan placed it at the Tribeca Film Festival and we won best documentary there in 2004. We co-won it. And it's a funny story. Glenn Close and Whoopie Goldberg were on the judging panel. I got to know Glenn Close because she came to see the film and stayed behind to tell me that she absolutely loved it. She then took us out for dinner. I met her again and she agreed to do a little tag for our DVD to say how great the film was, so I went back to her house to film that. She told me that there were eight judges and four of them wanted my film to win, and the other four wanted a great Palestinian film to win. They fought it out for hours and in the end they decided to award both films. Winning at Tribeca took us into another zone. Suddenly there was a lot more interest in the film. Jan had already made the sale to the Sundance Channel but winning confirmed the sale. The film has done very well at festivals and really helped us internationally. It went on to win best documentary in Australia in that year at our IF Awards. As a result of that we got into over 20 festivals all over the world and it won many other awards.

Q – Have you seen any revenue back from the film yet?

Cathy – Yes! We just got a big check the other day! $23k AUS. We have to pass on most of that to our funding partners as that's part of our contract but we do keep 20%. It never occurred to me that there would be revenue in the back end for a film like this. I made this film because I wanted to get justice for my mother and I wanted to tell a story that's been burning away in me for twelve years. I never imagined in my wildest dreams that one, it would help my mother so profoundly and two, that it would have the impact that it's had on audiences around the world. Millions of people have seen it now and many of them write to us! I got an email just yesterday from a woman talking about her own case and how profoundly the film had helped her. We created a website for the film and that gets an incredible amount of visits and attention from people. It's ongoing and not over yet.

Q – What advice would you give a new documentary filmmaker?

Cathy – Build teams. That's very important. Find creative people around you that you can work with. Think big but keep your overheads small. I'm not interested in becoming a huge big company, but I want my ideas to be big. Nurture the relationships you have with your DPs, your production managers, and your crew because they are vital to everything. Always adhere with passion and conviction to the heart of the project. Don't give away the heart, the kernel of it and don't compromise that. Don't compromise your own personal integrity and your own personal ethic when you're making a film.

*Help stop sexual assault against women. Go to Cathy's website **www.hatchling.com.au** to learn more about her film and her story.*

Ellen Perry

THE FALL OF FUJIMORI

Q – What's your background and how did you get into documentaries?

Ellen – I studied film at USC School of Cinema and Television and I started developing my last documentary while I was in school. It was on the Three Gorges Dam in China. An article by Patrick Tyler, who was at the time, the Beijing Bureau Chief at *The New York Times* inspired me.

Q – When you were at film school did you want to make documentaries?

Ellen – No. *Great Wall Across The Yangtze* completely fell into my lap. All of my friends in school were going to go work as PAs or assistants to agents or producers in Hollywood, whereas I had an opportunity to go make a documentary. It was an amazing story about an extremely controversial subject matter. It was China; it was the largest dam in the world, the largest displaced population ever in peacetime history...how could I refuse? I didn't know it was going to take me 4 years or that it wouldn't be a money making venture. *Great Wall* ended up airing on national PBS. So in the end, it was successful.

Q – Did you find that the struggle over the years wore you down?

Ellen – Yes not only because of the difficult subject matter but also because filmmaking was on the cusp of the digital revolution. I started shooting in 1996 and they'd just introduced the digital video camera at NAB. I knew good and well there's no way I was going to get past security in China with a Betacam. One of my professors told me about this little digital camera that produces better quality than broadcast resolution. Naturally, this little digital technology has changed the face of filmmaking, particularly documentary.

Q – So you didn't have many problems there?

Ellen – No, I had problems! I was kept under house arrest. I have to blame *Lonely Planet* for that. I was traveling to this nature reserve called Shennongjia and took the bus route *Lonely Planet* suggested. But it went right through a military zone. We got off the bus and all I saw were military trucks. My translator went to check into the only hotel when suddenly these military guys walk in full uniformed regalia and say in English – that's what really scared me, *"Do you have a travel permit?"* They stopped asking for travel permits in the late 80's. This was something left over from Deng Xiaoping and Mao Tse-Tung and there were only a few areas where they required that, such as nuclear testing sites, for instance, or along the Mongolian Border. So I knew I was in trouble. But we talked our way out of it...thank God!

Q – Did anything else like that happen?

Ellen – No. People didn't take me seriously because nobody had ever seen this camera before...it didn't look professional. Unfortunately, I probably destroyed any other chance of filmmakers going into China and filming surreptitiously. Ultimately, *Great Wall* was a national show with a website detailing how I penetrated China's interior. There were also screenings at the Woodrow Wilson Center and the Council on Foreign relations where, apparently, Chinese government officials attended. I want to go back to China, but I hear that if I did, I'd be turned away. It was a very objective film – that's my policy with political docs...objective filmmaking. It was the same with *The Fall Of Fujimori*. In fact, with *Fujimori*, I was in even more danger because I was dealing with the CIA, Peruvian secret police and a society still afraid of the Fujimori "mafia."

Q – Did they hassle you?

Ellen – When I was interviewing or taking meetings with individuals in public places who were involved in intelligence or the Fujimori government, there were always these lone guys very nearby to our tables drinking coffee for way too long. As a precaution my interviewees and I would always take out our batteries to our cell phones for fear that our conversations were being recorded. In terms of the CIA, I had gone to San Jorge Prison which is sort of a minimum security prison to do an off-camera interview with an individual implicated in an arms deal to the FARC rebels in Colombia, which some believe was one of the reasons the Fujimori regime ultimately collapsed. Vladimir Monesinos was Fujimori's intelligence guy and, apparently, Fujimori's henchman. Montesinos brokered a government-to-government arms deal with Jordan. But instead of the arms going to Peru, they were, in fact, air dropped over Columbia into FARC stronghold territory.

The US had recently passed a bill called Plan Columbia where the US and the EU had invested billions of dollars in curtailing arms and narco-trafficking in Colombia. After that, the State Department said to the CIA (Montesinos was on the CIA's payroll), *"That's it. We don't want to hear anymore about our man in Latin America. Vladimiro Montesinos crossed the line. He's got to go."* This isn't in the film because it's way too complicated, but literally a week later a video was leaked out to the media showing Montesinos bribing an opposition congressman. But, going back to my interviewee in San Jorge prison, he was allegedly the moneyman behind this arms deal to FARC and is currently imprisoned in Peru…much to his dismay. It was an incredible amount of information. And as soon as I left the prison, my phone rang and it was the US Embassy. And they were on me for the rest of the time.

Q – What did they say to you?

Ellen – What am I doing here? What kind of film am I making? What kind of interviews do I want? I told them I was focusing on the Fujimori presidency and his battles with terrorism. Once they got the information from me, they suggested people for me to interview – people that I wanted to interview and that I had tried contacting, but to no avail. Needless to say, after my conversation with the US Embassy, those same people returned my phone calls right away. The fact is, the US Embassy/ CIA could have made my life miserable, but instead they helped. I suppose I didn't pose a real threat to their agenda. I was very honest and letting them know that I wasn't trying to uncover some nasty arms deal.

Q – Why did you choose Fujimori as a subject?

Ellen – While editing *Great Wall*, I flipped on CNN and Fujimori was giving his victory speech after the commando raid. I was like, *"What just happened in the world?"* I also wondered why a Japanese man was President of Peru. The next day, *The New York Times* had a front-page article about the hostage crisis and the commando raid. Even at that point, a red flag had been raised about why all of the guerillas were killed. There were rumors that some of them had surrendered and were executed. So then it was like, did Fujimori give the word to take no prisoners? I cut out the article, filed it away and thought that maybe I'd make a film about it one day. In 2000, Fujimori's regime collapsed. Montesinos was on the run and Fujimori fled Peru to Japan, the land of his ancestry, amidst allegations of corruption and murder. This is a great Shakespearian story. But it's also a very relevant story to our current political climate. After 9/11, I realized that the Fujimori story and his battle with terrorism was relevant to the world, not just Peru. In the end, the film ended up being a really powerful cautionary tale.

Q – Did you get any funding this time because of Great Wall?

Ellen – No. It doesn't get any easier. I put a proposal together and tried to raise money from the NEH, ITVS, ect… and was turned down. I was actually approached by one private investor who wanted to give me seed money, but in turn, he wanted editorial control. Of course, I refused to do that. So he pulled funds and took my story to another producer, claiming it as his own. But it didn't matter – I made the movie, he didn't. Looking back though it was a real bummer. I really needed that funding. I was completely broke. In fact, I had to paint ceilings to make my rent. I was slapping paint on ceilings in various apartments all the while saying to myself, *"Dammit, I was talking at the Woodrow Wilson Center last year – look at me now."* I'm sure every filmmaker can sympathize with that story. But I suppose in this business, or any business for that matter, that's how one separates the wheat from the chaff. You have to be willing to make sacrifices. In the end, Sundance stepped up to the plate. They gave me a small grant in the fall of 2003.

Q – In terms of the proposal, did you get any finance from that?

Ellen – It was a hard sell. Why would Americans care about a Latin American president? Was it a stretch to draw parallels to 9/11? Absolutely not. In fact, Seymour Hersh wrote an article in 2003 claiming that Rumsfeld approved death squads in Iraq. There's also the use of military tribunals at Guantanamo Bay. The way the capture of Saddam Hussein was handled. Using that amateur video, probing his mouth. They have the same footage of Abimael Guzman, Head of the Shining Path, in Peru. It was like Bush ripped off Fujimori.

Q – When did you shoot Fujimori?

Ellen – I started production in 2002. Went to Peru completely self-financed with help from the producer of *Great Wall*. It was really discouraging because nobody was returning my calls. Peru was in some ways harder than China to get people to talk because the threat and fear of Montesinos was still there. And even though he had been captured and was in prison, he had a lot of strength and power from the inside. I ended up having to go through the clergy first. This is very *Godfather*-esque, in order to get to individuals in the government.

Q – How did you know to do that?

Ellen – I didn't. I was learning as I was going. You listen. You let your gut be your guide. So my first interview was with Julio Wicht who was a hostage in a Japanese embassy and then Hubert Lanssier, who was a chaplain in the prison system. And then Gaston Garatea who was on the Truth and Reconciliation Commission. After those three interviews, who are all clergy, I was able to talk with the head of the intelligence apparatus and then members of Congress and the press. Then I started talking to Fujimori's brother and it was through him that I was able to get access to the Fujimori clan. But I had to go through this huge screening process.

After seven weeks, I left Peru with some good archival and decent interviews, but I didn't have a film. I came back and was able to cut together a trailer and sent it out to the Sundance Institute and they bit on it. They had just merged with George Soros Open Society so there was a clear interest in films of this nature.

Q – What was your process with the archival footage? What were you looking for?

Ellen – I had no idea what kind of footage existed. For instance, I didn't know about Guzman in his cage. I had read that he had been presented in a cage, but that didn't translate for me visually. When I actually saw that footage, it was like, *"Are you kidding me?"* And getting the footage was easy. People in Peru wanted this story told because they hate Fujimori and they want to bring him back to face justice. Fujimori wants it told because he wants to clear his name.

Q – Did you get the archival footage from Peruvian news sources?

Ellen – Yeah. I have very little footage from American news sources, almost none in fact.

It's all from Peruvian sources and the President himself. And most of the footage was donated because they don't have the rights thing down yet. Everyone owns the same footage. They don't have any archival libraries. I was very, very lucky.

Q – Was it only you going down there?

Ellen – Yes. I had assembled an advisory board because I went for the NEH grant, which they didn't fund because they wanted a more historical context. They wanted me to cover terrorism for the last 100 years, which wasn't something that I wanted to do. But the advisory board was great because they really helped me with a lot of connections. In fact, one of them was the one who lead me to Santiago Fujimori, who is President Fujimori's brother. Every documentary filmmaker should have an advisory board. Most grant institutions require them,

Q – So what happened with the Sundance Institute?

Ellen – I came back, put the trailer together and sent it off to Sundance. When I went back to Peru a few months later, I got an e-mail from the Sundance Institute saying that they were interested in funding the project, but that they needed more from me. So they asked me to write a script, and I did. When I came back to the States I let them know that I had secured the interview with Keiko Fujimori, Fujimori's daughter, and that she was approaching her father on my behalf. Diane Weyerman, who, at the time was head of the Sundance Documentary Fund, told me that when my project came up before the board, they all looked around the table and said, *"Do you think that Ellen can pull this off?"* And Diane said, *"I think she's going to do it."* Kudos to them for having the courage and the vision to fund this film.

I immediately contacted Keiko and said I had just been awarded a grant with the Sundance Institute, as in Robert Redford's Sundance Film Festival. They're the most important independent film organization in America and, of course, she relayed that to her father. I needed the money desperately, but I also needed the stamp of approval from an institution like Sundance. Fujimori being the savvy politician that he is thought that this is the project that I want to do because it is going to get made and there is a powerful entity backing it.

Q – How much was the grant?

Ellen – $25,000. It was enough for me to go to Washington, DC and do my interviews on Beta and enough to go to Japan and film Fujimori for over a month.

Q – What was the process for writing the script? What were you looking for in the story and did you write it specifically for Sundance's needs?

Ellen – I was writing the only story I knew how. I had my vision and my approach. I wrote it like a Shakespearian tragedy because that was the way I saw it. I even broke it up into a five-act structure.

Q – Did you know where the story was going while you were shooting or did it come when you were editing?

Ellen – I did at least 40 interviews not to mention with Fujimori, himself, which the formal interview was at least 16 hours. You never know what you're going to get. That's what is so difficult about funding documentaries up front, you have your idea and high concept and you want to believe that you can pull it off. But what if you can't? I brought my editor and dear friend, Kim Roberts in, who worked on *Lost Boys*

then said, *"I think I'm ready for you to look at something."* I looked at it and I started to cry - it was really special. That sort of set the tone for the rest of the film. We had a three-hour rough cut initially and then we whittled it down to an hour and a half. So we'd cut important sequences such as a scene in the Japanese Embassy crisis. The first cut of that sequence was 45 minutes, which we had to cut down to 15. You put in everything you want, everything you think is important and it is a fairly linear process and then you cut it down.

Q – How do you organize your footage and did you use a transcription service?

Ellen – I worked with over 10 translators. My transcripts ended up being 2,000 plus pages. And, no, I did not go to a service. They're far too expensive. I had students at Stanford University transcribe at a seriously discounted rate. Zack Anderson, who is one of the writers, was just dumbfounded by the process because he would see me every day making a little bit of progress with no money. People worked on this because they believed in the project.

Q – How did you approach writing the script?

Ellen – Kim and I put together a paper edit of the script and then we started editing in Final Cut. Once we had it down to a rough cut, I realized we were going to need voice over so I went to Zack Anderson for that. Then it was an issue of how we were going to bridge these complicated sequences where the interviewees could not.

Q – Is voice over used throughout the movie?

Ellen – It's used sparingly. There's one scripted page of narration, and I did the voiceover. Not because I wanted to, but because I ran out of time. Sundance makes that call and you've 8 weeks to finish. We finished a week before Sundance.

Q – What did you do for music?

Ellen – Mark Adler composed the music for this and it's an amazing composition. It's so beautiful. He worked with a Peruvian percussionist. It was a mixture of a western classical composition to indigenous Peruvian and Japanese instrumentation. I paid him a lot for my budget, but not nearly his going rate. Guys like Mark Adler and Kim Roberts like working on these projects because it is a much purer, cleaner form of cinema

Q – What instruction or theme did you give the composer?

Ellen – I had a temp track so my instruction was to be creative and original, but know that I want the same emotion I used in the temp track. He exceeded my expectations. I was in San Francisco and he was in LA, so he'd send me an FTP with a couple of tracks and I'd give it a thumbs up or thumbs down. Fortunately it was thumbs up most of the time because we had less than two months to put this together. Then he brought in the live instruments and it went beautifully.

Q – Did you have any money left over from the grants to pay for this?

Ellen – No, this was all out of my own pocket. I can't give you the exact budget amount but it was around $500,000.

Q – Did the film sell and what was that process like?

Ellen – Yes, we've sold to numerous territories worldwide, including the BBC and to P.O.V., a national series on PBS. The process was much easier since Fujimori premiered at Sundance.

Q – What advice would you give to a new filmmaker?

Ellen – My tip to any filmmaker is never give up. That's the key to your success.

Index

Symbols

A

B

C

D

E

F

G

H

W

X

Y

Z